TRAPPED IN A RELIGIOUS MARRIAGE

Human Rights Research Series, Volume 86.

The titles published in this series are listed at the end of this volume.

TRAPPED IN A RELIGIOUS MARRIAGE

A human rights perspective on the phenomenon of marital captivity

Benedicta Deogratias

INTERSENTIA

Cambridge – Antwerp – Chicago

Intersentia Ltd
8 Wellington Street
Cambridge | CB1 1HW | United Kingdom
Tel.: +44 1223 736 170 | Fax: +44 1223 736 169
Email: mail@intersentia.co.uk
www.intersentia.com | www.intersentia.co.uk

Distribution for the UK and Ireland:
NBN International
Airport Business Centre, 10 Thornbury Road
Plymouth, PL6 7 PP
United Kingdom
Tel.: +44 1752 202 301 | Fax: +44 1752 202 331
Email: orders@nbninternational.com

Distribution for Europe and all other countries:
Intersentia Publishing nv
Groenstraat 31
2640 Mortsel
Belgium
Tel.: +32 3 680 15 50 | Fax: +32 3 658 71 21
Email: mail@intersentia.be

Distribution for the USA and Canada:
Independent Publishers Group
Order Department
814 North Franklin Street
Chicago, IL60610
USA
Tel.: +1 800 888 4741 (toll free) | Fax: +1312 337 5985
Email: orders@ipgbook.com

Trapped in a Religious Marriage. A human rights perspective on the phenomenon of marital captivity

ISBN 978-1-78068-842-8 (paperback)
ISBN 978-1-78068-843-5 (PDF)
D/2020/7849/107
NUR 828

British Library Cataloguing in Publication Data. A catalogue record for this book is available from the British Library.

CONTENTS

LIST OF FREQUENTLY USED ABBREVIATIONS

ACHR	American Convention on Human Rights
ACHPR	African Charter on Human and Peoples' Rights
CEDAW	Convention on the Elimination of all forms of Discrimination Against Women
CEDAW Committee	Committee on the Elimination of Discrimination Against Women
CESCR	Committee on Economic, Social and Cultural Rights
CRC Committee	Committee on the Rights of the Child
CSW	Commission on the Status of Women
DEVAW	Declaration on the Elimination of Violence Against women
DCC	Dutch Civil Code
ECHR	European Convention on Human Rights
ECmHR	European Commission of Human Rights
ECtHR	European Court of Human Rights
HRC	Human Rights Committee
ICCPR	International Covenant on Civil and Political Rights
ICESCR	International Covenant on Economic, Social and Cultural Rights
IPV	Intimate partner violence
NGO	Non-Governmental Organisation
SGP	Staatkundig Gereformeerde Partij
VAW	Violence Against Women
VCLT	Vienna Convention on the Law of Treaties
UDHR	Universal Declaration of Human Rights

CHAPTER 1
INTRODUCTION TO MARITAL CAPTIVITY

1.1. A HUMAN RIGHTS APPROACH TO MARITAL CAPTIVITY

> Yehudis Smith: '*Imagine being locked up in a cell, not knowing when you will be released, if ever. Living day in and day out with the fear that you'll never be able to move on with your life, never be able to find true love, have children, have the life you always thought you'd have, and only being 22 years old. Your husband isn't lost at sea and he's definitely not mentally ill (he knows exactly what he's doing). He walks by your cell daily, dangles the keys in front of you, and walks away; the up-and-down emotional roller coaster of, "maybe today is the day... or maybe I'll die this way. This is how it feels to be an agunah... an "ungetted woman." And it doesn't matter if you're 22, 62, or 82... whether you're at the beginning of your life with no children, or fighting on your death bed. NOBODY can tell such a woman that she has a choice, for that is the very thing that her husband has taken from her.*'[1]

This extract depicts a woman's physical, emotional, psychological and legal struggles after futile attempts to have her religious marriage dissolved. As it turns out, she is forced to remain married against her will. This is a situation which evidently affects every aspect of her life. This peculiar situation is also known as marital captivity.

In contemporary times, the termination of a marriage has become an inevitable truth for an ever- increasing number of relationships. Divorce is generally considered and experienced as an undesirable outcome of the marriage and it is often followed by a tedious time and money consuming process. In many cases, the dissolution of the marriage is eventually realised. However, in certain instances, as illustrated in the case above, one or both couples may not be able to terminate the marriage by way of divorce. The dissolution of a marriage can be hindered by both legal and non-legal factors, such as financial restrictions, social and emotional pressure to remain married, fear of losing a residency permit, religion, and so on. This contribution examines situations in which religion forms a barrier to the dissolution of a marriage. The focus is placed on religious doctrines, convictions and practices that may form a barrier to the termination of a marriage and, thereby, create a situation of marital captivity. In this contribution, the term 'marital captivity' refers to:

1 Yehudis Smith,' In this story, the Agunah was me', *Collive Community News Service.*

'a situation wherein the dissolution of a religious and/or legal marriage is obscured for religious reasons, consequently forcing the spouse(s) to remain in the marriage against their will.'

Situations of marital captivity occur globally within different religions, and it is a phenomenon that disproportionately affects women, as is illustrated by the case above and for reasons that are elaborated upon in section 1.3.1. and Chapter 3.[2] Unfortunately, marital captivity is not a new social problem, as it can be traced back to the late 19th century.[3] Notwithstanding the fact that marital captivity is an issue that religious communities have struggled with for centuries, it is only in the past few decades that the issue of marital captivity has increasingly received public attention outside of the religious sphere.

The concerned spouses, civil society, religious authorities, professionals and scholars have all contributed to finding solutions, creating public awareness and pinning the issue on the political agenda of their respective governments. Within different legal systems, a variety of measures have been adopted to redress and prevent situations of marital captivity from arising in the first place. For example, reforms of personal laws, particularly in the area of family law, have been adopted in certain non-secular countries in order to the facilitate women's ability to divorce.[4] Civil divorce has also been introduced in some States so as to enable partners to divorce in accordance with civil law.[5] At times, even legislative and judicial intervention have been adopted in the efforts to facilitate the removal of religious barriers to the dissolution of the marriage. Some countries have opted to re-interpret existing legal mechanisms to cover situations of marital captivity.[6] For example, in the Netherlands judges have relied on tort-actions

2 See also Esther van Eijk, *Wel gescheiden, niet gescheiden? Een empirisch onderzoek naar huwelijkse gevangenschap in Nederland*, (Maastricht University, 2017), p. 90.; Eliane Smits van Waesberghe, et al., *Zo zijn we niet getrouwd: Een onderzoek naar omvang en aard van huwelijksdwang, achterlating en huwelijkse gevangenschap*, (2014), pp. 10,14.

3 French tribunals of northern African colonies (Algeria, Tunisia and Morocco) sough to resolve situations of marital captivity in Jewish communities in the late 19th century. H. Patrick Glenn, 'Where heavens meet: The compelling of religious divorces', 28 *The American Journal of Comparative Law* 1–38, (1980), pp. 13–15.; See also Haim Sperber, 'Wanted: Missing Jewish husband', *Hadassah-Brandeis Institute*, *at* <www. 614ezine.com/wanted-missing-jewish-husband/> last accessed 24 January 2017.; Anna R. Igra, *Wives without husbands: Marriage, desertion, and welfare in New York, 1900–1935* (2007), p. 4.

4 Such as Egypt, Israel, Morocco. On Israel: Weiss and Gross-Horowitz, *Marriage and Divorce in the Jewish State: Israel's Civil War*, p. 15.; *The property relations between spouses, 1973, at* <www.pereslaw.co.il/document/54,67,32.aspx> last accessed 04 February 2018.; Lenore J. Weitzman,' The Politics of Jewish Divorce Law Reform', *Franke Institute Annual*, p. 14. On Egypt: Pauline M. Kruiniger, Islamic divorce in Europe: Bridging the gap between European and Islamic legal orders, (2014) (Maastricht University), pp. 114–115, 120, 123–126. On Morocco: Id., p. 171–172, 179–181.

5 E.g. Ireland and Malta. Ireland introduced divorce in 1995 by the Fifth Amendment to the Constitution. Malta introduced divorce in 2011. David Sharrock, 'Malta votes yes to legalise divorce', *The Guardian* 2011.

6 E.g. France, Israel and the Netherlands. On France: Cour de Cassation, Chambre civile 2, 21 November 1990, 89–17.659.; Cour de Cassation, Chambre civile 2, 15 June 1988, 86–15.476. On Israel: Susan M.

to facilitate the dissolution of a religious marriage by compelling the non-cooperative spouse to cooperate in the religious divorce.[7] Some common law countries have adopted legislative measures that require the removal of religious barriers so as to enable the divorced spouses to remarry.[8]

So far, the dialogue on marital captivity has centred around finding solutions to end and prevent situations of marital captivity. More specifically, the emphasis has been placed on the role of religious communities in creating solutions (for example by way of re-interpretations of religious doctrines), the role of States and the implications of State intervention in a phenomenon that is perceived as a religious and private matter.

Remarkably, and as the literature review in subchapter 1.4. illustrates, reference to the human rights dimension of marital captivity has been scarce, despite this being a global phenomenon that negatively affects the trapped individuals in ways that do not necessarily concern or relate to their religious affiliation, membership and convictions. As the case above illustrates, marital captivity is a situation that negatively impacts the trapped spouses' autonomy to live a fulfilling life which is in accordance with their own free will and wishes. Notably, experts and professionals in the field as well as trapped spouses, are increasingly stressing that a situation of marital captivity infringes upon the human rights of the trapped spouses.[9] This notwithstanding, few inquiries have been made into the human rights that are alleged to be violated within a situation of marital captivity and even far less attention has been devoted to the implications of including a human rights discourse in relation to the phenomenon of marital captivity.

For this reason, the present contribution focuses on the human rights aspects of marital captivity. More specifically, this contribution seeks to contribute to the process of finding sustainable solutions to end and prevent this issue, by including and exploring human rights law as a tool for addressing marital captivity. Analysing the causes and consequences of marital captivity from a human rights perspective enables an understanding of how the trapped spouses are affected in the exercise and enjoyment of their human rights. More importantly, human rights contain obligations for States to respect, protect and ensure individuals' rights. Adopting a human rights-approach to marital captivity, thus, allows a study of the role of the State and its human rights obligations to respond to this phenomenon. In fact, elaborating on the role of the State

Weiss, *The tort of Get- abuse: How damage litigation has changed the course of family law in Israel*, (2011).

7 See also section 3.4.1. and paragraph 4.4.2.2.1.

8 *New York Domestic Relation Law*, paras. *236 and 253.*; United Kingdom Divorce (Religious Marriages) Act 2002, chapter 27.; Canadian Divorce Act, Section 21.1.; South Africa Divorce Act 70 of 1979, section 5A.
See also case law such as High Court Justice, *AI v. MT*, 30 January 2013, [2013] EWHC 100 (Fam).; Court of Appeal of the United Kingdom, *Brett v. Brett*, 5 December 1968, [1969] 1 All ER 1007.; Supreme Court of Canada, *Bruker v. Marcovitz*, 14 December 2007, 3 S.C.R. 607, 2007 SCC 54.

9 See also subchapter 1.4.

in complying with its human rights obligations is a key element, since States are, after all, the duty bearers in human rights law. Finally, inclusion and reference to human rights has also the advantage of attaching a degree of gravity and severity to situations of marital captivity.

Having said that, the principal question is: In what ways does a human rights approach contribute to the process of finding solutions to prevent and end situations of marital captivity?

This question warrants further elaboration, particularly since marital captivity is socially and legally a complex phenomenon. To begin with, besides the trapped spouses, marital captivity involves other multiple actors, i.e. the other spouses who may not want to divorce on religious grounds, the religious communities and authorities, the State and possibly multiple States where there are cross-border elements. On top of that each of these actors has different interests which, within the context of marital captivity, tend to be at odds. For example, on the one hand the State has an interest to intervene in order to protect trapped spouses and comply with its human rights obligations. Likewise, State intervention to facilitate the dissolution of a religious marriage is also within the interest of the trapped spouse, particularly where this leads to ending a situation of marital captivity. On the other hand, since the core problem concerns the inability to terminate a religious marriage, the implication is that religious normative systems govern the marriage including its dissolution. Thus, religious authorities that are tasked with the observance and enforcement of the rules on divorce have an interest in maintaining full control and presiding over such matters with little external interference. Similarly, the concerned State may also have an interest to not encroach upon religious affairs and thereby risk interfering with the religious freedom of the concerned spouses and religious communities. The ongoing debate in the Netherlands, that is elaborated in subchapters 3.3. and 3.4. illustrates this conundrum. Besides the different actors that are involved, account has also to be given to the fact that the legal status of religious marriages and divorces varies across jurisdictions. Consequently, the ways in which marital captivity manifests itself and the (legal) consequences that arise therefrom, for all the involved actors, will vary from one legal system to the other.

Answering the principal question requires taking the above factors into account, as these explain how marital captivity is manifested within a given national context, how trapped spouses are affected in the enjoyment of their human rights and the degree and manner in which States can and should intervene in situations of marital captivity. An understanding of how human rights law can serve as a tool to address marital captivity thus requires recognising the human rights that are involved, their implied State obligations, the multiple competing rights and interests and how these should be weighed against each other within a human rights framework. In other words, what human rights are at stake in a situation of marital captivity? What are the State obligations that arise from the affected human rights? How, should competing rights and interests within situations of marital captivity be balanced; which interests should be given precedence over the others and why? What are the implications of adopting a human rights-based approach and what is the relevance of a human rights discourse for the process of finding solutions? These are all questions that, to date, have remained largely unanswered and/or unaddressed and for which this contribution aims to provide some answers. Subchapter 1.5. elaborates further on and accounts for the specific human rights provisions that are investigated in the study. For now, it is more appropriate to elaborate briefly on the background of this contribution and the approach taken by the author.

The present contribution derives from a study that was part of a larger research project on marital captivity in the Netherlands (*NWO Marital captivity in the Netherlands-Bridging the Gap between religion and law*). This project aimed to bring clarity to the occurrence of marital captivity in the Netherlands and to contribute to finding (legal) solutions for ending or preventing situations of marital captivity.[10] It is for this reason that the present contribution addresses marital captivity as it it has been observed in the Netherlands within four religions: Christianity, Islam, Judaism and Hinduism.

Inclusion of the Netherlands is advantageous in that it enables an analysis of marital captivity within a national context. More specifically, it allows to clarify and illustrate the variety of situations of marital captivity and exemplify how a secular State, such as the Netherlands, accommodates and responds to a phenomenon that is inherently characterised by religious conditions. The religious dimension may, as mentioned above, form an additional hurdle for secular States, as they are challenged with finding a balance between competing human rights in such a way that aligns with their secular character. Furthermore, studying this phenomenon from a national context allows not only to illustrate the specific measures that have been adopted to counter marital captivity, but also allows to reveal the reasoning behind them and consider their respective advantages and limitations. Including a national context also allows for a comprehensive and realistic understanding of the potential that a human rights approach to marital captivity can bring. This can only contribute to the effective implementation and protection of human rights within situations of marital captivity.

To that end, and acknowledging the widespread occurrence of marital captivity, this contribution aims to offer a global perspective on the human rights dimension of marital captivity. Furthermore, the fact that most States are contracting parties to one or more of the human rights instruments, has as consequence that the questions raised in this contribution may be relevant and applicable to other States Parties to the human

10 *Marital Captivity: Bridging the gap between religion and law (MARICAP)*, (2014), *at* <www.maastrichtuniversity.nl/nl/over-de-um/faculteiten/rechtsgeleerdheid/capaciteitsgroepen/privaatrecht/projecten/echtscheiding-e-5> last accessed 24 January 2017.; Jamila Mejdoubi, *Factsheet- Wel gescheiden, niet gescheiden. Huwelijkse gevangenschap in Nederland*, (Universiteit Maastricht, Atria & Kennisinstituut voor emancipatie en vrouwengeschiedenis, 2016).; van Eijk, *Wel gescheiden, niet gescheiden? Een empirisch onderzoek naar huwelijkse gevangenschap in Nederland.*

rights instruments that are investigated in this contribution. Thus, the intended use of the results is not limited to the Netherlands or any other State for that matter. The circumstances that are specific for the Netherlands are discussed only insofar as these are necessary for highlighting the importance of integrating a human rights discourse within the phenomenon of marital captivity. Additionally, and where necessary, reference is also briefly made to developments in, and responses to, this phenomenon in other States, particularly in secular States.

Furthermore, a global perspective implies taking into consideration and assessing the implications of a human rights discourse for both secular and non-secular States. The relationship between the States and religious communities differs among States that are parties to the investigated human rights treaties. Consequently, the human rights obligations of States that incorporate religious laws within their legal system and recognise religious marriages and divorce may be different from the human rights obligations of secular States which do not recognise religious laws, marriages and divorces. It is thus, important to take this difference into account in order to ascertain a comprehensive picture of the role of States in addressing marital captivity.

In light of the foregoing, the following subchapter first explains some of the adopted terminologies in this contribution. Here after subchapter 1.3. elaborates further on marital captivity, its causes and consequences. This is followed up by an overview of the human rights discourse on marital captivity in subchapter 1.4. Subchapter 1.5. outlines the rights that will be investigated in this contribution. This is followed up by the methodology subchapter 1.6. Subsequently, subchapter 1.7 provides an outline of this contribution.

1.2. TERMINOLOGICAL CLARIFICATION

At this stage, it is crucial to first clarify several terminological concepts that will be used throughout this contribution. Within different legal systems, marriage and divorce can be established and obtained in different ways. Some States do not recognise civil forms of marriage, while other States only recognise civil forms of marriage and divorce. Some States also recognise religious marriages as legal and valid marriages. Thus, it is imperative to have an overview of the meaning that is attached to the concepts of 'marriage' and 'divorce' and how these may differ depending on the context.

'Marriage' refers to a formal marriage as well as an informal marriage. A formal marriage concerns a marriage that is given legal recognition. For example, only civil marriages have legal recognition in the Netherlands. Customary, traditional and religious marriages are not recognised and, other than the religious and social value attached thereto, they have no legal effect or meaning. Spouses can enter into both civil and religious, traditional or customary marriages. Spouses may also conclude only a civil marriage or only a religious, customary or traditional marriage. However, where they opt for the latter, spouses will not be considered married according to the law.[11] From the perspective of the Netherlands, these constitute informal marriages. In this contribution, reference is made to 'informal marriages' to indicate marriages that have no legal recognition.

The term 'religious marriage' refers to marriages conducted in accordance with religious rites. A religious marriage may be formal or informal and it will depend very much on the recognition that is given to such a marriage in each State. As mentioned, religious marriages that have been conducted in the Netherlands, in principle, constitute informal marriages. However, certain countries do acknowledge and give legal recognition to religious marriages.[12] Moreover, there are countries in which civil marriage has not been introduced and spouses can therefore only entertain a marriage in accordance with the various personal or customary laws.[13] Within such legal systems, religious marriages have the status of 'formal marriages', i.e. a legal and valid marriage.

Furthermore, religious marriages, may nevertheless be recognised in a legal system that, in principle, does not recognise religious marriages as formal marriages. This is the case when, for example, spouses to a religious marriage request the recognition of the religious marriage in that country, in accordance with the rules of private international law. Where the conditions are met, the formal religious marriage that has been concluded in one legal system, may then be registered as a legal and valid marriage in the other legal system, for example, the Netherlands.[14] In other words, a religious marriage may nevertheless constitute a formal marriage in the Netherlands, so long as it has been concluded in a legal and valid manner abroad and is recognised, as such, in the Netherlands.

---

11 Additionally, it is also prohibited to entertain a religious marriage prior to a civil marriage. *Dutch Civil Code (Burgerlijk Wetboek Boek 1, Personen- en familierecht)*, article 1:68.; Dutch Criminal Code *(Wetboek van Strafrecht)*, article 449 Sr.

12 For example, the United Kingdom, Italy, Spain or Syria. However, national laws may impose conditions (e.g. registration of the religious marriage) to the conclusion of a religious marriage. For a marriage to be valid within the country's legal system, the intended spouses have to comply with and meet the set conditions. van Eijk, *Wel gescheiden, niet gescheiden? Een empirisch onderzoek naar huwelijkse gevangenschap in Nederland*, pp. 15–16.

13 E.g. Iran, Israel, Jordan and Saudi Arabia to name but a few.

14 For example, a marriage concluded at the embassy in accordance with the personal laws of a State that grants legal status to religious and customary marriages, can be recognised in the Netherlands provided that neither of the spouses is Dutch. van Eijk, *Wel gescheiden, niet gescheiden? Een empirisch onderzoek naar huwelijkse gevangenschap in Nederland*, p. 16.

Scheme 1. Variations of marriage

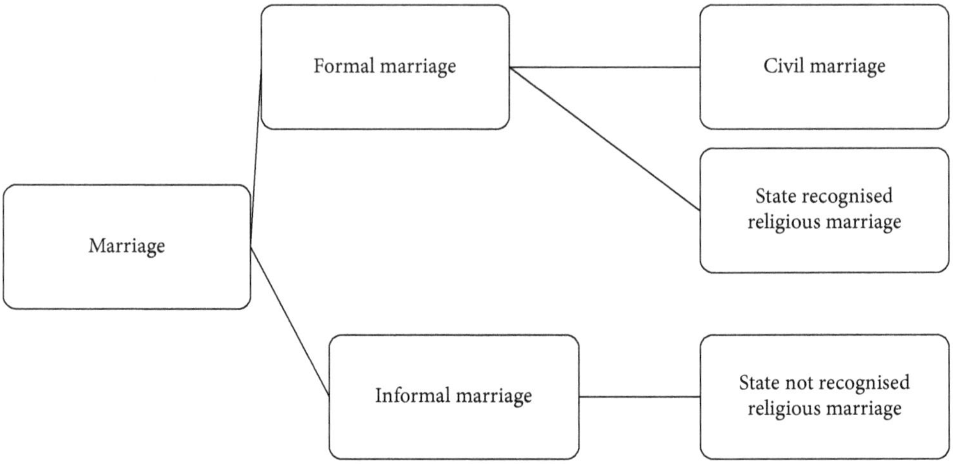

'Divorce' or 'the dissolution of a marriage' may also refer to the dissolution of a civil marriage, a religious marriage or both. It is therefore important to be aware of the marriage that is being terminated in a given situation, as the dissolution of each marriage may be governed by two separate normative systems i.e. civil law regulates the civil dissolution and religious laws regulate the religious dissolution. In principle, a civil divorce or annulment will not necessarily terminate a religious marriage. Consequently, spouses may be divorced civilly in accordance with the domestic laws, but they will still be married according to the religious laws and rules. This means that the concerned spouses will have to dissolve the marriage twice: once civilly and once religiously. However, there are some exceptions to this.

As will be seen in Chapter 2, in certain religious branches a civil divorce may also be recognised by and within the religious communities. In these circumstances, a civil divorce will then also impact the perceived religious union between the partners and they will no longer be considered married civilly and religiously. Furthermore, a civil divorce or annulment in one legal system, may also dissolve a State-recognised religious marriage in another legal system, once it has been recognised by that State. In this case, it will not only dissolve the religious marriage, but will also terminate the civil effects attached to such a marriage.

Similarly, a religious divorce or annulment will not, by definition, entail that the civil marriage ceases to exist. Spouses, who have performed both forms of marriage, may also be required to terminate the marriage legally, as well as in accordance with the religious rules on marriage. Where the marriage is governed by formal religious laws, a religious divorce or annulment will consequently terminate the religious marriage as well as the legal status attached thereto. It can then also be recognised in another State as terminating the recognised legal marriage there. The recognition of such a divorce in, for example, a another State, will then also mean that the civil effect awarded to the recognised religious marriage, by that State, will cease to exist.

Furthermore, in some countries a religious annulment may be recognised and enforced as terminating the formal legal marriage.[15] Additionally, a religious divorce conducted in a country that does not recognise religious divorces, may nevertheless be recognised in another country, provided that the laws of that country recognise foreign religious divorces.[16] Finally, where no State recognises a religious divorce or annulment, then this can be labelled as an informal divorce that has no legal status or effect. This mode of divorce only dissolves an informal religious marriage.

Scheme 2. Variations of divorce

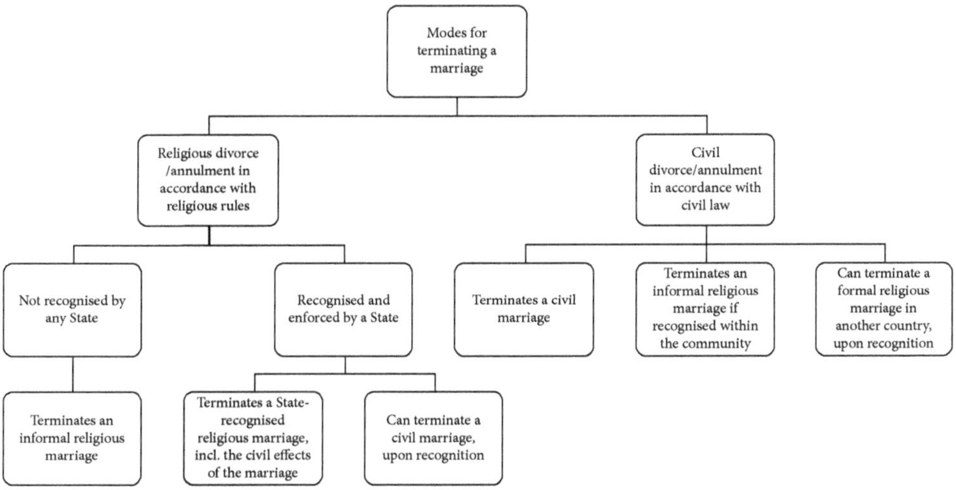

1.3. THE CAUSES AND CONSEQUENCES OF MARITAL CAPTIVITY

A situation of marital captivity arises as consequence of religious laws that either do not recognise divorce at all, are ambiguous on this matter, or afford one or both spouses very limited grounds for obtaining a divorce. Chapter 2 elaborates further on the religious doctrines that enable situations of marital captivity to arise and persist. Religious barriers may also include religious views and convictions on divorce that are upheld within the religious communities. These may trigger negative responses by

15 E.g. the Philippines. See also the case of European Court of Human Rights, *Pellegrini v. Italy,* 20 July 2001, Application No. 30882/96.

16 E.g. Saudi Arabia. See also the case *of Sulaiman v. Juffal* which involved Saudi nationals who performed a religious divorce (repudiation) on UK soil and had it registered at the Saudi Sharia Court. The religious divorce was, however, not recognised in the United Kingdom. High Court of Justice (Family Division), *Sulaiman v. Juffali,* 09 November 2001, [2001] EWHC556 (Fam), paras. 2, 8–11.

community members when these are transgressed (e.g. stigmatisation, social isolation, pressure from family and community members, religious sanctions etc.). As a result, these too may create barriers for the spouses in pursuing a religious or civil divorce (or both) and it may pressurise either of the spouses into remaining in a broken and at times even violent marriage. It should be born in mind that the religious barriers to divorce may also operate beyond the religious sphere, where religious laws are incorporated into State law. In these cases, spouses may then be trapped in a religious marriage which may also be legally recognised by the State (i.e. a formal marriage).

It is also important to point out that the degree of restrictions that trapped spouses experience in a situation of marital captivity, will partly depend on the importance that is attached to religious convictions concerning the institution of marriage by both or either of the spouses and their immediate religious community. Some spouses may attach less value and significance to the religious character of a religious marriage. This may, for example, be the case if they are not actively practising their faith, have changed or denounced their faith or are satisfied with a civil divorce and do not feel the need to dissolve the religious marriage. Therefore, while a situation of marital captivity may exist, in practice the problems experienced vary among trapped spouses and will very much depend on the significance and importance that is attached to the extant marriage by the spouses themselves and by their religious communities.

Apart, from the personal and social significance attached to a still existing marriage by spouses and their community, the recognition of a religious marriage may also have actual legal consequences in that country.[17] Therefore, the still existing religious marriage may affect the trapped spouse's status and rights in that country, irrespective of the personal and social significance which either or both spouses attach to that marriage.

1.3.1. MARITAL CAPTIVITY AS A WOMEN'S ISSUE

While both men and women can become trapped in a religious marriage against their will, practice reveals that marital captivity disproportionately affects women.[18] This is because women, in some religions, have limited options to initiate a religious divorce and have to secure the cooperation of their husbands in order to obtain a divorce.[19] Consequently, husbands can maintain control over their wives by withholding cooperation to the religious divorce thereby effectively holding their wives hostage in the religious marriage.

---

17 Van Eijk, *Wel gescheiden, niet gescheiden? Een empirisch onderzoek naar huwelijkse gevangenschap in Nederland*, p. 89.

18 Id., p. 90.; Eliane Smits van Waesberghe, et al., *Zo zijn we niet getrouwd: Een onderzoek naar omvang en aard van huwelijksdwang, achterlating en huwelijkse gevangenschap*, (2014), pp. 10,14.

19 The grounds for divorce within Catholicism, Protestantism, Hinduism, Islam and Judaism are described in Chapter 2.

On top of that, the existing power imbalance at the dissolution of the marriage between wives and husbands is reinforced by the fact that men are guaranteed social and religious privileges that women are not. For example, husbands may, in some religions, terminate the religious marriage unilaterally or may, under certain circumstances, have multiple wives.[20] This is particularly the case when certain communities and countries approve of or condone polygamy (e.g. in certain Muslim communities and countries) or bigamy (e.g. rabbinical law permitting, in limited circumstances, a trapped husband to remarry while the first religious marriage continues to exist).[21] Therefore, even in the event that husbands are trapped in a marriage, they are not limited in their rights and lives in the same way that women are.

The fact that marital captivity affects women disproportionately highlights the gender aspects inherent within situations of marital captivity. This is particularly observable in the existing power disparities between wives and husbands at the dissolution of the religious marriage, that are upheld in, and prescribed by, certain religions. Efforts to find solutions to prevent and end situations of marital captivity need to take the existing power imbalances between women and men into account.

For this reason, the present contribution addresses the gender dynamics and power imbalances that are inherent in situations of marital captivity. In this respect recognition is given to the fact marital captivity is primarily a women's issue since that women are disproportionately affected. This approach allows to study the inherent power imbalances between married women and men within a human rights framework, even though these are in fact prescribed by religion. Also, it enhances a gender sensitive approach to marital captivity which permits to study and recognise the specific ways in which women are affected by and victimized within situations of marital captivity. This in turn contributes to reaching sustainable solutions to end and prevent marital captivity that are tailored to the needs of trapped women. Thirdly, and related hereto, studying marital captivity as a women's issue enables to explore the phenomenon holistically by including societal factors and structures that increase the risks of women becoming trapped in a religious marriage (e.g. cultural and religious views and practices that undermine the trapped women's rights, domestic violence, inequalities in divorce rights etc.).

The focus on marital captivity as a women's issue, however, does not mean or imply that men are not or cannot be victims of marital captivity. Men too can be affected by a situation of marital captivity and may have to deal with the consequences of having to remain married against their will, although this occurs in far more limited instances. Additionally, the consequences and impact of marital captivity for trapped husbands

20 In general, at the dissolution of the marriage men are guaranteed privileges that women are not within the Islamic and Jewish faiths. For further details in the religious rules within these religions see subchapter 2.3. and 2.4.

21 See *supra* note 196 and 235

are, in some religious groups, mitigated somewhat by social and religious privileges (e.g. the capacity to remarry).[22] Where a situation of marital captivity infringes upon and obscures the trapped husbands' rights, the human rights framework adopted in this contribution is equally relevant and is largely applicable to their plight.

It should be borne in mind that the discriminatory aspects will not be present in all situations of marital captivity involving a trapped husband (e.g. when both the husband and the wife have restricted grounds to dissolve or annul the religious marriage). Therefore, it is important to point out that the passages of this contribution that address the discriminatory aspects of marital captivity, are mainly applicable for situations of marital captivity where there are power imbalances between wives and husbands.

1.3.2. THE CONSEQUENCES OF A SITUATION OF MARITAL CAPTIVITY

Laila, at the age of 19 marrieds a man in Palestine in accordance with the domestic personal laws. They moved to the Netherlands and years later they divorce in accordance with Dutch secular law, after the husband has left the familial home. According to Dutch law they are divorced, but according to Islamic law they are still married. Also, for her social environment Laila is still considered as being married even if this is not the case and everyone is aware of the fact that the former partner has left her. She wants to also end this religious marriage in Palestine, for which she needs cooperation from her husband but her former partner informs her that he has no intention to cooperate with this divorce. He has also accused her of adultery and is using the religious marriage as a means to blackmail Laila which makes obtaining the religious divorce in Palestine all the more difficult.[23]

This account, as well as the previous case of Yeuhudis, demonstrate the far-reaching consequences of marital captivity for trapped woman. A situation of marital captivity can have legal and social consequences for the trapped spouses and may be detrimental to the mental health and overall well-being of the trapped spouse. In fact, as the case of Laila demonstrates, trapped women may also be faced with legal and social consequences in their country of origin, where the religious marriage has not yet been dissolved. Although the extent, form, degree and severity of these consequences will differ from one case to case, the following paragraphs discuss these consequences in general.

1.3.2.1. Restrictions in establishing new relationships

A situation of marital captivity will primarily affect the trapped spouse's possibilities to form relationships with new partners. Remarriage or the formation of new relationships may be impossible or have negative social and/or legal consequences. New relationships,

22 See also subchapter 2.3. and 2.4.

23 Van Eijk, *Wel gescheiden, niet gescheiden? Een empirisch onderzoek naar huwelijkse gevangenschap in Nederland*, Annex II (translation Dutch to English by Benedicta Deogratias).

for example, may be considered as acts of adultery. As adultery is an offence in some States, trapped spouses who entertain new relationships with a significant other may additionally have to face the legal consequences, for having established a new relationship. The inability to remarry also implies that the prospective spouses cannot establish family life on the basis of marriage and take benefit from the legal and social advantages that arise from the status of being married. Consequently, the trapped spouse's quality of life is affected due to the limitations they may experience in moving on and shaping their lives freely.[24]

As already mentioned, the degree to which a trapped spouse experiences these limitations varies between the sexes. As a result of the social and religious privileges that men enjoy, trapped men may experience milder restraints as they are allowed to form new partnerships without being held accountable for committing adultery.[25] Whereas women who wish to engage in new partnerships experience far more restrictions as this may be perceived as an act of adultery within the community or even constitute an act of adultery in the country of origin.[26] The social reaction to an adulteress wife may range from gossip and stigmatisation to more far reaching sanctions, such as honour-related crimes and potentially even criminal prosecution in the country of origin. Fear of shaming, shunning and possible prosecution in the country of origin for committing adultery, may influence the woman's decision to abstain from establishing partnerships. Therefore, it is of paramount importance to recognise the different ways in which women and men experience and are affected by situations of marital captivity in their everyday choices and overall quality of life.

Leaving the religious community or exploring another religion could be an option. However, one must take into account the significance that religion may have for the adherent. Both religious dogmas and religious communities can serve as vital sources of emotional support as well as sources of encouragement, confidence and resilience in times of hardship. Membership of a religious community may also provide and reinforce a sense of belonging and identity of the adherent. The more prominent this significance is, the harder it becomes to detach oneself from the religion. In addition, having to relinquish one's own participation and involvement in a religious community, may nevertheless lead to social isolation from family, friends and other members of the religious community.[27]

1.3.2.2. Difficulties in leaving a violent environment

Marital captivity is a complex phenomenon that often involves additional factors that increase the vulnerability of, in particular, trapped wives to further abuse. A matter of

---

24 Id., pp. 68,71–72.

25 See sections 2.3.2. and 2.4.2.

26 Van Eijk, *Wel gescheiden, niet gescheiden? Een empirisch onderzoek naar huwelijkse gevangenschap in Nederland*, pp. 68,71–72.

27 Id., pp. 70–72.

great concern involves the presence of domestic violence between the spouses. More often than not women and girls are victims of domestic violence. In itself, the presence of violence and the fear of violence can discourage women who wish to terminate their marriage, thereby keeping them in a state of marital captivity for much longer.[28] Besides violence husbands can also go so far as to isolate their wives by limiting and excessively controlling their wives' activities and interactions outside of the familial house.[29] By physically and socially isolating the trapped wife, circumstances of dependency of the trapped wife on her husband, are created and reinforced. Besides fear and violence, factors of dependency also make it even harder for the wife to leave a violent and controlling partner.[30] On top of that, religious barriers to divorce, including any negative views and convictions on divorce that are prevalent within the religious communities, may also discourage spouses from leaving a violent relationship.[31]

In turn, an ongoing situation of marital captivity can facilitate the commission and escalation of violence.[32] This is more so where the wife is trapped in a violent marriage, which she is unable to terminate. The ongoing situation of marital captivity enables a potentially violent spouse to continue having a certain degree of control over the trapped wife. This controlling factor is only reinforced when the trapped wife needs to secure the cooperation of the violent spouse in order to dissolve the religious marriage. Thus, the victim of the ongoing violence may be required to confront and interact with their aggressor, which may increase the likelihood of further victimisation. Fear of having to confront the violent spouse and the fear of being victimised can, in turn, impair the trapped woman's efforts in securing a religious divorce and consequently ending all ties with a violent partner.[33] Essentially, this creates a dangerous situation for the trapped wives who are then unable to leave a violent relationship.

Additionally, where a woman does decide to go through with the divorce, this may be perceived as an act of transgression and a violation of the families and non-cooperative spouse's honour and reputation. In turn, this may incentivise the commission of acts of violence against that spouse as a response to the violated honour and reputation. In one such case, a man killed his ex-wife after she had divorced him and declined all and any interaction with him. The religious marriage had not yet been dissolved.[34] The perpetrator, as well as the *imam*, who was interrogated, continued

[28] Id., pp. 61, 65.

[29] In the 2014 research on marital captivity in the Netherlands it was discovered there are women who are forced to live isolated from society. These are referred to as 'hidden wives' (*verborgen vrouwen).* Thus, the wife may not only be trapped in the marriage against her will, but she may also be physically trapped in a violent and unsafe environment. van Waesberghe, et al., *Zo zijn we niet getrouwd: Een onderzoek naar omvang en aard van huwelijksdwang, achterlating en huwelijkse gevangenschap*, (2014), p. 14.

[30] Van Eijk, *Wel gescheiden, niet gescheiden? Een empirisch onderzoek naar huwelijkse gevangenschap in Nederland*, pp. 13, 63.

[31] Id., p. 27.

[32] Id., p. 65.

[33] See for example the case of Kirsten as described in: van Eijk, *Wel gescheiden, niet gescheiden? Een empirisch onderzoek naar huwelijkse gevangenschap in Nederland*, p. 50.

[34] Rechtbank Groningen, 11 October 2010, ECLI:NL: RBGRO:2010:BO0132. See also Hoge Raad, 24 June 2014, ECLI:NL:HR:2014:1500, para. 2.2.2.

to refer to the victim as the wife of the perpetrator. He could not accept that she had ended the relationship and refused to divorce her. In his opinion, a divorced man was not a man. Her persistence to be free from him not only incentivised his continual harassment but eventually led him to deliberately robbing her of her life.

It is also important to highlight how religious tribunals/authorities attend to violence occurring within a marriage, as trapped women may seek to secure a religious divorce via these agencies. Several studies have revealed, the responses of religious authorities to marital captivity and domestic/ partner violence within the marriage can complicate the dissolution of the religious marriage further and even facilitate the commission of further violence against the trapped wife.[35]

1.3.2.3. Exploitation of the weak position of the trapped wife

Another area of concern is the weak position that certain trapped women are in when have in effectuating a religious divorce. The unequal divorce rights between spouses that are prescribed in certain religions norms are prone to abuse by the husband. Religious norms that grant the husband an exclusive right to unilaterally terminate the marriage at will, consequently enable husbands to retain a degree of control over their wives, as they can withhold cooperation and delay the divorce process. Furthermore, a calculating husband may exploit this imbalance to make unfair, unjust and unreasonable demands in exchange for a divorce.[36] The recalcitrant spouse may, for

---

[35] On *Sharī'a Councils* in the United Kingdom see: Cerian C. Griffiths, 'Sharia and Beth Din courts in the United Kingdom: is legal pluralism nothing more than a necessary political fiction', 15 *Studia Iuridica Torniensia* 39–51, (2004), pp. 44–45.; Machteld Zee, *Choosing Sharia? Multiculturalism, Islamic Fundamentalism and Sharia Councils* (The Hague, 2016), pp. 123–143.; Colleen Shannon-Lewy and Valeria T. Dull, 'The response of Christian clergy to domestic violence: Help or Hindrance?', 10 *Aggression and Violent behaviour* 647–659, (2005).; Belinda Richardson, *Christian Clergy Response to Intimate Partner Violence: Attitudes, Training, Or Religious Views?*, (2007) (Purdue University), pp. 35–37.; Heidi M. Levitt and Kimberly N. Ware, 'Religious leaders' perspectives on marriage, divorce, and intimate partner violence', 30 *Psychology of Women Quarterly* 212–222, (2006), pp. 216–218.; Christine Rzepka-Hagion,' Religious views & domestic violence', *The Ripple Effect*. For example, where certain religious denomination and religious authorities uphold the right of, or condone husbands to discipline their wives, justifications for such practices may be alleged to derive from religious doctrines of male domination over women or may be condoned practices within certain religious communities and religious denominations. Some examples of these are found in all four religions: Eliyahu Touger, *The Rambam's Mishneh Torah (English translatoin by Eliyahu Touger)*, Sefer Nashim, Ishut para. 21.10.; *The Qur'an (English translation by Sahih International)*, An-Nisa 34.; *The Holy Bible, New International Version, 1 Corinthians 11:3.*; Bühler, *The laws of Manu*, chapter IX, paras. 2–3. See also, Rzepka-Hagion, *Religious views & domestic violence*. Religious courts may also at times jeopardise the safety of abused women or marginalise their experiences, by holding them responsible for the violence committed against them, encouraging them to go back into violent relationships or demanding that the spouses meet for reconciliation purposes. Lengthy or unsuccessful religious divorce processes may add difficulties for those women who want to leave a violent relationship and environment.

[36] Van Eijk, *Wel gescheiden, niet gescheiden? Een empirisch onderzoek naar huwelijkse gevangenschap in Nederland*, pp. 65, 72–74. The incident of a rabbi extorting lump sums from trapped women is another

example, exploit his privileged position to secure child custody rights, financial gains or demand that the trapped wife relinquishes her rights and financial claims in exchange for the divorce. This imbalance is further weakened by the little protection that *Sharia Councils* and *Beth dins* afford to the rights of women. These dispute settlement mechanisms have been criticised frequently for their discriminatory treatment of women and for not protecting women's rights adequately.[37]

1.3.2.4. Cross-border complications

Where both or either of the spouses has ties with more than one country, for example on grounds of being a national, citizen or originating from a foreign country, a situation of marital captivity can severely impair the cross-border movement of the trapped wife. One such complication is that of a 'limping' personal status, whereby spouses are married in one State yet divorced in another. The uncertainty of the marital status can restrict women when travelling to or leaving their country of origin. This is particularly the case when wife's ability to obtain travel documents or to travel to, from or within the country of origin is made conditional on the approval of the (ex-) husband. For example, in certain Muslim majority countries, such as Iran and Saudi Arabia, the husband or male guardian's approval/cooperation is necessary for the wife to travel. One may assume that if the husband is reluctant to cooperate with the religious divorce, he will most certainly exhibit a similar attitude in giving his approval to his 'wife's' travelling activities.[38] Therefore, where the trapped wife wishes to travel, she may encounter difficulties in travelling to or from the said destination/ country.

---

clear example of the weak position of trapped women and how the unequal bargaining positions can be exploited to take advantage of trapped women. Antonia Blumberg, 'Michel Gugenheim, French Chief Rabbi, Accused Of Extortion Over Religious Divorce', *Huffing Post* 12 May 2014, *at* <www.huffingtonpost.com/2014/05/12/michel-gugenheim-extortion_n_5309341.html> 27 December 2015. See also Rosenberg, *Praying for divorce: The abuse of Jewish women through Jewish divorce law*, pp. 238–239.; Rachael Charlotte Proudman, *Equal and free? Evidence in support of Baroness Cox's arbitration and dediation services (Equality) Bill*, (2012), pp. 17, 20–21, 29–30, 33.

37 Proudman, *Equal and free? Evidence in support of Baroness Cox's arbitration and dediation services (Equality) Bill*, pp. 17, 20–21.; Leichter, *The effect of Jewish divorce law on family law litigation*, p. 4.; Jane Corbin, *Secrets of Britain's Sharia Councils* (22 April 2013).; Radhika Coomaraswamy, *Report of the Special Rapporteur on violenc against women, its causes and consequences: Cultural practices in the family that are violent towards women*, (Economic and Social Council, 2002), [E/CN.4/2002/83], paras. 7, 66, 69; United Nations Secretary-General, *In-depth study on all forms of violence against women: Report of the Secretary-General*, (United Nations General Assembly, 2006), [A/61/122/Add.1], para. 78.; Riki Holtmaat, 'Article 5', in Freeman, et al. *The UN Convention on the Elimination of All forms of Discrimination against women: A commentary* (Oxford, 2012), pp. 156–157.

38 Oreste Rossi 'Question for written answer P-007842/12 to the Commission (Vice President/High Representative)', *Official Journal of the European Union*, 5 September 2012, p. 122.; 'Chiara Invernizzi: dieci mesi ostaggio del marito arabo ', *Blitz Quotidiano* 24 December 2012. In this case an Italian woman was trapped in Saudi Arabia after her former partner refused to give her the necessary approval to leave Saudi Arabia. This prevented her from returning to her home. This case is further discussed in subsection 6.2.3.2.

Other restrictions on travelling to the country of origin may find their roots in the fear of being prosecuted in the country of origin[39], where the recalcitrant husband has reported an act of adultery by the trapped wife, or the fear of losing custody over one's children, as the laws of that country may grant custody rights to the recalcitrant husband. Prior knowledge of such probabilities may influence the woman's decision to visit her country of origin. Such was the case of an Iranian woman who abstained from visiting her ill mother in Iran, out of fear of losing her children to the recalcitrant husband's family.[40] While divorced in the Netherlands, the registration of the divorce in Iran required cooperation from the husband, who turned out to be non-cooperative. Consequently, they were still considered married in Iran, as the requirements for divorce according to Iranian family law, which is based on Islamic religious rules, require the husband's cooperation.

1.4. MARITAL CAPTIVITY IN HUMAN RIGHTS DISCOURSE

The majority of studies on marital captivity have focused on this issue as it occurs in Islam and Judaism.[41] In this regard, prominent attention has been placed on exploring the rationale behind the religious interpretations, factors that account for marital captivity, creating/finding solutions within the religious communities and the impact of foreign religious normative systems in secular States. Notably, human rights are being invoked increasingly within the dialogue on marital captivity by grieving groups, civil society, scholars, legislators and national judiciaries. As such, reference has been made to, *inter alia,* the right to family life, the right to remarry, the right to privacy and the right to freedom and security.[42] Other implied rights that have been raised include the right to

---

39 Susan Rutten, Esther van Eijk, Lisanne Drost, Khadija Kadrouch-Outmany and Eliane Smits van Waesberghe, *Gewoon getrouwd: Een onderzoek naar kindhuwelijken en religieuze huwelijken in Nederland*, (2015), pp. 124–125. See also the case of Laila described in section 1.3.2.

40 Rechtbank Overijssel, 24 December 2013, ECLI:NL: RBOVE:013: 4269.
van Eijk, *Wel gescheiden, niet gescheiden? Een empirisch onderzoek naar huwelijkse gevangenschap in Nederland*, pp. 73–75.

41 Some examples are: Benjamin Shmueli, "Civil actions for acts that are valid according to religious family law but harm women's rights: Legal pluralism in cases of collision between two sets of laws", 46 *Vanderbilt Journal of Transnational Law* 823–897, (2012), pp. 823–897.; Leichter, *The effect of Jewish divorce law on family law litigation.*; Shamreeza Riaz, 'Shariah perspective on marriage contract and practice in contemporary Muslim societies', 3 *International Journal of Social Science and Humanity* 263–267, (2013).; Lynn D. Wardle, 'Marriage and religious liberty: Comparative law problems and conflict of laws solutions', 12 *Journal of Law & Family Studies* 315–364, (2010).; Susan M. Weiss and Netty C. Gross-Horowitz, *Marriage and divorce in the Jewish state: Israel's civil war* (2013).

42 Rutten, *Protection of spouses in informal marriages by human rights*, p. 90.; Guy Fitoussi, *Essai comparatif et critique du rôle du juge dans le procédure de divorce entre le système judiciaire français et israélien*, (2007) (University of Paris 8), pp. 84–85.; Supreme Court of Canada, *Bruker v. Marcovitz,* 14 December 2007, 3 S.C.R. 607, 2007 SCC 54, para. 82.; Weiss and Gross-Horowitz, *Marriage and divorce in the Jewish state: Israel's civil war*, p. 167–188.

culture, the right not to be a victim of one's own culture[43], the right to develop as a person, the right not to be humiliated[44], the right to due process in the rabbinical courts[45] and the (equal) right to divorce.[46] The latter are, however, not stated as such in most human rights treaties but they may, nonetheless, be implied in existing human rights provisions. The existence and scope of protection thereof, may thus require further inquiry.

Additionally, marital captivity has also been raised within the context of violence against women, although without necessarily making reference to human rights provisions or the human rights framework in general. Rosenberg for example conceptualises *get*[47] denial as a form of violence against women, which she coins as 'get abuse'. In her analysis, she underlines the nature of *get* denial as a *'coercive control tactic'* which husbands exploit in order to (maintain) control and even punish their wives. The link to violence against women is reflected by *'the husband's use of power and control during get denial which is extremely abusive in its intent and consequence for agunot, causing the women emotional anguish and sometimes physical pain as well as the marital constraint'*.[48] While this observation accurately describes a situation of marital captivity, the analysis stops there without any further reference to human rights law as such. In addition, the implications of classifying *get* denial as a form of violence against women, in terms of the State's and society's required responses is left largely unaddressed. Rather the aim seems to be the mere classification of *get* denial (marital captivity) as a form of violence against women and to demonstrate the underlying ideology that gives rise to such a classification (i.e. the husbands' power over their wives and the abuse thereof).[49]

No doubt, the inclusion and reference to human rights can have the advantage of attaching a degree of seriousness and importance to the issue of marital captivity. The inclusion of human rights language may also facilitate increasing public awareness and mobilising the political will to respond adequately. A refined human rights discourse, however, which not only provides for an in-depth analysis of the claimed human rights in terms of their scope and limitations, but which also attends to State's obligations to prevent, protect and fulfil these rights, may increase the impact and effectiveness of responses by all stakeholders and lead to sustainable solutions to prevent and end situations of marital captivity.

---

43 Ruth Halperin-Kaddari, *Agunot in Israel- A study*, (JOFA – NYU Tikvah Agunah Summit), *at* <https://www.jofa.org/Summit_Proceedings> last accessed 29 November 2016, p. 1.

44 Rutten, *Protection of spouses in informal marriages by human rights*, p. 90; Fitoussi, *Essai comparatif et critique du rôle du juge dans le procédure de divorce entre le système judiciaire français et israélien*, pp. 84–85.

45 Weiss and Gross-Horowitz, *Marriage and divorce in the Jewish state: Israel's civil war*, pp. 175–185.

46 Human Rights Watch, 'Divorced from justice- Women's unequal acces to divorce in Egypt', *at* <www.hrw.org/node/11887/section/6> November 2015.; Weiss and G ross-Horowitz, *Marriage and Divorce in the Jewish State: Israel's Civil War*, pp. 166–169.

47 A writ of divorce.

48 Rosenberg, *Praying for divorce: The abuse of Jewish women through Jewish divorce law*, p. 217.

49 Id., p. 228.

National courts and governmental bodies that have addressed the issue of marital captivity have also made reference to specific human rights of the trapped spouses which are at stake in a situation of marital captivity. Reference has been made to the notions of violence against women and domestic violence[50], gender equality, human dignity, and the ability to remarry.[51] This has occasionally taken place within the context of the scope and limitations of the freedom of religion. However, thus far national case law has provided little guidance in respect of the substance of these rights and principles, and even less with regards to the State's obligations that arise from these rights.

What can also be seen is the increasing attention that is being paid to the issue of marital captivity by human rights institutions on both international and regional levels. Initially, reference to situations of marital captivity were captured in statements concerning restrictive and discriminatory marital practices, customs and laws in a number of countries that adversely affect women or violate their rights. For example, the United Nations Committee on the Elimination of Discrimination Against Women (CEDAW Committee) has occasionally pointed out that the personal laws[52] of certain countries may impose discriminatory restrictions on women who seek a divorce, which would contravene the right of equality during the dissolution of the marriage (Article 16 (1) (c) CEDAW).[53] The Committee has also dealt with the *agunah* problem as occurring in Israel, in its 2011 concluding observations to the fifth periodic report of Israel.[54] Most notably, the issue of marital captivity was raised explicitly by the CEDAW Committee in its reaction to the 6th periodic report of the Netherlands, after this phenomenon had been brought to the attention of the Committee by means of shadow reports.[55] The Committee

50 Ministerie van Volksgezondheid Welzijn en Sport, *Huwelijkse gevangenschap - Huiselijk geweld,* (2014), *at* <www.huiselijkgeweld.nl/dossiers/campagne_huwelijksdwang/beleid/huwelijkse-gevangenschap> last accessed 27 December 2015.

51 Supreme Court of Canada, *Bruker v. Marcovitz,* 14 December 2007, 3 S.C.R. 607, 2007 SCC 54, paras. 63, 92.; High Court of South Africa, *Singh v. Ramparsad* (KZN564/2002) ZAKZHC 1, paras. 45, 53.

52 Some States include one or more personal laws within their legal systems. India and Israel are examples of States that incorporate personal laws. Family matters, marriage and divorce, matters of personal status are, for example, regulated in accordance with, Hindu law, Islamic, Jewish Law or Christian based laws. Consequently, Hindu Law will apply to the marriage and divorce of a Hindu couple, Islamic based law will apply to a Muslim couple, Jewish Law will apply to a Jewish couple and so on. Some countries provide also civil law as an option, for which individuals can opt instead of the personal laws. Thus, in States that enforce personal laws individuals may be subjected to different legal systems, as these are applied pursuant to the individuals' assigned religion.

53 Committee on the Elimination of Discrimination Against Women, *Concluding Observations Kazakhstan 2007,* (2007), CEDAW/C/KAZ/CO/2, para. 29.; Committee on the Elimination of Discrimination Against Women, *Concluding observations Zambia 2002,* A/57/38 part II, paras. 222, 230. See also Marsha Freeman, 'Article 16', in Freeman, et al. *The UN Convention on the Elimination of All Forms of Discrimination Against Women: A commentary* (New York, 2012), pp. 417–420.

54 Committee on the Elimination of Discrimination Against Women, *Concluding Observations Israel 2011,* CEDAW/C/ISR/CO/5, paras. 48–49.

55 See for example, *Netherlands Institute for Human Rights - Written Contribution to the 65th session of the UN Committee on the Elimination of Discrimination Against Women (CEDAW) on behalf of the consideration of the sixth periodic report of the Netherlands,* (College voor de Rechten van de Mens, 2016), p. 2.

has expressed its concerns on the little information that the State had provided concerning the application of the 'tort-action' by Dutch judges.[56] It recommended the State to '*conduct awareness raising campaigns and training on marital captivity for the judiciary and law enforcement officials in order to eradicate this phenomenon*'.[57]

Likewise, the Special Rapporteur on freedom and religion and belief concluded that the religious divorce restrictions imposed on women in certain States are discriminatory and infringe upon women's rights.[58] The Special Rapporteur has, in this regard, urged the competent (religious) authorities to ensure equal treatment of spouses during the dissolution of the marriage and to respect their human rights.[59] Similarly, the Special Rapporteur on violence against women added the practice of *get* denial within divorce procedures in Israel's Rabbinical courts to the list of '*cultural practices that are harmful to women*', therefore highlighting the link between marital captivity in a Jewish marriage and violence against women.[60]

The issue of marital captivity has also been identified, on two occasions, by both the African Commission as well as the Special Rapporteur on the rights of women.[61] In the Concluding observations to the 7th and 8th periodic report of Egypt, the Commission reserved concerns in respect of Egypt's divorce proceedings.[62] A clearer statement was made by the Special Rapporteur in the report of the Mission in Djibouti. This report briefly discussed situations in which women have poor defences when they cannot manage to dissolve the marriage. The Special Rapporteur established that lawyers did not appear when the case was being adjudicated by the *Cadi* (who judges on the basis of *Shari'a*). Unfortunately, the report did not go as far as to link this situation to any right, nor did it indicate whether the Government of Djibouti had the obligation to rectify this situation.[63]

In terms of jurisprudence, to date only one case related to the issue of marital captivity has been dealt with by the European Commission of Human Rights.[64] This case, *D. v.*

---

56 The tort-action is elaborated further in section 3.4.1.

57 Committee on the Elimination of Discrimination Against Women, *Concluding Observations to the Netherlands 2016*, CEDAW/C/NLD/CO/6, paras. 43(d), 44 (d).

58 Abdelfattah Amor, *Étude sur la liberté de religion ou de conviction et la condition de la femme au regard de la religion et des traditions*, (2002), paras. 120–122.

59 Id., p. 49.

60 Asma Jahangir, *Report of the Special Rapporteur on freedom of religion or belief Asma Jahangir – Mission to Israel and the Occupied Palestinian Territory*, (Human Rights Council, 12 January 2009), [A/HRC/10/8/Add.2], paras. 49,71.

61 The Special Rapporteur on Rights of Women is also mandated to assist the African Governments in the development and implementation of the Maputo protocol.

62 African Commission on Human and People's Rights, *Concluding Observations Egypt* 2005, 37th Ordinary Session of the African Commission on Human and People's Rights, para. 21.

63 African Commission on Human and Peoples' Rights, *Report on the Promotional Mission Undertaken by Commissioner Kamel Rezag Bara to the Republic of Djibouti, (African Commission on Human and Peoples' Rights*, (Kairaba 2005), [DOC/OS(XXVIII)/187/6], para. 32.

64 European Commission of Human Rights, *D. v. France*, 6 December 1983, Application No. 10180/82, p. 199.

France, was initiated by a recalcitrant spouse who had been ordered to pay reparations to his ex-wife, to whom he had denied a *get*. The plaintiff alleged that the French court's order to compensate his ex-wife with a monetary sum for the harm caused by his non-cooperation to a Jewish divorce violated his religious freedom. Therefore, the Commission did not address the issue of marital captivity as such and thus did not attend to it.[65] Neither did it indicate any specific human rights of the ex-spouse that might be infringed by a *get* denial. Notably, the more recent case of *Babiarz v. Poland*[66] concerned a situation of marital captivity that, however, was not founded on religious barriers to divorce. In this case, the situation of marital captivity was created by the Polish divorce laws. The details and relevancy of this case are discussed in Chapter 5.

The above shows a growing trend of engaging a human rights discourse. The inclusion of human rights considerations has engendered a degree of seriousness to the issue of marital captivity. This, in turn, facilitates advancing public awareness and mobilising the public debate on the issue of marital captivity. The dialogue, however, has rarely gone beyond referencing certain specific rights. Little interpretation and direction has been provided in respect of the alleged human rights that are infringed by a situation of marital captivity and little has been said about the role of the State in terms of preventing such violations and protecting the rights of the trapped spouse(s). Similarly, answers on how to then balance the seemingly competing rights (i.e. the trapped spouse's rights *vis-à-vis* the freedom of religion), have remained largely unaddressed.

1.5. ADOPTING A HUMAN RIGHTS APPROACH TO MARITAL CAPTIVITY

As previously mentioned, the research question of this contribution is:

In what ways does a human rights approach contribute to the process of finding solutions to prevent and end situations of marital captivity?

From this question the four sub-questions arise:
- What specific human rights are at stake in a situation of marital captivity?
- What are the State obligations that flow from the affected human rights?
- How should competing rights and interests within situations of marital captivity be balanced?
- What are the implications of adopting a human rights-based approach and what is the relevance of a human rights discourse for the process of finding solutions?

65 More on this case see subsection 4.4.2.1.
66 European Court of Human Rights, *Babiarz v. Poland,* 10 January 2017, Application No. 1955/10.

With regards to the first sub-question, a number of substantive human rights and principles are selected and studied. These are briefly discussed in the following sections. It is imperative to stress that this contribution does not aim or attempt to provide an exhaustive examination of all human rights that could possibly be affected within a situation of marital captivity or analyse the entire catalogue of human rights. Such an exercise would go beyond the purpose of this contribution which is to use human rights as a tool to address marital captivity. Rather, the aim of this contribution is to promote and include a human rights based approach in the efforts to find solutions to end and prevent marital captivity.

The second sub-question serves the purpose of outlining the State's obligations which derive from the rights under investigation. Establishing the corresponding human rights obligations permits the identification of what responses are expected from the State.

The third sub-question deals with the competing interests and rights that are at the heart of situations of marital captivity. It is commonly acknowledged that human rights are indivisible, interdependent and interrelated. This means that human rights are equal and that there exists, in fact, no hierarchy between the guaranteed rights. The fact that some rights have a peremptory character (such as the right to be free from torture and the prohibition from slavery), may not be derogated from under any circumstances (e.g. the right to freedom of religion)[67], should be realised immediately (e.g. non-discrimination) or rather progressively (e.g. economic, social and cultural rights), is not indicative of a hierarchy. Therefore, where there are competing interests and rights which demand protection, a fair balance has to be struck.

The fourth sub-question deliberates upon the benefits of a human rights approach to the process of finding solutions and underscores why it is relevant to involve a human rights approach to the ongoing discussions concerning marital captivity.

1.5.1. THE SELECTED HUMAN RIGHTS

In light of the first sub-question, a number of substantive human rights provisions have been selected and are examined in this contribution. These are:

- the freedom of religion,
- the right to divorce,
- the right to remarry,
- the right to respect for private life,
- the right to freedom of movement,
- the right to health, and
- the right to be free from violence against women

67 UN Human Rights Committee 'General Comment No. 22: Article 18 (Freedom of thought, conscience or religion)', 1993, CCPR/C/21/Rev.1/Add.4, para. 1.

The selection of these rights warrants further elaboration. Firstly, the religious aspects that are inherent in situations of marital captivity are factors that cannot simply be ignored, if there are to be any attempts to address marital captivity effectively. After all, it is the religious barriers that enable and cause situations of marital captivity to exist. Furthermore, besides the concerned spouses, there are other actors that may be involved and affected by a situation of marital captivity, such as the religious authorities and the religious community. All of these actors enjoy rights that are protected and guaranteed by the fundamental right to freedom of religion and these too are worthy of protection. Consequently, this raises the question as to whether State intervention in a principally religious affair (marital captivity) is compatible with the religious freedom of the involved spouses and the religious community. Thus, it is important to assess the scope and limitations of this right within the context of marital captivity. This contributes to a greater understanding of the boundaries for State intervention and responses to marital captivity. More importantly, studying the freedom of religion enables to strike a viable balance between the trapped spouse's rights and the freedom of religion.

With regards to the other rights, these are included from the perspective of the trapped spouse. It is important to bear in mind that each specific situation of marital captivity may involve other human rights that are not addressed by this contribution. Each specific situation should thus be approached with due care and by taking into consideration the specific circumstances of the trapped spouse and the rights that are involved. This contribution, however, does not focus on single cases but on the phenomenon as a whole. Thus, the rights that have been selected are those that are directly affected in most situations of marital captivity that occur in secular as well as non-secular countries. More importantly, they also contribute to developing an in-depth human rights perspective on the issue of marital captivity.

As marital captivity concerns the inability to dissolve a religious marriage, the most obvious and direct solution is to terminate the religious marriage. Thus, the question which arises is whether individuals have a right to divorce or at the very least whether the State has a duty to facilitate the dissolution of a religious marriage. In respect of the phenomenon of marital captivity, 'a human right to divorce' would be particularly useful because as it can offer a direct solution, namely the dissolution of the religious marriage. However, none of the investigated human rights treaties contains a provision that explicitly guarantees a right to divorce, albeit the UDHR, ICCPR and the CEDAW recognise women's and men's right to equality at the dissolution of the marriage. Notwithstanding, the fact that a right to divorce is not mentioned explicitly within a provision does not by definition mean that such a right could not be implied within existing provisions.

The right to marry subsequent to a divorce and the right to respect for private life are likely to be affected in all situations of marital captivity. Even where the spouse(s) might be able to remarry after a civil divorce, an undissolved religious marriage may still create social, practical and moral constraints on the trapped spouse's choices to engage in a new (civil) marriage. Engaging in new relationships or remarrying are, therefore, not always realistic options for trapped spouse(s), even when they are divorced civilly. Essentially, the ability of the trapped spouse(s) to fully and freely exercise their personal autonomy and to engage in certain relationships and shape their lives as they deem fit, are restricted.

The right to free movement primarily concerns those situations whereby the trapped wife is hindered from travelling between States due to additional requirements such as demanding the cooperation of the (ex-) husband for issuing travel documents and/or approval for travelling. Another deterrence to travel to the country of origin could be the fear of being prosecuted there. A report of adultery made to the authorities in the country of origin against the trapped wife can create unsafe and complicated conditions and may be perceived as reason enough to abstain from travelling to the country of origin.

Furthermore, the right to health is included within the analysis, since situations of marital captivity may negatively affect the trapped spouse's overall well-being. That a situation of marital captivity can have detrimental effects on both the mental and emotional well-being of the trapped spouses is well illustrated in the account of Yehudis.[68] The physical and mental well-being of the trapped spouse may also be a concern where factors, such as violence, are present.

With regards to the right to be free from violence against women, marital captivity has increasingly been identified as a form of violence against women and, at times, is even addressed as a form of forced marriage, in literature. Studying marital captivity within the context of violence against women not only stresses the seriousness of this issue, but also enables to place the focus on the power imbalances and gender dimensions between spouses and provides for another perspective. Additionally, this approach fosters a greater understanding of the human rights at stake, the underlying root causes and the societal impact of marital captivity. It also contributes to and strengthens claims for greater State compliance with human rights obligations to protect and guarantee the human rights of trapped spouses and to eradicate acts of violence against women more specifically.

Finally, in discussing these rights, other inter-related rights are briefly highlighted where these are relevant, although these are not addressed separately. For example, the right to family life is discussed in relation to the right to found a family by way of marriage and the right to physical and mental integrity is implied within the right to private life and the right to health. The notion of access to justice and the rights it compromises (e.g. the right to a fair trial and the right to an effective remedy) are also mentioned when discussing the State obligations and solutions to end marital captivity. Addressing these separately would require examining divorce proceedings as these are provided and occur within national courts, in order to determine how and to what extent these rights are affected. In other words, these rights are best studied within a national context (e.g. the right to effective remedies of the trapped spouse in the

68 See at *supra* note 1.

Netherlands). Given that this contribution adopts a global approach and considering the great number of different legal systems and differences in dispute settlement mechanisms it would not be feasible to study these rights in all national contexts.

1.5.2. OVER-ARCHING PRINCIPLES OF HUMAN RIGHTS LAW

Besides these rights, general principles of personal autonomy, equality between women and men and non-discrimination are also considered. The trapped spouses endure far-reaching consequences that restrict them from moving on with and shaping their lives in many ways. An ongoing situation of marital captivity affects and restricts their choices, plans, actions and their capacity to act freely and autonomously. Individual autonomy is a fundamental principle in human rights law that underlies the substantive human rights provisions that are investigated in this contribution. The essence of this principle is discussed briefly in Chapter 6.

As for the principles of equality between women and men and non-discrimination, these have been included in all human rights documents and are integral features of certain human rights treaties, such as the UN Convention on the Elimination of all forms of Discrimination against Women.[69] This document has as objective to ensure equality between women and men in all areas and to eliminate discrimination against women. Equality and the prohibition of discrimination are explicitly mentioned in relation to the substantive human rights provisions contained therein (e.g. Article 7 on the political participation of women, Article 8 on political representation, Article 9 on nationality, Article 10 on education, Article 11 on employment, Article 12 on health, Article 13 on economic life, Article 14 on rural women, Article 15 equality before the law etc.). Other examples are Articles 3 and 26 of the International Covenant on Civil and Political Rights[70], Articles 2 (2) and 3 of the International Covenant on Economic, Social and Cultural Rights[71] and Article 14 of the European Convention on Human Rights.[72]

Within this contribution, the right to equality and the prohibition of discrimination are dealt with within the context of, and in connection with, the above-mentioned substantive rights. This approach enables two things, namely; to study the scope of protection afforded by the rights and simultaneously to consider how the power imbalances and inequalities between women and men during a divorce affect the exercise of these rights. A general analysis of the right to equality and prohibition of

---

69 United Nations General Assembly, *Convention on the Elimination of All Forms of Discrimination Against Women*, 18 December 1979.

70 United Nations General Assembly, *International Covenant on Civil and Political Rights*, 16 December 1996.

71 United Nations General Assembly, *International Covenant on Economic, Social and Cultural Rights*, 16 December 1996.

72 Council of Europe, *European Convention for the Protection of Human Rights and Fundamental Freedoms, as amended by Protocols Nos. 11 and 14*, 4 November 1950.

discrimination, as guaranteed in the investigated human rights law instruments, would not offer many insights into how the discriminatory aspects affect the exercise and enjoyment of the investigated rights.

1.6. METHODOLOGY

The object of this contribution is to investigate the above enumerated human rights in order establish to what extent they are applicable to situations of marital captivity, identify the human rights obligations that rest on the States and resolve any existing conflict between competing human rights and interests that occur within situations of marital captivity i.e. answers to the first three sub-questions. This requires interpreting the scope, limitations and interrelation of the selected human rights provisions. For the purpose of treaty interpretation, the methodology adopted in this contribution is based on the methods of treaty interpretation prescribed in the Vienna Convention on the Law of Treaties (VCLT).[73]

1.6.1. METHODS OF INTERPRETING HUMAN RIGHTS INSTRUMENTS

Article 31(1) VCLT stipulates adhering to the 'ordinary meaning of the word' which implies a grammatical analysis of the text of the treaty, including its pre-ambles and annexes. This ensures objective interpretation and guarantees that the interpretation of a treaty does not merely rely upon the intentions of the parties.[74] Next to grammatical interpretation, Article 31 (1) VCLT also stresses a contextual analysis. This means that the text should not be taken in isolation but should be interpreted within the context of the treaty as a whole. The context of the treaty can be obtained by taking into consideration any formal agreements on the interpretation of the treaty concluded in connection with the conclusion of the treaty[75], any subsequent agreements and practices that have been agreed upon by parties and any relevant rules of international law.[76] A contextual analysis benefits the interpretation process as it acknowledges the dynamic and evolutive nature of treaties. In order to remain relevant and applicable

73 United Nations General Assembly, *Vienna Convention on the Law of Treaties*, 23 May 1969.

74 Alexander Orakhelashvili, 'Restrictive interpretation of human rights treaties in the recent jurisprudence of the European Court of Human Rights', 14 *European Journal of International Law* 529–568 (2003), p. 535.; Engelen, *Interpretation of Tax treaties under International Law*, p. 146.

75 This includes reservations and any interpretative statements and declarations made at the stage of ratification which may affect the interpretation of a treaty. Gardiner, *Treaty interpretation*, pp. 237–241.

76 Vienna Convention on the Law of Treaties, Article 31 (2–3).; Rudolf Bernhardt, 'Evolutive treaty interpretation, especially of the European Convention on Human Rights.' 42 *German Yearbook Book of International Law* 11–25, (1999), pp. 15–16.; Malgosia Fitzmaurice, 'Interpretation of human rights treaties', in Shelton, *The Oxford Handbook of International Law* (Oxford, 2013), p. 747.

to social realities, treaties have to 'evolve' over time to match social and legal developments. By acknowledging subsequent agreements and practices as elements of treaty interpretation, a contextual analysis, thus, enables to take into consideration legal and social developments along the life of a treaty. The VCLT also stipulates that a treaty needs to be interpreted in light of its 'object and purpose'. Essentially, this means that an interpretation should ensure the effective operation of the treaty that is in accordance with its object and purpose (i.e. the principle of effectiveness).[77] Thus, effective interpretation should not lead to the loss of the effect or to an effect that is inconsistent with the treaty's object and purpose.[78] Finally, Article 32 VCLT prescribes a supplementary method of interpretation, that complements the interpretation methods stipulated in article 31 VCLT. This article prescribes an analysis of the preparatory documents where it is deemed necessary to confirm or determine the intentions of the parties.[79]

Noteworthy, the VCLT articles on treaty interpretation do not create, explicitly or implicitly, a hierarchy in the methods of interpretation. These methods '*are not step- by step formulas for producing a conclusive interpretation in each and every case. These rules instead indicate factors of elements that one should take into consideration [...] Although the rules contain a certain inherent logical sequence, they should not all necessarily be used in every case, nor should they always be sequentially applied.*'[80]

Considering the above, the starting point is a textual analysis of the selected human rights. According to human rights monitoring bodies treaty texts should be given autonomous meaning instead of adopting existing meanings from the domestic laws of States.[81] The selected human rights are included in many international and regional

---

77 Engelen, *Interpretation of Tax treaties under International Law*, p. 172.

78 Id., p. 185.

79 Engelen, *Interpretation of Tax treaties under International Law*, p. 152.

80 Fitzmaurice, *Interpretation of human rights treaties*, pp. 746–745.

81 UN Human rights committee, *Gordon C. Van Duzen v. Canada*, 07 April 1982, Communication No. 50/1979, para. 10.2.; Fitzmaurice, *Interpretation of human rights treaties*, p. 769. In the case of *Engel v. The Netherlands*, the ECtHR elaborated briefly on the rational of autonomous interpretation of convention text. Having to determine the term 'criminal' within the context of Articles 6 and 7 ECHR, the Court explained that if '*Contracting States were able at their discretion to classify an offence as disciplinary instead of criminal, or to prosecute the author of a "mixed" offence on the disciplinary rather than on the criminal plane, the operation of the fundamental clauses of Articles 6 and 7 [articles providing minimum rights to those who are charged of a criminal offence] would be subordinated to their sovereign will. Latitude extending thus far might lead to results incompatible with the purpose and object of the Convention.*' European Court of Human Rights, *Engel and Others v. The Netherlands*, 8 June 1976, Application Nos. 5100/71; 5101/71; 5102/71; 5354/72; 5370/72, para.81. Similarly, the Inter- American Court of Human Rights has maintained that '*The terms of an international human rights treaty have an autonomous meaning, for which reason they cannot be made equivalent to the meaning given to them in domestic law.*' Inter-American Court of Human Rights, *Mayagna (Sumo) Awas Tingni Community v. Nicaragua*, 31 August 2001, Series C No. 79, para. 146.

treaties. In this contribution, however, the selected rights are analysed as they are contained in the following human rights instruments:

- The International Covenant on Civil and Political Rights (ICCPR)
- The International Covenant on Economic, Social and Cultural Rights (ICESCR)
- The Convention on the Elimination of All forms of Discrimination against Women (CEDAW)
- The European Convention on Human Rights (ECHR)

The selection of these human rights documents is based on factors such as their focus on women's issues and the abundance of available primary sources such as concluding observations, general comments and jurisprudence. Studying all four instruments allows to conduct a legal comparison between the UN human rights mechanism and the ECHR, develop a comprehensive and integrated understanding of the rights investigated, and identify developments on both the international and regional levels.

This list is further complemented with other human rights instruments on the specific subjects of violence against women, such as the Council of Europe Convention on Preventing and Combating Violence against Women and Domestic Violence (Istanbul Convention). Additional human rights law instruments such as the Universal Declaration of Human Rights (UDHR), the American Convention on Human Rights and the Protocol to the African Charter on Human, Peoples' Rights on the Rights of Women in Africa will be examined in so far as they are relevant to the subject of inquiry. Notably, the UDHR is a non-binding instrument. This notwithstanding, it remains an important document in human rights law and its declarative form should by no means overshadow its political, legal and moral significance.[82]

Besides, studying the text of the treaties a contextual analysis is included by involving all the sources that compromise the context of the treaties as well as any other sources that constitute subsequent agreements or practices within the meaning of Article 31(3 a-b) VCLT. In respect of the latter, reliance is prominently made on the subsequent agreements and practices that stem from international and regional human rights monitoring bodies and experts. Inclusion of subsequent practices appearing at a national level, in the form of, for example, consensus on a subject matter, is limited and only included where there are not sufficient sources that cover the subject matter at the international and regional level. The reason for this approach lies in the fact that it is not

82 For more on the status of the UDHR see also: Hilary Charlesworth, *Universal Declaration of Human Rights (1948)*, Max Planck Encyclopdedia of Public International Law, *at* <http://opil.ouplaw.com/view/10.1093/law:epil/9780199231690/law-9780199231690-e887> last accessed 08 February 2018.; Hurst Hannum, 'The status of the Universal Declaration of Human Rights in National and International Law.' *25 Georgia Journal of International & Comparative Law* 287–397 (1996), pp. 240–242, 322–323, 342–346.; Hilary Charlesworth, *Universal Declaration of Human Rights (1948)*.

feasible to conduct an analysis on how all the rights investigated in this contribution are interpreted and applied in relation to marital captivity on the national level, considering the global approach taken in this contribution.

As for the specific sources, these include preambles, relevant optional protocols, general comments, concluding observations, decisions of treaty bodies, case-law of human rights tribunals[83] explanatory reports[84] and practices that show an emerging consensus[85] on an issue (e.g. soft-law instruments, resolutions, statements, expert reports).[86] As Article 31(3) provides recourse may be made to the provisions and principles in other international and regional human treaties as well as general international law.[87] These sources expand further on the content of the human rights provisions as well as their implied human rights obligations. Furthermore, including and studying the documents of human rights monitoring bodies allows to examine how these expert bodies have dealt with situations involving competing rights. These are insights that are essential for the deliberation on which rights and interests ought to be given precedence specifically within situations of marital captivity.

83 *International Human Rights Law and Practice – Final Report on the impact of findings of the United Nation human rights treaty bodies* (International Law Association, 2004), pp. 5–7. States' positive/concurring responses or acquiescence of documents concluded by human rights monitoring bodies may establish 'subsequent practice' within the meaning of article 31(3b) VCLT. Such documents include, general comments, concluding observations and decisions of individual complaint. Where State's do not object to such documents or even apply these documents within other contexts this may then be considered as constituting 'subsequent practice'. By the same token decisions by regional human rights courts, governed to monitor regional human rights treaties can be understood to also fall within such 'subsequent practice'.

84 Engelen, *Interpretation of Tax treaties under International Law*, pp. 241–242.

85 This interpretation method analyses the level of consensus on a given matter or standard on the domestic level as well as in the international context. It has mostly been recognised and applied in the interpretation of the European Convention of Human Rights and is considered to emanate from the evolving nature of the treaty. It often involves a comparative analysis of how the subject matter of inquiry is regulated in member States. Where consensus can be established, this can be used to legitimise interpretations that introduce new standards as being implied within the treaty's provisions. The absence of such a consensus, similarly, legitimises an interpretation that the subject matter may not be implied within the treaty's provisions. *Interpretative mechanisms of ECHR case-law: the concept of European consensus*, Human Rights Education for Legal Professionals, *at* <https://www.coe.int/en/web/help/article-echr-case-law> last visited 15 October 2018. See also: Fitzmaurice, *Interpretation of human rights treaties*, p. 769.; European Court of Human Rights, *Demir and Baykara v. Turkey*, 12 November 2008, Application No. 34503/97, paras. 68, 76

On the method of consensus on the domestic level within the Inter-American Human Rights systems see: Lucas Lixinski, 'The Consensus Method of Interpretation by the Inter- American Court of Human Rights', 3 *Canadian Journal of Comparative and Contemporary Law* 65–96 (2017), pp. 75–82.

86 Magnus Killander, 'Interpreting regional human rights treaties', 7 *SUR-International Journal on Human Rights* 145–169, (2010), p. 148–149.; Gardiner, *Treaty Interpretation*, p. 287.

87 Killander, *Interpreting Regional Human Rights Treaties*, p. 149. See also: European Court of Human Rights, *Demir and Baykara v. Turkey*, 12 November 2008, Application No. 34503/97, paras. 65–86.; European Court of Human Rights, *Al-Adsani v. The United Kingdom*, 21 November 2001, Application No. 35763/97, para. 55. In this case the Court stipulates that the ECHR '*should be interpreted as far as possible in harmony with other principles of international Law which it forms a part of.*

The object and purpose of human rights treaties is to guarantee and protect the human rights of individuals from intrusion by State and private actors.[88] The requirement for interpretations to be 'in light of the object and purpose' taken together with the principle of effectiveness compels that any interpretation serves to ensure the practical and effective protection of individuals' human rights.[89] Thus, an interpretation of a human rights provision or concept may not be so narrow that it renders the enjoyment of human rights ineffective, superfluous, or inaccessible for individuals.[90] To that end, the analysis of the human rights provisions provided in this contribution adopts and builds upon this premise and seeks to produce an understanding of the investigated human rights, including their limitations, that is consistent with the object and purpose of the human rights treaties.

Last but not least, the supplementary method of interpretation provided in Article 32 VCLT, is also relevant for interpreting human rights treaties. Preparatory works may be studied where it is necessary to establish the State parties' intentions for the purpose of treaty interpretation. Thus, where the content of a right or its applicability to situations of marital captivity remains unclear, reference shall be made to the *travaux préparatoires.*

---

88 The European Commission of human rights followed a similar line of reasoning with regards to the object and purpose of the European Convention on Human Rights finding that, '*the obligations undertaken by the High Contracting Parties in the European Convention are essentially of an objective character, being designed rather to protect the fundamental rights of individual human beings from infringements by any of the High Contracting parties*'. European Commission of Human Rights, *European Commission of Human Rights, Austria v. Italy,* 11 January 1961 Application No. 788/60, p. 140. cited in Olivier de Schutter, *International Human Rights Law: cases, materials, commentary* (Cambridge, 2014), p. 119. In its General Comment No.24 the Human rights Committee has been very specific in defining the object and purpose of the ICCPR, which is: '*to create legally binding standards for human rights by defining certain civil and political rights and placing them in a framework of obligations which are legally binding for those States which ratify; and to provide an efficacious supervisory machinery for the obligations undertaken.* UN Human Rights Committee 'General Comment No. 24: Issues relating to reservations made upon ratification or accession to the covenant or the Optional Protocols thereto, or in relation to declarations under article 41 of the covenant', 1994, CCPR/C/21/Rev.1/Add.6, para. 7. Referring to both the Inter-American Convention of Human Rights as well as modern human rights treaties the Inter-American Court of Human Rights concluded that the '*their object and purpose is the protection of the basic rights of individual human beings irrespective of their nationality, both against the State of their nationality and all other contracting states*'. Inter-American Court of Human Rights, 'The effect of reservations on the entry into force of the American Convention on Human Rights, Advisory Opinion OC-2/82 of 24 September 1982 (Series A) No. 2,(1982)', para. 29. See also Alexander Orakhelashvili, 'Restrictive interpretation of human rights treaties in the recent jurisprudence of the European Court of Human Rights', 14 *European Journal of International Law* 529–568, (2003), p. 535.; Gardiner, *Treaty interpretation* (2015), pp. 167–214.; Kirsten Mechlem,'Treaty Bodies and the Interpretation of Human Rights', 42 *Vanderbilt Journal of Transnational* Law 905–947, (2009), p. 912.

89 European Court of Human Rights, *Chassagnou and Others v. France*, 29 April 1999, Application Nos. 25088/94, 28331/95, 28443/95, para. 100.; European Court of Human Rights, *Airey v. Ireland,* 9 October 1979, Application No. 6289/73, paras. 24, 26.

90 Fitzmaurice, *Interpretation of human rights* treaties, p. 752.; See also Inter-American Court of Human Rights, *Mayagna (Sumo) Awas Tingni Community v. Nicaragua,* 31 August 2001, Series C No. 79, para. 147.

Next to the primary sources mentioned above, secondary sources are also studied. This involves secondary literature on marital captivity and on related topics. The inclusion of secondary sources allow to follow the debates and developments on marital captivity and other themes that are relevant. Secondary sources are selected on the basis of their relevance to the subject matter and relevant topics. This includes a wide variety of sources, such as governmental documents, research reports, journal articles, newspaper articles, encyclopaedia entries, books and electronic sources etc.

Furthermore, as this contribution also aims to illustrate marital captivity within the national context of the Netherlands, additional sources include Dutch case law, bills, national laws, government documents and secondary literature such as previous studies, reports[91] and scholarly articles. Additionally, case law and national laws of the United Kingdom and France are also studied in order to further illustrate the challenges secular States face when responding to marital captivity. More specifically the inclusion of this material serves to illustrate the different ways in which all three secular States have dealt with the religious aspects inherent in situations of marital captivity.

1.6.2. SCOPE AND LIMITATIONS

As has been mentioned previously in subchapter 1.5. this contribution does not aim to provide an exhaustive examination of all the human rights that could possibly be affected by a situation of marital captivity or analyse the entire catalogue of human rights. Central in this contribution is demonstrating how human rights law can and should be included within the discussions on marital captivity. To this end the methodology applied in this contribution may also be extended to analyse rights, other than those investigated in this contribution. In particular, the third sub-question, which concerns resolving any competing interests and rights that are present within situations of marital captivity, remains equally relevant where other rights are involved, so that the answers to this sub-question remain relevant where rights, other than those investigated, are affected.

Secondly, this contribution will not focus on divorce implications caused by factors other than religion. In addition, any other religious norms, cultural practices, customs and traditions that do not fall within the religions under investigation are not included within this contribution. However, where situations similar to marital captivity may arise due to the application of such religious norms, cultural practices, customs and traditions, the analysis and findings of this contribution may be of relevance.

---

91 This includes reports emanating from the other sub-projects of the *NWO Marital captivity in the Netherlands- Bridging the Gap between religion and law.* van Eijk, *Wel gescheiden, niet gescheiden? Een empirisch onderzoek naar huwelijkse gevangenschap in Nederland.*; Pauline Kruiniger, *Niet langer geketend aan het huwelijk! Juridische instrumenten die huwelijkse gevangenschap kunnen voorkomen of oplossen*, (Maastricht University, 2018).

Thirdly, it is important to bear in mind that factors such as the States' organisational structure, cultural background, human rights commitment and reservations, developed solutions etc. may affect the shape that marital captivity takes within the State. These factors may also also affect a State's responses to marital captivity, its compliance with human rights obligations and the degree to which it can be held accountable for failing to comply with its human rights obligations. Notwithstanding, these factors are included to the extent that they enrich the global perspective that is offered in this contribution. In this contribution the phenomenon of marital captivity is considered both from the perspective of secular as well as non-secular systems. in order to identify how both secular and non-secular States should proceed in addressing marital captivity.

Fourthly, this contribution examines the human rights that are at stake within the State's jurisdiction. Although, recognition is given to the fact that some situations of marital captivity have transnational implications.[92] Whether States have human rights obligations to protect the trapped spouse beyond their own jurisdiction, requires studying the extra-territorial reach of human rights obligations as well as the relationship between the different protection mechanisms for individuals[93] that exist in international law. However, as aforementioned, this contribution primarily focuses on the rights that are at stake within the jurisdiction of the State and the obligations of States to protect those rights. Questions concerning extra-territoriality, diplomatic protection and the relation between various fields of international law are not examined in this contribution. Nonetheless, further studies on the extra-territorial reach of human rights law and human rights obligations for situations of marital captivity with transnational elements are needed and should be encouraged

Fifthly, this contribution seeks to identify the tools and measures that should be employed specifically for the issue of marital captivity. In other words, the intention is not to create a list of specific measures that national authorities should adopt at international, national and local levels. This is an exercise best left for the national authorities to design, assess and implement. Similarly, this contribution does not aim to assess whether existing measures and the current responses to marital captivity are (in)compatible with the State's human rights obligations. Rather it aims to provide insights into the conditions and obligations that arise from investigated human rights and, as a consequence, may serve as the starting point for follow-up studies for creating a framework and adopting indicators for assessing the implementation and effectiveness of State's measures to curb situations of marital captivity.

92 See subsection 1.3.2.4.
93 Such as diplomatic protection and consular assistance.

1.7. OUTLINE

As religion forms the context in which situations of marital captivity occur, it is important to have some understanding of the religious doctrines and practices that enable situations of marital captivity to exist and to persist. Therefore, prior to studying the selected human rights, the following Chapter 2 elaborates further on the religious rules and views on marriage and divorce in all four religions investigated in this contribution. This allows for a better understanding not only of the underlying rational behind these rules but more importantly also of the different ways in which situations of marital captivity manifest.

Considering that there are multiple interests and actors (State, religious community, non-cooperative spouse and the trapped spouse) involved within situations of marital captivity, it is important that this contribution addresses these in an orderly and coherent manner. Chapter 3, therefore, first focuses on the State and more specifically the secular State. This is achieved by studying marital captivity as it occurs in the Netherlands, which is a secular State. Besides the interests of complying with its human rights obligations, a secular State, such as the Netherlands, may also have other fundamental interests that affect the degree and manner in which it can intervene in situations of marital captivity. One such factor is the State- Church relationship that is upheld in a State. The prevailing State-Church relationship essentially sets the boundaries for the State and ensures that State authorities do not intervene in matters that are reserved for religious communities. Studying marital captivity as it occurs in the Netherlands, then, allows to demonstrate and examine the conflicting interests and values which a secular State has to address when intervening in an issue that is primarily perceived as a private and religious matter. Additionally, a national context enables to demonstrate the specific ways in which a secular State, such as the Netherlands, can respond to a phenomenon that is deeply inter-twined with religion.

Similarly, the right to freedom of religion, which follows from the religious dimension inherent in situations of marital captivity, also sets boundaries for State intervention in religious matters. The right to freedom of religion and the State-Church relationship are two sides of the same coin in that they determine the boundaries for State intervention in religious affairs. As such, the right to freedom of religion requires States to respect and guarantee individuals their religious freedom. Additionally, religious freedom is of particular relevance for the religious community and the involved spouses who may expect and want to dissolve the religious marriage in accordance with the religious rules and procedures with limited external intervention by the State. The right to freedom of religion is addressed in Chapter 4, which focuses on the interests of the religious community and the non-cooperative spouses to dissolve the marriage in accordance with religious customs. The scope of protection afforded by the right to freedom of religion as well as its limitations are examined in order to determine whether any State intervention to prevent and end situations of marital captivity may constitute an interference with the freedom of religion. In turn, this contributes to the exercise of delineating to what degree the State may limit this right in order to address situations of marital captivity and protect the trapped spouses' rights.

After having examined the interests and rights that place boundaries on State intervention in Chapters 3 and 4, the following Chapters 5–7, consider the rights that demand State intervention, namely the rights that may be affected on the side of the trapped spouse. Starting with the most direct solution for ending situations of marital captivity, Chapter 5 offers an examination of a 'right to divorce' in human rights law. The most sustainable solution for ending situations of marital captivity is to enable both spouses to initiate and obtain a divorce on equal grounds. For this reason, the effort is made to establish the position of a right to divorce in human rights law. As has been mentioned previously, none of the human rights instruments investigated in this contribution explicitly include a right to divorce. However, this in itself does not preclude that such a right may be or ought to be implied within existing provisions. Furthermore, where a right to divorce is established or can be argued, it is then important to gain an understanding of its sphere of protection and whether it extends to both civil as well as religious divorces.

Chapter 6 addresses the rights that are most likely to be affected by a situation of marital captivity on the side of the trapped spouse. These include the right to private life, the right to remarry, the right to freedom of movement and the right to health. Rather than discussing these rights separately, this Chapter places their analysis in a broader context that is centralised around the principle of personal autonomy. This is a fundamental core principle of human rights law that is protected and guaranteed by substantive human rights provisions. This approach not only enables to show how these rights are inter-dependent, but it also enables to reveal the core issues at the heart of a situation of marital captivity and to accurately depict the experienced restrictions that trapped spouse(s) encounter.

Chapter 7 provides an additional perspective on the human rights dimension of marital captivity by addressing marital captivity within the context of violence against women. This Chapter sets out to investigate whether marital captivity constitutes a form of violence against women and, if so, what such a qualification implies with regards to the State's obligations to eradicate violence against women in general and marital captivity more specifically.

Chapter 8 then concludes with a brief summary of the rights and State's obligations that are discussed in Chapters 3 to 7. This is followed by a discussion on how to balance the competing interests and rights that are investigated in this contribution.

Insights are provided on the weight that should be attributed to the competing rights and interests within the context of marital captivity. Finally, this Chapter closes with recommendations and guidelines that States should consider in their efforts to eradicate marital captivity and to afford greater protection to trapped spouses. These are deduced from State obligations implied in all rights investigated in this contribution that have been identified in the previous Chapters.

CHAPTER 2
RELIGIOUS BARRIERS TO DIVORCE

Maryam marries a man in accordance with religious customs. About a year later, a civil marriage is also concluded in accordance with the domestic law of the Netherlands. Years later the marriage starts to deteriorate, and this eventually leads to a civil divorce. However, succumbing to the pressure from her family and the church, Maryam decides to remain in and maintain the marital life with her former partner, despite being civilly divorced. Eventually, the couple stops living together. Wanting to also terminate the religious marriage Maryam also requests, from the competent religious authorities, documents confirming that the religious marriage has been terminated. Eventually, she manages to secure these documents. Now she expresses that she really feels that she is finally divorced from her ex-husband. For Maryam it was important to also have dissolved the religious marriage in accordance with the religious norms on divorce.[94]

As disheartening and draining as the process of going through a divorce may be, this extract shows the significance the involved spouses and their social community may attach to a religious marriage. Spouses may be expected, both by the religious community as well as by themselves, to abide by their marital obligations for as long as the religious marriage has not yet been terminated. Therefore, the ending of a marriage in accordance with religious rules does not only have significant meaning within the community and for the spouses, but it also has social and religious consequences. It liberates the spouses from the religious marriage and therefore dissolves any remaining marital ties that may exist between them. For this reason, spouses may feel inclined to obtain a religious divorce, even after they have obtained a civil divorce.

Marital captivity occurs in multiple religions. A study conducted in 2014 in the Netherlands, on the instructions of the Dutch Ministry of Social Affairs and Employment, revealed that most situations of marital captivity occur within Christian, Hindu, Jewish and Muslim communities.[95] What is noteworthy is that this contribution reported a general estimation of between 447 and 1687 cases of marital captivity, between 2011 and 2012 in the Netherlands and, thus, between 224 and 844 cases each year.[96]

---

94 Extracted from: van Eijk, *Wel gescheiden, niet gescheiden? Een empirisch onderzoek naar huwelijkse gevangenschap in Nederland*, Annex II. (Translation Dutch to English by Benedicta Deogratias).

95 Van Waesberghe, et al., *Zo zijn we niet getrouwd: Een onderzoek naar omvang en aard van huwelijksdwang, achterlating en huwelijkse gevangenschap*, (2014), pp. 10–12.; van Eijk, *Wel gescheiden, niet gescheiden? Een empirisch onderzoek naar huwelijkse gevangenschap in Nederland*, pp. 46–49.

96 Id., pp. 14, 73. It should be noted that this study adopted a broader definition of marital captivity which included other factors alongside religion, which may in turn cause situations of marital captivity to

Thus, marital captivity will be studied as occurring in Christian, Hindu, Jewish and Muslim belief systems. Due to the varying religious views on marriage and divorce and the diverging legal and religious normative systems regulating marriage and divorce, situations of marital captivity occur in a wide range of scenarios. For this reason, the following subsections summarise the different religious views on the institutions of marriage and divorce and the different variations of marital captivity that may arise within Christianity, Hinduism, Islam and Judaism respectively. What is provided are the general views and procedures adopted in each of these religions. However, it should be kept in mind that within each of the religions investigated in this contribution, there exist different schools of thought and diverging interpretations which lead to different rules on certain aspects and different degrees and forms of commitment to religious rules and scriptures. Consequently, the forms, causes and consequences of marital captivity may vary not only between different religions, but also within the religious denominations that are found within one religion. The differences and specificities within the large number of religious denominations and schools, however, will not be discussed in great length as this goes beyond the scope of this contribution. Furthermore, the term 'religious law/norms' in this section refers to social, ethical, religious and legal norms and/or practices which aim to reflect, and are derived from, the beliefs and doctrines of the religions being studied.

2.1. CHRISTIANITY, DIVORCE AND MARITAL CAPTIVITY

Within the Catholic and Protestant branches of Christianity, the institution of marriage is perceived as a part of the creation.[97] The book of Genesis reads as follows: '*Therefore shall a man leave his father and his mother, and shall leave unto his wife; and they shall be one flesh*'.[98] Its sacred significance flows from the Creators authentic design of unifying man and woman into 'one flesh'.[99] The significance and nature of marriage is also found in the comparison of the relationship of man and woman, which should be a reflection of the indivisible relationship between Christ and the Church.[100] Marriage,

arise. The provided numbers, therefore, include cases of marital captivity caused by both religious and non-religious factors.

97 Jay E. Adams, *Marriage, divorce, and remarriage in the Bible* (1986), p. 4.; John Witte, *From sacrament to contract: Marriage, religion, and law in the western tradition* (Louisville, 2012), pp. 32–35.

98 *The Holy Bible, New International Version* (2011), Genesis. 2:24, Mark 10: 6–9.; *Catechism of the Catholic Church* (2003), sect. 1603–1605, 2335. The Catechisms of the Catholic Church is the summarisation of principles, doctrinal statements and instructions of the Catholic faith and morals. According, to Pope John Paul II, it may be considered as a '*valid and legitimate instrument for ecclesial communion and a sure norm for teaching the faith*'.
Pope John Paul II, *Apostolic Constitution Fidei Depositum on the publication of the Catechism of the Catholic Church prepared following the Second Vatican Ecumenical Council* (1992).

99 Adams, *Marriage, divorce, and remarriage in the Bible*, p. 4.; *Catechism of the Catholic Church*, sec. 2364, 2382.

100 John Witte, *From sacrament to contract: Marriage, religion, and law in the western tradition* (Louisville, 2012), pp. 49–50. In this regard, reference is often made to the book of Ephesians 5:22–32 which provides

besides being part of the creation, is also one of the seven holy sacraments according to the Catholic faith.[101] Thus, the institution of marriage is held in high esteem. This is reflected in the common expression of '*what therefore God hath joined together, let no man put asunder*'[102], which implies the intended indissoluble nature of a religious marriage.[103]

However, this does not imply that all Christians live up to the bond of 'till death do us part'. The social reality is that there are exemptions and long-established practices that enable the termination of the marriage. Within both Catholicism and Protestantism, acts of separation, divorce and annulment are recognised and practised.[104] How the termination of marriage takes its form, however, differs largely between the different denominations. Depending on the religious branch, multiple normative systems (secular law and religious law) may govern the dissolution of the marriage. In other words, the effect that a civil divorce or annulment has on the religious marriage differs between Catholicism and Protestantism. Nonetheless, it should be noted that divorce or separation is, in general, discouraged in both Protestant and Catholic branches, particularly when there is no seemingly valid reason for terminating the marriage.[105]

2.1.1. MARRIAGE DISSOLUTION IN THE CATHOLIC FAITH

Separation in the Catholic faith, although discouraged, is legitimate in certain circumstances. These conditions are as follows: adultery, causing serious bodily and/or mental harm to the other spouse or children, desertion and circumstances that render communal life extremely difficult.[106] Separation leaves both the civil marriage and religious marriage intact, but has as its consequence that spouses are relieved from the duty '*to preserve conjugal living*' and they may thus live separately from one another.[107]

A civil divorce, although perceived as an immoral and '*grave offense against the natural law*', an offence to the sacramental conjugal bond and as disrupting the family unit and

---

the following comparison between the marriage of the spouses and the marriage of the church and Christ. '*Wives, submit to your own husbands, as to the Lord. For the husband is the head of the wife even as Christ is the head of the church, his body, and is himself its Saviour. Now as the church submits to Christ, so also wives should submit in everything to their husbands. Husbands, love your wives, as Christ loved the church and gave himself up for her, that he might sanctify her, having cleansed her by the washing of water with the word […]. This mystery is profound, and I am saying that it refers to Christ and the church*'.

101 For all seven sacraments of the Catholic faith, see part I of the Code of Canon Law.

102 *The Holy Bible, New International Version*, Matthew 19:6.

103 See also *Code of Canon Law* can. 1056.

104 *Code of Canon Law*, can. 1141–1165. 1671.

105 Adams, *Marriage, Divorce, and Remarriage in the Bible*, p. 23–25. Code of Canon Law, can. 115, reiterates the spouses' obligation to preserve the marriage, unless there exists a valid reason to suspend or terminate conjugal life.

106 *Code of Canon Law*, can. 1152–1153.

107 *Code of Canon Law*, can. 1151.

causing disorder in society, can nevertheless be tolerated in certain circumstances.[108] Where these circumstances are met, divorce becomes legitimate and, thus, it will may not constitute a moral offence. This is the case, when divorce is the only means by which certain legal rights can be protected or where it is in the best interest of the children from the union.[109] A civil divorce only affects the civil marriage. However, like separation, it leaves the religious marriage intact. Engaging in new relationships or even going so far as to contract a new civil marriage may, thus, result in a '*situation of public and permanent adultery*', since both spouse(s) are still married according to the laws of the Church.[110] Consequently, disciplinary measures against these 'adulterers' may be implemented, which could involve the exclusion from exercising certain ecclesial responsibilities and receiving communion.[111]

The religious marriage can be terminated by way of an annulment or be dissolved by the Church tribunal. The latter can only take place when the marriage has not yet been consummated voluntarily. However, where a marriage between baptised spouses has been consummated it cannot then be dissolved.[112] Other exceptions concern the dissolution of a marriage between unbaptized spouses. Where one of the spouses fully converts to Catholicism, and seeks to be baptised, the marriage entered before either of the spouses was baptised can be dissolved provided that the non-baptised spouse has left the marriage.[113] This is also known as the 'Pauline privilege'. The dissolution of the marital bond is different from the annulment in the sense that the dissolution of marriage absolves the spouses from their otherwise valid and irrevocable bond. Whereas, an annulment asserts the absence of a valid and irrevocable bond having ever been established. The rules on annulment, as recently amended under the leadership of Pope Francis on 15 August 2015 and which entered into force on 8 December 2015[114], provide a speeded-up process for annulment, whereby annulment by a single religious tribunal is sufficient. The requirement to seek a second decision, confirming the annulment by the first court, has been scrapped for the majority of the cases. Grounds for annulment include, among others, the establishment of defective consent due to mental illness, insanity, psychological abnormalities, minority of age or external pressure, a misunderstanding about the meaning and nature of marriage, adultery, impotence and where one or both spouses have no desire to procreate.[115]

---

108 *Catechism of the Catholic Church*, sec. 2384–2385.

109 Id., sec. 2383.

110 Id., sec. 2834. Similarly, the new partners are equally marked as adulterers due to their engagement with persons who are already married.

111 Id., sec. 1650.

112 *Code of Canon Law*, can. 1141–1142. Accordingly, a valid and consummated marriage '*cannot be dissolved by no human power and by no cause, except death*'.

113 Id., can.1143, section.1.

114 Stephanie Kirchgaessner, 'Pope reforms Catholic church's marriage annulment process', *The Guardian* 8 September 2015, *at* <www.theguardian.com/world/2015/sep/08/pope-radically-reforms-catholic-churchs-marriage-annulment-process> last accessed 7 July 2018.

115 Pope Francis, *Apostolic Letter Motu Proprio of the supreme pontiff Francis, Mitis iudex Dominus Iesus* (2015). This document amended, among others, the process of nullifying a marriage. For other

2.1.2. MARRIAGE DISSOLUTION AND MARITAL CAPTIVITY IN THE PROTESTANT FAITH

Within the Protestant churches, a civil divorce affects the religious marriage. This different approach to a civil divorce is the result of historical events, which are related to the formation of the Protestant churches. As early as the 16th century reformists such as Martin Luther and John Calvin, advocated theological reforms in the area of, among others, marriage. The traditional understandings of marriage as indissoluble were challenged, which diminished the sacramental nature of marriage. Marriage was re-interpreted as a gift to mankind, for both believers and non-believers. Marriage was perceived to be primarily an earthly social matter that, therefore, had to be subjected to earthly laws.[116] However, the general view remained that the institution of marriage was subjugated to Divine law. Divine law, then, was recognised to have been appropriated by civil law, of which the administration and implementation was entrusted to civil magistrates who, ultimately, derived their authority from God i.e. *'God's vice-regents to govern the earthly kingdom'*.[117]

Hence, all marital affairs were considered to be affairs of the State, which had to be governed by State law and recognised by the Church.[118] Furthermore, the reformed theological views acknowledged that divorce and subsequent remarriage was compatible with Scripture in certain circumstances.[119] All acts of marriage and divorce, however, had to be performed publicly.[120] Despite the fact that divorce is possible within Protestantism, it remains an act that is highly discouraged.[121] Where the marriage has

---

grounds see Article 14, para. 1. under the heading 'The way of proceeding in cases regarding the declaration of the nullity of a marriage'.

116 John Witte, *From sacrament to contract: Marriage, religion, and law in the western tradition* (1997), pp. 51–52.

117 Id., p. 70.

118 Id., pp. 70–71.

119 Id., pp. 65–66.

120 Id., pp. 52–53,70.

121 For example, the *Church Order of the Christian Reformed Church in the Netherlands (Christelijke Gereformeerde Kerken in Nederland) provides that the church may not encourage nor advise spouses to divorce. Rather the church ought to direct all its efforts in facilitating reconciliation between the spouses. Kerkorde van de Christelijke Gereformeerde Kerken in Nederland – het laatst gewijzigd en aangevuld door de de generale synode van Huizen/Nunspeet (2010)* (2011), *article 70 (4- f)*. The Protestant Church in the Netherlands is largely silent on the matter of divorce. The *dienstbook deel II* (prayer book) and the *Uitbreiding Gereformeerde Liturgie* (an annexed document to the prayer book), reaffirm the sanctity of marriage. Interestingly, the prayer book includes prayers, texts and recitations that divorced spouses and the religious communities may pray in the event of a divorce. However, the wording of the title '*(Keuze)teksten woorden en gebeden als de wegen scheiden*' (which may be translated in '(Option) texts, words and prayers when the roads separate') does not seem to suggest that it is these rites that dissolve the marriage or that these are mandatory. Rather this is a process by which the formal divorce is recognised by the spouses and community. *Kerkorde van de Protestantse Kerk in Nederland inclusief de ordinanties, overgangsbepalingen en generale regelingen* (2013), Ordinantie 5, article 3.; *Dienstboek II (*2004), digitaledition, *at* <https://www.preekwijzer.nl/liturgie/dienstboek-ii-pdf/7992> last accessed 03 April 2018, pp. 391–394.; P. van den Heuvel (red.), *De toelichting op de kerkorde van de Protestantse Kerk in Nederland* (2004), chapter 7.3.

become unduly difficult to maintain, the general rule was, and still is, to first exhort all means to reconcile the spouses and eliminate all factors that impede a peaceful and respectful conjugal life.[122] Where these efforts are futile, either of the spouses may then sue for a civil divorce.[123] In general, a civil divorce has the effect of relieving the spouses of the religious marriage, since marriage and divorce are recognised as a State's affair. However, in certain denominations, the religious authorities maintain the final word on the couples' marital status.[124] Subsequent remarriage after the implementation of a valid civil divorce, however, still is considered a grey area due to limited guidance from Scripture on this matter.[125]

Within the different Protestant denominations, different views exist in respect of remarriage. The more liberal denominations generally allow remarriage after a divorce, while the conservative denominations may allow remarriage only in limited circumstances or may not condone divorce and remarriage at all.[126]

2.1.3. MARITAL CAPTIVITY AND MULTIPLE NORMATIVE SYSTEMS

In Catholicism, marriage is divided in two categories and is governed by two authoritative normative systems. Marriage is governed by religious codes and doctrines while civil marriages are governed by State law. The civil judge is recognised as possessing the authority and jurisdiction to adjudicate over matters relating to the status of a civil marriage. At the same time, ecclesial tribunals enjoy authority and jurisdiction to govern and adjudicate on matters that are related to the status of the sacramental marriage. Consequently, a civil divorce will not affect an otherwise valid religious marriage. A situation of marital captivity may arise where spouses cannot annul or dissolve the religious marriage. This, essentially, results in both spouses remaining married, even if a civil divorce has been pronounced and regardless of their desire to stay married. While they are enabled to contract a new civil marriage, the spouses may still be considered as married according to the laws of the Church. Any additional relationships may be perceived as an act of adultery by the Church and therefore justify

---

122 *Kerkorde van de Christelijke Gereformeerde Kerken in Nederland – het laatst gewijzigd en aangevuld door de de generale synode van Huizen/Nunspeet (2010)* (2011), *Article 70 (4-f).*

123 *Initially, grounds for divorces were limited to situations of adultery and abandonment. However, other grounds for divorce found wider acceptance in the course of the 16th century, inter alia, impotence, deception, grave incompatibility, personal difference, violence and felonies.* Witte, *From sacrament to contract: Marriage, religion, and law in the western tradition*, pp. 66–69.

124 Kerkorde van de Gereformeerde Kerken in Nederland, C46. 5.; *Kerkorde van de Christelijke Gereformeerde Kerken in Nederland – het laatst gewijzigd en aangevuld door de de generale synode van Huizen/Nunspeet (2010), Article 70 (4-a).*

125 See for example, *Kerkorde van de Christelijke Gereformeerde Kerken in Nederland – het laatst gewijzigd en aangevuld door de generale synode van Huizen/Nunspeet (2010), Article 70 (4- d, e).*

126 William A Heth, 'Jesus on divorce: how my mind has changed', 6 *The Southern Baptist Journal of Theology* 4–29, (2002), pp. 5–12.

the proclamation of sanctions against the concerned spouses such as excluding the concerned spouse from participating in the Eucharistic communion.[127] In addition, the grounds for divorce may be far more limited in comparison to the grounds that are provided for in secular law. Such strongly held views on the institution of marriage as being indissoluble may inhibit the decision for either or both spouses to initiate a civil divorce. In fact, the religious conviction of marriage as being indissoluble has occasionally been put forward by an opposing spouse in civil divorce proceedings.[128] So far, however, such arguments have not been honoured.

Distinctively in Protestantism, marriage and divorce are subjected to State laws and in most cases a civil divorce will be recognised as dissolving the marital obligations and rights that exist between the spouses. However, the requirement to publicly announce the intention to divorce may form an obstacle for spouses who want to divorce, as it not only solicits the (undesired) involvement of the community and religious leaders, but it may also may facilitate stigmatisation, shunning and shaming within the community, particularly when divorce and remarriage are not condoned.[129] In addition, the perceived obligation to focus primarily on maintaining a (difficult) marriage may discourage spouses from pursuing a civil divorce. This notwithstanding, and assuming that civil divorce is still accessible, spouses may still be hindered in exercising this possibility and may feel pressurised to remain married.[130]

These conditions may contribute to the creation of a situation whereby one or both spouses remain married against their wishes and desires. However, once both or either of the spouses decide to initiate a civil divorce, State law will have to proceed irrespective of the religious convictions on the matter of divorce. In a State where irretrievable breakdown of the marriage is the only basis for divorce(e.g. the Netherlands), situations of marital captivity to a civil marriage are highly unlikely.[131] Notably, other legal systems may adopt stricter grounds which, for example, enable an

127 *Catechism of the Catholic Church*, sec. 1650.

128 See for example in the case Cour d'Appel de Reims, 27 June 2002, 2001/00587. Upon notification of a divorce petitioned by the husband, the wife filed an objection on the basis of an exceptional clause. This clause allowed a disadvantaged spouse to object to a divorce, if the divorce would be likely to bring about long-term material and mental harm for either of the spouses and/or their children. Additionally, the wife claimed that the sought divorce was impermissible due to the indissoluble character of the Catholic marriage. Her objections were not honoured by the court of appeal.

129 Witte, *From sacrament to contract: Marriage, religion, and law in the western tradition*, p. 70.

130 This is, for example, illustrated by the case of Maryam in Chapter 2.

131 One spouse can object to the civil divorce by arguing that the ground for divorce – irretrievable breakdown of the marriage- is not established. However, such an objection is rarely accepted. In one case the wife successfully, object to a divorce initiated by her husband on the grounds that the marriage had not broken down. In the case the husband had become unhappy and felt patronised by his wife, who was also his mentor and administrator. Other than that, the spouses continued to live together and continued to comply with their marital obligations towards one another. According to the court, the husband had filed for a divorce because he had felt patronised and not because the marriage had become unbearable for him. The Court of Appeal, honouring the objection, overturned the divorce judgment of the lower court. Gerechtshof Leeuwarden, 23 September 2008, LIJN: BF4943.

innocent spouse to oppose the application for a divorce by the party at fault.[132] This may then create a situation of marital captivity within a civil marriage.

Additionally, although a civil divorce terminates the religious marriage, some denominations may require recognition within the religious community before the spouses can be recognised as divorcees. Where such recognition is not confirmed by the religious authorities and within the religious communities, as the case of Maryam illustrates, spouses may be considered as being married within that community. Essentially, the continuation of the marriage is based on the religious convictions of the involved spouses, religious community and religious authorities, rather than on any legal basis.

2.2. HINDUISM, DIVORCE AND MARITAL CAPTIVITY

The ability to divorce, in Hinduism, is intrinsically attached to the nature and significance that is attributed to a Hindu marriage. Similar to Catholicism, marriage is a sacrament (*Samskāra).*[133] Every sacrament asserts a physical and spiritual transformation, which elevates the concerned individual further towards the higher goal of rebirth in a higher caste or becoming a proper ancestor to one's family.[134] Marriage is considered to be the most important and prominent sacrament.[135] It is considered to engender physical, spiritual and social transformation for the spouses. The physical and spiritual transformation involves the purification of the body[136] and the permanent joining together of the spouses into a single body. The woman becomes the half body of the husband and takes over his qualities.[137] The social aspect of the transformation is reflected in the change of social status, the social and moral duties of the spouses and the acquisition of new relationship qualities with the family (in-laws) and community members.[138] Together, the spouses carry social and moral duties to procreate, sustain family life and preserve the sacramental union.[139]

---

132 E.g. Poland and Bulgaria. See for example European Court of Human Rights, *Babiarz v. Poland,* 10 January 2017, Application No. 1955/10.; European Court of Human Rights, *Ivanov and Petrova v. Bulgaria,* 14 June 2011, Application No. 15001/04.

133 Werner Menski, *Hindu law: beyond tradition and modernity* (2012), p. 280.; Ralph W. Nicholas, 'The effectiveness of the Hindu sacrament (Samskära): Caste, marriage, and divorce in Bengali culture', in Harlan and Courtright *From the margins of Hindu marriage: Essays on gender, religion, and culture* (New York, 1995), p. 139.

134 Menski, *Hindu law: beyond tradition and modernity.* p. 280; Nicholas, *The effectiveness of the Hindu sacrament (Samskära): Caste, marriage, and divorce in Bengali culture*, p. 139.

135 Id., p. 140.

136 Id., p. 139.

137 Id., p. 141.; Patrick Olivelle and Suman Olivelle, *Manu's Code of Law* (2005), p. 191.

138 Menski, *Hindu law: beyond tradition and modernity*, p. 281.

139 Id.; Nicholas, *The effectiveness of the Hindu sacrament (Samskära): Caste, marriage, and divorce in Bengali culture*, p. 141.

A valid marriage is established by performing certain rites.[140] There is a great diversity of customs – among the different communities, tribal groups, castes and families- regarding which rites are essential for establishing a valid marriage.[141] As a matter of fact, there is no consensus on which specific rites or combinations of rites are essential for validly establishing a marriage. Although among scholars, the *saptapadi* (the spouses jointly taking seven steps before the sacred fire) is considered as an essential and indispensable ritual by which the spouses become united upon the seventh step.[142]

India's Hindu Marriage Act 1955, a codification of classical Hindu law and customary practices, reflects the flexibility and diversification of Hindu marriage customs. It provides in Article 7 thereof that '*A Hindu marriage may be solemnized in accordance with the customary rites and ceremonies of either party thereto.*' A 'custom' refers to '*any rule which, having been continuously and uniformly observed for a long time, has obtained the force of law among Hindus in any local area, tribe, community, group or family: provided that the rule is certain and not unreasonable or opposed to public policy; and provided further that in the case of a rule applicable only to the family it has not been discontinued by the family*'.[143] While no other rite is mentioned explicitly, the Hindu Marriage Act 1995 provides that '*where such rites and ceremonies include the saptapadi [...] the marriage becomes complete and binding when the seventh step is taken*'.[144] As on a side note, registration by a civil magistrate or the lack thereof, does not affect the validity of the marriage.[145] Therefore, the validity and legality of a Hindu marriage is dependent on the proper completion of Hindu marital customs, which the given community, group or family considers to be essential. Once concluded the marriage is considered to be indissoluble.[146]

2.2.1. NON-EXISTENT OR IMPOSSIBLE?

Aside from the nature of marriage, which suggests the impossibility of divorce -i.e. a ritual to reverse the physical and spiritual transformation-, the possibility of terminating a Hindu marriage is even more obscure due to the scarce references that are made to it in Hindu scriptural sources.[147] For these reasons, many scholars and writers on Hindu

140 Menski, *Hindu law: beyond tradition and modernity*, p. 280.
141 Id., pp. 283–284.
142 Id., p. 283.
143 Id.; *The Hindu Marriage Act*, Article 3(a).
144 Id., Article 7(2).
145 63 Id., Article 8(5).
146 Menski, *Hindu law: beyond tradition and modernity*. pp. 279, 434.
147 Nicholas, *The effectiveness of the Hindu sacrament (Samskära): Caste, marriage, and divorce in Bengali culture*, p. 141. Hindu sources consist of *Sruti* ('what is heard'; divine revelation), which includes the entire corpus of the *Vedic* and the *Smriti* ('recollection'; man made codification of doctrines and practices that are a product of studies and interpretations of Vedic literature). *Smriti* texts include the *Dharma-Sutras* and *-Shastras* (the texts of Hindu philosophers, which contain rules of conduct and rites), *Kalpa-sutras* (ancient myths, stories and history), Puranas *(Hindu* epics*)*, *Mahabharate*

marriage and divorce have concluded that the institution of divorce is either unknown or simply impossible in Hinduism.[148] In this respect, passages of the *Manusmrti*[149] are cited as re-affirming the non-availability of a religious Hindu divorce. In addition, the general sentiment towards divorce is one of contempt, as divorce is perceived as morally inappropriate and a grave violation of the sacrament of marriage.[150]

However, the occurrence of divorce within Hindu communities is not as alien as one initially might think. Accordingly, and similar to the rites for a Hindu marriage, there is no consensus on how to implement a Hindu divorce. Historically, however, there have been long-established practices of divorce or other forms of discontinuing the marital life and subsequent remarriage.[151] This has been found to occur more so in the lower castes[152] but it also occurs when divorce or separation can be found to serve a higher goal (e.g. in cases where either of the spouses is infertile).[153] Support for these practices can also be found in scriptural texts which describe, amongst others things, the remarriage of abandoned women and widows[154] and grounds that justify abandonment by the husband.[155]

In comparison to men, women enjoy limited grounds for divorce or separation.[156] For example, according to the *Manu-smriti*, the husband is entitled to confiscate the wife's inheritance and stop cohabitating with her if she loathes him and he has tolerated this for at least one year.[157] The wife may also be 'superseded', by way of a second

---

and *Ramayana* (poetical literature). Encyclopedia Britannica, *Manu-smriti*, Encyclopedia Britannica Online, *at* <www.britannica.com/topic/Manu-smriti> last accessed 7 June 2018.

148 Menski, *Hindu law: beyond tradition and modernity*, pp. 432–433.

149 The *Manu-smriti* (Laws of Manu) also known as *Manava-dharama-shastra* are considered to be the most authoritative texts of Hindu code. These includes passages such as '*Neither by sale nor by repudiation is a wife released from her husband; such we know the law to be, which the Lord of creatures [...] made of old*'

150 Menski, *Hindu law: beyond tradition and modernity*, p. 432.

151 Nicholas, *The effectiveness of the Hindu sacrament (Samskära): Caste, marriage, and divorce in Bengali culture*, p. 141.; Menski, *Hindu law: beyond tradition and modernity*, p. 432.

152 Nicholas, *The effectiveness of the Hindu sacrament (Samskära): Caste, marriage, and divorce in Bengali culture*, p. 156. This is because at times it may be considered that the most essential rituals are not properly carried out within the lower cases and, therefore, no proper physical and spiritual transformation has taken place. In addition, marriage among the lower castes is said to be more contractual in nature. Id., p. 142.

153 Menski, *Hindu law: beyond tradition and modernity*, p. 432, 435.

154 Such as those found in the Manu-smriti '*If a woman abandoned by her husband, or a widow, of her own accord contracts a second marriage and bears (a son), he is called the son of a re-married woman (Paunarbhava).*' Georg Bühler, *The laws of Manu* (1969), Chapter IX, para. 175. '*If she be (still) a virgin, or one who returned (to her first husband) after leaving him, she is worthy to again perform with her second (or first deserted) husband the (nuptial) ceremony*'. Id., Chapter IX, para 176. '*Having thus, at the funeral, given the sacred fires to his wife who dies before him, he may marry again, and again kindle (the fires)*'. Id., Chapter V, para. 168.

155 '*Though (a man) may have accepted a damsel in due form, he may abandon (her if she be) blemished, diseased, or deflowered, and (if she have been) given with fraud.*' Id., Chapter V, para. 72.; see also Menski, *Hindu law: beyond tradition and modernity*, p. 433.

156 Id., p. 436.

157 *Olivelle and Olivelle, Manu's Code of Law*, p. 194.

marriage; after eleven years where she bears only girls; after ten years if all her children die; after eight years if she is barren; at any time when she '*drinks liquor, is dishonest, cantankerous, sick, vicious or wasteful*' and at once if she is foul-mouthed. Any act of contempt against the supersession entitles the husband to either lock the wife up or repudiate her. On the other hand, the husband's long-term absence requires the wife to wait for eight years if he has left for religious/legal reasons; six years if he has left for educational or career purposes and three years if he has absconded for pleasure.[158] Whether any of these forms qualify as a divorce i.e. the permanent dissolution of the marriage or merely a separation, remains a disputed matter.[159]

Another method of terminating the conjugal life is the establishment of a default in the execution of the marriage rituals. The marriage may cease to exist when it is established that the marriage rites have not been carried out or that the unification and transformation of the spouses has not been accomplished. However, this form of terminating the marriage resembles that of an annulment rather than a divorce, since in essence it implies that the spouses were never validly married in the first place.[160] Divorce or separation can also be reached by mutual consent, through a unilateral act of the husband or by deed.[161] This may involve the intervention of a religious authority such as, the *panchayats* (a village council) or caste tribunals.[162] A *pandit* (Hindu priest and scholar) may also perform certain customary rites that are recognised within the specific community.[163] Yet in other cases, the public announcement of the spouses' wishes to discontinue the marital relationship before the community and elders may suffice.[164] A peculiar and rather uncommon avenue that is found in literature concerns the 'kidnapping' of a married woman for the purpose of remarriage to another man. After rituals of acceptance by the new in-laws, the public announcement of the marriage and settlement of the first marriage before the religious authority, the 'kidnapped 'bride may be considered as being released from her first marriage and to be validly married with the second husband.[165]

2.2.2. MARITAL CAPTIVITY AND COMPETING NORMATIVE SYSTEMS

From the above it can be concluded that the effective availability of a Hindu divorce depends on certain factors, such as the existence of divorce within the religious community and Hindu-majority countries, the existence of accompanying rites and the

158 Id.
159 Menski, *Hindu law: beyond tradition and modernity*, p. 435.
160 Nicholas, *The effectiveness of the Hindu sacrament (Samskāra): Caste, marriage, and divorce in Bengali culture*, p. 143.
161 Menski, *Hindu law: beyond tradition and modernity*, p. 437.
162 Id., pp. 437–438.
163 See documentary: Organisatie voor Hindoe Media, 'Scheiden binnen het hindoeïsme', broadcasted 25 May 2013, *NPO*.
164 Menski, *Hindu law: beyond tradition and modernity*, p. 437.
165 Livia Holden, *Hindu divorce: A legal anthropology* (Hampshire, Burlington, 2008), pp. 80–82.

perceived necessity for the spouses to perform a ritual that symbolises the termination of the religious marriage. The safest conclusion that can be drawn at this point is that where divorce and subsequent remarriage is available and recognised, both spouses are entitled to terminate the religious marriage and remarry in accordance with religious rites. Where divorce or separation rituals are recognised and practised spouses then have the possibility to terminate an unwanted marriage and can be relieved of their conjugal, social and moral obligations. Women, however, may be provided with far more limited grounds for initiating a religious divorce. For example, they are not equally entitled to 'supersede' their husbands by way of a second marriage.

However, the non- existence of divorce rites and/or the consideration of the religious marriage as indissoluble not only leads to much insecurity and confusion within Hindu communities, but it can also lead to situations whereby the spouses are divorced according to civil law, yet still married according to the religious doctrine. Put differently, the fact that a civil marriage can be dissolved does not affect the religious marriage, nor does the availability of a civil divorce create an outlet for the religious conjugal bonds. This point is illustrated in a Dutch documentary on divorce within the Dutch-Hindu Community, which follows a Hindu woman's efforts to end the religious marriage years after she had left a violent marriage and had obtained a civil divorce. Together with a *pandit*, she engages in a ritual to erase her *sindoor* and then releases her from the religious marriage.[166] Furthermore, a situation of marital captivity may also arise where the spouse(s) adhere(s) to the credo of marriage as indissoluble or as non-existent which may influence the spouse(s) decision to pursue a civil divorce.[167]

2.3. ISLAM, DIVORCE AND MARITAL CAPTIVITY

Similar to the way in which Hindu norms have been incorporated into the personal laws of countries, Islam has influenced the legal frameworks of several Muslim majority countries, although in various forms and to varying degrees. Religious norms that are legal in nature find their codification in the *Shari'a*.[168] However, it should be borne in mind that Islam is no exception to schism. There exist various schools of thought, which each have different and, sometimes diverging, interpretations of Islamic norms and doctrines. In addition, geographical, historical, political and cultural specificities are factors that contribute to further diversified interpretations, modifications and application of Islam-based rules within Muslim communities and Muslim-majority countries.[169] It would do great injustice to refer to Islamic law or *Shari'a* as a homogeneous normative system that is interpreted, implemented, and executed in a

166 Organisatie voor Hindoe Media, *Scheiden binnen het hindoeïsme*.
167 High Court of South Africa, *Singh v. Ramparsad* (KZN564/2002) ZAKZHC 1.
168 Id., pp. 47, 51–55.
169 Id.

uniform manner across all Muslim communities and Muslim majority countries.[170] Therefore, in terms of marriage and divorce there are many variations in the divorce process, the forms of divorce that are practised and the grounds which can be invoked. The following subsections, however, will not delve into the specificities of each of the existing schools or the variations that are found in countries that incorporate *Shari'a* within their legal frameworks.

Unlike the sacramental nature of Catholic and Hindu marriages, marriage in Islam is not attributed a similar status of being sacramental. For example, marriage is not explicitly mentioned in the five pillars of Islam.[171] That is not to say, however, that the institution of marriage enjoys little significance. Marriage is a devotional and highly recommended act. Marriage does not only pave the way to procreation and the establishment of a family, but it also permits condoned and lawful intimacy between the spouses.[172] In addition, marriage (*nikah)* is a contract that is established by the offer and acceptance of the intending spouses.[173] As any other contract, the valid establishment of a marriage creates obligations and rights between the spouses. Among others these include the husband's obligation of to pay to the wife a dowry and, to maintain the wife in her needs (food, clothing and lodging). In exchange, the wife submits to be obedient to the husband and she may not refuse sexual interaction, unless this is done for religious reasons.[174] Regarding the dowry, parties are left with the discretion to determine the value and moment of payment.[175]

2.3.1. REPUDIATION, DIVORCE BY MUTUAL CONSENT AND DIVORCE WITH THE INTERVENTION OF RELIGIOUS AUTHORITIES

Compared to Catholicism and Hinduism, where divorce is considered either impossible or non-existent, divorce is recognised and regulated in Islam. Reconciliation, however, should always be attempted first.[176] Divorce without a valid reason is reprehensible and considered to be a misconduct. The most common methods of divorce are unilateral repudiation by the husband, divorce by mutual consent and divorce pronounced by

170 Id., p. 48.

171 These are: *Shahadah* (witnessing/declaration of faith), *Salat, (*five daily prayers), *Zakat* (almsgiving/charity), *Sawm* (fasting during the month of Ramadan) and *Hajj* (pilgrimage to Mecca).

172 Sayyid Muammad Rizvi, *Marriage and morals of Islam* (2014), chapter 2.
Kruiniger, *Islamic divorce in Europe: Bridging the gap between European and Islamic legal orders*, pp. 58–59.

173 Id., p. 41.; Dawoud Sudqi El Alami and Doreen Hinchcliffe, *Islamic marriage and divorce of the Arab world* (1996), p. 5.

174 Id., p. 5.; Kruiniger, *Islamic divorce in Europe: Bridging the gap between European and Islamic legal orders*, p. 59.

175 Id., pp. 106–107.

176 Id., p. 41.

a judge (or a *Sharia Council* in countries that do not award religious institutions the status of State apparatus).[177]

Repudiation *(talaq)* by the husband is the most common mode of initiating a divorce.[178] It is an exclusive right which entitles the man to unilaterally terminate the marriage at will, without having to consult or obtain consent from the wife. The husband is not required to give a (valid) reason for his actions, nor is intervention by a competent authority necessary in order to validate the divorce.[179] The repudiation may be performed in writing, orally or in signs provided that the husband is deemed to be of sane mind and the form in which it is pronounced is sufficiently clear to demonstrate the husband's intention to repudiate his wife.[180] The husband is also entitled to delegate this right to his wife or a third party, although he may only do so under limited conditions. Once delegated, the exclusive right of repudiation can then be exercised by the wife or a third-party within a specified time frame. It may also be made conditional on the occurrence of specific events, such as solemnisation of a second marriage by the husband. Where these conditions arise, the woman or third party is then entitled to invoke the delegated right of repudiation.[181] Essentially, this implies that the wife is able to repudiate herself before the specified period has elapsed or upon the fulfilment of the specified conditions. Depending on the form of repudiation, a divorce may either be revocable or irrevocable. Where the repudiation is revocable, the man may revoke the repudiation before the waiting period has lapsed. Thereafter the conjugal life will resume unaffected. Whereas, an irrevocable divorce cannot be revoked by the husband and, therefore, it will dissolve the marriage permanently.[182]

The second method is divorce by mutual consent (*khul'*), i.e. offer and acceptance to divorce. Occasionally, this involves the woman having to provide compensation in exchange for the husband's repudiation. In general terms, compensation will take the form of a repayment of the dowry or of the proportion of the dowry that had already been satisfied and relinquishing the entitlement to the remainder. Compensation may also take the form of a payment of a monetary sum, a waiver of maintenance and child custody rights or a renouncement of remuneration for child care.[183] Divorcing spouses may also reach a mutual agreement to relinquish the husband's entitlement to the dowry and any other compensation.[184] Similar to the unilateral repudiation, divorce by mutual consent does not require the involvement of a religious authority.[185] However,

177 For other less common forms of marriage dissolution see Id., p. 43.
178 El Alami & Hinchcliffe, *Islamic marriage and divorce of the Arab world*, p. 22.
179 Id.
180 More on the formal and substantive requirements see Kruiniger, *Islamic divorce in Europe: Bridging the gap between European and Islamic legal orders*, pp. 72–78.
181 Id., pp. 93–95.
182 Id., pp. 78–79.
183 Id., p. 41.
184 Id., p. 43.
185 Id., p. 88.

unlike unilateral repudiation, this form of divorce provides a platform for the woman to express her will and desire to divorce by enabling her to initiate the divorce. Upon completion divorce by *khul'* is irrevocable.[186]

Alternatively, the third method involves the intervention of a competent judge or a *Sharia Council*. The woman can then petition for a divorce (*tatliq*) or an annulment (*faskh*).[187] This mode of divorce or annulment provides a solution in instances where the husband is unwilling or unable to cooperate and repudiate his wife in the form of either *talaq* or *khul'*. Provided that permissible grounds for divorce or annulment have been established, the judge can terminate the marriage on his own authority or by way of repudiating the woman on behalf of the husband.[188] Generally, however, the dissolution of the religious marriage via judicial intervention is made conditional on strict grounds, which makes it a mode of dissolution that is not easily accessible to trapped wives.[189] It should be reiterated that grounds for divorce vary to a great extent within the different schools of Islam.[190] Marriage dissolution by a judge safeguards the woman's entitlement to the entire dowry (where only a proportion had been paid), maintenance and child custody rights and entitlement to remunerations for child care.[191] The judicial divorce results, in general, in an irrevocable termination of the marriage. However, a judicial divorce granted on the basis of retrievable grounds, such as the failure to provide maintenance or the refusal to have sexual intercourse, produces a revocable divorce. The marital life can be resumed where the husband opts to rectify the invoked grounds for divorce.[192]

After the pronouncement of a repudiation or the granting of a judicial decision, whether revocable or irrevocable, a waiting period of three months follows this decision (or the period equivalent to three menses cycles).[193] This serves the purpose of ensuring the paternity of an unborn child, as the wife may potentially be with child.

---

186 Id., p. 89.

187 Id., pp. 82–83.

188 Within different schools there are multiple interpretations of how to classify the termination of the marriage by intervention of a judge (divorce or an annulment) and on whose authority the judge pronounces the termination (on his own or on behalf of the husband). For more details see Id., pp. 41–42, 83–84.

189 Id., p. 87.

190 Permissible grounds vary between the schools, with the Malaki school providing for more grounds for divorce (failure to pay the dower, prolonged absence of the husband, wrongful acts by the husband). The Hanafi school has far more limited grounds (the husband's total incapacity to consummate the marriage and non- conversion of a non-Muslim man married to a Muslim woman). For detailed elaboration on the grounds for divorce in Islamic schools see Id., pp. 82–84.; El Alami & Hinchcliffe, *Islamic marriage and divorce of the Arab world*, pp. 28, 30–31.

191 Kruiniger, *Islamic divorce in Europe: Bridging the gap between European and Islamic legal orders*, p. 87.; El Alami & Hinchcliffe, *Islamic marriage and divorce of the Arab world*, pp. 31–32.

192 Kruiniger, *Islamic divorce in Europe: Bridging the gap between European and Islamic legal orders*, p. 84.

193 *The Qur'an (English translation by Sahih International)*, At-Talaq 1, Al- Baqarah 228. Although the waiting period may differ depending on the specific conditions of the divorcing couple. For example, the waiting period for a pregnant woman is until the delivery of the child, for a girl (child) or a woman

Regarding a revocable divorce, the waiting period creates opportunities for the spouses to reconcile and resume their marital life.[194] During the waiting period, the husband may be obliged to continue to pay the entire or part the maintenance obligations towards the wife.[195] A revocable repudiation becomes irrevocable upon the lapsing of the waiting period, provided that the husband has not revoked the repudiation or resolved the retrievable divorce grounds. Thereafter, the husband is, in the case of a divorce by unilateral decision or judicial decision, obliged to satisfy the remaining dowry, and in some instances to offer a gift of consolidation.[196] Once the marriage has been terminated, both spouses are entitled to remarry.[197]

2.3.2. MARITAL CAPTIVITY AND COMPETING NORMATIVE SYSTEMS

In countries which adopt *Shari'a* in their legal system, religious norms do not only bind people in the religious and moral sense, but it also forms binding law. In other words, marriage and divorce conducted under *Shari'a* may have a legal character. Therefore, marriage and divorce arrangements in Muslim communities can be governed by the formal secular law of the country of residence, as well as by formal religious-based law of the country of origin. Where the marriage has been contracted or has been registered in the country of origin in accordance with *Shari'a* or Islamic personal laws, it may be the case that the secular divorce of the country of residence (e.g. a Dutch divorce judgment) is not recognised in that State. As a consequence, the spouses may have a limping personal status, whereby spouses are divorced in the country of residence but are still legally married in the country of origin. The spouses may then have to divorce twice: both in the country of residence and in the country of origin. This situation is prone to affect spouses that have active links with both their country of origin and their country of residence.

Similarly, even where the transnational aspect is less of a problem for spouses, the importance attached to a religious divorce within the religious communities may

in post-menopause the waiting period is three months, while divorcing a virgin does not invoke a waiting period. *The Qur'an Surah (English translation by Sahih International* Al- Ahzab 49 provides: '*O You who have believed, when you marry believing women and then divorce them before you have touched them, then there is not for you any waiting period to count concerning them. So provide for them and give them a gracious release.*' See also Kruiniger, *Islamic divorce in Europe: Bridging the gap between European and Islamic legal orders*, pp. 102–103.

194 Id., p. 102.; *The Qur'an (English translation by Sahih International*, Al- Baqarah 231.

195 Kruiniger, *Islamic divorce in Europe: Bridging the gap between European and Islamic legal orders*, pp. 100, 104–105.

196 Id., p. 109.

197 *The Qur'an (English translation by Sahih International)*, Al- Baqarah 230. In particular surah Al-Baqarah 232 provides that '*And when you divorce women and they have fulfilled their term, do not prevent them from remarrying their [former] husbands if they agree among themselves on an acceptable basis*'.

in itself provide a sufficient incentive for the spouses to pursue religious divorce by having recourse to religious authorities. In these instances, marriage and divorce are then perceived not only as a civil affair governed by formal law, but also as a religious affair that is governed by informal religious norms. A civil divorce promulgated by, for example, a Dutch judge will therefore not always be recognised by the religious communities as dissolving the religious marriage.

The situation of marital captivity arises where the husband refuses to repudiate his wife and the *Shari'a Council* or the State judiciary cannot dissolve the marriage on their own authority or on the husband's behalf, due to the lack of, or insufficient, evidence of grounds for divorce. This is even more so the case in communities and countries which adhere to schools that provide very limited grounds for divorce. Abstention from repudiation results in the continuation of the marriage, regardless of the wife's will, appeal or preferences. Consequently, she will not be able to remarry or enter into new relationships without committing adultery. The man does not face similar consequences since polygamy, in Islam and some Muslim- majority countries, is permitted, although under strict conditions, and is primarily a privilege that is reserved for men.[198]

Furthermore, the unilateral right of repudiation of one's wife creates imbalances in the bargaining powers of the divorcing spouses.[199] Essentially, divorce by mutual consent means the woman's dependency on the husband's will to divorce her, while the judicial divorce offers limited options to divorce without the husband's cooperation. The husband, on the other hand, can easily untie the religious marriage. Additionally, and as any amount of compensation may be fixed, divorce by *khul'* is prone to abuse by the husband who, in practical terms, is in the position to set exorbitant demands in exchange for the repudiation. Consequently, this can lead to situations where the wife has to literally buy her freedom. It is this imbalance in divorce rights that accounts for women being disproportionately affected and prone to becoming trapped in religious marriages. On the other hand, men have the availability to repudiate their wives, with relative ease.

Therefore, within Islam, a situation of marital captivity is facilitated by the combination of two conditions: religious norms that uphold unequal divorce rights between men and women and the non-cooperative spouse or the inability to dissolve the religious marriage with the intervention of religious authorities. Typically, the non-cooperative spouse will be the husband, since the cooperation of the wife is not a requirement for divorce by way of repudiation.

---

198 Often the following text are cited in relation to the practice of polygamy: *The Qur'an (English translation by Sahih International)*, An-Nisa 4: 3, 129.

199 Van Eijk, *Wel gescheiden, niet gescheiden? Een empirisch onderzoek naar huwelijkse gevangenschap in Nederland*, p. 56.

2.4. JUDAISM, DIVORCE AND MARITAL CAPTIVITY

Both the institutions of marriage and divorce are governed by Jewish law (*halakhah).*[200] In certain countries, such as Israel, *halakha* is incorporated into State law and primarily governs family matters and personal status for the Jewish population. This means that a marriage concluded in accordance with the religious rites may enjoy legal recognition. Once more, it is important to bear in mind that in practice, the implementation, interpretation and application of *halakhah* differs among the diverse Jewish communities as a consequence of geographical and cultural diversity, as well as diverging religious dogmas that exist in the various Jewish denominations.[201] Likewise, views on the requirements of, and the significance attached to, a writ of divorce (*get)* and remarriage in the absence of a *get,* differ among the various denominations.[202]

The Jewish marriage is both a religious, as well as, a private contractual affair. From a religious point of view, marriage is linked to the Creation.[203] Accordingly, the first human was androgynous being both male and female, and was later split in two halves: one male and one female.[204] Individual men and women are, therefore, but halves and incomplete beings, until the moment they form a unity and return to the natural state of one single body: the original design. Marriage symbolises this transformation.[205] In addition, marriage serves to create legitimate settings for intimacy. It brings about a change in personal status and implicates the acquisition of certain moral, legal and

---

200 Michael J. Broyde, *Marriage, divorce, and the abandoned wife in Jewish law: A conceptual understanding of the agunah problems in America* (2001), p. 44. The written Thora consists of the first five books of Moses codified in the Torah. The oral Torah consists of laws that are believed to have been given to Moses by God on Mount Sinai. These where then transmitted to others orally. Although as in every chain of orally transmitted information, changes and ambiguities in the transmitted rules occurred, which has led to disagreements among religious authorities regarding the rules, particularly where these are incompatible with the written Thora. David. D. Friedman, *Jewish Law: A very brief account, at* <www.daviddfriedman.com/Academic/Course_Pages/legal_systems_very_different_10/Jewish_Law_Summary.htm> last accessed 27 December 2015.

201 Hillel. C. Gray, *Foreign features in Jewish law: How Christian and secular moral discourses permeate Halakhah*, (2009) (University of Chicago), p. 14.

202 Within the Orthodox and Conservative denominations significant value is attached to the granting and receiving of a *get*. On the other hand, it is submitted that Reformist Judaism does not require a *get* in order to remarry where the marriage has been dissolved by a civil divorce. In practice, however, securing a *get*, may be recommended in order to secure the position of any children born out of the new relationship. This is done in order to avoid that such children are considered as illegitimate within the community. Lisa Rosenberg, 'Praying for divorce: The abuse of Jewish women through Jewish divorce law', in Fong *Out of the shadows: Woman abuse in ethnic, immigrant, and aboriginal communities* (Toronto, 2010), p. 216.; Alexandra Leichter, 'The effect of Jewish divorce law on family law litigation', 2 *Journal of the International Academy of Matrimonial Lawyers* 1–18, (2009), p. 16.

203 *'Therefore shall a man leave his father and his mother, and shall cleave unto his wife, and they shall be one flesh.' The Complete Tanakh -With Rashi commentary (Online english translation by Rabbi A.J. Rosenberg), The Judaica Press, at* <www.chabad.org/library/bible_cdo/aid/63255/jewish/The-Bible-with-Rashi.htm> last accessed 27 December 2015, Bereishit (Genesis) 2:24.

204 Michael Kaufman, *Love, marriage, and family in Jewish law and tradition* (New Jersey, 1992), p. 4.

205 Id., pp. 4–8.

religious duties towards one another as well as towards the community and the divinity (*Yahwhe*).[206] Marriage is also important, as it contributes to the religious duty of furthering the Creation by way of procreation (*mitzvah or piryah v'rivyah*).[207]

Marriage is regarded as a private contractual matter which only requires the consent of both spouses in order to be validly established. Intervention by the State and religious agencies to solemnise the marriage or to dissolve it is not necessary.[208] Rather, both Jewish law as well as religious authorities serve the purpose of resolving disputes which are related to the status of marriage.[209] The nature of the contract is often compared to a commercial contract or a purchase agreement.[210] Notably, although contracting the marriage involves both spouses, all actions relating to the status of the marriage are primarily and unilaterally executed by the man. This arrangement is considered to derive from the nature of marriage itself, whereby the husband is perceived as the active party, i.e. the outgoing party who 'acquires' the woman and is obligated, in accordance with the marriage contract (*ketubah*), to maintain the woman in all her needs. In return the wife, the passive party, then agrees to submit herself under the oversight of the husband.[211]

2.4.1. DIVORCE IN JUDAISM

The unequal distribution of power in Judaism means that spouses do not possess equal rights to terminate the marriage. The husband enjoys an exclusive right to unilaterally terminate the marriage. However, for this to be acceptable, both spouses must to give their consent.[212] The Torah provides that '*When a man takes a wife and is intimate with her, and it happens that she does not find favour in his eyes because he discovers in her an unseemly [moral] matter, and he writes for her a bill of divorce and places it into her hand, and sends her away from his house*'.[213] This is the basis of the practice of granting a writ for divorce, which is also referred to as a *get*. Thus, divorce is brought about by the husband expressing his free will to divorce his wife by the act of handing her a writ

---

206 Id., p. 11.

207 Id., p. 4.

208 Susan M. Weiss, *Divorce: The Halakhic perspective*, Jewish Women: A comprehensive historical encyclopedia (2009), *at* <www. jwa.org> last accessed 27 December 2015.

209 Broyde, *Marriage, divorce, and the abandoned wife in Jewish law: A conceptual understanding of the agunah problems in America*, p. 45.

210 Id., p. 1.; Weiss, *Divorce: The Halakhic Perspective*.; Kaufman, *Love, marriage, and family in Jewish law and tradition*, (1992) p. 229.; Gail Labovitz, 'Contemporary Approaches to Qiddushin', in Fishman *Love, Marriage, and Jewish Families: Paradoxes of a Social Revolution* (2015), p. 222.

211 Kaufman, *Love, marriage, and family in Jewish law and tradition*, (1992), pp. 154–155.; Labovitz, *Contemporary Approaches to Qiddushin*, p. 222.

212 Labovitz, *Contemporary Approaches to Qiddushin*, p. 222.; Kaufman, *Love, marriage, and family in Jewish law and tradition*, (1992), p. 234.

213 *The Complete Tanakh -With Rashi commentary (Online english translation by Rabbi A.J. Rosenberg)*, Devarim (Deuteronomy) 24:1.

of divorce (a *get*). A *get* produced under coercion or duress (*get me'useh*) is void.[214] This rule is interpreted as being implied in the Torah[215] and therefore enjoys a certain degree of biblical authority. As a result, the requirement of a *get* produced out of the husband's free will, may be given considerable weight and is examined with strict scrutiny by the religious authorities.[216] In essence, the dissolution of a Jewish marriage is placed entirely at the husband's discretion.

Initially, the consent and the will of the woman to divorce was not a requirement. As is provided in the Mishnah[217], 'a man who gives a divorce is not like a woman who is divorced. While a woman may be divorced with her consent, as well as without it, a man can give a divorce only with his full consent and therefore, since her consent is not necessary, a woman need not have mental competence in order to receive her divorce'.[218]

However, measures have been put in place in an effort to rectify this asymmetric division of power between the spouses and so as to better safeguard the rights of divorcing women. Measures include, inter alia, the introduction of the requirement of acceptance of the get by the woman. This has factually changed the nature of the divorce process from one of an exclusive right of unilateral divorce to one of divorce by mutual consent.[219] Furthermore, the integration of the ketubah enables women to better protect their rights. In the ketubah, spouses may decide to lay down their mutual obligations and conduct during the marriage, the maintenance obligations of the husband, a *get* clause and the financial rights of the woman in case the marriage is dissolved either by the death of the husband or by a divorce.[220] A ketubah, however, is not an essential pre-condition to a valid marriage and a marriage conducted in the absence of this may be valid nevertheless.[221] Additional measures include the prohibition of polygamy and a restriction of the husband's unilateral divorce right by requiring that it should not be exercised in the absence of any fault on the wife's part. Therefore, the husband may not divorce from his wife on the basis of obscure pretences and where she refuses to accept the *get*, this will result in the marriage not being dissolved.[222]

---

214 Labovitz, *Contemporary Approaches to Qiddushin*, p. 223.; Weiss, *Divorce: The Halakhic Perspective.*

215 David A. de Sola and Morris J. Raphall, *Eighteen Treatises from the Mishna* (1843), Yevamot 14:1.

216 Broyde, *Marriage, divorce, and the abandoned wife in Jewish law: A conceptual understanding of the agunah problems in America*, p. 13, 64.

217 The Mishnah is a compilation of the oral Torah, the written Torah and man-made legal contributions. It does not codify the existing law as such, but rather it provides guidance, commentaries and arguments of past historical interpretations. The texts of the Mishnah, on the other hand, have led to debates among scholars and religious authority. The compilation of debates and scholarly work of the Mishnah were later collected in the Babylonian Talmud and Jerusalem Talmud, the former having more authority. See also Friedman, *Jewish Law: A very brief account.*

218 De Sola and Raphall, *Eighteen Treatises from the Mishna*, Yevamot 14:1.

219 Broyde, *Marriage, divorce, and the abandoned wife in Jewish law: A conceptual understanding of the agunah problems in America*, pp. 18, 20–24.

220 Id., p. 18.

221 Labovitz, *Contemporary Approaches to Qiddushin*, p. 222.

222 Broyde, *Marriage, divorce, and the abandoned wife in Jewish law: A conceptual understanding of the agunah problems in America*, pp. 20–22.

In addition, women are able to sue for divorce in certain circumstances.[223] Generally, the implementation of a divorce does not require rabbinical intervention. Mutual consent by the divorcing spouses is sufficient in this regard. The rabbinical courts will intervene, however, if mutual agreement is lacking.[224] The grounds of divorce are not only limited to extreme circumstances such as adultery, incurable illness, desertion, or impotence but also include more lenient grounds such as marital dissatisfaction, spousal incompatibility and mutual agreement of the spouses to divorce.[225] However, just as in the other religions, divorce is discouraged.[226] A legitimate and moral divorce requires prior efforts of reconciliation. Fostering reconciliation is one of the prime tasks of the rabbinical courts. Measures that can be taken in this regard involve recommending the spouses to consider counselling, frequently summoning the spouses to the court and delaying the divorce process so as to extend the time available for reconciliation.[227]

Alternatively, the rabbinical courts can annul the marriage or apply the evidentiary rules on divorce in a lenient manner, particularly where the woman faces becoming an *agunah* (chained wife) for the rest of her life. This may be the case when the husband cannot divorce from his wife because his whereabouts are unknown and cannot be retrieved, or when the husband is missing and his passing cannot be confirmed.[228] Rabbinical courts, however, tend to reserve these remedies for exceptional cases and they are applied with great caution.[229] In addition, the degree of leniency is highly dependable on the prevailing philosophy within the particular rabbinical court.[230]

Provided that the grounds for divorce have been sufficiently evidenced and established, the rabbinical court can determine that the husband is to divorce from his wife by providing a *get* or it can compel the wife to accept the *get*. In the absence thereof, due to non-cooperation by the husband or wife, the rabbinical court is entitled to adopt sanctions against the recalcitrant spouse, which may include imprisonment, the revocation of travel

223 Id., pp. 18–22.

224 Kaufman, *Love, marriage, and family in Jewish law and tradition*, (1992), p. 236.

225 Michael Kaufman, *Love, marriage, and family in Jewish law and tradition* (New Jersey, 1996), pp. 265–268.; Weiss, *Divorce: The Halakhic Perspective*.

226 Kaufman, *Love, marriage, and family in Jewish law and tradition*, (1992), p. 235.; Aviad Hacohen, *Tears of the Oppressed: An Examination of the Agunah Problem: Background and Halakhic Sources* (Jersey City, 2004), p. 1.

227 Kaufman, *Love, marriage, and family in Jewish law and tradition*, (1996) pp. 262–263.

228 Hacohen, *Tears of the Oppressed: An Examination of the Agunah Problem: Background and Halakhic Sources*, p. 2. There is no consensus within the Jewish diaspora, on the subject of annulment of a Jewish marriage. For further discussion on the issue of annulment and divorce see, Weiss, *Divorce: The Halakhic Perspective*.; Broyde, *Marriage, divorce, and the abandoned wife in Jewish law: A conceptual understanding of the agunah problems in America*, pp. 5, 20.

229 [29] Hacohen, *Tears of the Oppressed: An Examination of the Agunah Problem: Background and Halakhic Sources*, pp. 2–3,7–16.

230 Mayer E. Rabinowitz,' Issues in Jewish ethics: *Agunot* – Abandoned wives', *Jewish Virtual Library*.

documents (e.g. driving licence, passport), monetary fines, exclusion from the synagogue and in very limited circumstances, physical violence.[231] The latter sanction is the subject of ongoing debate, particularly where physical violence is employed against the recalcitrant husband in the attempt to force him to grant a *get*. This is argued to generate a coerced divorce and thus, it runs a high risk of being labelled as an invalid *get*.[232]

2.4.2. MARITAL CAPTIVITY AND COMPETING NORMATIVE SYSTEMS

The Jewish divorce procedure exhibits similar implications of competing normative systems governing the dissolution of the marriage. Marriage and divorce are matters requiring the application of Jewish law and are therefore exclusively placed under the jurisdiction of rabbinical courts *(Beth din)*. Any divorce pronounced by a non-Jewish court and without prior recourse to a rabbinical court may be deemed invalid, due to the court's lack of authority to decide over a Jewish marriage.[233] Consequently, a civil divorce that is pronounced, for example by a Dutch court, will not imply that the religious marriage ceases to exist. Regardless of the existence of a civil divorce, spouses may still be compelled to also finalise a religious divorce. A Jewish divorce can only be ascertained in accordance with Jewish law by the spouses (by the husband granting a *get and* the wife accepting it) and occasionally through the intervention of a *Beth din*.

A situation of marital captivity may then arise where either of the spouses refuses to cooperate in the religious divorce or when the marriage cannot be dissolved or annulled by rabbinical decision. Where the woman refuses to accept the *get*, the marriage will continue to exist and she will in essence trap her husband in the marriage.[234] Likewise, the husband can restrain the woman in the marriage by refusing to grant her a *get*, thereby creating an *agunah* situation. Men faced with a situation of marital captivity, however, have the possibility to remarry or engage in new relationships in certain circumstances. However,

---

231 Kaufman, *Love, marriage, and family in Jewish law and tradition*, (1992), pp, 235–237.
In fact, Maimonides' rules (writings by Rabbi Moses ben Maimon in the 12th century) state: '*If one is obliged by law to divorce his wife and he refuses to do so, a Jewish court in every place and in every period, may even cause him to be beaten until he declares "I am willing". He then writes the get and it is a valid divorce contract*'.
Weiss, *Divorce: The Halakhic Perspective*.

232 Broyde, *Marriage, divorce, and the abandoned wife in Jewish law: A conceptual understanding of the agunah problems in America*, p. 20.; Weiss, *Divorce: The Halakhic Perspective*.

233 Kaufman, *Love, marriage, and family in Jewish law and tradition*, (1992), p. 237. However, if a divorce decision adopted by a non-Jewish court is preceded by a decision of a rabbinical court compelling the cooperation of either of the spouses, then the non- Jewish judge may adopt measures to pressurise the compliance and cooperation of the recalcitrant spouse.

234 Hacohen, *Tears of the oppressed: An examination of the agunah problem: background and Halakhic sources*, p. 1.

to do so rabbinical consent is required.[235] There are no similar possibilities for trapped women. Engaging in another relationship will constitute adultery. In addition, rabbinical courts can pressurise the woman to accept the *get*, whereas pressurising the man may (somewhat ironically) invalidate the *get*. Notably, the effectiveness of the sanctions that rabbinical courts are competent to adopt against the recalcitrant spouse have limited impact in secular countries. Rabbinical courts in secular countries have no legal or public authority to impose and execute some of the powerful sanctions that are available, such as threatening with imprisonment.[236] Thus, the wife is entirely dependent on the husband's willingness to divorce her, where the marriage cannot be annulled or where the rabbinical court cannot release the woman from a dead marriage. This asymmetrical arrangement of divorce rights between the spouses, whereby women have little to no effective modes of dissolving a religious marriage, is naturally prone to abuse by the husband. A *get* may, and frequently is, withheld with the intention of extorting the wife.[237]

To conclude, similar to the practices that are found in Islam, marital captivity in the Jewish communities is enabled by two conditions: religious norms that prescribe unequal divorce rights between the spouses and the non-cooperation of a spouse to the dissolution of the religious marriage. In addition, the unilateral right that husbands have and the very limited effective possibilities that women have to initiate and obtain a divorce, in turn account for the disproportional amount of women that end up in a situation of marital captivity.

2.5. MARITAL CAPTIVITY TO A RELIGIOUS MARRIAGE

The sections above demonstrate that a situation of marital captivity is primarily enabled by two factors. Firstly, marital captivity is enabled by religious rules that restrict the spouses' ability to divorce one another or prescribe unequal rights to divorce between women and men. Secondly where cooperation is a prerequisite to the dissolution of the marriage, marital captivity is enabled by the actual act of not cooperating with the dissolution of a religious marriage.

It is important to point out that not all religions require cooperation of either or both spouses to the dissolution of the marriage. The grounds for divorce in Catholicism and Protestantism, for example, do not require that either or both spouses cooperate in the dissolution of the marriage. The non-cooperation of the other spouse, therefore, does not form a barrier to the dissolution of the religious marriage. Thus, while the first factor will be present in all religions investigated, the second factor i.e. non-cooperation will materialize in those religions that require cooperation of the

235 Diana E.H. Russell and Nicole van de Ven, *Crimes Against Women: Proceedings of the International Tribunal*, (1990), pp. 50–52. This document demonstrates the practice whereby a trapped husband can take up a second wife if a hundred rabbis give their permission (*Heter meah rabbanim*).

236 Labovitz, *Contemporary Approaches to Qiddushin*, p. 237.

237 Id., p. 223.

other spouse (e.g. Judaism and Islam) in order to dissolve the religious marriage. The very act of not cooperating to the religious divorce, for whatever reasons, will then give rise to a situation of marital captivity, where the marriage cannot be dissolved in any other way.

Additionally, it should be borne in mind that not all religions investigated in this contribution prescribe power imbalances between women and men at the dissolution of the marriage. As an example, within Christian faiths the grounds for divorce are equal for women and men. Within these faiths both women and men are as likely to become trapped in a religious marriage, where the religious tribunals and communities are not able to dissolve the religious marriage, or do not recognise it as dissolved. The ambiguity concerning divorce rules and practices in Hinduism, makes it difficult to draw a definitive conclusion on whether similar power imbalances are present. This will be dependent on whether divorce is actually even recognised and where it is, how the rights to initiate and obtain a divorce are distributed between the spouses, and whether cooperation of either spouse is required in order to end the religious marriage.

The scheme below provides for an overview of situations of marital captivity as they occur within the different religions

Scheme 3. Marital captivity in a religious marriage by religion

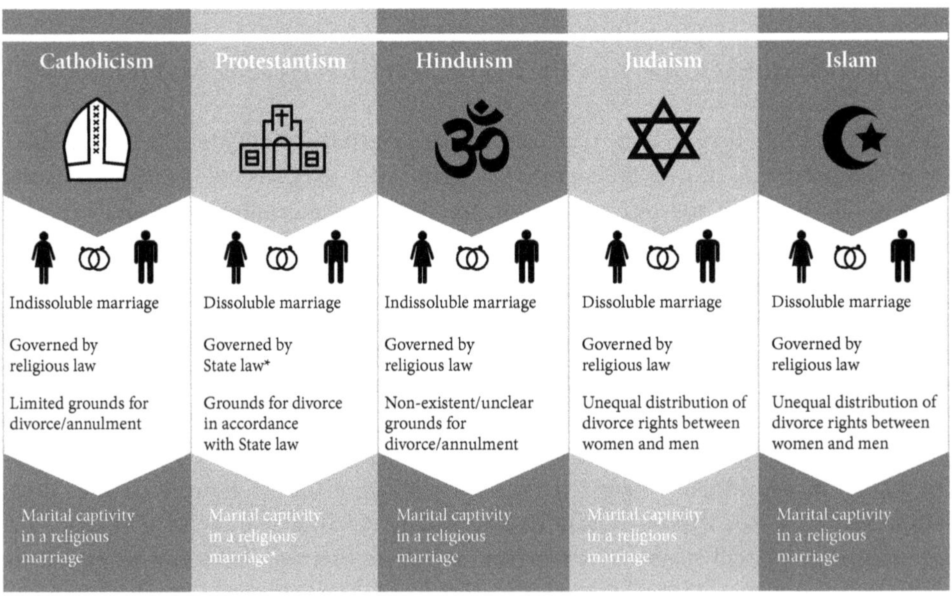

* Generally, it is acknowledged that a civil divorce dissolves all marital ties. In certain communities, however, the religious authorities proclaim to maintain the last judgment over the dissolution.[238]

238 See section 2.1.2.

CHAPTER 3
MARITAL CAPTIVITY IN THE NETHERLANDS

Marital captivity is, as previously noted, a phenomenon that is not bound to a specific territory, nation or community. A great number of secular and non-secular countries have already had experiences with this phenomenon and have tried to resolve and prevent situations of marital captivity in various ways.[239]

The extent and level with which religious authorities have been involved in redressing marital captivity, has also varied and is dependent on other factors such as the ongoing public discussion, the political climate and the State-Church[240] arrangements which are characteristic to each country. This not only illustrates the variety in how countries have responded to end and prevent marital captivity, but it also shows that countries might adopt different approaches in their efforts to protect trapped spouses' rights. Thus, country-specificities may also affect how human rights are protected and also the measures that States adopt within their territory to solve and end situations of marital captivity.

As such, being aware of the given national context contributes to a comprehensive and realistic understanding of the potentials that a human rights-based approach provides for addressing marital captivity within a given context. Additionally, understanding the difference in national contexts is also key to reaching country-specific solutions and ensuring the greater commitment of States and communities to preventing and ending situations of marital captivity.

Using the Netherlands as an example State, the following subchapters provide an oversight of marital captivity as it occurs in the Netherlands. This exercise enables to bring clarity to the phenomenon and also allows to demonstrate how marital captivity is perceived in the Netherlands and what factors have contributed to this perception. It also enables to demonstrate examples of specific measures that have been adopted, the reasoning behind them and their respective advantages and limitations. Above all, it enables to include and clearly illustrate aspects that are particularly relevant for

239 *Supra* notes 4–6.

240 In this Chapter the term 'Church' is used in a broad manner as referring to and including non-Christian religions. Therefore, it is not used restrictively as referring only to religions that are based on Christianity.

secular States. The religious dimension forms an additional challenge for secular States as they are challenged with balancing competing human rights in such a way that aligns with their secular character. This may result in conflicting State interests, which must be weighed up and which are highly relevant for the implementation and protection of human rights.

Therefore, the first two subchapters outline the social and legal context that is found in the Netherlands. Subchapter 3.2 provides an oversight of State-Church relations, its historical formation and the current trends. This is followed by subchapter 3.3 which provides a brief overview of the composition of religious communities in the Netherlands and it outlines how religious communities have organised themselves in the Netherlands. In particular, the activities and role of religious tribunals will briefly be elaborated upon. Subchapter 3.4. then follows with an explanation of the position of religious marriages and divorces in the Netherlands. The perceptions of marital captivity, which includes the framing of marital captivity in studies, case law and public discourse are also briefly discussed therein. This is complemented by subchapter 3.4 which demonstrates the measures that have been adopted in the Netherlands and touches upon their advantages and limitations. The chapter concludes with a reflective note on the State-Church model of the Netherlands, how the State's secular features have influenced the authority's perceptions and responses to marital captivity and why an approach that involves human rights is useful for generating holistic and country specific solutions.

3.1. STATE-CHURCH RELATIONS

Across the world the form of State-Church relations, diverges from country to country. For example, the Vatican is a theocratic State where religion dominates the State's political and legal apparatus. Countries such as Egypt, Saudi-Arabia and Iran, are not theocratic in the purest sense of word, nevertheless, religion and politics are intertwined in the legal order which is also reflected in the prominence of religion in State politics and in the inclusion of religion within their legal system. In other States, the separation of State and Church is the guiding principle. Even within secular States relations may differ. These may range from countries that adopt a strict separation of State and Church (e.g. France and Turkey) to countries that have an established church (the United Kingdom and Italy) as well as countries that recognise multiple religions and entertain cooperative relations with the religious communities (e.g. Belgium and the Netherlands).

As a result, the meaning given to the notions of 'secularism', 'separation of State and Church' and 'neutrality of the State' will vary from country to country. The different State-Church arrangements within countries may also account for the difference in how States have responded to a religious phenomenon, such as marital captivity, that negatively impacts certain individuals. Therefore, when seeking solutions to help end situations of marital captivity and in developing solutions for preventing new ones from arising, it is imperative to be aware and take into consideration the national context of a given country.

As aforementioned, the Netherlands is a secular State. However, a strict separation of the State and Church has never existed, and religion has always played a role in both the public and private sphere. The notion of the separation of State and Church, as it is understood currently, has undergone a long historical development. Understanding the peculiar interaction of State-and Church relations and the composition of Dutch society therefore warrants a brief account of the historical and social context.

3.1.1. THE HISTORICAL CONTEXT

Religious tolerance is, and has been, a historically consistent feature and a peculiarity of the Netherlands. As far back as the 16th century, Protestants and Catholics inhabited the provinces that would later become the Netherlands.[241] At the beginning of the 16th century, the northern provinces declared that all persons enjoyed a right to freely hold their own religion and not be persecuted on the basis of their religion.[242] This peculiar feature turned the northern provinces into a safe haven for those who were persecuted on the basis of their religion elsewhere. Consequently, the Republic attracted and accommodated Christians and Jews from other denominations which contributed to the further diversification of religious communities in the Netherlands.

The Calvinist Church enjoyed a privileged position, although this was not in the form of an established church. At the same time, the State could intervene in religious matters, including those of a theological nature, for the purpose of maintaining and protecting public order.[243] The Batavian Revolution, at the end of the 18th century, laid staged the foundations of secularism in the Netherlands. Influenced by the French Revolution, the ideas of separation of State and church and the notion of equality for all citizens, independent of their religion, were embraced throughout the provinces.[244] However, diverging from the French *laïcité*, recognised religions including the minority religions that had thus far been tolerated received equal protection from the State. The Calvinist Church was stripped of the privileged position that it previously enjoyed.[245] This notwithstanding, religion remained visible in the public and political sphere and

241 Hans Kippenberg, 'The changing relationship between State and Church/religion in the Netherlands', 67 *GEO journal* 317–330, (2006), pp. 318–319. Protestants predominantly inhabited the northern provinces, while Catholics mostly settled in the southern provinces.

242 This was declared in Article 13 of the Union of Utrecht. Kippenberg, *The changing relationship between state and church/religion in the Netherlands*, p. 318.

243 F.T Oldenhuis, J.G Brouwer, D.N.R Wegerif and F.E Keijzer, *Schurende relaties tussen recht en religie* (Assen, 2007), p. 7.

244 Kippenberg, *The changing relationship between state and church/religion in the Netherlands*, p. 319.; Oldenhuis, *Scheurende relaties tussen recht en religie*, p. 7.

245 Kippenberg, *The changing relationship between state and church/religion in the Netherlands*, p. 319.

the State remained competent to interfere in church affairs.[246] During the 19th century, however, religion began to be perceived more as a matter belonging to the private sphere. All churches received equal protection from the State; the previously required consent of the State on the spending of church money was abolished and churches no longer needed State approval for organising their internal affairs. The Protestant dominance in the public sphere further diminished as well.[247] There was a growing sense and desire to foster unity of the Dutch nation and its people, not necessarily based on one's religious affiliation but on ones citizenship of the Dutch State.[248] This was paralleled by progressively establishing a national system in the areas of education, and later spreading out to other domains such as social services, that were hitherto predominantly provided by organised institutions of the different religious communities.[249] By the end of the 19th century, the socialist movement, formed by individuals that had either loosely or entirely deflected from their religious community, began to make their voices heard within the public and political arena.

Going into the 20th century, religion regained prominence in the public and political arena, despite the ongoing secularisation process. There was a growing sense of religious identity which was further fuelled by the growing resistance to the French ideas of secularisation among orthodox Protestants and Roman Catholics. This encouraged Protestants and Roman Catholics to organise themselves and strengthen their position socially, economically and politically.[250] Eventually, this led to a division of society into four segments, also known as the '*verzuiling*' of the Dutch social order. Society was divided into four pillars consisting of the socialists, the liberals, the Roman Catholics and the orthodox Protestants. Social infrastructure for everyday private, public, economic and even political life was organised and institutionalised on the basis of these pillars.[251] Despite this development, the secularisation process continued to shape Dutch society and spread out into other areas. The State financing of churches

---

246 In fact, on the governmental level, Church affairs were managed by two separate departments: the Ministry of Roman Catholic Worship and the Ministry of Reformed Church and other public worship. Id., p. 320.

247 Id., pp. 320–321.

248 Id., p. 320.

249 Id.; Sophie van Bijsterveld, 'Religion and Law in the Netherlands', 17 *Insight Turkey* 121–141, (2015), p. 123.

250 Kippenberg, *The changing relationship between state and church/religion in the Netherlands*, pp. 321–322. The religious identity was further strengthened by an education related dispute in the latter half of the 19th century. The educational requirements were changed which consequently meant that public schools could easily meet the educational requirement, while religious affiliated schools could not. The education dispute that had up been building up since the 1850's, finally calmed in 1917, after it was established that both public and private (confessional) primary education would receive equal state financing.

251 Id., p. 322. In his article Kippenberg provides a clear example that encapsulates all aspects of life during this period. '*Living in a verzuilde ('pillarized') society meant that a Catholic married a Catholic boy or girl, sent her/his children to a Catholic school, listened to the program of a Catholic broadcasting cooperation, read a Catholic newspaper, rented a house from a Catholic housing association, was a member of a Catholic trade union, received Catholic medical care, voted for a Catholic political party and was eventually buried in a Catholic cemetery by a Catholic undertaker*'.

in other domains (e.g. financing of religious establishments) was loosened, and certain rights were lost.[252]

Halfway through the 20th century, the established confessional powers in the political arena decreased and the *de-pillarisation* of the Dutch society took hold. Increasing geographical mobility, prosperity, media participation and technological advancements were among the factors that set this shift into motion as they enabled an environment of individualism to foster. This enabled individuals to deflect from and feel less bound to their respective pillars. In addition, the financial ties with the State became more limited and certain rights were lost (e.g. the right to salaries and pensions for church ministers) over the years.[253] Regardless of this shift, religion remained represented in both the public and private life.[254] In addition, increased migration from colonial states and the labour force coming from among others, Turkey, Pakistan and Morocco, brought along hitherto largely unrepresented religions, primarily Islam and Hinduism. A combination of the institutional structures which had been adopted in the early pillarised climate and the prevailing norms of tolerance and equal protection of all religions consequently, enabled these 'new religions' to develop and become visible within Dutch society.[255] As such, places of worship, schools and certain media outlets sprouted. However, the influence of these 'new religions' in Dutch society, did not reach a level equitable to the 'domestic religions' as that which was entertained by the Christian communities. They did not form a pillar, and they did not influence social and legal structures, democratic values, decision-making processes and public discourse in the same manner and to the same extent as the 'domestic religions' (predominantly Christian) had done.[256]

3.1.2. SECULARISM AND STATE NEUTRALITY IN THE DUTCH CONTEXT

In the Netherlands, the current constitution neither mentions nor defines the terms 'neutrality', 'secular state', 'separation of State and Church' or any synonym thereof. The Constitution does not even mention the term 'Church'.[257] Despite this, the principle of State-Church separation is positive law in the sense that it is deemed to be expressed in

252 Id., pp. 321–322.

253 Id., pp. 323–324.

254 Id., p. 323.; Sophie van Bijsterveld, 'Religion and the Secular State in the Netherlands', *Neuere Entwiclungen im Religionsrecht europaeischer Staaten* 93–112, (2013), p. 524. For example, one of the leading parties that has been in the cabinet coalition (with the exception of the 1994 and 2012 coalition) since the 1980's is the *Christen-Democratisch Appèl* (CDA). This party consists of the former Roman Catholic and Protestant political representatives that were established either during or after the pillarization era. These consisted of The *Christelijke Historische- Unie* (CHR), the *Anti-Revolutionaire Partij* (ARP) and the *Katholike Volkspartij* (KVP) which fused to form the CDA in 1980. Notably, most of these parties had also partaken in the government coalition before they fused into the CDA.

255 Kippenberg, *The changing relationship between state and church/religion in the Netherlands*, p. 326.

256 Id., p. 326.

257 Van Bijsterveld, *Religion and the Secular State in the Netherlands*, p. 525.

the Dutch Constitution and treaties by operation of Articles 1, 6 and 23 of the Dutch Constitution.[258] In practice, the principle of separation of State and Church is generally adopted and applied as a self-evident and self-explanatory term.[259] Van Bijsterveld attributes the lack of a clear definition to the fact that it has not been codified and is thus not likely to be raised in disputes, resulting in the limited examination and revaluation it has received.[260]

However, guidance on the interpretation of this principle can be found in the 2004 parliamentary report on ensuring fundamental rights and religion in a pluralistic society.[261] This report reiterates the core values of the State-Church relations in the Netherlands as being those of tolerance, reciprocity and (religious) pluralism. These are regarded as invaluable features of the Dutch State and society.[262] According to the report, the separation of State and Church entails that the State as well as the Church are, respectively entitled to function independently from one another.[263] This is a two way street which implies that the State should not interfere in religious matters that are reserved for religious organisations, in as much as the latter should not interfere in State-attributed matters. Therefore, religious and belief system-oriented organisations may regulate internal affairs, such as the appointment of clerics, independently and autonomously. In principle, the State should refrain from directly interfering with religious matters that concern the religious community. However, this entitlement may be subjected to certain restrictions, particularly when it comes at the cost of the fundamental rights of others or societal core values and principles.[264] Likewise, preserving the independence of the State in its role as the organiser and protector of society entails that religious and belief system organisations, including their 'officials', do not possess any public or judicial competences.[265] In essence, this principle endows both the State and the Church independence in regulating matters that concern them and simultaneously sets boundaries for both the State and the Church.[266]

The complementary notion of 'neutrality' of the State provides that, in its operation, the State should treat all religions and belief systems in an equal manner. This, for example,

---

258 Sophie van Bijsterveld, 'Scheiding van Kerk en Staat: een klassieke norm in een moderne tijd', in van de Donk. et al. *Geloven in het publieke domein* (Den Haag, 2006), p. 248.; See also 'Grondrechten in een Pluriforme samenleving, Kamerstukken II 2003/2004, 29 614, nr. 2', p. 7.

259 Van Bijsterveld, *Scheiding van Kerk en Staat: een klassieke norm in een moderne tijd*, p. 248.; Kamerstukken II 2003/2004, 29 614, nr. 2, p. 7.

260 Van Bijsterveld, *Religion and Law in the Netherlands*, p. 125.

261 Kamerstukken II 2003/2004, 29 614, nr. 2.

262 Kamerstukken II 2003/2004, 29 614, nr. 2, p. 6.

263 Id., p. 7.

264 Id.; See also subchapter 4.5. on the subject of the State obligations in relation to religious freedom. Oldenhuis also provides that the principle of separation of State and Church entails a boundary for the State not to interfere directly in religious affairs (e.g. by directly financing religious activities). Oldenhuis, *Scheurende relaties tussen recht en religie*, p. 13.

265 Kamerstukken II 2003/2004, 29 614, nr. 2, p. 7.

266 Van Bijsterveld, *Scheiding van Kerk en Staat: een klassieke norm in een moderne tijd*, p. 248.

requires that religious communities are entitled to regulate their affairs autonomously, receive financial assistance and represent themselves in the private and public sphere on an equal basis. The State may not favour or privilege one over the other. Neutrality should also not be interpreted in the strictest sense as implying the exclusion of and non-involvement with all religions or belief systems. Rather the State may, in certain circumstances, interfere in religious matters, refer to religious sources or draw inspiration from belief systems or religious dogmas, in so far this is not incompatible with the principles of equality and the religious freedoms that are guaranteed to them by the Dutch constitution and international human rights instruments.[267] Therefore, both principles do not entail that there is to be a strict separation which requires limited State involvement in any religious matters. The guiding principles and approach to religions and their activities remain that of tolerance and equal treatment.

3.1.3. GROWING RELIGIOUS SUSPICION

As history has shown, religious tolerance and equal protection of all religions are key features of State-Church relations in the Netherlands. Religion is and always has played a role in both the public and private realm. However, declining religiosity among the Dutch population and changes in the cultural and religious composition of the Dutch society, which took place throughout the latter half of the 20th century, are developments that have steadily generated a climate of religious suspicion. In particular, this has taken place more so towards Islam as consequence of ongoing conflicts and new forms of threats.[268] Factors such as the radicalisation of youth in certain religious communities and other social issues that occur more frequently in certain religious communities, such as forced marriage, child marriage, marital captivity etc., have played a major role in the rise of suspicion towards religion and religious communities.

To illustrate this point, in 2009 a study on the presence of *Sharia Tribunals* in the United Kingdom, it was concluded that there were 85 active *Sharia Tribunals*.[269] These findings sparked political and public commotion on the presence of *Sharia Tribunals* and the application of *Shari'a* in the Netherlands.[270] Statements made by the Islamic scholar Hitham Al-Haddad in favour of introducing Sharia councils made headlines and only added fuel to the fire.[271] Many who perceived this as problematic expressed the incompatibility of certain provisions of *Shari'a* with Dutch fundamental principles

267 Kamerstukken II 2003/2004, 29 614, nr. 2, p. 7.

268 Joep de Hart and Paul Dekker, *Kerken in de Nederlandse civil society: institutionele grondslag en individuele inspiratiebron*, (Wetenschappelijke Raad voor het regeringsbeleid, Geloven in het publieke domein, Den Haag 2006), pp. 144–145; Kippenberg, *The changing relationship between state and church/ religion in the Netherlands*, p. 327–288; Oldenhuis, *Scheurende relaties tussen recht en religie*, pp. 10–11.

269 Denis MacEoin, *Sharia Law or 'one law for all?'*, (2009), p. 68.

270 Minister van Justitie 'Brief Tweede Kamer: Schriftelijk overleg over shariarechtbanken', Justitie, 1 Septmeber 2009.

271 'Ook Sharia raad in Nederland?', *NOS*, 11 January 2012, *at* <http://nos.nl/artikel/382653-ook-sharia-raad-in-nederland.html.

and core values. In their view, fundamental values such as gender equality were at risk of being undermined by the application of *Shari'a*. Furthermore, the application of *Shari'a* was perceived as undermining the supremacy of the legal system and weakening the governments supervisory role over its citizens.[272] Essentially, the raised concerns demanded for more insights and oversight on the activities of and within religious communities. By way of a reaction, in 2010 the government requested for a study to be conducted on the application of *Shari'*a in the Netherlands.[273] The study concluded that while there were various ways of settling dispute in Muslim communities and that religious laws were applied by these mechanisms, there were active no Sharia Tribunals in the Netherlands. However, and as Berger rightly pointed out in response to the highly politicised reactions, the occurrence of religious tribunals and the existence of internal dispute settlement mechanisms in the Netherlands are neither recent nor alien phenomena.[274] Christian and Jewish communities have their own establishments that deal with disputes which arise within their respective communities on the basis of their own religious normative systems. This is because in the Netherlands, religious communities are entitled to manage their internal affairs in accordance with their religious doctrines, within the limits set by the law. Subchapter 3.2. elaborates further on the organisation of Christian, Jewish, Islamic and Hindu communities in the Netherlands, and the role that religious tribunals play therein.

Other factors which have sparked this sentiment of suspicion are the increased attention that is attributed to issues such as same sex marriages, abortion and gender equality, which have in urn amplified the differences and conflicts between fundamental societal values and religious values. Topics that have been dominating the public discourse and political agenda, such as immigration and multiculturalism, have similarly revived the interests and concerns regarding the place of religion in the public domain and the prevailing understanding of the State-Church relations in the Netherlands.[275] There is growing support for shifting towards a stricter interpretation of secularism and neutrality of the State. This may include embracing the French notion of *laïcité* i.e., ensuring a religion-free public domain and curtailing religion predominantly to the private sphere.[276] Although this discussion is best left for other forums, it goes to show the revived interest of religion and the ongoing process of revaluating State-Church relations.[277]

---

272 Minister van Justitie 'Antwoorden kamervragen inzake shariarechtbanken', Justitie, 02 July 2009.; 'Pleidooi shariaraad stuit op verzet vrouwen', *de Volkskrant* 12 June 2012, *at* <www.volkskrant.nl/archief/pleidooi-shariaraad-stuit-op-verzet-vrouwen~a3269510/>.

273 Laurens G.H. Bakker, Anoushka J. Gehring, Krista van Mourik, Maurice M. Claessen, Chris Harmsen and Egbert Harmsen, *Sharia in Nederland: Een studie naar Islamitische advisering en geschillenbeslechting bij moslims in Nederland*, (Instituut voor Culturele Antropologie en Ontwikkelingsstudies, Instituut voor Rechtssociologie & Radboud Universiteit Nijmegen, 2010).

274 Maurits Berger, *Juist blokkeren van Shariaraad is dom*, (2012), *at* <http://leiden-islamblog.nl/articles/juist-blokkeren-van-shariaraad-is-dom> last accessed 02 February 2018.

275 For example, in relation to the wearing of headscarves by public officials and the proposed burqa ban.

276 Oldenhuis, *Scheurende relaties tussen recht en religie*, pp. 13–14.

277 Id., pp. 10–11.

3.2. RELIGIOSITY AND THE ORGANISATION OF RELIGIOUS COMMUNITIES

In the Netherlands, a 2014 study found that more than half of the Dutch population (53%) indicated that they were affiliated to a religion in 2013.[278] Ever since, these numbers have been decreasing by about one percent per year.[279] Comparing this data to previous years, an overall gradual decline of the religious population can be observed from 60% at the beginning of this century to 55% by 2010.[280] By 2015, 50.1% of persons indicated that they were not affiliated with any religion.[281]

Religions founded in Christianity account for the majority of the religious population in the Netherlands. The figures show that in 2015, the Roman Catholic church accounted for 23.7% of the population, followed by 15.5% that identified with the Protestant faiths. Islam[282] was the second largest religion (4,9% of the population), followed by Hinduism[283] (0,6%), Buddhism (0,4%) and Judaism[284] (0.1%). The following sections briefly outline the nature of the existing communities, their organisational structure, dispute settlement mechanisms and legal status.

3.2.1. CHRISTIAN COMMUNITIES

The Roman Catholic Church has the clearest hierarchal structure. All authority is concentrated in the Pope, who is at the head of the church.[285] Together with the College of Bishops the Pope possess both the doctrinal and organisational authority within the universal church and exercises the legislative, executive and judicial function.[286] The Netherlands forms one church province, which is subdivided in 7 dioceses: Rotterdam, Groningen, Breda, Roermond, 's-Hertogenbosch, Haarlem-Amsterdam and Utrecht. The latter is the archdiocese with the Archbishop as the head. The other diocese are

278 Hans Schmeets, *De religieuze kaart van Nederland, 2010–2013*, (2014), p. 4.

279 Hans Schmeets, *De religieuze kaart van Nederland, 2010–2015*, (2016), p. 5.

280 Schmeets, *De religieuze kaart van Nederland, 2010–2013*, p. 4.

281 Id., p. 5.

282 Ton Bernts, Gert De Jong and Hasan Yar, *Een religieuze atlas van Nederland*, (Wetenschappelijke Raad voor het regeringsbeleid, Geloven in het publieke domein, Den Haag 2006), pp. 91, 113–114, 116–117. Persons of Turkish (328 000) and Moroccan (296 000) descent accounted for two thirds of the Muslim population in 2006. The remaining one third consisted, primarily, of persons originating from Iraq, Afghanistan, Iran, Suriname and Somalia. The majority are Sunni, while the Shiite and Turkish Alevi form a minority representation of the Muslim population.

283 In 2006 the majority of Hindus originated from Suriname, India and Sri Lanka. Id., pp. 91, 126–127.

284 Id., pp. 132–133. It should be noted that there is a weak connection between religiosity to Judaism and membership of the Jewish community. In a study conducted in 2006, 62% of the members that indicated their affiliation with the Jewish community was on the basis of a self-perceived duty to keep the Jewish community viable, while 17% of those belonging to the community indicated that they were not affiliated with Judaism.

285 *Code of Canon Law*, can. 330–333.

286 Id., can. 330–338.

managed by the bishops together with their presbyter council (priests).[287] The bishops exercise the legislative, executive and judicial arms within their respective diocese, with the exception of matters that are reserved for the highest or other church authority.[288] On their turn, the dioceses are subdivided into parishes which are smaller community units which are led and guided by a priest, under the supervision of a bishop.[289] Each diocese has its own tribunal (*kerkelijke rechtbank*), with the bishop serving as the judge at first instance.[290] The church tribunal of another diocese fulfils the role of second instance tribunal, while the Apostolic Tribunal of the Roman Rota forms the highest appellate tribunal of the Roman Catholic Church.[291]

These courts have legal procedures in place for administrative appeals, sexual misconduct, employment-related disputes and for addressing instances of misconduct.[292] They also have the competence over religious matters, property and marital-related disputes.[293] Concerning the latter, about 200 requests for marriage annulments are initiated every year.[294] The judicial processes of the church tribunals are not open to the public. Canon law is the operating normative system, as it is codified in the *Codex Iuris Canonici*. This system applies universally over the entire church. Additional to the Canon law, there are also particular laws which are enacted by the bishops and apply only in the diocese for which they have been designated. Furthermore, the legislative power that is vested in the Pope and bishops also makes it possible to promulgate other laws that serve to give further interpretative guidance on the application of Canon law.[295]

Turning to the Protestant denominations, these are less hierarchal, when compared to the Roman Catholic Church. The merger of the Dutch Reformed Church, the Reformed Churches in the Netherlands and the Evangelical Lutheran Church in 2004 created the Protestant Church in the Netherlands which forms the largest Protestant community thereof.[296] This church is composed of various municipalities across the country and management occurs at different levels. The general synod governs church matters at the level of the church. The classis meetings regulate matters at the regional level, while

---

287 Id., can. 495.

288 Id., can. 381.

289 Id., can. 515.

290 Id., can. 1419.

291 Id., can. 1438–1444.

292 Oldenhuis, et al., *Schurende relaties tussen recht en religie*, pp. 97–108.

293 Code of Canon Law, can. 1400–1401. These provisions refer to a wide range of the subject matters over which the church tribunal has competence. Accordingly, church tribunals have the competence to pursue or vindicate the 'rights of physical or juridic persons', declare 'juridic facts' and impose 'penalty for delicts'. Tribunals adjudicate over a broad range of matters including 'cases which regard spiritual matters or those connected to spiritual matters' and 'violation of ecclesiastical laws and all those matters in which there is a question of sin, in what pertains to the determination of culpability and the imposition of ecclesiastical penalties.

294 Oldenhuis, et al., *Scheurende relaties tussen recht en religie*. p. 102.

295 Id., p. 97.

296 Id., p. 108.

the church council oversees its respective municipality.[297] Each of these three bodies have legislative and executive powers within their respective levels. The governing documents are the church statute (*Kerkorde van de PKN*) and fourteen ordinations.

There are dispute settlement mechanisms in place for solving internal matters, although these do not govern religious divorces. The judicial arm is situated within the supervisory boards (colleges), which are formed by individual religious members.[298] These boards are each appointed with competence over particular matters. These include, among others, disciplinary measures, disputes between the pastor and the church council, property-related disputes between municipalities, complaints of a managerial nature and disputes concerning the activities of church bodies, clerics or others in service of the church.[299] The decision of a regional supervisory board can be appealed to the general supervisory board.[300] Decisions are anonymised when made public and decisions concerning disciplinary matters are not disclosed.[301]

3.2.2. JEWISH COMMUNITIES

In the Netherlands, the various Jewish communities have organised themselves along the lines of affiliation, ancestry and commonly shared traditions.[302] The largest is the Dutch-Israeli Church community (*Nederlands-Israëlitisch Kerkgenootschap (NIK)*. The NIK is governed by the daily council (*permanente commissie*) and the general council (*centrale commissie*) which together deal with internal as well as external affairs which affect the Jewish communities.[303] There are a few Jewish municipalities across the country, the four largest of which are located in Amsterdam, Rotterdam, Utrecht and The Hague.[304] An appointed chief rabbi is entrusted with providing religious guidance to the community and representing the Jewish community in the public life.[305]

Religious tribunals (*Beth din)* are established in certain municipalities that have one or more rabbis. The *interprovicinciaal Opperrabbinaat*, foresees for *Halacha*-based decisions

297 *Kerkorde en ordinanties van de Protestantse Kerk in Nederland inclusief de overgangsbepalingen*, Article VI, 4.

298 Id., Ordinantie 12, Article 1 (2), Article XI (V).

299 Oldenhuis, et al., *Scheurende relaties tussen recht en religie*, p. 109.; *Kerkorde en ordinanties van de Protestantse Kerk in Nederland inclusief de overgangsbepalingen*, Ordinantie 12.

300 *Kerkorde en ordinanties van de Protestantse Kerk in Nederland inclusief de overgangsbepalingen*, Ordinantie 12, Article 8.

301 Oldenhuis, et al., *Scheurende relaties tussen recht en religie*, p. 114.

302 L. Evers and J. Stodel, *Jodendom in de praktijk* (2011), para. 10.2.

303 *Landelijke Organisatie, at* <www.nik.nl/dit-is-het-nik/landelijke-organisatie/> last accessed 13 March 2018.

304 Almere, Amersfoort, Arnhem, Breda, Bussum, Groningen, Noord-Holland, Noordwest (Heemstede), Leeuwarden, Limburg (Maastricht), Nijmegen, Rotterdam, Stedendriehoek, Twente, Utrecht, Zeeland and Zwolle *Joodse Gemeente, at* <www.nik.nl/joodse-gemeente/>.; Evers & Stodel, *Jodendom in de praktijk*, para. 10.2.

305 *Reglement betreffende de inrichting en het bestuur van het Nederland-Israeliëtisch kerkgenootschap*, Verordening no. 159, Article 77a.

for all the other townships which do not have a rabbi.[306] These tribunals are, amongst other things, charged with controlling and ensuring compliance with religious laws within the community, e.g., that store owners provide Kosher foods. They also provide religious council and education to community members and take part in solemnising marriages.[307]

The dissolution of a marriage in accordance with the *Halacha* is an activity that is entrusted with the *Opperabbinaat voor Nederland,* which is based in Amsterdam.[308] By way of contrast to Catholicism the competences of the *Beth dins*, their interpretations of the *Halacha* and their decisions only apply in relation to Dutch Jewish communities and have no universal recognition. Furthermore, there is no centralised authority similar to that which is found in the Roman Catholic Church.

3.2.3. MUSLIM COMMUNITIES

There is no prevailing nor consistent model of organisation within Muslim communities in the Netherlands, although many of the existing organisations are Mosque organisations.[309] This may, as Oldenhuis suggests, be related to the distinctive character that is attributed to the function of communities of adherents *(umma).* Religious law encourages an organisation structure that facilitates the social and political unity of the community and ensures compliance with religious laws in all aspects of life by community members. Politics and religion are therefore regarded as inseparable. Therefore, the form of organisation should follow its function.[310] While this is easily achievable in Muslim majority countries, this is more problematic in secular countries where general neutral laws apply to all individuals and abidance with the law is expected from all citizens, irrespective of one's religion.[311]

By way of contrast to Canon law, which provides clear and specific guidelines on the organisational structure of religious communities, *Shari'a* provides little guidance on the organisation structure of mosque organisations in secular States.[312] Additionally, there is no hierarchy or a central Islamic authority and there are different schools and denominations within Islam. These factors in turn partly account for the different ways in which Muslim communities have organised themselves in the Netherlands. It should also be pointed out that even in Muslim majority countries, the structural organisation of the religious community and the placed role of mosques within the communities varies greatly.[313]

---

306 *Interprovinciaal Opperrabinaat, at* <www.nik.nl/dit-is-het-nik/rabbinaten/interprovinciaal-opperrabbinaat-ipor/> last accessed 13 March 2018.

307 Evers and Stodel, *Jodendom in de praktijk*, para. 10.2.

308 *Interprovenciaaa Opperrabinaat, at* <www.nik.nl/dit-is-het-nik/rabbinaten/opperrabbinaat-voor-nederland/>.

309 Oldenhuis, et al., *Schurende relaties tussen recht en religie*, pp. 136–138.

310 Id., pp. 137.

311 Id., pp. 137–138.

312 Id., p. 138.

313 Id., pp. 138–139.

In the Netherlands, there are various forms of dispute settlement within Muslim communities. Disputes can be settled by family, friends[314], imams and/or the board of the organisation.[315] As a side note, while having the status of religious leaders within their communities, imams do not see dispute settlement as their primary task. Rather they are more frequently approached to provide council than to settle disputes.[316] Furthermore, there is no identifiable procedure for settling disputes, however certain customs/practices may be followed, such as the involvement of brothers, cousins, uncles and fathers.[317] Matters which are subjected to internal dispute resolution primarily concern marital disputes and divorce matters and, to a lesser, extent, familial problems. Financial issues can also be dealt with in this manner.[318] In theory, parties are not bound by these decisions but in practice they carry certain weight due to the perceived authority of the mediators. There is also a certain pressure from within the community to comply with these decisions. In addition, the status and role of religious law, as the governing normative system, within the dispute settlement mechanism remains vague. However, it has been submitted that religious law serves to provide guidance in the settlement of disputes and is therefore used to substantiate the decisions so as to ensure greater compliance with the ultimate decision.[319]

3.2.4. HINDU COMMUNITIES

The organisational structure, existing dispute settlement mechanisms and application of religious laws in Hindu communities is by far the least clear of the religions studied in this thesis. The majority of the Hindu population in the Netherlands originates from Suriname. The two major schools are the Sanatan Dharm and the Arya Samaj.[320] Similar to the Muslim communities, Hindus have organised their communities into associations and foundations. There are numerous Hindu associations and foundations in the Netherlands.[321] Noteworthy is the *Shri Sanatan Dharm Mahasabha Nederland*,

---

314 Settlement by friends is also an option where parties do not have family in the Netherlands.

315 Oldenhuis, et al., *Schurende relaties tussen recht en religie*, p. 143.; Bakker, et al., *Sharia in Nederland: Een studie naar Islamitische advisering en geschillenbeslechting bij moslims in Nederland*, pp. 72–80.

316 Bakker, et al., Sharia in Nederland: Een studie naar Islamitische advisering en geschillenbeslechting bij moslims in Nederland, p. 75. The tasks of imams are to lead the prayers in the mosque, to hold the service on Friday followed by the Friday prayers, to ensure abidance with to religious norms in the mosque, to provide Koran and Islamic education to children, youth and adults and to give council and advice in a way that is compatible with the Islamic scripture.

317 Id., pp. 77–78.

318 Id., pp. 72–80.

319 Id., pp. 80–83.

320 Bernts, et al., *Een religieuze atlas van Nederland,* pp. 91, 126–127.; Anja van Heelsum and Eske Voorthuysen, *Surinaamse organisaties in Nederland: Een netwerkanalyse*, (Amsterdam, 2002), p. 12. Within these branches' individuals, families and communities may hold diverging views, customs, rituals and practices.

321 Id., pp. 12–15.

which is an umbrella organisation that is made up of nine *mandirs* (Hindu-temples).[322] There is also the *Shri Sanatan Dharm Priestersraad Nederland* (SDPN), which is an independent national organisation for *brahman pandits*.[323] Founded in 2002, the SDPN fulfils the task of managing and coordinating the activities of the priests.[324] For the Hindus that follow the *Arya Samaj* school, there are the *Federatie Arya Samaj Nederland* and the *Pratinidhi Arya Sabha Nederland*. These are umbrella organisations of other *Arya Samaj* affiliated organisations.[325] However these, and other similar umbrella organisations, have not managed to serve the role as the overall umbrella organisation for the Hindu community in the Netherlands. There remains no clear and strong organisational structure within Hindu communities.[326] It has been submitted that this is the result of, amongst other things, a lack of strong leadership and realistic goal setting within the communities, strong competition, financial disagreement and distrust.[327] Notably, the existing fragmentation incentivised the government and Hindu communities to establish the *Hindoe Raad Nederland* in 2001. This organisation primarily aims to serve the interests of the Hindu community and to act on behalf of the Hindu community, as the negotiation partner with the Dutch government.[328]

The various existing organisations deal with both religious activities as well as cultural and social activities within the Hindu communities, such as coordinating the places of worship, managing the burial of Hindu adherents, promoting Hindu education and providing for Hindu-oriented media etc.[329]

The priests *(pandits)* serve multiple tasks for adherents and have, at least in the Netherlands, adapted to provide services that attend to the demands of adherents.[330] Activities include, providing guidance and council, presiding over rituals and ceremonies in the *mandir* and in adherents' homes and providing for lectures in the

---

322 More on this foundation can be found at: <www.mahasabha.nl/> last accessed 27 May 2018.

323 According to the caste system, *brahaman* are members of the highest caste. In general, priests who preside over religious rituals derive from this caste. Burg, Theo Damsteegt, Krishna Autar, *Hindoestanen in Nederland*, (Leuven, Apledoorn: 1990), p. 91.

324 Id., p. 135. For more see also 'Over de SDPN', *at* <https://sdpn.wordpress.com/over-de-sdp/> last accessed 27 May 2018.

325 Organisatie Hindoe Media, 'Hindoewijzer: 45 jaar Arya Samaj in Nederaland', *at* <www.ohmnet.nl/hindoewijzer/radio/45-jaar-arya-samaj-nederland/> last accessed 27 May 2018.; Van Heelsum and Voorthuysen, *Surinaamse organisaties in Nederland: Een netwerkanalyse*, p. 14.

326 Id., p. 13.

327 Id.

328 Corstiaan van der Burg, 'The Hindu diaspora in the Netherlands: Halfway between local structures and global ideologies' in Jacobsen, & Kumar, *South Asians in the Diaspora: Histories and Religious Traditions* (Leiden, 2004), p. 109.; van Heelsum and Voorthuysen, *Surinaamse organisaties in Nederland: Een netwerkanalyse*, p. 25.

329 For example, the Organisatie voor Hindu Media which attends television and radio broadcasts that involve and relate to Hinduism. For more on this organisation, see *<www.ohmnet.nl/over-ohm/>* last visited 27 May 2018. See also van der Burg, et al., *Hindoestanen in Nederland*, pp. 135–136.; van Heelsum and Voorthuysen, *Surinaamse organisaties in Nederland: Een netwerkanalyse*, p. 13.

330 Van der Burg, et al., *Hindoestanen in Nederland*, pp. 135–136.

mandir. *Pandits* are also involved in the rituals that solemnise religious marriages.[331] However, their role and involvement in the termination of a marriage is less clear. The much-criticised documentary on divorce in Hinduism is an example thereof.[332] In this respect, it should be borne in mind that the process for dissolving the religious marriage remains somewhat ambiguous in Hinduism. There is no common consensus on either the existence thereof or clarity on the nature of divorce rituals.

3.2.5. THE STATUS OF RELIGIOUS COMMUNITIES

As was demonstrated in the previous paragraphs, all four religions have viable and active religious organisations in the Netherlands. Although, in terms of possessing legal personality, the form which they take differs from one religion to the next. The aforementioned organisational structures of the Christian and Jewish communities partake in society as 'religious communities' within the sense of Article 2:2 of the Dutch Civil Code (DCC).[333] What is noteworthy, a more precise translation of the Dutch term '*kerkgenootschap*' would be *church society*. On the face of it, this would seem to imply a narrow interpretation which is limited to those religious communities with strong links to the Christian faith, due to the use of the term 'church'. However, when looking at the meaning that was attributed to this term during parliamentary discussions, and which was later confirmed in Dutch case law, this assumption could not be further from the truth. The prevailing understanding is that a church society concerns a permanent association of people which, on the basis of common religious conceptions, aim to enable theolatry in a community of its members.[334] To qualify as a church society, two factors are determinant in this regard: the existence of a structured organisation of individual members and a religion. In principle this means that non-Christian faiths fulfil these criteria, as is the case with Islam, Hinduism and Judaism. With this in mind adopting the term 'religious community' seems to be a more accurate description of the types of organisations that are referred to in Article 2:2 DCC.

A religious community does not require formal conditions to be met for the establishment thereof, as the first indent of Article 2:2 DCC recognises that they have legal personality. Secondly, they are managed and structured in accordance with

---

331 Pandits', *at* <www.sanatandharm.net/pandits/> last visited 27 May 2018.; Susan Rutten, et al., *Gewoon getrouwd: Een onderzoek naar kindhuwelijken en religieuze huwelijken in Nederland*, pp. 71, 80, 84.

332 Organisatie voor Hindoe Media, *Scheiden binnen het hindoeïsme.*

333 This provision reads as follows:
'1. Religious communities and their independent subdivisions and bodies in which they are united, have legal personality.
2. 'They are governed by their own charter insofar the rules thereof are not in conflict with law. With the exception of Article 2:5, the below listed Articles of the present Title (Title 2.1) do not apply to them. Nevertheless, these Articles may be applied accordingly as far as this is in agreement with the charter of the religious community and the nature of the mutual relationships within that community.

334 Oldenhuis, et al, *Schurende relaties tussen recht en religie*. pp. 84–86.

their own charters according to the second indent.[335] In other words, the law of legal persons does not stipulate which particular conditions the charter and organisational structure should meet, in the same way that it does for, by way of example, associations (Articles 2:26 – 28 DCC). However, despite being entitled to form religious communities within the meaning of Article 2:2 DCC, Muslims and Hindu organisations partake in society as associations or foundations. Consequently, these organisations do not enjoy the status of being religious communities, due to the fact that they have established their legal status as associations or foundations. In the Netherlands, it is not possible to have legal status on the basis of multiple forms of legal personality.[336] Thus, by establishing themselves as associations or foundations, the Muslim and Hindu organisations essentially forfeit their option to declare themselves as religious communities.

Oldenhuis submits several explanations for why Muslim and Hindu communities have opted to organise themselves as association or foundations, rather than establishing themselves as religious communities. A major factor is the lack of information or unclear information concerning the status of religious communities and how to declare and assert this status. It may also be the case that the founders of a Hindu or Muslim organisation are under the impression that the protection and freedoms afforded to both structures are the same. Furthermore, the absence of a formal registration process only adds to the ambiguity of this form of legal personality and therefore may be perceived as an obstacle, particularly where the religious community seeks to legitimise its legal personality to the public/society.[337] For these reasons, it is understandable why these communities may opt to establish an association or a foundation, so as to assert their legal personality and to be able to communicate this clearly to the public. Notably, certain mosque organisations have been registered as religious communities. However, this has been done for rather symbolic reasons because they had previously established legal personality either as associations or foundations, meaning that Article 2:2 DCC does not apply to them.[338]

Not having legal personality by way of Article 2:2 DCC has certain consequences. First, the second indent of Article 2:2 DCC acknowledges the freedom of religious communities to be governed by their own charters, as long as they remain within the limits set by the law. Furthermore, they are exempted from the general rules on legal persons. This means that the general provisions on legal persons, including those on the prohibition and dissolution of dangerous legal persons, do not apply to religious communities. Muslim and Hindu organisations which are not religious communities, at least within the meaning of Article 2:2 DCC, are therefore subjected to the general organisational, administrative and financial rules of legal persons. Secondly, Muslim organisations and Hindu organisations may be dissolved under Article 2:20 DCC, as

335 Van Bijsterveld, *Religion and Law in the Netherlands*, p. 127.
336 Oldenhuis, et a., *Schurende relaties tussen recht en religie*. pp. 138–139.
337 Id., pp. 140–141.
338 Id., p. 138.

the general rules on legal persons continue to apply to them. Thirdly, the extent and manner in which a secular judge examines and interferes in the matters related to a church society is marginal in comparison to interference in and examination of matters related to an association or foundation.[339] Although none of the decisions of religious tribunals have legal effect, those of religious community are examined marginally when they are challenged before a secular court. This is more so the case where the disputed matters are perceived as internal affairs, the fundamental procedural safeguards are guaranteed and the decision does not conflict with the law or public policy.[340]

3.3. MARRIAGE, DIVORCE AND MARITAL CAPTIVITY

In the Netherlands, religious marriages are not recognised. They also have no legal effects, create no legal rights and obligations between the spouses and do not affect the spouses' civil status. According to Article 1:30 (2) DCC, the law only recognises civil marriages. Thus, spouses that only celebrate a religious marriage are, by law, not considered to be legally married. These types of marriages therefore constitute informal religious marriages. However, one ought to keep in mind that certain religious marriages can nonetheless be recognised as formal marriages in the Netherlands. This may, for example, be the case when a religious marriage is conducted in a country where religious marriages constitute formal and legally valid marriages. To enjoy the same legal status as that of a married couple, the spouses can request to have their marriage recognised in conformity with the rules of private international law in the Netherlands.[341] Additionally, it should be kept in mind that an informal marriage conducted in the Netherlands may be recognised in that other State. Thus, an informal marriage in the Netherlands, may nevertheless constitute a formal marriage in another country.

The right to celebrate the marriage in accordance with one's religious beliefs is subjected to a restriction that requires a civil marriage be concluded prior to the conclusion of a religious marriage. Article 1:68 DCC prohibits the solemnisation of a religious marriage prior to a civil marriage. This has been found to be a legitimate restriction to both the right to freedom of religion and the right to marry, as the restrictions serve the aim of protecting the legal rights of the spouses and ensuring legal certainty.[342] As a religious marriage does not create any legal effects, the provision serves the purpose of ensuring that spouses are not under a false assumption that a religious marriage creates a change in their personal status and entitles them to spousal legal rights and obligations. In addition, this restriction serves to protect the weaker

339 Id., pp. 120–125.
340 Id.
341 Mejdoubi, *Factsheet- Wel gesheiden, niet gescheiden. Huwelijkse gevangenschap in Nederland*, (2016), p. 3.
342 Rechtbank Rotterdam, 06 January 2016, ECLI:NL:RBROT:2016:8, para 4.1.

parties (e.g. children of the union), by ensuring that the legal rights and obligations deriving from the civil marriage, are established and may be enforced upon termination of the marriage.

As for divorce, spouses have equal rights to initiate divorce proceedings. Articles 1:151 and 1:154 DDC provide 'irretrievable breakdown' as the only ground for dissolving a marriage.[343] Both or one of the spouses can invoke this ground and fault of either spouse is not a prerequisite. Upon examination and establishment that this is indeed the case, a civil judge will pronounce the divorce between the spouses. These articles only refer to the dissolution of a civil marriage and thus only the civil institutions of marriage and divorce are recognised. Secular family law is therefore the governing normative system in these situations. Therefore, a civil divorce dissolves the civil marriage, but it does not necessarily affect the religious marriage or the religious significance attached to marriage. However, certain religious communities may give recognition to a civil divorce, as is done within Protestant denominations. Additionally, a civil divorce, pronounced by a Dutch judge can also have the effect of dissolving a State-recognised religious marriage i.e., a formal marriage that is recognised or has been celebrated in another country. This can be achieved where the Dutch civil divorce is recognised in a country where, for example, the State-recognised religious marriage was celebrated. Recognition of a Dutch divorce, therefore, may result in the dissolution of the State-recognised religious marriage.

Similar to religious marriages, religious divorces are awarded no recognition. Similarly, the religious rules on divorce, as well as the divorce processes that religious tribunals maintain, have no legal meaning or effect. Legal pluralism is not acknowledged in these situations.[344] In other words, religious normative systems are not incorporated in State law and do not therefore constitute 'law' in a formal sense.[345] The dissolution of an informal marriage in accordance with religious laws does not affect a civil marriage. At the same time, divorce in accordance with the religious laws is not prohibited either. As a matter of fact, this typically occurs as religious communities are allowed to govern their internal affairs in accordance with their own normative systems.[346] However, this does not amount to formal legal pluralism.[347]

Again, there are exceptions to the rules. The recognition of a religious divorce may nevertheless occur where it concerns a foreign divorce that was promulgated in accordance with the governing religious law of the concerned country i.e., the

343 Dutch Civil Code (Burgerlijk Wetboek Boek 1, Personen- en familierecht), Articles 1: 151, 1:154.

344 Oldenhuis, et.al., *Schurende relaties tussen recht en religie*.p. 138.; Minister van Justitie, *Brief Tweede Kamer: Schriftelijk overleg over shariarechtbanken*, pp. 1–2.

345 See the reaction of the Minister of Justice on religious tribunals and the application of religious laws in the Netherlands. Id.

346 See Bakker, et al, *Sharia in Nederland: Een studie naar Islamitische advisering en geschillenbeslechting bij moslims in Nederland*, on the application of Islamic law in Muslims communities. See Oldenhuis, et al., *Schurende relaties tussen recht en religie*. pp. 83–126 on the application of religious laws in Christian communities.

347 Minister van Justitie, *Brief Tweede Kamer: Schriftelijk overleg over shariarechtbanken*, pp. 1–2.

dissolution of a State-recognised religious divorce. Spouses may then request the recognition of this religious divorce in the Netherlands in accordance with the rules of private international law. Another instance where a religious divorce may have formal recognition can occur where the Dutch judge has to apply foreign religious law to dissolve a formally recognised religious marriage. This may be the case when the judge establishes that, in accordance with private international law, the foreign law is applicable to the divorce proceedings.[348] The judge will then have to apply religious laws (e.g. Islamic law or Jewish law) in the divorce proceedings, in so far as the application thereof does not conflict with public policy.[349]

3.3.1. PUBLIC DISCOURSE ON MARITAL CAPTIVITY

While the oldest known case of marital captivity can be traced back to 1982[350], it is only since the 21st century that this phenomenon has been coined and received increasing public attention outside of the religious communities. Recent studies have also identified other factors that may also contribute to enabling and creating marital captivity, alongside the religious factors discussed in this contribution.[351]

Interestingly, within the public discourse and political debates[352], much attention has been paid to religious marriages or state-recognised religious marriages and the complications that come with the dissolution of a religious marriage. Consequently, the

---

348 Dutch Civil Code, Articles, 10:56–57.

349 Id., Article 10:59.

350 Hoge Raad, 22 January 1982, ECLI: NL:HR:1982:AG4319.

351 For example, abandonment in a foreign country and the incompatibility of two or more family law systems governing the marriage may create complications for spouses seeking a divorce. Lack of knowledge on the available means, insufficient financial, social and emotional pressure and the deprivation of liberty are all factors which may contribute to creating a situation of marital captivity. van Eijk, *Wel gescheiden, niet gescheiden? Een empirisch onderzoek naar huwelijkse gevangenschap in Nederland.*; Eliane Smits van Waesberghe, et al., *Zo zijn we niet getrouwd: Een onderzoek naar omvang en aard van huwelijksdwang, achterlating en huwelijkse gevangenschap*, (2014). pp. 24, 93.; See also the case of Maryam which is discussed in Chapter 2.

352 See for example, Susan Rutten, et al., *Gewoon getrouwd: Een onderzoek naar kindhuwelijken en religieuze huwelijken in Nederland*, pp. 124–128; Susan Rutten, 'Protection of spouses in informal marriages by human rights', 6 *Utrecht Law Review* 77–92, (2010), pp. 77–92.; Mattijs de Blois, 'Religious law versus secular law: The example of the Gett refusal in Dutch and English and Israeli law', Id., pp. 93–114. Marije van Beek, 'Vrouw in het nadeel bij religieuze scheiding', *Trouw* 30 June 2016, *at* <https://www.trouw.nl/home/vrouw-in-het-nadeel-bij-religieuze-scheiding~a4b20661/> last accessed 04 February 2018.;'Vragen gesteld door de leden der Kamer, met de daarop door de regering gegeven antwoorden, Kamerstukken II, 2016/ 2017, 1785' 2017.; 'Minister van Veligheid and Staatssecretaris van Veiligheid en Justitie 'Huwelijks- en gezinsmigratie; Brief regering; Reactie op de brief van de organisatie Femmes for Freedom inzake huwelijkse gevangenschap, Kamerstukken II, 2011/2012, 32 175, nr. 31', 2012. See also Statements by Femmes for Freedom, *Huwelijkse gevangenschap, at* <www.femmesforfreedom.com/themas/huwelijkse-gevangenschap/> last accessed 27 December 2015.; *Aanpak huwelijksdwang, at* <https://www.rijksoverheid.nl/onderwerpen/huwelijksdwang/huwelijksdwang-voorkomen> last accessed 02 Februrary 2017. *Huwelijksdwang en achterlating-Huwelijkse gevangenschap* (2013), *at* <https://www.huiselijkgeweld.nl/dossiers/huwelijksdwang/beleid/huwelijkse-gevangenschap> last accessed 03 February 2018; Ministerie van Volksgezondheid

discourse on marital captivity has tended to lean more towards the religious conditions as well as transnational factors which give rise to situations of marital captivity. The most frequently raised challenges and points of discussion have been, how and to what extent, the State ought to intervene and facilitate the cessation and prevention of situations of marital captivity. In particular, much attention has been attributed to marital captivity as it occurs in the Jewish and Muslim communities. This result may be partly attributed to the increasing body of case law that has dealt with marital captivity into a Jewish or Islamic marriage.[353] In addition, members within these communities have also shown more willingness to involve the public and national authorities in their efforts to find sustainable and effective solutions to ending and preventing marital captivity. Far more limited cases have involved Catholic spouses[354] and to date no case has been issued involving a Hindu marriage. In this regard, the engagement of and disclosure by Christian and Hindu communities has been minimal compared to the other two religions. The easier available and accessible insights and information of marital captivity as occurring in Muslim and Jewish communities, therefore, can partly help to explain why the narrative has mostly focused on marital captivity occurring within these communities.

In the case law, the religious dimension has largely been circumvented and is rarely addressed explicitly. Judges have primarily focused on establishing their jurisdiction over a case of marital captivity. The main position has been that the religious dimension does not preclude judges from having jurisdiction to consider the case. For example, spouses from the Christian faith, have at times challenged a request for divorce by the other spouse. In essence what they were attempting to create was a situation of marital captivity within a civil marriage, by requesting that the marriage could not be dissolved. In one case, the opposing spouse (the husband) argued, somewhat creatively, that the vows between the spouses implied an agreement to apply 'godly law' (i.e., the law given by God) to the marriage instead of secular law or religious law. According to this law, the spouse argued, the marriage could only be terminated upon death of either of the spouses. Essentially, he argued that the parties had made an agreement to deviate from civil law and in particular Article 1:151 DCC which provides 'irretrievable breakdown' of the marriage as a legitimate ground for divorce. The court dismissed this claim, as public policy and morality do not permit the circumvention, by an agreement between the parties, of the legal grounds for divorce.[355] In two other cases, the opposing spouses (the wives) objected to a civil divorce on the basis that a divorce was incompatible with

---

Welzijn en Sport, *Huwelijkse gevangenschap – Huiselijk geweld, at* <www.huiselijkgeweld.nl/dossiers/campagne_huwelijksdwang/beleid/huwelijkse-gevangenschap> last accessed 27 December 2015.

353 See section 3.4.1.

354 In these cases, one of the spouses attempted to obstruct a civil divorce by arguing that the marriage was indissoluble. So far, these arguments have not been accepted in any divorce proceedings. Hoge Raad, 29 April 2016, ECLI:NL:HR:2016:767.; Hoge Raad, Conclusion of the attorney general, 09 December 2005, ECLI:NL:PHR:2005:AU5285.

355 Hoge Raad, 29 April 2016, ECLI:NL:HR:2016:767, para. 4.

their religious convictions, namely that a marriage is indissoluble. In both cases, the Court concluded that the religious convictions of both women could not prevent the dissolution of the marriage.[356] Furthermore, the court held that this did not constitute a violation of the right to freedom of religion or the right to private and family life, as one of the spouses had alleged.[357] Therefore, the religious position that a marriage is indissoluble or is governed by religious laws has not precluded judges from deciding over civil divorce cases.

With regard to marital captivity in Jewish and Islamic marriages, judges have been able to establish jurisdiction on the basis of a tort-action i.e., whether a given situation of marital captivity constitutes a tort.[358] However, the lack of an explicit mention of the religious dimension does not imply that this factor has not influenced the outcome of a case. For example, one advocate general stressed the importance of a restrictive and judicious approach when dealing with religious matters.[359] Judges have at times taken into consideration the views of religious authorities on the matter of a 'coerced' *get*.[360] Likewise, in 2016 a civil judge reached the conclusion that trapping a spouse in an informal religious marriage, despite the fact that a civil marriage had never existed, did not constitute a tort and the judge proceeded to even recommend the applicant to visit the *Sharia Councils* in Europe.[361] This decision was eventually overturned by the Court of Appeal in 2017.[362]

3.3.2. THE ROLE OF THE STATE IN RELIGIOUS DIVORCES

An additional area of concern that has been raised in relation to marital captivity and religious marriages, relates to the religious divorce practices in religious tribunals. One argument that is frequently forwarded in this regard is the incompatibility of certain religious rules with fundamental norms and values of the State, such as the principle of equality between women and men.[363] In this regard, questions have been raised

356 Hoge Raad, Conclusion of the attorney general, 09 December 2005, ECLI:NL:PHR:2005:AU5285, para. 10. See also previous case involving the same parties, Hoge Raad, Conclusion of the attorney general, 27 June 2003, ECLI:NL:PHR:2003AF7681, paras. 9–10 and Hoge Raad, 12 July 2002, ECLI:NL:HR:2002:AE4037, para 3.3.

357 Hoge Raad, Conclusion of the attorney general, 09 December 2005 ECLI:NL:PHR:2005:AU5285, paras. 8–9.

358 Wetboek van Burgerlijke Rechtsvordering (Dutch Code of Civil Procedure), Article 6(e).; Burgerlijke Wetboek, (Dutch Civil Code), Article 6:162.

359 Hoge Raad, Conclusion of the attorney general, 10 November 1989, ECLI:NL:PHR:1989:AC1683, para 2.21.

360 Gerechtshof Amsterdam, 31 August 1989, ECLI:NL:GHAMS:1989:AD0874.; Rechtbank Haarlem, 17 February 1989, ECLI:NL:RBHAA:1989:AH2605.; Rechtbank Amsterdam, 17 November 1983, ECLI:NL:RBAMS:1983:AH0155.

361 Rechtbank Rotterdam, 06 January 2016, ECLI:NL:RBROT:2016:8. This case is discussed more in detail in para. 2.5.2.

362 Gerechtshof Den Haag, 21 November 2017, ECLI:NL:GHDHA:2017:3297.

363 See for example the reactions and debates related to the issue of *Sharia Tribunals* and *Shari'a* in the newspaper article *Pleidooi shariaraad stuit op verzet vrouwen* that was published in the Volkskrant in 2012.

concerning the permissibility of such activities and the role that the State should adopt in addressing these practices. As a response to these questions, the Minister of Foreign affairs submitted that individuals are free to submit themselves to the rules of the organisation they voluntarily choose to be a member of, including religious laws, even if these are not perfectly aligned with the secular laws on marriage and divorce.[364] This line of reasoning reflects the complex relationship between individuals and the religious communities they belong to. Within the context of the freedom of religion, religious communities are not obliged to preserve and protect all the rights of their adherents, as it is presumed that individuals voluntarily submit to the rules of the religion and community and are therefore, free to leave the religious community so as to recant their religion at any time.[365]

Similarly, the Minister and Secretary of Security and Justice have, in their responses to Femmes for Freedom[366], acknowledged that so long as those submitting to the religious laws are not coerced to do so, the legislator has no business in interfering with their religious affairs.[367] It was also suggested to ensure that the fundamental principles and values of Dutch law on divorce are appropriated in religious laws on divorce; however this was rejected. This suggestion was perceived, by the Minister and Secretary of Security and Justice, as encroaching upon the religious affairs and was considered to be incompatible with the secular principles of the Netherlands.[368] Additionally, it was submitted that the State cannot be held accountable for religious rules on divorce that are not in line with gender equality principles, as these have not been enacted or implemented by the State.[369]

3.4. MEASURES FOR ADDRESSING MARITAL CAPTIVITY

How to address marital captivity is still an ongoing debate. The measures in place, although effective to some extent, have not provided sustainable solutions to marital captivity.[370] In the legal domain, several initiatives have been proposed which are briefly summed up in the following paragraphs.

One proposal that was put forward in 2012 by the non-governmental organisation (NGO) Femmes for Freedom, involved the adoption of legislative measures that

---

364 'Vragen gesteld door de leden der Kamer, met de daarop door de regering gegeven antwoorden', Kamerstukken II, 2011/2012, nr.3114, aanhangsel', 2012, pp. 1–2.

365 See Secion 4.3.2.

366 Kamerstukken II, 2011/2012, 32 175, nr. 31, pp. 5–6.

367 Id., p. 6.

368 Id., pp. 5–6.

369 Id., p. 5.

370 'Brief van de Minister van Sociale Zaken en Werkgelegenheid, Kamerstukken II, 2014/2015, 32 175, nr. 53', 2014.; 'Motie van het lid Yücel c.s. over voorkomen dat een vrouw gevangen blijft in een religieus huwelijk, Kamerstukken II, 2015/2016 33 836, nr. 9', 2016.;'Motie van de Leden van Nispen en Karbulut, Kamerstukken II, 2016/2017, 33 836, nr. 11', 2016.

would make obtaining a civil divorce conditional on the dissolution of the religious marriage.[371] In essence, this proposition mirrored the existing legal measures which have been adopted in some common law countries such as the United Kingdom and Canada. However, the transformation of this proposition into a bill did not come about. A major area of concern was that such a law could obstruct or unnecessarily delay obtaining of a civil divorce. So long as the religious barriers remain, particularly where spouses cannot divorce (e.g. Catholic marriages) or do not want to do so, the civil divorce could be withheld. This was found to be an undesirable outcome.[372] Another area of concern with regard to this proposal was that the proposed measure would not contribute to advancing legal certainty. It was argued that the legal system in the Netherlands, being a civil law system, was not comparable to that of a common law system. The role which judges play in both systems differs extensively. In the common law system, judges influence and contribute to the creation and development of the law. This approach was considered to increase the likelihood of legal uncertainty within the Dutch system.[373] The proposal was, therefore, not adopted as there was no perceived need for such a measure. The only ground for divorce is and had to remain that of the irretrievable breakdown of the marriage in accordance with Article 1:151 DCC. In addition, it was submitted that the existing measures to tackle marital captivity were sufficient.[374]

Another proposal was to facilitate the recognition of Dutch divorces abroad. For example, where foreign law was the designated law, according to the rules of private international law, the Dutch judge should then have to take into account all the specificities that are required in the concerned country. This would then facilitate the recognition of the judgment in that particular country. Regarding this proposal, the government stressed that judges were already aware of this option and were implementing this to the best of their abilities.[375] However, at the same time, the government did stress that not much can be done when the non-recognition is, for example, based on the view that a secular judge has no authority to dissolve a religious marriage. Furthermore, on the basis of their sovereignty and dependent on the treaties they are party to, third countries have the discretion to establish the grounds for recognising or not recognising foreign divorce decisions.[376]

There have been also proposals for increasing extra-territorial engagement of Dutch embassies to protect and assist trapped spouses abroad, by way of offering

---

371 Kamerstukken II, 2011/2012, 32 175, nr. 31, p. 2. See also the new proposal by Kruiniger that is discussed in Kruiniger, *Niet langer geketend aan het huwelijk! Juridische instrumenten die huwelijkse gevangenschap kunnen voorkomen of oplossen*, pp. 69–71.

372 Kamerstukken II, 2011/2012, 32 175, nr. 31, p. 2.; 'Brief Motie Kooiman', Justitie, 10 July 2013, p. 2. See Kruiniger who counters these arguments in: Kruiniger, *Niet langer geketend aan het huwelijk! Juridische instrumenten die huwelijkse gevangenschap kunnen voorkomen of oplossen*, pp. 66–68.

373 Kamerstukken II, 2011/2012, 32 175, nr. 31, p.2.

374 Id., pp. 2–3.

375 Id., p. 8. See also 'Brief Motie Kooiman', Justitie, 10 July 2013, pp. 2–3.

376 'Antwoorden op de Kamervragen van het lid Bergman (D66) over huwelijksdwang en huwelijkse gevangenschap', Werkgelegenheid, 26 September 2016, p. 5.; Brief Motie Kooiman, p. 3.

legal assistance and consular protection. Accordingly, it has been submitted that the relevant authorities have been engaged and deployed the where Dutch embassies have been made aware of situations of marital captivity abroad.[377] However, it is not clear how many cases this concerns and what specific measures were adopted in any of these cases. On the subject of extra-territorial protection, the main position is that Dutch embassies are to respect the local legal orders and are in no position to enforce the human rights obligations of, among others, the Women's' Convention and the ICCPR in these countries.[378] With regard to providing legal assistance so as to facilitate the divorce processes abroad, it has been pointed out that the local means would have to be employed. In such an event, the matter would then be subjected to the national normative system, particularly more so if it involves individuals with dual nationality. The case may then be considered entirely as a local matter and legal assistance would then have to be obtained from the concerned country as well. Furthermore, it is also submitted that financial assistance cannot be provided by the Dutch embassies, as financed legal assistance is reserved for legal cases that occur in the Netherlands.[379] In addition, consular protection is reserved for situations where a Dutch citizen is detained abroad and is facing criminal charges.[380] Furthermore, it has also been pointed out that while, under international law, States have a right to protect their citizens abroad, States are not obliged to do so.[381] That being said, these factors restrict the extent to which Dutch embassies can provide extra-territorial protection and the means they can deploy to protect a trapped spouse abroad.[382]

Noteworthy, in 2017 there was growing support for proposing a bill that would enable trapped spouses to request a penalty for a spouse who refuses to cooperate in the dissolution of a religious divorce. However, as it stands, no official proposal or bill has been drafted and it remains to be seen what the outcome will be.[383]

More recently, the Minister of Legal Protection has confirmed to follow-up on one of the recommendations that was provided in the 2018 report of Kruiniger. This has resulted in the pending bill *wetsvoorstel tegengaan huwelijkse gevangenschap.*[384] In this bill, the possibility to request a judge to compel a spouse to cooperate in the dissolution

377 Kamerstukken II, 2011/2012, nr. 3114, aanhangsel, p. 2.; Antwoorden op de Kamervragen van het lid Bergman (D66) over huwelijksdwang en huwelijkse gevangenschap, p. 5.

378 Kamerstukken II, 2011/2012, 32 175, nr. 31, p. 8.

379 Kamerstukken II, 2011/2012, 3114, aanhangsel, p. 2.; Antwoorden op de Kamervragen van het lid Bergman (D66) over huwelijksdwang en huwelijkse gevangenschap, p. 5.

380 Kamerstukken II, 2011/2012, 32 175, nr. 31, p. 8.

381 Id.

382 Kamerstukken II, 2011/2012, 3114, aanhangsel, p. 2.; Antwoorden op de Kamervragen van het lid Bergman (D66) over huwelijksdwang en huwelijkse gevangenschap, p. 5.

383 Joyce Boverhuis and Ferry Stoop, *CDA en GroenLinks willen boete voor mannen die vrouwen gevangen houden in Islamitisch huwelijk* (2017).

384 'Wet van xxxx tot wijziging van met name het Wetboek van Burgerlijke Rechtsvordering en het Burgerlijk Wetboek (tegengaan huwelijkse gevangenschap)', 2018, WGK009515.

of a religious marriage is included as an ancillary provision in article 827e of the Dutch Code of Civil Procedure.[385] This provision would enable partners who are in the process of a civil divorce to request the judge to also adopt measures that can facilitate the dissolution of the religious marriage. Essentially, the proposed provision would apply to situations in which partners are married religiously and civilly.[386] Notably, in practice, and as is evidence by the existing body of case law[387], this possibility is already available via the tort action. However, to date this possibility is not mentioned explicitly in the law. The bill would, thus, ensure that this possibility is anchored in the law. This would also contribute to raising awareness on the fact that spouses may also have responsibilities to cooperate in the dissolution of the religious marriage upon a civil divorce. Additionally, the proposed provision would also remove a hurdle that spouses currently may face, namely having to conduct a separate tort- action proceeding against a non-cooperative spouse. The proposed provision would enable judges to consider a request to compel a (potentially) non-cooperative spouse to cooperate in the dissolution of a religious divorce as an ancillary provision in the main civil divorce proceedings.[388]

Finally, the studies conducted by van Eijk and Kruiniger reveal that solutions are also being sought by religious communities and professionals alike. They also reveal that in addressing marital captivity there are perceived roles for the State, experts and professionals respectively. Awareness-raising and prevention are regarded as important focal areas. Better preparation of the intending spouses by and within the religious communities has been put forward as one of the ways to prevent situations of marital captivity. As such, professionals as well as the religious community and authorities may play an important role in supporting and informing the intended spouses on the legal and religious aspects of marriage and divorce.[389] Similarly, increased preparation of divorcing spouses may prove to be another means for preventing situations of marital captivity from arising. Professionals, and in particular lawyers, can contribute to this goal by informing the spouse on the implications of a civil divorce and the potential transnational consequences.[390] Increased awareness-raising of one's rights and autonomy and the empowerment of the spouses as well as the religious community has been identified as another area that can be improved.[391] Another promising tool with much potential is the divorce settlement, in which spouses can choose to include

385 Id., p. 2.

386 Although, a step in the right direction, this measure has been criticized in the parliamentary debates as not providing solutions for trapped women that have only conducted a religious marriage. 'Huwelijkse gevangenschap, Kamerstukken II 2018/2019 nr. 79 9', 2019, pp. 1–2.

387 See section 3.4.1.

388 'Memorie van Toelichting – Wet van xxxx tot wijziging van met name het Wetboek van Burgerlijke Rechtsvordering en het Burgerlijk Wetboek (tegengaan huwelijkse gevangenschap), 2018 *at* <https://www.internetconsultatie.nl/huwelijksegevangenschaptegengaan> last accessed 23 January 2019.

389 Van Eijk, Wel gescheiden, niet gescheiden? Een empirisch onderzoek naar huwelijkse gevangenschap in Nederland, p. 77.

390 Id., p. 78.

391 Id.

an agreement to cooperate in the dissolution of the religious marriage upon a civil divorce.[392] Kruiniger, also promotes creative ways to use existing legal tools to prevent marital captivity and facilitate the dissolution of the religious marriage.[393] Other perceived areas that could contribute to addressing marital captivity include educating and training professionals that deal or may have to deal with marital captivity (e.g. social workers, lawyers, embassy staff); improved prevention of forced marriages, raising awareness within the communities to reduce the negative connotations attached to divorce and increased and better cooperation with the religious authorities that deal with religious divorces.[394]

When dealing with marital captivity, outside of the religious dispute settlement mechanisms, trapped spouses in the Netherlands have resorted to the secular judge to obtain a divorce. The civil tort action has been a prominent tool for facilitating the dissolution of a religious marriage. New developments include the criminalisation of certain situations of marital captivity. In addition, non-legal initiatives have also been developed and implemented. These have primarily aimed to facilitate an open dialogue within the religious communities on subjects that are considered taboo, such as marital captivity. These are briefly outlined in the following paragraphs.

3.4.1. CIVIL LAW

Judicial remedies to compel the cooperation of a recalcitrant spouse have been in place since 1982, after a tort action against a recalcitrant Jewish spouse was honoured by the Supreme Court.[395] The spouses already attained a civil divorce. However, the ex-husband had continued to withhold a writ of divorce from his ex-wife. Both the Court of First instance and the Court of Appeal declined the wife's request to compel the man to cooperate in a religious divorce. The lower courts concluded that there was no legal basis to establish jurisdiction for an issue over which the religious tribunals themselves had no factual power to enforce. The Supreme court, however, held the view that secular judges had jurisdiction over the matter. However, they did not entertain jurisdiction over the actual dissolution of a religious marriage. The court also held that the fact that the religious tribunal had no factual means to compel cooperation could not, in itself, be a reason for the secular court not to have jurisdiction over the matter. Nor did it mean that a secular court can or may not invoke the necessary means to compel the recalcitrant spouse's cooperation, particularly where the non-cooperation

392 Kruiniger, *Niet langer geketend aan het huwelijk! Juridische instrumenten die huwelijkse gevangenschap kunnen voorkomen of oplossen*, p. 48.

393 E.g. making use of mediation, prenuptial agreements or contractual agreements before, during or at the dissolution of the civil marriage. More detailed information can be found in: Id., pp. 45–59.

394 Id., pp. 42–44. van Eijk, *Wel gescheiden, niet gescheiden? Een empirisch onderzoek naar huwelijkse gevangenschap in Nederland*, pp. 78–79, 81–83.

395 Hoge Raad, 22 January 1982, ECLI: NL:HR:1982:AG4319.

constitutes a tort.[396] After all, and on the basis of Article 6:162 DCC, secular courts have jurisdiction to examine alleged tortious acts. For establishing whether the given situation constituted a tort, the court developed its own criterion. Whether the withholding of a religious divorce constitutes a tort is dependent on:

- The restrictions the trapped spouse faces upon continuation of the religious marriage;
- the nature and importance of the non-cooperative spouse's objections and
- the costs attached to the cooperation and willingness of the trapped spouse to compensate a part of or the entire costs.[397]

The outcome in the given case was in favour of the trapped spouse and the husband was consequently compelled to cooperate to the religious divorce or otherwise face a financial penalty for his failure to comply with the court's decision.

This case has paved the way for more cases being brought before the civil courts in relation to marital captivity within Muslim and Jewish communities. By 1989, the courts extended the tort action to compel a recalcitrant spouse to cooperate in the dissolution of an Islamic marriage at the Moroccan consulate in the Netherlands, so that the spouses would also be divorced under Moroccan law.[398]

In the subsequent cases, the court has ruled more frequently in favour of the trapped women.[399] In two cases, however, Dutch courts have ruled in favour of the recalcitrant spouse. In one case, the court came to this conclusion after finding that the husband could not be compelled to cooperate in a specific way. The trapped woman specifically requested her husband to cooperate in the form a repudiation (*talaq*). However, the husband refused to repudiate his wife, but he was willing to cooperate to the religious divorce by way of a divorce by mutual consent (*khul'*).[400] In the other case, the court ruled in favour of the recalcitrant spouse after establishing that the law applicable to the matrimonial property still had to be determined. The law governing the division of the matrimonial property in turn could point to either divorce by repudiation or divorce by mutual consent, as the type of divorce effected the property was to be divided among the spouses. Therefore, honouring the request of the woman (transferring of the repudiation right to herself) could not be honoured as this would affect the division of the matrimonial property. In addition, the court established that the woman had no urgent interest since she had no real prospects of travelling to a foreign country or remarrying.[401]

396 Hoge Raad, 22 January 1982, ECLI: NL:HR:1982:AG4319, para. 2. of the judgment on the merits.
397 Id.
398 Hoge Raad, 10 November 1989, ECLI:NL:HR:1989:AC1683.
399 Rechtbank Rotterdam, 8 December 2010, ECLI:NL:RBROT:2010:BP8396.; Rechtbank Amsterdam, 10 April 2012, ECLI:NLRBAMS:2012:BW2800.; Rechtbank Overijssel, 24 December 2013, ECLI:NL:RBOVE:013: 4269.; Rechtbank Den Haag, 21 October 2014, ECLI:NL:RBDHA:2014:14191.; Rechtbank Oost-Brabant, 03 August 2016, ECLI:NL:RBOBR:2016:4140.
400 Rechtbank Amsterdam, 2 April 2014, ECLI:NL:RBAMS:2014:1644.
401 Rechtbank Rotterdam, 09 September 2016, ELCI:NL:RBROT:2016:6943, para 4.2.

While a situation of marital captivity is more likely to affect women, the 1983 case illustrates that men too can be trapped in a religious marriage. In this case, the woman refused to accept the *get*. This provoked the man to invoke a tort action. He requested the court to establish that by not cooperating, the woman had committed a tort and thereby restricted him from remarrying. The court ruled in favour of the husband after establishing that the woman had no fundamental objections other than to attain financial advantages. The woman was, thus, compelled to cooperate in the religious Jewish divorce.[402]

More recently the tort action has also been applied to situations involving only a religious marriage. In these cases, the spouses had only conducted a religious marriage in the Netherlands and had not taken any effort to conclude a civil marriage. In the first case, the wife demanded the husband to be compelled to cooperate in the dissolution of the Islamic marriage by way of the *talaq* or *khul'*. However, as it only concerned a religious marriage, the court concluded that the religious marriage had no legal status. In the court's view, the wife had not been affected in her rights and interests under the Dutch legal order. More specifically, her rights to freedom of religion and to marry had not been restricted as she was eligible to conduct a formal marriage. On the basis of these factors, the court dismissed the claim and referred the applicant to bring her case before a *Sharia Council* in the United Kingdom.[403] This decision was overturned by the Court of Appeal which held that the fact that it concerned a religious marriage, did not preclude that the wife may have rights and interests which were being impaired by the continuation of a religious divorce. The Court of Appeal established that the continuation of the religious marriage would not only have a negative impact on the social life of the woman and restrict her in moving on and establishing new relationships, but it could also be exploited by the husband to gain rights over the children if she were to travel to her country of origin. She also risked being charged with committing adultery in the country of origin, if she were to entertain a new relationship. These were the interests for which she sought legal protection via the tort action, irrespective of whether or not a civil marriage had existed.[404] As the husband had not provided any valid justifications to restrict the woman's interest, the Court of Appeal ruled in favour of the wife, by compelling the recalcitrant spouse to cooperate in the dissolution of the religious marriage by way of repudiation. Remarkable is that, the court ordered the husband to provide the wife with a registered letter containing the formulation: '*The undersigned [the man] resident at [address] declares to want to divorce [the woman] and hereby expresses the talaq, talaq, talaq*'.[405]

Similarly, in a second case which also concerned a religious marriage, the wife demanded that the husband be compelled to cooperate in the dissolution of a religious

402 Rechtbank Amsterdam, 17 November 1983, ECLI: NL:RBAMS:1983:AH0155, para. 11.

403 Rechtbank Rotterdam, 06 January 2016, ECLI:NL:RBROT:2016:8.

404 Gerechtshof Den Haag, 21 November 2017, ECLI:NL:GHDHA:2017:3297, paras. 14–18.

405 The Dutch tekst reads as following: '*Ondergetekende [de man] wonende aan [adres] verklaart te willen scheiden van [de vrouw] en hierbij de talak,talak, talak uit te spreken*'. Id., judgment.

marriage. The court proceeded by first establishing the legal question pertaining to the case and its jurisdiction over the matter. As the wife had alleged a tort induced by the husband, the legal question was not whether the religious marriage or claim for its dissolution was valid, but rather whether the non-cooperation, by the husband, had constituted a tort. In the courts view, the non-legal character of a religious marriage does not imply that it cannot have factual consequences which can be qualified as tortious towards the other partner.[406] Thus, the wife was seeking legal protection on the basis of Article 6:162 DCC over which the court had jurisdiction to hear the matter. The court proceeded to rule in favour of the trapped spouse on the basis that she had or would experience far reaching restrictions to her fundamental rights, while the husband had not provided any fundamental objections to the divorce other than financial related issues.[407]

In a more recent case, the civil judge accepted jurisdiction over a Jewish marriage that was conducted in Amsterdam and that had later been recognised as a marriage by the regional rabbinical court of Tel Aviv in Israel. In this case, the court established jurisdiction over the matter and ruled in favour of the wife. Finding that by not cooperating to the Jewish divorce, the husband had committed a tort. The court ordered the husband to cooperate to a Jewish divorce in Amsterdam. The husband opposed this decision, where after establishing competence and jurisdiction over the matter, the court ruled in favour of the husband.[408] More details of this case are provided for in paragraph 4.4.2.2.1.

As case law shows, the tort action has proven to be quite successful for addressing cases of marital captivity. Generally, judges do not attempt or claim to preside over the dissolution of the religious marriage, rather they merely compel a non-cooperative spouse to cooperate in the dissolution of marriage. At times, the courts have specified the type of cooperation that is required from the recalcitrant spouse. There are, however, some drawbacks of this solution. The success rate is dependent on whether the recalcitrant spouse cooperates, and there is always a chance that the marriage can drag on where the recalcitrant spouse refuses to comply with the court's decision. In this regard, its effectiveness in terms of generating the actual dissolution of a religious marriage still needs to be assessed. The exact numbers of cases that have actually led to the termination of a religious marriage are facts that cannot be drawn from the cited case law. Furthermore, whether a situation of marital captivity constitutes a tort is to be decided upon on a case by case basis. In other words, a situation of marital captivity does not by definition constitute a tort.[409] In analysing a case, the judge will proceed to balance the interests of the disputing spouses, which will not automatically be in the favour of the trapped spouse.

---

406 Rechtbank Oost Brabant, 03 August 2016, ECLI:NL:RBOBR:2016:4140, paras. 4.3–4.6.

407 Id.

408 Rechtbank Amsterdam, 04 December 2017, ECLI:NL:RBAMS:2017:8910, paras. 2.1, 2.2, 2.5, 4.3.

409 Brief Motie Kooiman, p. 3.; Hoge Raad, 22 January 1982, ECLI: NL:HR:1982:AG4319, para. 2.

3.4.2. CRIMINAL LAW

On 26 July 2011, a bill was submitted by the Dutch Minister of Security and Justice. The bill proposed the broadening of the Dutch Criminal Code in order to criminalise practices of forced marriage, polygamy and female genital mutilation. This bill entered into force on 1 July 2013.[410] The issue of marital captivity was raised during the drafting phase by the NGO Femmes for Freedom. This organisation proposed broadening the definition of forced marriage so as to include semi-legal marriages (religious marriages) and marital captivity.[411]

The adopted amendment defines forced marriage as the '*coercing [of] a person to enter into a marriage. It is irrelevant whether this concerns a religious marriage or legal marriage (or both). The core factor is coercion. This coercion may, for example, occur in the form of tremendous psychological pressure, violence or threats of such violence, carried out by the intended spouse, parents, family or the community. The coercion can be directed at the victim, but can also be directed at third parties as long as the victim does not perceive any other options than to engage in the marriage*'.[412]

The offence of forced marriage has, therefore, been broadened so as to incorporate religious marriages. However, the legislator has pointed out that while the Istanbul Convention obliges States to criminalise the '*intentional conduct of forcing an adult or a child to enter into a marriage*', it does not oblige States to criminalise non-cooperation within divorce proceedings.[413] Thus, while forced marriage and marital captivity may lead to similar results, marital captivity is considered to revolve more around the difficulties of obtaining a divorce rather, than with the involuntary entrance into a marriage.[414] In addition, it was pointed out that the State is not obliged to criminalise the non-cooperation to a divorce as international human rights law does not guarantee a right to divorce. For these reasons, a general inclusion of marital captivity as a form of forced marriage within the meaning of Article 284 of the Criminal Code has not been accepted.[415] However, it has been maintained that situations of marital captivity which

---

410 'Besluit van14 mei 2013 tot vaststelling van het tijdstip van inwerkingtreding van de wet van 7 maart 2013 tot wijziging van het Wetboek van Strafrecht, het Wetboek van Strafvordering en het Wetboek van Strafrecht BES met het oog op de verruiming van de mogelijkheden tot strafrechtelijke aanpak van huwelijksdwang, polygamie en vrouwelijke genitale verminking ', 2013, Stb. 2013, 187.

411 Kamerstukken II, 2011/2012, 32 175, nr. 31, pp. 3–5.

412 Translation of the original text by Benedicta Deogratias.

413 Kamerstukken II 2011/2012, 32 175, nr. 31, p. 5.

414 Although in recent years, marital captivity is increasingly being defined as an extended form of forced marriage, i.e. forced to remain married. See for example, Boverhuis and Stoop, *CDA en GroenLinks willen boete voor mannen die vrouwen gevangen houden in Islamitisch huwelijk.*; *Response of the Kingdom of the Netherlands to the List of issues (CEDAW/C/NLD/Q/6) in relation to the sixth periodic report submitted by the Netherlands under Article 18 of the Convention on the Elimination of All Forms of Discrimination against Women*, pp. 11–12.

415 Id., p. 4.

fulfil the conditions of coercion[416], in accordance with Article 284 of the Criminal Code, can constitute a criminal offence. That means that, the recalcitrant spouse can be prosecuted and sentenced if found guilty. This will be the case where the non-cooperative spouse intentionally resorts to violence, threats or other hostile acts. One may think of a situation whereby the recalcitrant husband threatens to harm the wife or children, if the woman would try to seek a civil or religious divorce.[417]

Thus, as it stands marital captivity can constitute a criminal offence. Although this is a great effort and a step in the right direction for addressing marital captivity, there remains a lacuna for those situations of marital captivity which do not meet all the conditions of coercion. As submitted by the Minister and Secretary of Security and Justice in their responses, the mere non-cooperation to a religious divorce is not likely to reach the threshold of 'coercion' within the meaning of Article 284 of the Criminal Code.[418] Thus, the mere act of constraining the woman in a religious marriage against her will, for whatever reasons and motivations, is not a criminal offence.

As a final remark, this provision has yet to be applied in practice. In 2017, a woman sought to report a situation of marital captivity and polygamy against her husband and an imam who had enabled the husband to remarry a second wife. She had separated from her husband after a violent relationship and sought to divorce him as a result. The husband refused to dissolve the marriage and the religious authority was not able to facilitate the realisation of a religious marriage. The prosecutor, did not take any further action in this regard. Since it did not concern a civil marriage, but rather a religious and therefore non-recognised marriage, it was held that no criminal offence had been committed. Therefore, the actual effectiveness of Article 284 Criminal Code for addressing situations of marital captivity, besides functioning as a deterrence, remains to be seen.

3.4.3. ALTERNATIVE MEASURES

In 2012, a platform was established, *Platform Eer &Vrijheid,* in order to facilitate the exchange of information between social workers, professionals and relevant authorities, which in turn is supposed to lead to timely and adequate response by the relevant institutions.[419] Education on human rights has been encouraged at the local municipality levels. In addition, information on human rights has been made available digitally and is distributed to professionals and during campaigns.

Other measures in place to address marital captivity are of a non-legislative nature. In January 2015, the Ministry of Social affairs and Welfare proposed the *Actie plan-*

416 These conditions are: there is an intention to coerce someone, the coercion is unlawful, the coercion is enabled by violence, threats of violence and other hostile acts and there is a causal link between the coercive acts and the acts of the victim.

417 Id., p. 4.

418 Id., pp. 4–5.

419 Kamerstukken II, 2011/2012, 32 175, nr. 31 1, p. 7.; Kamerstukken II, 2015/2016, 32 175, nr. 60, p. 4.

zelfbeschikking 2015–2017.[420] This was a two-years action plan which aimed to prevent, among others, situations of forced marriages, abandonment, honour-related violence, forced solitude and marital captivity from arising. The main aim was to empower individuals to exercise their personal autonomy and encourage them to make decisions which enable them to circumvent situations that exacerbate the likeliness of being victimised within their community. Central to this plan was raising awareness of these phenomena, encouraging mentality changes within certain communities and educating individuals of their fundamental human rights, personal autonomy and opportunities. This was achieved by facilitating the exchange of information and cooperation between migrant groups, refugees and civil society. Activities also included the training of 160 persons, also referred to as ambassadors, from within the targeted communities. These, ambassadors were tasked with fostering a dialogue within the community on the above-mentioned subject matters and other taboo subjects such as the acceptance of homo sexuality. By 2016, these ambassadors had managed to organise 1,000 dialogue meetings within twelve communities and thereby had reached a great number of individuals within their respective communities.[421]

More recently, the issue of marital captivity has been included in existing awareness-raising initiatives such as *Verandering van Binnenuit*[422] and *(H)echt Verbonden*.[423] These initiatives not only target affected groups but in generating awareness they also involve multiple stakeholders such as professionals, experts, social workers, community leaders, religious authorities, scholars, law-enforcement etc.

3.5. CONCLUDING REMARKS

Existing State efforts and in particular the tort- action reveal that national authorities have readily used secular means to facilitate the dissolution of the marriage. The religious dimension inherent in a situation of marital captivity has not withheld State authorities to act within their competences to facilitate the dissolution of a religious marriage.

---

420 'Brief van de Minister van Sociale Zaken en Werkgelegenheid, Kamerstukken II, 2014/2015, 32 175, nr. 54', 2015.; 'Brief van de Minister van Sociale Zaken en Werkgelegenheid, Kamerstukken II, 2015/2016, 32 175, nr. 60', 2016.

421 Id., p. 3.

422 This initiative targets persons with a migrant background and refugees. Its main aim is te promote, security, equality and acceptance of women and LGBTQ individuals within migrant communities. For more information see: <https://www.movisie.nl/verandering-binnenuit> last accessed 17 November 2019.

423 This project focused specifically on the issue of marital captivity. It aimed at generating a dialogue between relevant stakeholders on marital captivity. In order to facilitate the exchange of information, good practices and experiences, several expert meetings were organized with religious authorities from different communities, experts, lawyers, social workers and scholars. This project produced, among others, a publication on the various aspects of religious and civil marriages, leaflets for professionals and victims and a series of short videos wherein religious leaders elaborate on the views and rules concerning marriage and divorce. More information about this project can be found *at* <https://www.rotterdam.nl/wonen-leven/hecht-verbonden/> last accessed 17 November 2019.

Having said that, the religious dimension has also been a prominent feature in the discussions concerning the phenomenon of marital captivity, in the Netherlands. This perception has, at times, influenced the position that the national authorities (e.g. politicians, law makers and judges) have taken in their effort to address marital captivity. While it is clear that measures are needed to redress and solve situations of marital captivity, it remains unclear the extent to which the State can intervene and via which means. This is reflected in the somewhat questionable statements that have been made by politicians, law makers and judges. While concerns have been raised about the negative consequences that a situation of marital captivity involves for the trapped spouses, national authorities have, nonetheless, at times adopted a restrictive approach thereto. The main arguments in this regard are that individuals are free to submit themselves to the rules and decisions of their respective religious community, even if these are not entirely aligned with the fundamental core principles and values of the State. Additionally, the common understanding is that the State should not intervene in religious affairs, which the dissolution of a religious marriage is considered to be related to. Accordingly, an interference in the religious affairs would most likely be the case where a secular judge would, for example, claim to have the authority to dissolve a religious marriage. Similarly, compelling religious communities to assimilate the secular values related to a civil divorce law, within their own religious divorce may also cause frictions in the established State-Church relations.

Without taking a position on the propriety of this approach, several reflective conclusions can nevertheless be drawn from this exercise. Firstly, studying the national context of the Netherlands reveals that it is crucial to be judicious in the framing of a phenomenon, such as marital captivity, that takes effect and has negative impacts in the religious, private and public spheres. The framing of marital captivity depends not only on how marital captivity is presented, but also on many other factors such as the political climate, dominating topics in the public debate, available expertise and so on. It is important take into consideration how marital captivity is framed, as this affects how the phenomenon is perceived and received by the public and influences how the national authorities respond to this phenomenon. In this regard, it is important not to primarily frame marital captivity as predominantly a religious phenomenon, a private matter or an issue specific to certain migrant or minority communities. This not only diminishes the fact that marital captivity is a societal and wide spread issue, but it may also place religious, migrant or minority communities unnecessarily in a negative light.

Furthermore, how marital captivity has been received as well as how the State has responded to it, has been influenced by the prominent attention that has been given to the religious dimension of marital captivity. In this regard, the State has proceeded with great caution so as not to intervene in religious affairs. This, at times, has tended to restrict the State' s perceived possibilities to intervene and contribute to the creation of a social environment whereby cases of marital captivity are addressed appropriately and adequately.

Secondly, this exercise shows that there is great need to revaluate the State-Church relations within the discussions on marital captivity. So far, the main approach can be summarised as one of a restrictive approach due to the religious nature that is inherent in situations of marital captivity. However, looking at the context as a whole actually reveals that the State already intervenes in religious affairs by, for example, restricting the right to celebrate religious marriages, as it protects spouses and ensures certain fundamental principles, e.g. legal certainty. Likewise, the tort action enables the State to remedy and to end tortious conduct by a non-cooperative spouse. This has been considered as not trespassing the set boundaries of the State as it often merely compels cooperation to a religious divorce by a non-cooperative spouse. However, the fact that it has been a successful tool is only further evidence that the State can and has the means to influence the religious divorce process, albeit indirectly, without acting in contravention of its secular principles. Furthermore, the principle of separation of State and Church is interpreted as one of tolerance and equal treatment of all religions. It does not preclude all and any State interference and religion is neither excluded from the public sphere.

Additionally, religious communities do not have a *carte blanche* to do anything they want within their internal sphere. This is, for example, reflected in Article 2:2 (1) DCC. Religious communities are entitled to be governed by their own charter in so far as this does not conflict with the law. As such, this entitlement may be subject to certain restrictions where certain activities conflict with the law. The boundaries and interactions between the State-Church are, thus, not precisely defined. In order to establish and define the State- Church boundaries a constant balancing is necessary.

That being said, there is no reason why the State should not adopt a similar approach when it comes to the phenomenon marital captivity. The State has the discretion and means to manoeuvre and regulate aspects that directly and indirectly affect religious communities and affairs. Doing so requires appropriately weighing and balancing the competing rights and interests. For marital captivity, this should also include the impediments and restrictions that are incurred by the trapped spouses and the negative social impacts of marital captivity. These aspects need to be taken into consideration and weighed accordingly against the individual and collective religious freedom and the State's secular character and human rights obligations.

Thirdly, looking at the national context of the Netherlands, it ia important to create clarity on the States position and obligations *vis-à-vis* the trapped spouse and the religious communities. The rights of religious members and communities to organise themselves as they deem fit and the religious freedom they enjoy with regards to their internal affairs, do not by definition entail that the State is discharged from all of its obligations. It also does not mean that the State cannot condition these rights to the preservation of fundamental values and norms. Article 2:2 DCC is a clear example that this is possible. While it is true that the State cannot be held responsible for religious norms it has not enacted, the State still has obligations to prevent and protect the human rights of its people, as this contribution aims to demonstrate. In other words, the fact that the State has not enacted or conducted practices which violate human rights does not, by definition, alleviate the State from discharging its human rights obligations.

Finally, this exercise has shown that the inclusion and involvement of human rights has been minimal in both the case law as well as in relation to the responses by national authorities. A human rights-centred approach is therefore necessary as it not only adds a new dimension to the existing debate, but it also stimulates active government action as opposed to the religious dimension which, at times, seems to stimulate passive governmental (re)action. Seeking to contribute to the discourse on marital captivity in the Netherlands and elsewhere, this contribution promotes another perspective to the phenomenon. Namely, one that takes human rights as the starting point for any discussion on marital captivity irrespective of the States specific model or religious composition. This does not, however, entail a dismissal of the religious dimension of marital captivity. By way of contrast, the implications of the religious dimension for the State, spouses and religious community are also taken into account and studied. The following Chapters, therefore, not only provide a framework of the human rights that are at stake in a situation of marital captivity, but it also examines the implications brought about by the religious dimension that is inherent in marital captivity.

CHAPTER 4
MARITAL CAPTIVITY AND THE FREEDOM OF RELIGION

The religious aspects inherent in the phenomenon of marital captivity also need to be given consideration. Religious communities have an interest in solving the issue in accordance with prevailing religious rules and values. Where the religious rules require the cooperation of the other spouse to the divorce, cooperating or not cooperating to a religious divorce may be considered as a reflection of the concerned spouse' s religious convictions. Besides the State-Church relations that prevail within the respective State, it is also important to take the religious matters into account when considering means and measures to address marital captivity.

Particularly for secular States, State-Church relations are a critical factor that should be taken into consideration when considering how the State can respond to the phenomenon of marital captivity. There are three principles underlying the notion of secularism, namely: the separation of State and Church, neutrality of the State and the freedom of religion. These principles apply in parallel to one another and shape the boundaries of the State's discretion, competences and jurisdiction *vis à vis* those of the Church. The first two principles have been elaborated upon within the context of the Netherlands in Chapter 3 above. The mere understanding of the principles of 'separation of State and Church' and 'State neutrality', however, does not sufficiently answer the question of whether State intervention in cases of marital captivity is, or is not, permissible, particularly more so for secular States. The notions of 'separation of state and church' and 'neutrality of the State' merely define the power arrangements between the State and the Church. Thus, a complementary inquiry is necessary in order to establish whether the State's intervention is permissible. In this respect, the right to freedom of religion plays an important role as it provides a framework for analysing the obligations, competences and boundaries of the State. It enables to determine the permissibility of State intervention in religious matters. Understanding the right to freedom of religion, its scope and limitations is thus crucial for the process of finding solutions to marital captivity.

This Chapter, therefore, elaborates further on the scope and limitations of the right to freedom of religion and whether a State's intervention to prevent and end situations of marital captivity may constitute an interference with this right. Both the situation where it concerns a religious marriage that is considered as indissoluble as well as situations in which the cooperation of both spouses or of the husband is required, are addressed. The first situation relates to religious rules that do not regulate or do not allow spouses to divorce. Situations of marital captivity then arise as a consequence of restrictive religious rules. Notably, spouses in this category not only oppose a religious divorce but may also oppose the dissolution of a civil marriage on the grounds that a civil divorce goes against their religious conviction of marriage as indissoluble in nature. In the course of this Chapter, these spouses are referred to as the 'opposing spouses'. The second situation relates to religious rules that do allow spouses to divorce but also require the cooperation of both spouses or of the husband. Situations of marital captivity then arise where cooperation with the religious divorce is withheld and a religious divorce cannot be obtained in another way. In the course of this Chapter, the spouses that refuse to cooperate to the dissolution of a religious marriage are referred to as 'non-cooperative spouses'.

Subchapter 4.1. first provides some background on the reasons and motives of non-cooperative and opposing spouses. This is followed by a textual analysis of the provisions that guarantee the right to freedom of religion in subchapter 4.2. For both situations, it is necessary to understand and study how the right to freedom of religion is involved. More specifically, this subchapter considers whether the right to freedom of religion protects religious rules and religious divorce practices that create situations of marital captivity and that impair the trapped spouses' rights. In particular, as the religious divorce process occurs by and within the religious communities, it is essential to study the freedom which religious communities have to regulate and to enforce the religious rules on divorce within their communities. Subchapter 4.3., therefore, addresses the collective religious freedom in relation to the application, by religious communities, of rules that limit both spouse's ability to dissolve the religious marriage as well as rules that predominantly limit the possibilities of married women to dissolve the religious marriage. Are these matters that are protected within the right to freedom of religion? And if so, to what extent can the State then intervene in order to redress and remedy the negative effects of religious rules and practices that result in the violation of individuals rights?

Subchapter 4.4. considers whether the act of non-cooperation with a religious divorce or opposition to a civil divorce on the basis of one's religious convictions constitutes a religious manifestation within the meaning of the article 18 ICCPR and article 9 ECHR. If answered in the affirmative, does a court order compelling the recalcitrant spouse to cooperate in the dissolution of a religious marriage or a decree of (civil) divorce then constitutes an interference with the non-cooperative and opposing spouse's religious freedom? Because marital captivity has scarcely been addressed by international and human rights monitoring, the sources that specifically deal with these questions are limited. For this reason, where necessary the practices of States on a national level are included. This serves the purpose of providing insights into how the right to freedom of religion has been considered in situations of marital captivity within these States. More specifically, have national States found the act of opposing or not cooperating to a religious divorce to constitute a religious manifestation? Similarly, is State intervention in situations of marital captivity considered as an infringement of this right? In this respect, an analysis is provided of the laws and case law of the Netherlands, France and the United Kingdom. These countries have been selected on the basis of the available sources. It is also important to note that all three States are secular States, have all dealt with situations of marital captivity and are State parties to the human rights documents investigated in this contribution.

Subchapter 4.5. addresses the State obligations that arise from the freedom of religion and also outlines the criteria for permissible restrictions of this right within the context of marital captivity. The main findings are summarised in subchapter 4.6.

4.1. REASONS AND MOTIVES TO OPPOSE THE DISSOLUTION OF A RELIGIOUS MARRIAGE

Before analysing the scope of protection of the right to religious freedom, it is most appropriate to first set out the different situations and motives for opposing or not cooperating with a (religious) divorce. The dissolution of a civil and or religious marriage could be hampered by a spouse who, for non-religious reasons (e.g. economic incentives), opposes the dissolution of the marriage. As an example:

Naseem took the initiative to dissolve both the civil and religious marriages after being married for three years. The civil divorce was granted after she was divorced in accordance with religious procedures. Her (ex-) husband refused to cooperate in the religious divorce and so she initiated civil proceedings against him in an attempt to compel him to cooperate with the religious divorce. She recounts: '*Knowing him…the moment that I would [re]marry…because I made it so difficult for him- according to him (…) I am sure that he would use that against me (…) I have already heard from multiple people that he has said "well, she made me grieve because of the divorce, now I let her feel how it feels if she comes to me for an Islamic divorce, because she has to come to me [for that]"*'.[424]

Reasons for not cooperating could, as the case of Naseem illustrates, be motivated by sheer bad faith to harm the other spouse. Financial motives could also be reasons for not cooperating, particularly where the husband wants to reclaim or does not want to pay off the dowry.[425] Other examples of this behaviour by non-cooperative spouses can also be found in the national case law that is discussed in subsection 4.4.2.2 below. In most cases, this will concern a non-cooperative husband due to the inequality in divorce

424 Van Eijk, Wel gescheiden, niet gescheiden? Een empirisch onderzoek naar huwelijkse gevangenschap in Nederland, p. 51.

425 Van Eijk, Wel gescheiden, niet gescheiden? Een empirisch onderzoek naar huwelijkse gevangenschap in Nederland, p. 69.

rights that women and men have in certain religions. The unequal power distribution then enables the husband to exploit religious rules and constraints on divorce to their advantage by refusing to provide the necessary cooperation to dissolve the religious marriage. It is also conceivable that the non-cooperative spouse or the opposing spouse to a divorce, genuinely does not want to dissolve the marital ties and sincerely invokes religious grounds for opposing or refusing to cooperate with the religious divorce. Such was the situation in the previously discussed case of *Rechtbank Amsterdam 2 April 2014*, whereby the husband refused to cooperate with a religious divorce by way of a repudiation as this did not reflect his religious judgement of the divorce.[426]

4.2. THE LEGAL FRAMEWORK

The freedom of religion has been codified in both the ICCPR and the ECHR. Article 18 of the ICCPR states:

> '1. *Everyone shall have the right to freedom of thought, conscience, and religion. This right shall include freedom to have or to adopt a religion or belief of his choice, and freedom, either individually or in community with others and in public or private, to manifest his religion or belief in worship, observance, practice and teaching.*
> 2. *No one shall be subject to coercion which would impair his freedom to have or to adopt a religion or belief of his choice.*
> 3. *Freedom to manifest one's religion or beliefs may be subject only to such limitations as are prescribed by law and are necessary to protect public safety, order, health, or morals or the fundamental rights and freedoms of others.*'

Similar wording can be found in Article 9 ECHR, which provides:

> '1. *Everyone has the right to freedom of thought, conscience, and religion; this right includes freedom to change his religion or belief and the freedom, either alone or in community with others and in public or private, to manifest his religion or belief, in worship, teaching, practice, and observance.*
> 2. *Freedom to manifest one's religion or beliefs shall be subject only to such limitations as are prescribed by law and are necessary in a democratic society in the interests of public safety, for the protection of public order, health or morals, or for the protection of the rights and freedoms of others.*'

While the focus is primarily on these two instruments, other international and regional instruments are referred to where necessary. These include the Universal Declaration of Human Rights (UDHR)[427], the Declaration on the Elimination of All Forms of

426 Rechtbank Amsterdam, 2 April 2014, ECLI:NL:RBAMS:2014:1644.

427 Uinted Nations General Assembly, *Universal Declaration of Human Rights*, 10 December 1948, UN Doc. A/RES/3/217 A. The freedom of religion in the UDHR is found in article 18 taken in conjunction with the Article 29.

Intolerance and of Discrimination Based on Religion or Belief[428] and the European Union Charter of Fundamental Human Rights[429](EU charter). The declaratory nature of the first two sources does not undermine their legal significance. The importance and significance of the UDHR has been briefly addressed in subchapter 1.6..The Declaration on the Elimination of All Forms of Intolerance and of Discrimination Based on Religion or Belief is the first document to set standards of the rights pertaining to the freedom of religion and it has been relied on for the purposes of interpreting Article 18 ICCPR.[430] As for the EU Charter, Article 10 thereof, on the freedom of religion, guarantees not only the same rights as Article 9 ECHR but also adopts the same meaning and scope as Article 9 ECHR.[431] Nonetheless, there are some differences between both provisions. For example, while the EU Charter explicitly recognises the right to conscientious objection, a similar formulation is not found in the ECHR.[432]

4.3. RELIGIOUS RULES AND PRACTICES THAT ENABLE MARITAL CAPTIVITY

The article 18 ICCPR and Article 9 ECHR contain four constituent components, namely; 'thought', 'conscience', 'religion' and 'belief'.[433] In practice, no precise distinction is drawn between these concepts. Neither the Human Rights Committee (HRC) nor the ECtHR and the European Commission of Human rights (ECmHR) have discussed the contents of these concepts at great length. Often, these concepts have been dealt with jointly without necessarily drawing clear distinctions between the activities that each one of them protects. Attempts to draw distinctions tend only to reveal the interrelated nature of these concepts rather than substantiating their distinctness and differences. That being said, the provisions 9 ECHR and 18 ICCPR extend to cover a broad range of intellectual conceptions.[434] Furthermore, all four components are not only protected

---

428 United Nations General Assembly, *UN General Assembly, Declaration on the Elimination of All Forms of Intolerance and of Discrimination Based on Religion or Belief, 25 November 1981*, 25 November 1981, UN doc. A/RES/36/55, Articles 1 and 8.

429 European Union, *European Union, Charter of Fundamental Rights of the European Union, 26 October 2012*, 26 November 2012, 2012/C 326/02, Article 10.

430 Julian Rivers, *The law of organized religions: between establishment and secularism* (2010), p 44.

431 Steve Peers, Tamara K. Hervey, Jeff Kenner and Angela Ward, *The EU Charter of Fundamental Rights: A commentary* (Oxford, 2014), p. 291.

432 Article 10 (2) of the EU Charter provides: '*The right to conscientious objection is recognised, in accordance with the national laws governing the exercise of this right.*'

433 Despite the first part only referring to 'thought', 'conscience', 'religion', the freedom to hold and change one's 'beliefs' (i.e. ideological value systems) is also considered to be protected. This is mentioned in Article 9 ECHR and emphasised by the HRC in *General Comment No. 22: Article 18 (Freedom of thought, conscience or religion)*, para. 1.

434 HRC, *General Comment No. 22: Article 18 (Freedom of thought, conscience or religion)*. para.2.; Jean-François Renucci, *Article 9 of the European Convention on Human Rights*, (Human Rights Files, No 20, 2005), p. 12.; Christoph Grabenwarter, *European Convention on Human Rights: Commentary* (München, Oxford, Baden-Baden, Basel, 2014), p. 238.

equally but should be taken as interactive elements that appertain to the right to freedom of thought, conscience, religion and belief as a whole. This is also reflected and indicated by the fact that these concepts have been codified in one single provision.[435]

Nevertheless, do the Articles 18 ICCPR and 9 ECHR protect all types of belief systems even when these enforce rules and practices that lead to the violation of other people's rights and are discriminatory towards women? The following sections examines firstly whether the right to freedom of religion also extends to protect those religious rules and practices that give rise to situations of marital captivity. Secondly and related hereto is whether the enforcement of such rules within the religious community is protected by the right to freedom of religion.

4.3.1. RELIGIOUS RULES THAT LIMIT BOTH SPOUSES' OR WOMEN'S POSSIBILITIES TO DISSOLVE THE RELIGIOUS MARRIAGE

Human rights monitoring institutions have generally evaded defining the term 'religion' or establishing which belief systems are included within this notion. Instead, the approach has been to consider the term as self-explanatory and, where the issue has been raised the tendency has been to assume the existence of a religion.[436] Despite the absence of a clear and concise definition, there are common acknowledgements in relation to the scope and substance of the terms 'religion' and 'belief'.

Firstly, the freedom of religion and belief is submitted to be an invaluable feature of a pluralist society and it therefore significantly affects individuals in many aspects of their lives.[437] Secondly, both religious and non-religious beliefs fall within the scope of application of both the ECHR and the ICCPR.[438] The inclusion of the term 'belief' ensures that other non-religious belief systems, such as agnostic, atheist or rationalist beliefs are equally protected.[439] Both terms are to be interpreted broadly and are not

---

435 De Jong, The freedom of thought, conscience and religion or belief in the United Nations (1946–1992), pp. 22–23.

436 Richard Clayton and Hugh Tomlinson, *The law of human rights* (Oxford, 2000), para. 14.40.; Elizabet. O. Benito, *Elimination of all forms of intolerance and discrimination based on religion or belief: Study of the current dimension of the problems of intolerance and of discrimination on grounds of religion or belief*, (Sub-Commission on Prevention of Discrimination and Protection of Minorities, 31 August 1986), [E/CN.4/Sub.2/1987/26], para. 19.

437 European Court of Human Rights, *Kokkinakis v. Greece*, 25 May 1993, Application No. 14307/88, para. 31. In the words of the ECtHR, the religious dimension of Article 9 ECHR, is *'one of the most vital elements that go to make up the identity of believers and their conception of life, but it is also a precious asset for atheists, agnostics, sceptics and the unconcerned'.*

438 Manfred Nowak, *U.N. Covenant on Civil and Political Rights: CCPR commentary* (Arlington, 2005), p.414.

439 European Court of Human Rights, *Kokkinakis v. Greece*, 25 May 1993, Application No. 14307/88, para. 31. In the case of *Kokkinakis v. Greece* the ECtHR explicitly extended the protection of Article 9 ECHR to also cover agnostics and atheists and the unconcerned. See also HRC, *General Comment No. 22:*

limited to traditional religions or institutionalised beliefs, but they should also extend to include emerging and unconventional belief systems, such as Rastafarianism, pacifism, veganism, atheism, as well as political ideologies such as communism.[440] Thirdly, a restrictive approach is recommended when dealing with questions pertaining to the legitimacy and authenticity of a religion or belief. This obligation also extends to a restrictive approach when assessing the legitimacy, forms and ways in which individuals express and manifest their religion or belief.[441] In fact, during the discussion of general comment No. 22 of the HRC, Higgins stressed that States, as well as the committee itself, should not have absolute leeway to determine the contents of what constitutes a religion or belief nor to assess what constituted a manifestation. Rather this should largely be left for the adherent and believers to determine the content of their religion/belief and how to express this.[442]

However, despite such a broad interpretation, it does not mean that any and all beliefs and 'self-proclaimed' religions fall within the scope of protection of Article 18 ICCPR and Article 9 ECHR. Under the ECHR system, religions and beliefs that are incompatible with the rule of law, human rights or the principles and values of democracy are excluded from the protection of Article 9 ECHR.[443] Equally, belief systems that do not have a clear and identifiable structure may be excluded from the ambit of Article 9 ECHR.[444] To fall within the scope of protection of Article 9 ECHR, a belief needs to be more than just opinions and ideas, which are instead protected under Article 10 EHCR on the freedom of expression. Furthermore, these need to reflect views that have '*attained a certain level of cogency, seriousness, cohesion, and importance*'.[445] However, what this level actually is remains largely unanswered. At the time of writing, there has not been a single case that resulted in the exclusion of a religion or belief from

---

Article 18 (Freedom of thought, conscience or religion).; Arcot Krishnaswami, *Study of discrimination in the matter of religious rights and practices*, (United Nations, 1960), [E/CN.4/Sub.2/200/Rev. 1], p. 1 in footnote.; Nowak, *U.N. Covenant on Civil and Political Rights: CCPR commentary*, p. 414.; Grabenwarter, *European Convention on Human Rights: Commentary*, p. 237.

440 Human Rights Committee, *Prince v. South Africa*, 31 October 2007, Communication No. 1474/2006, para. 6.5.; Jim Murdoch, *Freedom of thought, conscience and religion: A guide to the implementation of Article 9 of the European Convention on Human Rights*, (Council of Europe, 2007), [Human Rights handbooks No. 9], p. 11.

441 Schabas, *The European Convention on Human Rights: A commentary*, p. 425.; Jean-François Renucci, *Article 9 of the European Convention on Human Rights*, (Human Rights Files, No 20, 2005), p. 23. Asma Jahangir, *Civil and Political Rights, including the question of religious intolerance*, (Commission on Human Rights, 8 March 2006), [E/CN.4/2006/5/Add.4], para. 41.

442 Id.

443 Robin C.A. White and Clare Ovey, *The European Convention on Human Rights* (New York, 2010), p. 407.

444 Renucci, *Article 9 of the European Convention on Human Rights*, p. 12. For example, in the case of individualised religion or beliefs. More on this subject see: Carolyn Evans, *Freedom of religion under the European Convention on Human Rights* (2001), pp. 58–59.

445 European Court of Human Rights, *Campbell and Cosans v. the United Kingdom*, 25 February 1982, Application No. 7511/76; 7743/76, para. 36.

the protection of Article 9 ECHR.[446] In most cases, the ECmHR and ECtHR have, without further notice, presumed to assume the existence of a religion or belief.

Remarkably, the HRC has been less reserved on establishing whether a religion or belief systems constitutes a 'religion' within the meaning of Article 18 ICCPR. In the case of *M.A.B. W.A.T. and J.-A.Y.T. v. Canada*, the HRC excluded the 'Assembly of the Church Universe' – which claimed that the use of cannabis was a central aspect of their belief – from the protection of Article 18 ICCPR.[447]

Where it concerns religious rules and practices that enable situations of marital captivity to arise and persist the conclusion may be drawn that Christianity, Hinduism, Islam and Judaism are religions. This is a fact that has been accepted globally. Their existence as religions within the meaning of the articles 18 ICCPR and 9 ECHR is therefore not contested in this contribution, despite the fact that they prescribe religious rules that enable situations of marital captivity and as a result impair upon the trapped spouses' human rights.

4.3.2. APPLICATION AND ENFORCEMENT OF RESTRICTIVE AND DISCRIMINATORY RULES WITHIN THE RELIGIOUS COMMUNITY

Besides the involved spouses, marital captivity is also a phenomenon that involves the religious community in the sense that it is within the community that the consequences of marital captivity are experienced and reinforced. The establishment and dissolution of a religious marriage is primarily a matter reserved for the religious authorities both in secular States as well as in States where religious tribunals have jurisdiction over the matter.

Both the ICCPR and ECHR recognise that the right to freedom of religion has a collective aspect. The phrase '*individually or in community with others*' provides that the freedom of religion is not only limited to individual rights but also includes collective elements. In *Metropolitan Church of Bessarabi v. Moldova*, the ECtHR underscored the importance of the collective dimension as following: '*the autonomous existence of religious communities is indispensable for pluralism in a democratic society and is thus an issue at the very heart of the protection which article 9 affords*'.[448] The collective dimension forms a fundamental basis for the freedom of religion as it

---

446 White and Ovey, *The European Convention on Human Rights*, p. 407.

447 Human Rights Committee, *M.A.B., W.A.T. and J.-A.Y.T. v. Canada*, 8 April 1994, Communication No. 570/1993, para. 4.2. Members of this church alleged that the '*care, cultivation, possession, distribution, maintenance, integrity and worship of the "Sacrament"*', i.e. cannabis, were integral and central aspects of their belief. The HRC, however, concluded that a '*belief consisting primarily or exclusively in the worship and distribution of a narcotic drug cannot conceivably be brought within the scope of article 18 of the Covenant (freedom of religion and conscience).*

448 European Court of Human Rights, *Metropolitan Church of Bessarabia and Others v. Moldova*, 13 December 2001, No. 45701/99, para. 58.

enables individuals to exercise certain individual rights.[449] Its protection is crucial for guaranteeing religious freedom in its entirety.[450] As a matter of fact, this symbiosis of the individual and collective freedoms has been underscored in the *Hasan & Chaush v. Bulgaria*, case where the ECtHR considered that *'participation in the life of the community is [...] a manifestation of one's religion protected by Article 9 of the Convention'*.[451]

The collective dimension, additionally, involves more than the mere enabling of individuals to exercise their freedom of religion. This is illustrated in article 6 of the Declaration on the Elimination of All Forms of Intolerance and of Discrimination Based on Religion or Belief, which also recognises aspects that concern the organisation and structuring of religious communities. For example, Article 6 of this declaration recognizes the freedom to solicit and receive voluntary financial and other contributions from individuals and institutions; the freedom to train, appoint, elect or designate by succession appropriate leaders called for by the requirements and standards of any religion or belief and the freedom to establish and maintain communications with individuals and communities in matters of religion and belief at the national and international levels.[452] Likewise, both under the ECHR scheme as well as the ICCPR, religious communities are acknowledged to enjoy the freedom to autonomously regulate their internal affairs without impermissible interference by the State.[453]

The freedom to autonomously regulate internal affairs covers all doctrinal matters such as determining the content and modes of manifestations as well as organisational aspects concerning management and structural matters. This includes, *inter alia*, *'freedom to choose their religious leaders, priests and teachers, the freedom to establish seminars or religious schools, the freedom to prepare and distribute religious texts or publications'*[454], the right not to be discriminated against, freedom to have a capacity to operate autonomously, the freedom to structure themselves in accordance with the laws

---

449 Yildirim provides that in matters concerning State-Church relations, States do enjoy a wide margin of appreciation. Mine Yildirim, *The collective dimension of freedom of religion or belief in international law: The application of findings to the case of Turkey*, (2015) (Åbo Akademi University), pp. 30–31.

450 Yildirim, *The collective dimension of freedom of religion or belief in international law: The application of findings to the case of Turkey*, pp. 31,46.; European Court of Human Rights, *Svya Mychaylivska Parafiya v. Ukraine*, 17 June 2007, Application No. 77703/01, paras. 123–124. According to the ECtHR case law, ensuring that individuals can exercise the right to manifest one's religion requires the protection of the community, its members and its assets. Despite, it has been submitted that in comparison to the individual rights, the collective aspects of the freedom of religion have received far less attention and protection.

451 European Court of Human Rights, *Hasan and Chaush v. Bulgaria*, 26 October 2000, Application No. 30985/96), para. 62.

452 Such as freedom to establish and maintain places for worship; the freedom to establish and maintain appropriate charitable or humanitarian institutions; the freedom to solicit and receive voluntary financial and other contributions from individuals and institutions.

453 Grabenwarter, *European Convention on Human Rights: Commentary*, p. 240.

454 HRC, *General Comment No. 22: Article 18 (Freedom of thought, conscience or religion)*, para. 4.

of the country, the freedom to worship and assemble and the freedom to establish places for these purposes.[455]

The degree to which the State can interfere in internal affairs is dependent on whether it concerns doctrinal matters or internal management matters. Doctrinal affairs enjoy a higher level of protection in the sense that the State should exercise greater restraint for interfering in doctrinal matters. The freedom religious communities enjoy to govern internal affairs related to their management and structure (e.g. sales contracts, appointment and dismissal of clergy and employees), however, is relative in the sense that a State can interfere in these matters if it is in accordance with the limitation clauses of article 9 ECHR and 18 ICCPR.[456]

It is noteworthy that religious institutions and communities may and do impose certain views, rules, and standards on their adherents. Women may, for example, be denied certain positions within the religious organisation. Within the religious community, men and women may be ascribed roles that do not necessarily conform to the equality standards set by international human rights standards. Adherents and individual members may not agree with or find themselves in the imposed rules, conduct and behaviour. In these circumstances, the religious freedom that religious communities and organisations enjoy managing their internal affairs takes precedence over the religious freedom of individual community members. Thus, where there is a clash between religious freedom of the religious community and that of an individual member (e.g. when an individual member disagrees with doctrinal related matters that prevail within the religious community), it is unlikely that the individual's religious freedom shall be given precedence.[457] The reasoning behind this is that, individuals have, by their membership of a certain religious community, made a choice to obey the rules and practices of the religious authorities. In fact, so long as the individual can effectively exercise his or her right to leave or recant the religion, the religious community is not

455 See also the 1989 Vienna Decision principle 16 *Concluding Document of the Vienna Meeting 1986 of Representatives of the participating States of the Conference on Security and Co-operation in Europe, held on the basis of the provisions of the final act relating to the follow-up to the conference.* (19 January 1989) p. 3.; Mauro Gatti, 'Autonomy of religious organisations in the European Convention on Human Rights and in the European Union Law', in Rossi and Di Federica *Fundamental rights in Europe and China- Regional identities and universalism* (2013), pp. 3,6.; Yildirim, *The collective dimension of freedom of religion or belief in international law: The application of findings to the case of Turkey*, pp. 115–118.

456 Sylvie Langlaude Doné, 'Religious organisations, internal autonomy and other religious rights before the European Court of Human Rights and the OSCE', 34 *Netherlands Quarterly of Human Rights* 8–40, (2016), p. 12. de Jong, The freedom of thought, conscience and religion or belief in the United Nations (1946–1992), p. 424. See also; European Court of Human Rights, *Staatkundig Gereformeerde Partij v. the Netherlands*, 10 July 2012, Application No. 58369/10, paras. 67–72.; European Court of Human Rights, *Refah Partisi (The Welfare Party) and Others v. Turkey*, 31 July 2001, Application Nos. 41340/98, 41342/98, 41343/98, paras. 70–85. In both cases the Court found that State interference in the organisation of religious based political parties was justified.

457 Karl Hanson, 'Vrijheid van gedachte, geweten en godsdienst, in Lanotte & Haeck *Handboek EVRM-Deel 2 Artikelsgewijze commentaar*, (Antwerpen, Oxford 2004), pp. 811.-812.

required to grant him/her religious freedom.[458] This however, does not mean that the collective freedom and autonomy of religious communities are absolute. These may still be subjected to restrictions, where for example the activities of religious communities and organisations are harmful to the population or public safety.[459]

4.3.2.1. The regulation of religious divorces as internal affairs

Whether the freedom to regulate their internal affairs includes the dissolution of religious marriages within the religious tribunals is not that self-evident. Human rights discourse on the autonomy of religious organisations, both in literature as well as in primary sources, has primarily focused on the structural and management matters of religious organisations (e.g. matter and disputes relating to contracts, property, employment, education, and organisational structure).[460] Little attention has been given to the activities of religious authorities related to family and marital matters and whether such matters concern doctrinal or management matters. Yildirim and Norton are both supportive of the application of religious laws by and within religious communities to solve internal matters, including those related to family disputes.[461] At the core of their argument is the symbiosis between individual rights and the collective entitlements that are included in the right to freedom of religion. Both authors defend the position that the application of religious laws by religious tribunals supports and serves to fulfil the individual right to religious freedom as well as the communal aspects that are recognised in human rights law. Among others, religious tribunals and authorities provide individuals with the possibility to live according to and abide by the religious laws; they provide religious knowledge and guidance for adherents; they enable individuals to change and recognise their personal status (e.g. member, non-member, married, divorced); they support the religious community and communal aspects (e.g. development of doctrinal discourse) and they provide for religious adjudication. Therefore, the inclusion of activities of religious tribunals to adjudicate over domains analogous to civil law, including marital matters, would seem to be included and protected within the freedom of religion either as falling within the collective dimension or as ensuring that individuals can exercise their rights to manifest and live according to their religion.[462] Notably, Yildirim also rightfully notes that the use of religious laws or religious dispute settlement mechanisms has not been recognised or ever

458 Id., p. 812.; Schabas, *The European Convention on Human Rights: A commentary*, p. 430.; Evans, *Freedom of religion under the European Convention on Human Rights*, p. 129.

459 Schabas, *The European Convention on Human Rights: A commentary*, pp. 429–430.

460 Doné, *Religious organisations, internal autonomy and other religious rights before the European Court of Human Rights and the OSCE.*; Gatti *Autonomy of religious organisations in the European Convention on Human Rights and in the European Union Law.*

461 Jane. C. Norton, *Freedom of religious organizations* (Oxford, 2016).

462 Yildirim, The collective dimension of freedom of religion or belief in international law: The application of findings to the case of Turkey, pp. 146–149.

been identified as a religious manifestation in practice.[463] Where the dissolution of a marriage in accordance with one's religion can be considered as a religious manifestation, then it may be argued that a religious divorce process, by religious tribunals, is necessary and should be protected as it enables individuals to exercise their religious freedom also in matters related to divorce.

Reality shows religious divorces do occur both in secular as non-secular States. Religious tribunals/authorities govern over family and marital matters, whether as informal settlement mechanism, formal mechanism. (i.e. as state apparatus) or where their decisions are recognised and enforced by secular authorities. The case of *Pellegrini v. Italy* is an example of the latter, whereby an annulment of the religious marriage by the Roma Rota, was recognised and enforced in Italy.[464] In doing so religious authorities apply the religious rules on divorce, including those that disadvantage the position of married women. Moreover, secular authorities that have intervened within situations of marital captivity have tended to acknowledge the religious dimension of situations of marital captivity as well as the roles religious authorities partake in the dissolution of religious marriages.[465] For example, in the cases *Rechtbank Rotterdam 06 January 2016*[466] and *Rechtbank Amsterdam 17 January 1983*[467], judges made reference to the respective religious authorities as having the authority and competency over religious divorces. In France, the main line of reasoning is that the State does not preside over matters concerning the religious divorce.[468] Beyond creating new means to facilitate the realization of a religious divorce, secular authorities have largely left it up to the spouses and religious authorities to bring about the religious divorce.

In the case of Jewish and Muslim divorces, the religious laws on divorce already provide the spouses with unequal rights to initiate a divorce. In Catholicism, the indissolubility of marriage is emphasised in Canon Law and in Hinduism the dissolubility of a marriage is unclear.[469] The interpretation and application of religious provisions on divorce are acts that are, thus, closely intertwined with doctrinal matters and are matters that are reserved for the religious authorities in both secular and non-secular States. Having established that, this leads to the next question. Namely, do State efforts to facilitate the dissolution of a religious marriage or prevent situations of marital captivity interfere with collective religious freedom?

463 Id., p. 149.
464 European Court of Human Rights, *Pellegrini v. Italy*, 20 July 2001, Application No. 30882/96.
465 See the national case law discussed in subsection 4.4.2.2.
466 Rechtbank Rotterdam, 06 January 2016, ECLI:NL:RBROT:2016:8.
467 Rechtbank Amsterdam, 17 November 1983, ECLI:NL:RBAMS:1983:AH0155. See also Hoge Raad, 22 January 1982, ECLI:NL:HR:1982:AG4319.
468 Cour d'Appel Paris,16 March 2011, [10/01413].
469 See sections 2.1.1. and 2.2.1.

4.3.2.2. State interference in religious affairs related to divorce

The question as to whether intervention in the religious divorce processes constitutes an interference with the collective dimension is not really a relevant consideration when the intervening body is the religious authority (e.g. religious tribunals). This is because religious authorities have the competence to do so and are guaranteed their freedom to manage their internal affairs. The situation is different, however, when the intervening body is a non-religious institution (e.g. a civil court or the national legislator). Not only do non-religious bodies have no authority in relation to religious affairs, but the autonomy that religious communities are entitled to under Article 18 ICCPR and Article 9 ECHR, requires for a restrictive approach to be adopted by the State in interfering in internal affairs of religious communities. Thus, whether interventions by non-religious State bodies interfere with the collective freedom of religion requires further examination in respect of how exactly these measures operate and affect the religious divorce processes.

In some secular States measures to address and resolve marital captivity have been developed and implemented.[470] These have predominantly, sought to resolve situations of marital captivity that are the result of a recalcitrant spouse refusal to cooperate in the religious divorce. Generally, the facilitation of a religious divorce and/or prevention of a situation of marital captivity has been reached by developing a mechanism to increase pressure on the non-cooperative spouse.[471] In other words, these measures have mostly involved indirect solutions to resolve situations of marital captivity (e.g. tort action, sanctions, legislation that requires the removal of barriers to remarry).[472] It is important to recognise that where successful, these measures essentially influence the outcomes of a religious divorce process, albeit indirectly.

It is equally important to recognise that all these measures are within the competences of State legislators and courts, i.e. national courts do have jurisdiction over tort and liability claims and legislators have the competence and authority to regulate civil, family and divorce laws. In all the measures that have been adopted by secular States, the actual dissolution of the religious marriage has remained a matter that secular authorities have refrained from interfering in. To date, none of these measures has involved dictating to religious communities how to end a situation of marital captivity or to provide for a divorce where the religious rules do not allow or recognize a divorce. State measures have not interfered with the doctrinal affairs since these do not directly or indirectly seek to enforce particular interpretations, doctrines or practices within a given religious community.

In sum, although secular measures have the potential to indirectly influence the process of dissolving a religious marriage, these measures do not amount to an

[470] These measures have been summarised in Chapter 1.1. *Supra* notes 4–6. See also section 3.4.1. and subsection 4.4.2.2.

[471] Id.

[472] Id.

interference with the internal affairs of the religious communities. Religious authorities continue to enjoy the autonomy and competence to preside over the religious divorce procedure in accordance with the prevailing religious norms and practices.

Notably, the more recent case law of the Netherlands[473] is somewhat remarkable, however, as at times courts have directed spouses to cooperate in a particular form of divorce: the repudiation. For example, in a case that was heard in November 2017, the Court of Appeal commended the recalcitrant to cooperate in the repudiation and went even further by dictating the precise way (a registered letter) and formulation (*'The undersigned [the man] resident at [address] declares that he wants to divorce [the woman] and hereby expresses the talaq, talaq, talaq'*).[474] This approach goes further than the court's previous decisions, where the non-cooperative spouses were compelled to cooperate in the dissolution of the religious marriage. It is questionable whether by dictating the formulation and type of the religious divorce, the court, in fact, is not interfering with the religious autonomy of both the individual and the religious community. A specific order to cooperate in a certain form of divorce not only influences the outcome, but it also influences the religious divorce process, which is a matter that, in principle, should be dealt with by the appropriate religious authorities.

Even if it can be assumed that a judicial decision requiring a husband to repudiate their wife may constitute an interference in religious affairs, it should also be borne in mind that the entitlement which religious communities enjoy to regulate their internal affairs autonomously is not absolute and may be subject to restrictions. The limitation clauses of Article 18 ICCPR and Article 9 ECHR allow for such restrictions and provide the criteria for permissible interference by the State.[475] Where the tipping point is cannot be asserted with certainty. However, as previously noted the nature of the interference (i.e. in doctrinal or management matters) influences the extent and way in which States may intervene.[476] Account should also have to be taken of any overriding interests that justify such an interference. In the case of marital captivity, these include protection of the trapped spouse's rights, promotion of equality between spouses, and the prohibition of discriminatory practices. Where the balance should be found is elaborated in Chapter 8. However, several observations can be drawn from the case of *Staatkundig Gereformeerde Partij v. The Netherlands*. It should be borne in mind, however, that this case involved a religious political body. In other words, the political nature of the *Staatkundig Gereformeerde Partij* (SGP), entails that the case concerned a religious body that operated in the public and political settings as opposed to a purely religious body, such as a religious tribunal, which is primarily concerned with the internal religious affairs of the religious community. Going forward it is, therefore, imperative to keep this distinction into account. Nonetheless, the case does

473 Rechtbank Oost Brabant, 03 August 2016, ECLI:NL:RBOBR:2016:4140, paras. 3.1–3.2, 5.1.

474 Gerechtshof Den Haag, 21 November 2017, ECLI:NL:GHDHA:2017:3297.

475 The criteria and legal framework of the limitation clauses are elaborate further in section 4.5.2.

476 See section 4.3.2.

provide guidance on where to place the weight in situations where religious groups, in exercising their religious autonomy, violate and restrict other fundamental rights.

In short, the conservative protestant political party SGP, barred women candidates from being included on its electoral list for parliamentary elections. The party was in receipt of subsidies from the Dutch government, which led to the initiation of litigation on the basis of the State's alleged failure to comply with its human rights obligations under Article 7 CEDAW and Articles 2 *juncto* 25 ICCPR. Both the Court of the First Instance and the Supreme Court established that the State had acted unlawfully by not adopting measures against the SGP's discriminatory practices. In complying with these decisions the Minister of Interior Affairs withheld the grant of subsidies to the SGP.[477] Eventually, the case was heard by the ECtHR, which began its reasoning by reiterating that the Convention promotes the ideals and values of a democratic society and that any interference with, *inter alia*, Article 9 ECHR, can only be justified by a necessity that '*spring[s] from a "democratic society"* '.[478] It then followed up by establishing that the principle of equality between women and man and the advancement of this principle is, at current times, '*a major goal in the member States of the Council of Europe*'.[479] According to the ECtHR, '*weighty reasons would have to be advanced before a difference of treatment on the ground of sex could be regarded as compatible with the Convention*'.[480] According to the Court, these principles and practices implied that '*States are prevented from 'lending support to views of the man's role as primordial and the woman's as secondary*'.[481] While the Court did not produce a final decision (as the case was declared inadmissible), it nevertheless gave an indication as to which interests should prevail, by siding with views of the national courts. The national courts had found that the '*SGP's position is unacceptable regardless of the deeply-held religious conviction on which it is based*'.[482]

What this case shows is that the State may not remain inactive or allow for views and practices that subordinate women to go unchallenged, particularly in the political and public settings. Additionally, in contemporary democratic societies of member States of

---

477 Hoge Raad, 09 April 2010, ECLI:NL:HR:2010:BK4549, paras. 4.5.5.- 4.6.1.; Gerechtshof 's-Gravenhage, 20 December 2007, LIJN: BC0619, para. 7.2.; Raad van State, 05 December 2007, LJN: BB9493. Notably, the Administrative Jurisdiction Division of the Council of State (*Raad van State*) on the other hand was more judicious and refrained from drawing a conclusion on whether or not the State had acted in contravention of Article 7 CEDAW. Instead, it directed its attention on whether the minister, by denying to grant subsidies to the SGP, had acted in accordance with the Law on subsidising political parties (*Wet subsidiëring politieke partijen*). The Council of State reached the conclusion that the Minister had to grant the SGP subsidies as it had met the conditions set forth by the law. In the meantime, so as not to lose its financial privileges, the SGP amended its rules so that women can be included on the party's list.

478 European Court of Human Rights, *Staatkundig Gereformeerde Partij v. the Netherlands*, 10 July 2012, Application No. 58369/10, para. 70.

479 Id., para. 72.

480 Id.

481 Id., para. 77.

482 Id., para. 73.

the Council of Europe, the principle of gender equality is held in high regard and carries significant weight. From this case, it seems that the principle of gender equality is a value that is weighty enough to justify interferences by the State in the ways in which religious-based institutions organise themselves, particularly where such institutions bar the advancement of gender equality within the public and political spheres.

In conclusion, States have shown that it is possible to intervene in situations of marital captivity without interfering with the internal affairs of trapped spouses. Furthermore, the collective religious freedom does not guarantee religious communities unconditional and unrestricted free rein. The entitlement which religious communities enjoy to autonomously regulate their internal affairs is not absolute and may be subject to restrictions. States may be required to intervene where the application and enforcement of religious rules lead to disadvantaging women and violating their rights.

4.4. INDIVIDUALS' RIGHT TO FREEDOM OF RELIGION

As aforementioned the right to freedom of religion contains collective as well as individual guarantees. In this subchapter, the focus is on the individual right to freedom of religion of the non-cooperative and opposing spouses.

Both Article 18 ICCPR and Article 9 ECHR comprise two dimensions: the internal and external dimension, also known as the *forum internum* and the *forum externum*. The protection afforded to each dimension differs, however. The *forum internum* refers to the individuals' uttermost private sphere i.e. judgements, convictions and ideas occurring within the individual's conscience as well as expressions made within the individuals' inner private sphere, so long this does not affect the rights of others or the outer world.[483] The *forum internum* is absolute, which implies that under no circumstances, even in a situation of State emergency, may the State take measures that infringe or limit the exercise of this freedom.[484] This is provided for in Article 18 (2) ICCPR in conjunction with Article 4 (2) ICCPR, which confirms that the freedoms and rights guaranteed in the first limb, cannot be derogated from.[485] In theory, and in accordance with Article 15 (1) ECHR, the rights and State obligations enshrined in Article 9 ECHR may be derogated from in times of emergency. The specificities related to such a situation, however, remain unclear.[486]

483 John P. Humphrey, 'Political and Related Rights', in Meron *Human Rights in International Law: and Policy Issues* (Oxford Scholarship Online 1986), p. 179.; H. Bielefeldt, N. Ghanea and M. Wiener, *Freedom of Religion or Belief: An International Law Commentary* (Oxford 2016), p. 76.

484 Brems, *Article 14: The Right to Freedom of Thought, Conscience and Religion*, p. 19.

485 HRC, *General Comment No. 22: Article 18 (Freedom of thought, conscience or religion)*, 30 July 1993, para. 1. For example, the HRC has referred to the freedom of conscience as an example of a right that cannot be derogated from.

486 Schabas, *The European Convention on Human Rights: A commentary*, p. 420.

The *forum internum* includes the right to freely and autonomously adopt, maintain or change one's religion or belief without impermissible external influences, and the right to be free from coercion.[487] The freedom of religion and belief, as provided for in Article 18 (1) ICCPR and Article 9 ECHR, guarantees the freedom to adopt, maintain and change one's religion or belief autonomously, without impermissible external influences, i.e. the freedom from coercion.[488] It is comprised of different elements and rights, including but not limited to, the right to freely and autonomously choose to adhere (or not) to a religion or belief, the right to convert to another religion or belief, the right to withdraw from or not belong to a religious group, the right to choose not to reveal/disclose one's affiliation with a religion or belief, as well as the right to refrain from activities that would require an individual to recant or change their held religion or belief.[489] The freedom from coercion, as it is enshrined in Article 18(2) ICCPR, guarantees a right not to be coerced to adhere, recant or maintain a certain religion or belief.[490] It is worth noting that Article 9 ECHR does not contain a provision on the freedom from coercion, similar to that of Article 18 (2) ICCPR. However, case law exhibits that the freedom from coercion is included implicitly within the freedom to change one's religion or belief. On several occasions, both the ECmHR and ECtHR have concluded that adopting coercive measures or forcing individuals to maintain or change their belief is incompatible with Article 9 ECHR.[491]

The *forum externum* refers to expressions that occur within or which extend to the public sphere. It concerns the externalisation of one's thoughts, convictions, and beliefs to the outer world, which may, therefore, affect the rights of others.[492] The second part of the freedom of thought, conscience and religion confers on individuals the '*freedom*

487 Krishnaswami, *Study of discrimination in the matter of religious rights and practices*, p. 24.; Nowak, *U.N. Covenant on Civil and Political Rights: CCPR commentary*, p. 417.; Schabas, *The European Convention on Human Rights: A commentary*, p. 420.

488 Krishnaswami, *Study of discrimination in the matter of religious rights and practices*, pp. 16, 24; Nowak, *U.N. Covenant on Civil and Political Rights: CCPR commentary*, p. 417.; Schabas, *The European Convention on Human Rights: A commentary*, p. 420.

489 Nowak, *U.N. Covenant on Civil and Political Rights: CCPR commentary*, p. 414.; de Jong, The freedom of thought, conscience and religion or belief in the United Nations (1946–1992), p. 61. See case European Court of Human Rights, *Sinan Işık v. Turkey* 2 February 2010, Application No. 21924/05, para. 41. Notably, within the ECHR system, the freedom not to disclose or reveal one's religious affiliation has been dealt with as falling within the right to freedom of manifestation, which may then be subjected to restriction i.e. individuals may be required to reveal, disclose or substantiate their religious/non-religious affiliations in certain contexts. See also Grabenwarter, *European Convention on Human Rights: Commentary*, pp. 238–239.

490 The HRC has specified the term 'coercion' to include any treatment or conduct that compels individuals to adhere to, change or recant a certain religion or belief, the practice of sanctioning individuals that hold certain religions or beliefs and other indirect coercive practices that may impair the freedom to have, maintain and change one's religion (e.g. by way of restricting access to certain facilities). HRC, *General Comment No. 22: Article 18 (Freedom of thought, conscience or religion)*, paras 3,5,8.; Renucci, *Article 9 of the European Convention on Human Rights*, pp. 20–22.

491 European Commission of Human Rights, *Knudsen v. Norway*, 8 March 1985, Application No. 11045/84, p. 258.; European Court of Human Rights, *Ivanova v. Bulgaria*, 12 July 2007, Application No. 52435/99, para. 79.

492 Bielefeldt, et al., *Freedom of Religion or Belief: An International Law Commentary*, p. 76.

to manifest one's religion or belief in teaching, practice, worship and observance, alone or in community with others and in private or in *public*'.

Opposition to or non-cooperation with a religious divorce falls within this dimension. Within the Islamic and Jewish faiths, the act of not cooperating is not only a requirement for a valid religious divorce, but it is also a right that spouses are entitled to use according to their own discretion. Thus, it could be said that a recalcitrant husband who refuses to cooperate in a religious divorce is exercising his God-given right. For religions that consider marriage as indissoluble, this may be less clear since no specific action is needed on the part of the spouses for a situation of marital captivity to arise. However, divorcing spouses have, as the case law discussed in 4.4.2.2. will reveal, at times attempted to hinder a civil divorce by invoking the religious nature of an indissoluble marriage as argument to oppose the effectuation of civil divorce. Where (religious) divorce is deemed as incompatible with the spouses' religious and personal convictions, the concerned spouses may then refrain from, oppose or not want to engage in any activities that would result in the dissolution of the (religious) marriage. These considerations then raise the question as to whether withholding or not cooperating with a religious divorce, by a recalcitrant spouse, constitutes a religious manifestation within the meaning of Article 18 ICCPR and Article 9 ECHR. Is a spouse who opposes or objects to cooperate in a (religious) divorce on the basis of her or his religious convictions entitled to do so? If so, is compelling her or him to divorce or requiring him to cooperate in a religious divorce a restriction of her/his rights. Related hereto, does the right to freedom of religion include a right to object complying to an obligation to cooperate in a (religious) divorce? In other words, can a recalcitrant spouse invoke a right to conscientious objection as a way to countermand a legal obligation to cooperate in the dissolution of a religious marriage? It is, thus, imperative to establish whether these practices constitute religious manifestations within the meaning of the right to freedom of religion. This requires examining the protected sphere of Article 9 ECHR and Article 18 ICCPR

4.4.1. RELIGIOUS MANIFESTATIONS

States must approach questions concerning the legitimacy, forms and ways in which a religion or belief is manifested restrictively.[493] Both the ICCPR and ECHR have, by way of case law and specific provisions, excluded certain activities and behaviour from the protection of the right to freedom of religion and belief. For example, States not only have the possibility to limit, but they may well be obligated to prohibit activities

493 Evans, *Freedom of religion under the European Convention on Human Rights*, p. 104.; Asma Jahangir, *Civil and Political Rights, including the question of religious intolerance*, (Commission on Human Rights, 9 January 2006), [E/CN.4/2006/5], para. 41. Bielefeldt, et al., *Freedom of Religion or Belief: An International Law Commentary*, p. 111.; Schabas, *The European Convention on Human Rights: A commentary*, p. 425.; Renucci, *Article 9 of the European Convention on Human Rights*, p. 23.

and behaviour, where they are immoral in nature and when they endanger the rights and freedoms of others (e.g. in case of human sacrifice, widow burning, mutilation etc.), in accordance with Article 18 (3) ICCPR.[494] Likewise, there are certain activities that are more likely to be excluded from the protection of the freedom to manifest a religion or belief. For example, manifestations of a religion or belief that amount to discrimination against women are not likely to receive protection. Article 18 ICCPR cannot be relied upon to justify discrimination against women. This also extends to discrimination against women in respect of their freedom of religion.[495] Furthermore, manifestations that amount to propaganda for war, advocate national, racial or religious hatred or incite discrimination, hostility or violence, should not only be prohibited by law, in accordance with Article 20 ICCPR, but they should also be excluded from the protection that is granted by Article 18 ICCPR.[496]

The ECmHR and ECtHR have adopted a rather distinctive and pragmatic approach in this regard. Case law reveals that certain manifestations may be excluded from the protection of Article 9 ECHR, in the sense that they do not constitute religious manifestations. For example, in the case of *Arrowsmith v. the United Kingdom*, the ECmHR concluded that the distribution of leaflets by a pacifist, which contained, among others, information on the procedures of objecting, refusing, discharging from or leaving military posts in Northern Ireland, did not constitute a religious manifestation. In the ECmHR's view, the leaflets '*did not express pacifist views*' as their content did not convey '*the idea that one should under no circumstances, even not in response to the threat of or the use of force, secure one's political or other objectives by violent means*'[497], and thus did not '*further pacifist ideas*'.[498] In *Kosteski v. The former Yugoslav Republic*, the refusal to work a particular day because it was a religious holiday was not considered to be a religious manifestation.[499] Other examples of practices that fall outside the scope of Article 9 ECHR are the marketing of goods[500], assisted suicide[501] and certain burial practices.[502]

Notwithstanding the foregoing, the four modalities (worship, teach, observe and practice) of manifestations that are stated in both the ICCPR and the ECHR should be

494 Bielefeldt, et al., *Freedom of Religion or Belief: An International Law Commentary*, p. 111.; Krishnaswami, *Study of discrimination in the matter of religious rights and practices*, p. 29.

495 UN Human Rights Committe '*General Comment No. 28: Article 3 (The equality of rights between men and women)*', 2000, CCPR/C/21/Rev.1/Add.10, para. 21.

496 HRC, *General Comment No. 22: Article 18 (Freedom of thought, conscience or religion)*. para. 7.

497 European Commission of Human Rights, *Arrowsmith v. the United Kingdom*, 16 May 1977, Application No. 7050/75, para. 72.

498 Id., para. 74.

499 European Court of Human Rights, *Kosteski v. the former Yugoslav Republic, 13 April 2006*, Application No. 55170/00, paras. 37–38.

500 European Commission of Human Rights, *X. and Church of Scientology v. Sweden*, 5 May 1979, Application No. 7805/77.

501 European Court of Human Rights, *Pretty v. the United Kingdom*, 29 July 2002 Application No. 2346/02, para. 82.

502 European Commission of Human Rights, *X. v. the Federal Republic of Germany*, 10 March 1981, Application No. 8741/79, p. 138.

interpreted in an inclusive manner so as to ensure that different types of manifestations of religion or belief are protected.[503] Furthermore, practice by the respective monitoring bodies shows that activities which amount to a manifestation can be categorised differently within each or several of the four modalities. In fact, human rights monitoring bodies often discuss these modes simultaneously, without making a clear distinction as to their specific elements and distinctions. The parameters of where one mode ends and the other begins will not always be easily identifiable. Rather, these modalities should be regarded as forming interactive elements of one right.[504] The following subsection addresses each one of these modes briefly.

4.4.1.1. Manifestation in worship, teaching, observance and practice

The concept of 'worship' concerns acts and rituals that are integral to or are a direct expression of one's religion or belief.[505] Conventional examples are praying and preaching, but the wearing of a beard can also be considered as an act of worship according to the HRC's case of *Boodoo v. Trinidad and Tobago*.[506] Additionally, the freedom to manifest in worship includes the right to assemble and connect with others for the purpose of carrying out such expressions, as well as the right to maintain a place of worship and to perform the necessary rites and rituals with the necessary objects.[507]

Teaching refers to the transmission of the prescriptions, dogmas and doctrines of a religion or belief.[508] In terms of Article 9 ECHR, teaching is to be understood as the '*general communication of religious knowledge*'.[509] This includes, among others, the freedom to choose religious leaders, the freedom to establish religious schools, the freedom to distribute texts and publications, as well as the freedom to attempt to persuade others to join one's religion or belief.[510] Attempts to convert others will not necessarily constitute a violation of the 'receiver's' religious freedom.[511]

---

503 Grabenwarter, *European Convention on Human Rights: Commentary*, p. 238.

504 De Jong, The freedom of thought, conscience and religion or belief in the United Nations (1946–1992), p. 79.

505 HRC, *General Comment No. 22: Article 18 (Freedom of thought, conscience or religion)*, para. 4.; UN Human Rights Committe *Clement Boodoo v. Trinidad and Tobago*, 15 April 2002, Communication No. 721/1996, para. 6.6.; Evans, *Freedom of religion under the European Convention on Human Rights*, p. 107.

506 UN Human Rights Committe *Clement Boodoo v. Trinidad and Tobago*, 15 April 2002, Communication No. 721/1996. See also Nowak, *U.N. Covenant on Civil and Political Rights: CCPR commentary*, p. 420.

507 HRC, *General Comment No. 22: Article 18 (Freedom of thought, conscience or religion)*, para. 4.; Declaration on the Elimination of All Forms of Intolerance and of Discrimination Based on Religion or Belief, 6(a) and (h).; Carolyn Evans, p. 107.

508 Nowak, *U.N. Covenant on Civil and Political Rights: CCPR commentary*, p. 420.

509 Grabenwarter, *European Convention on Human Rights: Commentary*, p. 238.

510 HRC, *General Comment No. 22: Article 18 (Freedom of thought, conscience or religion)*, para. 4.

511 European Court of Human Rights, *Kokkinakis v. Greece*, 25 May 1993, Application No. 14307/88, para. 3.1. Whether the ICCPR contains a similar right to 'try and convince one's neighbour', is not clear. The *travaux préparatoires* show that the article was intended to deal '*only with the right to change one's own religion or belief, nor that of the other persons*. At the same time, discussions on the term of 'coercion'

As for the terms 'practice' and 'observance', HRC's general comment No. 22 refers to both 'observance' and 'practice', as including, the wearing of religious clothing, observing dietary restrictions and participating in rituals associated with certain stages of life.[512] In the ECHR, the term 'observance' refers to ritual customs such as pilgrimages, observing dietary rules, a particular dress code, headwear etc.[513] As for the term 'practice', in the case of *Arrowsmith v. the United Kingdom*[514], the ECmHR developed a criterion for determining whether certain acts constitute 'practice'. It held that not all conduct that is motivated or influenced by a religion or belief will qualify as 'practice'. In order for acts to fall within the scope of the freedom to manifest in practice, they need to be an actual expression of the concerned belief or religion.[515] This is the case when there is a direct link between the religion or belief practised and the act alleged to be a manifestation in practice. This means that individuals need to objectively showcase that the necessity to engage in the respective activities arises from their religion or belief.[516] In other words, the alleged activity should be required by the religion or belief according to an objective assessment of, for example, experts, religious leaders or religious rules. Neither the ECmHR nor ECtHR have been inclined to place substantial weight on the subjective claims of individuals who allege a manifestation in practice.[517]

4.4.1.2. Conscientious objection

In everyday life, believers may have to obey certain religious days (e.g. Sabbath and Sunday), practice and preserve certain rites and rituals (e.g. daily prayers and wearing certain clothing) or refrain from certain activities (e.g. consuming certain foods). To ensure compliance with the religious prescriptions adherents can then, for example, request temporary leave from work in order to celebrate and obey the religious prescriptions or they may ask to be exempted from having to partake in specific activities that are deemed incompatible with their religious convictions. However,

---

show a certain acknowledgement to the permissibility of '*moral and intellectual persuasion*' by others, though a proposal to include a passage including the freedom to '*persuade other persons of full age and sound mind of the truth of his beliefs*' was eventually rejected. Citations from UN doc. A/C.3/SR.576, para. 37, A/2929, para.116 Commission on Human Rights, 5th Session (1949), 6th Session (1950), 8th Session (1952) in Bossuyt *Guide to the "Travaux Prếparatiores" of the International Covenant on Civil and Political Rights* (1987), pp. 358,363.; see also Krishnaswami, *Study of discrimination in the matter of religious rights and practices*, pp. 26–28.;

512 HRC, *General Comment No. 22: Article 18 (Freedom of thought, conscience or religion)*, para. 4.

513 Grabenwarter, *European Convention on Human Rights: Commentary*, p. 239.

514 Separate Opinion, in part dissenting of Mr. Opsahl in European Commission of Human Rights, *Arrowsmith v. the United Kingdom*, 16 May 1977, Application No. 7050/75, para. 3. Noteworthy are the views of Mr. Opsahl in his dissenting opinion. He recommends that this criterion be interpreted and applied in a broad manner. A broad understanding, he argues, enables many acts to still fall within the scope of Article 9 ECHR, even those that, *prima facie*, are not deemed as manifestation of belief or religion, provided that they are expressed genuinely and consistently within the context of the particular case.

515 Id., para. 71.

516 Evans, *Freedom of religion under the European Convention on Human Rights*, p. 115.

517 Id., pp. 120–121.

where this is not possible, frictions may then exist between having to comply with religious convictions *vis a vis* having to comply with legal obligations that derive from general laws or contractual obligations. The latter may then oblige religious individuals to engage in activities that they perceive as conflicting with their religious obligations. The question is therefore whether objecting to comply with the legal obligations is an act that ought to receive protection within the scope of the right to freedom of religion. In other words, does the right to freedom of religion guarantee a right to conscientious objection to legal obligation?

The subject of conscientious objection is very relevant, in particular, for those situations of marital captivity that involve a non-cooperative spouse who is compelled, by way of legal obligation (e.g. a tort action), to cooperate in the dissolution of a religious divorce. A non-cooperative spouse may not want to comply with such a legal obligation out of religious considerations. For example, a recalcitrant spouse may not want to cooperate with a court order that compels him to cooperate in a *talaq* procedure, where he, out of religious considerations finds a *khul'* divorce to be more appropriate[518] or simply does not want to divorce from his wife. Thus, can a non-cooperative spouse refuse to cooperate with a legal obligation that demands his cooperation by invoking his religious freedom?

4.4.1.2.1. ICCPR

During the drafting process of the ICCPR, the inclusion of a right to conscientious objection was proposed twice. One proposal advocated the inclusion of a provision on conscientious objection which recognised that individuals should not be required to act contrary to their '*religious observance or practice*'. The second proposal limited the recognition of conscientious objection to military service. Ultimately, however, neither of these proposals were adopted.[519]

Whether Article 18 ICCPR contains a general right to refrain from acts that conflict with one's conscience, including a right not to be compelled to do so, is still a matter of an ongoing debate. Conscientious objection relating to military service, on the other hand, has been recognised and is protected under Article 18 ICCPR. Initially, the existence of a right to conscientious objection to military service was dismissed.[520] However, this changed with the 1993 general comment No. 22, which recognised the existence of such a right, despite the fact that Article 18 ICCPR makes no reference

[518] This was for example the case Rechtbank Amsterdam, 2 April 2014, ECLI:NL:RBAMS:2014:1644. For more on this case see section 3.4.1.

[519] Bossuyt, *Guide to the "Traveaux Préparatiores" of the International Covenant on Civil and Political Rights*, p. 364.

[520] Human Rights Committee, *L. T. K. v. Finland*, 9 July 1985, Communication No. 185/1984, para. 5.2. This case concerned a conscientious objector to military service. The Committee concluded that '*The Covenant does not provide for the right to conscientious objection; neither article 18 nor article 19 of the Covenant, especially taking into account paragraph 3 (c) (ii) of article 8, can be construed as implying that right*'.

to a right to conscientious objection for military service. General comment No. 22 affirms that a right to conscientious objection can be derived from Article 18 ICCPR, where an obligation to use *'lethal force'* is experienced as conflicting with the freedom of conscience and the right to manifest one's religion or belief.[521] Notably, some authors see a problem with the wording, since it can be interpreted narrowly as only covering those instances that actually involve the use of lethal force and thus excluding other military activities from its scope.[522] Nonetheless, the Committee has, via subsequent concluding observations and decisions, consistently reaffirmed that a right to conscientious objection to military service, for both religious and non- religious reasons, can be derived from Article 18 ICCPR.[523] Whether or not alternative civilian services are provided and objectors are required to undergo these in order to substitute their military obligations is a matter that the HRC has left to the discretion of States. However, where States do provide for alternative services, the HRC recommends that these then ought to be *'outside the military sphere and not under military command'*.[524]

The question remains whether, beyond the military context, a general right to conscientious objection exists or may develop, as has been the case for the right to conscientious objection to military service. In this regard, the HRC has had the opportunity to deal with objectors in other domains. In *J.P v. Canada*, the Commission

---

521 HRC, *General Comment No. 22: Article 18 (Freedom of thought, conscience or religion)*. para.11.

522 Brems, *Article 14: The right to freedom of thought, conscience and religion*, p. 15.; Nowak, *U.N. Covenant on Civil and Political Rights: CCPR commentary*, p. 424.

523 Office of the United Nations High Commissioner for Human Rights, *Conscientious objection to military service: Analytical report of the Office of the United Nations High Commissioner for Human Rights*, (Human Rights Council, 2017), [A/HRC/35/4], para. 8.; Human Rights Committee, *Concluding Observations Ukraine 2001*, CCPR/CO/73/UKR, paras. 20–21.; Human Rights Committee, *Concluding Observations Kyrgyzstan 2014*, CCPR/C/C/KGZ/2, para. 32. In more recent cases, the HRC has firmly established that a *'right to conscientious objection to military service inheres in the right to freedom of thought, conscience and religion. It entitles any individual to an exemption from compulsory military service if such service cannot be reconciled with that individual's religion or beliefs'*. On top of that, the HRC has also clarified that the freedom from coercion applies to this right, thus any measures to coerce and individual to act against her or his conscience is incompatible with Article 18 ICCPR. Human Rights Committee, *Uchetov v. Turkmenistan*, 15 July 2016, Communication No. 2226/2012, paras. 7.6–7.7.; Human Rights Committee, *Nurjanov v. Turkmenistan*, 15 July 2016, Communicaton No. 2225/2012, paras. 9.3–9.4.; Human Rights Committee, *Nasyrlayev v. Turkmenistan* 15 July 2016, Communication No. 2219/2012, paras 8.7–8.6.; Human Rights Committee, *Yegendurdyyew v. Turkmenistan*, 14 July 2016, Communication No. 2227/2012, paras. 7.7–7.6.; Human Rights Committee, *Japparow v. Turkmenistan*, 17 December 2015, Communication No. 2223/2012, paras. 7.6–7.7.; Human Rights Committee, *Mahmud Hudaybergenov v. Turkmenistan*, 22 December 2015, Communication No. 2221/2012, para. 7.5–7.6.; Human Rights Committee, *Abdullayev v. Turkmenistan*, 19 May 2015, Communication No. 2218/2012, paras. 7.7–7.8.; Human Rights Committee *Min-Kyu Jeong et al. v. the Republic of Korea*, 27 April 2011, Communications No. 1642–1741/2007, paras. 7.4–7.5.

524 Human Rights Committee, *Uchetov v. Turkmenistan*, 15 July 2016, Communication No. 2226/2012, paras. 7.6–7.7.; Human Rights Committee, *Nurjanov v. Turkmenistan*, 15 July 2016, Communication No. 2225/2012, paras. 9.3–9.4.; Human Rights Committee, *Nasyrlayev v. Turkmenistan*, 15 July 2016, Communication No. 2219/2012, paras 8.7–8.6.; Human Rights Committee, *Yegendurdyyew v. Turkmenistan*, 14 July 2016, Communication No. 2227/2012, paras. 7.7–7.6.

had to answer whether the refusal to pay taxes was protected under Article 18 ICCPR.[525] The Committee found that although the right to '*hold, express and disseminate opinions and convictions*' was protected, the refusal to abide by her tax obligations on the basis of her convictions was not protected by Article 18 ICCPR. In a subsequent and similar case, *J.v.K. and C.M.G.v.K.-S. v. The Netherlands*, the Committee reaffirmed that Article 18 ICCPR did not extend so far as to protect individuals who refuse to pay taxes. Thus, the refusal to pay taxes on the basis that this contravenes one's personal or religious beliefs does not fall within the scope of Article 18 ICCPR.[526]

From the foregoing, it may be concluded that the freedom of conscience and the right to manifest one's religion or belief, guarantees a right to conscientious objection, albeit it has only been recognised within the context of compulsory military services.[527] The HRC has not recognised a right to conscientious objection in other domains. Furthermore, the Committee has reiterated that both the right to manifest one's religion or belief as well as the freedom of conscience, do not imply the '*right to refuse all obligations imposed by law*'.[528] In addition, the right to manifest one's religion can provide '*protection, consistent with article 18, paragraph 3, against being forced to act against genuinely held religion and beliefs*'.[529] In essence, this comes down to a balancing exercise, whereby if the conditions of Article 18 (3) are met, the State may impose restrictions by compelling individuals to act against their conscience.

Additionally, the recognition of a right to conscientious objection within the military context, reaffirms that the ICCPR is a living and flexible instrument that is able to be interpreted within constantly changing societies. The ICCPR is adaptable to new developments and unforeseen challenges that the original drafters may not have been able to forsee or include.

---

525 Human Rights Committee, *J.P. v. Canada*, 7 November 1991, Communication No. 446/1991*/, para. 4.2. The case concerned a Canadian Quaker who, alleging a violation of her freedom of conscience and religion under Article 18 ICCPR, refused to pay a percentage of her taxes that were reserved for the Canadian military and defence efforts. She considered that engaging in such activities was contrary to her religious convictions.

526 Human Rights Committee, *J.v.K. and C.M.G.v.K.-S. v. the Netherlands*, 31 July 1992, Communication No. 483/1991, para. 4.2.

527 The HRC observes that the use of lethal force '*may seriously conflict with the freedom of conscience and the right to manifest one's religion or belief*'. See also HRC, *General Comment No. 22: Article 18 (Freedom of thought, conscience or religion)*. para 11.

528 The HRC has concluded that '*the right to manifest one's religion or belief does not as such imply the right to refuse all obligations imposed by law*'. Furthermore, in the case of *Paul Westerman v. the Netherlands*, the HRC held the freedom of conscience does not '*imply the right to refuse all obligations imposed by law, nor does it provide immunity from criminal liability in respect of every such refusal*'. Human Rights Committee *Yeo-Bum Yoon and Myung-Jin Choi v. Republic of Korea*, 23 January 2007, Communications Nos. 1321/2004 and 1322/2004, para. 8.3.; Human Rights Committee *Paul Westerman v. the Netherlands*, 13 December 1999, Communication No. 682/1996, para. 9.3.

529 Human Rights Committee *Yeo-Bum Yoon and Myung-Jin Choi v. Republic of Korea*, 23 January 2007, Communications Nos. 1321/2004 and 1322/2004, para. 8.3.

4.4.1.2.2. ECHR

The recognition of a right to conscientiously object in the ECHR has, so far, been limited to individuals who have objected to participate in military service. The long established practice was that Article 9 ECHR neither protects nor guarantees a right to conscientious objection, even within the context of military service.[530] However, this position changed following the case of *Bayatyan v. Armenia*.[531] Despite the fact that Article 9 ECHR does not explicitly refer explicitly to conscientious objection, the court in this case concluded that opposition to military service may in certain instances '*constitute a conviction or belief of sufficient cogency, seriousness, cohesion*' that is protected by Article 9 ECHR. This is the case when there is a '*serious and insurmountable conflict between the obligation to serve in the army and a person's conscience or his deeply and genuinely held religious or other beliefs*'.[532] Thus not only must the conflict be serious and insurmountable, but there is also a requirement of genuineness on the part of the objector.

Similar to the HRC, both the ECtHR and the ECmHR have had to deal with cases of conscientious objections in other domains. These cases reveal that the recognition of conscientious objection to military service is the exception rather than the rule. In the case of *Blumberg v. Germany*, the applicant refused to conduct a medical examination on an apprentice, as he had found this to conflict with his personal interests. This served as reason to dismiss the applicant from his work. The applicant then alleged a violation of his freedom of conscience. The case was declared inadmissible. The refusal to examine the apprentice, which served as the ground of dismissal, was found not to '*constitute an expression of coherent views on a fundamental problem*', and therefore the applicant could not enjoy protection under Article 9 ECHR.[533]

In another case, *C. v. UK*, a Quaker refused to pay taxes as they were partially also intended for military expenditure.[534] The Commission reached the conclusion that the obligation to pay taxes, being a general and neutral one, did not have any links with individual's beliefs and hence did not have conscientious implications in and of itself. This was supported by the fact that the competences to impose tax are recognised in Article 1 of the First Protocol to the ECHR.[535] Therefore, Article 9 ECHR did not

---

530 This was also rejected by State parties during the drafting of the ECHR. European Commission of Human Rights, *Preparatory work on article 9 of the European Convention on Human Rights*, (1956), [DH(56)] 14, p. 23, *at* <https://www.echr.coe.int/Documents/Library_TravPrep_Table_ENG.pdf> last accessed 12 October 2018.

531 European Court of Human Rights, *Byatyan v. Armenia*, 27 July 2011, Application No. 23459/03, paras. 110–128.

532 Id., para. 110.

533 European Court of Human Rights, *Klaus Blumberg v. Germany*, 18 March 2008, Application No. 14618/03, p. 4.

534 European Commission of Human Rights, *C. v. the United Kingdom*, 15 December 1983, Application No. 10358/8 3, pp. 143–146.

535 Id., p. 147.

protect or include a right to refuse to abide by legal obligations to pay taxes, as these apply '*generally and neutrally*' in the public sphere.

Likewise, in the case of *Revert and Legallais v. France*, the applicants sought protection under Article 9 ECHR by alleging that the obligation to join a professional association of architects, which could potentially offend his conscience as an architect, constituted a violation of his rights under Article 9 ECHR. Reaching the same conclusion, the ECmHR found that the obligation applied to all architects on a neutral basis and had no links with their personal beliefs.[536] Noteworthy is the case of Skugar *and Others v. Russia* in which the Court established that Article 9 ECHR does not contain a negative obligation towards conscientious objectors.[537] In this case, the Court held that the State, in designing and implementing its internal procedures, cannot be required to take into account the way in which individual citizens could interpret legal obligations and duties on the basis of their religious beliefs.[538] This essentially implies, that in the course of its regulatory activities, the State is not bound to take into account the fact that certain laws and measures may conflict with the conscience of certain individuals or groups.

From the above it may be concluded that a general right to refuse to comply with legal obligations on the basis that these are incompatible with one's personal or religious convictions cannot be derived from Article 9 ECHR.[539] Legal obligations cannot be evaded by alleging that they are in conflict with an individuals' conscience. Beyond the military context, Article 9 ECHR cannot be said to protect all outward conduct and behaviour that reflects an individuals' conviction and certainly not where the evasion of legal obligations would be the result thereof.[540] Both the ECmHR and ECtHR have upheld the 'neutral and general legal obligations' criteria, which provide that since such obligations primarily aim at regulating public life in general and do not have any links to individuals religion or beliefs, it follows that they do not impact the individual's convictions and hence cannot cause an interference with the freedom of conscience, religion or belief.[541] Nevertheless, general legal obligations may still be challenged under a combination of the articles 9 and 14 ECHR.[542] This may, for example, be the case if the imposed obligations are found to disproportionately affect individuals of certain specific faiths in the observance of their religious convictions (e.g. State laws

536 European Commission of Human Rights, *Paul Revert and Denis Legallais v. France*, 8 September 1989, Application Nos. 14331/88, 14332/88, para. 2, at p. 317.

537 European Court of Human Rights, *Skugar and Others v. Russia*, 3 December 2009, Application No. 40010/04, p. 7. Additionally, the Court also acknowledged that variance may exist between an individual's religious interpretation and the prevailing interpretation within the denomination he or she is an adherent to. In such an event, the concerned individual may still receive the protection of Article 9 ECHR if he or she sincerely holds a different understanding of her/his religion or belief.

538 Id., p. 9.

539 Grabenwarter, *European Convention on Human Rights: Commentary*, pp. 238–239.

540 Renucci, *Article 9 of the European Convention on Human Rights*, pp. 23–24.

541 Id.

542 Clayton and Tomlinson, *The law of human rights*, para. 14.51A.

that require registrars of marriages to officiate a same-sex marriage may affect State officials that adhere to faiths that prohibit same-sex marriage[543]).

Furthermore, although artikel 9 ECHR does not contain a general right to conscientious objection, the ECtHR has come to recognise that a right to conscientious objection to military service can be derived from this article. Similar to the ICCPR, this development demonstrate that ECHR is also a living and flexible instrument that is adabptable to the contemporary contexts of changing societies. Situations that the drafters have not explicitly included may still be found to be implied within treaty.

4.4.2. OPPOSITION AND NON-COOPERATION TO DIVORCE AS A RELIGIOUS MANIFESTATION

As previously mentioned, the practices and conduct that give rise to a situation of marital captivity are linked to the religious doctrines and views which unevenly distributed divorce rights between the spouses or either restrict spouses' ability to divorce by establishing indissoluble marriages or not allowing the practice of divorce. Thus, in a way, those acting in accordance with the religious rules on divorce are expressing their observance of these rules. This then begs the question as to whether the refusal to cooperate in a divorce and opposing a divorce are religious manifestations that are protected by Article 18 ICCPR and Article 9 ECHR. In order to answer this question, the following paragraphs provide an analysis of how situations of marital captivity have been dealt with by human rights monitoring bodies and national courts and legislators. More specifically, the focus is on the freedom of religion and how this right has been interpreted and applied in cases concerning marital captivity, and whether the non-cooperation or opposition to a divorce has been considered as a religious manifestation.

4.4.2.1. International and regional case law

The HRC has yet to deal with a case of marital captivity where the applicant alleges a violation of his freedom of religion as consequence of having to accept a civil divorce or having to cooperate in a religious divorce. Beyond statements, primarily found in concluding observations, that discriminatory divorce practices are incompatible with the treaty, the HRC has, to date, not addressed the phenomenon of marital captivity

543 See for example the case of European Court of Human Rights, *Eweida and Others v. the United Kingdom* 15 January 2013, Application Nos. 48420/10, 36516/10, 51671/10, 59842/10, paras. 102–105. In this case the third applicant, Ms. Ladele (the registrar) alleged a violation of Articles 9 jo. 14 ECHR on the account that having to participate in the 'creation of same-sex civil partnerships' and not being exempted from having to do so, constituted discrimination against her on the basis of her Christian beliefs. However, a violation was not found after the Court found that the requirement of registrars to officiate same sex-marriage served a legitimate aim and the State enjoyed a wide margin of appreciation in how they regulated the officiation of same sex-marriages.

directly.[544] Other human rights monitoring bodies have also still to be confronted with a case of marital captivity. This notwithstanding, the CEDAW Committee was the first treaty body to explicitly address marital captivity in its 2016 concluding observations on the Netherlands.[545] The right to religious freedom, however, was not mentioned in connection to marital captivity.

At the regional level, only one case concerning a situation of marital captivity has been dealt with by the European Commission of Human Rights. This was the 1983 case of *D. v. France*. The facts are as follows:

The marriage between the applicant (husband) and his partner (wife) was terminated on the initiative of the applicant by way of a civil divorce in 1975. Both the applicant and his wife were devoted to the Jewish faith. Consequently, the wife found it important to also terminate the religious marriage in accordance with the Jewish custom of delivering and accepting the *Get*. The husband, however, refused to provide his (ex-)wife with the *Get*. The (ex-)wife then initiated civil proceedings; demanding that she be compensated for the damages she had suffered as a result of the persistent withholding of the *get* by the applicant.[546] The husband alleged that he wished to retain the possibility to reassume the marital life with his (ex-)wife and could not divorce her due to his personal status. As a Kohen[547], under Mosaic law he was not permitted to marry a divorced woman.[548] Thus, he argued that by divorcing her, he would, in essence, forfeit the possibility to reassume marital life with her in the future, as he would then not be able to remarry her. However, the Supreme Court of France established that the applicant had never undertaken any efforts to reconcile with his (ex-) wife since the civil divorce had been pronounced. Notably, the Supreme Court of France did recognise that the withholding of the *get* had been an '*option of exercising his conscience*'. Nonetheless, the Supreme Court of France, as well as the lower courts, reached the conclusion that the husband had denied his ex-wife the *get*, purely in order to prevent her from remarrying another man and thus was driven by mal-intentions. The husband was found to have abused his privileged position and had inflicted damage on his (ex-)wife.[549] He was ordered to pay 2500 francs in damages. Eventually, the case was brought to the ECmHR by the husband. He alleged that the French court order to pay damages was an '*infringement*

544 See subchapter 1.4. on the extent to which human rights monitoring bodies have specifically addressed the phenomenon of marital captivity.

545 Committee on the Elimination of Discrimination Against Women, *Concluding Observations on the sixth periodic report of the Netherlands*.

546 Cour de Cassation, Chambre civile 2, 21 April 1982, [81–11.775].

547 Jewish priest. This status is obtained through one's patrilineal lineage to Aaron (Moses's older brother) Jacqueline Shields, *Modern Jewish History: The Tribes Today – Kohens, Levis &Yisraels, at* <www.jewishvirtuallibrary.org/jsource/Judaism/tribes1.html> last accessed 20 May 2016.

548 '*They shall not marry a woman who is a prostitute or who is desecrated, and they shall not marry a woman who is divorced from her husband for he [the kohen] is holy to his God.' The Complete Tanakh -With Rashi commentary (Online English translation by Rabbi A.J. Rosenberg),* Leviticus 21:7.

549 Cour de Cassation, Chambre civile 2, 21 April 1982, [81–11.775].

of his freedom of conscience and religion [as] he was ordered to pay damages by the courts for having manifested his religion or belief by the practise or accomplishment of the rites of the Jewish faith'.[550] Notably, the manifestation that the applicant referred to, both before the Supreme Court of France as well as the Commission, was not the refusal to grant a *get* as such, or even that his free consent was lacking, which is considered a prerequisite to the validity of a *get*. Instead, the applicant referred to the observance of Jewish law that prohibited him from marrying a divorced woman. In essence, the withholding of the *get* from his (ex)wife served as a means to ensure that he could re-engage in marital life with his (ex)wife without violating Jewish law on this matter.

The Commission had to establish whether the French court order constituted an infringement of the applicant's freedom to manifest his religion in observance or practice and thus, whether his refusal to grant the *get* was a religious manifestation. It concluded that the refusal to hand over a *get* did not constitute a manifestation of his religion in observance or practice. In this regard, two factors influenced the Commission's assessments towards this conclusion. First, divorce by way of a *get* delivery was in fact regulated by Jewish law. Second, delivering a *get* after the civil divorce had been pronounced was the common practice within the religious community. In the Commissions view, '*no man with genuine religious convictions would contemplate delaying the remittance of this letter to his ex-wife*'.[551] Thus, the refusal to grant a *get* was found not to constitute a religious manifestation and the French court order did not, therefore, infringe the applicant's religious rights. There was, accordingly, no violation of Article 9 ECHR.[552]

4.4.2.2. National case law

Since it is a global phenomenon, various secular and non-secular countries have undertaken efforts to address and resolve situations of marital captivity. Investigating their approaches to marital captivity and, in particular, how they have dealt with the religious aspects that are inherent in the phenomenon, contributes to a better understanding of the non-cooperative/opposing spouse's right to freedom of religion in situations of marital captivity. This section outlines how three countries in Europe – the Netherlands, France and the United Kingdom – have addressed the freedom of religion in relation to marital captivity.

4.4.2.2.1. The Netherlands

Starting with the situations whereby a spouse opposes the dissolution of a civil divorce, the jurisprudence discussed in section 3.4.1. demonstrates that the judiciary has not

550 European Commission of Human Rights, *D. v. France*, 6 December 1983, Application No. 10180/82, p. 201.
551 Id., p. 202.
552 Id.

been willing to concede to the demands of the opposing spouse. This notwithstanding, in the case of *Hoge Raad 09 December 2005*, the court did recognise that the freedom of religion could be affected by the pronunciation of a civil divorce. In that case, the appellant (the wife) opposed the effectuation of a civil divorce. She submitted that dissolving the otherwise indissoluble marriage would result in a violation of her right to private and family life (Article 8 ECHR and Article 17 ICCPR) and her freedom of religion (Article 9 ECHR and Article 18 ICCPR).[553] The Supreme Court upheld the Court of Appeal's decision, in which it had implicitly accepted that a civil divorce may constitute a restriction to the freedom of religion, which nevertheless was justifiable as it pursued the legitimate aim of protecting the rights of others.[554]

Concerning the situation of a non-cooperative spouse to a religious divorce, the Advocate General in the case *Hoge Raad of 10 November 1989*, acknowledged the religious nature of the act of repudiation. Compelling a spouse to cooperate in a religious divorce would affect the religious convictions of all the involved parties. Therefore, the Advocate General recommended a restrictive approach and higher standards of motivation when dealing with situations of marital captivity in which the judiciary is requested to compel the recalcitrant spouse to cooperate in a religious repudiation.[555] Due to the religious aspects that are inherent in situations of marital captivity, the courts have at times even had recourse to religious authorities and experts.[556] Furthermore, it has been acknowledged that the dissolution of a religious marriage or involvement in religious matters would go well beyond the competence of the courts.[557] Consequently, and pursuant to Article 1:30 of the Dutch Civil Code, a secular judge cannot dissolve a religious marriage, as their competences only extends to the legal aspects of the marriage. Nevertheless, judges maintain the competence to rule over cases of marital captivity and to determine whether non-cooperation to a religious divorce constitutes a tort within the meaning of Article 6:162 of the Dutch Civil Code. Where this is the case, the courts can order the husband to cooperate in the dissolution of the religious marriage and to adopt measures where he fails to do so.[558]

Regarding whether non-cooperation has been considered as a religious manifestation, the existing body of case law does not provide a conclusive answer to this question.

---

553 Hoge Raad, Conclusion of the attorney general, 09 December 2005, ECLI:NL:PHR:2005:AU5285, paras. 8–10. See also previous case with the same parties; Hoge Raad, Conclusion of the Advocate General, 27 June 2003, ECLI:NL:PHR:2003:AF7681, paras. 9–10.

554 Hoge Raad, Conclusion of the attorney general, 09 December 2005, ECLI:NL:PHR:2005:AU5285, paras. 8, 10.

555 Hoge Raad, Conclusion of the attorney general, 10 November 1989, ECLI:NL:PHR:1989:AC1683, para 2.21.
See also Rechtbank Haarlem, 17 February 1989, ECLI:NL:RBHAA:1989:AH2605, para 3.8.

556 Rechtbank Amsterdam, 17 November 1983, ECLI:NL:RBAMS:1983:AH0155.

557 Rechtbank Haarlem, 17 February 1989, ECLI:NL:RBHAA:1989:AH2605, para 3.4.; Hoge Raad, 22 January 1982, ECLI:NL:HR:1982:AG4319.

558 Id., O.II, paras. 4–6.

In a recent case involving a Jewish marriage, the husband argued that he had refused to comply with a previous court order to cooperate in the dissolution of the religious marriage because of the financial disadvantages he would incur, as the wife did not want to provide compensation. He also maintained that he had, on the basis of Jewish doctrine, principal objections to the divorce.[559] Ruling in favour of the husband, the judge found that it could not be established that he had committed a tort against his wife by refusing to cooperate in the religious divorce. In reaching this conclusion, the court considered the husband's financial and principal objections in order to establish whether his conduct was tortious. In so doing, it did not involve or examine this objection in relation to the right to freedom of religion, either explicitly or implicitly.[560]

In another case of the Court of Appeal of Amsterdam, the husband prevented the dissolution of a Jewish marriage by admitting to the religious tribunal (*Beth din)* that he had been compelled to provide the *get* by a court order of the civil judge.[561] In other words, he suggested that he was not acting upon his free will to deliver a *get* but was compelled to do so by the court. This would have resulted in a coerced *get*, which is a factor that may consequently invalidate the *get*. Thence, the *Beth din* refrained from drafting a *get* and therefore the entire process came to a halt and a religious divorce did not come about. The Court of Appeal concluded that by reporting on the fact that he had been compelled to cooperate in a religious divorce, the husband had prevented the dissolution of the religious marriage and had, therefore, committed a tort. It reasoned that it is an established practice for a *Beth din* to cooperate in the dissolution of a marriage, even when either party has been compelled to cooperate in the religious divorce by way of a court order.[562] The only reason that the *Beth din* would decline a *get* delivery, was if it was clear that the husband's free will was lacking. The court held that the *Beth din* had reached this conclusion on the basis of the recalcitrant spouse's explicit statements and external behaviour.[563] Furthermore, the court concluded that a court order compelling a spouse to cooperate is not necessarily incompatible with the voluntary character that is inherent in the Jewish divorce.

Noteworthy, in a previous case the Court of First Instance of Amsterdam had established that the *Beth dins* hold different views on the validity of a *get* that is produced under the influence of a court order.[564] This knowledge may have influenced the Court of Appeal' s conclusion that, in practice, the *Beth din* is willing to cooperate in the dissolution of a marriage, even if one of the spouses has been compelled by a secular judge to cooperate in the religious divorce. Therefore, in the court's view the dissolution of the religious marriage had been prevented, not due to its voluntary character that is inherent in a religious divorce, but due to the husband's statements.[565] The court considered that the admission by the husband to the *Beth din* that he had been compelled

559 Rechtbank Amsterdam, 04 December 2017, ECLI:NL:RBAMS:2017:8910, para 3.2.
560 Id., para 4.4.
561 Gerechtshof Amsterdam, 31 August 1989, ECLI:NL:GHAMS:1989:AD0874.
562 Id., para. 4.5.
563 Id., paras. 4.5, 4.7.
564 Rechtbank Amsterdam, 17 November 1983, ECLI: NL:RBAMS:1983:AH0155, para. 13.
565 Gerechtshof Amsterdam, 31 August 1989, ECLI:NL:GHAMS:1989:AD0874, para. 4.7.

to cooperate in the religious divorce, was not necessary nor required for the dissolution of the religious marriage. Notwithstanding the foregoing, it should be noted that beyond these facts, the court established that the husband had acted inconsistently in the past by admitting that he would cooperate on two occasions. He was also shown to be driven by financial motives and material gains.[566] Similar to the other case, the non-cooperation was not considered within the context of the right to freedom of religion or as an act of observing the interpretations of religious scripture that require a non-coerced *get*.

To conclude, although it has been shown that (at times) non-cooperative spouses have provided their religious convictions as a reason for refusing to cooperate in the dissolution of a religious marriage, the right to freedom of religion has not been invoked specifically and directly by the recalcitrant spouses. In addition, in most cases the motives and/or objections for non-cooperation that are provided by the recalcitrant spouse were not even of a religious nature. Consequently, the link to the right to freedom of religion has yet to be made. Courts have yet to deal with the specificities of the right to freedom of religion and to establish whether non-cooperation in a religious divorce may be considered as a religious manifestation.

4.4.2.2.2. France

The involvement of French courts in religious affairs (Jewish and Muslim) already occurred during its colonisation of, among others, Algeria, Tunisia and Morocco. In 1879, the Court of Appeal of Algeria handed down a decision concerning a situation of marital captivity. This concerned the *Darienté* case in which the husband remarried another woman in a civil ceremony, all the while refusing to give his first wife, with whom he had only been religiously married, a *get*.[567] The trapped spouse started legal proceedings against the recalcitrant spouse and requested that the non-cooperative spouse be compelled to deliver a *get*. The Court of Appeal of Algeria observed that the religious marriage was a "*fact' which could give rise to prejudice and found the plaintiff unjustifiably deprived of her liberty to marry and suffering injury to her freedom of conscience*'.[568] Finding that the delivery of the *get* was a non-religious '*civil act of ordinary nature*', the conclusion was reached that the husband could be compelled to grant a *get*. On appeal, the *Cour de Cassation* (the Supreme Court of France) drew the final conclusion that protecting the liberty of marriage and the freedom of conscience of the trapped spouse outweighed all the other conflicting interests and therefore the husband could be compelled to grant a get.[569] The *Darienté* decision was subsequently applied uniformly in Algeria and in most North-African colonies.[570]

566 Id., paras. 4.5–4.7.
567 Glenn, *Where heavens meet: The compelling of religious divorces*, p. 14.
568 Id.
569 Id.
570 Id., pp. 14–15, South African Law Commission, *Working paper 45- Project 76: Jewish* Divorces, pp. 72–73.

A similar approach was adopted in mainland France by the judiciary when cases of marital captivity presented themselves halfway through the 20th century.[571] In 1959, the Court of Appeal of Paris held that the execution of a *get* lacks religious meaning and that the *get* proceedings were of a civil nature that required neither attendance at a synagogue nor the taking of oaths.[572] Therefore, the court could compel a husband to deliver a *get* despite the fact that his religious convictions had changed and he had converted to another religion.[573] Likewise, in 1972 the Court of Cassation came to the conclusion that the civil enforcement of an order to cooperate in a Jewish divorce did not violate the French understanding of the separation of State and Church.[574] In more recent cases, French courts have dealt with two types of religious-based objections to the dissolution of marriage.

The first concerns marital captivity that is the result of a non-cooperative spouse. French courts have slightly deviated from the earlier case law and given certain recognition to the religious aspects that are inherent in the dissolution of a religious marriage. The act and motives underlying the granting or withholding of a *get* have been recognised as constituting relevant aspects of the freedom of conscience for the recalcitrant spouse.[575] In addition, the *Cour de Cassation* has consistently reiterated that an examination of the motives to deliver or withhold a *get*, are beyond the jurisdiction of the civil courts.[576] For example, the demand of a trapped spouse (the wife) to, among others, compel the husband to relieve her from the religious marriage by cooperating in the religious divorce, was rejected by the court on the basis that the 'Civil code does not provide a rule/position on this point'.[577] In more recent cases, judges have even taken into account the custom of dissolving the religious marriage subsequent to a civil divorce within Jewish communities. Expertise from religious leaders has also been sought at times.[578]

Significantly, the competence of the courts has been challenged in a number of cases, where a recalcitrant spouse alleged that the penalty imposed by the courts, on the basis of Article 1382[579] of the French Civil Code, constituted a violation of the principle of separation of State and Church and violated the recalcitrant spouse's religious freedom. Without addressing these objections on their merits, the *Cour de Cassation*

571 Glenn, *Where heavens meet: The compelling of religious divorces*, p. 15.

572 Id.; South African Law Commission, *Working paper 45- Project 76: Jewish Divorces*, (1992), p. 74.

573 Glenn, *Where heavens meet: The compelling of religious divorces*, p. 15.

574 Id., pp. 15–16.

575 Cour de Cassation, Chambre civile 2, 21 November 1990, [89–17.659].

576 Cour de Cassation, Chambre civile 2, 15 June 1988, [86–15.476].

577 Cour d'Appel Paris,16 March 2011, [10/01413].

578 In a case, a grand rabbi was summoned during the civil divorce process, who in fact confirmed that since the civil divorce had been effected, the recalcitrant spouse could not refuse to terminate the religious marriage by withholding a *get* from his ex-wife. Cour d'Appel de Versailles, 16 February 2012, [10/04809.

579 Article 1382 reads: '*Every act whatever of man that causes damage to another, obliges him by whose fault it occurred to repair it.*' French Civil Code, translated by David W. Gruning, Alain A. Levasseur, Paul M. Hebert, John R. Trahan & Juriscope, *at* <https://www.legifrance.gouv.fr/Media/Traductions/English-en/code_civil_20130701_EN> last accessed 11 February 2018.

has maintained that courts have the competence to establish whether the withholding of a *get* is an abuse of power (i.e. an abuse of the spouse's divorce rights) and to establish the responsibility arising from an abuse of power. This has also been found to be compatible with the principle of separation of State and Church.[580] Thus, while the French judges have been willing to recognise that dissolving a religious marriage forms a relevant aspect of the freedom of conscience of the recalcitrant spouse, the exercise of religious rights, i.e. the power that the husband has to trap or free the woman, may nonetheless be subjected to review by the civil judge. In conclusion, beyond recognising the religious aspects inherent in a situation of marital captivity, the French courts have refrained from fully addressing whether non-cooperation in a religious divorce constitutes a religious manifestation.

The second cases involve opposition to a civil divorce by a spouse. Most of these cases have concerned Catholic women. Article 240 of the French Civil Code has been invoked occasionally by an opposing spouse. This article enables a civil judge to reject a petition for divorce when the spouse who did not petition for the divorce, provides evidence that the divorce would have '*material or moral consequences of exceptional harshness*'.[581] In such cases, opposing spouses have undertaken efforts to meet the conditions that are found in Article 240 of the French Civil Code, by stating that a civil divorce was incompatible with their religious convictions or that a divorce would adversely affect their family, social environment or moral condition.[582] In none of these cases, however, did the French courts establish that a divorce would have exceptionally harsh material or moral consequences.

Moreover, in 1990, a spouse (the husband) appealed a divorce decree, alleging that in pronouncing a civil divorce, the Court of Appeal violated Article 9 ECHR and Article 10 UDHR (right to a fair trial).[583] He argued that the Court of Appeal had failed to consider the possibility of annulling the marriage by an ecclesiastic institution, prior to establishing its jurisdiction over the case in accordance with Article 242 of the Civil Code.[584] The Supreme Court rejected the appeal without addressing whether Article 9 ECHR and Article 10 UDHR entitled the applicant a right to apply religious laws to annul the marriage. Instead, the court focused on the factors that justified the

580 Cour de Cassation, Chambre civile 2, 15 June 1988, [86–15.476].; Cour de Cassation, Chambre civile 2, 13 December 1972, [71–12.043].

581 John H. Crabb, *The French civil code: Revised Edition (as amended to 1 July '994)* (Deventer, 1994).

582 Cour de Cassation, Chambre civile 1, 17 January 2006, [03–19.879].; Cour de Cassation, Chambre civile 2, 13 March 2003, [01–14.616].; Cour de Cassation, Chambre civile 2, 24 October 2002, [01–12.431].; Cour d'Appel de Reims, Chambre civile 2e section, 27 June 2002, [**2001/00587**]; Cour de Cassation, Chambre civile 2, 20 January 2000, [97–14.750].

583 Cour de Cassation, Chambre Civile 2, 21 May 1990, [89–12.512].

584 Article 242 states: '*A petition for divorce may be filed by a spouse when the facts which constitute a serious or renewed violation of the duties and obligations of marriage are ascribable to the other spouse and render unbearable maintaining the community life*'. French Civil Code translated by David W. Gruning, Alain A. Levasseur, Paul M. Hebert, John R. Trahan & Juriscope, at <https://www.legifrance.gouv.fr/Media/Traductions/English-en/code_civil_20130701_EN> last accessed 11 February 2018.

dissolution of the civil marriage (i.e. his abandonment of the marital home for several months, forbidding his wife to receive and entertain family members and friends and refusing to lead a 'normal' married life) and the designated competence of the Court of Appeal to dissolve the civil marriage.[585]

As it appears, French courts have not been inclined to accept complaints, on both religious and non-religious grounds, from opposing spouses which would, in essence, hinder a civil divorce. Objections to a civil divorce based on one's religious convictions have not been accepted by the French courts. The *Cour de Cassation* has tended to conclude that a civil divorce does not affect a religious marriage and that in pronouncing the divorce, the civil judge – acting within her or his competence – is not bound to follow the parties in all their argumentation.[586] The question of whether opposing a civil divorce, on the basis of there being a conflict with religious convictions, constitutes a religious manifestation has remained largely unanswered hitherto.

4.4.2.2.3. The United Kingdom

Prior to the adoption of the Divorce (Religious Marriages) Act 2002, UK judges also had to deal with situations of marital captivity in the Jewish communities. In the leading case of *Brett v. Brett*, the recalcitrant husband, who had withheld a writ of divorce from his wife, was ordered to pay a lump sum to his wife. Finding that the husband had attempted to exploit his position so as to obtain a bargaining advantage, the court awarded the wife a lump sum of 5,000 pounds to be paid by the husband on the condition that he had failed to provide a *get* after a period of three months had lapsed.[587]

Attempting to find sustainable solutions to the problem of marital captivity, the Orthodox Jewish community took the initiative, in 1996 and once again in 2000, to propose a bill that would enable the secular courts to influence the completion of a religious divorce. This resulted in the Divorce (Religious Marriages) Act which was passed and adopted in 2002 and applies in England and Wales. The inclusion of section 10A into the Matrimonial Causes Act 1973[588], enables the court to abstain

585 Cour de cassation, Chambre Civile 2, 21 May 1990, [89–12.512].

586 See among others the findings of the court in Cour de Cassation, Chambre civile 1, 17 January 2006, [03–19.879].; Cour de Cassation, Chambre civile 2, 13 March 2003, [01–14.616]; Cour d'Appel de Reims, Chambre civile 2e section, 27 June 2002, [**2001/00587**]; Cour de cassation, Chambre civile 2, 20 January 2000, [97–14.750].

587 Court of Appeal of the United Kingdom, *Brett v. Brett*, 5 December 1968, [1969] 1 All ER 1007, at *494, 496.

588 Matrimonial Cause Act 1973, *at* <https://www.legislation.gov.uk/ukpga/1973/18> last accessed 11 February 2018, Chapter 18, Section 10A. The Section reads as follows:
'*(1) This section applies if a decree of divorce has been granted but not made absolute and the parties to the marriage concerned –*
(a) were married in accordance with –
(i) the usages of the Jews, or
(ii) any other prescribed religious usages; and
(b) must co-operate if the marriage is to be dissolved in accordance with those usages.

from formalising a decree of divorce until the actions that are necessary to complete a religious divorce have been completed.

During the discussions of the bill, the question was raised as to whether the proposed bill interfered with religious matters and freedoms. From the offset, it was emphasised that the bill did not seek to interfere with religion, nor did it attempt to reinterpret or change religious laws. There was no intention or aim to introduce a right to civil and religious divorce, where it had not previously existed. This particular concern was raised by the Catholic communities.[589] Instead, the bill was '*framed to enable civil authorities to deal with a technical problem that has arisen within the Jewish community*'. Among the aims of this initiative were to place men and women on an equal footing and to prevent the abuse of the religious conditions that should be met at the dissolution of the marriage.[590] Notably, the court may only employ this discretion when dealing with an application for a civil divorce.[591] Thus, the Act does not extend to situations where only a religious marriage exists. Nor does it aim to solve the problem of religious divorce within the Jewish community or any other religious communities.[592]

Regarding the freedom of religion, it was concluded that the bill was compatible with, *inter alia*, Article 9 ECHR.[593] In fact, it was argued that there were positive obligations on the State to protect the trapped spouse's rights and that the bill would contribute to fulfilling this obligation. In Lord Lester of Herne Hill's view, '*unless such provision is brought into force, there will be breaches by the Government of their positive obligation under the convention to remove unjustifiable obstacles to the right of "chained" spouses to remarry in accordance with their religious belief and conscience, with equality of rights and responsibilities, and to provide effective remedies*

(2) On the application of either party, the court may order that a decree of divorce is not to be made absolute until a declaration made by both parties that they have taken such steps as are required to dissolve the marriage in accordance with those usages is produced to the court.
(3) An order under sub-section (2) –
(a) may be made only if the court is satisfied that in all the circumstances of the case it is just and reasonable to do so; and
(b) may be revoked at any time.
[...]
(6) 'Prescribed' means prescribed in an order made by the Lord Chancellor after consulting the Lord Chief Justice and such an order –
(a) must be made by statutory instrument;
(b) shall be subject to annulment in pursuance of a resolution of either House of Parliament'.

589 House of Commons debate on the Divorce (Religious Marriages) Bill, Hansard Debates text for Friday 12 Apr 2002, vol. 383, *at* <www.publications.parliament.uk/pa/cm200102/cmhansrd/vo020412/debtext/20412-02.htm#20412-02_spnew0> last accessed 23 September 2016, cc. 266–267.

590 Id., c. 281.

591 Id., c. 284.

592 House of Lords debate on the Divorce (Religious Marriages), Lord siting of 30 June 2000, vol. 614, *at* <http://hansard.millbanksystems.com/lords/2000/jun/30/divorce-religious-marriages-bill-hl l> last accessed 23 September 2016, c. 1244.

593 Id., c. 1246.

for breaches of their convention right'.[594] The only potential point of incompatibility that was noted, was that the bill may contravene the non-discrimination principle pursuant to Article 14 ECHR, where it would only apply to religious divorces in Jewish communities but not, for example, in Muslim communities. However, it was concluded that the differences in divorce procedures within the Muslim communities differed from divorce procedures carried out in accordance with Hebrew law, in that according to Islamic law, women have a possibility to divorce without the husband's cooperation.[595] Nonetheless, it was provided that the bill would also apply to religious marriages that are carried out in accordance with the laws of other faiths, provided that the circumstances are the same i.e. where next to a civil divorce, cooperation to a religious divorce is necessary and there is a risk that one of the spouses will refuse to cooperate and remove the religious barriers to remarriage. Therefore, although the Act came into existence on the initiative of the Anglo-British Orthodox Jewish community, it can equally be applied to religious marriages of other faiths that require the cooperation of both spouses in order to dissolve the religious marriage.[596] Finally, it should be noted that the fact that the initiative of the bill came from the Jewish community strengthened the argument for intervention by secular courts in situations of marital captivity and also had the effect that the legislative initiative was perceived as a desirable solution.[597]

To conclude, in the United Kingdom there is a certain degree of recognition of the religious aspects that are inherent in a situation of marital captivity. The act of dissolving a religious marriage in accordance with religious laws is a matter which judges and legislators do not envisage nor seek to interfere in. Nonetheless, the bill was found to be compatible with the right to freedom of religion. That being said, this does not indicate whether the act of cooperation or non-cooperation to a religious divorce is considered as a religious manifestation.

---

594 Id., cc. 1246–1247.; House of Commons debate on the Divorce (Religious Marriages) Bill, Hansard Debates text for Friday 12 Apr 2002, vol. 383, c. 266.

595 House of Lords debate on the Divorce (Religious Marriages), Lord siting of 30 June 2000, vol. 614, c. 1246–1247.; House of Commons debate on the Divorce (Religious Marriages) Bill, Hansard Debates text for Friday 12 Apr 2002, vol. 383, cc. 268–269.

596 See also House of Lords debate on the Divorce (Religious Marriages) Bill, Lords sitting of 10 June 2002, vol. 634, *at* <http://hansard.millbanksystems.com/lords/2002/may/10/divorce-religious-marriages-bill > last accessed 23 September 2016, c.1412.; Charlotte Proudman, 'Religious Marriages: Staying a decree absolute in order to increase the chances of obtaining a religious divorce', *Family Law week*, *at* <www.familylawweek.co.uk/>.
Section 10A (1) now applies to marriages conducted in accordance with the usages of Jews or '*any other prescribed religious usages*'. Though, at the time of writing, the act does not officially apply to Muslim marriages. The Anglo-Muslim community has not made use of this section or indicated that it wants to make use of it.

597 House of Commons debate on the Divorce (Religious Marriages) Bill, Hansard Debates text for Friday 12 Apr 2002, vol. 383, c. 269.; House of Lords debate on the Divorce (Religious Marriages) Bill, Lords sitting of 10 June 2002, vol. 634, c.1403.

4.4.2.3. *A right to oppose or withhold cooperation in a religious divorce?*

As it stands, the HRC has not provided much guidance on the question of how to classify the non-cooperation or opposition to a (religious) divorce. Under the ECHR, not cooperating to the dissolution of a religious marriage does not constitute a religious manifestation within the meaning of Article 9 ECHR.[598] State intervention in a situation of marital captivity, by imposing a legal obligation on the non-cooperative spouse to remedy the damages caused to the trapped spouse, does not constitute a violation of Article 9 ECHR. The inquiry on the practice within the three States reveals that national authorities do not explicitly recognise the acts of non-cooperation or opposition to a (religious) divorce as religious manifestations. At the same time, the religious nature pertaining to the act of not cooperating to or opposing a religious divorce has been recognised by the national authorities of all three States. So, does this mean that the act of not-cooperating with or opposing a (religious) divorce does not constitute a religious manifestation that is worthy of the protection guaranteed by Article 18 ICCPR and Article 9 ECHR?

Considering the foregoing, several conclusions can be drawn. Firstly, whether opposition to civil divorce is or is not a religious manifestation does not really carry implications for the State in relation to the dissolution of a civil marriage. This is because a civil divorce decree does not actually interfere with or restrict the opposing spouse's freedom of religion. A civil marriage is governed by civil law and is not indissoluble in nature. Conducting a religious indissoluble marriage does not change or affect the character of the civil marriage and *vice versa*. After all, in secular countries such as the Netherlands, France and the UK, the institutions of marriage and divorce are governed by two separate normative systems. Therefore, and as the French courts have highlighted, a civil divorce does not affect the religious marriage or its indissoluble nature i.e. it does not affect or dissolve the religious link between the spouses. An interference would be the case if the judges were to surpass the boundaries of their discretion by dissolving or annulling the religious marriage. In reality, therefore, a civil divorce leaves the religious marriage intact and does not attempt to dissolve or annul the religious marriage or even require the opposing spouse to undertake any such actions. The opposition in itself may genuinely be an expression of the spouse's religious convictions. However, a civil divorce can hardly constitute an interference with the religious freedom of the opposing spouse as it does not restrict or interfere with the religious freedom of the opposing spouse in respect of their religious convictions and beliefs regarding marriage and divorce.

Secondly, as was evidenced in both the *D. v. France* and national case law, non-religious factors do not deserve and are not awarded the protection of the right to freedom of religion. Even in the cases where a direct or indirect reference was made to the religious convictions of the recalcitrant spouse, the adopted discourse has so

[598] See subsection 4.4.2.1.

far been that non-cooperation founded mainly on bad faith, financial or other gains cannot be tolerated. National courts have, in such circumstances, intervened in favour of the trapped spouse. Likewise, the Commission in *D. v. France* refrained from acknowledging the recalcitrant spouse's actions as worthy of protection by the right to freedom of religion. Therefore, whether the recalcitrant spouse's actions or inactions are deserving of the protection under the right to freedom of religion is dependent on all the circumstances of the case and the true motives and intentions for not cooperating. Although, in reality, and particularly in the case of marital captivity, establishing the true motives let alone separating these from one's religious convictions and motivations may be a task that is not easily realisable. Nevertheless, the withholding of a religious divorce for reasons of personal or financial reasons can hardly be considered as a religious manifestation within the meaning of Article 18 ICCPR and Article 9 ECHR. Not cooperating, in such circumstances, will not be a genuine expression of one's religion.

But what about those spouses that genuinely do not want to divorce their spouse for religious reasons? Can the argument still be maintained that this too does not constitute a religious manifestation; especially given that the entire procedural regulation of the divorce process, including the rights that each spouse enjoys, directly derives from the religious tenets and scriptures?

Under both the ICCPR and ECHR systems, the general understanding is that a religious manifestation in observance or practice refers to acts that are either prescribed by religion or acts that have an 'obvious' link with the concerned religion and are actual expressions of that religion. For marital captivity, this means that there needs to be an obvious link between the spouse's acts/behaviour with the concerned religion so that these are also an expression of that religion (the necessity to engage in the respective activities is induced by the religion or belief). There is an obvious link between the religious doctrine and the actions of spouses who genuinely and sincerely oppose or withhold cooperation to a (religious) divorce. After all, the individually held religious convictions regarding the issue of divorce, find their basis in religious scripture and interpretations that prescribe a marriage either as indissoluble or that require free and wilful cooperation from the divorcing spouses. In fact, within the Islamic and Jewish faiths, spouses are entitled to a divorce, even though women are largely dependent on the cooperation of their husbands to do so. Thus, there is a link between the religious doctrines on divorce prescribed above and the observance of these doctrines by adherents. Furthermore, in certain denominations, much weight is attributed to religious scripture, rules and interpretations that require voluntary cooperation in a religious divorce, or that provide for limited grounds for divorce by mutual consent. Adherents may equally place significant importance to these provisions and requirements, meaning that non-cooperation or opposition to a (religious) divorce is an expression of one's genuine religious conviction. It should also be borne in mind that

States should act restrictively in assessing the authenticity and legitimacy of an alleged manifestation. Adherents to a religion or belief enjoy discretion in determining the manner in which they express their religion.

As for the argument given in *D. v. France*, namely that cooperation in a religious divorce, subsequent to a civil divorce is common practice, it should be pointed out that within the different religious communities, denominations and schools there are diverging practices and views on the subject of divorce. As is illustrated in the relevant case law, literature and practice, cooperation in a religious divorce subsequent to a civil divorce will not always be the case. Generalisations of 'common practices' within religious communities should thus be made with caution.

Taking all these factors into account, the conclusion can be drawn that the opposition to or the withholding of a (religious) divorce can be linked to and may be motivated by religious doctrine. Where this is the case, such practice may then be considered as actual expressions of and abidance with religious norms and may, therefore, constitute religious manifestations within the meaning Article 9 ECHR and Article 18 ICCPR. However, and as explained above, the recognition of opposition to civil divorce as a religious manifestation does not mean that this right is affected where a judge dissolves the civil marriage. As for the situation involving a non-cooperative spouse, the conclusion that non-cooperation in a religious divorce can constitute a religious manifestation should not be generalised to all situations of marital captivity. Instead only where the non-cooperation is motived and is an expression of the concerned spouse's religious convictions, can it be argued to be a religious manifestation.

4.4.2.4. *The implications of recognising divorce denial as a religious manifestation*

Considering the conclusion reached in the previous subsection, attention needs to be given to the implications of recognising the withholding of cooperation to a religious divorce as a religious manifestation within the meaning of Articles 18 ICCPR and 9 ECHR. Is such practice worth the protection of Articles 18 ICCPR and 9 ECHR?

By giving recognition to a religious manifestation that essentially allows husbands to deny their wives a divorce bears the risk of upholding and reinforcing religious doctrines and underlying ideologies that promote inequality between women and men at the dissolution of the marriage. This is particularly the case where the accessibility of divorce takes the form of being a men's prerogative and where women enjoy little to no possibilities to initiate a religious divorce. In addition, such a recognition would also imply protecting a practice that leads to the violation of the trapped spouse's rights.

There are two ways that one may consider the act of not cooperating to a religious divorce in relation to Articles 18 ICCPR and 9 ECHR. Firstly, considering the negative consequences of withholding a divorce, non-cooperation to a divorce may be considered as not constituting a religious manifestation that is worthy of the protection of Articles 18 ICCPR and 9 ECHR. In other words, such practices would be excluded from the scope of Articles 18 ICCPR and 9 ECHR. The HRC interpretation of Article 18 would be in support of this approach. The HRC has explicitly stressed that Article 18 ICCPR may not be relied upon to justify discrimination against women. In other words, the freedom of religion should not be relied upon where it leads to infringing women's rights. However, an interpretation of Article 18 ICCPR and 9 ECHR that recognises non-cooperation in a religious divorce as a religious manifestation would do exactly that. The freedom of religion would then used in way that enables the non-cooperative spouse to enforce religious norms, interpretations and practices that prescribe and promote unequal rights to the detriment of married women and impair women who want to end their marriage. Such an interpretation is thus hard to reconcile with the statements of the HRC. Similarly, such an interpretation would also be difficult to reconcile with the object and purpose to protect the human rights of individuals. As a reminder, the object and purpose of the investigated human rights treaties are to protect the human rights of individuals from infringements and ensure that individuals are guaranteed the effective enjoyment and exercise of their human rights. There are, thus, strong arguments against considering these practices as manifestations that are protected. Rather, these practices ought to be excluded from the protection of Articles 18 ICCPR and 9 ECHR.

The second approach is to consider non-cooperation to a divorce as a religious manifestation that is protected by Articles 18 ICCPR and 9 ECHR. This, however, does not mean that any interventions to compel the cooperation to a divorce, by a non-cooperative spouse, would constitute a violation of Articles 18 ICCPR and 9 ECHR. After all, the right to manifest one's religion is a relative right that may be subjected to restrictions in accordance with the limitation clauses contained in Article 18 (3) ICCPR and 9 (2) ECHR. Thus, even where non-cooperation to a religious divorce is recognised as a religious manifestation, there still remains the possibility to restrict the exercise and effects of such manifestations. Section 4.5.2 elaborates further on the limitation clauses and whether, in the case of marital captivity, restricting the religious freedom of the recalcitrant spouse to withhold cooperation, would be permissible.

As a final point of remark, the 1959 case of the Paris Court of Appeal, in which the court compelled the husband to deliver a *get* even though his religious convictions had changed, raises an important question. Can a non-religious or converted spouse be obliged to cooperate in the dissolution of a religious marriage? If so, would this interfere with his religious freedom (e.g. the right not to be religious, the right to have, maintain or change one's religion and the right to not partake in perceived religious activities)? It should be borne in mind that apostasy can serve as a ground for divorce or annulment in certain religious denominations and schools.[599] Where apostasy

599 Francis, *Apostolic Letter Motu Proprio of the supreme pontiff Francis, Mitis iudex Dominus Iesus*, Article 14, para. 1.; Jamal J. Ahmad Nasir, *The Status of Women under Islamic Law and Modern Islamic Legislation* (3 2009), pp. 154–155. In Catholicism, the amended process for annulling a marriage includes, '*the defect of faith which can generate simulation of consent or error that determines the will*' as grounds for annulling the marriage. In Hinduism there is not much clarity on the divorce

is a ground for divorce, then this does not consequently hinder the attainment of a religious divorce. Where this is not the case and the concerned spouse is required to cooperate, the right to freedom from coercion must then be borne in mind, particularly where non-cooperation is motivated by the fact that the spouse is non-religious or does not adhere to the religion within which the marriage should be dissolved. It is questionable whether compelling the concerned spouse to cooperate is of such a coercive nature that it infringes upon his right to have, maintain or adopt a religion. The compulsion to cooperate in a religious divorce is unlikely to reach this threshold of being coercive to the extent that the non-cooperative spouse feels compelled to change or recant his beliefs or adopt the religion within which the marriage was celebrated.

4.4.3. CONSCIENTIOUS OBJECTION TO DIVORCE

While the previous section dealt with non-cooperation as a religious manifestation, the remaining question is whether a non-cooperative spouse can borrow from a right to conscientious objection, from Articles 9 ECHR and 18 ICCPR, where he/she is compelled by court order to cooperate in the dissolution of the religious marriage. In other words, can a non-cooperative spouse refuse to cooperate in a legal obligation that demands his cooperation by invoking his religious freedom?

Firstly, to date a right to conscientious objection has not been recognised beyond the context of military services. From this alone, it is highly unlikely that the refusal to abide by the legal obligation to cooperate to a religious divorce falls within the recognised scope of conscientious objection.

Secondly, even if a right to conscientious objection can be developed to expand to other domains, the recalcitrant spouse may then have to show that he has serious, insurmountable and genuine objections that prohibits them from cooperating in a religious divorce. The non-cooperative spouse must then demonstrate that having to do so generates a conflict between his conscience or deeply held religious convictions and the required conduct. Furthermore, under the ECHR scheme, the objection must be an expression of coherent views on a fundamental problem. In the case of marital captivity, the 'coherent views' would refer to the religious rules and interpretations concerning the

---

practice itself. See section 2.2.2. Notably, the Indian Hindu Marriage Act provides apostasy as a ground for divorce in Article 13, ii of the Hindu Marriage Act. In Islam, some schools adhere to the notion that an act of conversion to atheism or taking on another religion (in some instance taking on a *non-kitabi* religion i.e. a religion other than one that is founded in Christianity or Judaism) dissolves the marriage. In other schools (*Hanafi*) and national laws (e.g. Kuwaiti law) it follows that only the apostasy of the husband automatically dissolves the marriage. In Judaism, there are different views on apostasy of the husband as a circumstance that justifies the annulment of a marriage. See Susan Weiss, *Divorce: The Halakhic Perspective, at* <www.jwa.org/encyclopedia/article/divorce-halakhic-perspective> last accessed 05 December 2016.

'fundamental problem', i.e. divorce.[600] In addition, it is hard to draw any conclusions regarding the extent to which religious laws on marriage and divorce have a significant impact on or serve as guidelines for the non-cooperative spouse's way of living. Whether the objection to cooperating in a divorce reaches the required threshold of being serious, insurmountable and genuine is not easy to establish. The weight attributed to the personal or religious convictions would have to be assessed on a case by case basis, in light of the limitation clauses and taking into account the rights of trapped spouses. However, where bad faith is present in a case of marital captivity it must be concluded that an objection to cooperate in a religious divorce would not amount to a serious, insurmountable and genuine objection which deserves the protection of Article 18 ICCPR and Article 9 ECHR.

Thirdly, a general right to conscientious objection would also be subjected to restriction in accordance with the limitation clauses of Articles 18 ICCPR and 9 ECHR. The right to conscientious objection, to the extent that it has been recognised, is also a relative right. Thus, where there are competing rights, as in the case of marital captivity, the exercise thereof may be subject to restrictions in order to guarantee the other rights.

4.5. STATE'S OBLIGATIONS AND LIMITATIONS TO THE FREEDOM OF RELIGION AND BELIEF

The previous subchapters reveal that the instances where the right to freedom of religion will be affected by the State's measures to address marital captivity are very unlikely. Even where an interference with the right to religious freedom can possibly be argued, then this is limited only to those situations involving a non-cooperative spouse. As aforementioned, in certain very limited circumstances, non-cooperation in a religious divorce can be argued to constitute a religious manifestation. This concerns situations wherein non-cooperation is founded in a spouse's genuine and sincere religious considerations. Compelling the non-cooperative spouse to cooperate may then arguably constitute an interference with their religious freedom

However, the right to manifest one's religion individual and collectively is a relative right and may be subjected to restrictions in accordance with the limitation clauses of Article 18 (3) ICCPR and 9 (2) ECHR respectively.[601] This means that State's interference with this right, in order to end situations of marital captivity, may be permissible. The following sections, therefore, elaborate on the limitation clauses of Articles 18 ICCPR and 9 ECHR, and examine whether State intervention, within the context of marital captivity, is permissible.

600 It is debatable whether divorce is a fundamental problem, although considering the perceived negative connotations that are attributed to divorce in current society, and particularly within religious communities, there is an argument to be found that divorce may be perceived as a problem.

601 Nowak, *U.N. Covenant on Civil and Political Rights: CCPR commentary*, p. 411.; Humphrey *Political and Related Rights*, p. 179.

4.5.1. STATE'S OBLIGATIONS

In principle, the ICCPR and ECHR do not advocate a certain model of State-Church relations. States with an official religion or an established Church do not by definition violate or impede the freedom of religion.[602] Compliance with the principle of non-discrimination would, after all, mean that other religions receive similar entitlements that are given to, for example, a State religion or church.[603] Likewise, secular States are by definition not in a better position to guarantee and protect the freedom of religion. The ICCPR and ECHR merely require that the freedom of religion is guaranteed, implemented and protected on the basis of the principles of equality and non-discrimination, irrespective of the State-Church relations. The respect and full protection of the freedom of religion requires the State to act in a neutral and impartial manner and to ensure religious pluralism and tolerance.[604]

The right to freedom of religion includes both negative as well as positive obligations. The negative obligations require the State to refrain from coercing individuals to adhere to or maintain a certain religion or belief. Equally so, the State is to refrain from compelling individuals to participate in religious activities to which the individual does not wish to adhere to[605], or to engage in religious activities against their will.[606] Furthermore, in accordance with the non-discrimination principle, the State is expected to refrain from discriminatory conduct towards any particular group that is devoted to a religion or belief. Likewise, the State should not disadvantage or provide undue advantages to a certain group or its members on the basis of a particular religion or belief.[607]

States have positive obligations to prevent and suppress conduct that is incompatible with the rights of others (e.g. the religious freedom of others, protection of minority religions

602 HRC, *General Comment No. 22: Article 18 (Freedom of thought, conscience or religion)*, paras. 9–10.

603 De Jong, *The freedom of thought, conscience and religion or belief in the United Nations (1946–1992)*, p. 283.
Under the ECHR, this might may not always be the case. For example, if an established church is entitled to State funding, it will not necessarily mean that another religious institution is entitled to State funding. This outcome is possible by the application of the margin of appreciation that States enjoy in certain circumstances. Yildirim provides that in matters concerning State-Church relations, States do enjoy a wide margin of appreciation. Yildirim, *The collective dimension of freedom of religion or belief in international law: The application of findings to the case of Turkey*, p. 437.

604 Yildirim, *The collective dimension of freedom of religion or belief in international law: The application of findings to the case of Turkey*, p. 437.

605 Grabenwarter, *European Convention on Human Rights: Commentary*, p. 239.

606 Carolyn A. Kapinus and Daniel R. Flowers, 'An Examination of Gender Differences in Attitudes Toward Divorce', 49 *Journal of Divorce & Remarriage* 239–257, (2008), pp. 73–74.

607 Krishnaswami, *Study of discrimination in the matter of religious rights and practices*, p. 53.; Nowak, *U.N. Covenant on Civil and Political Rights: CCPR commentary*, p. 416.; Sarah Joseph, Jenny Schultz and Melissa Castan, *The International Covenant on Civil and Political Rights- Cases, materials and commentary* (New York, 2004), p 505.; HRC, *General Comment No. 22: Article 18 (Freedom of thought, conscience or religion)*, para. 9.

that are threatened by opposing groups, protection from blasphemy etc.), or that is of an immoral nature.[608] States are also expected to ensure that individuals enjoy the actual possibility to recant or leave their respective religion or to abstain from engaging in certain religious expressions or manifestations.[609] In addition, there also rests a positive obligation on the State to actively work towards eliminating discrimination on the basis of religion or belief. In his study, Krishnaswami broadened this obligation by holding that States should equally *'prevent any individual, or group of individuals from making such adverse distinctions [against] or giving such undue preferences [to individuals or a group of individuals]'*. In other words, this entails an obligation on the State to eliminate discrimination that occurs in horizontal relationships between private actors.[610] Thus, the State is required to protect individuals from coercive acts that are carried out by private actors, especially where they restrict or influence the freedom to have, maintain or change a religion or belief of other individuals.[611] Under the ECHR, States have, among others, a positive obligation to ensure that individuals can leave a certain religion or belief, to create a peaceful atmosphere whereby individuals can exercise their religious freedom and receive protection against proselytism from the State as well as from private actors.[612]

4.5.2. INTERFERENCE WITH THE RELIGIOUS FREEDOM

An interference by the State, in the most conventional sense, involves the active involvement of the State, its agencies or officials, in a manner that restricts or obliterates the rights contained in both the ICCPR and ECHR. When it comes to marital captivity, it is thus crucial to identify which authority is involved. Where it concerns religious authorities, it suffices to submit that this is not likely to constitute an interference or violation of the non-cooperative spouse who belongs to the same religious community. In principle, the approach adopted by the ECtHR is that by their membership of a certain religious community, members have made a choice to obey the decisions and judgments of the religious authorities. In fact, so long as the individual can effectively exercise their right to leave or recant the religion, the religious community is not required to grant them their religious freedom.[613] Therefore, acceptance by the spouse

608 Clayton & Tomlinson, *The law of human rights*. para. 14.52.

609 Krishnaswami, *Study of discrimination in the matter of religious rights and practices*, p. 50.; Nowak, *U.N. Covenant on Civil and Political Rights: CCPR commentary*, p. 451.; Grabenwarter, *European Convention on Human Rights: Commentary*, p. 249.

610 De Jong, *The freedom of thought, conscience and religion or belief in the United Nations (1946–1992)*, p. 296.; Joseph, et al., *The International Covenant on Civil and Political Rights- Cases, materials and commentary*, p. 505.

611 Id.

612 Grabenwarter, *European Convention on Human Rights: Commentary*, p. 249. On proselytism, see also the following cases: *European Court of Human Rights, Kokkinakis v. Greece, 25 May 1993, Application No. 14307/88.; Europen Court of Human Rights, Larissis and Others v. Greece, 24 February 1998, Application Nos. 23372/94, 26377/94, 26378/94.*

613 Evans, *Freedom of Religion Under the European Convention on Human Rights*, p. 129.

of membership in the concerned religious community and the submission of the divorce before a religious tribunal or authority, in principle, implies acceptance of the religious authority's decisions. Where religious authorities are recognised by the State and where personal laws are the governing legal system, States should ensure that all religions and belief systems, as well as their followers, are protected and treated equally.[614] This may then entail creating other means to obtain a divorce for religious and non-religious individuals or individuals adhering to minority religions or belief systems (e.g. by introducing the institutions of civil marriage and divorce).

What is noteworthy is that this approach is simplistic in that it underestimates the complex relationship between individuals and the religious community they belong to, as well as the significance and social implications of possessing membership in a religious community. These are factors that may frustrate one's decision to leave a dead marriage. Furthermore, extending this line of reasoning to the trapped spouse results in unsustainable outcomes that do not contribute towards alleviating situations of marital captivity. A situation of marital captivity cannot simply be evaded by recanting one's religion or by leaving the religious community. The religious marriage will continue to exist within the religious community. Similarly, requiring the trapped spouse to recant or change religion as a 'solution' does not result in equal protection of the right to freedom of religion. This would, essentially, entail that the spouse has to forfeit her or his individual right to the freedom of religion in order to be released from an unwanted marriage. Additionally, other rights and freedoms may nevertheless continue to be impaired by an ongoing situation of marital captivity. This is especially so when the religious marriage continues to be perceived as still existing, morally binding and perhaps even legally binding in the country of origin.

The situation is different when the decision, requiring the recalcitrant spouse to cooperate, is taken by a secular State actor (e.g. courts or legislators). State actors, are obliged to respect, protect and fulfil human rights, including the right to freedom of religion. They may not limit individual's human rights beyond the permissible grounds. It is, therefore, relevant to assess how and, if so, to what extent the non-cooperative/opposing spouse's religious freedom is affected by secular intervention.

4.5.2.1. The limitation clauses

To ensure that State interference does not occur in an arbitrary manner and that restrictions occur with due process of the law, Article 18 ICCPR and Article 9 ECHR each contain a limitation clause to the freedom of religion. According to general comment No. 22, limitations must not be applied '*in a manner that would vitiate the rights guaranteed in article 18*', nor should they be imposed in a discriminatory manner.[615] Furthermore, the limitation clause should be interpreted strictly and

614 Krishnaswami, *Study of discrimination in the matter of religious rights and practices*, p. 47.
615 HRC, *General Comment No. 22: Article 18 (Freedom of thought, conscience or religion)*, para. 8.

consistently with the grounds that are provided in the limitation clause. Other grounds such as restrictions in the interest of the 'public security', that have been included in other provisions, may thus not serve as grounds for restricting the freedom of religion.[616] The rights protected in Article 18 ICCPR may not be subject to constraints that are not provided for in Article 18 (3) ICCPR (e.g. interference by relatives or imposing permission from third parties).[617] Whether interference by the State is permissible should be determined in accordance with the criteria set out in the limitation clause: the interference needs to be prescribed by law, to pursue a legitimate aim and to be necessary. These notions are briefly addressed in the following paragraphs.

4.5.2.1.1. Prescribed by law

With regard to the first criterion, the ICCPR and ECHR provide the exact same formulation of 'prescribed by law'. Further analysis, however, shows that this formulation is interpreted differently within each of these systems. Within the ECHR, the formulation 'prescribed by law' is broader and goes beyond formal laws to also include statutes, regulations and case law i.e. substantive law as well as international conventions.[618] Furthermore, the ECmHR and ECtHR have, via case law, included additional criteria that the concerned 'law' should meet. In particular, the law needs to be accessible, clear, precise and foreseeable in its effects and consequences so as to enable individuals to adjust their behaviour and conduct.[619]

By contrast, the formulation 'prescribed by law' within the ICCPR system is to be understood in the strict sense, meaning a '*general-abstract parliamentary act or an equivalent unwritten norm of common law, which must be accessible to all those subject to the law*'.[620] Beyond the qualitative requirement that the law should be accessible, it is also a requirement that the law should impose specific restrictions with '*adequate certainty*'[621], i.e. be clear in its formulation as imposing limitations. It has been submitted that a broad interpretation, which would include executive and administrative provisions, is inconsistent with the purpose of the limitation clause and the drafter's intention.[622] Therefore, executive and administrative provisions will meet these criteria only when they derive from the enforcement of a formal law that imposes restrictions.[623] In addition, the executive and administrative provisions need to be foreseeable and consistent with the rationale of that law.[624] Notably, the practice by

---

616 Id., para. 8.

617 UN Human Rights Committee, *General Comment No. 28: Article 3 (The equality of rights between men and women)*, para. 21.

618 Renucci, *Article 9 of the European Convention on Human Rights*, pp. 43–46.; Schabas, *The European Convention on Human Rights: A commentary*, p. 435.

619 Renucci, *Article 9 of the European Convention on Human Rights*, pp. 43–45. Schabas, *The European Convention on Human Rights: A commentary*, pp. 435–436.

620 Nowak, *U.N. Covenant on Civil and Political Rights: CCPR commentary*, pp. 272, 424.

621 Id., pp. 272–273.

622 Id.

623 Id.

624 De Jong, *The freedom of thought, conscience and religion or belief in the United Nations (1946–1992)*, p. 86–87.

the HRC shows that the Committee is willing to interpret this criterion to also include restrictions that have indirectly been prescribed by formal law, including case law.[625] For example, in the case of *Malcolm Ross v. Canada*[626], the HRC concluded that the dismissal of a school teacher was prescribed by law, by referring to the '*legal framework for the proceedings which led to the author's removal from office*'.[627]

4.5.2.1.2. Pursuing a legitimate aim

The second criterion requires that the interference pursues a legitimate aim. The wording of Article 18 ICCPR and Article 9 ECHR differs slightly in this regard. Where the ECHR refers to the protection of the rights and freedoms of others, the ICCPR refers to the 'fundamental' rights and freedoms of others. This peculiar formulation implies that it concerns rights of significant value and importance that are awarded stronger protection and are, for example, codified in national constitutions. International human rights standards, as provided for in the International Bill of Rights, meet this criterion, thereby meaning that limitations for reasons of protecting any of the rights and principles (e.g. the respect for gender equality) will constitute a legitimate aim. For State parties to the ICCPR, this will also be the case even when the particular right does not have the status as a constitutional right within national law.[628] The criteria of 'public order' extends to cover limitations that serve the purpose of preventing public disorder.[629] It may, for example, be invoked where the State implements or enforces a legal order that, although having restrictions on the religious freedom of individuals or of religious communities, is aimed at protecting the general public from potential harmful practices.[630] Protection of 'public safety' involves the adoption of measures

---

625 Paul M. Taylor, *Freedom of Religion: UN and European Human Rights Law and Practice* (2005), p. 300.

626 This case concerned a school teacher in Canada who was dismissed because he had expressed his extreme ideologies and opinions against the Jewish faith. He alleged that he had been prohibited from expressing his religious convictions freely and that, therefore, this constituted a violation of Articles 18 and 19 ICCPR. Even though Canada did not have any formal laws that prohibited expressions that denigrate religious faiths, the HRC concluded that the restriction (the dismissal from work) was nonetheless prescribed by law.

627 UN Human Rights Committee *Malcolm Ross v. Canada*, 26 October 2000, Communication No. 736/1997, paras. 11.3–11.4. The 'legal framework' refers to the legal provisions that were relied upon by the local authorities that sued the school for discriminating against Jewish students as well as the legal provisions that provided the basis for the applicants' dismissal.

628 Nowak, *U.N. Covenant on Civil and Political Rights: CCPR commentary*, p. 430.

629 Id., p. 428; Schabas, *The European Convention on Human Rights: A commentary*, p. 422.

630 Grabenwarter, *European Convention on Human Rights: Commentary*, p. 244. Notably, while the English texts of both the ICCPR and ECHR refer '*to protect public order*' and '*for the protection of public order*', the French texts refer to '*la protection de l'ordre*' in the ICCPR and '*l'ordre*' in the ECHR instead of the otherwise equivalent translation '*l'ordre public*'. During the drafting of the ICCPR, this issue of different wording was raised. It was submitted that '*the English expression 'public order' was not equivalent to and indeed was substantially different from the French expression 'l'ordre public' [...]. In civil law countries 'l'ordre public' is a legal concept used principally as a basis for negating or restricting private agreements, the exercise of police power or the application of foreign law. In common law countries, the expression 'public order is ordinarily used to mean the absence of public disorder. The common law counterpart of 'l'ordre public' is public policy rather than 'public order'*. Excerpts from UN

that aim to remove or prevent (threatening) situations that jeopardise the security, life, physical integrity or health of people or things.[631]

As for the concept of 'morals', the HRC in general comment No. 22 provided that; '*the concept of morals derives from many social, philosophical and religious traditions; consequently, limitations on the freedom to manifest a religion or belief for the purpose of protecting morals must be based on principles not deriving exclusively from a single tradition*'.[632] The religious freedom can also be restricted by State measures that aim to protect the health of individuals, including the persons whose religious rights are restricted. For example, in a case involving the mandatory wearing of helmets, the right to wear religious clothing (a turban) by a Sikh, was found to be a legitimate restriction because it also protected the health of the Sikh.[633]

4.5.2.1.3. Necessary (in a democratic society)

The third criterion requires that any limitation to the freedom of religion should be necessary. This criterion serves the purpose of assessing whether a fair balance between the competing interests of the individual, on the one hand, and of the society and public, on the other, has been struck.

This consists primarily of two elements.[634] The first is the necessity of the restriction. It must meet a pressing social need, which means that it not only needs to be sufficient and fitting for achieving the goal, but it also needs to be relevant. Whether there is a need is a matter that must be determined on a case by case basis. The second element requires that the adopted measure is proportionate to the legitimate aim it pursues and the rights it restricts.[635] This means that the restriction needs to be the least intrusive means available to pursue the legitimate aim. In other words, if there are less intrusive means to reach the pursued aim, the requirement of proportionality will not have been reached.[636] Finally, the adopted measure must be compatible with the 'democratic spirit', meaning that the adopted measure needs to be consistent with principles such as pluralism, tolerance and broadmindedness, which are invaluable foundations in a democratic society.[637]

---

doc. A/2929 Chapt. VI para 113. Bossuyt, *Guide to the "Traveaux Prέparatiores" of the International Covenant on Civil and Political Rights*, p. 365.

631 Nowak, *U.N. Covenant on Civil and Political Rights: CCPR commentary*, p. 427.

632 HRC, *General Comment No. 22: Article 18 (Freedom of thought, conscience or religion)*, para. 8.

633 European Commission of Human Rights, *X. v. the United Kingdom*, 12 July 1978, Application No. 7992/77, p. 2.; Human Rights Court, *Karnel Singh Bhinder v. Canada*, 25 October 1988, Communication Nos. 208/1986, para. 6.2.; Grabenwarter, *European Convention on Human Rights: Commentary*, p. 245; Nowak, *U.N. Covenant on Civil and Political Rights: CCPR commentary*, p. 429.

634 Renucci, *Article 9 of the European Convention on Human Rights*, pp. 47–48.

635 Id.

636 Schabas, *The European Convention on Human Rights: A commentary*, p. 438.; de Jong, *The freedom of thought, conscience and religion or belief in the United Nations (1946–1992)*, pp. 85–86.

637 Renucci, *Article 9 of the European Convention on Human Rights*, pp. 47–48.; Schabas, *The European Convention on Human Rights: A commentary*, p. 438.; European Court of Human Rights, *S.A.S. v. France*, 1 July 2014 Application No. 43835/11, para. 128.

4.5.2.1.4. Margin of appreciation

The notion of 'margin of appreciation' is a principle that has been developed within, and which is peculiar to, the ECHR system. This can be found in the 6th Recital of the Preamble of the ECHR.[638] The margin of appreciation refers to the degree of discretion that national courts and authorities have to determine the necessity and proportionality of implemented restrictions. The underlying reasoning is that the national authorities are in a far better position to assess the relevant factors and needs for their own national contexts than the ECHR and ECmHR are. Therefore, they should enjoy a certain degree of discretion when assessing the necessity for limiting rights that are guaranteed by the convention, as well as the means to implement such restrictions.[639]

The scope of the margin of appreciation doctrine is dependent on multiple factors. The nature of the rights in question, the context of the case, whether it concerns an interference by the State or interference by private non-State actors, as well as the existence of a consensus among the States Parties on a particular matter, are all factors that affect the States' margin of appreciation in a given case.[640] For example, measures involving economic and social policies and strategies (e.g. housing and urban planning strategies) are likely to be given a wider margin of appreciation. Where the infringed rights are crucial for the effective exercise of human rights or where they concern the individuals' existence or identity, the margin of appreciation may be less wide. Equally, consensus on a given matter may limit the margin of appreciation. However, even when there is a consensus on a matter, the Court may place less value on this factor, particularly where it concerns moral and ethical matters such as divorce.[641] States also enjoy a wide margin of appreciation in matters related to the organisation of State-Church relations, and in particular where this concerns the balancing of private interests.[642]

4.5.2.2. State interference in situations of marital captivity

As previously concluded, even where non-cooperation can be argued to constitute a religious manifestation[643], there still remains the possibility to restrict the exercise and effects of such a manifestation. The following paragraphs apply the above criteria and examine whether State interventions that compel a recalcitrant spouse to cooperate in a religious divorce are permissible.

---

638 Council of Europe, *Protocol No. 15 amending the Convention on the Protection of Human Rights and Fundamental Freedom*, Article 1.

639 Council of Europe, *Explanatory Report to the Protocol No. 15 amending the Convention for the Protection of Human Rights and Fundamental Freedoms*, (2013), para. 9.

640 Schabas, *The European Convention on Human Rights: A commentary*, p. 81.

641 See European Court of Human Rights, *Johnston and Others v. Ireland*, 18 December 1986, Application No. 9697/82, pp. 81–83.

642 Yildirim, *The collective dimension of freedom of religion or belief in international law: The application of findings to the case of Turkey*, pp. 37–38. See also European Court of Human Rights, *S.A.S. v. France*, 1 July 2014 Application No. 43835/11.

643 See subsections 4.4.2.3 and 4.4.2.4.

The first two criteria will not be too difficult to fulfil. With regards to the first criterion, under the ECHR system a court order is substantive law. The case of *Malcolm Ross v. Canada*[644] illustrates that the legal framework on the basis of which restrictive measures have been adopted, meets the criteria of 'prescribed by law' in the ICCPR.[645] Therefore, the criterion of 'prescribed by law' will be met, for example, where a court compels the recalcitrant spouse to cooperate in the dissolution of a religious marriage. So too will a legislative measure such as the Divorce (Religious Marriages) Act 2002 and laws that courts apply to compel a spouse to cooperate with the religious divorce.

As for the second criterion, a situation of marital captivity restricts and deprives the trapped spouse of her personal autonomy in many aspects of her life. The trapped spouse is not only kept hostage in an unwanted marriage but is also restricted in exercising her free choice to remarry or to establish new socially and legally legitimised relationships. The trapped spouse may also be restricted in her travelling arrangements. These are some of the rights that national courts have taken into consideration and which will be discussed, in detail, in the following Chapters. Safeguarding and preventing further impediments to the trapped spouses' freedom and rights serves a legitimate aim, i.e. the (fundamental) freedoms and rights of others.

Turning to the third criterion, from the perspective of both the trapped spouse and the religious community, there is a pressing need not only to end situations of marital captivity, but also to have sustainable solutions in place which prevent situations of marital captivity from arising. Additionally, this need has been echoed by religious communities and trapped spouses, who besides seeking solutions within the private and religious sphere, have in recent years also sought solutions from secular courts and the legislator. As a result, judicial and legislative measures have been developed as a response to the requests of religious communities and/or their members to find sustainable solutions to situations of marital captivity.[646] Furthermore, a restriction is relevant within the broad sense of its meaning, insofar as marital captivity is a problem that is increasingly gaining recognition, both within the religious communities as well as by the State and human rights monitoring bodies. This notwithstanding, holistic and sustainable solutions to end and prevent situations of marital captivity have yet to be found. Additionally, restricting the freedom of religion in order to enforce measures that facilitate the dissolution of a religious marriage, provides the trapped spouse with an additional means for enforcing cooperation in a religious divorce.

Notably, it may be argued that State intervention, particularly by a secular court and legislator, is neither adequate nor appropriate as it does not concern or deal with the religious divorce itself. After all, despite a fine or a court order to cooperate in a religious divorce, a spouse may continue to refuse to end the religious marriage. The religious

---

644 Human Rights Committee, *Malcolm Ross v. Canada*, 26 October 2000, Communication No. 736/1997.

645 Id., paras. 11.3–11.4.

646 See subchapter 3.4. and subsection 4.4.2.2. For more detail in this regard. See also *supra* notes 4–6.

marriage, thus, continues to exist. Legislative measures, such as the Divorce (Religious Marriages Act), also have their limitations in that a judge might be faced with a situation where the withholding of a civil divorce does not result in the envisaged cooperation. However, at the same time, this limitation in efficacy should not be overestimated and exaggerated. Courts in the Netherlands, France and the United Kingdom have, as the national cases above demonstrate, applied the legal mechanisms in place to incentivise non-cooperative spouses to cooperate in the dissolution of a religious marriage. In all three countries that have been considered, the pressure exercised by the civil courts have led to some success in this regard.

Finally, a fair balance also needs to be struck between the competing interests of all involved parties in a situation of marital captivity (including the trapped spouses' rights and interests and the State's and community's interests in finding solutions and respecting religious freedom). On which side the balance will tip needs to be determined on a case by case basis, taking into account the extent to which the non-cooperative spouse's religious rights have been restricted. Chapter 8 elaborates further on this balancing exercise, after considering what rights are at stake for the trapped spouses in Chapters 5 to 7. For now, it suffices to establish that State intervention in a situation of marital captivity is not likely to amount to an interference with the non-cooperative spouse's right to freedom of religion, as only very limited instances of non-cooperation constitute a religious manifestation. Even in the limited instances where non-cooperation does constitute a religious manifestation, State intervention is likely to be compatible with the limitation clauses and thus justified.

4.6. CONCLUDING REMARKS

This Chapter set out to identify the religious aspects that are inherent in a situation of marital captivity and to asses the legal implications and boundaries for States when responding to situations of marital captivity. The freedom of religion is involved due to the fact that opposition and non-cooperation to a religious divorce is grounded in the religious doctrines on divorce. In addition, the religious dimension of marital captivity means that it is an issue that not only concerns and affects the involved spouses, but it also involves the religious community as a whole. The actual dissolution of the religious marriage occurs within and in accordance with the rules of the religious communities. It is perceived as a religious affair over which the religious authorities maintain the ultimate autonomy and authority. Any State interferences that aims to facilitate the realisation of a religious divorce should, therefore, take into consideration the religious components that are inherent in situations of marital captivity and include judicious and sufficient motivation to that effect.

From the previous subchapters, the conclusions may be reached that the collective aspects of the freedom of religion and the entitlements religious groups enjoy to regulate and manage their internal affairs without any State interference are hardly at stake, where the State intervenes in situations of marital captivity. In particular, civil interventions, mostly by secular States, have aimed to facilitate the realisation of a religious divorce. These have neither been designed nor sought to take precedence over or govern the dissolution of religious marriages. The dissolution of a religious marriage is generally considered as a matter that is reserved for the religious groups themselves. In responding to marital captivity, States have not intervened with the organisational or doctrinal affairs of religious groups. However, where repudiation is dictated by non-religious public bodies, such as some civil judges have done in the Netherlands, this could constitute a far-reaching encroachment on the religious freedom of religious groups. In itself, this does not mean that the State should never intervene in situations of marital captivity or that any intervention in religious affairs is impermissible. After all, the collective freedoms and entitlements that are implied in the right to freedom of religion may be subjected to restrictions in accordance with the limitation clauses that are found in Article 18 ICCPR and Article 9 ECHR.

Where it concerns the subject matter of conscientious objection, a successful objection to an obligation to cooperate in a religious divorce, based on one's religious convictions, is highly unlikely. To begin, within the ICCPR and the ECHR, conscientious objection has not expanded beyond the context of compulsory military service. Secondly, whether the threshold of a serious, insurmountable and genuine conflict between the religious convictions and the obligation to cooperate in a religious divorce is ascertained in situations of marital captivity, is questionable. Thirdly, even if this were the case, conscientious objection must then be considered in light of the limitation clauses and may require balancing the trapped spouse's freedoms and rights against the opposing spouse's interest.

The exercise of analysing the scope and limitations of the freedom of religion has shown that not all forms of non-cooperation or opposition to a divorce constitute religious manifestations which deserve the protection of Article 18 ICCPR and Article 9 ECHR. As the discussed case law reveals, often non-religious related reasons and at times even bad intentions are the motives for refusing to cooperate in a religious divorce. In these instances, non-cooperation in a religious divorce should not be considered as a religious manifestation according to Article 18 ICCPR and Article 9 ECHR. However, non-cooperation to a religious divorce or the opposition to a civil divorce can, in certain limited circumstances be argued to constitute a religious manifestation. This may be the case where the opposition to or non-cooperation with a divorce is based on the genuine and sincere religious beliefs and convictions of the opposing or non-cooperative spouse. Notably, for a spouse who opposes a civil divorce, however, the effectuation thereof by a civil judge is not incompatible with her/his religious convictions and does not affect her/his religious freedoms. A civil divorce does not affect the religious nature of an indissoluble religious marriage or attempt to dissolve it. Where it concerns a non-cooperative spouse who withholds cooperation out of genuine religious considerations, this chapter has elaborated upon two approaches.

The first approach concludes that the non-cooperation is not worthy the protection of Articles 18 ICCPR and 9 ECHR and, thus, ought not to be recognised as a religious manifestation within the meaning of these Articles. The reasoning behind this being that, the freedom of religion may not be relied upon to justify discrimination against women. Additionally such an interpretation would not align with the object and purpose of the ICCPR and ECHR to guarantee and protect individual's human rights. Recognition of non-cooperation as religious manifestation on the other had would imply giving protection to conduct that impair the trapped spouse's rights (often women) and risk exacerbating inequality between women and men. Following this approach, it is then difficult to assert that the non-cooperation in a religious divorce, by relying on religious norms, interpretations and practices that prescribe or encourage discriminatory treatment of women, constitutes a religious manifestation that is worthy of the protection provided in Article 18 ICCR and Article 9 ECHR.

The second approach allows to consider non-cooperation as a religious manifestation and also invites to examine whether State imposed restrictions to this manifestation are permissible. After all, right to freedom of religion is not an absolute right and this right that may be subjected to limitations where there are more impending and weighty interests that require protection. State authorities should, then, resolve to balance the competing rights in accordance with the limitation clauses. Any intervention should meet the criteria of legitimacy, legality, subsidiarity and proportionality (and, for the purposes of the ECHR, they should be within the margin of appreciation). With regards to the (im)permissibility of State intervention in situations of marital captivity, the first two criteria (legitimacy and legality) are fulfilled in all cases. Alongside the freedom of religion, there are other rights and interests that also demand attention and protection. Additionally, there is a growing need to identify and develop holistic solutions to prevent and end all situations of marital captivity. In this regard, State intervention – be it by legislative or judicial measures – has proven to be an effective and appropriate tool to pressurise non-cooperative spouses into granting a divorce. The proportionality of State intervention in relation to the potential restriction of the right to freedom of religion for the non-cooperative spouse requires further examination. In this regard, competing rights and interests must be considered and included in this exercise. This requires taking into account and balancing the trapped spouse's rights, the State's compliance with its human rights obligations and, depending on the prevailing State-Church relations, the State's secular principles *vis á vis* the right to freedom of religion. This will be discussed in more detail in Chapter 8.

CHAPTER 5
THE RIGHT TO DIVORCE

'[I need the religious divorce], because I need our relationship to be over in every way.'[647]

'[S]ymbolically, [religious divorce] is very important given the place it took in our marriage, given that it was, you know, the sine qua non [of our marriage], [...] We must undo all the ties that bind us, including the religious. [...] [If he had refused to give the get], I would have experienced that as an act of war.'[648]

'He wasn't bent on [religious principles], and neither was I. But I had a conscience problem, I told myself: "I can't do this to God," you know! [...] So we went to what they call a rabbinical court, where there are many rabbis. [...] We had to have a get. It is a very important element for the woman to be freed from the husband and eventually remarry religiously.'[649]

These accounts demonstrate another important and crucial factor that lies at the core of situations of marital captivity: the importance that religious adherents – the trapped spouses, the non-cooperative spouse and the religious community – attach to complying with religious rules, including those on divorce. Alongside religious motivations, a religious divorce may carry significant symbolic value and meaning for all involved. Its very pronunciation is perceived and experienced as bringing an end to the marriage, the marital life of the spouses and all and any ties between the spouses. It should not be forgotten that a situation of marital captivity can also have legal implications in other countries, which only adds to the perceived necessity of also dissolving the religious marriage in accordance with the religious rules.

Marriage and divorce are profound fundamental social structures that are prevalent in most societies. However, the roles attached thereto, their societal consequences and regulation differ from one country to the next. The institution of marriage is closely related to the foundation of family life. The very act of marriage establishes the basic family unit i.e. the spouses. It also encourages and legitimises the cohabitation and intimacy between the spouses, both socially and legally. In its turn, the family is the cornerstone of society. In human rights treaties, the family is described as '*the natural*

---

647 Pascale Fournier, 'Secular portraits and religious shadows: An empirical study of religious women in France', in Berlinerbau, et al. *Secularism on the edge: Contemporary Church-State relations in the United States, France and Israel* (New York, 2014), p. 223.

648 Id.

649 Id., p. 224.

and fundamental group unit of society'.[650] After all, it is within the family that the growth, well-being and development of all family members, and in particular of the children, is expected to occur. Stability in the family structure reassures a stable continuation of the qualities and conditions that are necessary for ensuring safety and order, developing qualities such as tolerance, individuality and enabling the personal growth and well-being of the individual family members. Stable families contribute to society and have a significant social role in structuring a viable and orderly society.[651] It is therefore unsurprising that human rights provisions specifically provide that the family unit should not only be protected by the State, but also by other societal stakeholders.[652] As the foundation for the establishment of a family unit, marriage also has an equally imperative social role. It is important, for the sake of the family unit, that the spouses in the marriage uphold their marital obligations. The social role that the institution of marriage serves, therefore, makes marriage not only a private matter between the spouses, but to some degree it is also a matter of public interest: '*Stability of marriage is a legitimate aim which is in the public interest*'.[653] Both society and the State have to facilitate and protect the institution of marriage. In addition, marriage involves public festivities and celebrations of the union of two people. It is therefore not surprising that, generally speaking, marriage is regarded positively and held in high regard, from both a social and religious perspective, as well as from a human rights perspective. To date, no country prohibits or has ever outlawed marriage by law and all the religions under investigation celebrate marriage.

Divorce threatens to dismantle not only the marriage between the spouses, but also the family unit that has arisen from the marriage. From this point of view, divorce does not serve the public interest. By way of contrast, divorce signifies covert hardship and is experienced as an undesirable outcome of the (marital) life that threatens the family life and society as a whole.[654] As a matter of fact, scientific studies have conclusively identified the many negative aspects and effects of divorce that occur to the involved spouses, children and society.[655] In light thereof, it will come as no surprise that divorce is regarded negatively. This is also reflected by how divorce has been regulated across

---

650 This formulation has been adopted in for example, Article 18 UDHR, Article 10 ICESCR, Article 23 ICCPR, Article 17 ACHR and Article 18 ACHPR.

651 Grégor Puppinck, *Third party intervention- Submission to the Fourth Section of the European Court of Human Rights in the cases Babiarz v. Poland, Gajewski v. Poland, and Piotrowski v. Poland* (2014), paras. 3–4.

652 Universal Declaration of Human Rights, Article 18; International Covenant on Civil and Political rights, Article 23; American Convention on Human Rights, Article 17.

653 European Court of Human Rights, *F. v. Switzerland,* 18 December 1987, Application No. 11329/85, para. 36.

654 William A. Schabas, *The Universal Declaration of Human Rights: The Travaux Préparatoires,* p. 2464 extracted from UN. Doc. A/C. / SR.125, p. 368.

655 See among others, Frederick Lorenz, K. Wickrama, Rand Conger and Glen Elder, 'The short-term and decade-long effects of divorce on women's Midlife Health, 47 *Journal of Health and Social Behavior* 111–125, (2006).; Neil Kalter, 'Long-term effects of divorce on children: Religious organisations, internal autonomy and other religious rights before the European Court of Human Rights and the

the world in different jurisdictions. While the institution of marriage is practically regulated in all different normative systems (legal, religious, customary etc.), divorce on the other hand, is not always regulated, may be prohibited or is made contingent on certain grounds. For example, only a half century ago there were more countries that had no legal provisions on divorce.[656] At the time of writing the divorce is not possible in the Vatican and for the majority of the population of the Philippines.[657] However, it should be noted that over the past decades public discourse and sentiments towards divorce have been shifting. The increased occurrence of divorce and the rise of divorced couples within society have had the effect that divorce has become more acceptable in many western States.[658] Despite being an undesirable and unfortunate turn out of events, divorce is still and has always been a societal reality.

Human rights treaties are no exception in terms of regulating marriage and divorce. Almost all of the treaties discussed in this thesis contain a provision on the right to marry. States are encouraged to guarantee both the possibility of celebrating a religious and a civil marriage. The fact that human rights law recommends both forms of marriage signifies their importance and value in society. However, while the existence of a religious or customary marriage is a self-evident fact in most countries, this is not the case for the civil marriage. In fact, not all countries provide for this form of marriage.[659] When dealing with such countries, human rights treaty bodies have frequently expressed their concerns in respect of the absence of a civil marriage in certain jurisdictions.[660] For example, in one of its general comment[661] the HRC

OSCE', 57 *American Journal of Orthopsychiatry* 587–600, (1987).; L. Zagorsky Jay, 'Marriage and divorce's impact on wealth', 41 *Journal of Sociology* 406–424, (2005).

656 For example, Ireland, Malta, Italy, Portugal, Spain and India.

657 However, the Philippines does allow divorce for the Muslim population and for Filipinos residing abroad.

658 Paul R. Amato and Irvin Shelly, 'Historical trends in divorce in the United States', in Fine and Harvy *Handbook of divorce and relationship dissolution*, p. 69. Although this study is primarily focused on the US, similar attitudes can be observed in the legislative processes of many countries. Some countries such as Chile, Ireland, Italy, Malta, Portugal and Spain that initially did not recognise or which even outlawed divorce have, in the past half century, introduced civil divorce into their legal systems. Other countries have moved from fault-based divorce systems to no fault-based system or have introduced the possibility to unilaterally initiate divorce proceedings (e.g. Canada, France, Greece Luxembourg and the United Kingdom). See also: Libertad González and Tarja K. Viitanen, 'The effect of divorce laws on divorce rates in Europe', 53 *European Economic Review* 127–138, (2009), pp. 127–129.; United Nations Division for Social Policy and Development- Programme on the Family, *Major trends affecting families: A background document* (2003).

659 This is usually the case for non-secular States, in which marital matters are regulated by religious rules. A marriage will then be conducted by the concerned religious authorities. The marriage may then be registered with the civil authorities, where this option exists. Examples are Indonesia, Libya, Mauritania, Saudi Arabia and Yemen.

660 See subsections 5.2.1.1 and 5.2.1.3.

661 Human Rights Committee 'General Comment No. 19: Article 23(The Family) Protection of the Family, the Right to Marriage and Equality of the Spouses', 1990.; see also the Human Rights Committee's response to the absence of civil marriage in Israel. Human Rights Committee, *Concluding Observations Israel 1998*, A/53/40 vol. I (1998) 45, para. 325.

advocates for the availability of civil marriages. In this regard, the Committee holds that 'the *right to freedom of thought, conscience and religion implies that the legislation of each State should provide for the possibility of both religious and civil marriages*'.[662]

Introducing a civil marriage is important because it provides non-believers or devotees of other minority religions with an optional way to contract a valid marriage. As a result, many countries have introduced the possibility to contract a valid civil marriage, next to the religious marriage.[663] The right to marry, whether religious or civil, is thus undisputedly a fundamental human right.

The same cannot be said for divorce. A quick glance through the treaties under investigation reveals that the 'right to divorce'[664] is not explicitly mentioned in any treaty. Nevertheless, the fact that there is no explicit mention of a right to divorce does not mean that such a right exists. The only reference to divorce is found in the provisions concerning the right to marry.[665] Notably, the subject of dissolving a marriage is only discussed in relation to the principle of equality which requires that equality between women and men is ensured in all matters relating to the marriage and its dissolution. However, whether a right to divorce can be deduced as implied within existing human rights provisions requires further inquiry.

The inability to divorce is the main problem pertaining marital captivity. Whether or not a right to divorce exists is thus an essential question, the answer to which is very much relevant for the ongoing efforts to resolve and end situations of marital captivity. For if such a right is implied within human rights law it would offer trapped spouses a strong basis to demand protection of this right by the State and seek remedies where this right has been violated. It would enable trapped spouses to demand the dissolution of a marriage and possibly facilitate in alleviating the religious barriers to divorce.

Therefore, this Chapter primarily sets out to examine the existence of a human right to divorce and whether it is implied in the existing human rights provisions. The articles on the right to marriage, contained in the investigated human rights treaties are first outlined in subchapter 5.1. Subchapters 5.2. and 5.3. follow up with an analysis and a discussion on whether human rights law guarantees or should guarantee a right to divorce. In this respect, it is important to keep the two dimensions of marriage and divorce (religion and law) in mind. Where such a right exists, does it also extend to both the religious and civil divorce? Or is it only limited to the civil divorce? Where a right to divorce exists and it extends to the religious aspects of the marriage, it could then serve as basis for some degree of State involvement in the realisation of a religious divorce. Subchapter 5.4 summarises the findings and conclusions of this Chapter.

---

662 HRC, *General Comment No. 19: Article 23(The Family) Protection of the Family, the Right to Marriage and Equality of the Spouses*, para. 4.

663 With the 1954 Special Marriage Act, India has made it possible for nationals to contract a civil marriage, irrespective of their religion. The Act also contains provisions for a civil divorce in sections 27–28 thereof.

664 Or other synonyms such as the right to dissolution of marriage or the termination of marriage.

665 See for example the Articles 16(1) UDHR, Article 23(4) ICCPR, Article 16 CEDAW, Article 17(4) ACHR and Article 7(second indent) of the Maputo Protocol.

5.1. THE LEGAL FRAMEWORK ON MARRIAGE AND DIVORCE

As previously noted, reference to divorce is made in terms of '*equal rights [between women and men] at the dissolution of the marriage*'. In many international and regional human rights documents, this formulation is found within the provisions that concern the right to marry.

The UDHR provides in Article 16 (1) thereof that:

> *'Men and women of full age, without any limitation due to race, nationality or religion, have the right to marry and found a family. They are entitled to equal rights as to marriage, during marriage and at its dissolution.'*

The ICCPR contains similar wording. Articles 23 (2) and (4) thereof stipulate that:

> *'[...]*
> *(2) The right of men and women of marriageable age to marry and to found a family shall be recognized*
> *(3) States Parties to the present Covenant shall take appropriate steps to ensure equality of rights and responsibilities of spouses as to marriage, during marriage and at its dissolution. In the case of dissolution, provision shall be made for the necessary protection of any children.'*

The ICESCR, on the other hand, does not contain a separate provision on marriage. Rather, the ICESCR contains a broader provision that covers the right to family life. Article 10 (1) thereof provides that:

> *'The States parties to the present Covenant recognize that:*
> *The widest possible protection and assistance should be accorded to the family, which is the natural and fundamental group unit of society, particularly for its establishment and while it is responsible for the care and education of dependent children. Marriage must be entered into with the free consent of the intending spouses.'*

The CEDAW provides in Article 16 thereof that:

> *'States Parties shall take all appropriate measures to eliminate discrimination against women in all matters relating to marriage and family relations and in particular shall ensure, on a basis of equality of men and women:*
> *(first indent) the same right to enter into marriage [...].*
> *(third indent) the same rights and responsibilities during marriage and at its dissolution.'*

At the regional level, the ECHR provides in Article 12 thereof that:

> *'Men and women of marriageable age have the right to marry and found a family, according to the national laws governing the exercise of this right.'*

Article 12 ECHR is complemented by the seventh Protocol to the Convention (Protocol No.7)[666] which contains a provision on marital affairs. Article 5 of this protocol reads as follows:

> *'Spouses shall enjoy equality of rights and responsibilities of a private law character between them, and in their relations with their children, as to marriage, during marriage and in the event of its dissolution [...]'.*

Similar provisions are also contained in other regional human rights documents. The American Convention on Human Rights (ACHR)[667], also known as the Pact of San José, provides in Article 17 (4) thereof that:

> *'The States Parties shall take appropriate steps to ensure the equality and the adequate balancing of responsibilities of the spouses as to marriage, during marriage, and in the event of its dissolution.'*

By way of contrast, the African Charter on Human and Peoples' Rights (ACHPR)[668] does not contain a provision on marriage. However, the Guidelines and Principles on Economic and Social and Cultural Rights in the African Charter on Human and Peoples' Rights that was issued by the African Commission provide that Article 18 (1–2) ACHPR[669], on the protection of family and vulnerable groups, contains an implied right to marry. States are, therefore, obliged to ensure the equality between partners in marriage.[670] This obligation extends to ensuring:

> *'separation, divorce or annulment of a marriage or other form of family partnership shall be effectuated by judicial order[...], [that] all spouses enjoy the same rights in case of separation, divorce or annulment of marriage or any other form of family partnership [and that] all spouses have the same rights to seek separation, divorce or annulment of marriage or other form of family partnership'*.[671]

---

666 Council of Europe, *Protocol No. 7 to the European Convention for the Protocol of Human Rights and Fundamental Freedoms.*

667 Organization of American States (OAS), *American Convention on Human Rights, 'Pact of San Jose', Costa Rica*, 22 November 1969.

668 Organization of African Unity (OAU), *African Charter on Human and People's Rights*, 27 June 1981.

669 Article 18 ACHPR reads:
'The family shall be the natural unit and basis of society. It shall be protected by the State which shall take care of its physical health and moral.
The State shall have the duty to assist the family which is the custodian of morals and traditional values recognized by the community. (...).

670 African Commission on Human and Peoples' Rights 'Principles and Guidelines on the implementation of economic, social and cultural rights in the African Charter on Human and People's Rights', 2010, p. 55.

671 Id., pp. 55–56.

Furthermore, the Protocol to the African Charter on Human and Peoples' Rights on the Rights of Women in Africa, also referred to as the Maputo Protocol[672], also addresses the dissolution of marriage. Article 7 of this Protocol states that:

> *'States Parties shall enact appropriate legislation to ensure that women and men enjoy the same rights in case of separation, divorce or annulment of marriage. In this regard, they shall ensure that:*
> *(first indent) separation, divorce or annulment of marriage shall be effected by judicial order.*
> *(second indent) women and men shall have the same rights to seek separation, divorce or annulment of marriage [...]'.*

A comparison of all these articles shows that all treaties, save the ICESCR, have provisions on the right to marry and to found a family. The ICESCR only mentions the condition required in order to enter into marriage (free consent). Furthermore, all treaties, save the ICESCR and ECHR, include a reference to the dissolution of a marriage. However, this reference is made in relation to the equality principle. None of the instruments explicitly provide that spouses have a right to dissolve the marriage as such.

Notably, the Maputo Protocol as well as the Guidelines, go a step further and have a clearer position on the subject of divorce. Similar to the other treaties, both documents mention the dissolution of marriage in relation to the equality principle. On top of that, both documents refer to how divorce should be effectuated. According to these documents States have an obligation to ensure the ability of divorce via judicial bodies.

In addition, the ICCPR, CEDAW, ACHR and the Maputo Protocol call upon States to take appropriate steps to ensure equality in matters relating to the dissolution of the marriage. This choice of formulation indicates that the States Parties to these treaties and protocol are obliged to take action, where necessary, to provide that the principle of equality is complied with in matrimonial affairs, including the dissolution of marriage. This is in contrast with the somewhat inactive formulation that is found in the UDHR and ECHR Protocol No. 7, both of which only recognise that women and men are entitled to equal rights at the dissolution of the marriage.

5.2. A RIGHT TO DIVORCE

As concluded above, none of the human rights under investigation contain a right to divorce. However, this does not mean that such a right does not exist or can be implied in the provisions found above. It also does not mean that such a right cannot develop in human rights law, where it has not yet been recognised. For this reason, it is imperative to first determine whether such a right exists.

672 African Union, *Protocol to the African Charter on Human and People's Rights on the Rights of Women in Africa*, 11 July 2003.

5.2.1. DIVORCE IN HUMAN RIGHTS LAW

As provided in subchapter 1.6., there are several sources that can be used for the interpretation of treaty provisions. Among these are the practices and statements made by treaty bodies. The following subsection will, therefore, revise the general comments, case law, concluding observations and *travaux préparatoires* of the concerned treaties in order to determine the status of a right to divorce in human rights law.

5.2.1.1. General comments

The HRC has expressed its views regarding Article 23(4) ICCPR in two general comments. In general comment No. 19, the Committee asserted that spouses are entitled to equal rights and responsibilities in all matrimonial matters, including arrangements concerning legal separation or the dissolution of the marriage.[673] In a similar manner, general comment No. 28 on equal rights of men and women provides that '*States must also ensure equality in regard to the dissolution of marriage, which excludes the possibility of repudiation. The grounds for divorce and annulment should be the same for men and women [...]*'.[674] In this regard, it has also held that discriminatory treatment in relation to divorce grounds or during the divorce or separation procedures is prohibited.[675] Where it concerns State recognised divorce or separation, then State officials will be involved in the divorce or separation, thereby meaning that they have to comply with the prohibition of discrimination. The CEDAW Committee does not provide further clarity on the subject of the availability and accessibility of divorce in its general comments. In general comment No. 21, the Committee briefly noted that relying on religious or customary laws in marital affairs may have '*wide-ranging consequences*' for women. In particular, the Committee has expressed its concerns towards religious and customary rules that disfavour women. Accordingly, relying on such rules might diminish women's rights to equal status and responsibility within the marriage. As a matter of preference, the Committee has thus encouraged States to respect the Convention's principles when determining and conferring rights and responsibilities in marital matters.[676]

What is apparent from these general comments, is that State's procedures in matters of divorce and separation should be available and accessible to women and men on an equal basis. The HRC does not suggest that individuals have a right to divorce, but it merely asserts that States have an obligation to ensure equality in the dissolution

---

673 HRC, *General Comment No. 19: Article 23(The Family) Protection of the Family, the Right to Marriage and Equality of the Spouses*, paras. 8–9.

674 HRC, *General Comment No. 28: Article 3 (The equality of rights between men and women)*, para. 2.

675 HRC, *General Comment No. 19: Article 23(The Family) Protection of the Family, the Right to Marriage and Equality of the Spouses*, paras. 8–9.

676 UN Committee on the Elimination of Discrimination Against Women, 'General Recommendation No. 21 on Equality in marriage and family relations', para. 1.

of marriage, as is required by the principle of equality. Whether this obligation also extends to the dissolution of religious marriages, is discussed further in section 5.2.3.

5.2.1.2. Case law

At the time of writing this contribution there have been no decisions, by the respective treaty bodies, concerning the availability or accessibility of divorce. On the regional level however, there have been far more developments in this area. The ECtHR has had to rule on multiple cases involving spouses who were not able to dissolve their marriage. The following paragraphs outline the developments in a chronological order.

The 1972 case of *Airey v. Ireland* concerned an applicant (wife) who wanted to be released from her marriage. She did not want to remarry but wanted to escape the abusive marriage and to protect her children and herself from her partner's violence. Although Ireland did not permit divorce[677], it did have provisions on annulment and separation.[678] The common practice was for parties to separation proceedings to be represented by a lawyer. In this case, the applicant had little financial means to obtain legal aid and was not able to start the separation proceedings as she was not in the position to effectively represent herself.[679] Eventually, her case reached the ECmHR which referred it to the ECtHR. The applicant alleged, among others, a violation of Article 6 ECHR. The combination of the prohibitive costs of proceedings, the inability to receive legal aid while she had no financial means and the inability to represent herself had impaired her of the right to access the courts.[680] Furthermore, she alleged that the inaccessibility of legal procedures to determine her rights and obligations in family matters was a violation of Article 8 ECHR.[681] She did not claim a violation of Article 12 ECHR, nor did she claim that she had a right to divorce or a right to separation.

After reiterating that Article 8 ECHR contains both negative as well as positive obligations, the ECtHR concluded that the protection of family life may, in certain circumstances (e.g. abusive marriage) '*require that spouses are relieved from their duty*

---

677 Article 41.3.2° of the Constitution at the time, provided that '*No law shall be enacted providing for the grant of a dissolution of marriage*'.
European Court of Human Rights, *Airey v. Ireland,* 9 October 1979, Application No. 6289/73, para. 10.

678 There was a possibility to apply for separation via a court decree. Despite the fact that such a decree was legally binding, it did not have any effect on the existence of the marriage.

679 European Court of Human Rights, *Airey v. Ireland,* 9 October 1979, Application No. 6289/73, paras. 8–11.

680 With regard to Article 6 ECHR, the ECtHR held that there was no obligation for States to provide legal aid '*for every dispute relating to a 'civil right*'. In the ECtHR's opinion, alleging that there is an obligation to provide legal aid would '*sit ill*' with the wording of the Convention, as it does not contain any provision on legal aid. However, the ECtHR held that Article 6 ECHR may in certain circumstances require that legal assistance be affordable, especially '*when such assistance proves indispensable for an effective access to court [...].* Id., para. 26.

681 Id., para. 13.

to live together'.[682] Ireland had the obligation to '*make this means of protection effectively accessible, when appropriate, to anyone who may wish to have recourse thereto*'.[683] Thus, by failing to provide Mrs. Airey with the means to achieve a separation from her husband, the ECtHR found that Ireland violated Article 8 ECHR.

The case of *Johnston v. Ireland*[684] is the earliest case in which the ECtHR was confronted with the subject matter of divorce. The case concerned an applicant (husband), who after 13 years of marriage, decided by mutual consent to separate from his first wife.[685] The couple had three children. After a while, the applicant started living with the second applicant (new partner) and had a child with her (third applicant). The first and second applicant had wanted to marry. Ireland at the time did not permit divorce and did not allow for any law that '*enacted providing for the grant of a dissolution*'.[686] Consequently, as the first applicant could not divorce from his first wife, he was not permitted to marry the second applicant as this would have been incompatible with the principle of monogamy.[687] Hence, the applicants brought the case before the ECtHR claiming, among others, that the absence of provisions on divorce and the non-recognition of family life outside the marriage constituted a violation of Articles 8 and 12 ECHR by the Irish authorities.[688] The non-recognition of divorce effectively hindered the first applicant and his new partner from remarrying. The ECtHR was thus faced with the question of whether Articles 12 and 8 (private life) EHCR contained an implied right to divorce and consequently, whether the non-recognition of divorce amounted to a violation of this right.

The Court found that the ECHR was not only silent on this matter but in fact, the drafters had deliberately omitted any provisions on divorce. In other words, the intention was only to protect the right to marry, but not the '*right to have the ties of marriage dissolved by divorce*'.[689] Furthermore, the Court pointed out that following the enactment of Protocol No. 7 in 1984, the opportunity to include a right to divorce was once again not taken. Therefore, Article 5 of Protocol No. 7 did not contain a right to divorce according to the court. Notably, the ECmHR, which had dealt with the case before it had been examined by the ECtHR, already held that there was no breach of Articles 8 and 12 ECHR as the '*right to divorce and subsequently to remarry was not guaranteed by the Convention*'.[690]

---

682 Id., paras. 32–33.
683 Id., para. 33.
684 European Court of Human Rights, *Johnston and Others v. Ireland,* 18 December 1986, Application No.9697/82.
685 A formal separation had been issued only after the first and second applicant indicated their desire to marry.
686 European Court of Human Rights, *Johnston and Others v. Ireland,* 18 December 1986, Application No.9697/82, para. 16.
687 Id., paras. 10–16.
688 Id., para. 38.
689 Id., para. 53.
690 European Commission of Human Rights, *R. Johnston and others against Ireland,* 5 March 1985, Application No. 9697/82, paras. 88–103.

The Court reached the conclusion that a right to divorce could not be derived from Article 12 or 8 ECHR and that the regulation of marriage and divorce was principally a matter for the State to determine.[691] In the separate opinion to this case, Judge De Meyer sided with the courts by finding that a right to divorce was not implied in any of the Convention's provisions. Even in the event that a right to divorce does exist, De Meyer concluded that it cannot be classified as a fundamental right.[692] Additionally, De Meyer hinted at the distinction between the religious and legal dimensions of marriage and divorce and asserted that the *Johnston v. Ireland* case only concerned the legal aspects of marriage and divorce. According to De Meyer, Ireland did not have jurisdiction over religious marriages that were solemnly concluded in the Church. In his view, marriages falling within the State's jurisdiction were only limited to marriages that were recognised by the State and which have legal effect.[693]

Twenty-five years after the ruling in *Johnston v. Ireland*, a rather similar case, *Ivanov and Petrova v. Bulgaria*, was brought before the ECtHR once more. Four years after entering into a marriage, the respondent (wife) and the children separated from the applicant (Ivanov). Alimentation arrangements were established. Shortly thereafter, the first applicant met the second applicant (new partner). After nine years, the new couple decided to live together and conceived a child. Eventually, the first applicant filed for a divorce. The first and second applicant wanted to solemnize their relationship in matrimony. The divorce of the first marriage was demanded on the ground of irretrievable breakdown. The applicant argued that this had been caused by the lengthy absence of the first wife and that she, in fact, had left him. During the session before the Court of First Instance, the wife objected the application for divorce and argued that she was not responsible for the separation as, in fact, she was not the one who had abandoned the first applicant. She maintained that she always expected him to join the family and that reconciliation between herself and the first applicant was still attainable. The Court of First Instance rejected the first applicant's petition, holding that his allegation was ill-founded. The first applicant appealed this decision, which was rejected on the ground that no divorce could be granted where the innocent spouse opposed the divorce.[694] Before the ECtHR, the first and second applicant claimed, among others, that this decision was a violation of the right to a fair hearing (Article 6 ECHR), the right to family life (Article 8 ECHR) and the right to marry (Article 12 ECHR).[695]

The Court accepted the fact that the denial of a divorce, combined with the prevailing principle of monogamy in Bulgaria, had effectively led to the inability

691 European Court of Human Rights, *Johnston and Others v. Ireland,* 18 December 1986, Application No.9697/82, paras. 49–57.

692 Id., separate opinion of judge De Meyer, para. 6.

693 Id., separate opinion of judge De Meyer, para. 4.

694 European Court of Human Rights, *Ivanov and Petrova v. Bulgaria,* 14 June 2011, Application No. 15001/04, paras. 6–24.

695 Id., paras. 38, 55.

of the first and second applicant to marry.[696] It continued by reaffirming that the administration of marriage and divorce are primarily State matters. In addition, the ECtHR rightly pointed out that the present case differed from the *Johnston v. Ireland* case. In the present case, divorce was allowed by the State. The spouses in *Johnston v. Ireland* were prevented from marrying because Ireland did not permit couples to divorce. Whereas, the first and second applicants were prevented from marrying each other by virtue of the rejected petition. Simply put, where *Johnston v. Ireland* concerned a right to divorce, the present case concerned the ability to obtain a divorce.

Following the *Johnston* reasoning, the Court established that Articles 8 and 12 ECHR cannot be interpreted as guaranteeing the exercise of a right to divorce, nor do they guarantee a favourable outcome in divorce proceedings.[697] However, it did point out that excessively long divorce procedures, as well as situations where the consent of the innocent spouse forms an insurmountable obstacle that prevents the dissolution of an irreparable marriage, could pose an issue under Article 12ECHR.[698] In this case, however, the ECtHR concluded that the inability of the first applicant to remarry, as a consequence of the rejected divorce application, was not an unreasonable restriction of Article 12 ECHR. Thus, the ECtHR declared the case inadmissible in respect of Articles 8 and 12 ECHR.[699]

In the most recent cases, the ECtHR has not diverted from this reasoning and has asserted that Article 12 ECHR contains a right to remarry, though both Articles 8 and 12 ECHR cannot be interpreted as including a right to divorce or a right to obtain a divorce. The case of *Piotrowski v. Poland* arose as a consequence of a provision in Polish law that granted the innocent spouse to a divorce, a right to refuse consenting to a divorce that was initiated by the party at fault.[700] The applicant (husband) wanted to divorce the respondent (the wife) on the ground that both parties were at fault. The domestic court established that only the applicant was at fault for the irretrievable breakdown of the marriage. The refusal to consent to the divorce by the respondent was considered to be her right and could, as such, not be presumed to be against the '*principles of social coexistence*'.[701] Before the ECtHR, the applicant claimed that the refusal to grant him a divorce violated his private life and made it impossible for him to remarry, which consequently amounted to a violation of Articles 8 and 12 ECHR.[702] The ECtHR reiterated its stance: a right to divorce or a right to a favourable outcome in divorce proceedings could not be deduced from both provisions, and that Article 12

696 Id., para. 60.
697 Id., para. 64.
698 Id., para. 61.
699 Id., para. 67.
700 The Polish provisions provided that that a divorce could not be granted if: it had been requested by the party who was at fault, the other party refused to give consent to the divorce and the refusal of the innocent party was not contrary to the reasonable principles of social coexistence. Id., para. 21.
701 European Court of Human Rights, *Piotrowski v. Poland*, 22 November 2016, Application No. 8923/12, paras. 4–15.
702 Id., para. 28.

ECHR guaranteed a right to marry for divorcees. Furthermore, it reiterated that in '*the area of framing divorce laws and implementing them in concrete cases, contracting States enjoy a wide margin of appreciation in determining the steps to be taken to ensure compliance with the Convention*'.[703] Following this line of reasoning, the ECtHR concluded that neither of these provisions were violated, as Article 8 ECHR could not be read as imposing a duty to accept the applicant's petition for divorce on the national authorities.[704] In addition, the Polish authorities had not prevented him from marrying as he had not demonstrated that there existed a stable and long-lasting relationship with the new partner, nor had he shown to have any concrete plans to remarry. In fact, the applicant had made an explicit statement of his wish not to remarry. Therefore, the ECtHR found that the applicant had not sufficiently demonstrated that the '*legal fiction of his continuing marriage prevent him from enjoying his personal life to the full*'.[705]

In the quite similar case of *Babiarz v. Poland*, the ECtHR once more declined to re-evaluate the *Johnston v. Ireland* interpretation of Articles 8 and 12 ECHR. The applicant (husband) left the respondent (wife) to live with a new partner. One year prior to petitioning for divorce, the applicant conceived a child with the new partner. There were no children of the marriage between the applicant and respondent. The divorce was filed in 2006. Similar to the *Piotrowski* case, the respondent (wife) – being the innocent spouse – was entitled to refuse to give consent to the divorce, which is exactly what she did. This was because she had wanted to reconcile with the applicant. Despite coming to the conclusion that the marriage had irretrievably broken down, that reconciliation was unlikely and that the applicant had been with the new partner for a long while, the national courts, nevertheless, reached the conclusion that the respondent was rightfully entitled to refuse to consent to the divorce. The national courts declined to accept the petitioned divorce. Instead, they reached the conclusion that the respondent's refusal to the divorce was presumed to be compatible with '*those universally accepted principles*' and that she had not acted out of bad faith or to vest the applicant.

In addition, the duration of the applicants' new relationship was by itself not considered to be a sufficient reason that would invoke an exception to this rule.[706] Before the ECtHR, the applicant claimed that the refusal to grant him a divorce by the national courts prevented him from marrying the new partner and founding a family with her. In so doing, the national authorities violated his rights under Articles 8 and 12 ECHR.[707] The Court proceeded to establish that Polish divorce law, which designed to protect the weaker party against the '*machinations and bad faith of the other party*'.[708] In the Court's view, divorce is a weighty matter that should not be allowed injudiciously

703 Id., para. 44.
704 Id., para. 54.
705 Id., para. 51.
706 European Court of Human Rights, *Babiarz v. Poland,* 10 January 2017, Application No. 1955/10, paras. 5–19.
707 Id., para. 32.
708 Id., para. 52.

when a '*person simply [decides] to leave his or her spouse and have a child with a new partner*', irrespective of the procedural and substantive rules of the domestic divorce law.[709] In the given case, the ECtHR concluded that the applicant had not shown that he faced an absolute impossibility to obtain a divorce, even though it was evident that the spouses had been separated for over a decade, their marriage was irreparable, the respondent continued to oppose the divorce and the applicant had been living with his new partner and child throughout that period.

Seemingly, the underlying reasoning for this conclusion was the fact that the applicant had not been prevented from submitting a new petition for divorce at a later stage. Furthermore, the Court found no violation of Article 8 ECHR, as the applicant's paternity rights – over the child born between him and his new partner – were recognised.[710] In respect of the right to family life, the ECtHR concluded that while Article 8 ECHR provides protection to de facto families, this protection does not imply a duty on the State to give legal recognition to de facto families or a duty to accept a petition for divorce.[711]

5.2.1.3. Concluding observations

In their concluding observations to State reports, UN treaty bodies have been clear on the subject matter of divorce, especially when dealing with countries that either outlaw(ed) divorce or apply discriminatory divorce laws. While the HRC and CESCR have not gone so far as to assert a right to divorce, they have occasionally referred to the devastating consequences that arise from the non-recognition of divorce.[712] For example, the HRC held that the lack of a divorce law in Chile 'could amount to a violation of article 23(2)', as this subjects married women to discriminatory property laws, even when the marriage has broken down irretrievably.[713] Concerns have also been expressed towards States that rely on personal and religious laws in matrimonial affairs; particularly, when such laws do not accord spouses equality in the dissolution of the marriage.[714]

---

709 Id., para. 54.

710 Id., para. 55.

711 Id., para. 57.

712 Human Rights Committee, *Concluding Observations Ireland 1993*, A/48/40 vol. I (1993) 119, para. 608.; Committee on Economic, Social and Cultural Rights, *Concluding Observations Philippines 1995*, E/C.12/1995/7, para. 11.; Human Rights Committee, *Concluding Observations Philippines 2012*, CCPR/C/PHL/CO/4, para. 12.

713 Human Rights Committee, *Concluding Observations Chile 1999*, CCPR/C/79/Add.104, para. 17.

714 Human Rights Committee, *Concluding Observations India 1997*, A/52/40 vol. I (1997) 67, para. 432.; Human Rights Committee, *Concluding Observations Israel 1998*, A/53/40 vol. I (1998) 45, para. 325.; Human Rights Committee, *Concluding Observations United Republic of Tanzania 1998*, A/53/40 vol. I (1998) 57, para. 396.; Human Rights Committee, *Concluding Observations Libyan Arab Jamahiriya 1999*, A/54/40 vol. I (1999) 32, para. 137.; Human Rights Committee, *Concluding Observations Morocco 2000*, A/55/40 vol. I (2000) 24, para. 98.; Committee on Economic, Social and Cultural Rights, *Concluding Observations Israel 2003*, E/C.12/1/Add.90, para. 23.

Along similar lines, the CESCR has also expressed concerns about the fact that the Philippines prohibits divorce.[715] In its concluding observations regarding the Philippines, the CESCR submitted that the introduction of civil marriage and divorce by the State would provide latitude for the '*individuals concerned to determine the duties that religion imposes on marriage and divorce*'.[716] This is an interesting statement as it hints to a distinction between the religious institutions of marriage and divorce *vis à vis* the legal institutions of marriage and divorce. The former should, as per the view of the CESCR, be left to individuals to decide if and to what extent they wish to be observant to religious norms and values related to marriage and divorce. In a way, the religious aspects of marriage and divorce are regarded as private matters and limited State intervention seems to be commended. Regulating marriage and divorce civilly contributes to this goal as it allows for the individuals concerned to abide by their religious rules on marriage and divorce.

Similar to the other two treaty bodies, the CEDAW Committee has frequently addressed its concerns regarding personal and religious rules that disfavour women in divorce proceedings, as well as legal systems that have no provisions on divorce.[717] Up until 2004, Chile did not have any provisions on divorce. In its concluding observations to the report submitted by Chile in 1995, the Committee encouraged the authorities of Chile to '*introduce legislation opening up the rights to legal divorce*'[718], so as to allow women to remarry after they had been divorced and to ensure equality of women and men in instituting divorce.[719] However, it should be borne in mind that the CEDAW Committee does not encourage legal divorce. In fact, the Committee has occasionally expressed its concerns for those countries that have high divorce rates.[720]

5.2.1.4. Preparatory works

The preparatory works of a treaty are a supplementary means of treaty interpretation in accordance with article 32 of the VCLT. Where there remains uncertainty on the interpretation of a specific subject matter, recourse may be had to these sources in

---

715 Committee on Economic, Social and Cultural Rights, *Concluding Observations Philippines 1995*, E/C.12/1995/7, para. 11.

716 Id.

717 Committee on the Elimination of Discrimination Against Women, *Concluding Observations Indonesia 1998*, 53/38/Rev.1 part I (1998) 24, paras. 284.; Committee on the Elimination of Discrimination Against Women, *Concluding Observations Algeria 1999*, A/54/38/Rev.1 part I (1999) 12, para. 91.; Committee on the Elimination of Discrimination Against Women, *Concluding Observations Pakistan 2013*, CEDAW/C/Pak/CO/4, para. 28.

718 Committee on the Elimination of Discrimination Against Women, *Concluding Observations Chile 1995*, A/50/38 (1995) 35, para. 155.

719 Committee on the Elimination of Discrimination Against Women, *Concluding Observations Chile 1999*, /54/38/Rev.1 part II (1999) 64, para. 222.

720 Committee on the Elimination of Discrimination Against Women, *Concluding Observations Czech Republic 1998*, A/53/38/Rev.1 part I (1998) 16, para. 198.; Committee on the Elimination of Discrimination Against Women, *Concluding Observations Pakistan 2013*, CEDAW/C/Pak/CO/4, para. 28.

order to establish or confirm whether a specific interpretation aligns with the drafters' intention. As the implied existence of a right to divorce cannot be confirmed via the above sources, the *travaux préparatoires* may provide crucial information on the drafters' intentions on this subject matter.

Starting with the UDHR, the draft text of the UDHR was set up for discussion during the ninth meeting of the Commission on the Status of Women in 1948. This draft introduced 'the right to marry and equal freedom in respect of marriage'. Lacking any specific mention of equality in respect of the dissolution of marriage, the Commission on the Status of Women (CSW) stressed the indispensability of explicitly extending this right to equal freedom in respect of marriage dissolution.[721] The amendments proposed by the CWS were transmitted to the Commission on Human Rights. This amendment reads: *'Men and women shall have equal rights to contract or dissolve marriage in accordance with the law'*.[722] Likewise, the Australian delegate expressed that the article should contain a provision on divorce. According to the delegate's view, such an inclusion would rectify incidents whereby women are divorced for a minor pretext or cannot obtain a divorce in a similar way that men can.[723] The United Kingdom proposed to insert, in the then Article 13, the following text: *'Men and women are entitled to equal rights as to marriage'*.[724] These amendments were discussed during the 58th Meeting of the Commission on Human Rights, which was held in June 1948. According to the United States delegate, the phrase *'as to marriage'* implied the right to dissolve a marriage.[725] Both the CSW, as well as the (at the time) Byelorussian Soviet Socialist Republic, opposed this draft and expressed their preference for a text that plainly stated the principle of equality of men and women in marriage and its dissolution.[726] By way of a response to this critique, the delegate from the United Kingdom stressed that the proposed amendment was intended to cover all phases of marriage and thus comprised *'all questions pertaining to marriage, such as the right to contract marriage, relations between spouses during marriage and the dissolution of marriage'*.[727] India also proposed the addition of the words *'and to dissolve marriage'*.[728] Interestingly, this amendment was adopted by 11 votes.[729] What is noteworthy is also the amendment proposed by the Union of Soviet Socialist Republics (USSR), which stated that *'men and women shall enjoy equal*

721 Schabas ed. The Universal Declaration of Human Rights: The Travaux Préparatoires, p. 1355 extracted from UN Doc. E/CN.6/ SR.28, p. 3.
722 Id., p. 1390 extracted from UN.Doc. E/737.
723 Id., p. 1359 extracted from UN.Doc E/CN.6/SR. 28, p. 7.
724 Id., p. 1621 extracted from UN.Doc E/CN.4/99, p. 4.
725 Id., p. 1745 extracted from UN.Doc. E/CN.4/SR.58, p. 8.
726 Id., pp. 1476–1747 extracted from UN.Doc. E/CN.4/99, pp. 10–12.
727 Id., p. 1747 extracted from UN. Doc. E/CN.4/99, p. 12.
728 Id., p. 1359 extracted from UN Doc. E/CN.6/ SR.28, p. 7. Which then would have read *'Men and women are entitled to equal rights as to marriage and to dissolve marriage'*.
729 Id., p. extracted from UN. Doc. E/CN.6/SR.28, p. 7.

rights both during marriage and when divorced'.[730] The USSR stressed the need for making divorce available and accessible, stating that the *'refusal to grant divorce, in the case of a family crisis, was tantamount to a flagrant denial of freedom'*.[731] While acknowledging that divorce should not be encouraged, the USSR nonetheless deemed it highly important to ensure the equality of women and men in respect of access to and the exercise of divorce.[732] This motion was, however, rejected on the basis that it was too limited and referred to divorce as the only form of marriage dissolution. Whereas, marriage dissolution can occur in various ways (e.g. marriage annulment, separation, death by partner etc.).[733] As per the view of the Commission on Human Rights, it was best to refrain from specifically mentioning divorce. Rather, it favoured retaining the words *'as to marriage'* as, at the time, divorce did not exist in some countries.[734] This sentiment was also echoed by some of the delegates, who found the mention of *'divorce'*, in the then Article 14, to be too problematic. It was feared that the explicit mention of *'the equal rights of both spouses as to divorce'*, would be interpreted as setting divorce on an equal footing with marriage. In addition, it was considered that such terminology could be misunderstood as encouraging individuals to divorce. This in turn would amount to unnecessarily endangering the cornerstone of society: the family.[735] As it turned out, the US delegate reaffirmed its view that the term *'as to marriage'* covered all stages: including a right to divorce.[736] Attempts to provide for a clearer provision were disregarded at the time. The overall position was that progress in relation to the availability and accessibility of divorce for women was a proper task for the CSW.[737] The phrase *'equal rights as to marriage, during marriage and at its dissolution'* was thus retained.

While the prevailing position was to preserve much leeway for countries in matters concerning divorce[738], the UDHR aimed to encourage States to enact compatible legislation in matters relating to divorce and to introduce the possibility of divorce within their legal systems. Furthermore, the UDHR was intended to have a dynamic and flexible interpretation, which would permit the progressive recognition and evolvement of rights that were not explicitly mentioned or rights that were not (yet) recognised by States at its adoption. On this matter, the Third Committee of the United Nations General Assembly argued that the international declaration of principles could not afford to be limited to what, at the time, already existed in the various

---

730 Id., p. 1979 extracted from UN. Doc. E/800, p. 41.

731 Id., p. 2469 extracted from UN. Doc. A/C. / SR.125, p. 373.

732 Id.

733 Id., p. 2459 extracted from UN.Doc. E/800, pp. 41, 365.

734 Id., p. 2463. extracted from UN.Doc. A/C.3/ SR. 124, p. 367.

735 Id., p. 2464 extracted from UN. Doc. A/C./ SR.125, p. 368.

736 Id., p. 2468 extracted from UN. Doc. A/C./ SR.125, p. 373.

737 Id., p 2459 extracted from UN. Doc. A/C./ SR.124, pp. 363–364.

738 *'The whole question of divorce was a matter of slow evolution...it should be left to the countries themselves to progress at their own rates of evolution'*. Id., extracted from UN. Doc. A/C./SR.124, pp. 363–364.

legal systems.[739] Despite the discussions on the inclusion of a right to divorce within the UDHR, whether such a right was or could be implied, as well as its content, were matters that were eventually left unanswered.

In light thereof, whether a right to divorce has evolved is also a subject matter that necessitates further inquiry. What is certain is that where the right to divorce already exists in a legal system, it should be accessible to both men and women on equal footing.

Noticeably, the legislative history of the ICCPR, ICESCR, CEDAW and ECHR[740] repeatedly refer to the UDHR. This peculiarity, throughout the *travaux préparatoires* of these treaties, may explain the somewhat minimal discussion on marriage dissolution. It seems as if Article 16 UDHR was taken for granted and incorporated as such, with only minor changes to the wording.

The provision on marriage in the ICCPR for example, is largely an extract from Article 16 UDHR.[741] There was some discussion on whether a provision on marriage and dissolution of marriage was to be inserted in the ICESCR rather than in the ICCPR. The ICESCR was intended to be implemented in a progressive manner and hence would have been a better instrument for the realisation of a right concerning marriage and the dissolution thereof. Progressive implementation would allow leeway and discretion for countries to regulate and change their legislation over time and at their own pace. Regardless, the provision was included in the ICCPR and to a lesser extent in the ICESCR.[742]

As for divorce, little attention was paid to this subject matter. Discussion on this issue was, rather, concentrated on the various forms of marriage dissolution. The death of either spouses as well as divorce were acknowledged to fall within the scope of the 'dissolution of marriage'. Again, divorce was labelled as an unfavourable way to end a marriage.[743] Furthermore, the participating countries did recognise that where divorce exists in a country, the spouses are entitled to equal rights in matters relating to divorce.[744] This was considered to be reflected in the formulation '*equality of rights and responsibilities*' that can be found in Article 23(4) ICCPR.[745] As for the CEDAW, divorce or the dissolution of marriage was barely discussed.[746] Notably, during the drafting of what was to become Article 16 CEDAW, Austria proposed to include the requirements

739 Id., p. 2461 extracted from UN. Doc. A/C./SR.124, p. 365.

740 The UDHR served as a source of inspiration for the provision on marriage contained in Article 12 ECHR. Council of Europe, *Collected edition of the "Travaux Préparatoires" of the European Convention on Human Rights* (The Hague, 1985), pp. 194–196 extracted from UN. Doc. A.290, para. 7.

741 Bossuyt, *Guide to the "Travaux Préparatiores" of the International Covenant on Civil and Political Rights*, pp. 447–448.

742 Id.

743 Id., pp. 449–450.

744 Id.

745 Id., p. 449.

746 A limited number of the original documents on the drafting of the CEDAW were accessible.

of *de facto* and *de jure* equality of the grounds for divorce for men and women. This motion, however, was withdrawn and was not voted upon.[747]

Turning to the ECHR, the drafters envisaged drafting a clear provision on marital affairs i.e. an improved Article 16 UDHR. Hence, from early on the provision only mentioned a right to marriage. The reference to the 'dissolution of marriage' or even 'equal rights in the dissolution of marriage' was deliberately omitted. The Legal Committee to the Consultative Assembly asserted its preference to only preserve the first part of Article 16 UDHR (*They are entitled to equal right as to marriage).*[748] The second part on '*equal rights as to marriage, during marriage and at its dissolution*' was thus excluded. The Legal Committee had no intention to include any matters relating to the dissolution of marriage.

Nevertheless, three decades after the adoption of the ECHR, matters relating to the dissolution of marriage were included in the seventh Protocol to the ECHR. The explanatory report of the protocol provides that the equality principle mentioned in Article 5 only covers 'the *relations between the spouses themselves, in regard to their person or their property and in their relations with their children*'.[749] On the subject of divorce, the report provides a salient answer on the existence of an implied right to divorce. It asserts that '*the words "in the event of its dissolution" do not imply any obligation on a State to provide for dissolution of marriage or to provide any special forms of dissolution*'.[750] This statement rules out the possibility of an implied right to divorce, whether in the legal or religious sense, under the ECHR or the Protocol thereto.

As for the other regional human rights treaties, the scope of Article 17 ACHR, in respect of divorce, was hardly discussed at all during the drafting process. Perhaps the wording was taken for granted or as self-explanatory; either way no discussion arose on this matter other than a reference to the equivalent provisions in the UDHR and ICCPR.[751] Following the wording of the texts, the provision clearly emphasises the equality of the spouses in the event of dissolution. Hence, it appears that the provision on marriage does not contain an implied right to divorce as such.[752] Likewise, as the formal records of the preparatory work leading to the ACHPR or the Maputo Protocol are not easily

747 Lars Adam Rehof, *Guide to the travaux préparatoires of the United Nations Convention on the Elimination of All Forms of Discrimination Against Women* (Dordrecht, 1993), p. 175 extracted from UN. Doc. A/32/218, para. 125.

748 Id., p. 218 extracted from Doc.77, para. 7.

749 Council of Europe 'Explanatory Report of Protocol No. 7 to the Convention for the Protection of Human Rights and Fundamental Freedoms' (1985), para. 35.

750 Id., para. 39.

751 *Draft Inter-American Convention on the protection of Human Rights*; 2–3 'Report of the US delegation to the Inter-American conference on protection of human rights', in Buergenthal & Norris *Human Rights: the Inter-American System* (Dobbs Ferry, 1982). p. i.

752 2–3 'Draft IAC working document prepared by the Secretariat of the Inter-American Commission on Human Rights', in Buergenthal & Norris *Human Rights: the Inter-American System* (Dobbs Ferry, 1982).; Corinne A. A. Packer, *Using human rights to change traditions and practices that are Harmful to women's reproductive rights* (Antwerp, Oxford, 2002), p. 110.

traceable[753], uncovering the drafters' intentions and whether these documents contain an implied right to divorce cannot be asserted with certainty.

5.2.2. EQUALITY AT THE DISSOLUTION OF MARRIAGE

Although none of the investigated provisions indicate that they contain a right to divorce, Articles 23 ICCPR, 16 UDHR and 16 CEDAW do require that States guarantee equality of spouses in all family matters, including equality at the dissolution of the marriage. In this respect, State's recognised laws (including written and unwritten, customs and religious laws) that discriminate against women in matters of marriage and divorce as well as the practice of repudiation have been condemned on multiple occasions.[754]

The right to equality at the dissolution of the marriage has several implications for non-secular States which incorporate personal laws that award spouses unequal rights during the divorce, annulment or separation. For these States, human rights treaty bodies and human rights experts have not shied away from disapproving of these practices and asserting that these discriminate against women, even if these find their basis in religious scripture, doctrines or interpretations.[755] For example, reporting on the multiple legal systems that govern marriage and divorce in Israel, the Special Rapporteur on freedom of religion or belief stressed the importance of ensuring equality and non-discrimination against women also in the realm of personal status of individuals.[756] According to the Special Rapporteur, the fact that religious courts have jurisdiction over matters of marriage and divorce did not '*absolve the authorities from*

---

753 Several informal records of the drafting sessions of part II and II have been published by one of the participants of the African Commission. See Frans Viljoen, 'The African Charter on Human an People's Rights: The Travaux Préparatoires in the light of subsequent Practice', 24 *Human Rights Law and Journal* 313–326, (2004), p. 322.

754 Schabas, *The European Convention on Human Rights: A commentary*, pp. 543–544.; Freeman *Article 16*, pp. 439–440.; Committee on Economic, Social and Cultural Rights, *Concluding Observations Israel 2003*, E/2004/22, para. 266.; Committee on the Elimination of Discrimination Against Women, *Concluding Observations Israel 2011*, CEDAW/C/ISR/CO/5, paras. 48–49.

755 HRC, *General Comment No. 19: Article 23(The Family) Protection of the Family, the Right to Marriage and Equality of the Spouses*, para.9.; CEDAW, Committee on the Elimination of Discrimination Against Women, *Concluding observations Zambia 2002*, A/57/38 part II, para. 222.; Committee on the Elimination of Discrimination Against Women, *Concluding Observations Israel 2011*, CEDAW/C/ISR/CO/5, paras. 48–49.; CEDAW, *General Recommendation on article 16 of the Convention on the Elimination of All Forms of Discrimination against Women (Economic consequences of marriage, family relations and their dissolution)*, para. 14.; Committee on Economic, Social and Cultural Rights, *Concluding Observations Israel 2003*, E/2004/22, para. 266.; Amor, *Étude sur la liberté de religion ou de conviction et la condition de la femme au regard de la religion et des traditions*, paras. 120–123.; Jahangir, *Report of the Special Rapporteur on freedom of religion or belief Asma Jahangir – Mission to Israel and the Occupied Palestinian Territory*, paras. 49,71.

756 Jahangir, *Report of the Special Rapporteur on freedom of religion or belief Asma Jahangir – Mission to Israel and the Occupied Palestinian Territory*, para. 49.

their responsibility to ensure equal treatment and the implementation of human rights for all individuals'.[757]

Essentially, States that have personal laws in place which provide women and men unequal rights to divorce and which treat women and men differently during the divorce, annulment or separation procedures are acting contrary to their human rights obligations. Discrimination on the grounds of divorce, annulment or separation as well as discrimination within the procedures for divorce, annulment or separation is prohibited.[758] States are encouraged to ensure that the grounds for divorce (as well as annulment and separation) are the same for both partners.

Similarly, the practice of repudiation has been frequently condemned by human rights monitoring bodies. Repudiation is a form of marriage dissolution that is incompatible with the principle of equality. Considering that general comment No. 28 refers to marriage and divorce that is enabled, enforced and/or recognised by the State, it may be concluded that the reference to repudiation is also made in this context. Therefore, this form of ending a marriage should be prohibited and States are obliged to exclude the possibility of repudiation in their legal systems.[759]

Equality between men and women should also be guaranteed in all affairs which are related to the termination of the marriage (e.g. distribution of property, custody rights over the children, visiting rights, inheritance etc.).[760] States that only allow for marriage dissolution in accordance with personal laws are also recommended to introduce the possibility of a civil divorce, where this does not yet exist. Additionally, the CEDAW Committee requires that personal laws on marriage and divorce, that discriminate against women, are harmonized with human rights provisions, and in particular Article 16 CEDAW. More specifically, on marital captivity, in its concluding observations to Israel's fifth periodic report, the CEDAW Committee addressed the problem of the *agunah* within the State. It recommended the State of Israel to bring its laws in line with Article 16 CEDAW '*by 'prohibiting the possibility of extorting concessions from women in return for the "get" as well as the practice of retroactive invalidation of divorces [...], limiting the scope of rabbinical courts' jurisdiction to matters of marriage and divorce alone [and by] prohibiting current exceptions under which it is allowed and polygamous marriages [...]*'.[761] However, it should be noted that States

757 Id.., para. 71.

758 HRC, *General Comment No. 19: Article 23(The Family) Protection of the Family, the Right to Marriage and Equality of the Spouses*, para. 9.

759 HRC, *General Comment No. 28: Article 3 (The equality of rights between men and women)*, para. 2.; Committee on Elimination of Discrimination Against Women, *Concluding Observations Israel 2011*, CEDAW/C/ISR/CO/5, paras. 48–49.; Committee on Economic, Social and Cultural Rights, Concluding Observations Israel 2003, E/2004/22, para. 266.; Schabas, *The European Convention on Human Rights: A commentary*, pp. 543–544.; Freeman *Article 16*, pp. 439–440.

760 HRC, *General Comment No. 28: Article 3 (The equality of rights between men and women)*, para. 26.

761 Committee on the Elimination of Discrimination Against Women, *Concluding Observations Israel 2011*, CEDAW/C/ISR/CO/5, para. 49.

may have placed reservations on the provisions that require the realisation of equality between women and men at the dissolution of the marriage. Although, the CEDAW Committee has considered reservations on article 16 CEDAW to be impermissible and incompatible with the Convention.[762] Nonetheless, within national contexts, such reservations should always be taken into account.

As for States that do not incorporate or recognise religious normative systems, the position is different. Individuals may need to dissolve the marriage in accordance with the religious rites and may thus resort to religious authorities that are not recognised or regulated by the State. The inequality between women and men in the dissolution of marriage is found in religious norms, interpretations and practices. Similarly, certain religious authorities can and do condone the condemned practice of repudiation as a means of dissolving a marriage. Repudiations do occur even when such practices are not recognised by the State.[763] This raises the question as to whether the obligation to ensure equality between spouses at the dissolution of marriage also includes informal forms of marriage dissolution that are not recognised by the State. For example, does the Netherlands have an obligation to ensure equality in the dissolution of an informal Jewish or Islamic marriage?

Firstly, States are recommended to protect the rights of women who engage in relationships that are not necessarily recognised by the State, such as *de facto* unions.[764] In its general recommendation No. 21, the CEDAW Committee recommends that States protect the equality between women and men in *de facto* unions, and to recognise 'consensual unions' as a source of rights.[765] The Committee's understanding of the relationships that are protected by Article 16 CEDAW is therefore not limited only to State sanctioned marriages.[766] This broad interpretation therefore guarantees that Article 16 CEDAW extends to include women that are in various forms of relationships. That being said, States are not obliged to recognise *de facto* unions as formal marriages or to treat them as such.[767] Where informal religious marriages, as is suggested by

762 Committee on the Elimination of Discrimination against Women, *Report of the Committee on the Elimination of Discrimination Against Women (Eighteenth and nineteenth sessions)* (UN General Assembly, 1998), [A/53/38/Rev.1], para 17.

763 For example, in religious tribunals in the Netherlands or the United Kingdom. Both States do not recognise or regulate the practice of repudiation.

764 Freeman *Article 16*, p. 417. *De facto* unions are not marriages in the formal sense. There exists no consensus on the definition of *de facto* unions and States adopt various definitions and criteria for establishing whether a relationship qualifies as a *de facto* union or not.

765 UN Committee on the Elimination of Discrimination Against Women 'General Recommendation on article 16 of the Convention on the Elimination of All Forms of Discrimination against Women (Economic consequences of marriage, family relations and their dissolution)', 2013, CEDAW/C/GC/29, paras. 26, 28, 31.; CEDAW, *General Recommendation No. 21 on Equality in marriage and family relations*, para. 18.; Freeman *Article 16*, pp. 418–419.

766 CEDAW, *General Recommendation on article 16 of the Convention on the Elimination of All Forms of Discrimination against Women (Economic consequences of marriage, family relations and their dissolution)*, para. 19.

767 Freeman *Article 16*, pp. 418–419.

Freeman[768], can be considered as *de facto* unions, this then has the effect that States are obliged to protect the rights of women in such relationships and to ensure that women's rights are not left unprotected against religious laws which may put them at the disadvantage in family and property matters.[769] Where it concerns marital captivity, it is questionable whether such a situation can be labelled as a *de facto union* for the purposes of Article 16 CEDAW. To begin with, the trapped spouse has no intention and no desire to remain in the marriage and is in fact forced to stay married against her/his will. The fact that they may be civilly divorced also does not make it realistic to classify marital captivity as a *de facto* union, as the divorce indicates the decision of one (or both) spouse(s) not to form a union.

Secondly, Article 2(e) CEDAW obliges States Parties to '*condemn discrimination against women in all its forms*' and adopt '*all appropriate measures to eliminate discrimination against women by any person, organisation of enterprise*'. States are, thus, obliged to exercise due diligence so as to prevent and protect from any discrimination against women by private parties.[770] The obligation to exercise due diligence is further expanded upon in subchapter 7.6. Similarly, the HRC interprets Article 26 ICCPR, which contains the general provision on equality, as requiring States to adopt measures to prohibit discriminatory practises by private actors in all fields. In this respect, the HRC refers to the fields of 'employment, education, political activities and the provisions of an accommodation, goods and services'.[771] This is not an exhaustive list, however. Nevertheless, the lack of an explicit reference to discrimination by private parties in the areas of marriage and family makes this statement vulnerable to criticism.[772] As the issue of marital captivity suggests, inequality of rights between women and men and discrimination also occur within the family and religious context. The exercise and enjoyment of certain human rights may, therefore, be obscured by a private person, the religious community or the recalcitrant spouse.

That being said, it should firstly be borne in mind that States are not obliged to give legal status and recognition to religious marriages and divorces nor to give religious marriages and divorces the same legal status and rights as the civil institutions of marriage and divorce.[773] States are also not obliged to recognise *de facto* unions as formal

768 Id.
769 Id., p. 418.
770 Id., p. 87.
771 HRC, *General Comment No. 28: Article 3 (The equality of rights between men and women)*, para. 31.
772 Ivana Radačic, 'Human Rights of women and the private/public divide in International Human Rights Law', 3 *Croatian Yearbook of European Law and Policy* 443–468, (2007), pp. 443, 445. Critics argue that the lack of articulating the occurrence of discriminatory practices within the family is reflective of the perception and ideas that this is a sphere that commends minimal State intervention of the State. This in turn hinders the progressive development of human rights standards within the family and facilitates the perpetuation of human rights breaches within the family.
773 J.H. Gerards, A. W. Heringa, J. G. C. Schokkenbroek and J. van der Velde, *Europees Verdrag voor de Rechten van de Mens: Rechtspraak & Commentaar* (Den Haag 2006), pp. 12–13.

marriages or to treat them as such. Additionally, religious communities are entitled, as was established in section 4.3.2., to regulate their internal affairs autonomously. Therefore, where the obligation to ensure equality at the dissolution of marriage can be extended to informal religious marriages, it is important to bear in mind the autonomy that religious communities are entitled to and to ensure that any adopted State measures do not encroach upon the doctrinal matters of religious communities. This notwithstanding, does not mean that the right to regulate internal religious matters is absolute and cannot be subjected to restrictions where necessary. As aforementioned, the fact that the discriminatory practices in the dissolution of an informal marriage are imbedded in religious doctrines and practices does not alleviate the State from its obligation to address discrimination and harmful practices that occur as consequence of these practices. In fact, and as demonstrated in subsection 4.3.2.2., States have the means to respond to discriminatory practices that occur within so-called private settings, to facilitate the dissolution of an informal religious right and to protect the rights which are impaired by a situation of marital captivity. Thus, even though secular States do not adopt, implement and enforce religious laws, doctrines and practices, States are, as will be demonstrated in subchapter 7.6., obliged to address discrimination which arises within these settings.

5.2.3. NO IMPLIED RIGHT TO DIVORCE

Having regarded, the drafting history, general comments, concluding observations and decisions of human rights monitoring bodies, several conclusions can be drawn:

Firstly, all treaties, with the exception of the ECHR, contain a provision that guarantees equality between spouses at the dissolution of marriage. States that incorporate personal laws that restrict women's rights to initiate and obtain a divorce or allow the possibility of repudiation are failing to comply with their human rights obligations to ensure equality of spouses at the dissolution of marriage. Discrimination against women in respect of the grounds for divorce and during the divorce procedure is prohibited. States are obliged to put an end to such practices and to harmonize their personal laws to ensure equality between women and men during marriage and at its dissolution. The situation is less clear for States that do not incorporate or recognize religious normative systems as it is not clear if the principle of equality between spouses at the dissolution of marriage also extends to informal divorces. Nevertheless, the general provisions on equality require States to protect women from discrimination by private actors and within private settings, so that the religious dimension inherent in situations of marital captivity does not alleviate secular States from this obligation.

Secondly, none of the instruments intends or aims to encourage the act of divorce or to set it on an equal footing as marriage. None of the human rights bodies on international and regional level have revealed explicitly that there is a right to divorce. The reluctance to clarify whether there is an implied right to divorce during the drafting process, reflects the sentiment in respect of the subject matter of divorce that prevailed at the time. This was considered as a matter which should be left up for the States' discretion to regulate. Furthermore, as some States did not even have any provisions on divorce, the introduction thereof was considered as a matter that should be realised progressively. Developments in this area have not deviated too far from this attitude. All the UN treaty bodies have only gone so far as to encourage civil divorce where it did not exist and stressed the need for addressing of discriminatory personal laws and practices in the dissolution of marriage. Creating the possibilities for both a civil divorce and marriage creates an alternative for spouses to circumvent otherwise discriminatory provisions or undue restrictions that may be contained in personal laws. In introducing a possibility for civil marriage and divorce, though, the principle of equality must be upheld, including equality of spouses in the initiation of a divorce. At best this can be seen as an obligation for States to introduce and recognise a civil divorce within their systems, rather as a right to divorce as such.

Thirdly, under the ECHR both the right to divorce and the right to exercise one's right to divorce (and obtain a divorce) have been explicitly excluded as protected rights within the articles 8 and 12 ECHR. States have a wide margin of appreciation in the measures they adopt in family matters and the conditions they adopt for divorce matters. They are not obliged to allow or guarantee the possibility of a civil divorce and not doing so, is not incompatible with the Convention as provided in the *Johnston v. Ireland* and subsequent cases.[774] UN treaty bodies have been less explicit in denouncing the existence of a right to divorce. Rather their approach has been to encourage States to introduce the possibility of legal divorce, where there is none.

5.3. A RIGHT TO DIVORCE OR NOT TO DIVORCE?

As already concluded a right to divorce has not been recognised in any of the human rights treaties that have been investigated. However, since the drafting of these treaties, society has moved on, divorce rates have increased and the sentiments and views on divorce are slowly shifting. Considering the contemporary views on the subject of divorce, the fact that nearly all countries allow divorce and the increasing recognition of marital captivity as widespread issue, can it still be maintained that a right to divorce should not exist or be developed within the human rights system?

The question of whether there is a right to divorce should be separated from the question of whether there is a human right to divorce. Concerning the former, nearly all States have provisions that enable married couples to petition for a divorce, with the exception of the Vatican City and the Philippines. In nearly all countries the right

[774] See cases that are discussed in subsection 5.2.1.2.

to petition for a divorce has become rather a matter of fact than a legal question. Whether a human right to divorce should be recognised on the other hand is a question that needs to be revaluated not only in the ordinary meaning of the treaties, as done by the ECtHR, but also with due consideration of the context, object and purposes of these treaties. This requires adopting multiple interpretation methods rather than centralising one above the others. Any interpretation should serve to guarantee that individual's human rights are practical and effective and should not render the enjoyment of human rights ineffective or inaccessible for individuals.[775] Taking the drafters intentions into considerations reveals exactly what the Contracting States had intended to be bound to and this is a relevant method of treaty interpretation as provided in article 32 VCLT. While there is an ongoing debate on whether a hierarchy of sources and interpretation methods can be deduced from the articles 31 and 32 VCLT, the conclusion can at least be drawn that the preparatory works are not the main or conclusive sources for treaty interpretation.[776] This interpretation method cannot be taken in isolation without equally taking into consideration the context of the treaty, its object and its purpose to protect individuals against violations of their rights by the State and private parties alike. Therefore, the following sections will attempt to adopt an integrated interpretation of the treaties provisions on the subject of divorce. By taking contemporary developments and re-evaluating the arguments provided in the ECtHR's case law, there are arguments to be found for acknowledging a right to divorce or at the very least an obligation to adopt adequate measures to solve a situation of marital captivity.

5.3.1. ACKNOWLEDGING A RIGHT TO DIVORCE

As has already been pointed out there are multiple interpretation methods that ought to be taken into account in an integrate manner. The society is in constant change, as consequence of political shifts, economic fluctuation, cultural exchanges and technological advancements. In this sense societal norms, values and morals are also subject to change over time. Similarly, human rights are not static and their interpretation should follow and reflect the changes and needs of society. The ECtHR has through its case law frequently asserted that the ECHR Convention ought to be '*interpreted in the 'light of present-day conditions*', that it is '*designed to safeguard the individual in a real and practical way as regards those areas with which it deals with*' and that it intends '*to guarantee not rights that are theoretical or illusory but rights that are practical and*

775 See *supra* note 89–90.

776 See among others Julian Davis Mortenson, 'The Travaux of Travaux: Is the Vienna Convention Hostile to Drafting History?', 107 *American Journal of International Law* 780–822, (2013).; Ulf Linderfalk, 'Is the hierarchical structure of articles 31 and 32 of the Vienna Convention real or not? Interpreting the rules of interpretation', 54 *Netherlands International Law Review* 133–154, (2007).; European Court of Human Rights, *Babiarz v. Poland,* 10 January 2017, Application No. 1955/10, Dissenting opinion Judge Pinto Dealbuqeurque, para. 13.

effective[777]'. This supposes an evolutive interpretation of the treaty, that may lead to establishing rights that are not explicitly contained therein. Evolutive interpretation is, thus, not an alien method of interpretation. As demonstrated in subchapter 1.6., treaty interpretation methods do allow for developments along the life of a treaty to be taken into account by way of Articles 31 (2–3) VCCLT. In fact, human rights monitoring bodies have occasionally used this method of interpretation to recognise implicit rights within human rights provisions. Some examples here of are the earlier discussed recognition of a right to conscientious objection to military services in the ICCPR and more recently in the ECHR, as well as the right to be free from violence against women in the CEDAW.[778] Remarkably on the subject matter of divorce, the ECtHR has instead on relying on the drafters' intentions and has ruled out the possibility to apply an evolutive interpretation. Since the *Johnston* case it has consistently maintained that it cannot '*by means of an evolutive interpretation, derive from these instruments a right that was not included therein at the outset. This is particularly so here where the omission was deliberate.*'[779]

Considering that in other areas the ECtHR has established rights and duties that were not contained in the Convention, the ECtHR approach in the divorce cases seems to be somewhat inconsistent. On this point judges Sajó and Dealbuqerque, argue that the exclusion of an expression from within the text does not necessarily imply that a right cannot be derived from another principle and social developments on the particular matter.[780] The recent acknowledgement of the right to conscientious objection to military services within the Convention is not a single sporadic case. As both Judges Sajó and Dealburquerque, reveal in their dissenting opinions, the ECtHR has been inconsistent in the interpretation methods adopted by the Court in other areas. For example, in *MBH v. Hungary*[781] the court established that article 10 could in fact be interpreted to contain a right to access to State-held information. This right is not explicitly mentioned in the concerned provision. In reaching this conclusion the Court, among others, expressed that the *travaux préparatoires* are not '*delimiting for the question whether a right may be considered to fall within the scope of an Article of the Convention if the existence of such a right was supported by the growing measure of common ground that had emerged in a given area*' and that '*the consensus emerging from specialised international instruments and from the practice of Contracting States may constitute a relevant consideration for the Court when it interprets the provisions of the Convention in specific cases.*'[782] Similarly, in the case of *Sigurdur A. Sigurjónsson*

---

777 European Court of Human Rights, *Airey v. Ireland,* 9 October 1979, Application No. 6289/73, paras. 24, 26.

778 See subchapter 6.1.

779 European Court of Human Rights, *Johnston and Others v. Ireland,* 18 December 1986, Application No.9697/82, para. 31.

780 European Court of Human Rights, *Babiarz v. Poland,* 10 January 2017, Application No. 1955/10, Dissenting opinion Judge Sajó, para. 3, Dissenting opinion Judge Pinto Dealbuqeurque, para. 13.

781 European Court of Human Rights, *Magyar Helsinki Bizottság v. Hungary,* 08 November 2016, Application No. 18030/11.

782 Id., para. 124–125.

v. Iceland[783] the Court acknowledged the negative freedom of association as being guaranteed by Convention. Noteworthy, the preparatory works of the ECHR indicated that a negative freedom of association was deliberately omitted from Article 11 ECHR on the freedom of assembly and association.[784] In explicitly acknowledging the negative freedom of association in *Sigurdur*, the court relied among others on the growing number of countries that guaranteed such a right in their national law as well as the growing consensus of the importance of such a right in the international community and other international human rights documents.[785] The right to be free from violence against women, which is discussed further in Chapter 7, is another example a right that has been found to be implied within the ECHR and CEDAW. The CEDAW committee considers that the Convention may include implicit rights and cover certain matters, including violence against women, even when they have not been explicitly mentioned within the text of the Convention. In this regard, the CEDAW Committee has confirmed that the '*spirit of the Convention covers other rights, which are not explicitly mentioned in the Convention but which have an impact on the achievement of equality of women with men and which represent a form of discrimination against women*'.[786]

Considering the foregoing and taking into account the impairments created when spouses are denied divorce and the fact that divorce is allowed in almost all countries, there is nothing standing in the way of the ECtHR to revaluate its position on the subject of divorce. After all, the fact that all Contracting States have provisions on divorce in their national law means a consensus of the State parties to legalize and regulate divorce. However, it should be noted that there is little evidence to support that there is a common ground on the right to divorce in international treaties, since these have, so far, predominantly concentrated on the subject of equality of men and women in the dissolution of marriage. Nonetheless, acknowledging the State's practice of legalizing divorce means that States enjoy a narrow margin of appreciation in respect of making divorce available. Rightly so, judges Sajó and Dealbuquerque also argue that the margin of appreciation is not wide, from the very fact that there is a European consensus on the issue of divorce.[787] However, in respect of the specificities, grounds

783 European Court of Human Rights, *Sigurdur A. Sigurjónsson v. Iceland*, 30 June 1993, Application No. 16130/90.

784 '*On account of the difficulties raised by the 'closed-shop system' in certain countries, the Conference [of Senior Officials to the Committee of Ministers] in this connection considered that it was undesirable to introduce into the Convention a rule under which 'no one may be compelled to belong to an association' which features in the United Nations Universal Declaration*'. European Commission of Human Rights, *Preparatory work on article 11 of the European Convention on Human Rights*, (1956), DH (56) 16, p. 11. <https://www.echr.coe.int/LibraryDocs/Travaux/ECHRTravaux-ART11-DH(56)16-EN1693924.PDF> last accessed 12 October 2019.

785 Id., para. 35.

786 UN Committee on the Elimination of Discrimination Against Women 'General Recommendation No. 28 on the core obligations of States Parties under Article 2 of the Convention on the Elimination of All Forms of Discrimination against Women', 2010, para. 7.

787 European Court of Human Rights, *Babiarz v. Poland*, 10 January 2017, Application No. 1955/10, Dissenting opinion Judge Sajó, para 7.; European Court of Human Rights, *Babiarz v. Poland*, 10 January 2017, Application No. 1955/10, Dissenting opinion Judge Pinto Dealbuqeurque, para. 16.

and restrictions to divorce, a wide margin of appreciation can be argued considering the diverging approaches taken by Contracting States.

5.3.2. MORAL BARRIERS AND COMPETING INTERESTS

In the cases of *Piotrowski* and *Babiarz,* the national authorities argued among others that the restrictions contained in the national laws served two legitimate aims i.e. the rights and freedoms of others (the interests and well-being of the divorced spouse) and the protection of morals (as they counteract the '*menace of arbitrary and unilateral terminations of marriages*'[788]).[789] Similarly, the European Centre for Law and Justice, which intervened in support of the Polish government, argued that recognising a right to divorce would be contradictory as article 12 ECHR aims to protect the marital link rather than harm it. It submitted that such a right would favour an '*individualist conception of freedom*', that would enable one spouse to deprive the other spouse of '*possession of their marital estate*'.[790] Likewise the Court seemed eager to save the institution of marriage itself, regardless of the specific situation of the applicant. In its view the recognition of a right to divorce would not only have the consequence of underestimating the procedural and substantive regulation of divorce by national states, but would also work in the favour of granting a divorce to '*a person [who] simply decides to leave his or her spouse and have a child with a new partner*'.[791] As provided, the Court also readily accepted that national laws had aimed to protect the weaker party (the opposing spouse) against the '*machinations and bad faith of the other party*'. Thus, despite the ongoing changes in society and increasing acceptance of unconstitutional forms of relationship (e.g. cohabitation, registered partnership, de facto union etc.), there still remains a strong moral argument and need to protect the institution of marriage. This sentiment is reflected in some countries, such as Poland, where the protection of morality is perceived to be reason enough to restrict divorce laws.

While these are profound fundamental issues that should not be taken lightly, the other side of the coin is that by withholding a divorce, national courts are essentially enabling and maintaining a situation of marital captivity to a formal marriage. Additionally, the question is also whether there is any moral justification in keeping an individual in a marriage against their will and, whether indeed an opposing spouse

---

788 European Court of Human Rights, *Piotrowski v. Poland,* 22 November 2016, Application No. 8923/12, para. 37.

789 European Court of Human Rights, *Babiarz v. Poland,* 10 January 2017, Application No. 1955/10, para. 39.

790 In opposing the recognition of a right to divorce, the ECLJ, went even further by equating the recognition of a right to divorce to the recognition to a right to death in article 2 ECHR. Puppinck, *Third party intervention- Submission to the Fourth Section of the European Court of Human Rights in the cases Babiarz v. Poland, Gajewski v. Poland, and Piotrowski v. Poland,* paras. 18–22.

791 European Court of Human Rights, *Babiarz v. Poland,* 10 January 2017, Application No. 1955/10, para. 54.

has a right to remain married with a person against their will. The situation becomes even dire when there are other parties involved such as a new partner or children from the new relationship. In other words, when the concerned individual has left the first marriage, has already established a new *de facto union* and family lifeand demands legal recognition of this new relationship, is it morally correct to deny them this right, simply because they have not lived up to their obligations to the first marriage which has broken down? Is the trapping of one or both spouses in a formal marriage against their will the most appropriate tool to protect the institution of marriage? It would rather seem that national divorce laws that enable to the innocent spouse to trap the other spouse in a marriage, seek to impose a sanction on the spouse who is at fault for the brake down of the marriage, instead of protecting the prevailing morals on marriage and divorce.

Likewise, judge Sajó contended that forcing an individual to 'maintain a legal relationship with a person no longer out of choice, is not a moral'.[792] He did not to find a moral in '*upholding a de jure fiction marriage to the detriment of a de facto family which seeks recognition*'.[793] In his view, the morals protected in the *Johnston* case and subsequent case law are no longer profoundly deeply embedded in the 'fabric of society' as consequence of the global recognition of divorce.[794] Likewise, the effectiveness of the Polish divorce laws in enforcing these morals is also questionable. According to judge Sajó the proper tool for enforcing morals is not forcing individuals to remain married involuntarily.[795] Dealbuquerque followed a similar reasoning and asserted that a spouse who does not respect the duties and morals of marriage can be sanctioned by other tools of civil law (e.g. in the division of matrimonial property). Additionally, in respecting the principle of State neutrality, State policy and laws should refrain from imposing certain religious or ethical morals.[796]

Furthermore, competing interests should also be taken into account. As shown in the cases of *Ivanov and Petrova* as well as *Babiarz*, the unavailability of a legal divorce may severely impede on the private and family life of those related to the trapped spouse. There is, thus, critic to be given to Courts finding that the unavailability or inaccessibility does not violate or seriously impede the rights guaranteed in article 12 ECHR, as it deprives both partners to give legal recognition to their relationship by way of marriage.[797] Similarly, marriage establishes the family. The family life is protected in article 8 ECHR. Therefore,

792 Id., Dissenting opinion Judge Sajó, para. 6.
793 Id., Dissenting opinion Judge Sajó, para. 16.
794 Id., Dissenting opinion Judge Sajó, para. 21.
795 Id., Dissenting opinion Judge Sajó, para. 14.
796 Id., Dissenting opinion Pinto Dealbuquerque, para. 21.
797 See for example Kathleen M Dillon, 'Divorce and Remarriage as Human Rights: The Irish Constitution and the European Convention on Human Rights at Odds in Johnston v. Ireland', 22 *Cornell International Law Journal* 63–90, (1989).; Nancy Johnson, 'Recent Developments: The Breadth of Family Law Review Under the European Convention on Human Rights', 36 *Havard International Law Journal* 513–570, (1995).

the right to family life of the new partner and any children involved should be balanced fairly against the rights of the opposing spouse to maintain a fictive marriage and family life with the trapped spouse. Put in this perspective it becomes unlikely to argue that the opposing spouses interest to remain married and to maintain a fictive family life with the other spouse against their will, should prevail over the rights of the new partner to legally marry and establish family life with the trapped spouse, even when the trapped spouse carries the fault of damaging the first marriage. This is an outcome that impairs the relationship and autonomy of both the intending spouses for the sake of protecting a relationship that is unlikely to be redeemed. It is certainly not beneficial for the intending spouses, and highly unlikely that it will lead to favourable outcome for the innocent spouse in terms of mending the broken relationship. In this respect, judge Sajó also argues that under article 8 ECHR individuals are guaranteed the '*right not to be forced to live with in a marital union with another person [...]* '. In his view, the opposing spouse's right to family life does not mean '*the right to family life with a specific person against their will*'.

5.3.3. DIVORCE AND THE RIGHT TO MARRY

Despite the fact that the right to divorce has not been recognised in human rights law, the right to marry subsequent to a divorce has been recognised in the UN treaties as well as in the ECHR.[798] The right to marry is a fundamental and intimate right. The provisions on the right to marry have been found to also include a right for divorcees and widow(ers) to remarry. Section 6.2.1. elaborates further on the right to remarry. The right to marry it is a relative right in that it may be restricted by domestic laws. Restrictions may include material conditions (e.g. attained marriageable age, free and full consent, prohibited types of marriages[799] etc.) as well formal conditions (e.g. formalisation requirements, civil marriage prior to a religious ceremony, registration etc.). Thus, national laws that impose restrictions and conditions, such as being of marriageable age or the requirement that any pre-existing marriage has to be dissolved, are permissible.[800] Restrictions, however, may not be unreasonable or render the right inaccessible entirely.[801] National laws that impose a waiting period for female divorcees or widows to remarry have been found to be incompatible with human rights guarantees.[802] Unreasonable restrictions, that impair the very essence of the right to

---

798 The right to remarry is discussed further in section 5.2.1.

799 Such as polygamy, marriage of convenience or consanguineous marriages, which are prohibited in some countries.

800 UN Committee on the Elimination of Discrimination Against Women 'General Recommendation No. 19 on Violence against women', 1992, para 16. Article 12 ECHR explicitly subjects the right to marry to the national laws of contracting States.

801 Schabas, *The European Convention on Human Rights: A commentary*, p. 533; Freeman *Article 16*, p. 422.; European Court of Human Rights, *F. v. Switzerland*, 18 December 1987, Application No. 11329/85, para. 38.

802 Human Rights Committee, *Concluding Observations Japan 1998*, CCPR/C/79/Add.102, para. 16.; Committee on the Elimination of Discrimination Against Women, *Concluding Observations*

remarry for divorcees are, therefore, to be eliminated and equality to the right to remarry should be guaranteed for both women and men.[803]

Depending on the conditions set in the domestic laws of States Parties, the right to remarry may also be dependent on the whether any existing marriage has been or can be dissolved. This is particularly more so for States that adhere to the principle of monogamy and allow for individuals only to be married to one person at a time. Where divorce is inaccessible, the spouse who is denied divorce as well as the new partner can then not exercise the right to (re)marry. The case of *Babiarz v. Poland, Ivanov and Petrova v. Bulgaria* and *Johnston v. Ireland*, illustrate that such a situation can be created by national laws on divorce that either prohibit divorce or enable an opposing spouse to obstruct the pronunciation of a divorce. Although, these cases do not strictly fit the definition of marital captivity adopted in this contribution, as they are created by secular national laws. Nonetheless, it cannot be denied that the applicants, in these cases, were in fact trapped in the formal marriage, forced to remain married civilly and experienced similar restrictions to their rights as the situations of marital captivity studied in this dissertation.

On a side note, all the above cases dealt marriage and divorce in their formal sense, i.e. State recognised marriage and divorce. In all these cases the applicants were unable to terminate a formal marriage and were thus unable to remarry formally. Within the context of marital captivity, however, it is important to bear in mind that the inability to terminate a formal as well as an informal religious marriage can inhibit the spouses from exercising their right to remarry both legally as well as religiously.[804]

The act of marrying is an essential aspect of individuals' personal autonomy in respect their choices to marry and found a family. The States Parties have to guarantee the effective enjoyment and accessibility to this right also by divorcees. The underlying principle of effectiveness[805], prompts the question whether the effective exercise of the right to remarry may imply the removal of any unreasonable restrictions and barriers to remarry. If this is the case, does the right to remarry include a duty on the State to remove unreasonable restrictions and barriers to remarry, including religious barriers?

5.3.3.1. The ECtHR position on divorce and the right to remarry

In the cases of *Babiarz v. Poland, Piotrowski v. Poland, Ivanov and Petrova v. Bulgaria,* and *Johnston v. Ireland,* the ECtHR had to deal with situations where a pre-existing

---

Luxembourg 1997, A/52/38/Rev.1 part II, paras. 212, 223.; Committee on the Elimination of Discrimination Against Women, *Concluding Observations Japan 2003,* A/58/3 (Supp No. 38), para. 371.

803 Freeman *Article 16,* p. 422.; Committee on Economic, Social and Cultural Rights, *Concluding Observations Israel 2003,* E/2004/22, para. 266.; ECHR European Court of Human Rights, *F. v. Switzerland,* 18 December 1987, Application No. 11329/85, paras. 32, 38, 40.

804 For the consequences of marital captivity see: section 1.3.2. For the *scope of the right to remarry and the corresponding obligations in relation to marital captivity see section 6.2.1 and subchapter 6.3.*

805 See subchapter 1.6.

marriage and the inability to dissolve that marriage prevented both the trapped spouses as well as their new partners to exercise their right to remarry. In all four cases, national authorities had adopted conditions in their divorce laws that, in practice, prevented spouses from divorcing and consequently created situations of marital captivity to a legal marriage. Analysing these cases, thus, provide valuable insights on how the ECtHR has evaluated the relation between restrictive divorce laws and the right to remarry and whether the former are compatible with article 12 ECHR.

In the case of *Babiarz v. Poland,* the Court asserted that the condition of consent by the innocent spouse in the divorce, could raise issues under article 12 ECHR where the consent formed an '*insurmountable obstacle*' for granting a divorce to the guilty party.[806] The ECtHR did not define with much words, what could be considered as an 'insurmountable obstacle'. However, it did consider that '*excessive length of divorce proceedings*' or '*insurmountable legal impediments on the possibility to remarry*' may qualify as insurmountable obstacles.[807] Nonetheless, the ECtHR and ECmHR have, in this case and other the other cases[808], concluded that the inability to divorce in accordance with national laws does not necessarily constitute a restriction of the very essence of article 12 ECHR.[809] In this case, it took into account that the trapped spouse was not prevented in initiating new divorce proceedings[810] In addition, individuals may also have to show the '*existence of a stable and long-lasting relationship with another (...) or concrete marriage plans that would be frustrated by the refusal to obtain a divorce*'.[811]

Consequently, the ECtHR has established a worrisome precedence, presumably, in a misguided effort to respect the prevailing position that divorce is not a guaranteed human right. The result is a regrettable situation whereby the right to remarry is guaranteed in theory but may not be accessible in reality. As it stands, laws that enable

806 European Court of Human Rights, *Babiarz v. Poland,* 10 January 2017, Application No. 1955/10, para. 50. See also European Court of Human Rights, *Ivanov and Petrova v. Bulgaria,* 14 June 2011, Application No. 15001/04, para 61.

807 European Court of Human Rights, *Babiarz v. Poland,* 10 January 2017, Application No. 1955/10, para. 50.

808 European Court of Human Rights, *Piotrowski v. Poland,* 22 November 2016, Application No. 8923/12.; European Court of Human Rights, *Ivanov and Petrova v. Bulgaria,* 14 June 2011, Application No. 15001/04.; European Court of Human Rights, *Johnston and Others v. Ireland,* 18 December 1986, Application No.9697/82.

809 European Court of Human Rights, *Babiarz v. Poland,* 10 January 2017, Application No. 1955/10, paras. 51, 55.; European Court of Human Rights, *Piotrowski v. Poland,* 22 November 2016, Application No. 8923/12, para.52.; European Court of Human Rights, *Ivanov and Petrova v. Bulgaria,* 14 June 2011, Application No. 15001/04 para. 64; European Court of Human Rights, *Johnston and Others v. Ireland,* 18 December 1986, Application No.9697/82, paras. 53–54.

810 European Court of Human Rights, *Babiarz v. Poland,* 10 January 2017, Application No. 1955/10, paras. 51, 55. In the *Babiarz* case the argument was reached that the domestic courts and laws had not made it impossible for the applicant to obtain a divorce as he maintained the possibility to reapply for a divorce at a later stage. See also European Court of Human Rights, *Piotrowski v. Poland,* 22 November 2016, Application No. 8923/12, para.52.

811 Id., para 51.

one spouse to hold the other in a situation of marital captivity to a legal marriage, are permissible. Accordingly, such laws and the condition of marital captivity to a legal marriage do not constitute unreasonable restrictions to the right to remarry. In reality, however, the right to remarry is then inaccessible for individuals who want or intend to remarry another partner. On top of that, the new partners are also deprived of this right as long as their intended spouse continues to remain trapped in the first marriage.

5.3.3.2. *Effective protection of the right to remarry*

International treaties, including those investigated in this contribution, aim to effectively protect individual's human rights against infringements by the State and private persons, encourage the realisation and observance of human rights by States and guarantee the effective access to human rights.[812]

As established the ability to divorce may in certain circumstances become a precondition to the right to remarry. Consequently, where a divorce is not available or is not accessible as in the cases of *Johnston, Ivanov and Petrova, Piotrowski and Babiarz,* the right to marry is not accessible for both the spouses who wish to marry each other.[813] It is, therefore, undeniable that a situation of marital captivity, whether to a formal or informal marriage, constitutes a barrier to the trapped spouses right to remarry as well as the right to marry of the new partners. Judge Sajó reached a similar conclusion in his dissenting opinion in the *Babiarz* case. On this subject, he concluded that in '*denying the applicant a divorce the national authorities had violated the essence of his right to marry.*[814] Dealbuquerque also submitted that national laws should not be constructed in a way that they impair the very essence of the right to marry. He went even further by arguing that, particularly for countries that adhere to the principle of monogamy, '*the right to remarry presupposes the right to divorce*[815]'. Similarly, in his partly dissenting and partly concurring opinion to the *Johnston* case, judge De Meyer held the view that the impossibility to have the legal marriage dissolved constituted a violation of the applicants' rights guaranteed in the articles 8, 9 and 12 ECHR.[816] De Meyer argued that the effective exercise of the right to marry and right to private and family life may imply that individuals are allowed '*to apply to be completely released in civil law from their marital ties, by means of legal recognition of their definitive separation.*'

Therefore, despite the lack of an explicit right to divorce, all three judges point out that national divorce laws that deny individuals a divorce, may in fact violate the very

---

812 On the object and purpose of human rights treaties see subchapter 1.6..

813 In the cases of *Ivanov, Piotrowski* and *Babiarz,* however the Court did not consider the impact of the restrictive national divorce laws as encroaching upon the right to marry of the husband and the new partner, despite the fact that the legal divorce had been withheld for a lengthy period of time and the new partner's right to marry was being restricted by the continuation of the legal marriage.

814 European Court of Human Rights, *Babiarz v. Poland,* 10 January 2017, Application No. 1955/10, Dissenting opinion Judge Sajó. para. 21.

815 Id., Dissenting opinion Judge Pinto Dealbuqeurque, para. 26.

816 European Court of Human Rights, *Johnston and Others v. Ireland,* 18 December 1986, Application No. 9697/82, separate opinion of judge De Meyer, para. 5.

essence of a right to remarry. The effective protection of this right may thus require the removal of such obstacles. What this entails is that, the provisions on marriage may contain duties for States to ensure that individuals can remarry, without necessarily implying that a right to divorce exists. In fact, the ECtHR has shown to be willing to acknowledge the existence of implicit duties within certain provisions. For example, in the discussed *Airey* case[817], the Court established that the State may be compelled to provide free legal services to the applicant, '*when such assistance proves indispensable for an effective access to court […]*'.[818] The Convention however does not contain a provision on legal aid and the Court has declined from acknowledging such a right as implied in article 6 ECHR. Similarly, in light of the effective respect for private and family life, the Court considered that the positive obligations within article 8 ECHR included the duty, for the State, to allow for couples to be relieved from their duty to live together.[819] In doing so however the court did not suggest that a right to separation could be derived from within the Convention.

Following this line of reasoning several conclusions can be drawn. Firstly, State's measures or the lack thereof, that have as consequence that spouses are essentially deprived from their right to marry, due to the fact that they cannot or may not dissolve the marriage, are incompatible with the right to remarry and may even obscure this right. A situation of marital captivity that arises from the application of restrictive divorce laws, violates not only the trapped spouse's right to remarry, but also the right to marry of the new partner.

Secondly, human rights, including the right to remarry, should be accessible and effective. States have to ensure effective exercise and enjoyment of the right to remarry by individuals. This means that States have a duty to guarantee the effective exercise and access to the right to remarry by individuals, protect this right from impermissible infringements (including those created by private persons) and abstain from imposing restrictions that are unreasonable and render the right ineffective.

Thirdly, there is an interdependence between the ability to dissolve a marriage and the effective enjoyment of the right to remarry, that should not be ignored. In cases where one of the spouses is stuck in an irreparable marriage and the new partner is unable to marry that spouse, the ability to dissolve the first marriage is thus the only way that both partners can effectively exercise their right to marry. Although a right to divorce has yet to be recognized, in such circumstances guaranteeing the right to remarry demands the removal of any barriers that hinder the effective exercise of this right. This is particularly more so, where both intending spouses have already established a long-term stable relationship, intend to remain with each other and the first marriage has broken-down. The concerned individuals should then have a possibility to have the first marriage dissolved in order to secure and exercise their

817 See subsection 5.2.1.2.

818 European Court of Human Rights, *Airey v. Ireland,* 9 October 1979, Application No. 6289/73, para. 26.

819 Id., paras. 32–33.

rights. The effective protection of the right to marry implies at the very least a duty on the State to ensure that spouses to an irreparable marriage are not deprived of their right to establish a new voluntary and legal marriage, as consequence of rigid and strict divorce regimes or any other barriers that may impair this right. This could, for example, be achieved by adopting exceptions to the national divorce laws (e.g. when the trapped spouse has established a new relationship or family life, marital life has ceased to exist for a long time and the opposing spouse has not made any evident efforts for reconciliation), and balancing all the competing interests adequately.

5.4. CONCLUDING REMARKS: THE RIGHT TO DISSOLVE A RELIGIOUS MARRIAGE?

The above exercise leads to the following findings:

Firstly, in most countries the right to divorce is secured and guaranteed to spouses. Countries that do not permit divorce have been encouraged to make divorce possible for their citizens. Countries that only provide the possibility of divorce in accordance with personal laws, have been recommended to introduce the possibility of a civil divorce, so as to better guarantee individuals' rights and ensure equality for individuals belonging to minority religions or beliefs and non-believers.

Secondly, States have an obligation to ensure equality between women and men at the dissolution of marriage. This obligation applies for all State recognised laws and practices. This means that States that guarantee women and men unequal rights to initiate a divorce, unequal rights in relation to any other matters related to the divorce (e.g. custody and property rights) or enable the practice of repudiation of wives, are not complying with their human rights obligations. States should thus, eliminate discriminatory laws and practices in matters of marriage and divorce and adopt measures to bring their laws and actions, in compliance with the equality principle.

Thirdly, the fact that secular States have not incorporated religious norms and do not recognize or regulate religious marriage and divorces, does not mean that they are alleviated from their human rights obligations to ensure equality within the family, and protect from discrimination by private parties occurring in the private spheres. As also elaborated upon in the following Chapters 6 and 7, States have obligations to protect any infringed rights of trapped spouses and are required to exercise due diligence to eliminate discrimination against women and ensure equality.

Fourthly, a right to divorce has yet to be recognized in human rights law. So far human rights monitoring bodies have refrained, both explicitly as implicitly, from recognizing a right to divorce. The underlying reasons can be summarized in three main arguments, namely:

1) the drafters had not intended to include and recognize a right to divorce and, therefore it cannot derive from the articles on the right to marry or the right to private and family life,
2) the recognition of a right to divorce may have negative effects as it may be perceived as encouraging divorce or setting divorce on an equal footing as marriage and
3) Protecting of family life, the institutions of marriage and the morals pertaining to marriage are also important interests that may impede the effectuation of a divorce.

Further consideration of these arguments, however, reveals that these arguments are flawed. With regards to the first argument, it is well established in the VCLT that treaty interpretation requires multiple interpretation methods, including but not limited to the assessing the drafters' intentions. Human rights treaties are flexible and living instruments that should be interpreted in a manner that aligns with their object to protect and guarantee individual's fundamental rights in a constantly changing society. This requires, taking the context, aim and purpose of human rights treaties, within cotemporary societies into account. Consequently, this implies that the content of human rights provisions will change and evolve over time, and cannot remain solely fixed on the ideas, values and principles that prevailed at the time of their drafting. In fact, the evolvement of human rights and recognition of new implied rights, is not an alien development in human rights law. Previously non-included rights and even rights that were at first explicitly excluded (such as the right to conscientious objection to military services in the ECHR system)[820], have at later moments been found to fall within the human rights provisions. Therefore, the mere fact that the drafters' intention was not to recognise a right to divorce or were hesitant of its inclusion, does not necessarily imply that such a right cannot develop in the future.

As for the second argument, it is questionable whether the recognition of a right to divorce has the effect of encouraging divorce or sets divorce on an equal footing as marriage. It is true that divorce rates have increased globally in the past decades, but there is no evidence that this trend is predominantly the consequence of nearly all States having introduced the possibility of divorce or having removed restrictions to this right (e.g. the Netherlands switched from fault-based to no fault-based divorce in with the amendment of the civil code in 1971[821]). Even as human rights monitoring bodies have recommended the introduction of civil divorce, where it does not exist, this has been done for the purpose of ensuring the principle of equality of individuals and protecting

820 See subsection 4.4.1.2.

821 Prior to this amendment divorce was permitted only on grounds of: adultery, wilful abandonment, criminal conviction and sever abuse of the other spouse. Spouses could also divorce after five years of being separated and divorce by mutual consent was prohibited. Mariken Lenaerts, 'De voorstellen tot herziening van het Nederlandse echtscheidingsrecht tijdens de Duitse bezetting', Family & Law 2013, pp. 214–216.

individuals' human rights. The intention behind these recommendations is not and cannot be taken as implying an encouragement of divorce or as equating divorce with marriage.

With regards to the argument of morality, this contribution does not argue against the value and significance attached to marriage or the underlying morals and reasons for protecting the institution of marriage and the family. However, the solutions for protecting the institution of marriage and the family cannot be found in trapping spouses who seek to dissolve an irreparable marriage. There are other appropriate and more suited means to protect the institution of marriage and the family than forcing one or both individuals to remain married. In fact, it is rather immoral to create and condone situations of marital captivity and force spouses to remain married against their will. In the same light, it is questionable whether individuals have a right to remain married to a person against that person's will and wishes. The basic premise of any legitimate relationship is that they are reciprocal and consensual. It is hard to imagine that human rights law would promote, enable or even protect any activities that violate this basic premise and imposes relationships on individuals against their will, thereby allowing for their human rights to be violated.

In conclusion, at current times, there are reasons to argue for the recognition of a right to divorce human rights law. Firstly, in almost all States, individuals have a right to initiate divorce and consequently the right and possibility to divorce are facts in all these States. Although, in reality substantive equality between men and women has not yet been realized in many countries, where women still experience far more restrictions in initiating and obtaining a divorce. Nonetheless, as human rights treaties dictate and as has been emphasised by human rights monitoring bodies, where a right to divorce is recognised the principle of equality should also be guaranteed at the dissolution of the marriage.

Particularly, where new strong and viable relationships have been established with a new partner and children are involved it is more important, appropriate and morally correct to protect the new bonds, instead prioritizing relationships that have become irreparable.

Furthermore, the right to remarry, which is a fundamental civil right that pertains the social identity and personal autonomy of all individuals, may in certain circumstances become conditional to the availability and accessibility of a divorce. The aim and purpose of human rights law is not only to ensure greater respect and protection of human rights and freedoms of individuals but also to guarantee that these are practical and accessible in real life situations. There is no point in guaranteeing rights but denying the practical means to access and exercise them. Therefore, the right to remarry ought to be recognised as entailing, at the very least, a duty to ensure that any rigid restrictions and any other barriers (including religious barriers) to this right are removed. This implies that where the inability to remarry is caused by a still existing marriage or any other obstacle (e.g. an informal religious marriage) States have a duty to facilitate in the removal of such an obstacle or restriction.

Finally, what is the added value of a right to divorce for situations of marital captivity? A right to divorce empowers and enhances the trapped spouse's possibilities to demand for a situation of marital captivity to be brought to an end. For non-secular States, where religious laws are an integral part of the States' legal system, the right to divorce implores State authorities to ensure that religious based laws and religious prescribed practices are compatible with this right. Additionally, the underlying principle of equality implies that non-secular States have to harmonize and reconcile both normative systems so that women and men can initiate and obtain a divorce on equal grounds.[822] Furthermore, within non-secular States, national authorities are more involved with and may undertake measures that directly involve, affect or concern the religious laws and practices within the State's legal system (e.g. the amendment of religion-based family laws). This close relationship between the State and the religious communities comes not only with greater competence for States to control, regulate and influence religious laws and practices by religious authorities, but also with greater accountability when the States fails to bring these laws and practices in compliance with their human rights obligations. Notably, how States go about it, as in the measures they would have to implement to harmonize religious based laws and practices on divorce, remains a matter over which States have discretion. In this regard, it imperative to keep in mind that the State's organisational structure and unique relationship with religious communities will affect the impact and implications of a right to divorce for its subjects. Additionally, the recognition of a right to divorce for situations of marital captivity, would still have to be regulated by the State, which may impose conditions to this right. However, such condition should then not be incompatible with the principle of equality and should not impair the very essence of both the right to (re)marry and the right to divorce.

For States that do not incorporate or regulate religious marriages or divorce, the position is different. As established, a formal divorce does not necessarily end an (informal) religious marriage, which may nevertheless lead to a situation of marital captivity to a religious marriage. In other words, even when the State does guarantee a right to divorce, enforcement of this right will not directly contribute to facilitating the dissolution of a religious marriage. Where the State only recognizes and regulates the civil forms of divorce, the question that then first needs to be answered is whether the right to divorce also extends to informal non-recognized divorces. Can a spouse, who is trapped in an informal religious marriage, claim the right to divorce and inversely is the State obliged to secure a right to an informal marriage?

There are several complications that need first to be pointed out. Firstly, as religious laws and religious authorities are not recognised and are considered informal. Therefore, claiming a right to an informal religious divorce would amount to claiming a right to a construction that does not exist within the respective legal system. It would require the State to give some form of recognition to the otherwise non-existent construction of a

822 States may also opt to place reservations on provisions they deem irreconcilable with their national laws and values.

religious divorce. At the same time, States retain the discretion to determine which forms of marriages and divorces they recognize and which they do not. States are also not under the obligation to give legal recognition to informal relationships. Secondly, certain religions clearly prescribe that divorce is impossible while others prescribe restrictions for women to initiate and obtain a divorce. Therefore, the right to divorce informally and the right to equality during divorce would have to be reconciled with the religious norms. Thirdly and related to the previous point, religious groups are entitled to regulate their own internal affairs, which includes doctrinal matters, interpretations of religion and enforcement of religious norms and values within the community. This is in fact guaranteed and protected within the collective freedom of religion. The State should respect this right and may only intervene when this is provided by the law, legitimate and necessary. Fourthly, peculiar to secular State is the notion of separation of State and Church, which may materialize in various forms and defines the boundaries of the State *vis-à-vis* religious groups. All these factors taken together have the effect is that secular States have far more limited direct control over the operation of religious groups within their territory, in comparison to non-secular States that incorporate religious laws within their legal system.

Extending the right to divorce to informal religious marriages would entail that the secular State has to ensure that the right to divorce is respected and guaranteed in religious divorce processes and interpretations. The State would also have to reconcile the religious laws and views that deny or prohibit divorce with the right to divorce. Essentially, the secular States would somehow have to ensure that religious communities adopt divorce within their normative system and practices, where they do not. The State would also have to ensure the enforcement of the principle of equality within the religious divorce processes, so that women and men can divorce on equal grounds. This means that, the State would have to impose certain values and views on divorce, that may not always align with the prevailing religious views and convictions on divorce, upon the religious communities. It is then important to contemplate whether imposing the right to divorce within religious communities does not go beyond the competences of the secular State and disregards the human rights provision and domestic laws that protect the freedom of religious communities to regulate their doctrinal and internal affairs.

Notwithstanding the foregoing, there are other ways to encourage and stimulate compliance with human rights and the principle of equality within religious communities and by religious groups without imposing a right to divorce. As has already been established, even secular States, have obligations to address human rights violations and discriminatory practices occurring within the private spheres, which may include religious communities. States have also the obligation to modify cultural and traditional practices that are discriminatory towards women. In other words, it may be too far reaching to impose a right to divorce on religious communities, however States do have to actively encourage and foster cultural changes within the conduct and practices of religious communities to comply with human rights principles. The obligations of the States to protect the trapped spouses' rights and the measures States may adopt for realising these obligations are elaborated further in sections 6.3.2., 7.6.2. and in Chapter 8.

CHAPTER 6
THE TRAPPED SPOUSE'S RIGHTS

As the aforementioned national case law illustrates[823], situations of marital captivity come in many different forms. The severity, legal and/or social impact and lived experiences, thus, are unique to each single case of marital captivity. The acquired social and legal status of 'married' or 'divorcee' are not merely expressions and confirmations of one's legal identity, but they are also social constructions that continuously shape an individual's social identity and status. A limping personal status or having the status of being legally and or religiously married thus affects the way in which individuals navigate through their social environment and interact with their community members. Consequently, the unsettled marital status of a trapped spouse may produce unnecessary restrictions for their effective participation in social and community life and it may impair their personal development. So long as the still existing (religious) marriage has significant legal and/or social significance, it will continue to undermine the trapped spouse(s)' ability and capacity to autonomously shape their lives. The autonomy of a trapped spouse, or rather the lack thereof, is the main and recurring deprivation in all situations of marital captivity.

In the following subchapters, the autonomy and the human rights of trapped spouses are discussed. As the trapped spouses are primarily restricted in their autonomy in respect of shaping their lives, subchapter 6.1. opens with an explanation of the notion of 'personal autonomy'[824] and how it translates into specific human rights provisions. The substantive human rights provisions are then given further attention in subchapter 6.2. In this regard, the right to remarry, the right to respect for private life, the right to freedom of movement and the right to health are analysed, as these are all likely to be affected by a situation of marital captivity. The inclusion of the selected substantive human rights is an imperative step for generating a better understanding of the State's role in addressing situations of marital captivity. The State's obligations inherent within these rights and the extent of these obligations to protect the trapped spouse(s)' rights are outlined in subchapter 6.3. The findings are, then, summarised in subchapter 6.4.

---

823 See the case law described in section 3.4.1. and subsection 4.4.2.2.

824 For pragmatic reasons and to avoid confusion, in the course of this Chapter the terminology 'individual autonomy' and 'personal autonomy' (which are used interchangeably) are adopted instead of 'self-determination', as this latter term, in international law, concerns a collective right of a political nature i.e. the right of people to determine their own political arrangements in a given territory.

6.1. PERSONAL AUTONOMY

Various definitions of autonomy exist both between and within disciplines, whereby their premise and content differ. Providing an exhaustive list of the many different definitions and understandings of autonomy goes beyond the purpose and scope of this contribution. However, the various ways in which autonomy is understood in (legal) philosophy and has developed in human rights law deserves a brief mention.

In general language, 'autonomy' may be defined as the '*freedom from external control or influence; independence*' or '*the right or condition of self-government*'. The term derives from the Greek '*autonomous*' (having its own laws).[825] Similarly, autonomy may also be described as the capacity of being self-legislative, the creator of one's own moral laws i.e. moral autonomy.[826] Autonomy may also be perceived as a neutral individual trait, free from questions of morality and moral obligations i.e. personal autonomy.[827] The underlying suppositions are that individuals are authentic and self-governing, they independently and critically asses and reflect their own laws, preferences, judgments and ends and they act in accordance therewith.[828]

Autonomy is also frequently described as 'the right to be left alone'.[829] In other words, individual autonomy is respected where there are no external interferences and restrictions by others or the State. This conceptualisation of autonomy underscores the interrelatedness of autonomy and freedom in its negative sense.[830] Personal autonomy, thus, requires a degree of freedom which may expand or contract depending on the degree of present interventions and restrictions or the absence thereof.

Personal autonomy, in a broader sense, involves the acknowledgement that being the best experts of their own interests, individuals should be able to make and live according

---

825 *Oxford Dictionary of English* (Third 2010). '*auto-*'(self) and '*-nomos*' (law).

826 This understanding of autonomy flows from what has largely been presented as Kant's concept of 'moral autonomy'. Moral autonomy can be understood as the '*capacity to subject oneself to objective moral principles*' instead of acting '*under influence of desire*'. Jill Marshall, *Personal freedom through human rights law? Autonomy, identity and integrity under the European Convention on Human Rights* (2009) p. 58.; Robert Johnson and Adam Cureton, *Kant's Moral Philosphy,* Stanford Encyclopedia of Philosophy, *at* <https://plato.stanford.edu/cite.html> 17 February 2018.;Mark Piper, *Autonomy: Normative,* Internet Encyclopedia of Philosphy- A peer reviewed academic resource, *at* <www.iep.utm.edu/autonomy/> last accessed 17 February 2018.; Jane Dryden, *Autonomy, at* <www.iep.utm.edu/autonomy/> last accessed 17 February 2018.See also *Oxford Dictionary of English.*

827 Marshall, *Personal freedom through human rights law? Autonomy, identity and integrity under the European Convention on Human Rights*, p. 58.

828 Piper, *Autonomy: Normative.*

829 Jaunius Gumbis, Vytaute Bacianskaite and Jurgita Randakeviciute, 'Do human rights guarantee autonomy?', *Cuadernos constitucionales de la Cátedra Fadrique Furió Ceriol* 77–93, (2008), p. 80.

830 Marshall, *Personal freedom through human rights law? Autonomy, identity and integrity under the European Convention on Human Rights*, pp. 16–17. Freedom can be understood in a negative and positive sense. Negative freedom (i.e. 'freedom from') suggests that one is free when unobstructed by others. A positive understanding of freedom suggests internal liberation and implicates guaranteeing conditions that permits and enables individuals to make their own choices and plan of actions i.e. 'free to'.

to their own laws.[831] Personal autonomy then entitles individuals the freedom '*to make choices and to take actions based on personal values and beliefs*'.[832] This approach to autonomy also acknowledges that there are external[833] and internal[834] conditions that affect the degree of autonomy individuals can exercise. Furthermore, the autonomy of individuals is limited where it obstructs the autonomy of others. Interference to protect third persons is then described, by Gumbis, as a '*normal phenomenon*'.[835]

Autonomy can also be described as '*a capacity that has to be developed- it can flourish through human relationships or lie underdeveloped*'.[836] This approach to autonomy highlights and includes the social context and conditions, in which autonomous individuals operate and it acknowledges that social contexts and conditions can inhibit or foster individual autonomy.[837] Consequently, the dependency of autonomy, social conditions and human relationships with others motivates individuals to respect the autonomy of others as this guarantees a healthy and beneficial environment for all.[838]

In all of these definitions, the reoccurring theme is that individuals are self-governing agents and that they are entitled to freely shape their lives and develop their personalities in accordance with their own rules.[839] The idea that individuals should be guaranteed to be their own person, not only in their actions, decisions and behaviour but also more in general in their being, is thus inherent within the notion of personal autonomy.[840] As a quality that is beneficial to all, personal autonomy is, therefore, worthy of respect and protection. This may not only require non-interference but also requires guaranteeing conditions in which individuals can develop and exercise free and full autonomy.

---

831 Nicole Hassoun,' Human rights, needs, and autonomy', *Kilthub Carnegie Mellon University*, p. 3.; Gumbis, et al., *Do human rights guarantee autonomy?*, p. 79.

832 Id., pp. 79–80. Gumbis includes an additional factor and considers autonomous acts to be only those actions which '*the agent gives preference*' to and which are taken independently and correspond to the individuals' plan of action.

833 Hassoun, *Human rights, needs, and autonomy*, p. 3. The external conditions refer to factors that are unlikely to be controlled by individuals but are nevertheless necessary in order to facilitate the realisation of these interests by the individual, e.g. external freedom, favourable environment and resources.

834 Id. The internal conditions refer to the knowledgeability of the individual of their own interests and control over their bodies, including possessing instrumental reasoning ability to make considerations, judgements and choices etc.

835 Gumbis, et al., *Do human rights guarantee autonomy?*, pp. 80–81.

836 Marshall, *Personal freedom through human rights law? Autonomy, identity and integrity under the European Convention on Human Rights*, p. 65.

837 Id., pp. 60–63, 65–66. Indeed, there is critique to be found to the underlying assumption of 'freely' choosing 'authentic' individuals that is common in many of the definitions of autonomy. It should be borne in mind that social constructions, relationships and interactions shape the 'authentic self' including the actions judgements and commitments individuals undertake and the values and considerations these are founded upon.

838 Id., p. 65.

839 Hassoun, *Human rights, needs, and autonomy*, p. 3.

840 Citation of Chrisman and Anderson in Marshall, *Personal freedom through human rights law? Autonomy, identity and integrity under the European Convention on Human Rights*, p. 58.

6.1.1. THE NOTION OF PERSONAL AUTONOMY IN HUMAN RIGHTS LAW

Substantive human rights have evolved from and are reflective of the values and ideas that dominated a particular age. The first wave of rights[841], in the Enlightenment era, is submitted to have been founded on the values of liberty, autonomy and justice. During that period, the proclamation of freedom and liberty of individuals from unwarranted restriction and interferences by State authorities were popular topics and were widely recognised.[842] Building on this wave, the second wave of rights evolved around the ideas of dignity and equality post the Second World War. Similar to the first wave of rights, the protection of individuals and guaranteeing of their liberty was a central tenet thereof. However, a new aspect was the inclusion of a globalised purpose to protect and guarantee human rights. Human rights were no longer only focused on the relationship between States and their citizens, but were also focused on securing global peace by creating a '*sense of moral purpose for all humankind*'.[843] Finally, the third wave of rights, gaining prominence in the post-Cold War era, is distinct from the previous waves due to its emphasis on the protection of human rights in a greater and complex internationalised society. Participation in the protection of human rights is extending to a growing number of agents, including private entities such as corporations and private individuals.[844] Thus, responsibility, dignity, equality, liberty, justice and autonomy are among the core concepts and values that form the foundation of the human rights system.[845]

Although personal autonomy is submitted to be among the values protected by and underlying human rights law[846], the notion is not mentioned in any human rights law documents that are investigated in this contribution. The existing literature on this subject matter tends to perceive personal autonomy either as a principle of human rights law (as a value protected by substantive human rights provisions) or as a human right in itself. The Convention on the Rights of Persons with Disabilities (CRPD) is the only

---

841 Francesca Klug, 'The Human Rights Act – a "third way" or "third wave" Bill of Rights', *European Human Rights Law Review* 361–372, (2001), p. 363. Klung proposes the term 'wave', rather than the traditional terminology 'generations of human rights' as this does justice to '*capture the dynamism involved in change*' and the evolution of human rights norms. First generation rights involve civil and political rights, second generation rights involve positive social and economic rights and third generation rights include collective and environmental rights.

842 Id., pp. 363–364.

843 Id., p. 364.

844 Id., p. 369.

845 See also Marshall, *Personal freedom through human rights law? Autonomy, identity and integrity under the European Convention on Human Rights*, p. 4.; Gumbis, et al., *Do human rights guarantee autonomy?*, p. 93.

846 Hassoun, *Human rights, needs, and autonomy*, p. 2.; Gumbis, et al., *Do human rights guarantee autonomy?*, p. 82.; N R. Koffeman, *(The right to) personal autonomy in the case law of the European Court of Human Rights*, (Leiden University, Leiden 2010), pp. 6–8. See also ECtHR case law: European Court of Human Rights, *Evans v. the United Kingdom* 10 April 2007, Application No. 6339/05, para. 57.; European Court of Human Rights, *Pretty v. the United Kingdom*, 29 July 2002, Application No. 2346/02, para. 61.

instrument that refers to the principle of individual autonomy as a guiding principle. Article 3 thereof contains eight guiding principles among which is the '*respect for inherent dignity, individual autonomy including the freedom to make one's own choices, and independence of persons*'.[847] The principle of autonomy is then recognised to be grounded in both civil and political rights (e.g. the right to privacy and freedom of thought) as well as socio-economic rights (e.g. the right to accessibility and support services).[848]

Another approach views autonomy as an expression of dignity as well as a component of liberty/freedom, in that individuals should exercise their autonomy free from State interference.[849] Individual autonomy is then considered to be a much narrower principle or even a right that derives from the broader notions of human dignity and freedom.[850] At times, personal autonomy is also equated to the notion of dignity.[851] As an aspect of human dignity and freedom, personal autonomy is thus an implicit concept within both the ICCPR and ICESCR.[852] Within the ICCPR and ICESCR, human freedom and dignity are described as foundations and guiding principles of substantive human rights. Similarly, the ECtHR has acknowledged that personal autonomy is '*an important principle underlying the interpretation of the Convention guarantees*'.[853] As a principle, autonomy may then be defined as the '*ability to conduct life in a manner of one's own choosing*', which may include actions that are dangerous and harmful to oneself.[854]

---

847 The others are: non-discrimination, full and effective participation and inclusion in society, respect for difference and acceptance of persons with disabilities as part of human diversity and humanity, equality of opportunity, accessibility, equality between men and women and respect for the evolving capacities of children with disabilities and respect for the right of children with disabilities to preserve their identities. UN General Assembly, *Convention on the Rights of Persons with Disabilities*, 24 January 2007, Article 3.

848 Valentina D. Fina, 'Article 3 [General Principle]', in Fian, et al. *The United Nations Convention on the Rights of Persons with Disabilities: A commentary*, (Springer International Publishing, 2017), p. 124.

849 Koffeman, *(The right to) personal autonomy in the case law of the European Court of Human Rights*, p. 5.; Norman Dorsen, András Sajó and Susanne Baer, *Comparative constitutionalism: cases and materials* (St. Paul, Minnesota, 2010), p. 536.; citation of Andrew Clapham in Christopher McCrudden, 'Human dignity and judicial interpretation of human rights', 19 *The European Journal of International Law* 655–724, (2008), p. 686.

850 Koffeman, *(The right to) personal autonomy in the case law of the European Court of Human Rights*, p. 7.; Mirko Bagaric and James Allan, 'The Vacuous Concept of Dignity', 5 *Journal of Human Rights* 257–270, (2006), p. 264.; Gumbis, et al.; *Do human rights guarantee autonomy?*, p. 88.

851 For example, Koffeman concludes to an understanding that equates autonomy or even submerges autonomy within human dignity and human freedom. He submits that '*perhaps the finding that personal autonomy is a principle underlying the interpretation of the Convention guarantees, in effect boils down to the finding that the very essence of the Convention is respect for human dignity and human freedom*'. Koffeman, *(The right to) personal autonomy in the case law of the European Court of Human Rights*, p. 7. See also Marshall, *Personal freedom through human rights law? Autonomy, identity and integrity under the European Convention on Human Rights*, p. 27.

852 International Covenant on Civil and Political Rights, preamble.; International Covenant on Economic, Social and Cultural Rights, 3, preamble.; S. Peers, T. Hervey, J. Kenner and A. Ward, *The EU Charter of Fundamental Rights: A commentary* (2014), paras. 01.06, 01.33.

853 European Court of Human Rights, *Jehovah's witnesses of Moscow and Others v. Russia*, 10 June 2016, Application No. 302/02, para. 135.

854 European Court of Human Rights, *Pretty v. the United Kingdom*, 29 July 2002, Application No. 2346/02, paras. 61–62.; Koffeman, *(The right to) personal autonomy in the case law of the European Court of Human Rights*, p. 16.

However, it should be noted that personal autonomy is not a limitless individual entitlement. Particularly where the acts are physically and/or morally harmful and dangerous to others or the environment, a balance between personal autonomy and public health, safety and rights of others has to be struck.[855]

At times, the ECtHR has also referred to personal autonomy as a right that is contained in Article 8 ECHR on the right to respect for private and family life.[856] However, in this regard it should also be noted that the ECtHR's decisions on this point have not been consistent. The ECtHR has, in various cases, resorted to using different terminology. In the context of Article 8 ECHR, 'personal autonomy' has been addressed both as a 'notion'[857], a 'principle'[858] and as a 'right'.[859] It has been discussed extensively in the context of the right to respect for private life and is considered as an aspect of the right to social and physical identity.[860] However, other than the rather broad definition of '*the ability to conduct life in a manner of one's own choosing*', the decisions of the ECtHR have not specified the contents of a right to individual autonomy. Koffeman, therefore, suggests that the unclear content, in combination with the small number of cases in which the court has asserted 'a right to individual autonomy', leads to the conclusion that the notion of individual autonomy has not yet evolved into a right and should instead be regarded as an underlying principle.[861]

The notion of autonomy is reflected and is protected in substantive human rights law. It has been discussed in relation to, among others, the right to develop one's personality, the right to actively participate in the political process, the right to privacy, the right to integrity, the right to be included in community life, the right to liberty, the right to legal recognition of gender assignment, the right to respect for one's sexual orientation and activities, the right to respect for the decision to become a genetic parent or not, the right to conceive a child, the prohibition of slavery, the freedom to travel, the freedom of religion and the freedom of association and assembly.[862] On the basis of this principle, the ECtHR has developed and extended existing human rights norms to assert the existence of some implied rights. For example, by invoking the notion of personal

---

855 Koffeman, *(The right to) personal autonomy in the case law of the European Court of Human Rights*, pp. 20, 25–27.

856 European Court of Human Rights, *Evans v. the United Kingdom* 10 April 2007, Application No. 6339/05.

857 European Court of Human Rights, *Pretty v. the United Kingdom,* 29 July 2002, Application No. 2346/02.

858 Id.

859 European Court of Human Rights, *Evans v. the United Kingdom* 10 April 2007, Application No. 6339/05.; European Court of Human Rights, *Kalacheva v. Russia,* 07 May 2009, Application No. 3451/05.

860 Koffeman, *(The right to) personal autonomy in the case law of the European Court of Human Rights*, p. 57.

861 Id., pp. 8, 10.

862 Fina, *Article 3 [General Principle]*, pp. 123–124.; European Court of Human Rights, *Sorensen and Rasmussen v. Denmark,* 11 January 2006, Application Nos. 52562/99, 52620/99, para. 54.; Koffeman, *(The right to) personal autonomy in the case law of the European Court of Human Rights*, pp. 57–58, 62–64.

autonomy, the ECtHR recognised that the right to private life, includes the right to form relationships with others. The latter right is, however, not explicitly mentioned in the article on the right to private life. Subsection 6.2.2.2. elaborates further on the evolution and contents of the right to establish relationships with others.[863]

Therefore, substantive human rights norms not only promote and protect, among others, the values of autonomy, dignity and freedom, but they are also founded on and ought to be constructed to reflect these values.[864] The construction and interpretation of substantive human rights, thus, should be conducted in a manner that promotes personal autonomy. Additionally, personal autonomy is a prerequisite for the effective exercise and enjoyment of all fundamental human rights and freedoms. The denial or obstruction of personal autonomy consequently results in the deprivation and restriction of substantive human rights.[865]

6.1.2. THE TRAPPED SPOUSE'S PERSONAL AUTONOMY

A situation of marital captivity inhibits the personal autonomy of the trapped spouse to shape and give full meaning to her/his life. This is reflected in the social and legal inhibitions and hurdles that trapped spouses, whom mostly are women, may encounter. An existing situation of marital captivity creates barriers for a trapped woman when she seeks to establish new intimate relationships and subsequently remarry or when she seeks to travel to her country of origin. A situation of marital captivity, therefore, infringes upon a fundamental principle of human rights law and violates the very essence of the values that are sought to be protected by the human rights regime. For a long time, however, marital captivity has been considered as a religious and private matter which should be solved within the religious and family sphere. Consequently, the deprivation and violation of a trapped spouse's autonomy and rights have and continue to pass largely unchallenged. It is, therefore, imperative that marital captivity is conceived and recognised as a human rights issue which requires the State's attention, and to recognise that it is more than merely a religious or spousal issue.

6.2. THE TRAPPED SPOUSE'S HUMAN RIGHTS

The previous subchapter identifies the fundamental problem that is at the heart of situations of marital captivity. Marital captivity encroaches upon and deprives the

863 See also Fina, *Article 3 [General Principle]*, pp. 123–124.

864 Koffeman, *(The right to) personal autonomy in the case law of the European Court of Human Rights*, p. 5.; Peers, et al., *The EU Charter of Fundamental Rights: A commentary*, paras. 01.06, 01.33.; Marshall, *Personal freedom through human rights law? Autonomy, identity and integrity under the European Convention on Human Rights*, p. 27.

865 Gumbis, et al., *Do human rights guarantee autonomy?*, pp. 81–82.

trapped spouses from their autonomy to shape and dictate their lives, future and identities as they deem fit. Some of the areas in which they are limited are illustrated in the earlier discussed national cases.[866] They are, among others, restricted in obtaining a divorce, establishing new relationships with new partners, remarrying, maintaining family life, participating within their social environment and religious community and travelling. Often violence may also be involved which affects their physical and mental well-being. Financial extortion and exploitations by a non-cooperative spouse may also negatively affect the trapped spouse financial situation. A situation of marital captivity, thus, affects multiple substantive human rights which are at the risk of being perpetually impaired where solutions remain limited or inaccessible. The following sections of this Chapter outline more in detail some of the rights that are most likely to be impaired by a situation of marital captivity. These are the right to remarry, the right to respect for private life, the freedom of movement and the right to health. Each of the selected rights protects a broad range of aspects. However, the focus shall primarily be placed on those aspects that are relevant for situations of marital captivity. The right to freedom from violence against women is addressed in Chapter 7.

6.2.1. THE RIGHT TO REMARRY

'Anneke married civilly as well as religiously. Her husband was violent and mentally ill. After being persuaded by her children, she sought help and decided to end the marriage by a civil divorce. Anneke was left disappointed by the reaction from the church: "I had no support, not from anyone. They left me hanging". She and her children were confronted with negative reactions, for example when she as a divorced woman wanted to participate in the communion ceremony. After she had met a new partner and wanted to marry him, she cut ties with the church because – "when people tell me 'God does not allow you to remarry, then they are using God to frustrate your life…in essence you are being ostracized'.[867]

A situation of marital captivity has shown, at times, to impair trapped spouses who want or intend to remarry. To begin with, the trapped spouse(s) may be prevented from remarrying due to the still existing formal marriage. The termination of a formal religious marriage may be hindered by religious laws and practices that prohibit divorce or that prescribe unequal rights to divorce between women and men. Consequently, and particularly in those States that uphold the principle of monogamy, spouses that are trapped in a formal marriage cannot entertain a new marriage. However, it should be kept in mind that some legal systems condone polygamy or reserve the possibility of bigamy for men. This creates further inequality between women and men in respect of the right to marry. This inequality also reinforces the likelihood of more women becoming trapped in a marriage than men. Basically, it enables a recalcitrant husband

[866] See the case law described in section 3.4.1. and subsection 4.4.2.2.

[867] Van Eijk, Wel gescheiden, niet gescheiden? Een empirisch onderzoek naar huwelijkse gevangenschap in Nederland, p. 27. (translation from Dutch to English by Benedicta Deogratias).

to hold the first wife hostage in the marriage and simultaneously to circumvent the consequences of marital captivity, as he is able to remarry and move on with his life.

Furthermore, a situation of marital captivity to a formal civil marriage may also arise due to national laws that enable opposing spouses to veto a divorce and thereby force the other spouse to remain married. This was the case in the earlier discussed cases of *Johnston, Ivanov and Petrova, Piotrowski and Babiarz.*[868] Admittedly, in these cases marital captivity was caused by the application of civil laws on marriage and divorce, which either prevented or restricted the ability of the spouse at fault to obtain a divorce by making it conditional on the innocent spouse's consent. The factors that barred obtaining a legal divorce were thus not necessarily founded in religious laws, doctrines and interpretations. Nevertheless, the inability to dissolve the legal marriage barred the trapped husbands as well as their intended spouse from their right to (re)marry.

A situation of marital captivity may also impair spouses from remarrying religiously, particularly where the religious marriage continues to exist and has social and religious significance within the religious community. The celebration of the new marriage in accordance with religious rites may be impossible for as long as the first marriage still exists. In Catholicism, for example, individuals cannot remarry a second partner without annulling or dissolving the first marriage.[869] Similarly, in Judaism and Islam women may only be married to one man at a time. Spouses may then be considered as still married or be expected to maintain the marital life, irrespective of whether they are civilly divorced. Consequently, remarrying religiously may be impossible and even prohibited.

Furthermore, as the case of Anneke and Maryam[870] illustrates, even if there has been a legal divorce, the religious community may continue to expect the divorcees to maintain the marital life or to abide by the religious views that do not allow divorcees to remarry.[871] A new marriage, either civilly and/or religiously, will not only be frowned upon but it may be considered as an act of adultery or a transgression of the religious norms and views on marriage and divorce. Consequently, the religious, social and/or moral ties created by the existing religious marriage may form considerable constraints on the trapped spouse's ability to remarry religiously. It may also discourage them from remarrying civilly.

6.2.1.1. *The right to remarry subsequent to a divorce*

It is important here to first provide clarification of the terms 'remarry' and 'the right to remarry' as is used in this contribution. The term 'remarry' is synonymous to the term

---

868 These cases were discussed in subsection 5.2.1.2.

869 *Catechism of the Catholic Church*, sec. 1645, 1664.

870 For the case of Maryam see Chapter 2.

871 Different Christian denominations hold different views on the subject of remarrying after a divorce. Remarriage, subsequent to divorce is allowed in some denominations, while in others it may be allowed only in restricted circumstances or not allowed at all. William A Heth, 'Jesus on divorce: how my mind has changed', 6 *The Southern Baptist Journal of Theology* 4–29, (2002).

'marry'. Both acts of marrying and remarrying involve the same act, that is subject to the conditions and formalities set by national legislation, and if valid results in changing the personal status of the involved individuals(married/unmarried). The terms 'remarry' and 'right to remarry', are used here for the sole purpose of accurately describing situations in which the involved individuals are still (forced) to stay married with the first partner but wish or intend to marry another partner. The right to remarry and the right to marry are thus not two distinct rights. The conditions prescribed within the provisions on the right to marry apply equally where individuals remarry, subsequent to a divorce. For the legal framework on the right to marry, reference is made to subchapter 5.1.

The right to remarry subsequent to the dissolution or termination of a marriage has been found to be implied within the provisions in article 12 ECHR which concerns the right to marriage by ECtHR. In the case *of F. v. Switzerland,* the ECtHR found that Article 12 ECHR '*secures for divorced persons the right to remarry without unreasonable restrictions on part of the state*'.[872] Thus, Article 12 ECHR affords all individuals a right to marry, and to all divorcees a right to remarry. The UN human rights monitoring bodies have not been as explicit on a right to remarry following a divorce. However, within the context of marriage and divorce, States have been encouraged to enable divorced women to remarry.[873] In addition, UN human rights monitoring bodies have occasionally, expressed concerns where State legislation impose discriminatory restrictions on women to remarry.[874] Divorced women may not be subjected to restrictions that divorced men do not face. Under Articles 12 ECHR and 16 CEDAW divorcees are, thus, entitled to remarry subsequent to a divorce.

In brief, the right to marry entitles individuals to freely and fully decide if and with whom they wish to marry.[875] Free and full consent is a constituent element of the right to marry and is reflective of individual's autonomy. Although the right to marry may be subjected to conditions and restrictions under national law (e.g. material and formal conditions), such conditions should not render the right ineffective and inaccessible. For example, laws that impose a longer waiting period on women before they can remarry have been found to be incompatible with the human rights obligations to ensure equality of women and men in marital life.[876] States that adopt such restrictions have been directed to review and amend such laws. Any unreasonable restrictions that

872 European Court of Human Rights, *F. v. Switzerland,* 18 December 1987, Application No. 11329/85, para. 33.

873 Committee on the Elimination of Discrimination Against Women, *Concluding Observations Chile 1999,* A/54/38/Rev.1 part II (1999) 64, para. 222.; Human Rights Committee, *Concluding Observations Japan 1998,* CCPR/C/79/Add.102, para 16.; Human Rights Committee, *Concluding Observations Mexico 1999,* CCPR/C/79/Add.109, para. 18.

874 *Supra* notes 802, 803.

875 Universal Declaration of Human Rights, Article 16 (2).; International Covenant on Civil and Political Rights Article 23(3).; International Covenant on Economic, Social and Cultural Rights, Article 10 (1).; Convention on the Elimination of all forms of Discrimination Against Women, Article 16 (1).

876 *Supra* note 802.

impair the very essence of the right to remarry for divorcees are, therefore, should be eliminated.[877] Furthermore, the right to remarry should be guaranteed on the basis of the principle of equality. Women and men must be able to remarry on the same basis as each other. Any unjustified differentiation in the exercise of this right between women and men is incompatible with the principle of equality.[878]

Notably, in some countries it follows that men are allowed to marry multiple women at the same time (polygamous marriages). Human rights monitoring bodies have taken a firm stance on this subject matter. Polygamous marriages have been found to be incompatible with human rights law. Polygamy not only maintains and reinforces inequality between women and men, but it is also a harmful practice that negatively affects women's rights.[879] Therefore, polygamy should be prohibited and the practice thereof should be brought to an end. Similarly, domestic laws that require a male guardian to give consent to the marriage, that prohibit women from marrying men that adhere to other religions or that enable rapists to evade criminal responsibility by marrying their victims have been found to also undermine the woman's right to marry. Such laws and practices should be abolished and eradicated in order to better secure the right to marry and to guarantee equality within the marriage.[880]

In order to fully assess the human rights that are at stake in a situation of marital captivity, it is imperative to establish whether the right to remarry guarantees individuals a right to remarry civilly, as well as religiously. After all, a situation of marital captivity may prevent trapped spouses from marrying civilly, as well as religiously. More specifically, does the right to remarry extend to formal State recognised marriages i.e. civil or religious), as well as to informal religious marriages? If so what, implication does this have for the States that do not recognise or acknowledge religious marriages?

6.2.1.2. *Religious, formal and informal marriages*

The CEDAW Committee has adopted a broad interpretation of the notion of marriage within the context of Article 16 CEDAW. This includes civil marriages, religious marriages, customary marriages, unregistered marriages, polygamous marriages[881] and

---

877 Freeman *Article 16*, p. 422; Committee on Economic, Social and Cultural Rights, *Concluding Observations Israel 2003*, E/2004/22, para. 266; ECHR European Court of Human Rights, *F. v. Switzerland*, 18 December 1987, Application No. 11329/85, paras. 32, 38, 40.; Committee on Economic, Social and Cultural Rights, *Concluding Observations Israel 2003*, E/C.12/1/Add.90, para. 23.; Freeman *Article 16*, p. 422.

878 Id.

879 CEDAW, *General Recommendation No. 21 on Equality in marriage and family relations*, paras. 14, 49.; CEDAW, *General Recommendation on article 16 of the Convention on the Elimination of All Forms of Discrimination against Women (Economic consequences of marriage, family relations and their dissolution)*, para. 28.

880 Id., paras. 23–26.

881 Although these are condemned, and States are recommended to eliminate these. UN Committee on the Elimination of Discrimination Against Women 'General Recommendation on article 16 of the Convention on the Elimination of All Forms of Discrimination against Women (Economic

de facto unions.[882] All of these forms of unions will not be recognised and sanctioned in each State. States have the discretion to determine how to classify the different types of unions between partners. In certain States, customary and religious marriages are considered to be legal marriages (i.e. formal marriages[883], while in others they are not recognised and have no legal status (i.e. informal marriage)).[884] Similarly, in many States polygamous marriages are prohibited, while in others polygamous marriages are allowed and are recognised as formal marriages.

Irrespective of the various forms of relationships that exist, the CEDAW Committee has recommended that States protect women's rights and promote the principle of equality in the various types of relationships, including unconventional relationships or relationships that may not have legal recognition or effect, such as *de facto* unions.[885] States ought to protect the rights of women in such relationships and ensure that women are not left vulnerable to religious laws which may put them at a disadvantage in family and property affairs.[886] States should recognise consensual unions as a source of rights.[887] However, States are not obliged to recognise *de facto* unions as formal marriages or to treat them as such.[888] Additionally, the CEDAW Committee has recommended that States register '*all marriages whether contracted civilly or according to custom or religious law*' for the purposes of ensuring the protection of spouses in accordance with human rights standards. The CEDAW Committee does not explicitly stress that such marriages be legally recognised, but it only seems to consider registration as a means that would facilitate the State to comply with its obligations to ensure equality between the spouses, control the marriageable age, counter polygamous marriages and to protect the rights of any involved children.[889]

More specifically on the subject of religious marriages, States may not prevent or prohibit individuals from celebrating the marriage in accordance with their religion or belief (negative obligation), as this is likely to amount to discrimination against religious individuals.[890] As an expression of one's religion, individuals may thus lend a

consequences of marriage, family relations and their dissolution) ', 2013, CEDAW/C/GC/29, paras. 26, 28, 31.; CEDAW, *General Recommendation No. 21 on Equality in marriage and family relations*, paras. 24, 39.

882 CEDAW, *General Recommendation on article 16 of the Convention on the Elimination of All Forms of Discrimination against Women (Economic consequences of marriage, family relations and their dissolution)*, paras. 19–31.

883 For example, Iran, Israel, Pakistan, Saudi-Arabia, South-Africa.

884 For example, Belgium, France, the Netherlands.

885 Freeman *Article 16*, pp. 418–419.

886 Id., p. 418.

887 Id., pp. 418–419.

888 European Court of Human Rights, *Savez crkava "Riječ života" and Others v. Croatia*, 09 December 2010, Application No. 7798/08, para. 56.; Freeman *Article 16*, pp. 418–419. See also section 5.2.2 at *supra* note 773.

889 CEDAW, *General Recommendation No. 19 on Violence against women*, para. 6.

890 Krishnaswami, *Study of discrimination in the matter of religious rights and practices*, p. 37.

right to marry in accordance with the religious customs and rites. As aforementioned, however, States are not obliged to give legal recognition to such a marriage or to give it the same status as a formal marriage. Informal religious marriages may, however, be considered as *de facto* unions.[891] Where this is the case, the implications are then that the State has an obligation to protect the rights of women whom have solely engaged in an informal religious marriage. Notably, while the Committee has not yet made a clear distinction between formal and informal marriages in the context of the right to (re) marry, the ECtHR had the opportunity to deal with an informal religious marriage in the cases of *Khan v. the United Kingdom*[892] and *X. v. Federal Republic of Germany*.[893]

The case of *X. v. Federal Republic of Germany* concerned an applicant who conducted a special ritual of marriage (i.e. an informal marriage). He requested for this marriage to be recognised by the registrar. Recognition was denied as the applicant had not conducted the marriage formally, in accordance with the national laws applicable in Germany. Before the ECmHR, the applicant alleged a violation of his rights under Article 9 ECHR as consequence of the State authority's refusal to recognise the informal marriage. In the Commission's view, marriage could not be '*considered simply as a form of expression of thought, conscience or religion but is governed by the specific provision of Article 12 which refers to the national laws governing the exercise of the right to remarry*'. As the spouse had not been prevented from marrying but was merely required to conduct the marriage in accordance with national law, the ECmHR did not find a violation of Article 12 ECHR and Article 9 ECHR.[894]

The case of *Khan v. the United Kingdom* involved an applicant who had conducted an Islamic marriage ceremony in the United Kingdom with a young girl of 14.5 years. He was prosecuted for the offences of abduction of and sexual intercourse with the minor child and was subsequently sentenced to imprisonment. Before the ECmHR, the applicant argued that his imprisonment had violated his right to manifest his religion, through the Islamic marriage (Article 9 ECHR) as well as the right to consummate his marriage (Article 12 ECHR). The fact that the case concerned an informal non-registered marriage was not raised nor was it considered to be an issue. Again, the Commission found that Article 12 ECHR was engaged.[895] By blurring formal and informal marriages, the Commission concluded that the internal domestic law set the minimum marriageable age at 16 years. Therefore, the Islamic marriage was invalid. A violation of Articles 12 and 9 ECHR was not established.

891 Freeman *Article 16*, pp. 418–419.
892 European Court of Human Rights, *Khan v. the United Kingdom*, 17 July 1986, Application No. 1579/85.
893 European Court of Human Rights, X. *V. Federal Republic of Germany*, 18 December 1974, Application No. 6167/73.
894 Id., p. 65.
895 European Court of Human Rights, *Khan v. the United Kingdom*, 17 July 1986, Application No. 1579/85, p. 255.

In both cases, the Commission seems to have implied that Article 12 ECHR guarantees individuals a right to conduct a valid marriage in accordance with the applicable domestic laws. By conditioning the validity and existence of informal marriages to national domestic law, the reasoning thus seems to be as follows: informal marriages that do not satisfy the material and formal conditions of domestic family laws are invalid and therefore do not fall within the scope of Article 12 ECHR. In other words, entirely informal marriages are unlikely to fall within the scope of Article 12 ECHR.[896] Individuals, it seems, cannot lend a right to conduct a marriage in ways that are not recognised or officiated by the State. Nor do they have a right to have such a marriage recognised as a valid form of marriage.

From the foregoing, several observations can be drawn. To begin with, the right to remarry extends to all forms of relationships that are recognised by the State as constituting a marriage. Where the State sanctions religious or customary marriages, individuals may not be denied the right to conduct a legal and formal marriage by way of a customary or religious marriage.[897] Where they do, the concerned State may not deny recognising this marriage unless there are objective and reasonable justifications to do so (e.g. where the spouses have not fulfilled the material or formal conditions). Regarding countries that allow and recognise polygamous marriages, human rights monitoring bodies have urged States to prohibit and discontinue these practices.

Furthermore, States may not prevent nor prohibit individuals from marrying in accordance with their religion or from conducting religious ceremonies to celebrate the marriage. The right to freedom of religion allows individuals to marry in accordance with religious practices. Notwithstanding, whether the provisions on marriage cover informal religious marriages in particular is a matter that has not been confirmed. While individuals may always engage in informal marriages, neither the UN monitoring bodies nor the ECtHR has explicitly granted individuals a right a right to remarry informally in accordance with one's religion. Rather, the ECtHR's case law suggests that Article 12 ECHR does not regulate the religious dimension of marriage and cannot be extended to informal religious marriages. Article 12 ECHR is therefore limited to formal marriages. Individuals cannot derive a right to informally remarry from Article 12 ECHR.

Even if a right to marry informally according to one's religion can be argued, it is important to assess and consider the implications of such a right in relation to the corresponding State obligations, particularly for secular States. There are several fundamental issues that need to be considered in this regard. Similar to the discussion

896 See also Jurisconsult, *Guide to article 9 – Freedom of thought, conscience and religion*, (2015), para. 82.

897 See also European Court of Human Rights, *Savez crkava "Riječ života" and Others v. Croatia*, 09 December 2010, Application No. 7798/08. This case contained a discriminatory content in that Croatia recognised religious marriages of certain religions and refused the recognition of religious marriages of other religions. The ECtHR found this to form discrimination against those religious groups and individuals whose marriages were denied recognition.

concerning the existence a right to a religious divorce, elaborated in section 5.2.1., the proposition of a right to marry informally would imply that the State would have to ensure that individuals can remarry informally. Essentially, this would require the State to guarantee that individuals can entertain a construction (i.e. the religious marriage) that does not exist within its legal system. This is an unsettling proposition in terms of the enforceability of such a right, particularly when religious laws and authorities prohibit or restrict individuals from remarrying. Related hereto is the fact that the State does not regulate the process or conditions for a valid religious marriage. This is a matter for the religious leaders, authorities and groups to interpret, apply and enforce within the given religious community. Evidently, this leads back to the question as to whether and how far the State can and should interfere in the marital affairs of religious communities. Would this amount to an interference with doctrinal matters and the autonomy that religious communities have to regulate their internal affairs? How is the State to guarantee that spouses can remarry religiously when the very same religion prescribes or restricts their possibilities to remarry? Is this a reasonable and realisable obligation for the State? These are questions that are not easily answered but demand thorough consideration if a right to marry informally is to be considered as implied within the Articles 12 ECHR and 16 CEDAW.

6.2.1.3. The right to remarry for trapped spouses

As previously established, the right to remarry concerns the right to formally remarry in accordance with the laws of the State. Thus, a situation of marital captivity that impairs the ability of the spouse or spouses to formally marry impairs their right to remarry. Furthermore, women and men should enjoy and be able to exercise this right on an equal basis as each other. State laws and practices that bar or restrict trapped women from remarrying, as well as the practices of polygamy are incompatible with this right and should be eliminated and prohibited.

Where it concerns informal religious marriages, however, the right to remarry does not seem to cover these types of marriages. The case law of the ECtHR on this matter seems to indicate that Article 12 ECHR cannot be extended to cover informal religious marriages and that it does not contain a right to marry informally.[898] It is unlikely that the provisions on marriage contain a right to marry informally in accordance with one's religion, and that it contains obligations on States to ensure this right is upheld irrespective of the religious laws on the ability of divorcees to remarry. Additionally, while States may not prohibit or prevent the establishment of a religious marriage, States are not obliged to recognise religious marriages or any other type of formed relationships that have no legal status within the given State.

[898] European Court of Human Rights, *Khan v. the United Kingdom*, 17 July 1986, Application No. 1579/85.

6.2.2. THE RIGHT TO PRIVATE LIFE

As already established, personal autonomy manifests itself in various substantive human rights, including the right to private life. In broad terms, the right to private life or the right to privacy guarantees that individuals can be themselves and can freely undertake any decisions concerning their private and social lives. Besides the perceived inability to remarry, trapped spouses may experience difficulties participating in social life as single or divorcees, and they may experience restrictions in autonomously shaping their lives and establishing intimate relationships with others.[899]

Furthermore, by not cooperating to the dissolution of the religious marriage, the recalcitrant spouses in essence exercises and retains a degree of control over the trapped spouses' social and private lives. The spouses' social environment may reinforce the experienced lack of control. Particularly where there is a strong social pressure to control the conduct and behaviour of married, divorcing or divorced women, trapped wives may experience far more restrictions when it comes to moving on with their lives, shaping their futures and establishing new partnerships. In other words, the trapped wife's autonomy to freely take decisions concerning her private and social life is inhibited by the continuation of a situation of marital captivity. The following subsections, therefore, study the right to private life in order to identify which specific rights are impaired by a situation of marital captivity.

6.2.2.1. *The legal framework*

The ICCPR regulates the right to respect for private life in Articles 17 thereof, which reads:

> *'1. No one shall be subjected to arbitrary or unlawful inference with his privacy, family, home or correspondences, nor to unlawful attacks on his honour and reputation.*
> *2. Everyone has the right to the protection of the law against such interference or attacks.'*

The wording of this article is almost identical to the wording of Article 12 UDHR:

> *'1. No one shall be subjected to arbitrary interference with his privacy, family, home or correspondence, nor to attacks upon his honour and reputation. Everyone has the right to the protection of the law against such interference or attacks.'*

The ICESCR does not contain a provision on the right to privacy. Article 10 ICESCR is only concerned with marriage and it also extends to cover the family unit. A similar provision is also lacking in the CEDAW, which has a different aim than reintroducing the already established human rights that are contained in the International Bill of Rights. Rather than being a stand-alone treaty, the CEDAW complements the UN's

899 See subsection 1.3.2.1.

human rights system, in that its aim and purpose is to assert the equality of women and men and eliminate discrimination against women in all spheres. Thus, the CEDAW does not contain a specific provision on the right to private life. However, the previously discussed Article 16 CEDAW does oblige States to '*eliminate discrimination against women in all matters relating to marriage and family*'. While the primary focus in this subsection is on the trapped spouse's private life, it is important to bear in mind that a situation of marital captivity may also affect the family life, particularly where children are involved.

Turning to the ECHR, the provision on private life is found in Article 8 thereof which states:

> '*1. Everyone has the right to respect for his private and family life, his correspondence and his home.*
> *2. There shall be no interference by a public authority with the exercise of this right except such as is in accordance with the law and is necessary in a democratic society in the interests of national security, public safety or the economic well-being of the country, for the prevention of disorder or crime, for the protection of health or morals, or for the protection of the rights and freedoms of others.*'

Article 11 of the American Convention on Human Rights guarantees the right '*to have his honour respected and dignity recognized*'. It also prohibits arbitrary interference with the right to privacy and stipulates that everyone has the right to protection of the law against attacks or interferences of their honour and reputation. The ACHPR does not, explicitly, set out the right to privacy in Article 18. However, Article 18 ACHPR attaches particular importance to the State's duty to protect the family.

6.2.2.1.1. 'Privacy' and 'private life'

Where the ECHR refers to 'private life', the UDHR and ICCPR both opt for the use of the term 'privacy'. The different use in terminology may raise questions as to whether the range of protection afforded differs and whether the right to privacy and the right to respect for private life are synonymous and interchangeable concepts. In reality, the spheres protected by the ICCPR and UDHR are not that different from those that are protected by Article 8 ECHR. Similarly, the ECmHR acknowledged in the case of *X. v. Iceland*, that '*for numerous Anglos Saxon and French authors the right for 'private life' is the right to privacy, the right to live as far as one wishes protected from publicity*'. Thus, the difference in the terminology used does not indicate that Article 17 ICCPR and Article 8 ECHR are two distinct rights.[900]

---

900 Schabas, *The European Convention on Human Rights: A commentary*, p. 369. Schabas provides that the difference in terminology is related '*to the important role of the French language in the drafting of the European Convention, 'private life' being a somewhat awkward rendering of 'vie privée'*'.

6.2.2.1.2. The physical and social dimensions

The right to respect for private life protects two dimensions which are essential for the free and full development of individuals. Firstly privacy, in its classical sense as a negative freedom, is a right that is held against others and it may be defined as the *'inviolability of the home and personal communications [...]; a private space, within which people can both be themselves and communicate privately with one another'*.[901] In this form, privacy is associated with securing that individuals are protected against unwarranted and unauthorised intrusions in their most private sphere.[902] It also ensures that individuals have access and control over their personal information and that they should enjoy a sphere in which they can seclude themselves from public scrutiny and opinion.[903] This focus on personal information and a zone of seclusion is the outcome of how 'the right to privacy' developed.[904]

Secondly, the right to privacy also extends to include the social context and it aims to guarantee individual development and autonomy.[905] Nowak describes this as a right *'of individual existence and autonomy in which human beings strive to achieve self-realisation by way of actions that do not interfere with the liberty of others'*.[906] In the same light Article 8 ECHR, alongside protecting a zone of seclusion and secrecy, also guarantees that individuals should be able to develop themselves and maintain relationships with others. Both the HRC and ECHR institutions have interpreted the right to privacy (right to respect of private life) to guarantee, among others, a sphere

---

901 Dorsen, et al., *Comparative constitutionalism: cases and materials*, p. 533.
Joseph describes this as a zone *'where one may withdraw from others to 'shape one's life according to one's own (egocentric) wishes and expectations.* Joseph, et al., *The International Covenant on Civil and Political Rights- Cases, materials and commentary*, p. 477.

902 Dorsen, et al., *Comparative constitutionalism: cases and materials*, p. 532.

903 Id.

904 Initially, privacy related conflicts were frequently treated as breaches of contract or trust or as breaches of property rights. For example, the unauthorised use of one's correspondence may have been considered as a matter involving stolen property, in that the author has property rights in her/his written words or the recipient had become the rightful owner. However, technological advancements in photography, filmography, telecommunication and new media formats have brought about more complex modes of unauthorised publications of personal material, slander and offences against the identity and personhood of individuals. Consequently, the notion of 'privacy' gained more recognition as an independent individual right that, despite its links to property law, was not a matter of property law. Eventually this led to the affirmation and recognition that individuals were entitled to have control over their personal data, including that which may have fallen in other hands, and are entitled to a zone of seclusion and isolation i.e. the right to be let alone. Within this sphere individuals could freely be themselves in their choices, actions and behaviours. Their communications, both the means of communication as well as the substantive content, were equally protected from the prying eyes of the public. Honour and reputation were also considered as objects worthy of protection against attacks by others (e.g. protection against putting someone in a false light). Morris L. Ernst and Alan U. Schwartz, *Privacy: The right to be let alone* (1977), pp. 5–6, 28,44, 46–70.; Nowak, *U.N. Covenant on Civil and Political Rights: CCPR commentary*, p. 379.; Dorsen, et al., *Comparative constitutionalism: cases and materials*, pp. 532–533.

905 Marshall, *Personal freedom through human rights law? Autonomy, identity and integrity under the European Convention on Human Rights*, pp. 54, 69.

906 Nowak, *U.N. Covenant on Civil and Political Rights: CCPR commentary*, pp. 385, 388.

in which individuals can freely express and develop their personality and identity (e.g. the right to change one's name, the right to obtain information necessary to discover important aspects of one's identity and their sexual life)[907], a right to personal development and a right to establish and develop relationships with other human beings and the outside world.[908] Personal autonomy then serves as the '*overarching principle and common denominator*' of these two dimensions.[909]

To summarise, the 'right to privacy' and, respectively, the right to respect for private life, ought to be interpreted broadly so as to include both the physical spheres that secure individuals' secrecy, seclusion and control over their personal information, as well as the social spheres of individual existence in which individuals can strive to develop themselves.

6.2.2.1.3. Limitation grounds

While the ECHR follows the common criteria that an interference should be 'in accordance with the law', serve a legitimate aim and be 'necessary in a democratic society', the ICCPR contains the distinctive criterion of 'arbitrary' and 'unlawful' interference. An interference is unlawful when it is not envisaged by or is in violation with the law.[910] The criterion 'unlawful' is to be constructed broadly as referring to conduct that conflicts with the national legal system and not solely with formal State laws.[911] It flows from Article 17(2) ICCPR that an interference can only be justified if it is provided in a clear and accessible law (law in the formal sense).[912] In this sense, the applied terminology corresponds with the criteria found in Article 8(2) ECHR, which requires that an interference is in accordance with the law. The difference is that 'law' in terms of Article 8(2) ECHR refers to both formal as well as material law.

A lawful interference may constitute an arbitrary interference where it is incompatible with the '*provisions, aims and objectives of the Covenant*', is not predictable and is not 'reasonable' in the particular circumstances.[913] The legitimate aims pursued

907 Bart van der Sloot, 'Privacy as human flourishing: Could a shift towards virtue ethics strengthen privacy protection in the age of Big Data?', 5 *Journal of intellectual property, information technology and electronic commerce law*, 230–244, (2014), paras. 25–26, 37.; Bart van der Sloot, 'Privacy as Personality Right: Why the ECtHR's focus on ulterior interests might prove indispensable in the age of 'Big Data', 32 *Utrecht Journal of International and European Law* 25–50, (2015), p. 25.; Human Rights Committee, *Coeriel and Aurik v. the Netherlands*, 31 October 1994, Communicatin No. 453/1991, para. 10.2.; Human Rights Committee, *Leonid Komarovski v. Turkmenistan*, 05 August 2008, Communication No. 1450/2006, para. 8.2.

908 European Court of Human Rights, *Pretty v. the United Kingdom*, 29 July 2002, Application No. 2346/02, para. 61.

909 Marshall, *Personal freedom through human rights law? Autonomy, identity and integrity under the European Convention on Human Rights*, p. 52.

910 Nowak, *U.N. Covenant on Civil and Political Rights: CCPR commentary*, p. 382.

911 Id.

912 Id.

913 UN Human Rights Committee 'General Comment No. 16', 1988, para, 4.; Nowak, *U.N. Covenant on Civil and Political Rights: CCPR commentary*, pp. 382–383.

by such an interference are not defined like they are in other provisions (e.g. Article 12 (3) and Article 18 (3) ICCPR). Nowak submits that the aim and purposes that are provided in the other provisions, as well as those provided for in Article 8(2) ECHR can be drawn upon, but he notes that not all the aims can be invoked as justifying an interference with Article 17 ICCPR.[914] The notion of 'reasonableness' corresponds with the criteria of proportionality, as it requires an assessment of all the circumstances of the case and a determination as to whether the interference is proportional to envisaged purposes.[915]

6.2.2.2. *Interpersonal relationships, social life and personal development*

As situations of marital captivity affect the trapped spouse's interaction with his or her social environment, this contribution, therefore, places more attention on the social dimension of the right to private life.

Different types of interpersonal relationships, both familial as well as non-familial, are essential for maintaining a viable social life. Interpersonal relationships are also essential and integral to the formation of an individual's social life, development, identity and personal growth. Pursuing, developing and maintaining interpersonal relationships are also among the most intimate and personal choices that individuals will make over the course of their lives. Effective participation in social life and establishing and maintaining relationships with others is, thus, imperative for the overall formation and development of individuals.

Article 17 ICCPR and Article 8 ECHR protect individuals' social life and guarantee that different types of social interactions can be developed and be maintained.[916] The right to establish relationships with others and the right to undertake activities that contribute to their free and full personal development are implied and guaranteed in these provisions. The following paragraphs address these subjects briefly.

6.2.2.2.1. The right to establish relationships with others

The HRC has established that one's connection with their ancestors constitutes a relationship that is worthy of the protection of Article 17 ICCPR, as it is a necessary aspect of their identity.[917] In other cases, the importance of human relationships and interactions to the development of an individual's identity and personhood have been underscored. For example, in the case of *Coeriel and Aurik v. The Netherlands*[918] and

914 Id., p. 383.
915 Id., pp. 383–384.
916 Kilkelly Ursula, *Handbook No.1: The Right to respect for private and family life*, (2001), p. 12.
917 Human Rights Committee, *Hopu and Bessert v. France,* 29 July 1997, Communication No. 549/1993, para. 10.3.
918 Human Rights Committee, *Coeriel and Aurik v. the Netherlands,* 31 October 1994, Communicatin No. 453/1991, para. 10.2.

Rhaiman v. Latvia[919], the HRC expressed that '*the notion of privacy refers to the sphere of a person's life in which he or she can freely express his or her identity, be it by entering into relationships with others, or alone*'.[920] The ECtHR and ECmHR have also developed the right to private life to include a right to establish and develop relationships with others. This right was first established in *X. v. Iceland*, whereby the Commission established that the right to private life extends '*to a certain degree, the right to establish and to develop relationships with other human beings, especially in the emotional field for the development and fulfilment of one's own personality*'.[921] In a subsequent case concerning the relationship between a detainee and his fianceé, the Commission established a positive obligation on the State to assist in the possibilities for detainees to develop and maintain relationships with persons outside the prison facility in '*order to facilitate their reintegration into society*'.[922] In *Niemietz v. Germany*, the ECtHR expanded upon this right further when it concluded that it '*would be too restrictive to limit the notion [of private life] to an "inner circle" in which the individual may live his own personal life as he chooses and to exclude therefrom entirely the outside world not encompassed within that circle*'.[923] In the ECtHR's view, activities of a professional or business nature, even when taking place in the 'outside world', may nevertheless fall within the ambit of private life. The Court reasoned that it is '*in the course of their working lives that the majority of people have a significant, if not the greatest, opportunity of developing relationships with the outside world*'.[924] Similarly, in *Bruggman v. Germany*, the ECtHR emphasised that, in line with its purpose, Article 8 ECHR protects a '*zone of interaction of a person with others, even in a public context*'.

However, in the ECtHR's view, the broad construction of Article 8 ECHR does not mean that all social interactions undertaken for establishing or developing interpersonal relationships with others fall within the scope of protection of the right to private life.[925] To begin with, as established in the case of X. v. *Iceland* the Commission one's relationship with their pet, even if such a relationship is kept only within the private sphere, is excluded from the protection of Article 8 ECHR.[926] Additionally, interpersonal relationships are, by their very nature, largely reciprocal and consensual. That is, their premise lays in the consensus and acceptance between individuals to

---

919 Human Rights Committee, *Rhaiman v. Latvia*, 30 October 2010, Communication No. 1621/2007.

920 Id., para. 8.2.; Human Rights Committee, *Coeriel and Aurik v. the Netherlands*, 31 October 1994, Communication No. 453/1991, para 10.2.

921 European Commission of Human Rights, *X. v. Iceland, 18 May 1976*, Application No. 6825/74, p. 87.

922 European Commission of Human Rights, *Wakefield v. the United Kingdom of Great Britain and Nothern Ireland*, 1 October 1990, Application No. 15817/89, p. 259. Notably, the relationship between the detainee and his fianceé was found to fall within the category of private life rather than family life.

923 European Court of Human Rights, *Niemietz v. Germany* 16 December 1992, Application No. 13710/88, para. 29.

924 Id.

925 European Court of Human Rights, *Friend, Countryside Alliance and Others v. the United Kingdom*, 24 November 2009, Application Nos. 16072/06, 27809/08, para. 41.

926 European Commission of Human Rights, *X. v. Iceland, 18 May 1976*, Application No. 6825/74, p. 87.

establish and maintain a level of interactions and exchanges that provide some form of mutual benefits for all involved parties. It follows therefore that relationships founded on fear, manipulation or other mal-practices are likely to fall outside the scope of the right to private life. A recalcitrant spouse, for example, cannot attempt to claim a right to maintain a relationship with the trapped spouse by virtue of Article 8 ECHR. Rightly so, as judge Sajó put forward in his dissenting opinion in the *Babiarz v. Poland* case, Article 8 ECHR cannot be interpreted as protecting an opposing or non-cooperative spouse's right to remain married with another person against the latter person's will.[927]

Similarly, relationships that are '*too broad and indeterminate that there can be no conceivable direct link between the requested measure and the applicant's rights*'[928] are considered to go beyond the scope of protection of Article 8 ECHR. This was concluded in the case of *Botta v. Italy* in which the applicant, a disabled man, claimed a violation of Article 8 ECHR due to the State's failure to adopt measures that would enable him to access the beach for recreational, leisure and social purposes at the location of his holiday accommodation.[929] Notably, in reaching this conclusion the ECtHR did take notice of the fact that the place for which the right was sought was far from the applicant's residence.[930] In the case of *Friend, Country Alliance and Others v. The United Kingdom*[931], the ECtHR further limited the social activities that are protected by Article 8 ECHR. Siding with the observations of the national courts, the ECtHR agreed that a distinction must be drawn between the situation in which activities are carried out for '*one's own enjoyment and the development of one's personality*' and a situation in which the same activities are carried out for a public purpose and where the concerned individual could '*not be said to be acting for personal fulfilment alone*'. The former would fall within the scope of protection of Article 8 ECHR, whereas the latter would not. Additionally, in order to fall within the protection of Article 8 ECHR, the undertaken social activities and interactions should not '*be too far removed from the personal autonomy*' of individuals.[932]

Several conclusions can be drawn from the *Botta v. Italy* and *Friend, Country Alliance and Others v. the United Kingdom*. Firstly, it seems that the right to establish relationships with the outside world contains elements of proximity and actuality. In addition, the public context in which the relationship is established and developed

---

927 European Court of Human Rights, *Babiarz v. Poland*, 10 January 2017, Application No. 1955/10, dissenting opinion judge Sajó, paras. 6–7.

928 European Court of Human Rights, *Botta v. Italy*, 24 February 1998, Application No. 21439/93, para. 35.

929 Id., paras. 8–19.

930 Id., para. 35.

931 European Court of Human Rights, *Friend, Countryside Alliance and Others v. the United Kingdom*, 24 November 2009, Application Nos. 16072/06, 27809/08, para. 43.

932 Id.. In this case, the ECtHR found that an undertaken activity (fox hunting) was to a great extent, a public activity, that had a public purpose and attracted a broad range of participants and spectators, and therefore was '*too far removed from the personal autonomy of the applicants*'. Additionally, the interpersonal relationships the applicants claimed to be impaired by the ban on fox hunting, were found to be too broad and indeterminate in scope.

affects the extent of protection that is guaranteed under Article 8 ECHR. Generally, the right to respect for private life '*is automatically reduced when the individual himself brings his private life into contact with public life or into close connection with other protected interests*'.[933] This general limitation thus also applies to the right to establish relationships with others. Although as shown in *Niemietz v. Germany* and *Bruggman v. Federal Republic of Germany*[934], activities in public life that form an essential aspect of one's private life and in particular with their right to establish relationships with others, may still fall within the scope of protection of the right to private life.

Secondly, relationships and activities that are uncertain, broad and vague may exceed beyond the protection that is afforded by Article 8 ECHR. Additionally, only activities undertaken solely for the purpose of personal fulfilment will fall within Article 8 ECHR. This position is, however, hard to reconcile with the earlier case of *Niemietz v. Germany,* in which the activities undertaken within the context of employment were deemed to be within the sphere of protection of Article 8 ECHR. After all, activities taken within the context of employment can arguably have a public purpose and the concerned individuals will not always engage in these activities purely for the purpose of personal fulfilment and development.

Thirdly, the link between the obligatory State action and an individual's private life seems to be a decisive factor in determining the scope of protection of Article 8 ECHR. In the *Botta v. Italy case,* the claimed right (i.e. access to the beach by disabled persons for recreational, leisure and social purposes) was found to fall outside of the scope of protection of Article 8 EHCR. This was concluded, not on the basis of an analysis of the scope of protection of Article 8 ECHR, but rather on the basis that the ECtHR and ECmHR had not established a positive obligation or a direct link between the requested State action and the applicant's claimed right. In other words, the ECtHR seems to have connected the scope of protection of Article 8 ECHR to the obligations contained therein. However, it is questionable whether the scope of human rights provisions (i.e. the protected activities, values and interests) are determined by the existence of corresponding obligations (i.e. expected actions by the State in a specific case). For example, even when a positive obligation can be established, there may be circumstances that justify State's inaction (e.g. protection the rights and freedoms of others or other State interests). This, however, does not mean that the claimed right, in the specific case, would ceases to exist as such. Rights can still exist even when the requested State's action/intervention goes beyond what is necessary to guarantee the protected interest. The fact that the requested State's action exceeds the positive obligations, and therefore that there is no direct link between the requested State's action and the claimed human rights, does not necessarily mean that claimed human rights do not exist.

---

933 European Commission of Human Rights, *Bruggman and Scheuten v. the Federal Republic of Germany,* 17 July 1977, Application No. 6959/75, para. 56.

934 European Court of Human Rights, *Niemietz v. Germany* 16 December 1992, Application No. 13710/88, para. 29; European Commission of Human Rights, *Bruggman and Scheuten v. the Federal Republic of Germany,* 17 July 1977, Application No. 6959/75, para. 56.

6.2.2.2.2. Personal development

Turning to the notion of 'personal development' within the ECHR system, the ECtHR has established that '*article 8 of the Convention primarily intended to ensure development, without outside interference, of personality of each individual in his relations with other human beings*'.[935] The Court has found a right to personal development to be included in Article 8 ECHR.[936] The ICESCR mentions the free and full development of individuals in relation to the right to education in Article 13 thereof, while the ICCPR does not contain an explicit reference to personal development. However, the UDHR contains provisions that guarantee individuals the right to personal development. Article 22 UDHR entitles individuals to realise the '*free and full development of [individuals'] personality*' and highlights the importance of social, economic and cultural rights for the realisation of this entitlement.[937] Article 22 UDHR is complemented by Article 29 (1) UDHR, which highlights the importance of community life for the full development of individuals.[938]

The content of the entitlement to realise free and full development of one's personality, however, is not clearly defined. The ECtHR has established a close link between individual identity and personal development. It has held that an individuals' identity and the details related thereto, information about one's identity and ancestry are matters that are relevant to one's personal development.[939]

On a side note, the ECtHR's terminology on this subject is varied and confusing. On different occasions, it has referred, to 'personal development', 'development of personality', self-fulfilment' and 'personal autonomy'. At times, these concepts have been equated and used interchangeably without providing clarity on their relation and differences.[940] For example, in the case of *K.A. and A.D. v. Belgium*, the ECtHR established that Article 8

---

935 European Court of Human Rights, *Botta v. Italy*, 24 February 1998, Application No. 21439/93, para. 32.; See also European Court of Human Rights, *Pretty v. the United Kingdom*, 29 July 2002, Application No. 2346/02, para. 61.

936 European Court of Human Rights, *Pretty v. the United Kingdom*, 29 July 2002, Application No. 2346/02, para. 61.

937 Johannes Morsink, *The Universal Declaration of Human Rights: Origins, drafting, and intent* (Philadelphia, 2010), pp. 210–212.

938 Article 29 (1) provides that: '*Everyone has duties to the community in which alone the free and full development of his personality is possible*'.

939 European Court of Human Rights, *Pfeifer v. Austria*, 15 November 2007, Application No. 12556/03, para. 33.; European Court of Human Rights, *Odievre v. France*, 13 February 2003, Application No. 42326/98, para. 29.; van der Sloot, *Privacy as personality right: Why the ECtHR's focus on ulterior interests might prove indispensable in the age of 'Big Data'*, p. 25.; van der Sloot, *Privacy as human flourishing: Could a shift towards virtue ethics strengthen privacy protection in the age of Big Data?*, paras. 25–26.

940 See for example European Court of Human Rights, *Odievre v. France*, 13 February 2003, Application No. 42326/98, para 29.; European Court of Human Rights, *Fernández Martínez v. Spain*, 12 June 2016, Applicaton No. 56030/07, para. 126.; European Court of Human Rights, *K.A. et A.D. v. Belgium*, 06 July 2005, Application Nos. 42758/98 and 45558/99, para. 83.; European Commission of Human Rights, *X. v. Iceland*, 18 May 1976, Application No. 6825/74, p. 87. See also Koffeman, *(The right to) personal autonomy in the case law of the European Court of Human Rights*, p. 29–30.

ECHR protects '*the right to self-fulfilment, whether it be in the form of personal development or as an aspect of personal autonomy [...]This right implies the right to establish relationships with other human beings and the outside world[...].*'[941] The conclusion may then be reached that personal autonomy, personal development and the right to establish relationships are all component parts of the right to self-realisation. Whereas, the formulation adopted *in X. v. Iceland* may lead to the conclusion that the establishment of relationships with others is among the preconditions for full personal autonomy and development and fulfilment of personality. Whether the ECtHR is deliberately using different wording or it is simply not being careful in its use of the different terminology or equates personality with personal development (or personal autonomy with personal development) cannot be clearly deduced from the foregoing case law.[942]

6.2.2.2.3. Concluding remarks

Effective participation in the community and entertaining social interactions and relationships are essential conditions for enabling individuals to realise their personal development and fulfilment. The right to private life, therefore, guarantees that individuals can establish and entertain various types of relationships with the outside world and thus participate in social life. The right to private life also guarantees that individuals can engage in social activities that enable the right to establish, develop and maintain relationships with others. The undertaken activities do not necessarily need to be entirely within private settings, although the public context may be decisive as to whether or not such activities are protected by the right to private life. The right to private life, however, does not seem to contain an obligation for States to ensure that individuals can indefinitely establish relationships with others.

Furthermore, despite the somewhat confusing terminology, personal autonomy, personal development, development of personality and interpersonal relationships are all interrelated, essential and fundamental aspects of an individual's overall functioning. Thus, these aspects fall well within the protection of the right to private life.

---

941 Translation by B. Deogratias from the original text: '*L'article 8 de la Convention protège le droit à l'épanouissement personnel, que ce soit sous la forme du développement personnel [...] ou sous l'aspect de l'autonomie personnelle [...]*'. European Court of Human Rights, *K.A. et A.D. v. Belgium*, 06 July 2005, Application Nos. 42758/98 and 45558/99, para 53. Noteworthy, a cross examination of translations of cases on this subject matter reveals that the ECtHR has adopted different translations of the notions of '*épanouissement personnel*' and '*développement personnel*'. The ECtHR has yet to establish whether and how these two French terms differ. At times the ECtHR has translated '*épanouissement personnel*' in 'personal development' and in other cases as 'self-fulfilment'. In the joint dissenting opinion of judges Wildhaber, Bratza, Bonello, Loucaides, Cabral Barreto, Tulkens and Pellonpää, reference was made to the terms '*developpement de la personnalité et à l'épanouissement personnel.*' In the English translation, this has been translated as 'personal development and self-fulfilment'.

942 Koffeman, *(The right to) personal autonomy in the case law of the European Court of Human Rights*, p. 30.

6.2.2.3. *The trapped spouse's private life*

Trapped spouses have a right to establish or entertain activities that enable them to establish and develop relationships with others for the purposes of developing their personality and identity. The right to respect for private life guarantees trapped spouses an effective participation in social life, the right to establish relationships with others and the outside world and the right to personal development. For trapped spouses, these rights are particularly crucial where it concerns establishing relationships with potential partners. However, a situation of marital captivity prevents the formation of intimate relationships. Engaging in a new intimate relationship may be considered to be religiously, legally, morally and socially deplorable within the social environment and by the (ex-) husband.

This is particularly more so for trapped wives, as certain religions permit trapped husbands to entertain new relationships with other women. This is a privilege that trapped wives are not given. Instead, the trapped woman may be expected and required to comply with the religious rules and views that require compliance with the existing religious marriage. The pressure that spouses experience in this area, as consequence of a continuing situation of marital captivity, limits them from fully participating in social life as single women or divorcees and from shaping their private and social lives as they deem appropriate. Trapped wives may not be free to move on with their lives, establish relationships with whomever they choose to and, more specifically, to establish relationships with potential new partners, for as long as they are still considered to be married. This impairs the personal development of trapped women as they are restricted in moving on with their lives and they are constantly reminded that they 'belong' to their former partner, so long as the religious marriage has not been dissolved. Although case law has established that Article 8 ECHR does not require States to secure that individuals can establish and maintain '*interpersonal relations of such a broad and indeterminate scope*'[943], a situation of marital captivity involves a far-reaching restriction to a specific type of relationship, so that this does not concern interpersonal relationships that are too broad and certainly not indeterminate in scope. The continuation of a situation of marital captivity restricts this right, irrespective of the location where the trapped spouses wish to establish such relationships.

Therefore, the trapped wife may be deprived of her autonomy to fully and freely make plans, take decisions and actions to direct and shape their lives as she sees fit. This, in turn, impairs her personal development. A situation of marital captivity thus amounts to an interference with the trapped spouse's right to respect for private life.

[943] European Court of Human Rights, *Botta v. Italy,* 24 February 1998, Application No. 21439/93, para. 35.

6.2.3. THE FREEDOM OF MOVEMENT

Both case law as well as the described case studies, repeatedly show that a situation of marital captivity may deprive women of the possibility to travel to the country of origin/nationality in order to visit relatives. Spouses may also face travel restrictions when seeking to return to their country of residence. As aforementioned, the restrictions that trapped spouses incur may differ from one case to the next. This is not any different in respect of the restrictions to free movement that trapped spouses, and in particular trapped women, may be faced with. For this reason, it is pertinent to first outline the different scenarios of marital captivity in which restrictions to free movement are experienced, and to highlight the contributing factors, involved actors and consequences.

6.2.3.1. *Terminological clarifications*

With individuals becoming increasingly more mobile and engaging in cross-border activities, an overview of the terms used to indicate the involved States and how these relate to spouses, for example by way of their nationality, residence and origin, is important. Now more than ever, spouses to a marriage have connections with multiple countries. For example, spouses may possess the nationality of multiple States or may originate from another country than the State of their permanent residence and they may regularly travel between both States. Spouses may also have contracted a formal (religious) marriage in one country and have registered in other countries with diverging legal systems. Therefore, to avoid confusion, the 'country of origin' is used here in a broad sense to include a country to which either or both spouses have ties to, by way of nationality or origin, and in which an existing religious marriage has legal recognition. This will also include the foreign country where a State recognised religious marriage has been concluded and to which the spouses still have ties to. The 'country of residence' this contribution is used to reference the country of their current residence, which is not the same as the 'country of origin'.

6.2.3.2. *Transnational aspects of marital captivity*

A trapped wife may not be able to travel to her country of origin. This may be the case when the national authorities of the country of origin require, in accordance with the national law, the approval of the husband prior to issuing the necessary travel documents. Women with a dual nationality or a foreign nationality (i.e. a different nationality than of the country of their residence) are mostly affected since certain countries require their nationals to enter on the country's nationality and the issuance of travel documents may be made conditional on the husband's approval.[944] Where this

[944] See also Rechtbank Rotterdam, 09 September 2016, ELCI:NL:RBROT:2016:6943.; Rechtbank Den Haag, 21 October 2014, ECLI:NL:RBDHA:2014:14191.; Rechtbank Amsterdam 2 April 2014,

is lacking, the trapped wife will face difficulties in travelling to the country of origin or travelling back to the country of residence. This is best illustrated by the case study of Farzaneh.

> *Farzaneh, a Dutch- Iranian, planned a family trip to Iran. Although she had obtained a civil divorce in the Netherlands, under Iranian law she was still considered to be married to her (ex) husband. At the Iranian embassy in the Netherlands, she was informed that she needed the approval of her husband for her application for a new Iranian passport. She also wanted to end the Iranian marriage so that she could travel freely. Obtaining a divorce in Iran turned out to be difficult, particularly as Farzaneh needed her (ex-) husband's approval in order to travel to Iran and she did not know of his whereabouts. She does not desire to start divorce proceedings again 'but I know that I have to (...) the fact that he controls that small part of my life (i.e. the passport), is so frustrating! It is as if I am inferior*[945] *(...) it is his way of putting me under pressure...he is abusing the situation, it is really frustrating, extremely frustrating (...).*[946]

As this case shows, an obtained divorce in one country (e.g. the Netherlands), may not be recognised in another country (e.g. Iran). Spouse(s) may then have to initiate divorce proceedings in both countries. However, as the case of Farzaneh illustrates, initiating divorce proceedings in the country of origin may also be a predicament, particularly when the woman seeking the divorce is prevented from travelling to the country of origin. In some countries, such as Iran, the national laws may impose conditions that require a woman to secure the approval of her husband for her travelling activities. The (ex-) husband can then restrict the woman's ability to travel by withholding the necessary approval. It may also be that the (ex-) husband cannot be found, in which case the movement of the trapped wife is also restricted.

A trapped wife may also be restricted from travelling back to the country of residence, due to not being in possession of the necessary travel documents. This is, for example, the case when the trapped wife needs an exit-visa or approval to leave the country but cannot obtain it or when her travel documents have been confiscated by the (ex-) husband or family members. The cases of Chiara and Sarah illustrate these scenarios which are briefly described here.

> *Chiara married a Saudi Arabian man. She relocated to Saudi Arabia to start their lives together. The marital life deteriorated and after five years, the marriage ended with a repudiation by her husband in accordance with Shari'a. Initially, the husband had refused to repudiate her and demanded the return of his dowry of two million euro, which was returned. Despite this, she remained trapped in Saudi Arabia as her travel documents were*

ECLI:NL:RBAMS:2014:1644.; Rechtbank Overijssel, 24 December 2013, ECLI:NL:RBOVE:013: 4269.; Rechtbank Rotterdam, 8 December 2010, ECLI:NL:RBROT:2010:BP8396.

945 Van Eijk, Wel gescheiden, niet gescheiden? Een empirisch onderzoek naar huwelijkse gevangenschap in Nederland, p. 42.

946 Id., p. 74.

confiscated by the local authorities on account of accusations instigated by the ex-husband of her having committed adultery. In an attempt to counter Chiara's report of domestic violence, the husband accused her of having committed adultery, an act that is punishable by death. The Italian embassy issued Chiara with the necessary travel documents to leave Saudi Arabia. Despite this effort, she could still not leave as she needed an exit-visa. Although the man was no longer her husband[947]*, she nevertheless needed his approval to apply for an exit-visa as he remained her sponsor, who can only be a Saudi Arabian national. While in Saudi-Arabia, she was not able to travel and drive alone. She was only able to do so because her father was staying with her and would travel with her. Finally, her plight was picked up by the Italian authorities as well as the Italian EU parliamentarian Rossi who requested the Commission to employ EU intervention to secure the safe return of Chiara to Italy.*[948] *Eventually, after quiet diplomatic intervention, the husband approved the exit-visa and Chiara was able to return to Italy.*

Sarah, a Dutch teenage girl of Somali descent, was lured under false pretences to Somalia, where she was forced to marry her uncle. Upon arrival, her passport was confiscated by her relatives. Eventually, she managed to escape to neighbouring Ethiopia where she, being a Dutch national, went to the Dutch embassy requesting that she be issued travel documents and be helped to return to the Netherlands. However, as she was still a minor (17 years) and was seemingly travelling without her parents she was informed to either return back to her parents or otherwise, the embassy would have to inform her parents of her whereabouts. Her parents managed to track her down and took her back to Somalia. Eventually, she managed to get her passport in her possession and came in contact with the Dutch-based NGO Femmes for Freedom, which facilitated her journey back to the Netherlands. The marriage to her uncle still needs to be dissolved. He has voiced threats that he will not divorce her.[949]

The case of Chiara and Sarah shows that spouses cannot only be trapped in an unwanted marriage but can simultaneously be trapped in a foreign country. Another aspect that is illustrated is that within a situation of marital captivity, the trapped wife may also be limited from travelling within the territory of the State they are in. In particular, this is likely to be the case where the national State imposes travel restrictions on women in respect of their travelling activities within the State. Companionship or approval of husbands, a male guardian, or parent (in case of a minor) may be required. This results in a far-reaching restriction to women's right to free movement and is an almost absolute control over the mobility and social life of women.

947 Oreste Rossi 'Question for written answer P-007842/12 to the Commission (Vice President/High Representative)', *Official Journal of the European Union*, 5 September 2012, p. 122. Silvana Mossano, 'Vi racconto il mio inferno di sequestrata in Arabia', *La Stampa Italia* 12 September 2012.; Silvana Mossano, 'Ostaggio del marito in Arabia Saudita libera dopo 10 mesi', *La Stampa Italia* 24 December 2012.The sources are not clear on her marital status. The local newspapers report that Chiara remained married to the Saudi husband, whereas the question by EU Parliamentarian Rossi suggests that a repudiation had been put into effect, while she was still trapped in Saudi Arabia.

948 Id.

949 'Holiday in Somalia turns into nightmare', *Radio Netherlands WorldWide* 18 August 18 2012.; 'Nederlandse ambassade laat bruidslavinnnen in de steek', *Joop Vara* 13 August 2012.

6.2.3.3. *The legal framework*

At the international level, the freedom of movement is regulated in Article 12 ICCPR and Article 15(4) of the CEDAW.

The ICCPR, in Article 12 thereof, follows similar wording to that of the UDHR.[950] However, it includes a limitation clause to the right to movement within the territory of a State and the right to leave a country:

> '1. Everyone lawfully within the territory of a State shall, within that territory, have the right to liberty of movement and freedom to choose his residence.
> 2. Everyone shall be free to leave any country, including his own.
> 3. The above-mentioned rights shall not be subject to any restrictions except those which are provided by law, are necessary to protect national security, public order (ordre public), public health or morals or the rights and freedoms of others, and are consistent with the other rights recognized in the present Covenant.
> 4. No one shall be arbitrarily deprived of the right to enter his own country.'

Article 15 (4) CEDAW provides that:

> *'States Parties shall accord to men and women the same rights with regard to the law relating to the movement of persons and the freedom to choose their residence and domicile.'*

Notably, the inclusion of Article 15 (4) was objected by some States. This was because in some States women do not have the full freedom of movement and choice of residence.[951] Several States have also placed reservations on this right[952] which the CEDAW committee has found to be incompatible with the object and purpose of the Convention.[953]

At the regional level, the freedom of movement is included in Articles 2 and 3 of the Fourth Protocol to the ECHR. Article 2 thereof reads:

> *'1. Everyone lawfully within the territory of a State shall, within that territory, have the right to liberty of movement and freedom to choose his residence.*
> *2. Everyone shall be free to leave any country, including his own.*

---

950 Article 13 UDHR States:
'1. Everyone has the right to freedom of movement and residence within the borders of each state.
2. Everyone has the right to leave any country, including his own, and to return to his country.'

951 Savitri W.E. Goonesekere, 'Article 15', in Freeman, et al. *The UN Convention on the Elimination of All Forms of Discrimination Against Women: A commentary* (New York, 2012), p. 391. Among others, Egypt, Indonesia and Iran. *Commission on the Status of Women: report on the 26th and resumed 26th sessions (13 September – 1 October and 6–17 December 1976)*, (1976), para. 134.

952 Some of which still maintain reservations, anno 2017: Algeria, Morocco, Tunisia, Bahrain, Jordan, Niger, Oman, Syria, United Kingdom and China in respect of Hong Kong. *Declarations, Reservations and Objections to CEDAW, at* <www.un.org/womenwatch/daw/cedaw/reservations-country.htm> last accessed 18 August 2017.

953 Goonesekere, *Article 15*, p. 406.

3. *No restrictions shall be placed on the exercise of these rights other than such as are in accordance with law and are necessary in a democratic society in the interests of national security or public safety, for the maintenance of ordre public, for the prevention of crime, for the protection of health or morals, or for the protection of the rights and freedoms of others.*
4. *The rights set forth in paragraph 1 may also be subject, in particular areas, to restrictions imposed in accordance with law and justified by the public interest in a democratic society.'*

The right to entry and the prohibition of expulsion are contained in Article 3 as follows:

'1. *No one shall be expelled, by means either of an individual or of a collective measure, from the territory of the State of which he is a national.*
2. *No one shall be deprived of the right to enter the territory of the state of which he is a national.'*

Other instruments that have a provision guaranteeing the freedom of movement are, among others, Article 45 of the EU Charter, Article 25 ACHR, Article 12 ACHPR and Article 13 UDHR.

As a point of notice, this contribution addresses the freedom of movement within the human rights context. States, however, may adopt bilateral treaties to further regulate or facilitate the movement of persons between the contracting States. These treaties and their implications for the movement of the trapped women, however, will not be addressed any further. Similarly, the rights and guarantees that European Union citizens have under European law will not be included. The purpose of this exercise is to establish the minimum standards that States are obliged to respect and protect under international and regional human rights law.

6.2.3.4. Three freedoms

If there is one thing that human beings, both individually as collectively, have done since time immemorial and that can be assured to be a constant in human evolution: then it is movement. Humans have and will always be on the move, whether it is for the sake of escaping hostile environments (e.g. war or environmental disasters), finding more suitable environmental habitats, exploration, commercial and economic reasons, for leisure and so on. In fact, one of the most important decisions individuals make in their lifetime is where they will live, plant their roots, settle down and take on employment, which may require commuting between different territories and States. The act of freely and purposely changing one's physical whereabouts is thus reflective of the notion of free and full personal autonomy and as individuals are in a constant flow of movement, the freedom of movement is pertinent to an individuals' liberty, development and the enjoyment of other human rights.[954]

[954] UN Human Rights Committee 'General Comment No. 27: Freedom of movement (article 12)', 1 November 1999, para. 1.; Chama L.C. Mubanga- Chipoya, *Analysis of the current trends and*

With the creation of States and borders, however, new interests have been called into existence that may require the restriction of an individual's movement (e.g. respect for State sovereignty and the protection of national security). For example, the right to leave and enter may be restricted in times of State emergencies, as this is a derogable right.[955] The movement of individuals within and between States is subjected to rules and procedures that differ from country to country. In the following paragraphs, the minimum standards that should be guaranteed are briefly addressed.

6.2.3.4.1. Movement within the territory of a country

There are three constituent elements to the freedom of movement. Movement within the territory of a State and transnational movement which contains two sides: i.e. the act of leaving a State and the act of entering a State. Individuals are entitled to move freely and reside in a location of their choice within the territory of the State of their nationality, citizenship or residence. For federal States, this right confers free movement in all the constituent territories.[956] However, only individuals, nationals as well as non-nationals that are considered as being lawfully resident within the concerned territory of a State are guaranteed this right. This includes individuals who, although having entered the territory unlawfully have obtained a lawful status (e.g. as a refugee or resident).[957] In other words, persons who are or remain unlawful in a territory are not included within this provision.[958] More specifically for non-nationals that are lawfully resident within the country, States in principle may award such individuals different or restricted rights to free movement than their citizens or nationals, provided that such measures are justifiable pursuant to the limitation clauses.[959] The right also implies that individuals or groups should not be subjected to forced displacement.[960] While lawful presence within and entrance to a State's territory are matters that are determined and subject to domestic law, States have to act in compliance with international law and the State's international obligations.[961]

---

developments regarding the right to leave any country including one's own, and to return to one's own country, and some other rights or considerations arising therefrom: final report prepared by C.L.C. Mubanga-Chipoya, (Economic and Social Council, 20 June 1988), [E/CN.4/Sub.2/1988/35], paras. 30, 55.

955 Id., para. 33. For example, Article 12 is not mentioned in Article 4 (2) ICCPR.

956 HRC, *General Comment No. 27: Freedom of movement (article 12)*, para. 5.

957 Id., para. 4.

958 Nowak, *U.N. Covenant on Civil and Political Rights: CCPR commentary*, p. 261.; HRC, *General Comment No. 27: Freedom of movement (article 12)*, para. 4.; Schabas, *The European Convention on Human Rights: A commentary*, p. 1057.

959 HRC, *General Comment No. 27: Freedom of movement (article 12)*, para. 4.; Joseph, et al., *The International Covenant on Civil and Political Rights- Cases, materials and commentary*, p. 352.

960 Id., para. 7.

961 HRC, *General Comment No. 27: Freedom of movement (article 12)*, para. 7.

6.2.3.4.2. The right to leave

Next to free movement within the territory of a State, human rights law also recognises a right to leave the territory of a State. The right to leave entails that individuals, nationals and aliens alike, ought to be free in their choice of destination i.e. the right to determine one's destination.[962] However, this right does not include a right to be admitted by the destination State.[963] The right to leave includes both the freedom to travel abroad as well as the freedom to emigrate.[964] As such, it is not conditional on the intended duration of one's stay abroad. Unlike the freedom of movement within the territory, the right to leave also provides guarantees to persons that do not have lawful residency within the territory (e.g. persons who have been lawfully expelled from that country).[965] They are entitled to depart to a destination of their choice. Notably, the HRC in its general comments seems to subject this right to the agreement of admission by the State of destination.[966]

Furthermore, international mobility, and at times even internal mobility, requires that individuals provide the necessary travel documents (e.g. a passport or identity card) which are issued by the authorities of their State. The right to leave implies, thus, a corresponding right to obtain travel documents.[967] As the issuance of travel documents is a matter of State sovereignty, the very nature of this right entails that even when nationals are abroad, they are still within the jurisdiction of the State of nationality for these matters.[968] Thus, and as has been confirmed by the HRC, the refusal to issue travel documents or the confiscation of travel documents by State authorities deprives individuals of their right to leave.[969]

The right to move within the territory and the right to leave may be subjected to restrictions, provided that these do not impair the very essence of the guaranteed rights and are justifiable pursuant to the limitation clauses of the respective provisions. A violation of these right arises where no proper justification can be established in accordance with these limitation clauses. The individuals' right to move and reside within a territory may, for example, be restricted for certain areas (e.g. military basis or industrial zones for processing radioactive material etc.). The right to move within

962 Id., para. 8.; Schabas, *The European Convention on Human Rights: A commentary*, p. 1060.

963 HRC, *General Comment No. 27: Freedom of movement (article 12)*, para. 8.

964 Nowak, *U.N. Covenant on Civil and Political Rights: CCPR commentary*, Nowak, p. 267.

965 HRC, *General Comment No. 27: Freedom of movement (article 12)*, para. 8.

966 Id.

967 Id., para. 9.

968 Human Rights Committee, *Sophie Vidal Martins v. Uruguay*, 23 March 1982, Communication No. R.13/57, paras. 7, 9–10.

969 HRC, *General Comment No. 27: Freedom of movement (article 12)*, para. 9.; Human Rights Committee, *Sophie Vidal Martins v. Uruguay*, 23 March 1982, Communication No. R.13/57.; Human Rights Committee, *Mabel Pereira Montero v. Uruguay*, 31 March 1983, Communication No. 106/1981.; Human Rights Committee, *Samuel Lichtensztejn v. Uruguay*, 31 March 1983, Communication No. 77/1980.

a territory and the right to leave for both nationals as well as non-nationals may also be restricted by the State for various of reasons, such as the performance of national service[970], pending criminal proceedings[971], execution of criminal sanctions[972], pending debts[973] etc. Exist-visas may also form restrictions to the right to leave, as was illustrated by the case of Chiara.[974] On this subject matter, the HRC has expressed its condemnations of such policies and urged States for these practices to be eliminated.[975] Nationals of another State may also be restricted from returning to their State of nationality or travel to another country. This may be the case when the hosting State imposes a temporary travel ban for the purpose of serving their sentence, where they have committed a criminal offence in the host State.

6.2.3.4.3. The right to enter

Finally, nationals are guaranteed the right to enter and remain in the State of their nationality.[976] This, however, does not include a right to residence upon entry.[977] Noteworthy, the right to enter for nationals is submitted to be part of customary law. A broad consensus for a similar status of the right to leave is crystallising.[978]

The category of 'nationals' also includes persons born outside the territory of their State of nationality and whom may be seeking to enter or repatriate to their country of origin for the first time.[979] Notably, while Article 3 (2) of Protocol No. 4 to the ECHR

970 Human Rights Committee, *Peltonen v. Finland,* 26 July 1994, Communication No. 492/1992.

971 European Court of Human Rights, *Antonenkov and Others v. Ukraine,* 22 November 2005, Application No. 14183/02.; Human Rights Committee, *Miguel Gonzalez del Rio v. Peru,* 28 October 1992, Communication No. 263/1987, para. 53. In the second case, the HRC established a violation of Article 12 as it considered the judicial proceedings to be unduly delayed and therefore unjustifiable.

972 Human Rigts Committee, *Salah Karker v. France,* 26 October 2000, Communication No. 833/1998.; European Court of Human Rights, *Miazdzyk v. Poland,* 24 January 2012, Application No. 23592/07. Although in this case the ECtHR found that the restriction of the French national in Poland was disproportionate in relation to his right to family life and right to medical care, which he could only receive in France.

973 European Court of Human Rights, *Luordo v. Italy,* 17 July 2003, Application No. 32190/96.; European Court of Human Rights, *Khlyustov v. Russia,* 11 July 2013, Application No. 28975/05.

974 Human Rights Committee, *Concluding Observations Sudan 1995,* CCPR, A/53/40 vol. I, para. 125.; Human Rights Committee, *Concluding Observations Ukraine 1995,* A/50/40, para. 320. See also subsection 5.2.3.2.

975 Human Rights Committee, *Concluding Observations Gabon 1996,* CCPR/C/79/Add. 71, para. 16.

976 HRC, *General Comment No. 27: Freedom of movement (article 12),* para. 19.; Council of Europe, *Explanatory Report to Protocol No. 4 to the Convention for the Protection of Human Rights and Fundamental Freedoms, securing certain rights and freedoms other than those already included in the Convention and in the First Protocol thereto,* (1963), p. 10.; Nowak, *U.N. Covenant on Civil and Political Rights: CCPR commentary,* p. 201.

977 Nowak, *U.N. Covenant on Civil and Political Rights: CCPR commentary,* p. 261.; UN Human Rights Commitee 'General Comment No. 15: The Position of Aliens Under the Covenant', (HRC), 11 April 1986, para. 5.

978 Vincent Chetail, *The transnational movement of persons under general International Law. Mapping the Customary Law foundations of International Migration Law* (Cheltenham, 2014), pp. 22–26.

979 HRC, *General Comment No. 27: Freedom of movement (article 12),* para. 19.

specifically guarantees the right to enter for nationals, the ICCPR seems to include a wider group as it refers to 'his own country' instead of 'nationality'. The inclusion of 'nationality', within Article 3 of Protocol No. 4 to the ECHR was favoured over a formulation similar to that of the ICCPR, as it was considered to contain clear and precise legal language.[980]

By way of comparison, the HRC's general comment No. 27 as well as the *travaux préparatiores* show a hesitation as to the coverage of Article 12(4) ICCPR. At first State parties referred to a right of nationals to enter.[981] However, as this would exclude non-nationals who had permanently established themselves in their host state, the formulation of the right to enter 'in his own country' was adopted instead. This formulation was understood to mean the country of which an individual is a national or citizen.[982] A wider interpretation of the right to enter was advocated in the 1999 general comment on Article 12 ICCPR. Besides nationals, the category of persons that should be included within the right to enter should include non-nationals and stateless persons who have strong ties to the concerned State so that it constitutes a '*close and enduring connection between the person and [the] country*' so that such persons cannot be considered to be '*mere alien[s]*'.[983] Long-term residents, including but not limited to stateless persons who arbitrarily have been deprived of the right to acquire the nationality of the country of such residence, are the categories of persons that the general comment would seem to refer to.[984] However, the HRC in the case of *Stewart v. Canada* adopted a narrower interpretation of 'his own country' to refer to persons who are nationals or others who '*while not nationals in a formal sense, are also not "aliens" within the meaning of article 13, although they may be considered as aliens for other purposes*'.[985] One may then think of nationals of a country who have been unlawfully stripped of their nationality, individuals whose country of nationality has been incorporated or transformed into another national entity and where the new nationality is being denied to them, or stateless persons who have been arbitrarily denied the acquisition of nationality of the State of their residence.[986] In this case, the HRC thus seems to have departed from the wider category of persons with strong ties. Instead, a much narrower category of persons has been introduced. This concerns persons who

980 *Explanatory Report to Protocol No. 4 to the Convention for the Protection of Human Rights and Fundamental Freedoms, securing certain rights and freedoms other than those already included in the Convention and in the First Protocol thereto*, para. 24.

981 HRC, *General Comment No. 27: Freedom of movement (article 12)*, para. 20.; Nowak, *U.N. Covenant on Civil and Political Rights: CCPR commentary*, p. 216.

982 Mubanga- Chipoya, *Analysis of the current trends and developments regarding the right to leave any country including one's own, and to return to one's own country, and some other rights or considerations arising therefrom: final report prepared by C.L.C. Mubanga-Chipoya*, para. 39.

983 HRC, *General Comment No. 27: Freedom of movement (article 12)*, para. 20.

984 Id.

985 Human Rights Committee, *Stewart v. Canada*, 01 November 1996, Communication No. 538/1993, para. 12.4. Article 13 ICCPR sets the conditions for the expulsion of aliens that are lawfully resident within the State.

986 Id.

were nationals at some earlier point in time or stateless persons who have for a long period of time resided in that country but have arbitrarily been denied the possibility to acquire the nationality of that State.[987]

Finally, procedures that require nationals to be able to identify themselves upon entering the country are not, by definition, considered as an unnecessary restriction of the right to enter. The right to enter does not entail that persons who claim to be nationals of a State are relieved from presenting and proving their nationality.[988] Interestingly, the provisions on the right to enter do not contain a limitation clause similar to those that accompany the right to movement within a State's territories and the right to leave. Article 3(2) of Protocol No. 4 to the ECHR does not seem to contain a limitation clause, as it only provides that nationals should not be deprived of their right to enter their State of nationality. However, the HRChas expressed that '*in no case may a person be arbitrarily deprived of their right to enter his or her own country.*[989] The inclusion of the word 'arbitrarily' in Article 12 ICCPR confirms that this right is not an absolute right and that there may be lawful reasons to deprive a national or citizen from their right to enter. The HRC requires that any imposed restrictions, as well as the process of their enforcement, are designated in laws, administrative actions or judicial decisions that are lawful, clear and precise.[990] Furthermore, restrictions on the right to enter should also be '*in accordance with the provisions, aims and objectives of the Covenant and should be, in any event reasonable in the particular circumstances*'.[991]

Similarly, within the ECHR system it has been acknowledged that the right to enter is not an absolute right and that there are limited circumstances whereby entry may be refused.[992] The explanatory report gives as an example criminals who have been extradited by their State of nationality and attempt to find refuge in their own country after having escaped from detention in the other country.[993] Similarly, persons in exile or persons whose nationality has been lawfully stripped may be prevented from re-entering the State of nationality.

---

987 However, eight judges to this case expressed, in their concurring and dissenting opinion, that they could not find themselves in the narrow interpretation of Article 12 (4).
Nowak, *U.N. Covenant on Civil and Political Rights: CCPR commentary*, p. 286.

988 *Explanatory Report to Protocol No. 4 to the Convention for the Protection of Human Rights and Fundamental Freedoms, securing certain rights and freedoms other than those already included in the Convention and in the First Protocol thereto*, para. 26.; Mubanga- Chipoya, *Analysis of the current trends and developments regarding the right to leave any country including one's own, and to return to one's own country, and some other rights or considerations arising therefrom: final report prepared by C.L.C. Mubanga-Chipoya*, para. 49.

989 HRC, *General Comment No. 27: Freedom of movement (article 12)*, para. 21.

990 Id.

991 Id.

992 *Explanatory Report to Protocol No. 4 to the Convention for the Protection of Human Rights and Fundamental Freedoms, securing certain rights and freedoms other than those already included in the Convention and in the First Protocol thereto*, para. 28.

993 Id.

6.2.3.5. *The freedom of movement in situations of marital captivity*

The inability to travel to the country of origin, to the country of residence or even within a country that is caused by a situation of marital captivity clearly affects the free movement of trapped spouses. Legal systems that restrict or require the husbands' approval to any travelling activities undertaken by wives deprive women of their right to freedom of movement. Furthermore, the right to leave includes the right to acquire the necessary travel documents. This right is restricted when it is subjected to the approval of the husband and it may even be entirely obliterated where approval by the (ex-) husband cannot be obtained. In particular, where it concerns entry into the country of origin of a trapped spouse who is a national of that country and who is required to travel on the passport of that country, the refusal to issue the travel documents will also impact their right to enter. Additionally, the confiscation of travel documents by private parties will also result in a restriction of the spouse's right to exercise free movement to travel between States.

6.2.4. RIGHT TO THE HIGHEST ATTAINABLE STANDARD OF HEALTH

A situation of marital captivity may cause different degrees of physical and psychological harm, the effects of which should not be overlooked. Feelings of despair, inferiority and of being trapped in a mental prison are not uncommon traits among trapped wives.[994] Women may suffer physical harm where violence is involved. Domestic violence and, at times, honour-related violence are often committed within a situation of marital captivity.[995] Non-cooperative spouses may still feel entitled to the trapped spouse whom they continue to perceive as their legitimate spouse. Obedience and subordination of, in particular, the (ex-) wife may be expected. The absence thereof or non-compliance by the trapped wife may trigger violence as a means to police her. The physical and psychological duress that a trapped spouse may have to endure can have serious health implications. Thus, it is equally important to take into account the health-related issues that may arise from a situation of marital captivity, alongside finding solutions to prevent and end situations of marital captivity. The following subsections will provide a brief outline of the right to health for the purposes of generating a greater understanding of the contents of this right and why it is imperative to acknowledge and include the right to health within the discussions on marital captivity.

---

994 See for example Smith, *In this story, the Agunah was me.*; Case study of Farnazeh in van Eijk, Wel gescheiden, niet gescheiden? Een empirisch onderzoek naar huwelijkse gevangenschap in Nederland, p. 105.

995 Rechtbank Groningen, 11 October 2010, ECLI:NL:RBGRO:2010:BO0132.; Rechtbank Rotterdam, 04 February 2016, ECLI:NL:RBROT:2016:898.; Case of Yasmeen in 'Voorkomen geweld tegen vrouwen, Kamerstukken II, 2014/2015, nr. 91', 2015, p. 6. See also casestudies of Anneke, Aya, Fariba, Kirsten and Sandra in van Eijk, *Wel gescheiden, niet gescheiden? Een empirisch onderzoek naar huwelijkse gevangenschap in Nederland*, pp. 104–106.

6.2.4.1. *The legal framework*

The right to health is generally recognised in international human rights law. In the ICESCR the provision on the right to health is found in Article 12(1) ICESCR, which prescribes that:

> *'States Parties to the present Convention recognize the right of everyone to the enjoyment of the highest attainable standard of physical and mental health'*

The second paragraph sums up several steps that States can adopt to ensure the realisation of the right to health. However, this is not an exhaustive list of all the steps that ought to be taken.

The CEDAW recognises that women have an equal right to healthcare in Article 12. The first paragraph provides:

> *'States Parties shall take all appropriate measures to eliminate discrimination against women in the field of health care in order to ensure, on a basis of equality of men and women, access to health care services, including those related to family planning.'*

Notably, by referring specifically to healthcare instead of 'physical and mental health', as article 12 ICESCR does, the scope of Article 12 CEDAW seems to be much narrower.[996] The right to health is also provided for in Article 25 UDHR which provides that:

> *'everyone has the right to a standard of living adequate for the health of himself and of his family, including food, clothing, housing and medical care and necessary social services (…)'.*

At the regional level, the ECHR contains no specific provision on the 'right to health'. However, it has been recognised to be contained in multiple ECHR provisions. Health-related issues have also been dealt with in relation to Article 2 (the right to life), Article 3 (the freedom from torture), Article 5 (liberty and security), Article 6 (fair trial), Article 8[997] and Article 14 (the principle of non-discrimination).[998] It is worth noting that the Council of Europe European Social Charter[999] and the European Union Charter on Fundamental Human Rights (EU Charter) also contain provisions on the right to health. Article 11 ESC contains a 'right to protection of health'. In the EU Charter this right is addressed only within the context of working conditions (Article 31

---

996 Brigit C. A. Toebes, *The right to health as a human right in international law,* (1999) (Intersentia/Hart), p. 5.

997 Jurisconsult, *Thematic Report: Health-related issues in the case-law of the European Court of Human Rights,* (Council of Europe, European Court of Human Rights 2015), p. 5.
Within Article 8 ECHR, the right to health has been recognised as an aspect of private life and, more in particular, as embedded within the right to physical and moral integrity.

998 Id., pp. 5–6.

999 Council of Europe, *European Social Charter (Revised)*, 3 May 1996.

EU Charter), youth labour (Article 31 EU Charter) and health care (Article 35 EU Charter). Both the ACHR and the ACHPR contain provisions on the right to health in Articles 10 and 11 ACHR and article 16 ACHPR.

6.2.4.1.1. Defining 'health'

The concept of 'health', as well as the scope of interpretation of the 'right to health', are matters over which there are diverging definitions and interpretations. These have ranged from broad interpretations that refer to notions of 'moral and social well-being' and include socio-economic and environmental conditions, to much narrower interpretations that limit health to deviations of normal functioning, diseases and illnesses.[1000] In human rights law, the ICESCR Committee has not attempted to further define the notion of 'health', nor has the ECtHR attempted to do so in its case law where health-related issues were raised. However, under the ICESCR it has been acknowledged that the right to health covers more than just physical functioning, diseases and health care aspects. The right to health also covers mental health aspects as well as decisive conditions of a socio-economic and environmental nature, such as violence, war, resource distribution, access to primary essentialities and environmental pollution.[1001]

While there are varying definitions of 'health' or a 'right to health', there is a wider consensus on what aspects are excluded from its scope. The right to health does not guarantee individuals a right to be healthy, neither does it fix a standard on what good health is or maintain that such a standard should be provided by all States in all circumstances.[1002] It has been recognised that the standard of attainable health will also be dependent on biological and socio-economic factors, as well as the resources of each specific State.[1003] In addition, not all forms related to an individuals' health can be prevented or protected by the State, particularly those that are beyond the control of the State (e.g. biological and genetic factors that impact an individuals' health, individuals' personal choices to engage in activities that could be detrimental to their health, an unhealthy lifestyles etc.).[1004]

1000 John Tobin, *The Right to Health in International Law* (2012), pp. 122–123,125–130.; Toebes, *The right to health as a human right in international law*, pp. 20–23. The WHO Constitution, for example, defines 'health' as: '*a state of complete physical, mental and social well-being and not merely the absence of disease or infirmity*'. World Health Organization, *Constitution of the World Health Organization as amended at the forty-fifth World Health Assembly*, October 2006, preamble.

1001 UN Committee on Economic, Social and Cultural Rights '*General Comment No. 14 (2000) – The right to the highest attainable standard of health (article 12)*)', 11 August 2000, E/C.12/2000/4, paras. 4, 10–11.

1002 Id., para. 8.; UN Office of the High Commissioner for Human Rights, *The Right to Health – Fact sheet No. 31*, (2008), p. 5. Notably, Article 11 of the European Social Charter does provide that States parties should '*remove as far as possible the causes of ill-health [...] [and] prevent as far as possible epidemic, endemic and other diseases, as well as accidents.*'

1003 CESCR, *General Comment No. 14 (2000) – The right to the highest attainable standard of health (article 12)*, para. 10.; *The Right to Health – Fact sheet No. 31*, p. 5.

1004 CESCR, *General Comment No. 14 (2000) – The right to the highest attainable standard of health (article 12)*, para. 9.

6.2.4.1.2. Limitations to the right to health

The ICESCR contains a general limitation clause in Article 4 ICESCR which requires that any limitations to the rights recognised in the Covenant, are '*determined by law only in so far as this may be compatible with the nature of these rights and solely for the purpose of promoting the general welfare in a democratic society*'. On this point, the ICESCR stressed that this limitation clause '*primarily intended to protect the rights of individuals rather than to permit the imposition of limitations by* States'.[1005] Notably, instead of adopting an exhaustive list of pursued aims, the ICESCR contains the rather broad concept of 'general welfare'. According to the Committee's general comment No. 14, 'general welfare' includes national security and public order.[1006] Furthermore, the Committee asserts that where States take deliberate retrogressive measures that relate to the right to health, then they carry the burden of proof to show that such measures have '*been introduced after the most careful considerations of all alternatives and that they are duly justified by reference to the totality of the rights provided for in the Convention in the context of the full use of the State party's maximum available resources*'.[1007] This, in essence, includes a proportionality test. Furthermore, violations or interferences with the right to health are also subjected to the criteria of unwillingness and inability of the State to protect and promote the right to health. The unwillingness of the State implies that the State has not made use of its maximum available resources to further the right to health and this thus constitutes a violation of its obligations under Article 12 ICESCR. Whereas, where the State is unable to comply with its obligations of Article 12 ICESCR, it then carries the burden of proof to provide that, with the resources it has, it has taken every possible measure to comply with its obligations.[1008]

6.2.4.2. The right to attain the highest standard of health

The right to the highest attainable standard of health covers both the physical and mental health of individuals, however, mental health is an aspect that has remained underdeveloped, partly due to the limited amount of attention States pay to this subject in their periodic reports and the little case law that relates to mental health.[1009] The right to health contains both freedoms and entitlements.[1010] Accordingly, '*the freedoms include the right to control one's health and body, including sexual and reproductive freedom, and the right to be free from interference, such as the right to be free from torture, non-consensual medical treatment and experimentation. Entitlements include the right to a system of health protection which provides equality of opportunity for*

[1005] Id., para. 28.
[1006] Id.
[1007] Id., para. 32.
[1008] Id., para. 47.
[1009] Toebes, *The right to health as a human right in international law*, p. 132.
[1010] CESCR, *General Comment No. 14 (2000) – The right to the highest attainable standard of health (article 12)*, para. 8.

people to enjoy the highest attainable level of health'.[1011] The description afforded to the 'freedoms' reflects a negative interpretation of freedom, whereby the focus is on non-intervention. Acknowledgement is given to the personal autonomy that is inherent in the right of physical integrity that awards individuals control over and responsibility for their own bodies. The entitlements align with a broader understanding of autonomy and give recognition to the importance of an infrastructure for health protection as an essential precondition for fostering the right to health. Entitlements can be categorised in healthcare-related matters and preconditions for health.[1012] With regards to the preconditions for health, these concern the primary necessities to an individual's life, such as access to clean and safe water, food, essential nutrition and housing, access to adequate sanitation and health-related information, as well as safe environmental conditions.[1013] Both healthcare-related aspects as well as preconditions for health need to be available[1014], accessible[1015], acceptable[1016] and of good quality.[1017]

The State's available resources are taken into account in determining the ability of the State to ensure and guarantee individuals freedoms and entitlements related to health. Thus, the right to health, as it is contained in Article 12 (1) ICESCR, guarantees that the necessary goods, facilities, services, socio-economic and environmental conditions are pursued and secured to the maximum ability of the State, so that individuals are able to pursue the highest attainable standard of physical and mental health.[1018] Similar to most second-generation rights, the right to health is a right that should be progressively realised. However, the right to health also contains immediate measures, such as guaranteeing equality in the implementation and protection of the right to health and actively working towards its realisation.[1019]

Finally, the right to health is interdependent, interrelated and indivisible from other human rights. The interpretation of health-related issues in other provisions of the ECtHR illustrates this link between the right to health and other human rights. In the same light, the CESCR acknowledges that Article 12 ICESCR is related and dependent

---

1011 Id.

1012 Toebes, *The right to health as a human right in international law*, pp. 243–258.

1013 CESCR, *General Comment No. 14 (2000) – The right to the highest attainable standard of health (article 12)*, para.11.; See also European Social Charter, Article 11.

1014 Id., para. 12. Availability means that '*functioning public health and health-care facilities, goods and services, as well as programmes, have to be available in sufficient quantity within the State party*'.

1015 Id. The requirement of accessibility has four dimensions. First, health care must be accessible without discrimination on any of the prohibited ground. Secondly, the provided facilities, services or goods need to be physically accessible in the sense that they '*must be within the safe physical reach for all sections of the population*'. Thirdly, these must be affordable to all. Lastly, informational accessibility means that individuals must be able to '*seek, receive and impart information and ideas concerning health issues*'.

1016 Id. The criterion of acceptability provides that health-care must be '*respectful of medical ethics and culturally appropriate*'.

1017 Id. Provided health-care, goods and services must be '*scientifically and medically appropriate and of good quality*'.

1018 Id., paras. 9–11.

1019 Id., para. 30.

on, *inter alia,* the principles of human dignity, non-discrimination and equality, and the substantive rights and freedoms of privacy, movement and access to information.[1020]

6.2.4.3. Health and marital captivity

In certain circumstances, a situation of marital captivity can have far-reaching consequences for the physical and mental health of the trapped spouse. While it should be borne in mind that, in reality, not all situations involving marital captivity will impact the trapped spouse's health to the same degree, the right to health or even the right to adequate and appropriate health care is a subject that has received little to no attention in the debates on marital captivity, even in cases that have involved domestic violence or honour-related crimes. How the trapped spouse's physical and mental integrity are affected by an ongoing situation of marital captivity, are subjects that remain largely unaddressed in studies on marital captivity as well as in judicial and legislative efforts that address marital captivity. However, the right to health and the guarantees it contains in relation to physical and mental health are very much relevant for trapped spouses. Further inclusion of this right in the dialogue on marital captivity is necessary. It is also important to assert the State obligations that arise from this right so as to better safeguard trapped spouses' rights.

6.3. STATES' OBLIGATIONS TO PROTECT THE TRAPPED SPOUSE'S RIGHT

As the previous subchapters have illustrated, a situation of marital captivity, essentially, impairs the autonomy of the trapped spouse. In particular, this is more so for women, as in some religious schools women have far more limited rights to initiate and obtain a divorce and they need to secure the cooperation of their husbands in order to obtain a divorce. A situation of marital captivity interferes with, among others, the right to remarry, the right to private life, the freedom of movement and the right to health. It is important to keep in mind that depending on the specific circumstances of each case, some of these rights may not be affected. The freedom of movement, for example, will not be affected where trapped spouses can freely travel without needing their (partners) approval.

Whether and to what extent the State is responsible for the interference with the trapped spouses' rights is dependent on whether the conditions that give rise to a situation of marital captivity can be attributed to the State. In States where religious laws, authorities and tribunals have no legal recognition or significance, such as in the Netherlands, a situation of marital captivity is created by private non-State actors. The

---

[1020] CESCR, *General Comment No. 14 (2000) – The right to the highest attainable standard of health (article 12)*, para. 3.

religious doctrines and views on divorce that do not allow divorce or that restrict the woman's right to initiate a divorce and enable a situation of marital captivity to arise are therefore not recognised and regulated by the State. Rather, these are interpreted, enforced and applied by the religious authorities within the religious communities. Religious tribunals and authorities are private actors and, in their operation, they do not represent the State. Additionally, where the dissolution of a religious marriage requires the cooperation of one of the spouses, the non-cooperative spouse too has a role in the creation and continuation of marital captivity. Again, this concerns a private actor.

Thus, in a secular State such as the Netherlands, it is not the State but rather the religious tribunals, community and/or recalcitrant spouse who create and maintain situations of marital captivity which, in turn, infringes upon the trapped spouse's rights. However, this does not necessarily mean that a secular State is alleviated from its human rights obligations to respond adequately and appropriately to the interferences with the trapped spouse's rights. Even if human rights violations are not directly attributable to the State, there may still be positive obligations on the State to secure and protect the trapped spouse's rights.

The situation is different in States where religious laws, authorities and tribunals are incorporated within the national legal system, such as in Israel for example. Restrictive and discriminatory religious laws on divorce then serve as domestic national laws and their implementation and application is recognised and regulated by the State. Religious authorities have the jurisdiction to adjudicate upon family matters, including those related to divorce. Their decisions have legal recognition and effects. Therefore, the conditions that enable situations of marital captivity to arise and persist are directly attributable to the State, even if a situation of marital captivity is factually created by a recalcitrant spouse's refusal to cooperate in the dissolution of a marriage. After all, it is the State's legal system and authorities that enable a non-cooperative spouse to hold the other spouse hostage to a marriage against their will. The human rights violations arising from a situation of marital captivity, thus, may be directly attributed to the State.

To make matters more complicated, multiple States may also be involved in situations of marital captivity, particularly where spouses are divorced in one country but still married in another country. This can have serious implications, particularly on the trapped women's freedom to travel to and from the country of origin. As was established in subsection 6.2.3.2., domestic laws and practices in other countries may make the issuance of travel documents conditional on the husband's approval and this will, therefore, restrict married women's rights to travel. Consequently, a trapped wife, in for example the Netherlands, may be unable to travel back to her country of origin, for example Iran, so long as she is still considered to be legally married in Iran as she will need the approval of her husband in order to obtain the necessary travel documents. Thus, the national laws of another State may set conditions that restrict and interfere with the trapped spouse's rights, even if the trapped spouse is in another State that does not impose similar restrictions.

Considering the foregoing, it is thus imperative to assess and distinguish, in each specific case, the role of all involved actors and to what extent violations of the trapped spouse's human rights are attributable to the State. This is necessary as it has implications for the extent of the State's obligation to effectively respect and guarantee the trapped spouse's rights. After all, in human rights law it is the States that are obliged to guarantee and protect individuals' human rights. In the following sections, therefore, the human rights obligations arising from each of the investigated rights are first elaborated upon. This is then followed by a discussion on the State obligations within the context of marital captivity, taking into account the different scenarios and their implications for the State.

6.3.1. TYPES OF OBLIGATIONS

In general, State obligations are categorised as negative or positive obligations. Negative obligations impose a duty on the State not to interfere with and to abstain from violating individual human rights.[1021] Positive obligations, on the other hand, impose a duty on the State to effectively secure and ensure the guaranteed human rights. These require that appropriate and suitable measures are taken to protect individual rights from being violated and to guarantee that individuals can genuinely enjoy and exercise their rights.[1022] The obligation to protect against violations by others implies, *inter alia*, that States have to regulate their observance with treaty rights by individuals and in particular within horizontal relationships. However, it should be borne in mind that human rights obligations are only binding only on States and, as such, do not have direct horizontal effect.[1023] In other words, they cannot be directly enforced in relationships between individuals.

1021 Dinah Shelton and Ariel Gould, 'Positive and negative obligations', in Shelton *The Oxford handbook of international human rights law* (Oxford, 2013), p. 563.

1022 Id., p. 563.; Jean-François Akandji-Kombe, *Positive obligations under the European Convention on Human Rights – A guide to the implementation of the European Convention on Human Rights* (No. 7 2007), pp. 7, 9–11. Notably, the legal basis for positive obligations derives from, Article 2 ICCPR, Article 2 ICESCR, Article 2 CEDAW and Article 3 ECHR respectively, taken in conjunction with the obligations implied in substantive provisions. *CEDAW,General Recommendation No. 28 on the core obligations of States Parties under Article 2 of the Convention on the Elimination of All Forms of Discrimination against Women*, paras. 5–8.; UN Human Rights Committee 'General comment No. 31 [80] The nature of the general legal obligation imposed on States Parties to the Covenant', 26 May 2004, CCPR/C/21/Rev.1/Add.13, paras. 5–6.; UN Committee on Economic, Social and Cultural Rights 'General Comment No. 3: The Nature of States Parties' Obligations (Art. 2, para. 1, of the Covenant)', 14 December 1990, E/1991/23, paras. 1–9.

1023 HRC, *General comment No. 31 [80], The nature of the general legal obligation imposed on States Parties to the Covenant*, para. 8.

6.3.1.1. Negative obligations

All of the rights that have been investigated in this Chapter (the right to remarry, the right to private life, the freedom of movement and the right to health) contain positive and negative obligations. The negative obligations inherent in the right to remarry require States to refrain from enacting, maintaining or preserving laws, policies and practices that undermine equality and sustain gender inequality in marital affairs, including divorce.[1024] States should also refrain from imposing restrictions that are unreasonable or which make it impossible to exercise and enjoy the right to remarry.[1025] In this regard, the practices of repudiation and polygamy have been condemned by human rights monitoring bodies. These practices undermine the position of women within the marriage and at its dissolution, and they exacerbate inequality between women and men within the family. Therefore, States that condone and regulate repudiation and polygamy have been instructed to bring these practices to an end and to amend the laws that allow and regulate repudiation and polygamy.[1026] Likewise, laws that, among others, impose waiting periods on divorced women for being eligible to remarry have been found to be incompatible with the woman's right to marry and the principle of equality. States that adopt such laws have been requested to review and amend these.[1027]

Furthermore, negative obligations require the State to abstain from interfering with individuals' right to private life.[1028] In general, the State has an obligation not to interfere with this right and should refrain from adopting measures that would interfere with individuals' enjoyment of their right to private life and the other rights protected therein. Laws and practices that interfere with an individuals' private life should, therefore, be eliminated. Similarly, laws and State condoned practices that enable private parties to violate privacy rights of women (e.g. requesting from female candidates a pregnancy test prior to hiring) should be eliminated.[1029] The individual's right to form relationships both within their private settings as well as within certain public settings should be respected. However, this does not mean that all measures that result in limiting or prohibiting the establishment of certain relationships or which affect an individuals' social life, by definition, constitute a violation of Articles 17 ICCPR and 8 ECHR. Restrictive measures may still be justifiable in accordance with the limitation clauses of these articles.[1030]

As for the freedom of movement, States are obliged to refrain from enacting any measures or conduct that would result in unreasonably or entirely restricting the

---

1024 Freeman *Article 16*, p. 440.
1025 HRC, *General Comment No. 28: Article 3 (The equality of rights between men and women)*, para. 24.
1026 See section 5.2.2 and subsection 6.2.1.1.
1027 HRC, *General Comment No. 28: Article 3 (The equality of rights between men and women*, paras. 23–26. See also section 5.3.3. at note 830.
1028 HRC, *General Comment No. 16*, paras. 1, 9.
1029 HRC, *General Comment No. 28: Article 3 (The equality of rights between men and women)*, para. 20.
1030 For example, the prohibition of sexual relationships with minors.

rights contained in the freedom of movement. The HRC has among others condemned laws that condition the married woman's free movement rights to the approval of their husbands.[1031] Restricting the right to free movement, particularly for women, by subjecting its exercise to the consent of others (e.g. the husband or relatives) is, in fact, incompatible with the rights contained in Article 12 ICCPR and the equality principle.[1032] Women's rights to free movement should also not be made conditional on their marital status. Both, the HRC and CEDAW Committee have found that subjection, by law or practice, of women's right to travel to the approval of others violates women's freedom of movement. States are required to end biased laws and practices of male guardianship over women's travelling activities.[1033] Furthermore, Article 15 CEDAW, which prescribes the equality of women and men before the law, contains a specific and immediate obligation which requires the promotion and implementation of equality by formal law and reform of laws in order to remove limitations to women's freedom of movement and to ensure women's rights.[1034] Thus, restrictions or discriminatory laws and practices that affect a married woman's freedom to travel within, to and from the State are incompatible with the obligations implied in the freedom of movement. Additionally, States should also refrain from frustrating an individuals' ability to travel by refusing to issue travel documents or by unreasonably frustrating the procedure to obtain travel documents.[1035]

Finally, the right to health also contains negative obligations. These require State actors to refrain from adopting measures or practices that impair an individual's health.[1036] This includes retrogressive measures that would increase risks to an individual's health (including environmental conditions) or which would limit or deny their access to information, goods, services and facilities that are beneficial for their health standards or which result in discriminatory practices. In general, such measures are presumed to be impermissible, unless the concerned State can prove justifications for the adoption and enforcement of measures that jeopardise an individual's right to health.[1037]

1031 See for example the observations of the HRC in Human Rights Committee, *Concluding Observations Lebanon 1997*, CCPR/C/79/Add.78, para. 18.; Human Rights Committee, *Concluding Observations Sudan 1997*, CCPR/C/79/Add.85, para. 14.

1032 HRC, *General Comment No. 27: Freedom of movement (article 12)*, para. 6.; Human Rights Committee, *Sandra Lovelace v. Canada*, 29 December 1977, Communication No. R.6/24.

1033 HRC, *General Comment No. 27: Freedom of movement (article 12)*, paras. 6, 18.; Goonesekere *Article 15*, p. 400.

1034 Id., p. 404.; CEDAW, *General Recommendation No. 21 on Equality in marriage and family relations*, para. 49.

1035 HRC, *General Comment No. 27: Freedom of movement (article 12)*, para. 9.; Nowak, *U.N. Covenant on Civil and Political Rights: CCPR commentary*, pp. 267–270.

1036 Schabas, *The European Convention on Human Rights: A commentary*, p. 370.; CESCR, *General Comment No. 14 (2000) – The right to the highest attainable standard of health (article 12)*, paras. 34, 50.

1037 CESCR, *General Comment No. 14 (2000) – The right to the highest attainable standard of health (article 12)*, paras. 32.

6.3.1.2. Positive obligations

All of the rights investigated in this Chapter also contain positive obligations. States are obliged to ensure the effective enjoyment of the right to remarry and to equality in all marital affairs, the right to private life, the freedom of movement and the right to health by individuals. This includes adopting measures to secure these rights, even within horizontal relationships, and to protect these rights from violations by non-State actors.[1038] Notably, the precise content of the State's positive obligations remains, largely, unspecified. To a lesser extent, human rights treaties explicitly contain and specify the positive obligations contained therein.[1039] Human rights monitoring bodies have resolved to clarifying the scope and content of positive obligations on an ad hoc (e.g. in the general comments and concluding observations) or on a case by case basis. Courts and human rights monitoring bodies have tended to apply the criteria for establishing compliance with negative obligations (legality, legitimacy and proportionality tests) analogously so as to establish the existence and scope of positive obligations.

The protection of the individual's rights from violations by others and guaranteeing that individuals can enjoy and exercise their rights obliges States to regulate the observance of human rights by individuals and in particular within horizontal relationships. For example, the HRC directs States to introduce legislative measures that ensure that the right to privacy is not interfered with by natural and/or legal persons.[1040] Similarly, the obligation to prohibit discrimination, ensure equal protection before the law[1041] and to adopt an adequate legal framework to combat certain practices that constitute violence against women[1042], require that measures be adopted to regulate the behaviour and conduct of individuals. This can for example be realised by, anti-discrimination,

---

1038 On the right to private life: HRC, *General Comment No. 16*, paras. 1, 9.; European Court of Human Rights, *Botta v. Italy,* 24 February 1998, Application No. 21439/93, para. 33. On the freedom of movement: HRC, *General Comment No. 27: Freedom of movement (article 12)*, para. 6.; Joseph, et al., *The International Covenant on Civil and Political Rights- Cases, materials and commentary*, p. 349. On the right to health: Schabas, *The European Convention on Human Rights: A commentary*, p. 370.; CESCR, *General Comment No. 14 (2000) – The right to the highest attainable standard of health (article 12)*.; ECtHR conclusion in the case of *Bevacqua and S. v. Bulgaria* as cited in: Lee Hasselbacher, 'State obligations regarding domestic violence: The European Court of Human Rights, due diligence, and international legal minimums of protection', 8 *Northwestern Journal of Human Rights* 190, (2009), p. 207.

1039 Some examples are found in the provisions that require the adoption of legislative measures against discrimination in the ICCPR and CEDAW. See John H. Knox, 'Horizontal Human Rights Law', 102 *American Journal of International Law* 1–47, (2007), pp. 24–25, 27–31.; Covenant on Civil and Political Rights, Article 26.; CEDAW, *General Recommendation No. 19 on Violence against women*, para. 24.

1040 HRC, *General Comment No. 16*, para. 9.

1041 Convention on the Elimination of All Forms of Discrimination Against Women, Article 2 (a, b, e).; International Covenant on Civil and Political Rights, article 26.; HRC, *General comment No. 31 [80], The nature of the general legal obligation imposed on States Parties to the Covenant*, para. 8.

1042 CESCR, *General Comment No. 14 (2000) – The right to the highest attainable standard of health (article 12)*, paras. 35, 51.

criminal and administrative laws.[1043] States are, furthermore, obliged to protect women from discrimination by non-State actors within the family, marriage and during the dissolution of the marriage.[1044] This should involve prohibiting, preventing and effectively addressing activities and practices that impair women's human rights, such as, honour-related crimes, forced marriage, marital rape, polygamy and forced abortions to name but a few.[1045] Measures should also include persecuting perpetrators of acts of violence against women and discouraging harmful and traditional practices that negatively impact the health of women and young girls.[1046]

States are also obliged to assess whether their domestic laws are compliant with the standards set out in Article 15 CEDAW. In doing so, States must assess whether '*religious or private law or custom*' conflict with the domestic laws and Convention rights and obligations.[1047] Implemented laws should not only aim to promote equality in public life, but they should endeavour to do so also in the private sphere, thereby requiring and encouraging private actors to conform to the equality standards found within domestic laws. The effective implementation and enforcement thereof requires that complementary mechanism for effective remedies to human rights infringements are in place.[1048] This includes securing judicial means to hold States and non-State actors responsible for human rights violations, as well as enabling constitutional and public interest litigations.[1049] In respect of public interest litigations, human rights groups should be enabled to represent aggravated individuals in accordance with the Optional Protocol.[1050] Finally, Article 15 CEDAW also obliges States to monitor and assess the impact and effectiveness of the remedies that are in place.[1051]

States are also obliged to enact laws and to adopt measures that ensure the equality of women in all matters relating to marriage and *de facto* relationships and to ensure that gender stereotypes and roles are not perpetuated or reinforced.[1052] In this regard, States should actively deploy their resources to challenge social and cultural attitudes and beliefs that limit women's roles to their reproductive capabilities and prescribe women the sole purpose of being married.[1053] State obligations related to eliminating gender

---

1043 Danwood M. Chirwa, 'The doctrine of State responsibility as a potential means of holding private actors accountable for human rights', 5 *Melbourne Journal in International Law* 1-36, (2004), pp. 11-12.; HRC, *General Comment No. 16*, para. 9.

1044 European Convention on Human Rights, Article 12 *juncto* Article 14.; Convention on the Elimination of All Forms of Discrimination Against Women, Article 2 (e) *juncto* Article 16.; International Covenant on Civil and Political Rights, Article 26.; HRC, *General Comment No. 28: Article 3 (The equality of rights between men and women)*, para. 31.; Freeman *Article 16*, p. 440.

1045 Freeman *Article 16*, p. 440.; CEDAW, *General Recommendation No. 21 on Equality in marriage and family relations*, paras. 14, 49. See also CESCR, *General Comment No. 14 (2000) – The right to the highest attainable standard of health (article 12)*, paras. 35, 51.

1046 Id.

1047 CEDAW, *General Recommendation No. 21 on Equality in marriage and family relations*, para. 47–50.

1048 Goonesekere *Article 15*, p. 405.

1049 Id., pp. 404–405.

1050 Id., p. 405.

1051 Id.

1052 Marsha Freeman *Article 16*, p. 440.

1053 Id., pp. 440–441.

stereotypes and roles are elaborated further in paragraphs 7.6.1.1.3. Furthermore, ensuring equality of women in all matters relating to marriage and *de facto unions* requires that States review any domestic laws that may prevent women from freely marrying. Additionally, the implemented measures should not only aim to promote equality in all matters relating to the marriage, but they should, as aforementioned, aim to promote and encourage private actors to conform to the equality standards that are found within domestic laws and human rights treaties.[1054] Conditions that enable women to enjoy their rights should also be secured. This includes establishing an effective infrastructure that enables women to enforce their right to marry or seek remedies and reparations via qualified, trained and accessible courts or other independent bodies.[1055] Noteworthy, States are recommended to establish a system for the registration of all marriages '*whether contracted civilly or according to custom or religious law*'.[1056] However, this recommendation does not entail that the registration of all marriages should also imply the legal recognition of such marriages. States have the discretion to determine the legal status and formalities of the various relationships that individuals may engage in.[1057]

States are also required to protect and secure conditions whereby individuals can exercise their right to private life, establish and maintain social life and realise their personal development. However, according to the cases of *Friend, The Country Alliance and Others v. the United Kingdom* and *Botta v. Italy,* this positive obligation does not extend so far as to require States to secure, by positive actions, that individuals can establish and develop relationships that are too broad and indeterminate in nature.[1058]

The link between the right to enter and the right to leave entails that each State has a positive obligation to issue travel documents, as these are a prerequisite for exercising the right to leave.[1059] Where the national is abroad, as was illustrated by the passport cases, both the host State and the State of nationality have obligations in relation to the national that is seeking to leave the host State.[1060] The country of nationality has a positive duty to ensure that their nationals can travel abroad and the State is, therefore, required to issue the necessary travel documents to that effect. It also has a negative duty not to refuse the national from returning. The host State, on the other hand, has a negative to refrain from restricting or interfering with the national's right to leave.[1061] Whether the host State has also a positive obligation to protect the

---

1054 CEDAW, *General Recommendation No. 21 on Equality in marriage and family relations*, paras. 47–50.

1055 Freeman *Article 16*, p. 440.

1056 Id., p. 440.; CEDAW, *General Recommendation No. 21 on Equality in marriage and family relations*, para. 39.

1057 See section 5.2.2.

1058 See subsection 6.2.2.2.

1059 Nowak, *U.N. Covenant on Civil and Political Rights: CCPR commentary*, p. 268.; HRC, *General Comment No. 27: Freedom of movement (article 12)*, para. 9.

1060 HRC, *General Comment No. 27: Freedom of movement (article 12)*, para. 9.

1061 Nihal Jayawickrama, *The judicial application of Human Rights Law: National, regional and international jurisprudence* (Cambridge, 2002), p. 474.; Nowak, *U.N. Covenant on Civil and Political*

concerned individual's freedom of movement, in the event that the State of nationality fails to, for example, issue the necessary travel documents, is something which has yet to be addressed by human rights monitoring bodies.[1062] Similarly, where the host State deprives a national of another State the freedom of movement (e.g. refusal to grant an exit-visa or imposing a travel ban), it remains uncertain the extent of human rights obligations that rest upon the State of nationality for as long as the national remains in the territory of the host State. Thus, while the State of nationality and the host State have obligations to guarantee the freedom of movement, it nevertheless remains unclear what these obligations include and what specific measures States may be expected to take so as to comply with these obligations. Notably, Jayawikrama submits that where an individual is detained abroad, the State of nationality then has a positive obligation, to '*deal with the state in which [its] citizen is detained with a view to securing the enjoyment of this right, since no citizen on his or her own can act with equal legal status with the governmental authorities of a foreign state. Where no such action was taken by the state of nationality, this right was infringed*'.[1063] The specificity of such actions is left unaddressed. However, this proposition raises several questions. Firstly, does such a the positive obligation have extra-territorial reach? Secondly, how would this State obligation then relate to other existing mechanism of international law such as diplomatic protection? Can human rights law serve as a legal basis to demand a State to exercise its right to diplomatic protection on behalf of its nationals that are abroad? Essentially, this would boil down to demanding the State to take measures that will undoubtedly encroach upon the territory, jurisdiction and sovereignty of the other State.

Further inquiry on this subject matter requires, among others, an assessment of the extra-territorial reach of the obligations of States under international human rights law. State's human rights obligations may have extra-territorial reach as is, for example seen, in the passport cases. The State of nationality continues to carry the obligation to ensure that its nationals are issued with the necessary travel documents and to ensure that they can travel abroad and back, irrespective of whether the nationals are in the territory of another State or not. The extra-territorial reach of human rights is a relevant subject matter for those situations of marital captivity where women are not only trapped in the religious marriage but are also trapped in another State.

Diplomatic protection and consular assistance are other mechanisms of protection worthy of consideration for such situations. On that note it is important to stress that,

---

Rights: CCPR commentary, p. 269. See also the passport cases: Human Rights Committee, *Mabel Pereira Montero v. Uruguay*, 31 March 1983, Communication No. 106/1981, para. 9.4.; Human Rights Committee, *Sophie Vidal Martins v. Uruguay*, 23 March 1982, Communication No. R.13/57, para. 7.; Human Rights Committee, *Samuel Lichtensztejn v. Uruguay*, 31 March 1983, Communication No. 77/1980, para. 6.1.

1062 Nowak, *U.N. Covenant on Civil and Political Rights: CCPR commentary*, p. 270.

1063 Jayawickrama, *The judicial application of Human Rights Law: National, regional and international jurisprudence*, p. 474.

human rights treaties do not guarantee individuals a right to diplomatic protection and consular assistance. In fact, in international law diplomatic protection and consular assistance are recognised as rights of the State[1064], although they are exercised on behalf of individuals i.e. it is the harm to individuals that serves as the basis for the application of these rights.[1065] The prevailing view is that States exercise these rights at their own discretion. States do not have a duty to employ these means and although nationals in distress have the privilege to request for such intervention, they do not have a right to diplomatic protection by the State of their nationality. The traditional approach to diplomatic protection and consular assistance as State rights, however, continues to be challenged. Discussions in this area have focused on the role of the injured individual, how to better protect the rights of individuals that are stranded in a host State, and whether States have or ought to have a duty to exercise these instruments.[1066]

Having said that, it is important to stress here that this contribution does not delve into the subject matter of extra-territorial application of human rights or the relationship between the various fields of international law as was explained in subchapter 1.6. It is clear, however, that this is an important subject, particularly in situations of marital captivity that have transnational elements, and where a trapped wife is prevented from leaving the host country. In seeking solutions, for such situations it is thus relevant to analyse the extent of protection which a trapped woman can expect from international human rights mechanisms (e.g. by way of the extra-territorial application of human rights) as well as through other means in international law that are aimed at protecting individual's rights (e.g. diplomatic protection and consular assistance).

The positive obligations that are implied in the right to freedom of movement also require protection from the conduct of private actors that may result in restricting an individuals' freedom to travel within, to and from a particular country. More specifically, within the context of migrant workers, the HRC has found that the confiscation of identity and travel documents of migrant workers, by their employer, is incompatible with Article 12 ICCPR. Therefore, in complying with their obligations,

---

1064 International Law Commission, *Draft articles on diplomatic protection with commentaries 2006* (2006), [A/61/10], Commentaries draft articles, p. 28–29.; United Nations, *Draft articles on diplomatic protection*, 2006, Article 2 *juncto* Article 19.

1065 International Law Commission, *Draft articles on diplomatic protection with commentaries 2006*, pp. 28–29.; Anna Maria Helena Vermeer-Künzli, *The protection of individuals by means of diplomatic protection: diplomatic protection as a human rights instrument*, (2007) (Leiden University), pp. 31–32.

1066 Article 19 of the ILC's Draft articles on diplomatic protection, for example, encourages States to 'take into account, wherever feasible, the views of injured persons with regard to resort to diplomatic protection and the reparation to be sought'. International Law Commission, *Draft articles on diplomatic protection with commentaries 2006*, Article 19. On these topics see also: David Leys, 'Diplomatic Protection and Individual Rights: A Complementary Approach', 57 *Harvard International Law Journal Online 1-14*, (2016). Chittharanjan F. Amerasinghe, *Diplomatic Protection*, (Oxford, 2008), pp. 80–90.; Mohamed Bennouna, *Preliminatry Report on diplomatic protection,* (1984), [/ CN.4/484], paras 80–87.; John R. Dugard, *First Report on Diplomatic Protection*, (2000), paras. 61–74; Anna Maria Helena Vermeer-Künzli, *The protection of individuals by means of diplomatic protection: diplomatic protection as a human rights instrument*, (2007) (Leiden University), pp. 175–205, 214–215.

States are recommended to adopt '*effective measures to protect the right of these foreign workers by preventing such confiscation and by providing an accessible and effective means for the recovery of passports*'.[1067]

Finally, despite the recognition that the right to health should be realised progressively, there are also immediate and core obligations that are inherent within the right to health. These set a minimum standard that States must comply with.[1068] The obligation to protect includes, *inter alia*, the active and effective protection of vulnerable and marginalised groups and ensuring that access to information and services are not limited by private parties.[1069] States should also adopt measures to prevent and remedy violations to the right to health by private actors.[1070] They should also create conditions that enable non-State actors to discharge their responsibility to respect and contribute to realising the right to health.[1071] The obligation to fulfil goes one step further by requiring the State to implement the necessary measures on its own initiative rather than as a response to violations by private actors.[1072] Measures may include information and awareness campaigns on matters that affect the health of individuals. Besides information dissemination and awareness campaigns, the furthering of health requires that health care workers are well trained to the various types and social contexts of health-related matters that occur within vulnerable groups.[1073]

By guaranteeing the right to health, States must also to take into account the special ways in which certain vulnerable groups experience health-related issues, and ensure that goods, facilities and services meet their specific needs.[1074] More specifically for women, States should implement appropriate services in the areas related to reproductive health, family planning and pregnancy and actively and effectively address violence against women by State agents as well as by private persons.[1075] This means, among others, ensuring that those working in the field of healthcare are trained to identify and respond appropriately to the consequences of violence against women.[1076] States are, additionally, obliged to take preventive, promotive and remedial actions to protect women from harmful, traditional and cultural practices that jeopardise

1067 Human Rights Committee, *Concluding Observations Lebanon 1997*, CCPR/C/79/Add.78, para. 22.

1068 CESCR, *General Comment No. 14 (2000) – The right to the highest attainable standard of health (article 12)*, paras. 30, 43. The core-obligations include, *inter alia,* the obligation to ensure: the right of access to health facilities, goods and services on a non-discriminatory basis; access to the minimum essential food and the freedom from hunger; access to basic shelter, housing, sanitation; adequate supply of safe and potable water; provisions of essential drugs and equitable distribution of all health facilities, goods and services. See also the Alma-Ata Declaration.

1069 Id., para. 35.

1070 Id., para. 51.

1071 Id., para. 42.

1072 Id., para. 36.

1073 Id., para. 37.

1074 Id., paras. 21–27.

1075 Id., para. 21.; UN Committee on the Elimination of Discrimination Against Women ' General Recommendation No. 24 on Article 12 of the Convention (Women and Health)', 1999, para. 2.

1076 CEDAW, *General Recommendation No. 24: Article 12 of the Convention (Women and Health)*, para. 15.

women's health.[1077] Furthermore, the CESCR has found that States have obligations to improve the health care that is provided to women, including its accessibility, quality and affordability and to reduce health risks such as maternal mortality and domestic violence.[1078]

On top of that

In addition, States also have international obligations to strengthen cooperation and provide assistance in order to secure the rights that are guaranteed in the ICESCR, including the right to health. International obligations not only require States to respect the right to health in other countries, but also to prevent third-parties from violating the right to health in other countries '*if they are able to influence these third parties by way of legal or political means, in accordance with the Charter of the UN and applicable international law*'.[1079]

6.3.2. MARITAL CAPTIVITY AND STATES' OBLIGATIONS

More specifically on marital captivity, in its 2016 concluding observations to the sixth periodic report of the Netherlands, the CEDAW Committee specifically recommended States provide '*training on marital captivity for judiciary and law enforcement officials in order to eradicate [marital captivity] this phenomenon*'.[1080] Additionally, the CEDAW Committee has also recommended the Netherlands to devote resources to facilitating awareness-raising efforts *vis-à-vis* marital captivity.[1081] In the 2011 concluding observation to Israel, the CEDAW Committee also recommended the State to '*ensure that rabbinical court judges are provided with training on the Convention, with special emphasis on article 16 as well as domestic violence*'[1082], with the aim of addressing situations of marital captivity occurring in Israel.

In this respect, it is particularly important that the judges are made aware of the human rights that are or are likely to be impaired by a situation of marital captivity. Including human rights law within the judicial process concerning situations of marital captivity is beneficial in that it directs judges to focus their attention on protecting human rights that are violated by ongoing situations of marital captivity. In turn, this

---

1077 CESCR, *General Comment No. 14 (2000) – The right to the highest attainable standard of health (article 12)*, para. 21.

1078 Id., para. 14.

1079 Id., para. 39.

1080 Committee on the Elimination of Discrimination Against Women, *Concluding Observations the Netherlands 2016*, CEDAW/C/NLD/CO/6, para. 44.; See also Celeste Montoya, *From Global to Grassroots: The European Union, Transnational Advocacy, and Combating Violence Against Women* (New York 2013), p. 218. On the training of professionals, including judges, on violence against women in the Council of Europe members.

1081 Committee on the Elimination of Discrimination Against Women, *Concluding Observations the Netherlands 2016*, para. 44.

1082 Committee on the Elimination of Discrimination Against Women, *Concluding Observations Israel 2011*, CEDAW/C/ISR/CO/5, paras. 48–49.

would help to eliminate erroneous conclusions such as those that were reached in the cases of *Rechtbank Rotterdam 06 January 2016* and *Rechtbank Amsterdam 12 April 2014*, where the involved judges did not consider the negative consequences of marital captivity on the trapped rights. Instead, they dismissed the trapped wife on account of the fact that there had only ever been a religious marriage and that she had no intention to travel or remarry in the near future. Centralising human rights within the judicial proceedings concerning marital captivity would, thus, enable judges to take appropriate consideration of the rights that are at stake, irrespective of the trapped woman's future plans and irrespective of whether or not there is a civil marriage.

Having said that, the following subsections elaborate further on the positive and negative obligations that have been outlined in section 6.3.1. within the context of marital captivity. The purpose hereof is to further specify what obligations States have to protect trapped spouses' rights and to prevent them from being violated. Where possible, particular examples and inspiration are drawn from the already existing measures found in certain States.

6.3.2.1. Protection from violations of the State and private actors

States have positive obligations to secure the trapped spouses' right to remarry and the right to private life. The specific obligations may vary and are dependent on whether a situation of marital captivity is directly attributable to the State. A situation of marital captivity may be enabled by State's laws (including personal laws) and practices that discriminate against women in matters of marriage and divorce (e.g. laws and practices that restrict women's rights to initiate and obtain a divorce, allow husbands to repudiate their wives, restrict the women's ability to remarry and condone polygamy). Furthermore, a situation of marital captivity is exacerbated by domestic laws that restrict women's mobility and access to an active social life. These laws foster discrimination against women and maintain inequality between women and men within the marriage, family life and before the law and impair the trapped women's rights. These impairments are, therefore, directly attributable to the State. Human rights obligations require that such laws are reviewed and, where necessary, abolished or adapted so as to ensure the equality of men and women in all marital affairs. The fact that this may concern personal laws, religious laws and religious dispute settlement mechanisms does not alleviate the State from its human rights obligations to protect the trapped spouses' rights and ensure equality of women and men. The equality principle should also find effect in the religious divorce procedures and the religious tribunals' decisions, where these are recognised and regulated by the State.[1083]

Furthermore, where women are deprived of their right to remarry and the right to establish relationships with others, as consequence of a situation of marital captivity,

[1083] Amor, *Étude sur la liberté de religion ou de conviction et la condition de la femme au regard de la religion et des traditions*, (2002), p. 49.

States should take the necessary steps to ensure that trapped wives can enforce and remedy the experienced restrictions to their rights. The judicial tort action found in Israel is an example of remedial measures that States may adopt in this respect. The development of remedial measures also affects the inherently unequal power arrangements that exist between divorcing spouses, as it effectively creates a new avenue for women to exert pressure on recalcitrant spouses.

Where the right to remarry is impaired by the actions of private parties and religious laws that are not recognised by the State, the State continues to carry the obligation to protect the trapped spouses' rights to remarry and right to private life from infringements by private actors. In this regard, States are obliged to protect women from discrimination by private actors. They are also obliged to develop an adequate legal framework to combat harmful practices against women. This requires, among others, that trapped spouses are enabled to enforce their rights and have access to effective remedies where their rights are infringed by the non-cooperative spouse. States should also regulate the behaviour and conduct of non-cooperative spouses. The tort- action and liability actions that have been adopted in a number of secular States are examples of how States can adopt measures to influence the behaviour of the non-cooperative spouse. Similarly, legislative and judicial measures have been adopted in, *inter alia*, Canada[1084], France[1085], the United Kingdom[1086] and the United States[1087] so as to resolve situations of marital captivity and to end the violation of trapped women's rights. Legislative measures such as those that require the removal of religious barriers to remarrying are another example of how States can mitigate marital captivity by influencing the conduct of spouses. Therefore, in realising its positive obligations, it can be argued that the State is required to take the necessary steps – including legislative initiatives – to ensure and facilitate the dissolution of the religious marriage. On this aspect, Lord Lester of Herne Hill's comments on the Bill that was later to become the Divorce (Religious Marriages) Act are accurate in that the right to remarry, in the ECHR, contains a positive obligation to remove unjustifiable obstacles to the right of *'"chained" spouses to remarry [...]'*.[1088]

Finally, States have also been encouraged by the CEDAW Committee to design a system for registering all marriages, including those that are contracted according to religious laws. This may prove to be a necessary and useful tool, particularly for addressing marital captivity. It should be borne in mind that the registration of all marriages does not imply the recognition of all types of marriages. By registering all marriages, States

1084 Canadian Divorce Act, Section 21.1.; Supreme Court of Canada, *Bruker v. Marcovitz*, 14 December 2007, 3 S.C.R. 607, 2007 SCC 54.

1085 See paragraph 4.4.2.2.2.

1086 See paragraph 4.4.2.2.3.

1087 New York Domestic Relation Law, paras. 236 and 253.

1088 House of Lords debate on the Divorce (Religious Marriages), Lord sitting of 30 June 2000, vol. 614, c. 1246.

are in a better position and have an oversight of both formal and informal marriages. Such knowledge may facilitate the State's efforts to ensure equality between partners within the private sphere, to identify and adequately respond to situations of marital captivity and to inform spouses of their rights, as well as the legal significance and implications that flow from formal and informal marriages.

6.3.2.2. Addressing the causes of marital captivity

States Parties to the investigated human rights treaties are obliged to also secure conditions that allow women to exercise their rights, irrespective of the prevailing State-Church model. Factors that increase or exacerbate situations of marital captivity, such as stigmatisation, negative attitudes towards divorcees, persistent gender stereotypes, inequalities within the private spheres and economic restrictions and dependency should be addressed and progressively eradicated. This requires policy initiatives to structurally address marital captivity on multiple levels and domains and it also requires the promulgation of strategies to involve all stakeholders in order to deal with situations of marital captivity. Taking the Netherlands as an example, measures could and should include awareness-raising campaigns on the issues and its underlying causes, training programmes, strategies to foster dialogue within religious communities on marital captivity[1089], research and advisory bodies that support and advise municipalities, policymakers, civil society and politicians on how to prevent and respond to marital captivity[1090] and a platform for facilitating the exchange of information between social workers, professionals and the relevant authorities.[1091]

Awareness-raising and educational campaigns for professionals as well as religious community members should not be underestimated. In particular, these should focus

[1089] For example, in the Netherlands State authorities have implemented the 'Self- Determination Action Plan 2015–2017' (*Actie plan-zelfbeschikking 2015–2017).* This national action plan includes providing a training programme on sensitive topics, including marital captivity, to information officers belonging to various migrant communities. Upon finishing this training programme, the information officers organised several meetings within their community on these issues. This has helped not only to raise awareness on sensitive topics within the religious communities, but also to facilitate opening the dialogue on these issues.; *Platform Eer &Vrijheid.* More information on this platform can be retrieved at <https://www.eerenvrijheid.nl/> last accessed 23 August 2017.

[1090] The Integration and Society Knowledge Platform (Kennisplatform Integratie en Samenleving). More information on this initiative is available at <https://www.kis.nl/english> last accessed 22 August 2017.

[1091] For example, via institutions such as Platform Eer &Vrijheid and Landelijke Knooppunt huwelijkse dwang en achterlating. The Landelijke Knooppunt huwelijkse dwang en achterlating is the national institute that provides expertise, support and advice to professionals, health care takers and politicians on matters related to forced marriage and abandonment, including marital captivity. It also facilitates bringing the appropriate institutions to the attention of cases of forced marriage or abandonment that occur abroad and it facilitates the cooperation between national, regional and local institutions that are tasked with responding to forced marriage and abandonment. More information is available at: <www.huwelijksdwangenachterlating.nl> last accessed 26 February 2018.; See also <www.leceergerelateerdgeweld.nl/> last accessed 26 February 2018.

on the training of civil servants, the judiciary and divorce lawyers to be sensitive to the effects of existing religious marriages, their potential extra-territorial effects and the available legal and non-legal means to end situations of marital captivity. Likewise, awareness-raising within religious communities should not only be limited to the issue of marital captivity but should also incorporate human rights education so as to foster change within the religious communities.

The conditions that enable marital captivity to persist find their basis in religious laws. Religious authorities and communities shape maintain and enforce the rules and practices that enable marital captivity. They have the authority and discretion to direct the views and practices on divorce in a manner that is accepted by and within the community. This makes their input in the process of finding solutions all the more valuable. Therefore, efforts to reach sustainable solutions to end and prevent situations of marital captivity should include and encourage cooperation with religious authorities and communities. Similarly, efforts undertaken within religious communities to find solutions to marital captivity should be encouraged.

6.3.2.3. *Ensuring the freedom of movement*

Firstly, States that adopt laws and practices that restrict a woman's ability to travel outside and within the territory of the State, or which make the exercise of this right conditional on the approval of their partner or family members, should be reviewed and amended so as to guarantee women their right to travel within, to and from the State. States are also required to provide trapped wives who have their nationality with the necessary travel documents to allow them to travel. States may also not obstruct and interfere with a woman's right to leave and enter unless this is justified.

Furthermore, where a trapped wife is abroad, both the State of nationality and the host State are obliged to ensure the freedom of movement of the trapped wife to leave the host State and return back to her country of nationality/residence. The precise content and scope of these obligations, however, remain unclear and require further inquiry, particularly in the field of the extra-territorial reach of human rights and on diplomatic protection and consular assistance. The relevance of such an inquiry for situations of marital captivity with transnational elements is not contested. However, as provided in section subchapter 1.6., this contribution does not delve into the extra-territorial application of human rights or the relationship between the various fields of international law so that the raised questions should be the subject of future studies on marital captivity.

States are also obliged to protect intrusions of this right by private parties. In fact, the indirect horizontal effect of the freedom of movement has been established within the context of migrant workers. Recognition of a similar effect can also be argued for situations of marital captivity. Interferences by private individuals who confiscate the trapped wife's travel documents or attempt to restrict their freedom of movement by other means, such as intentionally refusing to give consent to the wife's travelling undertakings do occur. States should, therefore, provide protection from such interferences, especially when they are the result of mal-intentioned spouses and family members. In this respect, preventing confiscation and providing accessible and effective means for the recovery of passports has been recommended.[1092] Remarkably, there is little specificity and directions on the execution of States' obligations to protect against violations of the freedom of movement by private parties. Developing laws that regulate the behaviour and conduct of individuals to refrain from violating the right to free movement of others and developing remedies for trapped spouses to enforce their freedom of movement is, therefore, a step in the right direction. For example, administrative or criminal sanctions can be imposed on those who confiscate the travel documents and the existing tort action may also be extended to pressure non-cooperative husbands to give approval and cooperate to the issuance of the travelling documents. Furthermore, as the cases of Sarah shows, the restrictions to travel may in themselves hinder the trapped women's ability to take the appropriate steps to enforce their right to free movement, particularly when they are in coercive relationships. Thus, in executing the State's obligations to secure the trapped spouse's rights, States should take due care to ensure that the adopted protective and remedial measures are not only effective but that they are also accessible to trapped spouses.

6.3.2.4. Guaranteeing the trapped spouse's health

In respect of the right to health, States are required to implement measures to protect against and to remedy violations of the trapped spouses' right to health by the State as well as by private actors. Specifically, for marital captivity, attention should not only be placed on the physical impairments but also on the mental implications and duress that trapped spouses endure. States are required to develop preventive, promotive and remedial actions to protect women from harmful practices that negatively affect their health, including marital captivity.[1093] States are also obliged to ensure that access to information on marital captivity, the various consequences of marital captivity and the available services and solutions are not restricted by private actors. Similarly, access to the existing legal and non-legal solutions and services (e.g. women's shelters) should be guaranteed. Healthcare facilities and services should be accessible and should accommodate the needs of trapped spouses, whom next to their health may require safety guarantees and assistance in the dissolution of the religious marriage. This requires taking into account and addressing the conditions that may prevent women from using the available facilities and services, such as safety, lack of information, inadequacy to accommodate children who may accompany the trapped wife etc. Furthermore, health care workers should be trained and educated on the phenomenon of marital captivity so that they are better equipped to identify and respond to marital captivity and other health-related issues, such as domestic violence and violence against women.

1092 *Supra* note 1067.
1093 See also complementary State obligations in subchapter 7.6.

6.4. CONCLUDING REMARKS

The previous subchapters have established that situations of marital captivity impair several human rights principles and freedoms of the trapped spouse. Four substantive rights have been addressed that are most likely to be impaired by a situation of marital captivity, namely: the right to remarry, the right to respect for private life, the right to free movement within and between States and the right to the highest attainable health.

All of the rights discussed in this Chapter contain both negative and positive obligations. These require the protection of the above-mentioned rights against violations by the State and by private persons i.e. the recalcitrant spouse and/or the religious community. Therefore, domestic laws and practices that enable and sustain situations of marital captivity or which discriminate against married women violate the trapped spouses' rights and are incompatible with the human rights obligations of States. These laws and practices should be eliminated and replaced by laws that guarantee and protect the trapped spouses' human rights. States are, furthermore, obligated to regulate the behaviour and conduct of individuals so as to ensure the non-violation of the specified human rights within horizontal relationships. This can be achieved by legislative, judicial as well as other measures. Additionally, the implied obligations require States to guarantee the exercise and enjoyment of these rights by the trapped spouse. States should also enable, support and facilitate trapped spouses to enforce their rights and seek remedies or reparations where their rights have been impaired by a situation of marital captivity.

It is essential to address the religious, cultural and traditional customs that are harmful or discriminatory towards women, as well as the stereotypes and prejudices related to the phenomenon of marital captivity. In this regard, the fact that marital captivity occurs, takes form in and is condoned within the private sphere and within the religious community does not alleviate the obligations on the State to contribute and facilitate in the creation of a society in which human rights are respected and enjoyed by all individuals. Therefore, alongside legislative and judicial measures, non-legislative measures should at least include further investment in awareness-raising campaigns, training programmes and information dissemination. Continuous effort is needed to address social, cultural and religious practices, stereotypes and beliefs that exacerbate marital captivity. Such efforts ought to encourage the inclusion of religious authorities within the dialogue on marital captivity, so as to guarantee a holistic approach to addressing marital captivity.

CHAPTER 7
VIOLENCE AGAINST WOMEN

The inability of women to initiate and obtain a divorce and the dependency on the husbands' cooperation to the dissolution of the religious marriage naturally places women in a vulnerable position. The unequal power arrangements between wives and husbands on divorce matters, enables husbands not only to gain control over their (ex-) wives ability to leave the relationship, but it also enables husbands to abuse and exploit their wives. The case of Aya illustrates the vulnerable position of trapped women:

> *Aya married against the wishes of her parents at the Moroccan consulate in the Netherlands. It was not a happy marriage. In fact, it was a violent marriage. Eventually, she managed to escape the violent marriage. She says about this situation: 'it was a very traditional family, a religious family too (…) divorce…that was just something you did not do, if your husband hit you, then you just had to accept that'. For years her husband refused to cooperate to the Moroccan divorce. Aya: 'I had then said: I don't care anymore, even if I never get divorced, I don't care'(…) and when I said 'leave it[the divorce]' he apparently realised that 'it [the divorce] doesn't interest her any more', and only then did he undertake action [to cooperate to the divorce]'. Eventually, the husband was compelled to cooperate to the divorce in Morocco. In the divorce agreement, Aya relinquished all her rights in exchange for the divorce- 'I had to give up everything because otherwise he would not cooperate.*[1094]

Trapped women are thus in a vulnerable position and are at risk of abuse, violence and other forms of harmful practices such as extortion, intimate partner violence, honour-related crimes and child abduction.[1095] Besides creating conditions that foster abuse of and violence against wives, situations of marital captivity may also create difficulties for spouses who attempt to leave a violent relationship and environment, as both spouses may still be expected to comply with their marital obligations. The existing marriage may then be used, by the violent spouse, to claim entitlements from the trapped wife. A situation of marital captivity may contribute to and exacerbate violence within the marriage. Furthermore, pressing for a divorce may also come at a high cost, particularly where this is perceived as an attack on the honour and reputation of the opposing

---

1094 Van Eijk, *Wel gescheiden, niet gescheiden? Een empirisch onderzoek naar huwelijkse gevangenschap in Nederland*, pp. 52, 104.

1095 See subsections 1.3.2.2. and 1.3.2.3. See also van Eijk, *Wel gescheiden, niet gescheiden? Een empirisch onderzoek naar huwelijkse gevangenschap in Nederland*, p. 13. See also the case of Sandra that is discussed in: Id., p. 45.; van Waesberghe, et al., *Zo zijn we niet getrouwd: Een onderzoek naar omvang en aard van huwelijksdwang, achterlating en huwelijkse gevangenschap*, p. 118.

spouse. Attempts to obtain a divorce may incite various forms of counter-measures by the other spouse, including resorting to lethal violence, as the following case of Yasmeen illustrates:

Yasmeen, a 25-year-old woman married her husband after the marriage had been arranged by her family. She ended up in a situation of marital captivity and wanted to leave her husband. However, she went missing. Her body was discovered three weeks after she had been reported as missing by her husband. As it turns out, she had most likely been strangled by her husband. He claimed it was an accident, however, it was quickly alleged to be a case of honour killing. The husband was sentenced to 10 years imprisonment.[1096] *Shortly before her death, Yasmeen had written to her niece about the fearful and dangerous situations she was facing. 'I am so afraid that something will happen to me! Sometimes I don't sleep the whole night'.*[1097]

In the 2014 joint general comment of the CEDAW Committee and the Committee on the Rights of the Child (CRC Committee), both monitoring bodies acknowledged that the act of demanding a divorce is, indeed, a factor that may incentivise honour-based violence against women.[1098] In turn, domestic violence, fear of violence or repetition of violent acts may discourage women from leaving the marriage or petitioning for a divorce.[1099] Moreover, divorce denial in the rabbinical court, as well as the practice of repudiation, have been identified by the CEDAW Committee and human rights specialised agencies as practices that are harmful to women.[1100] Likewise, the Special Rapporteur on violence against women has acknowledged that the restrictions imposed on women (e.g. the dependency on the husband's will to provide a *Get)* are factors which exacerbate The violent aspects and the controlling environment that are created by a situation of marital captivity are considered in this Chapter within the context of violence against women (VAW). Studying marital captivity within the context of VAW allows emphasis to be placed on the power imbalances that are inherent in situations of

1096 Nadia Berkelder, 'Adeel D. veroordeeld tot tien jaar cel voor dood Yasmeen', *Algemeen Dagblad* 09 May 2016.; Rechtbank Rotterdam, 04 February 2016, ECLI:NL:RBROT:2016:898.

1097 Saskia Belleman, 'Adeel D. blijft eerwraakmoord ontekennen', *Telegraaf* 21 January 2016. See also *Voorkomen geweld tegen vrouwen*, Kamerstukken II, 2014/2015, nr. 91, p. 6.

1098 Committee on the Elimination of Discrimination Against Women and Committee on the Rights of the Child 'Joint General Comment No. 31 of the Committee on the Elimination of Discrimination Against Women/ General comment No. 18 of the Committee on the Rights of the Child on harmful practices', 2014, CEDAW/C/GC/31-CRC/C/GC/18, para. 29.

1099 Van Eijk, *Wel gescheiden, niet gescheiden? Een empirisch onderzoek naar huwelijkse gevangenschap in Nederland*, pp. 61, 65.

1100 Jahangir, *Report of the Special Rapporteur on freedom of religion or belief Asma Jahangir – Mission to Israel and the Occupied Palestinian Territory*, paras. 49,71.; Coomaraswamy, *Report of the Special Rapporteur on violence against women, its causes and consequences: Cultural practices in the family that are violent towards women*, paras. 7, 66, 69.; United Nations Secretary General, *In-depth study on all forms of violence against women: Report of the Secretary General*, para. 78.; Committee on the Elimination of Discrimination Against Women, *Concluding Observations Togo 2006* (2006), CEDAW/C/TGO/CO/5, para. 14.; Dorcas Coker- Appiah, *The CEDAW Convention and harmful practices against women: the work of the CEDAW Committee*, (Committee on the Elimination of Discrimination Against Women, 2009), [EGM/GPLVAW/2009/EP.05], p. 7.; Holtmaat *Article 5*, pp. 156–157.

marital captivity, and it allows for a better understanding of the underlying mechanism, i.e. unequal power arrangements between the spouses during divorce. It also enables to analyse the social implications and impact of a situation of marital captivity for the spouses and for members of the religious community.

Central to this inquiry is whether marital captivity constitutes a form of violence against women (VAW), since it is a phenomenon that affects women disproportionately. Can, and if so, under which circumstances does the act of non-cooperation to a (religious divorce) or the inability to dissolve a religious marriage be classified as violence?

After providing a legal framework in subchapter 7.1, subchapter 7.2. provides terminological clarification on the concepts of 'violence against women', 'gender-based violence', 'women' and violence. Hereafter, Subchapter 7.3. follows with an in-depth analysis of what VAW entails. This includes studying the causes, consequences, function, settings and agents of VAW. This exercise is necessary in order to understand whether marital captivity can be qualified as VAW. By simply proclaiming that marital captivity is a form of violence, without giving sustainable reasoning does not guarantee that this is, in fact, the case nor does it contribute to an understanding of why marital captivity is or should be recognised as a form of VAW. The classification of marital captivity as VAW, as has been done in several scholarly works[1101], may have the advantage of attaching a degree of seriousness and gravity to this issue and thus attract more public and political attention. However, this advantage may be limited where the classification of marital captivity as VAW does not go beyond the mere classification of marital captivity as a form of VAW. There is also a risk in hastily classifying issues that affect women disproportionately as violence if this is done for the sole purpose of generating public discourse and interest on the matter. Therefore, the classification of marital captivity as a form of VAW should be drawn judiciously and complemented with an elaborative study on what the State's obligations are in relation thereto. Subchapter 7.4. then follows up with an analysis of the circumstances in which marital captivity qualifies as VAW. A comparison with other forms of VAW that bare much semblance to marital captivity is provided (forced marriage and intimate partner violence) in subchapter 7.5.. This has the purpose of identifying the unique traits of marital captivity which must be taken into account if effective solutions are to be ascertained. Subsequently, the State's obligations arising from the prohibition of violence against women are dealt with in subchapter 7.6., with subchapter 7.7. providing several concluding remarks.

7.1. THE LEGAL FRAMEWORK

Violence against women is a phenomenon that has received much attention in many fields, particularly in human rights law. Developments on the international level have yet to result in a binding instrument on the issue of VAW. Nonetheless, this

1101 Rosenberg *Praying for divorce: The abuse of Jewish women through Jewish divorce law*, p. 217.

phenomenon has been interpreted to be included in various UN treaties, including the CEDAW, the ICESCR and the ICCPR. Notably, during the drafting of the CEDAW, Belgium proposed the inclusion of '*attack on the physical integrity of women*' in the then Article 7 on trafficking and prostitution.[1102] This proposal, however, failed to find the necessary support. A second attempt by Portugal yielded the same result.[1103] Hence, the issue of VAW was dropped and was only brought up again later in 1989 in a general recommendation of the CEDAW Committee. This general comment articulates that Articles 2, 5, 11, 12 and 16 of the Convention contain positive obligations for States to protect women against acts of violence. As mentioned above in section 5.3.1. the CEDAW Committee has established that that the Convention covers VAW, despite this subject not being explicitly mentioned within the text of the Convention.[1104] States are, thus, required to report VAW in their periodic reports and to include information on what measures they have adopted to address VAW.[1105] The 1992[1106] and 2017[1107] general recommendations expand further on this subject. VAW is classified as gender-based violence and it also constitutes discrimination within the meaning of Article 1 CEDAW. These recommendations provide greater clarification as to the content and scope of the State's obligations in relation to VAW. Accordingly, gender-based violence is defined as:

> '*violence that is directed against a woman because she is a woman or that affects women disproportionately. It includes acts that inflict physical, mental or sexual harm or suffering, threats of such acts, coercion and other deprivations of liberty. Gender-based violence may breach specific provisions of the Convention, regardless of whether those provisions expressly mention violence.*[1108]

With this formula of VAW as gender-based violence, the CEDAW Committee was the first human rights treaty body to dismantle the private/public dichotomy in human rights law. For a long time, violence within the private sphere – which mostly affects women – remained largely or inadequately (un)addressed.[1109] By describing VAW

1102 Commission on the Status of Women, *International instruments relating to the status of women. Draft Convention on the elimination of Discrimination Against Women – Working Paper Prepared by the Secretary -General – Corrigendum*, (United Nations, 1976), [E/CN.6/591/Add. 1/Corr. 1], p. 2. The proposed provision provided the following wording: '*Each State party agrees to take all appropriate measures, including legislation, to combat all forms of traffic in women, exploitation of prostitution of women and attacks on the physical integrity of women*'.

1103 Christine Chinkin, 'Violence against Women', in Freeman, et al. *The UN Convention on the Elimination of All Forms of Discrimination Against Women: A commentary* (New York, 2012), p. 444.

1104 CEDAW, *General Recommendation No. 28 on the core obligations of States Parties under Article 2 of the Convention on the Elimination of All Forms of Discrimination against Women*, para. 7.

1105 UN Committee on the Elimination of Discrimination Against Women 'General Recommendation No. 12 on Violence against women', 1989.

1106 CEDAW, *General Recommendation No. 19 on Violence against women.*

1107 UN Committee on the Elimination of Discrimination Against Women '*General Recommendation No. 35* on gender-based violence against women, updating general recommendation No. 19', 2017.

1108 CEDAW, *General Recommendation No. 19 on Violence against women*, para. 6.

1109 Yakin Ertürk, *Integration of the human rights of women and the gender perspective: violence against women – The due diligence standard as a tool for the elimination of violence against women*, (UN

as gender-based discrimination, the CEDAW Committee, thus, created an avenue to shift public and States' attention on violence occurring within the private spheres. Discrimination, whether occurring in the private or public sphere, is a State affair. This flows from the human rights obligation to eliminate discrimination on the basis of protected criteria, including discrimination by private non-State actors. It is an obligation that primarily rests on the State and is included within the ICCPR[1110], ICESCR[1111] and the CEDAW.[1112]

Consequently, the affirmation that VAW constitutes discrimination has the effect that practices that were initially assigned to the private sphere are now considered as requiring State attention and intervention. States can now be held responsible for acts of VAW that are committed by private persons, by way of their failure to prevent or adequately respond to VAW. The link between gender-based violence and the non-discrimination principle, therefore, has proven to be a valuable one.[1113] Nonetheless, this approach has also been criticised for not sufficiently addressing the public/private dichotomy and for disparately addressing the way in which women are victimised.[1114] An additional point of critique to this approach by the CEDAW Committee has been the lack of an explicit recognition of VAW as a human rights violation in and of itself. The fact that VAW has been classified as discrimination, rather than calling it a human rights violation, tends to create differential treatment in the way that women experience violence, as opposed to other forms of violence that are considered as human rights violations. The CEDAW Committee has rectified this by recognising VAW as a human rights violation in the 2017 general recommendation No. 35.[1115] As it stands, the CEDAW recognises VAW as both a form of discrimination as well as a human right violation in and of itself.

Economic and Social Council, Commission on Human Rights, Report of the Special Rapporteur on violence against women, its causes and consequences, 20 January 2006), [E/CN.4/2006/61], para. 59.

1110 International Covenant on Civil and Political Rights, Article 26.

1111 International Covenant on Economic, Social and Cultural Rights, 3, Article 2(2).

1112 Convention on the Elimination of All Forms of Discrimination Against Women, Article 2.

1113 CEDAW, *General Recommendation No. 19 on Violence against women*, paras. 4–7.; Alice Edwards, *Violence against women under International Human Rights Law* (Cambridge, 2011), pp. 183–190.

1114 Id., p. 191–196. Edwards rightly points out that the link between VAW and discrimination is problematic in that responses and perceptions of discrimination cannot be assimilated and are not the same as those of violence. For example, the reasonable, objective and proportionality criteria may at times justify discrimination, which would inadvisably lead to the outcome that there could be circumstances in which the State's failure to address VAW as sex-based discrimination may justified. Similarly, account needs to be taken of the impact and effects that the used language has on the responses and remedies to VAW. The extent to which 'violence' is condemned in society is not the same as the extent to which discrimination against women is condemned. For example, certain forms of discrimination and, even violence against women, may be tolerated in some societies (e.g. honour-based murder) in a way that similar practices (murder) that are not based in discrimination are not. Reference to VAW as sex-based discrimination also creates an additional hurdle for victims who have to show that the violent acts they have endured are induced by discriminatory motives or ideologies.

1115 CEDAW, *General Recommendation No. 35 on gender-based violence against women, updating General Recommendation No. 19*, para. 1.

Other treaty bodies have also come to recognise VAW as a subject falling within their respective treaties. For example, the HRC has urged States, in their compliance with Article 7 ICCPR (prohibition of torture and other cruel, inhuman or degrading treatment) to protect against acts of female genital mutilation (FGM), forced abortions, domestic violence and other forms of violence against women, as well as to punish perpetrators and to provide remedies to victims.[1116] Similarly, the Committee Against Torture (CAT) has extended the obligation to act with due diligence in respect of some forms of VAW.[1117] The Committees have also, in several concluding observations, acknowledged and condemned violence against women[1118] and they encouraged States to prohibit and criminalise the practice of FGM.[1119] Furthermore, it has been suggested by the CEDAW committee that the prohibition of gender-based violence has evolved into customary international law. Thus, States that are neither party to regional instruments and the CEDAW would then be obliged to respond to and prevent such acts from occurring.[1120]

Beyond these instruments, there is no binding instrument on the international level that focuses specifically on violence against women. Notably, this normative gap came to the attention of the Special Rapporteur on Violence against Women. The Rapporteur stressed the '*need for a universal legally binding instrument on violence against women at the United Nations level*'.[1121] One instrument that addresses VAW comprehensively

1116 HRC, *General Comment No. 28: Article 3 (The equality of rights between men and women)*, para. 11.

1117 UN Committee Against Torture 'General Comment No. 2: Implementation of Article 2 by States Parties', 200, CAT/C/GC/2, para. 18.

1118 Committee Against Torture, *Concluding Observations on Greece 2004*, CAT/C/CR/33/2, paras. 4–5.; Committee Against Torture, *Concluding Observations on Ecuador 2006*, CAT/C/ECU/CO/3, para. 17.; Committee Against Torture, *Concluding Observations on Argentina 2004*, CAT/C/CR/33/1, para. 6.; Committee Against Torture, *Concluding Observations on Bahrain 2005*, CAT/C/CR/34/ BHR, paras, 6–7.; Committee Against Torture, *Concluding Observations on Nepal 2005*, CAT/C/NPL/CO/2, para. 27.

1119 Committee Against Torture, *Concluding Observations on Cameroon 2004*, CAT/C/CR/31/6, para 7.; Human Rights Committee, *Concluding Observations on Mali 2003*, CCPR/CO/77/MLI, para. 11.

1120 In its General comment no 35. the CEDAW committee establishes that: "*For over 25 years, the practice of States parties has endorsed the Committee's interpretation. The opinio juris and State practice suggest that the prohibition of genderbased violence against women has evolved into a principle of customary international law. General recommendation No. 19 has been a key catalyst for this process*". According to the CEDAW committee State practice can be found in the legal and policy measures State parties and non-parties have adopted to address diverse forms of gender-based violence (e.g. domestic legislations against VAW, invitations extended to the Special rapporteur on VAW (also by non-parties), non-parties' acceptance of recommendations on VAW through the Universal Periodic Review monitoring mechanism, the adoption of and endorsement by States of UN resolutions that address VAW, the adoption of regional treaties that address VAW and landmark documents such as the DEVAW and the Beijing Declaration and Platform of Action). CEDAW, *General Recommendation No. 35 on gender-based violence against women, updating General Recommendation No. 19*, para. 2. See also Ertürk, *Integration of the human rights of women and the gender perspective: violence against women – The due diligence standard as a tool for the elimination of violence against women*, para. 29.; Rangita de Silva de Alwis and Jeni Klugman, 'Freedom from violence and the law: A global perspective in light of the Chinese Domestic Violence Law', 37 *U. Pa. J. Int'l L.* 1–52, (2015), pp. 17, 20–21.

1121 Rashida Manjoo, *Report of the Special Rapporteur on violence against women, its causes and consequences*, (United Nations, 2014), [A/HRC/26/38], paras. 68–69.; Rashida Manjoo, *Report of the*

and explicitly recognises VAW as a human rights violation.[1122] Following upon this concern, a questionnaire was sent to all stakeholders in 2016. The purpose was to assess the need for a binding instrument on the global level.[1123] The responses consisted of submissions by international and regional human rights monitoring bodies, regional and national women's organisations and NGOs, legal experts and scholars. A majority of the responses (29 out of the 38) considered that there was a need for a separate and legally binding treaty or protocol to the CEDAW with a separate monitoring body. The main arguments for this initiative were that a new instrument would (a) contribute to structuring the fragmented framework on VAW, (b) address the existing normative gap on this topic and (c) encourage the monitoring of State's compliance with their due diligence obligations to address VAW.

Noteworthy, responses opposing the introduction of a new legally binding treaty on the international level came from, among others, the CEDAW Committee and the Council of Europe Group of action against violence against women and domestic violence (GREVIO).[1124] Arguments against the introduction of a new instrument focused on the fact that this would lead to further fragmentation of the legal framework on VAW and that it would not necessarily contribute to the existing challenges for ensuring greater implementation and compliance with human rights. It could also have the effect of increasing the burden on the State's reporting, resources and support. Furthermore, a lack of political support to endorse the enactment of such a treaty was predicted. Despite the diversity of perspectives on this subject matter, this exercise has highlighted an urgent need to direct attention and resources so as to ensure greater implementation and compliance with the already existing treaties and mechanisms on VAW.[1125]

On the regional level, the Council of Europe Convention on Preventing and Combating Violence against Women (Istanbul Convention) is the most recent regional human rights instrument to explicitly condemn violence against women. VAW is defined therein as:

Special Rapporteur on violence against women, its causes and consequences (United Nations, 2015), [A/HRC/29/27], pp. 9–18.

1122 Manjoo, *Report of the Special Rapporteur on violence against women, its causes and consequences (2014)*, paras. 68–69. An earlier recommendation for a new UN Convention by the Special Rapporteur on violence against women, in 2013, was met with support by the Deputy Executive Director of UN Women who stated that '*it would be a dream outcome of CSW*'. Rashida Manjoo, *Addendum to the Human Rights Council Thematic report of the Special rapporteur on Violence, its Causes and Consequences*, (United Nations, 2015), [A/HRC/29/27/Add. 5], pp. 5–6.

1123 Šimonović Dubravka, *Adequacy of the international legal framework on violence against women – Report of the Special Rapporteur on violence against women, its causes and consequences on the adequacy of the international legal framework on violence against women*, (United Nations General Assembly, 19 July 2017), [A/72/134].

1124 The monitoring body of the Council of Europe Convention on preventing and combating violence against women.

1125 Dubravka, *Report of the Special Rapporteur on violence against women, its causes and consequences on the adequacy of the international legal framework on violence against women*, pp. 19–20.

'[...] a violation of human rights and a form of discrimination against women and shall mean all acts of gender-based violence that result in, or are likely to result in, physical, sexual, psychological or economic harm, or suffering to women, including threats of such acts, coercion or arbitrary deprivation of liberty, whether occurring in public or private life.'[1126]

Gender-based violence is then defined as:

'violence that is directed against a woman because she is a woman or that affects women disproportionately.'[1127]

Within the ECHR, VAW has primarily been addressed in the case law of the ECtHR, as the ECHR does not contain a specific provision on VAW. Cases involving VAW have been dealt with, among others, under the provisions of Articles 2 (right to life), 3 (freedom from torture and ill-treatment), 4 (prohibition of slavery and forced labour), 6 (right to a fair trial), 8 (right to private life), 13 (right to an effective remedy) and 14 (prohibition of discrimination).[1128]

Other regional instruments that explicitly condemn VAW include the 2003 Protocol to the African Charter on Human and People's Rights on the Rights of Women in Africa (Maputo Protocol)[1129] and the 1994 Inter-American Convention on the Prevention, Punishment and Eradication of violence against women (Convention of Belém do Pará).[1130] Notably, both the Istanbul Convention and the Convention of Belém do Pará

1126 Council of Europe, *Convention on preventing and combating violence against women and domestic violence*, 11 May 2011, Article 3(a).

1127 Id., Article 3(d).

1128 European Court of Human Rights, *Airey v. Ireland,* 9 October 1979, Application No. 6289/73, involved a case of domestic violence and the failure of the State to ensure access to legal remedies and effective protection mechanisms. The ECtHR established a violation of Articles 6 and 8 ECHR. The case of European Court of Human Rights, *M.C. v. Bulgaria,* 4 December 2003, Application No. 3927/98, involved the rape of a minor and the failure of the State to prosecute the perpetrators. The ECtHR established a violation of Articles 3 and 8 ECHR. On the Articles 2,3 and 14 ECHR see the leading case of ECtHR, *Opuz v. Turkey,* 9 June 2009, Application No. 33401/01. This case involved ongoing domestic violence against mother and daughter, which escalated to the point that the perpetrator murdered the mother. The ECtHR established a violation of Articles 2, 3 and 14 ECHR, as the State failed take measures that would minimise the risks, had not prosecuted the perpetrator appropriately and had failed to protect women from violence. On the Articles 4, 6 and 13 ECHR see the case of European Court of Human Rights, *L.E. v. Greece,* 21 January 2016, Application No. 71545. This case involved a victim of human trafficking and sexual exploitation. The ECtHR established a violation of Articles 4, 6, and 13 ECHR due to the authorities' shortcomings in investigating the situation and acknowledging the applicant as a victim of trafficking.

1129 Maputo Protocol, Article 1: *'Violence against women' means all acts perpetrated against women which cause or could cause them physical, sexual, psychological, and economic harm, including the threat to take such acts; or to undertake the imposition of arbitrary restrictions on or deprivation of fundamental freedoms in private or public life in peace time and during situations of armed conflicts or of war'.*

1130 Organization of American States (OAS), *Inter-American Convention on the Prevention, Punishment and Eradication of Violence against Women ("Convention of Belém do Pará"),* 1994, Article 1: *'Violence against women shall be understood as any act or conduct, based on gender, which causes death or physical, sexual or psychological harm or suffering to women, whether in the public or the private sphere'.*

explicitly establish VAW as a human rights violation in itself.[1131] Both instruments also make a link between VAW and discrimination. The Istanbul Convention establishes VAW as both a human rights violation as well as a form of discrimination against women[1132], while the Convention of Belém do Pará includes the non-discrimination principle within the right to be free from violence.[1133] The Maputo Protocol, on the other hand, does not provide an explicit link between VAW and discrimination. Rather, VAW is discussed in the context of the respective rights to life, integrity and security in Article 4 (1) thereof.

Finally, there are various soft-law instruments on VAW, the most prominent being the 1995 Beijing Platform of Action[1134] and the 1993 UN General Assembly Declaration on the Elimination of Violence Against Women (DEVAW).[1135] This declaration is a valuable instrument, in particular, because it provides for a better understanding of VAW and the settings in which it occurs (the family, community and the State). It also provides a framework for action on both international and national level. VAW is defined as:

> *'[...] any act of gender-based violence that results in, or is likely to result in, physical, sexual or psychological harm or suffering to women, including threats of such acts, coercion or arbitrary deprivation of liberty, whether occurring in public or in private life.'*[1136]

The Beijing Platform of Action is a comprehensive soft-law document that has been adopted by 189 countries and which advances the goals of equality, development and peace by promoting the advancement and empowerment of women in all areas.[1137] VAW is described in the exact same wording as in Article 1 of the DEVAW.[1138] Additionally, VAW is recognised to be a '*human rights violation, resulting from harmful traditional or customary practices, cultural prejudices and extremism*'.[1139] VAW as a human rights violation has also been recognised by the Secretary-General in its '*In-depth study on all forms of violence against women*'.[1140]

1131 The Belém do Pará Convention in the preamble thereto states: '*Affirming that violence against women constitutes a violation of their human rights and fundamental freedoms, and impairs or nullifies the observance, enjoyment and exercise of such rights and freedoms*'.

1132 Istanbul Convention, Article 3 (a).

1133 Article 6 of the Belém do Pará Convention provides that the '*right of every woman to be free from violence includes, among others [...] the right of women to be free from all forms of discrimination [...]*.

1134 United Nations, *Beijing Platform of Action, adopted at the Fourth World Conference on Women, Fourth World Conference on Women*, 15 September 1995.

1135 United Nations General Assembly, *Declaration on the Elimination of Violence against Women.*; For a list of soft-law instruments on VAW see Manjoo, *Report of the Special Rapporteur on violence against women, its causes and consequences (2014).*

1136 Declaration on the Elimination of Violence against Women, Article 1.

1137 United Nations, *Beijing Platform of Action*, preamble.

1138 Id., para. 117.

1139 Id., para. 232 (g).

1140 United Nations Secretary General, *In-depth study on all forms of violence against women: Report of the Secretary General.*

Considering the provided legal definitions, VAW is characterised by:

a) the target of the violence, which are women and girls;
b) the presence of harmful acts (this involves an undefined range of acts which include threats of violence, coercion, arbitrary deprivation of liberty and fundamental freedoms);
c) the presence of harm and suffering which can be physical, psychological, sexual and/or economic in nature;
d) a causal linking between the concerned acts and the inflicted harm; and
e) a breach of human rights.

Despite the fact that certain instruments contain an enumeration of certain forms of VAW, these should not be considered as being exhaustive and encompassing all forms of VAW. Violence against women manifests itself in many different forms that are culturally specific, so that any attempt to draft an exhaustive list of all forms of VAW is futile and risks being too limited and static.[1141] New forms of VAW emerge over time as a consequence of changes in the political, social and economic climate, as well as through changes that are generated by technological innovations.[1142] One may think of contemporary forms of stalking and harassment, whereby modern technology can facilitate the perpetuation of such acts.[1143] Likewise, forms of VAW may diminish or change over time, in particular where they are actively addressed on the international, regional and national level.[1144] Instead, States must acknowledge the evolving nature of VAW and respond to new forms as they emerge.[1145]

This notwithstanding, the broadness of current definitions poses several uncertainties for analysing 'new' practices that are harmful to women. The range of acts that constitute VAW are undefined. There is no clear process by which certain acts and behaviours can be categorised as forms of violence against women. Therefore, following

---

1141 Id., para.105.

1142 Id., paras.104–105.

1143 Id., para.105. For example, the emergence of new communication fora such as social media can offer perpetrators additional means (e.g. information about the victim) to stalk or harass the victim. Similarly, acts of stalking and harassment are no longer limited to the physical realm, but are increasingly occurring in other settings including cyber life.

1144 For example, the slow shift towards the controversial symbolic forms of FGM or medicalisation of FGM. While cultural practices have progressively shifted towards the eradication of FGM, symbolic forms and the medicalisation of FGM have, at times, been seen as alternatives that inflict less harm and carry less risks for young girls and women. It nevertheless remains that symbolic forms of FGM are rooted in beliefs of controlling female sexuality and are forms of VAW. Alissa Koski and Jody Heymann, 'Thirty-year trends in the prevalence and severity of female genital mutilation: a comparison of 22 countries', *2 BMJ Global Health* 1–8 (2017), pp. 4, 6.; World Health Organisation, *Global strategy to stop health-care providers from performing female genital mutilation*, (2010).

1145 United Nations Secretary General, *In-depth study on all forms of violence against women: Report of the Secretary General*, para. 105.

subchapter, addresses the characteristics of VAW. This allows to gain an understanding of what VAW entails and, eventually, why marital captivity constitutes a form of VAW.

7.2. CONCEPTUAL CLARIFICATIONS

None of the international documents that have been investigated define the substance or scope of the notion of 'violence'. Scholarly attempts to define the content or scope of violence[1146], more in general, as well as VAW[1147] have been strenuous.[1148] Similarly, the seemingly interchangeable usage of the notions of 'gender-based violence' and 'violence against women', as adopted in some definitions of VAW, is somewhat misleading. In fact, these notions are not interchangeable. When speaking of violence against women, it is thus crucial to have an understanding of which persons fall within the category of 'women', how the concept of 'violence' is conceptualised and how VAW is different to other forms of violence. These notions are addressed in the following sections.

7.2.1. VIOLENCE AGAINST WOMEN AS GENDER-BASED VIOLENCE

Violence against women is considered to be a form of gender-based violence and at times it is referenced as a synonym thereof. However, while both notions contain overlap to a large extent, they are not synonymous in the sense that they describe the exact same phenomenon.

Gender describes social constructions of expected and appropriate behaviours, codes of conduct and activities for women and men.[1149] Gender, therefore, is a broader and fluid concept that is not limited to and transcends the biological differences between females and males. Both women and men can be targets of gender-based violence. For example, trans- and homophobic attitudes can trigger violence against homosexual or transsexual boys and men, as members belonging to this group may be perceived

1146 G. J. Abbink, 'Preface: Violation and violence as cultural phenomena', in Aijmer and Abbink *Meanings of violence: a cross cultural perspective* (Oxford, New York, 2000), p. xi. See also Elizabeth A. Stanko, 'Introduction: Conceptualizing the meaning of violence', in Stanko *The Meanings of Violence* (Taylor and Francis e-Library, 2005), p. 1.

1147 United Nations Secretary General, *In-depth study on all forms of violence against women: Report of the Secretary General*, para. 69.; *Ending violence against women: From words to action (Study of the Secretary-General)* (2007), p. 28.

1148 In fact, even among scholars there is no agreement on criteria or a definition of what 'violence' is. Stanko *Introduction: Conceptualizing the meaning of violence*, p. 3.; Pieter Spierenburg, 'Violence: Reflections about a word', in Body-Gendrot and Spierenburg *Violence in Europe: Historical and contemporary perspectives* (2008), pp. 13–14.; Willem de Haan, 'Violence as an essentially contested concept', in Body-Gendrot and Spierenburg *Violence in Europe: Historical and contemporary perspectives,* (2008), p. 28.

1149 See for example, Istanbul Convention, Article 3 (c).

as transgressors of the prevailing masculine roles and expected behaviours. Similarly, gender-based violence against women can be premised in misogynistic attitudes, a perceived transgression by women of their assigned gender roles or as the need to reinforce or maintain gender roles and identities. The definitions provided by the CEDAW Committee and Article 3(d) of the Istanbul Convention articulate a form of gender-based violence that has women as their main focus. The reference to 'gender-based violence' in the above-mentioned instruments is, thus, limited to violence that is directed towards women on the basis of their female gender and forms of violence that disproportionately affect women.[1150] In essence: VAW is a form of the larger phenomenon of gender-based violence.[1151]

The term 'women' also deserves some brief attention. It includes young girls[1152], although most documents on VAW tend to leave this term undefined. The Istanbul Convention does not include the terms 'gender' or 'sex' and it solely provides that the term 'women' includes girls under the age of 18 years.[1153] The CEDAW and Belém Pará Convention contain no provisions on the definition at all. Whereas, the Maputo Protocol defines 'women' as '*persons of female gender, including girls*'. The Special Rapporteur on violence against women follows a similar line of reasoning by addressing violence against transgender women as VAW.[1154] Therefore, the term 'women' includes more persons than adults and persons of the female sex. A broad conceptualisation of 'women' enables these instruments to protect young girls and any person who identifies as a woman – including trans individuals – from acts of VAW.

7.2.2. 'VIOLENCE' IN VIOLENCE AGAINST WOMEN

In defining the term 'violence', both narrow and broad definitions have been endorsed. Narrow definitions of violence have frequently been used in legal, criminological and anthropological studies.[1155] Legal definitions tend to refer to limited and precise forms of violence, such as physical assault[1156], or they focus on specific forms of violence and

1150 Istanbul Convention, Article 3 (d CEDAW, *General Recommendation No. 19 on Violence against women*, para. 6. Council of Europe, *Explanatory Report to the Council of Europe Convention on preventing and combating violence against women and domestic violence*, (2011), para. 44.

1151 Istanbul Convention, Article 3 (f).

1152 The Maputo protocol (Article 1), the Istanbul Convention (Article 3) and the draft CEVAWG (Article 2) contain provisions that include girls under the age of 18 within the meaning of 'women'. The Belém do Pará Convention and the DEDAW are silent on this matter.

1153 Istanbul Convention, Article 3 (f).

1154 Rashida Manjoo, *Advancement of Women- Note by the Secretary General: Report of the Special Rapporteur on violence against women, its causes and consequences*, (United Nations, 2011), [A/66/215], para. 33.

1155 Nancy A. Crowell and Ann W. Burgess, *Understanding violence against women* (Washington D.C., 1996), p. 9.

1156 Spierenburg *Violence: Reflections about a word*, pp. 13–14.

VAW such as harassment, coercion, threats, domestic violence and forced marriage.[1157] Within the narrowest of definitions, the human body (physical integrity) is central thereto, while other forms of infringements are largely excluded (e.g. the mental state and psychological integrity).[1158] Violence is primarily preserved to interpersonal interactions i.e. interpersonal violence. Furthermore, definitions on the narrow side of the spectrum tend to include elements of illegitimacy and intention.[1159]

One major advantage of a narrow definition of violence is that, particularly within the legal field, such definitions are clear and precise, rendering them operational in judicial systems. They ensure a degree of legal certainty. On the other hand, a major disadvantage of a narrow definition, particularly in respect of VAW, is that it is likely to exclude other forms of harm. For example, the exclusion of psychological suffering may trivialise women's lived experiences, whom may experience psychological suffering to be more injurious than the physical harm itself.[1160] In addition, the element of legitimacy can have the effect of disguising violent conduct. The explicit inclusion of this element asserts a false assumption that there are acts and behaviours that are inherently or objectively illicit and illegitimate.[1161] This, however, is far from reality, since there is a weak evidential link between injurious acts and the question of the illegitimacy of those acts. Whether or not an injurious act is illegitimate and unacceptable will depend on the prevailing political, social, cultural and legal context in which it occurs.[1162] In addition, the question of legitimacy of violent acts becomes highly problematic when the persons involved have a different understanding of the legitimacy of the act. This is particularly the case where the actor deems the act to be legitimate, but the victim, witnesses or community is/are of a different opinion or *vice versa*. n these cases, questions of legitimacy could then lead to unending discussions where no consensus can be reached and in the case of VAW, lead to far lesser protection where certain harmful practices are considered to be culturally and socially legitimate.

The definitions of VAW contained in the legal texts are broader and they cover also acts and behaviour that inflict non-physical harm.[1163] The elements of intention or legitimacy

1157 See for example the set of violent acts contained in Articles 33–41 of the Istanbul Convention, which States Parties are obliged to criminalise in their own national systems.

1158 Spierenburg *Violence: Reflections about a word*, p. 19.; de Haan *Violence as an essentially contested concept*, pp. 30–31.

1159 De Haan *Violence as an essentially contested concept*, pp. 27, 30–31.; Spierenburg *Violence: Reflections about a word*, p. 14. The inclusion of these elements serves the profound purpose of differentiating those acts that are conducted intentionally and cause physical harm or suffering, but are nevertheless legitimate, such as surgery and operations.

1160 Walter S. DeKeseredy and Martin D. Schwarz, 'Theoretical and methodological issues in researching violence against women', in Renzettie, et al. *Sourcebook on violence against women* (California, 2011), pp. 5–6.

1161 Id., pp. 5–6.

1162 De Haan, *Violence as an essentially contested concept*, p. 31.

1163 This has, however, not always been the case. Rather a shift from narrow definitions to broader definitions can be observed. The first forms of VAW to be addressed were trafficking and forced prostitution as early as 1949 in the UN Convention for the Suppression of the Traffic in Persons and

are not included.[1164] The use of the phrase 'such as', when defining the sources of violence, implies a non-exhaustive list of violent acts and behaviours other than those explicitly mentioned in the text. More recent developments in the field of VAW show a further broadening of the behaviour and practices that constitute violence. For example, In the 2011 report, the Special Rapporteur identified that VAW can be distinguished in two categories: interpersonal violence and institutional and structural violence.

Interpersonal violence includes economic, psychological, physical, sexual, emotional and verbal threats and actions.[1165] Physical violence covers physical behaviour, reliance on physical force, strength or weapons to inflict physical harm or suffering.[1166] More often than not, physical violence results in psychological harm (e.g. fear of repetition, continuous feeling of being threatened, feeling of helplessness) and it may also have detrimental economic consequences for the victim (e.g. unemployability as a consequence of severe physical harm). Psychological violence refers to non-physical acts such as coercive acts, threats, verbal abuse as well as any other acts that have the effect of humiliating, embarrassing or controlling the victim.[1167] Psychological violence

---

of the Exploitation of the Prostitution of Others. The 1975 World Conference of the International Women's Year briefly addressed the issue of violence experienced by women and girls and this resulted in the Declaration of Mexico on the equality of Women. This declaration urged global solidarity in the elimination of certain forms of VAW including '*mental cruelty*'. Likewise, the resolutions adopted during the same conference went a step further by encouraging States to be '*aware of the particular forms of violence and cruelty, both physical and mental, that are perpetuated against women*'. The International Tribunal on Crimes against Women, held in 1976 in Brussels, added yet more forms, including forced motherhood, forced sterilisation, woman/wife battering, femicide and female mutilation to the gradually growing list of recognised forms of VAW. By 1985, violence against women in the family received greater attention, including the physical and psychological effects of such violence. The third Conference on women held in 1985 recognised that VAW constitutes a *blow to [women's'] physical and moral integrity*' and that it has a universal and structural nature. Eventually, this led to one of the most important General Assembly resolution on violence against women, the Declaration on the Elimination of Violence against Women in 1993. United Nations, *Report of the World Conference of the International Women's year*, (1976), [E/CONF.66/34], pp. 78, 124.; Declaration of Mexico on the Equality of Women and their contribution to development and peace, 1975 in United Nations, *Report of the World Conference of the International Women's* pp. 2–7, para. 28.; Russell and van de Ven, *Crimes Against Women: Proceedings of the International Tribunal*, pp. 81–122.; United Nations General Assembly, *Resolution on domestic violence*, 1985. United Nations, *Report of the World Conference to review and appraise the achievements of the united nations decade for women: Equality, development and peace*, (1985), [A/CONF.116/28/Rev.1], paragraphs. 231, 258; United Nations General Assembly, *Declaration on the Elimination of Violence against Women* 1993 [A/48/104 (1993)].

1164 However, where it concerns acts of VAW that have been criminalised, the element of intent is often included as a constitutive element of the punishable act. For example in the Istanbul Convention, Articles 33–39 thereof prescribe forms that should be criminalised by States and the provision includes the element of intention.

1165 Rashida Manjoo, *Report of the Special Rapporteur on violence against women, its causes and consequences*, (Human Rights Council, 2011), [A/HRC/17/26], para. 25.

1166 Crowell and Burgess, *Understanding violence against women*, p. 14.; United Nations Secretary General, *In-depth study on all forms of violence against women: Report of the Secretary General*, para. 113.; Council of Europe, *Explanatory Report to the Council of Europe Convention on preventing and combating violence against women and domestic violence*, para. 188.

1167 United Nations Secretary General, *In-depth study on all forms of violence against women: Report of the Secretary General*, para. 113.

encompasses not only instant acts but also patterns of repetitive abusive, coercive or threatening acts that are spread over a period of time.[1168] Sexual violence refers to involuntary sexual acts that are committed or forced upon the victim as a means to exercise power and gain/maintain control over the victim.[1169] Sexual violent acts are to be understood in a broad sense to include non-consensual sexual conduct as well as all the kind of acts that have sexual connotations, including attempts to commit such acts[1170] and taking advantage of coercive or other advantageous circumstances in order to commit involuntary sexual acts.[1171] Victims of sexual violence are violated in their physical and/or psychological and moral integrity. Alongside severe injuries to the body, victims are left with psychological suffering (e.g. fear, shame and stigmatisation).[1172] Finally, economic violence consists of acts that extend to control or deny a woman access to and control over basic resources.[1173]

Institutional or structural violence is defined as 'any form of structural inequality or institutional discrimination that maintains a woman in a subordination position, whether *physical or ideological, to other people within her family, household or community*'.[1174] This category of violence is more focused on acts of an institutional nature, rather than acts that are committed between individuals. This includes ideologies of domination of women by men[1175]; religious and cultural practices that are harmful to women[1176]; policies, laws and practices that hinder or deny women access to essential resources[1177], land[1178], education, employment opportunities, participation in cultural and religious undertakings and the lack of laws that criminalise VAW.[1179]

Thus, this category of violence emanates from State institutions and processes, as well as practices of public and private entities in their application or reinforcement of institutionalised ideologies and beliefs on the roles of women and men. Structural

1168 Council of Europe, *Explanatory Report to the Council of Europe Convention on preventing and combating violence against women and domestic violence*, paras. 179–181.

1169 Id., paras. 189–191.

1170 Id., para. 190.; Inter-American Court of Human Rights, *Miguel Castro- Castro Prison v. Peru*, 25 November 2006, Series C No. 160, para. 306.; United Nations Secretary General, *In-depth study on all forms of violence against women: Report of the Secretary General*, para. 113.

1171 European Court of Human Rights, *M.C. v. Bulgaria*, 4 December 2003, Application No. 39272/98, para. 163.; International Criminal Tribunal for Rwanda, *Prosecutor v. Jean-Paul Akayesu*, 2 September 1998, ICTR-96-4-T, para. 688.; United Nations Secretary General, *In-depth study on all forms of violence against women: Report of the Secretary General*, para. 113.

1172 The Division for the Advancement of Women, *handbook for legislation on violence against women* (New York, 2010), p. 26. See also Inter-American Court of Human Rights, *Miguel Castro- Castro Prison v. Peru*, 25 November 2006, Series C No. 160, paras. 306–308.

1173 United Nations Secretary General, *In-depth study on all forms of violence against women: Report of the Secretary General*, para. 113.

1174 Manjoo, *Report of the Special Rapporteur on violence against women, its causes and consequences (2011)*, para. 26.

1175 Id., para. 26.

1176 Id., para. 35.

1177 Id., para. 30.

1178 Id., para. 29.

1179 Id., para. 27.

violence has the effect of increasing suffering and furthering gender inequalities.[1180] Interpersonal violence and institutional/structural violence operate simultaneously in all incidents involving interpersonal violence against women.[1181] This is due to the fact that interpersonal violence is founded on prevalent institutional (e.g. discriminatory policies and laws) or structural factors (e.g. unchallenged beliefs, ideologies and prejudices of women's inferiority and men's superiority) that condone, legitimise or justify abhorrence to such violence. Structural violence, however, can occur in the absence of interpersonal violence.[1182]

The advantages of broad definitions of VAW, which includes non-physical forms of injury and suffering, is that these accurately define and represent the lived experiences of women. In addition, the inclusion of the phrase 'such as' enables the definition to include more harmful acts, such as controlling behaviour. Additionally, the inclusion of institutional and structural violence draws attention to structural contributors of VAW which make women more likely to experience violence. This form of violence is equally as harmful as interpersonal violence.[1183]

Nevertheless, just like the narrow definitions, broad definitions also receive their fair share of criticism. Among this is the critique that is voiced over the inclusion of other types of injuries (e.g. psychological injury). This is deemed problematic because such type of injuries are hard to measure, establish and, to a great extent, are experienced subjectively.[1184] Opponents of a broad definition of violence argue that the idea of labelling acts that produce mental suffering as violence can lead to extreme circumstances, whereby people classify any behaviour they find unpleasant as violence.[1185] Similarly, the inclusion of 'structural violence' is also criticised for primarily serving particular political goals or moral ideologies. Labelling an act as constituting violence can, for example, have the effect of mobilising the political opinion to criminalise certain behaviours or to allocate more resources so as to reduce certain behaviours. Furthermore, the labelling of certain social phenomena and practices (e.g. discrimination and inequality) as violence has also been argued to incentivise and justify counter-violence that is targeted towards the primary violence e.g. protests.[1186] Therefore, opponents of broad definitions hold that these should be used tentatively and, where they are too broad, they should be abolished altogether.[1187]

1180 Id., paras. 26–35.

1181 Id., paras. 24, 26. As the Special Rapporteur on violence against women puts it '*No form of interpersonal violence against women is devoid of structural violence [...] therefore, when a woman is abused by a husband because he believes he has the right to physically assault her, the woman is experiencing interpersonal and structural violence simultaneously*'.

1182 Id., para. 35.

1183 Id., para. 66.

1184 Spierenburg *Violence: Reflections about a word*, p. 22.

1185 Id.; de Haan *Violence as an essentially contested concept*, p. 33.

1186 Spierenburg *Violence: Reflections about a word*, pp. 19–20.

1187 Id., pp. 19–21.

7.3. THE CHARACTERISTICS OF VAW

The previous subchapter explored the concepts of VAW and gender-based violence. It revealed that there is no agreed definition of what acts and behaviour constitute 'violence'. Likewise, there are no clear criteria for distinguishing VAW from other violent and harmful practices. How is VAW different to other forms of violence? Prior to establishing whether marital captivity constitutes VAW, it is thus important to understand what VAW is, as well as its characteristics and its impact on women and society at large. Therefore, the following sections will explore the root causes and consequences of VAW in order to gain a better understanding of what characterises certain acts and conduct as VAW.

7.3.1. THE ROOT CAUSE OF VAW

The widespread and complexity of violence against women is well-researched in the many studies that have attempted to identify its root causes. To date, there are a plethora of explanations of the underlying causes of VAW, which can be divided into two categories: the micro-level and macro-level causes and risk factors.

Micro-level explanations focus on identifying the internal and external root causes at the individual level by studying evolutionary, psychological, biological, neurophysiological, behavioural and personality factors of both the perpetrator and the victim. In relation to domestic violence, for example, there is evidence that individual characteristics (e.g. personality disorders, psychological instabilities, pathological abnormalities and behavioural deficits), as well as socio-economic factors (e.g. low educational achievement, occupational attainment and income), are factors that increase the likelihood of men engaging in domestic violence against women. Previously experienced abuse or witnessing abuse between parents during a child's formative years may also increase the likelihood of engaging in domestic violence as an adult.[1188] Risk factors for women include, *inter alia,* their geographical location (e.g. society where wife battering is condoned), level of education, employment situation, household size and marital relationships.[1189]

Despite being of high value in understanding the factors and conditions that aggravate VAW, studies that primarily focus on the individual run the risk of over-simplifying the nature and peculiarities of VAW by underestimating and/or

---

1188 For an extensive literature review on the empirical studies on individual factors that contribute to VAW see; Richard J. Gelles, 'Male offenders: Our understanding from the data', in Harway and O'Neil *What causes men's violence against women* (1999), pp. 40–44.; see also Steven R. Tracy, 'Patriarchy and domestic violence: challenging common misconceptions', 50 *The Journal of the Evangelical Theological Society* 573–594, (2007), p. 80.

1189 Manjoo, *Report of the Special Rapporteur on violence against women, its causes and consequences (2011)*, para. 22.

overlooking the societal context in which the violence occurs. Additionally, a micro-level focus tends to characterise instances of VAW as sporadic, incidental and isolated acts by violent individuals against women. Consequently, this approach is not the most appropriate and effective method to identify, study and understand the structural nature of VAW.[1190]

Macro-level studies focus on finding explanations of VAW at the societal level. These include social theories on the construction and institutionalisation of ideologies, beliefs and norms that exacerbate VAW.[1191] Feminist theories and explanations frequently designate 'patriarchy' or social systems that uphold male dominance and control over women as among the root causes of VAW.[1192] Biological theories seek answers from the internal physical processes, (e.g. hormone levels).[1193] Evolutionary and socio-biological theories, on their turn, reveal that the prevalence of certain individual and collective human behaviour are closely connected to survival reactions.[1194] Macro-level studies provide the necessary input for understanding the broader social context in which VAW occurs, its function and its agents. By the same token, ignoring the individual conditions, as discussed above, may result in an overly bias analysis, inaccurate generalisations of certain behaviours to a group of people and the simplification of the causes of VAW, as a result of excluding the realities and influences of psychological factors, past experiences, destructive behaviours and individual social conditions.[1195]

In human rights documents, the emphasis has primarily been laid on the societal and structural conditions that exacerbate VAW, although some acknowledgement has been made to the importance of taking into account individual conditions as well.[1196] In particular, reference is frequently made to certain 'root causes', these being: 'patriarchal structures/patriarchy', 'stereotypes', 'structural gender inequality', 'systemic

1190 United Nations Secretary General, *In-depth study on all forms of violence against women: Report of the Secretary General*, para. 73.; Gwen Hunnicutt, 'Varieties of patriarchy and violence against women: Resurrecting "patriarchy" as a theoretical tool', 15 *Violence against Women*, (2009), p. 556.

1191 James M. O'Neil and Rodney A. Nadeau, 'Men's gender-role conflict defense mechanisms, and self protective defensive strategies: Explaining men's violence against women from a gender-role socialization perspective', in Harway and O'Neil *What causes men's violence against women* (1999), pp. 89–96.

1192 Manjoo, *Report of the Special Rapporteur on violence against women, its causes and consequences (2011)*, para. 34.; Amy J. Marin and Nancy F. Russo, 'Feminist perspectives on male violence against women: Critiquing O'Neil and Harway's model', in Harway and O'Neil *What causes men's violence against women?* (1999), p. 25.; Hunnicutt, *Varieties of patriarchy and violence against women: Resurrecting "patriarchy" as a theoretical tool*, p. 25.

1193 Anthony F. Greene, 'Biological perspectives on violence against women', in Harway and O'Neil *What causes men's violence against women* (1999), pp. 53–60.

1194 Louise B. Silverstein, 'The evolutionary origins of male violence against women', in Harway and O'Neil, *What causes men's violence against women* (1999), pp. 61–84.

1195 United Nations Secretary General, *In-depth study on all forms of violence against women: Report of the Secretary General*, p. 29.

1196 Manjoo, *Report of the Special Rapporteur on violence against women, its causes and consequences (2011)*, para. 21.

discrimination' or any other terms which are synonymous thereto.[1197] The following subsections provide an analysis of these concepts and how they contribute to the prevalence of VAW

7.3.1.1. Patriarchy

Patriarchy has not only been a central theme in feminist studies on violence against women[1198], but it has increasingly been recognised as one of the primary root causes of violence against women by human rights monitoring bodies. Patriarchy is composed of two intertwined and complementary components. That is patriarchy as an ideology and patriarchy as an institution.[1199]

As an ideology, patriarchy sets out to define gender traits, roles and relations between women and men. In general, femininity encompasses, among others, virtues of passivity, obedience, ignorance, docility, and it is entrusted with activities such as domestic services and child rearing.[1200] Masculinity is portrayed as harbouring the virtues of aggression, violence[1201] and the toleration thereof, intelligence, ambition, qualities of leadership and it is associated with the activities of providing security, economic production, conflict resolution etc.[1202] These attributes are commonly reflected and formalised in stereotypes and prejudices of men and women such as the obedient, docile and submissive wife, the nurturing mother/wife[1203] *vis-à-vis* the man as the head of the household, the bread-winner, the heroic man etc. A patriarchal ideology, in essence, proclaims and creates a hierarchy between women and men. Men are ranked higher and placed in positions which enable them to exercise greater power within the given social unit (family, community, society), while women are placed in subordinate positions and are subjected to control and domination by men in many aspects of their lives.[1204]

1197 See for example Declaration on the Elimination of Violence against Women, Recital 6 of the Preamble.; Convention of Belém do Pará, preamble.; *Elimination and prevention of all forms of violence against women and girls: Focus on prevention of violence against women and girls – Moderator's summary*, (Commission on the Status of Women, 2013), [E/CN.6/2013/CRP.6], paras. 3–5.

1198 Marin and Russo, *Feminist perspectives on male violence against women: Critiquing O'Neil and Harway's model*, p. 21.

1199 Edward M. Akita, *Hegemony, patriarchy and Human rights: The representation of Ghanaian women in politics*, (2010) (University of Ohio), p. 45.; Hunnicutt, *Varieties of patriarchy and violence against women: Resurrecting "patriarchy" as a theoretical tool*, p. 557.

1200 Kate Millett, 'Theory of sexual politics', in *Sexual Politics*, (Granada Publishing, 1969).

1201 Hunnicutt, *Varieties of patriarchy and violence against women: Resurrecting "patriarchy" as a theoretical tool*, p. 566.

1202 Millett, *Theory of sexual politics*.; Marin and Russo, *Feminist perspectives on male violence against women: Critiquing O'Neil and Harway's model*, p. 31.

1203 Maternity is at times perceived as a trait which establishes female superiority and places women on a pedestal. However, the focus and limitation of women's social status, role and significance to their reproductive capacity adversely excludes their participation and inclusion in other spheres and decision-making positions in other fields. Holtmaat *Article 5*, pp. 147–148.

1204 United Nations Secretary General, *In-depth study on all forms of violence against women: Report of the Secretary General*, pp. 29–31.; Coomaraswamy, *Report of the Special Rapporteur on violence against*

As an institution, patriarchy refers to an established social system whereby society and social interactions on all levels are regulated on the basis of an ideology of male dominance. Men are the prime governors and benefactors of such a system.[1205] Patriarchal systems should be understood in a broad sense to include micro-level institutions (interpersonal interactions, the family unit) and macro-level institutions and structures (religious institutions, the economic market, bureaucracies, State's institutes, laws, practices and policies and other social organisational structures) in which these ideologies are entrenched, operate and eventually take effect.[1206] Within a patriarchal system, women are largely excluded from exercising and enjoying similar privileges and are placed in subordinate positions, i.e. they are the objects of control.[1207] Eventually, this accounts for the inequality in power arrangements that exist between women and men.[1208]

In sum, patriarchy refers to the systemic domination of women by men[1209] as a result of social systems that are founded on ideologies and beliefs that admit men greater authority to exercise primary power and control, while subordinating women to the control of and domination by men. This creates inequalities between women and men in both public and private life and it is also visible in the persisting political, social and economic inequalities between women and men.[1210] Thus, unequal power arrangements between men and women, that is inherent in patriarchy-based ideologies and institutions, are among the factors that contribute to the '*domination over and discrimination against women by men*' and to the occurrence and persistence of VAW.[1211]

Notwithstanding, it is important to bear in mind that patriarchal ideologies are not fixed and unalterable. Rather, the various ways in which patriarchal ideologies manifest, in the form of stereotypes or prejudices, varies across nations and cultures.

---

women, its causes and consequences: Cultural practices in the family that are violent towards women, p. 28.

1205 Akita, *Hegemony, patriarchy and Human rights: The representation of Ghanaian women in politics*, p. 45.

1206 Manjoo, *Report of the Special Rapporteur on violence against women, its causes and consequences (2011)*, para. 37.; Hunnicutt, *Varieties of patriarchy and violence against women: Resurrecting "patriarchy" as a theoretical tool*, p. 557.

1207 Akita, *Hegemony, patriarchy and Human rights: The representation of Ghanaian women in politics*, p. 45.

1208 Id.

1209 United Nations Secretary General, *In-depth study on all forms of violence against women: Report of the Secretary General*, para.69.; Millett, *Theory of sexual politics*.

1210 Akita, *Hegemony, patriarchy and Human rights: The representation of Ghanaian women in politics*, p. 45.; United Nations Secretary General, *In-depth study on all forms of violence against women: Report of the Secretary General*, pp. 28–30.; Coomaraswamy, *Report of the Special Rapporteur on violence against women, its causes and consequences: Cultural practices in the family that are violent towards women*, p. 28.

1211 United Nations Secretary General, *In-depth study on all forms of violence against women: Report of the Secretary General*, para. 69.

Patriarchal ideologies are subject to continuous reconstruction as societies change.[1212] Likewise, the manner in which patriarchal values/beliefs entrench themselves within social structures and institutions will vary across societies. Therefore, the degree and variation of patriarchal ideologies and arrangements that are found in any given society are highly dependent on the specific geographical conditions, historical events and cultural manifestations that exist. These are unique to each community, people and nation.[1213] Consequently, there is not one all-encompassing definition, model or ideology of patriarchy. Rather, the commonality is based on the inborn power disparity that exists between women and men. It reflects an unchallenged axiom that a functioning society requires some form of hierarchy and, therefore, that certain persons or groups of persons are entitled to have more power and control over others. Power disparities between women and men and maintaining control of such arrangements, therefore, forms the axis of patriarchy.

Furthermore, patriarchy does not manifest and operate in a vacuum. Neither is it the only form of power arrangements nor the dominant or only root cause of VAW.[1214] One can alternatively think of arrangements along lines of age, race, ethnicity, disability, nationality, religion, class etc.[1215] It is therefore important to recognise the synergy and intersection between different dimensions of power arrangements[1216] and how women navigate these as victims, mediators and agents of VAW. It is, therefore, crucial to take into account inequalities that are created by intersecting power arrangements in order to identify the multiple ways in which women experience violence and are discriminated against (e.g. on the basis of, race, class, ethnicity etc.).[1217]

7.3.1.2. Gender inequality

Gender inequality, just like patriarchy, is often construed as a major root cause of violence. The result of power disparities between women and men is that women are severely limited from operating equal power and authority. They are restricted in their autonomy from making choices that impact their social environment and their own lives, in particular, the choices and conduct that involves their sexual activities. This, in turn, generates a situation whereby women are systematically withheld from exercising

[1212] Hunnicutt, *Varieties of patriarchy and violence against women: Resurrecting "patriarchy" as a theoretical tool*, p. 559.

[1213] Akita, *Hegemony, patriarchy and Human rights: The representation of Ghanaian women in politics*, p. 45.; United Nations Secretary General, *In-depth study on all forms of violence against women: Report of the Secretary General*, para. 71.; Hunnicutt, *Varieties of patriarchy and violence against women: Resurrecting "patriarchy" as a theoretical tool*, pp. 554–559.

[1214] For a literature review see Tracy, *Patriarchy and domestic violence: challenging common misconceptions*, pp. 576–578.

[1215] Hunnicutt, *Varieties of patriarchy and violence against women: Resurrecting "patriarchy" as a theoretical tool*, pp. 557, 564.

[1216] Manjoo, *Advancement of Women- Note by the Secretary General: Report of the Special Rapporteur on violence against women, its causes and consequences*, para. 77.

[1217] Manjoo, *Report of the Special Rapporteur on violence against women, its causes and consequences (2011)*, paras. 28, 42–43, 49–50.

and enjoying certain fundamental rights and freedoms, and this consequently reinforces gender inequalities that further the perpetual cycle of VAW.[1218] It is widely accepted that a decrease in gender inequality, and an increase in women's economic independence, will translate into the eradication of VAW. The general proposition is that well-educated, economically and socially independent women are in better positions to leave violent relationships.[1219] Inequalities and discriminatory practices against women in areas such as employment, on the other hand, have the effect of limiting women's control over economic resources, and therefore they decrease the women's economic independence.[1220] This in turn, not only limits women's options and capacity to make autonomous decisions regarding their lives, but it also renders them more likely to be dependent on others, making it harder for them to leave violent environments.[1221] Despite that this is true to some extent, higher degrees of economic equality of women does not automatically translate into women experiencing less violence.[1222] In fact, in respect of wife battering, some studies have revealed that men are likely to abhor to violence against their partners, where the man's 'educational attainment, occupational attainment, and income are less than those of their partners'.[1223] This is because the changing roles of women can be a factor that increases the likelihood of intimate partner violence, where it is perceived as a transgression of women's roles and as a challenge to men's power, control and privileges.[1224] In addition, an increase in gender equality does not guarantee that the entrenched patriarchal values, that perceive women as submissive, will be automatically challenged or modified.[1225]

1218 United Nations Secretary General, *In-depth study on all forms of violence against women: Report of the Secretary General*, para. 68. Manjoo, *Advancement of Women- Note by the Secretary General: Report of the Special Rapporteur on violence against women, its causes and consequences*, para. 77.; United Nations Secretary General, *In-depth study on all forms of violence against women: Report of the Secretary General.*; Spierenburg *Violence: Reflections about a word*, pp. 28–30.

1219 Marin and Russo, *Feminist perspectives on male violence against women: Critiquing O'Neil and Harway's model*, p. 28.; CEDAW, *General Recommendation No. 19 on Violence against women*, para. 23. On this subject matter, the Special Rapporteur on violence against women states: '*Women that are empowered understand that they are not destined to subordination and violence. They resist internalizing oppression, they develop their capabilities as autonomous beings and they increasingly question and negotiate the terms of their existence in both public and private spheres*'. Manjoo, *Advancement of Women- Note by the Secretary General: Report of the Special Rapporteur on violence against women, its causes and consequences*, para. 77.

1220 United Nations Secretary General, *In-depth study on all forms of violence against women: Report of the Secretary General*, paras. 86–91.

1221 Manjoo, *Report of the Special Rapporteur on violence against women, its causes and consequences (2011)*, para. 29.

1222 Gelles *Male offenders: Our understanding from the data*, pp. 39–40.; Hunnicutt, *Varieties of patriarchy and violence against women: Resurrecting "patriarchy" as a theoretical tool*, p. 562.; Manjoo, *Report of the Special Rapporteur on violence against women, its causes and consequences (2011)*, para. 40.

1223 Gelles *Male offenders: Our understanding from the data*, p. 41.

1224 Marin and Russo, *Feminist perspectives on male violence against women: Critiquing O'Neil and Harway's model*, p. 27.

1225 Hunnicutt, *Varieties of patriarchy and violence against women: Resurrecting "patriarchy" as a theoretical tool*, p. 562. For example, during a visit of the CEDAW in Ciudad Juárez, Mexico, the committee found that the developments in the maquilas, created an unprecedented shift in the traditional gender roles as they provided increasing employment opportunities for women. This had

7.3.1.3. Practices that are harmful to women

Article 1 of the Maputo Protocol defines 'harmful practices' as '*all behaviour, attitudes and/or practices which negatively affect the fundamental rights of women and girls, such as their right to life, health, dignity, education and physical integrity*'. Cultural, traditional and religious practices that are harmful and discriminatory to women manifest in many different ways and are culturally specific.[1226] Such practices often aim to control women's choices, sexual activities and reproductive capacity[1227], and they are the very embodiment of patriarchal values. These include, inter alia, practices such as female genital mutilation, bride kidnapping, honour-related crimes, witch-hunting and practices that may not immediately be labelled as cultural phenomena but that are peculiar to a specific society/community (e.g. high date rape figures among college students in the United States).[1228] These practices are often legitimised, condoned or encouraged by the given cultural norms, traditional customs or religious norms. Cultural practices that are harmful to women also include practices that create conditions for violence to manifest and go unpunished, such as restrictions on women's access to economic resources within the family and limited rights enjoyed by women in the family and marriage.[1229]

7.3.1.4. Concluding remarks

The foregoing leads to the conclusion that, in essence, there is not one single cause that can be pointed out to be the main cause of VAW. Rather many different factors and combinations of factors may account for exacerbating VAW.[1230] Of more importance is recognising that VAW is universal, particular and structural.[1231] It is universal in

the effect of decreasing gender inequality, at least in terms of employment. At the same time, men did not experience a similar growth in employment opportunities. In an environment where VAW was condoned, the committee found that this change in gender roles gave rise to an environment of hostility towards the women that were employed in the maquilas. An explanatory factor that the Committee did take into account, was that although there was an increase in gender equality this did not happen in parallel with efforts to change patriarchal-based stereotypes, beliefs and attitudes within the community. These largely remained unchallenged. Consequently, the Committee concluded the attitudes toward the women that were employed, was partially driven by the perception that these women were transgressing their traditional social roles. Committee on the Elimination of Dicrimination against Women, *Report on Mexico produced by the Committee on the Elimination of Discrimination Against Women under article 8 of the Optional Protocol to the Convention, and reply from the Government of Mexico*, (2005), para. 25.

1226 United Nations Secretary General, *In-depth study on all forms of violence against women: Report of the Secretary General*, para. 84.

1227 Id.

1228 Id., para. 83.

1229 Id., para. 78.

1230 Id., pp. 27–28.; Crowell and Burgess, *Understanding violence against women*, p. 50.

1231 United Nations Secretary General, *In-depth study on all forms of violence against women: Report of the Secretary General*, para. 69.; Marin and Russo, *Feminist perspectives on male violence against women: Critiquing O'Neil and Harway's model*, pp. 21–22. This is also expressed in the preamble to the Istanbul Convention, which provides: '*Recognising the structural nature of violence against women as gender-based violence [...]*'.

the sense that it occurs globally and is persistent across all nations, cultures, peoples and classes.[1232] It is particular in the sense that VAW is culture-specific. Traditional, cultural, historical and geographical factors largely differ across societies and are particular to each society.[1233] This accounts for the many ways in which VAW can take form. It is structural in the sense that it is founded in structural factors, ideologies and normative systems that promote a hierarchy between the sexes.[1234]

Additionally, what the above-described causes of VAW have in common is that they restrict women's access to power in the public and private domains and inhibit women's personal autonomy and control of their bodies and lives. Harmful practices often have the purpose of restricting or depriving women of their autonomy by controlling women's choices and opportunities in respect of their (sexual) activities and reproductive capacity or depriving them of such choices (e.g. in the event of rape). Similarly, patriarchy prescribes power arrangements between women and men that entitle men more decision-making opportunities, including decisions that involve or concern women, while simultaneously denying women equal power. Promoting beliefs of women's subordination and male superiority and dominance over women essentially boils down to restricting women's autonomous agency, all the while asserting a degree of entitlement over women's lives, opportunities and activities. Control over women's bodies and choices and the restriction of women's autonomy is an inherent facet of the patriarchy-based power arrangements. This materialises itself in the prevailing gender inequalities within interpersonal and familial relationships, as well as the inequalities that exist on the societal level (e.g. pay gap, unequal representation in decision making positions and politics etc.). On its turn, gender inequality further restricts women's empowerment and advancement in all spheres of social life.

7.3.2. VIOLENCE AS A MEANS AND CONSEQUENCE

Expressions of violence can serve vital purposes within a community, such as ensuring social justice, survival and conflict resolution.[1235] Violence can also serve as a means to maintain certain power arrangements (e.g. between women and men) or it can be endorsed as a reaction to perceived threats to the existing power arrangements.[1236] For

---

1232 United Nations Secretary General, *In-depth study on all forms of violence against women: Report of the Secretary General*, para. 69.; Manjoo, *Report of the Special Rapporteur on violence against women, its causes and consequences (2011)*, para. 21.; *Ending violence against women: From words to action (Study of the Secretary-General)*, p. 28.; Declaration on the Elimination of Violence against Women, Recital 6 of the Preamble.

1233 United Nations Secretary General, *In-depth study on all forms of violence against women: Report of the Secretary General*, para. 69.

1234 Marin and Russo, *Feminist perspectives on male violence against women: Critiquing O'Neil and Harway's model*, p. 22.

1235 Coomaraswamy, *Report of the Special Rapporteur on violence against women, its causes and consequences: Cultural practices in the family that are violent towards women*, p. 28.

1236 Millett, *Theory of sexual politics*.

example, in certain communities violence against women or harmful practices may be regarded as a means to redeem or preserve male-honour. Male-honour may at times be connected with the ability to control and maintain control over women, particularly in respect of their sexual activities and reproductive capacities (e.g. in cases of honour-related crimes).[1237] Within this context, VAW serves as a means for punishing transgressors of gender norms and establishing control over the victims. It also serves as a mechanism for maintaining patriarchal values and systems that promote the subordination of women, male dominance and stereotyped roles of women and men.[1238] Abhorring violence in order to gain or maintain a degree of control over the victim's conduct and behaviour, be it physically, emotionally, mentally, economically or sexually, deprives the victim of their autonomy and agency to take measures that decrease their risk of being victimised. Notably, VAW is not the only means to uphold and enforce patriarchal values that preserve power disparities between women and men. Patriarchal values may also become entrenched within society through a process of socialisation.[1239]

At the same time, violence against women is also a consequence of social systems and harmful practices that are premised on patriarchy and gender inequality.[1240] As

[1237] Coomaraswamy, *Report of the Special Rapporteur on violence against women, its causes and consequences: Cultural practices in the family that are violent towards women*, p. 28.; United Nations Secretary General, *In-depth study on all forms of violence against women: Report of the Secretary General*, pp. 29–31. Notably, there is an observable correlation between societies that harbour patriarchal ideologies of aggression and violence as a male virtue and VAW. For example, evidence points to an increase in the rates of rape and domestic violence against women in societies which value toughness, power and domination as masculine attributes. Marin and Russo, *Feminist perspectives on male violence against women: Critiquing O'Neil and Harway's model*, pp. 28, 32.; see also Tracy, *Patriarchy and domestic violence: challenging common misconceptions*, p. 583.

[1238] United Nations Secretary General, *In-depth study on all forms of violence against women: Report of the Secretary General*, paras. 72–73. This is also expressed in the preamble of the Istanbul Convention, which shares the exact same wording: '*recognising (...) that violence against women and girls is one of the crucial mechanisms by which women are forced into subordination position compared with men*'. Marin and Russo, *Feminist perspectives on male violence against women: Critiquing O'Neil and Harway's model*, p. 31.; CEDAW, *General Recommendation No. 35 on gender-based violence against women, updating General Recommendation No. 19*, para. 10.; United Nations, *Beijing Platform of Action*, para. 117.

[1239] Socialisation here refers to the processes whereby beliefs, behaviours, attitudes and practices are consensually (without reference to force and/or coercion) accepted within a society and are considered to be normal, common conduct and beliefs. This process is facilitated by means such as upbringing, education and media representations. Patriarchal systems are, thus, largely self-sustaining and their survival and prominence is not merely dependent on the exploitation of violence. This also helps to partly explain why certain individuals/men will not engage in acts of VAW, despite being members of a community which upholds patriarchal values and is largely structured across patriarchal lines. Millett, *Theory of sexual politics*.; United Nations Secretary General, *In-depth study on all forms of violence against women: Report of the Secretary General*, para. 73.; Hunnicutt, *Varieties of patriarchy and violence against women: Resurrecting "patriarchy" as a theoretical tool*, p. 560.

[1240] *High-level round table on the elimination and prevention of all forms of violence against women and girls- Chair's summary*, (Commission on the Status of Women, 2013), para. 4.; CEDAW, *General Recommendation No. 19 on Violence against women* CEDAW, *General Recommendation No. 19:*

aforementioned, these are factors that contribute to the occurrence and the widespread persistence of VAW. The consequences of VAW are composed not only of physical, sexual, psychological or economic harm, but it also includes violations of fundamental human freedom and rights of the victims.[1241] Acts of VAW infringe upon the core values of human rights. Not only does the committed violence disregard the victim's human freedoms, dignity and integrity but it also cripples the victims' ability to fully function and act freely as an autonomous agent over their own bodies and lives. Furthermore, VAW – including the fear of repeated victimisation – places constraints on women's mobility and access to resources and support services.[1242]

7.3.3. SETTINGS AND AGENTS

Conventionally, VAW occurs in four settings, that is: violence in the family, violence in the community, violence perpetrated or condoned by the State and violence in the transnational arena.[1243] These settings are interwoven and coexist alongside each other. Power disparity on the lower private levels, the family, can overflow into power disparities in the public arena, for example.[1244] The following subsections highlight each of these settings as well as the actors within these settings that affect the prevalence of VAW.

7.3.3.1. Family, community and State level

Violence within the family refers to the perpetuation of violence within the context of interpersonal relationships, and it encompasses all forms of violence that women may

Violence against women, para. 11.; Council of Europe, *Explanatory Report to the Council of Europe Convention on preventing and combating violence against women and domestic violence*, para. 44.

1241 CEDAW, *General Recommendation No. 19 on Violence against women*, para. 6. These include, but are not limited to the right to life, freedom from torture, the right to marriage, the right to be free from VAW, the right to equal protection according to humanitarian norms in times of international or internal armed conflicts, the right to liberty and security of person, the right to equal protection under the law, the right to equality in the family, the right to the highest standard attainable of physical and mental health, the right to just and favourable conditions of work. Furthermore, there is growing recognition that VAW constitutes both discrimination, as well as a human rights violation in and of itself.

1242 United Nations, *Beijing Platform of Action*, para. 117.

1243 Manjoo, *Advancement of Women- Note by the Secretary General: Report of the Special Rapporteur on violence against women, its causes and consequences*, pp. 9–16.; United Nations Secretary General, *In-depth study on all forms of violence against women: Report of the Secretary General*, p. 23.

1244 United Nations, *Beijing Platform of Action*, paras. 29,185–186. In fact, it has been theorised that such power disparities started on the lower level of the family and were eventually adopted in the public arena as societies expanded. For example, stereotypical division of labour and household responsibilities have the effect of limiting women's chances and opportunities to enter the employment market. Consequently, women enjoy limited opportunities to develop the necessary skills and experiences to move up the ladder, thereby rendering them unfit for high decision-making positions compared to male competitors. This, in the end, contributes to the existing economic inequalities.

experience within the family throughout her life.[1245] This includes violence perpetrated by spouses/partners (e.g. domestic violence, marital rape etc.), as well as violence perpetrated by ex-spouses/partners.[1246] Violence within the family also encompasses other forms of non-spousal violence, i.e. violence perpetrated against a girl or woman by other family members[1247] (e.g. dowry-related violence, female infanticide, sexual abuse of girls and honour-based violence etc.), as well as violence perpetrated against domestic workers.[1248]

Violence occurring in the community involves interpersonal violence in both the private (e.g. neighbours, religious community, recreational/hobbies associations etc.) and public sphere (e.g. educational settings, workplace, hospitals, social institutions, public transportation, public places etc.).[1249] Unlike violence in the family, there may be no family ties between the victim and the perpetrator. One can think of forms of violence such as date-rape, femicide[1250] and harassment in public institutions.

The third setting concerns violence that is perpetrated and/or condoned by the State. This refers to violence perpetrated by State agents, i.e. all persons entitled to exercise State authority acting in their public capacity (e.g. such as humiliation and invasive body searches or violence against refugee and internally displaced women).[1251] Ineffective custody policies and practices, inadequate implementation of effective laws to protect victims and inadequate laws that lead to impunity for the perpetrators (e.g. cultural defences in criminal proceedings) are among the conditions that reinforce patriarchal beliefs of women's subordination, stereotypes and VAW.[1252] Impunity for acts of VAW may, in society, be perceived as an implicit condoning of such acts or, at the very least, they perpetuate the idea that one can 'get away with it'.[1253] Therefore, this

---

1245 United Nations Secretary General, *In-depth study on all forms of violence against women: Report of the Secretary General*, p. 37.; Council of Europe, *Explanatory Report to the Council of Europe Convention on preventing and combating violence against women and domestic violence*, para. 42.

1246 Id.

1247 Manjoo, *Advancement of Women- Note by the Secretary General: Report of the Special Rapporteur on violence against women, its causes and consequences*, para. 31.

1248 Yakin Ertürk, *Towards an effective implementation of international norms to end violence against women*, (Economic and Social Council, 2003), [E/CN.4/2004/66], para. 41. The Special Rapporteur extends the settings of violence in the family settings to include '*violence committed against domestic works and other forms of exploitation*'. Thus, violence in the family setting includes intimate relationships (partners/spouses), inter-generational relationships (where the perpetrator and victim share blood ties) and also business relationship (domestic workers).

1249 United Nations Secretary General, *In-depth study on all forms of violence against women: Report of the Secretary General*, para. 126.

1250 Femicide refers to the killing of women. It is not only limited to the context of the community, but it also includes, homicide by a partner, honour-related murder, female infanticide and dowry deaths. Noteworthy, is the Special Rapporteur's inclusion of '*certain deaths due to suicide*' i.e. self- inflicted violence as a form of VAW. Manjoo, *Advancement of Women- Note by the Secretary General: Report of the Special Rapporteur on violence against women, its causes and consequences*, para. 37.

1251 Id., paras. 39, 40.

1252 United Nations Secretary General, *In-depth study on all forms of violence against women: Report of the Secretary General*, para. 76.

1253 Id.

setting extends to also include institutional laws and policies, practices or attitudes that legitimise, condone or justify violence.[1254]

Individuals are becoming more and more mobile and are becoming increasingly connected to two or more countries. This cross-border element may create certain vulnerabilities for those who are active in a transnational continuum and for women in particular. The Special Rapporteur has therefore found that it is important to also address how this development affects women, by including a fourth setting. This concerns the transnational arena which covers '*a continuum of life experience across conventional State boundaries*'.[1255] Within this setting, women face specific challenges and new forms of vulnerabilities, from the very fact of their voluntary or involuntary relocation to States other than their State of origin or nationality. States' laws on migration and asylum may create conditions that exacerbate VAW. For example, in some countries the legal residence of a migrant spouse is made dependent on their marital status with a national or resident of the host State. The dependent position that migrant women are placed in, therefore, increases their risk of becoming victims of domestic violence and discrimination.[1256] In addition, the multiple actors involved (multiple States as well as private entities, such as private cooperation and organised crime), leads to women becoming vulnerable to a specific kind of violence. Paying attention to the factors that render women in the transnational settings more vulnerable to VAW is, therefore, crucial.

7.3.3.2. Agents of VAW: Perpetrators, victims, bystanders and the State

All individuals can reinforce or eradicate VAW, either individually or collectively. Violence against women, however, has predominantly been approached in terms of men's violence against women. In this respect, little attention has been paid to the role of women, whom are predominantly portrayed as the victims. It is a given that in the majority of scenarios women are victimised by male aggressors.[1257] Such a narration, however, should be made cautiously as it has the tendency to portray an undeserved display of women's positions and abilities.

Firstly the 'victim' label can reinforce patriarchal beliefs and stereotypes of women as passive, submissive and powerless beings. Secondly doing so not only obscures that VAW is also perpetrated and reinforced by women, but it also ignores the intersection between VAW and other systems of oppression. Within society, men and women enjoy certain statuses due to a combination of different factors such as age, race, class,

---

1254 Id., pp. 72, 76.

1255 Ertürk, *Towards an effective implementation of international norms to end violence against women*, paras. 42–43.

1256 See for example the case of *Jallow v. Bulgaria*. Committee on the Elimination of Discrimination Against Women, *Isatou Jallow v. Bulgaria*, 23 July 2012, Communication No. 32/2011.

1257 Marin and Russo, *Feminist perspectives on male violence against women: Critiquing O'Neil and Harway's model*, p. 22.

nationality etc. Consequently, individual women and men experience varying degrees of authority, privileges and subordination. Subordination in one line of arrangement (e.g. gender) does not mean subordination in another line of arrangement (e.g. age).[1258] Thirdly, there is also the danger of obscuring the reality that women possess the ability, not only to be catalysts in the eradication of VAW – as they, individually and/or collectively, resist against patriarchal roles and address VAW – but they can also reinforce patriarchal roles and other conditions that aggravate violence, in their capacity as perpetrators or by complying with internalised patriarchal beliefs and stereotypical roles.[1259] In fact, certain harmful practices involving girls are mostly perpetuated by women.[1260] Patriarchy may place women in subordination, but it is a misconception to assert that this renders women completely powerless as to their fate. Even within the constraints of subordination, women still maintain a certain degree of control and power.[1261]

In the same manner, men are complicit both passively or actively when they accept or reinforce patriarchal beliefs that justify, condone or legitimise VAW or when they engage in acts of VAW. However, men too can serve as a catalyst for the elimination of VAW, as they resist patriarchy-based stereotypes and systems, strive for equalised power arrangements and form solidarity with women in this pursuit. After all, both women and men are actors in the construction and deconstruction of cultural norms, gender identities and other social structures, including those that subordinate or emancipate women.[1262]

Besides individuals, the State has a major role in reinforcing VAW within society as well as in preventing and protecting against VAW. The reinforcement of the unequal power relations, patriarchal ideologies and systems, and structural violence occur not only where the State is directly involved in acts of VAW, but also when the State fails to respond or responds ineffectively to situations of VAW. There is a correlation between rates of VAW

1258 See for example a study by Nazli Kibri on patriarchal power dynamics among women in a Vietnamese community in the United States. She found that in the household, older women enjoy some degree of status and power. Young women, on the other hand, had the least status and power. Furthermore, the presence of male offspring was a variable that could increase women's status and power in the household. Therefore, she concluded that women had an incentive to comply with the patriarchal systems, as they were guaranteed an increase in status and power at an older age or when they bore male offspring. Nazli Kibria, 'Power, patriarchy, and gender conflict in the Vietnamese immigrant community', 4 *Gender & Society* 9–24, (1990), p. 12.

1259 United Nations Secretary General, *In-depth study on all forms of violence against women: Report of the Secretary General*, para. 8.

1260 Although accounting for far lesser numbers, women can also be perpetrators of violence against other women. An example is female genital mutilation, which is predominantly performed by women. UN Office of the High Commissioner for Human Rights, *Fact sheet No. 23, Harmful Traditional Practices Affecting the Health of Women and Children*, (1995).

1261 United Nations Secretary General, *In-depth study on all forms of violence against women: Report of the Secretary General*, para. 108.

1262 Id., para. 80.

and effective responses to VAW.[1263] The State may act as a driving force in shifting power relations, fostering social and cultural transformation in society and deconstructing social constructions. This can be achieved by, for example, eliminating laws and policies that are discriminatory towards women, encouraging education and training on VAW and engaging in awareness-raising efforts on VAW. Therefore, States' acts, or a lack thereof, may either weaken or reinforce the existing power relations and patriarchal structures.[1264]

Finally, increasingly public and private legal entities (e.g. International Governmental Organisations, Corporations and NGOs) and illegal networks have been added to the list of agents of VAW. In undertaking their activities, these agencies may not only be confronted with an environment whereby certain forms of VAW persist and are committed (e.g. sexual harassment and intimidation), but they may also commit or reinforce the commission of VAW. Likewise, legal entities may also be in a position to prevent and protect against certain forms of VAW.[1265]

7.3.4. THE NATURE OF VAW

The foregoing brings us to the following conclusions. First and foremost, VAW is a form of discrimination and it has been acknowledged as a human rights violation in and of itself. Secondly, the discussed human right instruments endorse a broad definition of VAW. Violence against women consists of many different forms of violent acts that harm women in multiple ways and that may be experienced by means of interpersonal interactions (interpersonal violence). Increasingly, attention has also been drawn to the structural factors that exacerbate or enable VAW to persist. These factors may be considered as constituting structural violence. Thirdly, there is not one root cause that can be singled out for the persistence of VAW. Rather there many different causes account for VAW. Patriarchy, gender equality and the persistence of harmful practices are among the major root causes of VAW. These create and maintain conditions whereby women are more susceptible to incidents of VAW. Nonetheless, it is imperative to understand that these causes cannot be defined as all-encompassing, comprehensive explanations of what actually causes VAW. Fourthly, VAW not only occurs within different settings, but its persistence or eradication is a process in which all individuals, States and private entities ought to contribute to.

Despite the wide range of actors, settings and actors involved, there are some common elements that are present within all forms of VAW. Firstly, VAW is a universal and

1263 Manjoo, *Advancement of Women- Note by the Secretary General: Report of the Special Rapporteur on violence against women, its causes and consequences*, para. 76.

1264 United Nations Secretary General, *In-depth study on all forms of violence against women: Report of the Secretary General*, paras. 72, 76.

1265 CEDAW, *General Recommendation No. 35 on gender-based violence against women, updating General Recommendation No. 19*, paras. 28, 69, 73, 96–99.

structural phenomenon which has the function and effect of maintaining inequality and power arrangements between women and men. It reinforces patriarchal values and ideologies that are detrimental to women. Structural discrimination and the subordination of women are among the results. Both are factors that contribute that enable VAW to persist. The controlling of women's behaviour, opportunities and activities and the power disparities between women and men, are, thus, essential and characteristic elements of VAW. This is primarily what makes VAW different from other forms of violence.

Secondly, VAW targets women's autonomy and agency. VAW, or the fear of victimisation, does not only alter the behaviour, perception of opportunities and conduct of women, but it also inhibits women in their capacity to exercise, freely and fully, their personal autonomy in all matters concerning their bodies, psychology and conduct, and it also restricts women from effectively advancing and participating in social life. Violence against women can then be summarised as involving personal and structural practices which, intended or not, have the effect of:

a) Inflicting physical, sexual, psychological and economic harm or suffering; and
b) Invading or inhibiting the personal autonomy of women to control and shape their own lives, whilst submitting them under the control of others.

Such actions may be founded in or incentivised by beliefs of women's subordination and/or inferiority. The result is that violence against women infringes upon the fundamental rights and freedoms of the victims, including the right to be free from violence.

7.4. MARITAL CAPTIVITY AS A FORM OF VIOLENCE AGAINST WOMEN

A situation of marital captivity does not only violate certain human rights, but it also inflicts harm and suffering to the trapped wife, as was illustrated in the case studies. It deprives trapped wife of the ability to exercise their personal autonomy and it may infringe on, among others, their freedom of movement, right to private life, right to remarry or right to health, particularly their physical and mental integrity.[1266] A situation of marital captivity also causes multiple forms of harm and suffering which may be physical, sexual, economic and psychological in nature. That being the case, it remains important to establish whether the mere act of non-cooperation or opposition to a (religious) divorce, or the inability to divorce can be qualified as a form of violence against women. This requires a closer look at the underlying causes and contributing

1266 An analysis of the scope and content of these rights, specifically for situations of marital captivity, is provided in Chapter 6.

factors of marital captivity, the settings in which it occurs and the effect of such a situation on women's autonomy.

Starting with the causes, a situation of marital captivity is created by a structural component. Often this is in combination with an interpersonal component.

The structural component relates to the religious norms and divorce procedures within the religious communities that create the conditions and condone the occurrence and continuation of situations of marital captivity. In certain religions (e.g. Catholicism and Hinduism), divorce is not recognised or may be non-existent. Spouses whose marriage breaks down have therefore very limited means to dissolve the marriage and are likely to end up in a situation of marital captivity within the religious marriage. A situation of marital captivity can arise at the moment either or both spouses wish to dissolve the religious marriage, irrespective of whether or not the other spouse opposes the divorce. Thus, where divorce is not allowed or is non-existent within the religion a situation of marital captivity may arise in the absence of an interpersonal component.

In other religions divorce is available. Within Islam and Judaism, men and women have several options for initiating and obtaining a divorce.[1267] However, within the internal processes of dissolving the marriage, women are likely to experience discriminatory treatment.[1268] On top of that, women are also provided with limited means to initiate and obtain a divorce due to the unequal divorce rights that are attributed to them by the prevailing interpretations of religious doctrines on divorce. Men are awarded more decision-making power regarding matters relating to the status of the marriage and, as a result, they can dissolve the marriage by way of a repudiation or by providing the woman with a writ for divorce.[1269] This creates a power imbalance between the spouses, whereby husbands are entrusted with more control over the marriage and over their wife's ability to terminate the marriage. As a result, in communities and countries where such interpretations of religious doctrines are socially, religiously and/or legally enforced, women are more likely to be affected by a situation of marital captivity than men. They are more likely to become a trapped in the marriage. Thus, women are then subordinated not only in terms of the ideological beliefs that men should have more rights at the dissolution of the marriage, but also in reality as their ability to divorce and freedom is made dependent upon the will of the (recalcitrant) husband. The power imbalance and inequality in divorce rights are, thus, not only prescribed but are also the underlying notions within the doctrines and interpretations of religious scripture and norms.

1267 See subchapters 2.3. and 2.4.

1268 See for example, Jahangir, *Report of the Special Rapporteur on freedom of religion or belief Asma Jahangir – Mission to Israel and the Occupied Palestinian Territory*, paras. 49, 71.; Zee, *Choosing Sharia? Multiculturalism, Islamic Fundamentalism and Sharia Councils*, pp. 129–140.; Corbin, *Secrets of Britain's Sharia Councils*.

1269 The inequality in divorce rights are based on the assumption and interpretations which consider husbands as the prime providers of their wives' needs and as prime obligators of their protection. See subchapter 2.3 and 2.4 for more detail in this regard.

The interpersonal component concerns the actual conduct that creates situations of marital captivity. i.e. the refusal of one spouse to cooperate to the religious divorce.[1270] There are various motives and intentions for withholding cooperation to a religious divorce. The non-cooperative spouse might resolve to such behaviour so as to prevent the trapped wife from moving on with her life or to inflict suffering, to exploit their status in order to guarantee advantageous outcomes in the divorce process or out of sheer spite. That being said, bad faith is not always a factor, as a recalcitrant or opposing spouse may have genuine and sincere religious and/or personal objections to the religious and civil divorce. A situation may also arise where the spouse simply cannot be found/reached or has gone missing and therefore cannot provide for the necessary cooperation. Nonetheless, the result is the same irrespective of the underlying motives and reasons for not cooperating to a religious divorce.

Furthermore, marital captivity is not only a consequence of the power disparities between wives and husbands, but it is als a phenomenon that keeps this arrangement in place. This concerns particularly religions that restrict women's ability to divorce and require women to secure the cooperation of their husbands, while simultaneously enabling men to unilaterally terminate the marriage or granting men privileges that exempt them from the negative consequences of marital captivity. This unequal power arrangements between women and men, essentially, subordinate women's ability to divorce and place women at the control and will of their husbands in matters concerning divorce. A situation of marital captivity is then not only a consequence hereof, but it also validates and reinforces the binding nature and legitimacy of religious rules and practices that prescribe unequal rights and privileges to women and men during a divorce, within the religious communities.

Notably, the situation is different for the religions where divorce is restricted for both spouses. The discriminatory aspect, whereby women's rights and ability to initiate and obtain divorce are restricted, is not present. For example, in Catholicism, the grounds for divorce and annulment apply for women and men equally and neither men nor women enjoy exclusive privileges at or after the dissolution of the marriage. Both women and men are restricted in their ability to obtain a religious divorce or an annulment and both women and men can oppose a divorce that is initiated by the other spouse.

As for the settings and involved stakeholders, the religious rules and practices that enable marital captivity are enforced by the religious tribunals within the religious communities. By complying with and enforcing the prevailing interpretations of religious rules on divorce and by condoning the discriminatory treatment within the divorce procedures, religious tribunals, leaders and community members – including both the trapped and recalcitrant spouse – enable situations of marital captivity to exist

[1270] As was illustrated in the respective national case law of the Netherlands and France, in paragraphs 4.4.2.2.1 and 4.4.2.2.2., To date, no opposition to a civil divorce has been successfully accepted by a secular court.

and persist. Furthermore, the settings are not only limited to the settings of the family and the community but also extend to State level, particularly, where religious tribunals operate as State institutions. Where this is the case, there is a direct link between the existence of a situation of marital captivity and State actions. In these scenarios, it is the State's institutions that implement and enforce the religious norms on divorce. Secular States are not exempted either, as situations of marital captivity do occur and persist. Omissions or inadequate responses to marital captivity may exacerbate existing situations and enable new situations to arise. Whereas, active responses to prevent and end existing situations may contribute to curtailing the issue and encourage the efforts to develop effective solutions for ending and preventing situations of marital captivity. The creation of a situation of marital captivity may then not be enabled by State organs, but a failure to address marital captivity adequately may lead to the persistence of marital captivity. The State may then be held liable for such a failure where it can be attributed to the State.

Essentially, a situation of marital captivity and the underlying power imbalances enable husbands to maintain a level of control, not only over the status of the marriage but also control over their wives' choices and ability to, among others, move on, establish new relationships, remarry and travel. Married women are dependent on the cooperation of their (former) spouse in a way that married men are not and, at times, they are at the mercy of their (former) husbands where external intervention, by secular judges or religious authorities, is not fruitful. Ultimately, the autonomy of the wives is made conditional on the cooperation of the husband.

Considering the foregoing, the conclusion can be reached that some cases of marital captivity do qualify as a form of violence against women. This concerns situations in which husbands impede the dissolution of the religious marriage, for whatever reason, and thereby trap women in a marriage against their will. Denying the wife a religious divorce, limiting her rights to initiate and obtain a divorce and holding her in the religious marriage against her will violates the trapped woman's rights and also inflicts harm and suffering upon the spouse. It also deprives wives of their autonomy in respect of many aspects of their life and it enables husbands to retain a degree of control over both the marriage and the trapped wife.

This is different where a situation of marital captivity arises due to the non-recognition or non-existence of a divorce. In this situation both spouses are not able to terminate the marriage and no spouse has more control over the status of the religious marriage than the other spouse. The indissolubility of the marriage is a condition that applies equally to both spouses. Husbands, then, do not have more rights during divorce than their wives and trapped wives are not placed under the control of others in a different manner than trapped husbands. There is no clear discriminatory element in the interpretation and application of the rules on divorce. In fact, the national case law discussed in subsections 4.4.2.2. and 5.2.1.2., illustrate that both women and men do actively attempt to oppose and object to the dissolution of a civil marriage by the secular judge, although all attempts to do so have hitherto been unsuccessful. Consequently, these forms of marital captivity, although restrictive and harmful, are less likely to be categorised as forms of VAW. These forms neither target nor affect women disproportionately. Nevertheless, this does not exclude the possibility that other acts of VAW could be facilitated and present within these forms of marital captivity (e.g. domestic violence as in the case of Anneke). It should be borne in mind that a situation of marital captivity can also incentivise other forms of violence such as domestic violence, extortion and honour killing.[1271]

In conclusion, not all situations of marital captivity constitute VAW. Forms of marital captivity that have the effect or purpose of submitting women's autonomy to the control of their husbands and which arise from religious rules and practices which prescribe unequal divorce rights and privileges to wives and husbands, constitute VAW and violate trapped women's fundamental rights and freedoms. The recognition of marital captivity as a form of VAW means that its very existence is a human rights violation i.e. the right to be free from VAW, and it constitutes a form of gender-based discrimination. Therefore, it is a matter that can no longer be ignored by the State or dismissed as being merely a private or religious issue.

7.5. MARITAL CAPTIVITY, INTIMATE PARTNER VIOLENCE AND FORCED MARRIAGE

In recent times, marital captivity has been addressed as a form of forced marriage.[1272] Situations of marital captivity may also include other forms of VAW such as intimate partner violence (IPV) and forced marriage. IPV also involves violence by a (former) partner, and thus, has much in common with marital captivity.

Linking marital captivity to recognised forms of VAW has the advantage that it immediately highlights the seriousness of marital captivity as a social phenomenon

1271 High Rabbinic Court, *Plonit v. Plonit*, 1995.; Supreme Court of Israel, *Plonit v. Plonit*, 1997. In these cases, both the High Rabbinic Court as well as the Supreme Court of Israel, held that the provision on divorce, *Shulchran Aruch (Medieval Compilation of Jewish law) Section 37 thereof, affirmed that the issuance of a Get depends only on the will of the husband. Provided that there is nothing that obliges the husband or requires the Rabbinic Courts to oblige the husband to divorce, although without force. In that case, there were no such conditions and the fact that the wife did not want to remain married to the man did not constitute a basis to oblige him to divorce her. Extracts of both decisions can be found at* <www.equalitynow.org/law/rabbinical_courts_jurisdiction_marriage_and_divorce_law_5713_1953> last accessed 03 December 2016.; van Eijk, Wel gescheiden, niet gescheiden? Een empirisch onderzoek naar huwelijkse gevangenschap in Nederland, p. 65.

1272 See for example *Netherlands Institute for Human Rights – Written Contribution to the Committee on the Elimination of Discrimination Against Women (CEDAW) on behalf of the consideration of the sixth periodic report of the Netherlands.*; CEDAW and CRC, *Joint General Comment No. 31 of the Committee on the Elimination of Discrimination Against Women.*; Committee on the Elimination of Discrimination Against Women, *Concluding Observations the Netherlands 2016.*

that warrants State attention. In addition, these two forms of VAW – IPV and forced marriage – bare much resemblance and overlap with situations of marital captivity. However, it is questionable whether marital captivity should be conflated with forced marriage or IPV. It is the authors view, that it is imperative not to conflate these phenomena, despite their semblance and overlap. Rather, studying and compering these phenomena enables not only to gain a better understanding of marital captivity in relation to these similar forms of VAW, but it also enables to understand the difference between them. Understanding their unique features, differences and causes, is crucial in terms of identifying and customising adequate responses to marital captivity.

7.5.1. INTIMATE PARTNER VIOLENCE

Intimate partner violence (IPV) is a form of domestic violence that is prevalent in the family setting. The Istanbul Convention defines domestic violence as 'all *acts of physical, sexual, psychological or economic violence that occur within the family or domestic unit or between former or current spouses or partners, whether or not the perpetrator shares or has shared the same residence with the victim*'. Under the Istanbul Convention, domestic violence is divided in two subcategories: IPV and intergenerational violence. The latter refers to violence within the context of parent-child relationships, which is more gender-neutral as it includes both girls and boys.[1273] The Special Rapporteur on violence against women takes a less gender-neutral approach and discusses domestic violence in terms of intimate partner violence and violence in interpersonal relationships (including former spouses/partners and domestic workers).[1274] Reference is made only to violence that targets women and girls. For example, reference is made to the sexual abuse of female children in the household and other traditional practices which are harmful to women and young girls.[1275] Domestic violence is therefore defined as:

> *'All acts of gender-based physical, psychological and sexual abuse by a family member against women in the family, ranging from simple assaults to aggravated physical battery, kidnapping, threats, intimidation, coercion, stalking, humiliating verbal abuse, forcible or unlawful entry, arson, destruction of property, sexual violence, marital rape, dowry or bride-price related violence, female genital mutilation, violence related to exploitation through prostitution, violence against household workers and attempts to commit such acts'.*[1276]

1273 Council of Europe, *Explanatory Report to the Council of Europe Convention on preventing and combating violence against women and domestic violence*, para. 4.

1274 Another differential point is that the Istanbul Convention does not include or establish violence against domestic workers as a type of domestic violence.

1275 United Nations Secretary General, *In-depth study on all forms of violence against women: Report of the Secretary General*, para. 25.

1276 Radhika Coomaraswamy, *A framework for model legislation on domestic violence*, (Commission on Human Rights, 1996), [E/CN.4/1996/53/Add.2]. Other legal sources which define domestic violence include: The United Nations General Assembly resolution on the Elimination of Domestic Violence against Women. This document provides that '*domestic violence can take many different forms,*

Intimate partner violence is thus a form of VAW that is primarily confined to the family setting and which concerns violence between (former)spouses/partners. In addition, this form of violence is not exclusively fixated on the home or joint residence, and it therefore also includes situations where there is no joint habitual residence as a consequence of a divorce or separation. The focus is primarily on the context in which the violence occurs, rather than on where the family unit is physically vested.[1277]

7.5.2. FORCED MARRIAGE

Both the CRC Committee and CEDAW Committee, in the 2014 joint general comment, prescribe forced marriage as '*marriages in which one and/or both parties have not personally expressed their full and free consent to the union*'.[1278] Furthermore, the definition of forced marriage was also broadened to include '*a marriage in which one of the parties is not permitted to end or leave it*'.[1279] Similarly, the CEDAW Committee considers marital captivity as constituting a form of forced marriage in its observations to the 6th periodic report of the Netherlands.[1280] In the 2014 report on preventing child and forced marriages, the Human Rights Council (UNHRC) adopted a similarly broad definition. Forced marriage is defined therein as a marriage '*which occurs without the full and free consent of one or both of the parties and/or where one or both of the parties is/are unable to end or leave the marriage, including as a result of duress or intense social or family pressure*'.[1281] Likewise, the Special Rapporteur on violence against women describes a forced marriage as 'a marriage lacking the free and valid consent of at least one of the parties'.[1282]

Situations of forced marriage often concern the coercion of women or young girls who are forcefully married off for a variety of reasons, such as abiding by and protecting cultural and traditional practices, strengthening family links or settling disputes between clans/tribes.[1283] Cultural and religious ideals on relationships, appropriate

---

including physical, psychological and sexual violence as well as economic deprivation and isolation. Such conduct may cause imminent harm to the safety, health or well-being of women'. CEDAW's general recommendation No. 19 defines domestic violence as '*that which inflicts physical, mental or sexual harm or suffering, threats of such acts, coercion and other deprivations of liberty*'.

1277 Council of Europe, *Explanatory Report to the Council of Europe Convention on preventing and combating violence against women and domestic violence*, para. 42.

1278 CEDAW and CRC, *Joint General Comment No. 31 of the Committee on the Elimination of Discrimination Against Women*, para. 23.

1279 Id.

1280 *Response of the Kingdom of the Netherlands to the List of issues (CEDAW/C/NLD/Q/6) in relation to the sixth periodic report submitted by the Netherlands under Article 18 of the Convention on the Elimination of All Forms of Discrimination against Women* (June 2016), pp. 11–12.

1281 Human Rights Council, *Preventing and eliminating child, early and forced marriage- Report of the Office of the United Nations High Commissioner for Human Rights*, (2014), [A/HRC/26/22], para. 6.

1282 Secretary General, *In-depth study on all forms of violence against women: Report of the Secretary General*, para. 122.

1283 *Vani*, also known as *Swara*, is practice whereby women are married off in order to resolve feuds between different tribes or to amend crimes committed by their male family members (blood price;

sexual behaviour and female sexuality may play a major role in this decision.[1284] Men and young boys too experience forced marriage, albeit, in lower ratio compared to women and girls.[1285] Forced marriage takes place primarily within the family setting.

The lack of free and full consent is thus a constitutive element of forced marriage. The use of force, coercion, threats or duress on one or both spouses are factors that are conducive to a forced marriage and are often present in some form or another. Such conduct serves to manipulate either or both spouses consent and are often perpetrated by parents and close relatives of the victim. However, a forced marriage can also arise where none of these factors are clearly present or visible. For example, coercion may occur in the form of unequivocal violent practices such as physical violence, abduction, rape, deprivation of liberty and threats of any such acts. However, coercion may also occur in more subtle and covert forms, such as relentlessly exercising social pressures, emotional blackmail or character assassination.[1286]

In addition, free and full consent may be presumed to be lacking in certain traditional practices (e.g. levirate marriage and child marriage[1287], marriage with one's rapist) or when the marriage is conducted in order to enable extended family members to migrate or live in a particular country.[1288]

Notably, UN human rights monitoring bodies have expanded the definition of forced marriage to include marriages in which one or both parties cannot end or leave the marriage. In other words, marriages in which one or both spouses no longer consent to

---

Arshad Munir and Ghulam Ali Khan, 'A Social Custom "Vani": Introduction and Critical Analysis', 28 *Al- Azwa*, (2013).

1284 Young girls can be married off as a way to ensure their virginity and to prevent them from engaging in any sexual misconduct, which could damage their reputation and disgrace the family's honour. Coomaraswamy, *Report of the Special Rapporteur on violence against women, its causes and consequences: Cultural practices in the family that are violent towards women*, para. 57.

1285 Id. Young boys too can be pressurised into marriages for the same reasons (e.g. strengthening the family links, controlling sexual behaviour and conduct, avoiding unsuitable matches etc.).

1286 Id.; United Nations Secretary General, *In-depth study on all forms of violence against women: Report of the Secretary General*, para. 122.

1287 Secretary General, *In-depth study on all forms of violence against women: Report of the Secretary General*, para. 121.; CEDAW and CRC, *Joint General Comment No. 31 of the Committee on the Elimination of Discrimination Against Women*, para. 20.; Gulnara Shahinian, *Report of the Special Rapporteur on contemporary forms of slavery, including its causes and consequences, Gulnara Shahinian -Thematic report on servile marriage.*, (United Nations General Assembly, 2012), [A/HRC/21/41], para. 27. The common stance for minor spouses is that they are presumed to lack the necessary physical and psychological understanding of the implications of a life decision such as marriage. Therefore, they lack the necessary capacity to provide free, full and well-informed consent to enter into a marriage due to their minor age. Furthermore, child marriages are considered to have far-reaching consequences on the development of the female child (e.g. health-related issues of child mothers, constraints to education etc.) and they impair the rights of young brides. However, in exceptional cases a marriage with a minor may be allowed when the child is at least 16 years-old and the exception is provided for by law.

1288 CEDAW and CRC, *Joint General Comment No. 31 of the Committee on the Elimination of Discrimination Against Women*, paras. 21, 23.

the continuation of the marriage. Expanding forced marriage to include marriages in which one or both spouses cannot end or leave the marriage, essentially, introduces a new element, namely: the inability to end or leave the marriage. This element, however, has been left undeveloped and undefined by the CRC and CEDAW Committees and the UNHRC. Nonetheless, it cannot be denied that this is a progressive development as 'forced marriages', then also includes situations of marital captivity.

That being said, it also important to reflect upon the implications of such an expansion. This expansion seems to imply that voluntary consent should always be present at the conclusion of the marriage and throughout the entire marriage. Thus, a marriage that has been entered into voluntarily and consensually, may at a later time, become a forced marriage when one spouse wishes to end or leave the marriage but is unable to do so.

The factors of duress or coercion also seem to play a lesser role as constitutive elements for the practice of forced marriage. Consent, during the marriage may cease to exist for a plentiful of reasons that do not involve coercion. Spouses may, for example, no longer want to stay married due to their incompatibility. Additionally, spouses may be unable to terminate the marriage due to other reasons that do not involve coercion. Restrictive and discriminatory religious doctrines on divorce and non-cooperation to a religious divorce, as the phenomenon of marital captivity shows, are also factors that can impair one or both spouses from initiating or obtaining a divorce. Similarly, spouses may also be unable to divorce due to restrictive divorce laws, as was illustrated in the cases of *Babiarz v. Poland, Piotrowski v. Poland, Ivanov and Petrova v. Bulgaria,* and *Johnston v. Ireland.*[1289] Additionally, including situations in which one or both spouses are unable to leave the marriage due to non-coercive factors (i.e. restrictive and discriminatory laws and practices that prevent spouses from initiating or obtain a divorce) within the definition of 'forced marriage', may have implications for States that do not permit divorce or that adopt restrictive and discriminatory divorce laws. The implications are, among others, that these States would then be directly accountable for enabling the commission of forced marriages.

7.5.3. SIMILARITIES AND DIFFERENCES

Similar to marital captivity, intimate partner violence (IPV) is a form of violence which can affect both female and male victims, although the majority of victims are women.[1290] However, marital captivity largely differs from IPV in the sense that it transcends the family realm. Members of the religious community will continue to treat the spouses as married, irrespective of whether a civil divorce has been put into effect. Moreover, community members can aggravate (e.g. where community members

---

1289 See subsection 5.2.1.2.

1290 United Nations Secretary General, *In-depth study on all forms of violence against women: Report of the Secretary General*, paras. 114–116.

condemn the trapped wife and leave her in a social isolation) or alleviate (e.g. through supportive friends and other adherents) a situation of marital captivity. Alongside the community, marital captivity may involve interference by religious authorities, particularly when the involvement of a religious tribunal becomes the only way for the trapped spouse to end a situation of marital captivity. Similarly, the same religious authority can and have shown to treat women unfairly and enforce religious norms and interpretations that disadvantage divorcing women.[1291] In fact, in certain countries these religious bodies are also State organs, which means that their actions are directly attributable to the State and thus a situation of marital captivity may be created and maintained by the State.

Marital captivity thus differs from IPV in the sense that it is not confined primarily to the family realm. The religious dimension, which involves the religious community, religious authority and at times the country of origin means that situations of marital captivity involve multiple settings. Consequently, marital captivity is a phenomenon that is not entirely reflected and represented within the category of IPV or domestic violence. Measures for addressing marital captivity, therefore, need to take into account the role and involvement of all involved actors in the family, community and on the State level. Both legal and non-legal measures should aim not only to address the interpersonal aspects of marital captivity, but they should also aim to tackle the structural factors than enable situations of marital captivity to arise and persist on all levels.

The concept of forced marriage has evolved to also include situations of marital captivity.[1292] The inclusion of marital captivity within the umbrella category of forced marriage is strategically meaningful. However, merely dubbing marital captivity as a form of forced marriage without distinguishing the differences between marital captivity and the traditional understanding of forced marriage, may not be the most effective way to address marital captivity.

While the final results are similar (i.e. lack of consent of either one or both spouses to get or remain married and being in a marriage against one's will), the root causes are not. The main important difference lies in the actions which impair the spouses' autonomy and eventually force them to get married or remain married against their will. In the case of forced marriage, the consent is lacking due to coercion i.e. consent is presumed to be lacking, in the presence of coercive acts or circumstances which infringe upon the personal autonomy of the concerned individual.[1293] The ability to choose one's

1291 Jahangir, *Report of the Special Rapporteur on freedom of religion or belief Asma Jahangir – Mission to Israel and the Occupied Palestinian Territory*, paras. 49, 71.; Zee, *Choosing Sharia? Multiculturalism, Islamic Fundementalism and Sharia Councils*, pp. 129–140.; Jane Corbin, *Panorama: Secrets of Britain's Sharia Councils*, BBC One broadcasted on 22 April 2013.

1292 The 2014 joint general comment of the CRC Committee and the CEDAW Committee found that the inability to end a marriage constitutes a forced marriage. CEDAW and CRC, *Joint General Comment No. 31 of the Committee on the Elimination of Discrimination Against Women*, para. 23.

1293 *Memorie van toelichting – Wijziging van het Wetboek van Strafrecht, het Wetboek van Strafvordering en het Wetboek van Strafrecht BES met het oog op de verruiming van de mogelijkheden tot strafrechtelijke*

spouse as well as the ability to choose whether or not to marry is limited to the extent that it is perceived to be entirely absent. While theoretically the intended spouse has the choice and ability to exercise such a choice, i.e. to not get married, the reality is that she cannot perceive another or better option. The perceived absence of alternative options is due to the presence of coercive acts and circumstances. Consequently, coercion has the effect of altering the behaviour and choices of the woman, driving her to act contrary to her free will and wishes and thus marrying against her will.

In the case of marital captivity, the lack of consent i.e. the wish and will to no longer be married may, as aforementioned, arise from multiple factors that are not coercive in nature, such as spousal incompatibility. However, the ability to act upon one's choice to terminate the marriage and the obligations arising therefrom, may be restricted by religious rules on divorce which afford women restricted and conditioned options to initiate and obtain a divorce. In essence, the lack of consent to continue a marriage has no social and legal consequences. Another crucial difference is that the trapped wife does not have any effective options to actually initiate and obtain a divorce, thereby ending the marriage. The experienced restrictions in the trapped wife's ability to end the marriage are prescribed by the prevailing religious norms. Therefore, the husband's cooperation or non-cooperation does not alter, limit or provide other alternative and feasible options. Even when there is no coercion, she will experience the exact same difficulties in terminating the marriage, as the premise of the experienced restrictions lays in the restrictive interpretations and enforcement of religious norms on divorce. This is equally the same where women are provided with limited, yet highly inaccessible, options for divorce without the husband's cooperation. The trapped wife's inability to end the marriage is then enabled by both the act of the husband's non-cooperation and the religious laws which require women to secure cooperation to the divorce with recourse to their husbands.

Therefore, while the end results are similar for both forced marriage and marital captivity, the difference lies in the fact that for situations of marital captivity, the forced conjugal relationship is the consequence of the inability to end or leave the marriage, rather than the trapped wife's lack of consent. It is, thus, imperative that any effort to address marital captivity takes into account the religious aspects that are inherent within this phenomenon.

To conclude, while situations of marital captivity share similarities with IPV and forced marriage and they are increasingly being addressed as forced marriage, this analysis has demonstrated that it is essential to acknowledge and consider the different aspects that are characteristic of each of these forms of VAW. Their cause, settings and constitutive elements differ. Marital captivity transcends the family sphere and involves multiple actors and, at times, even several legal systems. Furthermore, it is not the lack of consent that lies at the core of marital captivity, but rather it is the women's restricted options

---

aanpak van huwelijksdwang, polygamie en vrouwelijke genitale verminking, (Tweede Kamer der Staten-Generaal, 2011), [32840, nr. 3], pp. 1–4.

to initiate and obtain a divorce. By conflating these concepts, one runs the risk of not only diminishing the effectiveness of measures to address and prevent these social phenomena, but it may also create confusion, complicate any attempts to understand and study these issues and underestimate the seriousness of each of these forms of VAW. Therefore, strategies and policies as well as non-legislative measures to address each of these issues should take these differences into account, if they are to be effective in eradicating VAW. Doing so allows for an acknowledgement of the peculiarities and specificities of situations of marital captivity. Responses to marital captivity can then be tailored to address both the non-cooperation of the recalcitrant spouse, as well as the structural factors (i.e. the religious interpretations and practices) which enable marital captivity to exist.

7.6. STATES' OBLIGATIONS IN RELATION TO VAW

As was established in the previous subchapters, marital captivity qualifies as a form of VAW. This implies that the State has a role in responding to marital captivity in general as well as to specific situations. This subchapter, thus, considers the implications of recognising marital captivity as VAW. More specifically, it outlines the obligations that States have to respond to marital captivity as a form of VAW.

The CEDAW Committee categorises the obligations contained in the Convention in three types of obligations, namely obligations to respect, protect and fulfil.[1294] Under this convention, States are obliged to eliminate all forms of discrimination against women, including VAW.[1295] The general Article 2 CEDAW, which pertains the Convention as a whole, contains both negative as well as positive obligations to eliminate discrimination, including VAW.[1296] Article 2 specifically direct States to, among others, refrain from discriminating against women[1297], to condemn discrimination[1298], to repeal national penal laws that are discriminatory against women[1299] and to *'pursue by all appropriate means and without delay a policy of eliminating discrimination against women'*.[1300]

1294 *'The obligation to fulfil entails, that States take wide variety of measures to ensure de jure and de facto enjoyment of equal rights. This entails obligations of means or conduct and also obligations of result'.* CEDAW, *General Recommendation No. 28 on the core obligations of States Parties under Article 2 of the Convention on the Elimination of All Forms of Discrimination against Women*, para. 9.

1295 Convention on the Elimination of All Forms of Discrimination Against Women, Article 2–3.; CEDAW, *General Recommendation No. 19 on Violence against women*, para. 4.

1296 Committee on the Elimination of Discrimination Against Women, *A.T. v. Hungary*, 26 January 2005, Communication No. 2/2003, paras. 9.2–9.3.; CEDAW, *General Recommendation No. 28 on the core obligations of States Parties under Article 2 of the Convention on the Elimination of All Forms of Discrimination against Women*, paras. 9–13.

1297 Convention on the Elimination of All Forms of Discrimination Against Women, Article 2 (d).

1298 Id., Article 2.

1299 Id., Article 2 (g).

1300 Id., Article 2.

Similarly, the Istanbul Convention – in Articles 4 and 5 thereof – obliges States and their agents to refrain from engaging in any act of VAW and to '*take the necessary legislative and other measures to promote and protect the right for everyone, particularly women, to live free from violence in both the public and the private sphere*'.[1301]

The positive obligations to protect, as contained in Article 2 CEDAW, require, among others, that States protect women's rights and eliminate all forms of discrimination, including those committed by private parties.[1302] This is an immediate obligation, as States are required to act without delay so as to eliminate gender-based discrimination. Likewise, the Istanbul Convention not only prohibits acts of VAW by the State (a negative obligation), but it also ascribes positive obligations to States Parties in Article 5 thereof.[1303] States Parties are required to respond to acts of VAW that have been committed and they have a duty to '*exercise due diligence to, prevent, investigate, punish and provide reparations for acts of violence [...] that are perpetrated by non-State actors*'.[1304]

In principle, acts of VAW that have been committed by non-State actors are not directly attributable to the State. Nevertheless, the State 's accountability may still be established on the basis of the State's failure to comply with its positive obligations to protect women from acts of VAW that are committed by private actors.[1305] Failure to respond adequately may also have the effect of creating an environment of impunity, which may be perceived as encouraging VAW or at the very least as condoning the perpetuation of acts of VAW within society.[1306]

Furthermore, Article 2(f) taken in conjunction with Article 5(a) CEDAW contains an obligation on States to eliminate structural factors, on all levels, that are harmful, or which contribute to creating harmful conditions for women.[1307] Article 2(f) CEDAW

1301 Istanbul Convention, Article 4 (1).

1302 Convention on the Elimination of All Forms of Discrimination Against Women, Article 2 (e). The CEDAW Committee has asserted that, indeed, such obligations stem from Articles 2 (e)-(f) read in conjunction with Article 5 and it has specifically highlighted that Article 2 (e) requires States to eliminate discrimination by private parties CEDAW, *General Recommendation No. 19 on Violence against women*, paras. 9, 17, 24(a).

1303 See also Articles 12, 18, 49 and 62 which contain general positive obligations and principles for States Parties.

1304 Istanbul Convention, Article 5 (2).

1305 CEDAW, *General Recommendation No. 19 on Violence against women*, para. 9.; Council of Europe, *Explanatory Report to the Council of Europe Convention on preventing and combating violence against women and domestic violence*, para. 59.

1306 Rashida Manjoo, *Report of the Special Rapporteur on violence against women, its causes and consequences*, (United Nations, 2013), [A/HRC/23/49], para. 27; see also Inter-American Court of Human Rights, *Velasquez Rodriguez v. Honduras, 29 July 1988*, Series C No. 4, para. 175.

1307 CEDAW, *General Recommendation No. 35 on gender-based violence against women, updating General Recommendation No. 19*, para 26.; Andrew Byrnes, 'Article 2', in Freeman, et al. *The UN Convention on the Elimination of All Forms of Discrimination Against Women: A commentary* (New York, 2012), pp. 74–75.; CEDAW, *General Recommendation No. 28 on the core obligations of States Parties under Article 2 of the Convention on the Elimination of All Forms of Discrimination against Women*, para. 9.

directs States *'to take all appropriate measures, including legislation, to modify or abolish existing laws, regulations, customs and practices which constitute discrimination against women'*. Article 5(a) CEDAW requires States parties to take all appropriate measures to *'modify the social and cultural patterns of conduct of men and women, with a view to achieving the elimination of prejudices and customary and all other practices which are based on the idea of the inferiority or the superiority of either of the sexes or on stereotyped roles for men and women'*. An obligation on States to mobilise social and cultural transformation is also found in Article 4(j) DEDAW and Article 12 (1) of the Istanbul Convention, which largely echoes the wording contained in Article 5(a) CEDAW.

Remarkably, Article 5(a) CEDAW does not include a reference to religion and it only refers to culture in terms of 'cultural patterns'. However, the CEDAW Committee has adopted a broad interpretation of culture which includes religion, tradition, customs as well as other sources of societal norms and values such as economic arrangements, social and political structures and legal regulations.[1308] Moreover, it is submitted that Articles 2(e), (f) *juncto* 5(a) CEDAW impose *'an obligation on States Parties to intervene positively in the activities, and practices of religious, cultural, or ethnic groups that either directly or indirectly discriminate against women'*.[1309] As Holtmaat rightly observes, State parties' lack of *'[standing] up against religious authorities or community leaders who argue that their customs or religious prescriptions do not allow for women's equality'* ought to be considered as constituting direct discrimination against women, which is prohibited and incompatible with Articles 2(f) and 5(a) CEDAW.[1310] This provision, therefore, requires States to be critical of traditional, cultural, social structures and laws, as well as of religious practices that reinforce ideas of hierarchy between the sexes.[1311]

Furthermore, within the context of Article 5(a) CEDAW, the implied States' obligations have been broadened to include an obligation to eliminate systemic and structural inequalities of women, alongside eliminating gender-based ideologies and stereotypes.[1312] States are thus, also obliged to eliminate structural factors and practices which foster conditions of inequality and which exacerbate beliefs of women's subordination and inaction.[1313] In fact, the failure to address customs, traditions or religions that justify, condone or encourage acts of VAW may create accountability even in the absence of actual harm having taken place.[1314] The eradication of VAW is not

---

1308 Holtmaat *Article 5*, p. 150.; Frances Raday, 'Culture, religion and gender', 1 *International Journal of Constitutional Law* 663–715, (2003), pp. 677–680.

1309 Byrnes *Article 2*, p. 91.

1310 Holtmaat *Article 5*, pp. 155, 159.

1311 Frances Raday, 'Culture, religion, and CEDAW's article 5(a)', in Schöpp-Schilling and Flinterman, *The Circle of Empowerment* (New York, 2007), p. 71.

1312 Holtmaat *Article 5*, p. 144.

1313 Convention on the Elimination of All Forms of Discrimination Against Women, Article 2(f) jo. Article 5(a).; Istanbul Convention, Article 12(1).; Council of Europe, *Explanatory Report to the Council of Europe Convention on preventing and combating violence against women and domestic violence*, para. 85.

1314 Ertürk, *Integration of the human rights of women and the gender perspective: violence against women – The due diligence standard as a tool for the elimination of violence against women*, para. 88.

attainable without effective measures to redress sex-based discrimination and other structural factors that increase gender inequality. In complying with these obligations, States retain the flexibility to select the measures they adopt. This enables States to assess which measures are most effective and appropriate within their national context in order to address and eliminate discrimination and VAW.[1315]

More specifically on marital captivity, it is worthwhile noting here that the Special Rapporteur on freedom of religion or belief has included the practice of denying women '*the right to seek divorce and exposure to the threat of unilateral divorce*'[1316] as being among the list of practices that States should address in order to comply with Article 5(a) CEDAW. Thus, granting these practices the status of a religious manifestation[1317] may constitute a failure to comply with Article 5(a) CEDAW. In this respect, and as demonstrated in subsection 4.4.2.4. the conclusion that non-cooperation to a religious divorce constitutes a religious manifestation should be drawn cautiously.

That being, State intervention and efforts to foster social and cultural transformation, within religious communities may be perceived as encroaching upon the rights and entitlements (e.g. the freedom of religion) of communities and religious orders. Thus, how should State obligations in relation to VAW be weighed against any other competing interests?

Where cultural, traditional or religious attitudes and conduct undermine women's rights and equality, the CEDAW Committee has firmly established a precedence of giving priority to the protection of women's rights and freedoms.[1318] This approach aligns with and is reflected in the hierarchy that is implied in Article 5(a) CEDAW. In their efforts to ensure women's rights and equality, States are obliged to address cultural and traditional practices, ideological beliefs and stereotypes that undermine women's human rights and their right to equality. In other words, realising and guaranteeing women's rights and equality takes precedence over the obligations to respect cultural, traditional or religious norms and practices, particularly when these undermine women's rights and equality.

In the same light, in their case law on domestic violence, the CEDAW Committee and the ECtHR have established that women's lives, physical and mental integrity cannot be superseded by the perpetrator's rights.[1319] A similar hierarchy is prescribed by the Istanbul Convention. Article 12 (5) *juncto* Article 42 of the Istanbul Convention

1315 Byrnes *Article 2*, p. 77.

1316 Heiner Bielefeldt, *Interim report of the Special Rapporteur on freedom of religion or belief* (UN General Assembly, 7 August 2013), [A/68/290], para. 38.

1317 See also subsections 4.4.2.3–4.4.2.4.

1318 Id., p. 160.; Raday, *Culture, religion and gender*, p. 678.

1319 European Court of Human Rights, *Opuz v. Turkey*, 9 June 2009, Application No. 33401/01, para. 147.; Committee on the Eliminaton of Discrimination against Women, *Fatma Yildirim v. Austria*, 1 October 2007, Communication No. 6/2005, para. 12.1.5.; see also Committee on the Elimination of Discrimination Against Women, *A.T. v. Hungary*, 26 January 2005, Communication No. 2/2003, para. 9.3; Committee on the Elimination of Discrimination Against Women, *Goekce v. Austria*, 06 August 2007, Communication No. 5/2005, para. 12.1.5.

stresses that culture, custom, religion, tradition and custom may not be accepted in criminal proceedings as a justification for any acts of VAW. Similarly, the HRC concluded in one of its general comment, that the freedom of religion may not be relied upon to discriminate against women.[1320] The previously discussed ECtHR case of *Staatkundige Gereformeerd Partij v. The Netherlands* also confirms that the goals of advancing equality of the sexes and elimination of gender-based discrimination should be attributed considerable weight when these clash with the right to freedom of religion.[1321] As the ECtHR concluded, equality is a prominent goal in many countries and is enshrined in many treaties. Weighty reasons would, therefore, have to be given if this principle is to be subjugated and different treatment on grounds of gender is to be condoned.

State intervention in matters that are deeply entrenched in religion, although seemingly controversial to the collective freedom of religion, is possible without amounting to an infringement of religious freedoms. The case law on marital captivity is evidence of this. Additionally, next to judicial means of intervention, Cook proposes an alternative approach of financial intervention.[1322] She suggests that States may consider withholding tax privileges, or refuse to grant charitable immunity to religious institutions or groups that discriminate against women, bar women from participating in higher functions within their institutions or limit women's opportunities to exercise significant influence within the religious community and public sphere.[1323] An example where both judicial intervention and financial intervention contributed to eliminating discrimination within a religious group is that of the earlier discussed case of *Staatkundig Gereformeerde Partij v. The Netherlands.* During the civil proceedings, the domestic courts established that the State had acted unlawfully by not adequately addressing the discriminatory practices against women by the SGP. This led to a suspension of their subsidies by the State. In the meantime, while the decision was pending before the ECtHR, the SGP amended its rules so that women could be included on the party's list. This amendment was made in order to ensure that it would not lose its financial privileges. This case goes to show that States have effective means at their disposal to intervene in religious affairs that advance inequality and gender-based discrimination, without encroaching upon the religious freedom of religious groups.

To summarise, States can, therefore, be held accountable for failing to adequately respond to protect and prevent against acts of VAW i.e. responding to actual incidents of VAW, including those committed by private actors. In responding to and addressing VAW, States should refrain from acts which are discriminatory against women. Discriminatory, weak and inadequate responses may be directly attributable to the

---

1320 HRC, *General Comment No. 28: Article 3 (The equality of rights between men and women)*, para. 21.
1321 See subsection 4.3.2.2.
1322 Cook, *State Responsibility for Violations of Women's Human Rights*, p. 168.
1323 Id., p. 168.

State. The State can also be held accountable in respect of its obligation to appropriately address the structural factors that encourage and exacerbate the commission of acts of VAW. However, this leaves unanswered the question as to when a State's acts or omissions constitute a failure to comply with its positive obligations to protect and prevent. For example, does the mere existence of a form of VAW that has been committed by a private person constitute a failure of the State to prevent VAW? The following section, therefore, aims to provide clarity on the scope and content of the States' positive obligations to address and respond to VAW more generally and to marital captivity more specifically.

7.6.1. THE PRINCIPLE OF DUE DILIGENCE IN THE CONTEXT OF VAW

Within the context of VAW, the due diligence principle has served as a useful guiding tool to assess whether the State's efforts to protect from and prevent acts of VAW a compliant with its obligations. The principle of due diligence has evolved in international law and[1324], over the years, it has also emerged within the human rights discourse. It serves as a standard for assessing whether States have complied with their obligation to protect human rights.[1325] The due diligence standard in human rights law has been predominantly discussed in relation to the right to life and the right to be free from torture and ill-treatment.[1326] However, more recently this standard has also been applied in relation to other rights as well, including VAW.[1327]

With regards to the issue of VAW, the diligence principle has been adopted, both explicitly and implicitly, in various legal and quasi-legal instruments. The obligation to protect, enshrined in Article 2 CEDAW, requires that States respond with due diligence by means of preventing, investigating, prosecuting, punishing and providing reparations for acts of discrimination and VAW that are committed by private actors in both the public and private sphere.[1328] The duty to exercise due diligence has also

---

[1324] Ertürk, *Integration of the human rights of women and the gender perspective: violence against women – The due diligence standard as a tool for the elimination of violence against women*, para. 19. See also Timo Koivurova,' Due diligence', *Max Planck Encyclopedia of Public International Law*, paras. 4–7, 27, 35–36; International Law Commission,' Draft articles on Responsibility of Sates for Internationally Wrongful Acts, with commentaries', *at* <http://legal.un.org/ilc/texts/instruments/english/commentaries/9_6_2001.pdf> last acessed 12 September 2017, p. 39.

[1325] Chirwa, *The doctrine of State responsibility as a potential means of holding private actors accountable for human rights*, p. 17.

[1326] Inter-American Court of Human Rights, *Velasquez Rodriguez v. Honduras, 29 July 1988*, Series C No. 4.; European Court of Human Rights, *E. and Others v. the United Kingdom*, 26 November 2002, Application No. 33218/96.

[1327] See for example Istanbul Convention, Article 5 (2).

[1328] Id., para. 24.; CEDAW, *General Recommendation No. 28 on the core obligations of States Parties under Article 2 of the Convention on the Elimination of All Forms of Discrimination against Women*, paras. 10, 13, 19.; CEDAW, *General Recommendation No. 19 on Violence against women*, para. 9.

been extended in relation to the State's obligation to '*banish gender stereotypes*'.[1329] In fact, the CEDAW Committee considers that the obligation to exercise due diligence 'underpins the convention as a whole'.[1330] Likewise, Article 4(c) of the DEDAW explicitly commends States to '*exercise due diligence to prevent, investigate and, in accordance with national legislation, punish acts of violence against women, whether those acts are perpetrated by the State or by private persons*'. Reference to the obligation to exercise due diligence in relation to VAW is also made in the Beijing Platform of action which follows the exact same wording as that which is used in Article 4 (c) of the DEDAW.[1331] The Special Rapporteur on violence against women has also recognised that the adopted goal of preventing and eliminating VAW requires the State to act with due diligence on both the individual level (i.e. to adopt measures in each specific case to prevent and protect women from acts of VAW), as well as on the structural level (i.e. to adopt measures to tackle the root causes of VAW).[1332] Furthermore, States are obliged to exercise their due diligence obligations in good faith and in their commitment to prevent and protect against violence against women.[1333]

At the regional level, the Istanbul Convention also makes an explicit reference to the obligation to '*exercise due diligence to prevent, investigate, punish and provide for reparations of acts of violence[...] that are perpetrated by non-State actors*'.[1334] Article 4 (2) (b), (e), (f) and (i) of the Maputo Protocol requires States to prevent and eradicate violence against women, to punish perpetrators, to implement measures to provide rehabilitation and reparations for victims and to establish mechanisms for monitoring actions aimed at addressing VAW. Article 7(b) of the Convention of Belém do Para requires states to '*apply due diligence to prevent, investigate and impose penalties for violence against women*'. Similarly, in the leading case of *Velásqueze Rodriguez v. Honduras*[1335] the Inter-American Court of Human Rights interpreted the duty to exercise due diligence as being embedded in the general obligation to respect and ensure the guaranteed rights pursuant to Article 1(1) ACHR. According to the court, the duty to exercise due diligence requires the State to '*prevent, investigate and punish any violation of the rights recognized by the Convention and, moreover, if possible attempt to restore the right violated and provide compensation as warranted for damages*

1329 Committee on the Elimination of Discrimination Against Women, *Karen Tayag Vertido v. the Philippines,* 16 July 2010, Communication No. 18/2008, para. 8.4.

1330 CEDAW, *General Recommendation No. 35 on gender-based violence against women, updating General Recommendation No. 19* para. 24.

1331 United Nations, *Beijing Platform of Action*, para. 124 (b).

1332 Manjoo, *Report of the Special Rapporteur on violence against women, its causes and consequences (2013)*, para. 20.

1333 Ertürk, *Integration of the human rights of women and the gender perspective: violence against women – The due diligence standard as a tool for the elimination of violence against women*, para. 36.

1334 Istanbul Convention, Article 5 (2).

1335 The victim was arrested by State agents after his participation in activities that were considered by the State as being harmful to national security. The Inter-American Commission on Human Rights, which submitted the case on behalf of the victim, alleged violations to applicant's right to life, right to humane treatment and the right to personal liberty. Inter-American Court of Human Rights, *Velasquez Rodriguez v. Honduras, 29 July 1988*, Series C No. 4, para. 2.

resulting from the violation'.[1336] The duty to exercise due diligence is related to the State's obligations to prevent and protect from human rights violations committed by private persons.[1337] Noteworthy is also the 2002 document that was adopted by the Committee of Ministers of the Council of Europe on domestic violence.[1338] This document contains recommendations for members States on the protection of women from VAW, and it requires State parties to recognise their '*obligation to exercise due diligence to prevent, investigate and punish acts of violence*' that are perpetrated by the State or non-State actors.[1339]

The ECtHR also developed and incorporated a variation of the due diligence standard in the case of *Osman v. the United Kingdom*.[1340] In this case, the ECtHR asserted that the positive obligation to protect the right to life from being violated by non-State actors imposed a duty on the State to take preventative measures.[1341] However, this does not mean that the State is required to adopt measures to prevent each and every risk to the right to life from materialising, nor does it mean that the existence of a violation of the right to life, by definition, implies a failure of the State in respect of its duties.[1342] Such an interpretation would, in the ECtHR's view, '*impose impossible or disproportionate burdens on the State*'.[1343] A state may, thus, satisfy its duty to prevent by making general provisions, and it is not necessary to meet each individual claim.[1344] The duty to exercise due diligence is, therefore, an obligation of means and not an obligation of result.[1345] Furthermore, whether the State has failed to comply with its obligation to protect the right to life and its duty to prevent infringements to this right, will depend on whether the '*authorities knew or ought to have known at the time of the existence of a real and immediate risk to the life of an identified individual or individuals from the criminal acts of a third party and they failed to take measures within the scope of their powers which judged reasonably, might have been expected to avoid that risk*'.[1346]

1336 Id., para. 166.

1337 Id., paras. 172.

1338 Council of Europe 'Recommendation Rec (2002) 5 of the Committee of Ministers to member states on the protection of women against violence', Ministers, 30 April 2002.

1339 Id., para. II.

1340 Ertürk, *Integration of the human rights of women and the gender perspective: violence against women – The due diligence standard as a tool for the elimination of violence against women*, para. 22.

1341 European Court of Human Rights, *Osman v. the United Kingdom*, 28 October 1998, Application No. 87/1997/871/1083, para. 115.

1342 Id., para. 116.; European Court of Human Rights, *Opuz v. Turkey*, 9 June 2009, Application No. 33401/01, para. 129.; see also Chirwa, *The doctrine of State responsibility as a potential means of holding private actors accountable for human rights*, p. 17.

1343 European Court of Human Rights, *Osman v. the United Kingdom*, 28 October 1998, Application No. 87/1997/871/1083, para. 116. More generally on the obligations for the elimination of discrimination, see Byrnes *Article 2*, p. 87.

1344 Rebeca J. Cook, 'State Responsibility for Violations of Women's Human Rights', 7 *Havard Human Rights Journal* 125–175, (1994), p. 150.

1345 Koivurova, *Due Diligence*, paras. 3, 8.; Council of Europe, *Explanatory Report to the Council of Europe Convention on preventing and combating violence against women and domestic violence*, para. 59.

1346 European Court of Human Rights, *Opuz v. Turkey*, 9 June 2009, Application No. 33401/01, para. 130; European Court of Human Rights, *E. and Others v. the United Kingdom*, 26 November 2002,

In the case of *E. and others v. the United Kingdom*, the ECtHR further developed the obligation to protect, albeit within the context of the prohibition of ill-treatment (Article 3 ECHR). For there to be a failure, the ECtHR does not require that a violation of Article 3 ECHR could have been prevented, had the State responded reasonably and taken the appropriate measures. Rather, it is sufficient to establish that the State's active response to an existing risk or violation of Article 3 ECHR '*could have had a real prospect of altering the outcome or mitigating the harm*'.[1347] Moreover, the ECtHR seems also to have adopted the due diligence standard for assessing the extent of the positive obligations that are implied in Article 8 ECHR.[1348] The due diligence standard was also extended to cover domestic violence in the case of *Opuz v. Turkey*, where the ECtHR resorted to the conditions of knowledge and reasonableness in assessing whether the State had complied with its positive obligation to protect the victim's right to life.[1349] Thus, while the State's positive obligation is determined on a case by case basis, the ECtHR has established a duty on the State to respond reasonably where it is aware or can be expected to be aware of an infringement to the right to life and physical integrity, respectively.

Noteworthy, the CEDAW Committee has also endorsed the condition of knowledge in relation to domestic violence and the victim's right to life and personal security.[1350] The case of *Fatma Yildirim v. Austria*, for example, involved a deceased victim who had been abused and subsequently murdered by her husband. In assessing whether the Austrian authorities had responded with due diligence, the Committee weighed in the fact of whether the authorities had known about the victim's situation.[1351] The conclusion was that the authorities knew or should have known of the violent and unsafe situation that the victim was in. In the Committee's view, the victim's request to arrest the perpetrator should not have been denied by the public prosecutor.[1352] Thus, to establish a State's failure to exercise due diligence, it is important to show evidence that the State had knowledge or should have had knowledge about the commission of acts of VAW.[1353] This falls in line that with the ECtHR's view that not all acts of VAW constitute, by their very definition, a failure of the State's obligation. Nor does it show that positive obligation to eradicate VAW requires the absolute prevention of all forms of VAW.

Application No. 33218/96, paras. 88, 96.; European Court of Human Rights, *Osman v. the United Kingdom*, 28 October 1998, Application No. 87/1997/871/1083, para. 116.

1347 European Court of Human Rights, *E. and Others v. the United Kingdom*, 26 November 2002, Application No. 33218/96, para. 99.

1348 European Court of Human Rights, *Osman v. the United Kingdom*, 28 October 1998, Application No. 87/1997/871/1083, para. 128. The applicants also alleged a violation of Articles 2, 6, 8 and 13 ECHR.

1349 European Court of Human Rights, *Opuz v. Turkey*, 9 June 2009, Application No. 33401/01, para. 130.

1350 Committee on the Eliminaton of Discrimination against Women, *Fatma Yildirim v. Austria*, 1 October 2007, Communication No. 6/2005, para. 12.1.4.; See also Committee on the Elimination of Discrimination Against Women, *Goekce v. Austria*, 06 August 2007, Communication No. 5/2005, para. 12.1.4.

1351 Committee on the Eliminaton of Discrimination against Women, *Fatma Yildirim v. Austria*, 1 October 2007, Communication No. 6/2005, para. 12.1.4.

1352 Id.

1353 Lavrysen, *The scope of rights and the scope of obligations*, p. 170.

In light of the foregoing, the following conclusions can be drawn. The obligation to exercise due diligence within the context of VAW has become widely recognised in international and regional human rights law. In fact, it may even be concluded that the obligation to prevent and protect from VAW with due diligence has become a rule of customary international law.[1354] The due diligence standard requires States to protect victims of VAW by responding reasonably and adequately to acts of VAW and by adopting appropriate measures to prevent and protect women from VAW occurring in the first place.[1355] This does not mean that a State has to prevent all acts of VAW, nor does it mean that any act of VAW committed by a private actor implies a failure on the State to comply with its positive obligations. Whether the State has failed to exercise due diligence in responding to an act of VAW committed by a private person will be assessed on a case by case basis, taking into account all the circumstances of the case: including whether or not the State knew or ought to have known of the committed acts of VAW. Where the State is aware or is expected to be aware of instances of VAW that are perpetuated by private actors, it then has a duty to respond reasonably and appropriately so as to prevent or mitigate the harm. Finally, the due diligence standard consists of a set of duties: prevention, protection, investigation, punishment and the provision of reparations to victims of VAW. The following subsections will briefly address these duties more in detail.

7.6.1.1. The duty to prevent

In general, States have mostly relied on legislative interventions, awareness-raising campaigns and the training of professionals and officials who encounter cases of VAW.[1356] While these are all steps in the right direction, the Special Rapporteur on violence against women has identified and criticised the many programmes and policies that approach VAW as a stand-alone issue.[1357] This approach falls short of what is required and overlooks the fact that VAW is a complex social phenomenon that is related to and embedded in other social contexts, systems and structures. Therefore, in discharging their duty to prevent, States should adopt a comprehensive system that includes legal, political, administrative and cultural measures.[1358] A comprehensive approach to prevent VAW requires taking into account and linking VAW with other systems of power arrangement and oppression.[1359] Preventing VAW requires

---

[1354] Ertürk, *Integration of the human rights of women and the gender perspective: violence against women – The due diligence standard as a tool for the elimination of violence against women*, para. 29.

[1355] Chirwa, *The doctrine of State responsibility as a potential means of holding private actors accountable for human rights*, p. 15.

[1356] Ertürk, *Integration of the human rights of women and the gender perspective: violence against women – The due diligence standard as a tool for the elimination of violence against women*, para. 38.

[1357] Id.

[1358] Inter-American Court of Human Rights, *Velasquez Rodriguez v. Honduras*, 29 July 1988, Series C No. 4, para. 174.

[1359] Ertürk, *Integration of the human rights of women and the gender perspective: violence against women – The due diligence standard as a tool for the elimination of violence against women*, para. 38.

challenging and eliminating the structural factors, root causes of VAW and challenging the current power arrangements. This requires engaging and involving stakeholders on all levels in order to prevent VAW. Furthermore, a comprehensive system in itself is not sufficient where there is no commitment from State actors to implement and enforce such a system. Thus, the effective eradication of VAW requires the commitment of State actors, the inclusiveness of all stakeholders on multiple levels and addressing the structural factors and root causes of VAW. These conditions are further explained in the following paragraphs.

7.6.1.1.1. The commitment of the State

A comprehensive system to prevent VAW should be supported by committed State actors who, after all, are tasked with the adoption, implementation and enforcement thereof.[1360] At the legislative level, the legislator should not only prohibit all forms of VAW by law but should also criminalise sexual assault, violence within the family and all other forms of VAW that violate a woman's physical, sexual or psychological integrity.[1361] Proportionate sanctions should be imposed and civil remedies for victims against the perpetrator and the State should be introduced.[1362] The Istanbul Convention has taken the leading role in this regard and gone further than most instruments to direct Contracting States on the specific forms of VAW that should be criminalised. It has also directed States attention to other related aspects, such as ensuring that victims of VAW have a right to demand and receive reparations, regulating the legal consequences of forced marriages and enabling victims of forced marriages to dissolve or annul the marriage.[1363] Articles 33–41 thereof direct States to criminalise psychological violence through threats and coercion, stalking, physical violence, sexual violence (including rape), forced marriage, female genital mutilation, forced abortion and sterilisation and sexual harassment.

Alongside the criminalisation of certain acts of VAW, Article 2(f) *juncto* 5(a) CEDAW require States to repeal all laws, regulations and policies that discriminate against women (e.g. evidentiary rules in judicial proceedings that are discriminatory towards women).[1364] In particular, the CEDAW Committee has frequently expressed that discriminatory personal laws should be repealed, even in countries that have plural legal systems[1365], as victims of VAW should be protected at all times irrespective of

---

1360 Committee on the Elimination of Discrimination Against Women, *Goekce v. Austria,* 06 August 2007, Communication No. 5/2005, para.12.1.

1361 Article 2(b, c, e, f, and g) and Article 5(a) require States to *'adopt legislation prohibiting all forms of gender-based violence against women and girls'.* See also Recommendation Rec(2002)5 of the Committee of Ministers to member states on the protection of women against violence, pp. 11,1 3.

1362 CEDAW, *General Recommendation No 35 on gender-based violence against women, updating General Recommendation No. 19,* paras. 29, 33.; Istanbul Convention, Article 29.

1363 Istanbul Convention, Article 33.

1364 CEDAW, *General Recommendation No. 35 on gender-based violence against women, updating General Recommendation No. 19,* para. 31.; Byrnes *Article 2,* pp. 90–91.

1365 Byrnes *Article 2,* pp. 90–91.

the legal system of the country.[1366] Furthermore, State authorities have been directed to harmonise their legal systems with the various human rights treaties they partake in. More specifically, the CEDAW Committee directs States to harmonise '*any existing religious, customary, indigenous and community justice system norms (norms that are part of statutory, customary, religious, indigenous or common law, constitutional, civil, family, criminal or administrative law, evidentiary and procedural law) with its standards*'.[1367] Therefore, the fact that a State has a plural legal system does not alleviate the authorities from their duty to ensure that all personal laws within their domestic system protect victims of VAW and that these do not discriminate, burden or victimise women.[1368] Additionally, existing gender-neutral laws and policies should be examined and assessed to guarantee that these do not indirectly affect women in a negative manner.[1369]

At the executive level, authorities are required to design and adopt policies that are focused on addressing the structural factors and causes of VAW within society, as well as within State institutions, mechanisms and provided services. Monitoring mechanisms, which include competent national tribunals, should be developed and adequately funded. Furthermore, adequate funding should be reserved for victims of VAW, as well as for other diverse programmes and services that contribute to preventing incidences of VAW and which are designed to address the consequences of VAW.[1370] Additionally, measures should also be adopted to make public spaces safe and accessible to all women and girls.[1371] The allocation of resources and services should be conducted in such a way that women have access to critical resources and services whenever they are required.[1372]

At the judicial level, the authorities should – alongside ensuring that all legal proceedings are fair and impartial – also ensure that these are conducted free from gender-based discrimination, gender stereotypes and myths.[1373] Gender discrimination stereotypes and myths should be eliminated within the entire proceedings. This includes not only the procedural aspects of legal proceedings (e.g. evidentiary rules that attribute women's testimonies with less weight) but also judges' considerations

---

1366 CEDAW, *General Recommendation No. 35 on gender-based violence against women, updating General Recommendation No. 19*, para. 30.

1367 Id., para. 26.

1368 Id., para. 30.

1369 Id., para. 32.

1370 Id., para. 26.

1371 Id., para. 36.; Recommendation Rec(2002)5 of the Committee of Ministers to member states on the protection of women against violence, p. 9.

1372 United Nations, *Beijing Platform of Action*, paras. 124, 130.

1373 CEDAW, *General Recommendation No. 35 on gender-based violence against women, updating General Recommendation No. 19*, para. 26.; Committee on the Elimination of Discrimination Against Women, *Karen Tayag Vertido v. the Philippines*, 16 July 2010, Communication No. 18/2008, paras. 8.3–8.4.

and examinations of the alleged incidents of VAW[1374] and in their interpretation and application of the relevant domestic and international law.[1375]

Finally, the transnational level is a relatively new area that still needs to be developed in terms the States' duties to prevent VAW at this level. Currently, the main area of focus has been migration and human trafficking.[1376] Despite the fact that specific measures on this level need to be developed further, increased cooperation between States and cooperation between States and intergovernmental organisations to regulate and mitigate migration and human trafficking is generally perceived as an important first step in this regard.[1377] In this respect, the Special Rapporteur on violence against women has also assigned UN institutions with the duty to '*cooperate and to establish inter-agency strategies to work towards the elimination of VAW in close collaboration with local communities and civil society groups*'.[1378] Another area of focus concerns migration laws, asylum laws and policies that increases women's vulnerabilities to be subjected to VAW. States are, therefore, required to regularly examine the impact of their migration and asylum laws and policies.[1379]

7.6.1.1.2. Involvement of all stakeholders and sectors

In developing, implementing and evaluating preventative measures, States are encouraged to actively engage with all relevant stakeholders at all levels and in particular women's organisations.[1380] Awareness-raising efforts should target all stakeholders in society, which includes '*women and men at all levels of society, education, health, social services and law enforcement personnel and other professionals and agencies, traditional and religious leaders and perpetrators of VAW*'.[1381] Such efforts contribute to informing the public and victims of the harmful consequences of VAW and the available resources

1374 Committee on the Elimination of Discrimination Against Women, *Karen Tayag Vertido v. the Philippines*, 16 July 2010, Communication No. 18/2008, paras. 8.5–8.6.

1375 CEDAW, *General Recommendation No. 35 on gender-based violence against women, updating General Recommendation No. 19*, para. 26.

1376 Ertürk, *Integration of the human rights of women and the gender perspective: violence against women – The due diligence standard as a tool for the elimination of violence against women*, para. 95.

1377 Id.

1378 Id., para. 98.

1379 Id., para. 71.; Istanbul Convention, Chapter VII.

1380 Recommendation Rec(2002)5 of the Committee of Ministers to member states on the protection of women against violence, para. 5.; CEDAW, *General Recommendation No. 35 on gender-based violence against women, updating General Recommendation No. 19*, para. 48.; Istanbul Convention, Articles 12(4), 13 (1).

1381 Ertürk, *Integration of the human rights of women and the gender perspective: violence against women – The due diligence standard as a tool for the elimination of violence against women*, para. 87.; CEDAW, *General Recommendation No. 35 on gender-based violence against women, updating General Recommendation No. 19*, para. 35.; Recommendation Rec(2002)5 of the Committee of Ministers to member states on the protection of women against violence, pp. 7–8.

and services. They also facilitate to underscore the unacceptability of acts of VAW and to challenge the underlying gender stereotypes and power arrangements.[1382]

Similarly, preventative measures should also be included in the educational sector.[1383] Education, in a broad sense, plays a fundamental role in transmitting social norms and values within societies and it is crucial in the socialisation of gender constructions, identities and roles. Therefore, education and training programmes on VAW should be designed with a view of generating a comprehensive understanding of VAW as a complex social phenomenon that intersects and is intertwined with other social arrangements. Measures in this sector should include the removal of gender stereotypes from educational content, material and curricula, while simultaneously ensuring the further integration of gender equality content that promotes human rights.[1384] Furthermore, education and training programmes on VAW should be developed and provided recurrently. Participation in basic training programmes on VAW should be mandatory, particularly for '*judiciary, lawyers and law enforcement officers, including forensic medical, personnel, legislators, health-care professionals*'.[1385]

A strong alliance with all media is also imperative for advancing the State's positive obligations to prevent and protect against VAW.[1386] Preventative measures should involve and encourage all media outlets to eliminate discriminatory and stereotyped portrayals of women or specific groups of women in all their activities.[1387] Additionally, guidelines should be developed and provided to all media on the appropriate ways of covering and reporting incidents of VAW. A mechanism for monitoring and considering complaints of the discriminatory or stereotypical portrayal of women in the media should also be established.[1388]

1382 Ertürk, *Integration of the human rights of women and the gender perspective: violence against women – The due diligence standard as a tool for the elimination of violence against women*, para. 87.; Council of Europe, *Explanatory Report to the Council of Europe Convention on preventing and combating violence against women and domestic violence*, para. 91.

1383 Istanbul Convention, Articles 14–15.

1384 CEDAW, *General Recommendation No. 35 on gender-based violence against women, updating General Recommendation No. 19*, para. 35.; Recommendation Rec(2002)5 of the Committee of Ministers to member states on the protection of women against violence, p. 8.

1385 CEDAW, *General Recommendation No. 35 on gender-based violence against women, updating General Recommendation No. 19*, para. 38.; Recommendation Rec(2002)5 of the Committee of Ministers to member states on the protection of women against violence, p. 8. See also Council of Europe, *Explanatory Report to the Council of Europe Convention on preventing and combating violence against women and domestic violence*, para. 100.

1386 Holtmaat *Article 5*, p. 162.; Istanbul Convention, Article 17.

1387 Ertürk, *Integration of the human rights of women and the gender perspective: violence against women – The due diligence standard as a tool for the elimination of violence against women*, para. 87.; Recommendation Rec(2002)5 of the Committee of Ministers to member states on the protection of women against violence, p. 9.;

1388 [388] CEDAW, *General Recommendation No. 35 on gender-based violence against women, updating General Recommendation No. 19*, para. 37. Recommendation Rec(2002)5 of the Committee of Ministers to member states on the protection of women against violence p. 9.; Council of Europe,

Finally, the perpetrators of VAW are a category of actors that are rarely included. The role and impact that they can have on preventing VAW is often overlooked. Next to punishing perpetrators and enforcing the execution of assigned sanctions, States are recommended to develop training, rehabilitation and intervention programmes for perpetrators of VAW.[1389] These should not only aim to educate the perpetrators of the consequences of VAW and their own responsibilities, but they should also encourage perpetrators to adopt behaviours and patterns of conduct that do not rely on or involve violence.[1390]

7.6.1.1.3. Addressing the structural factors and eliminating the causes of VAW

Preventative measures should also address the structural factors that enable VAW and the underlying causes of VAW that were addressed in section 7.3.1.[1391] More specifically, Article 2(f) CEDAW in conjunction with Article 5(a) CEDAW impose on States the obligation to address structural factors that are discriminatory and harmful to women or that contribute to creating harmful situations for women.[1392] The obligation to exercise due diligence also pertains to Articles 2 (f) taken in conjunction with Article 5(a) CEDAW.[1393] Admittedly, this is not an easy undertaking and there is, generally, little evidence of States' active engagement in bringing about social transformation which deviates from patriarchal social structures and ideologies.[1394] In addition, there is the simple fact that social transformation and cultural change is a long and slow process that requires consistent and unrelenting efforts in order to be realised.[1395]

That being said, both Articles do require States to bring about cultural transformation and to implement a comprehensive system to identify, challenge and modify existing power arrangements, stereotypes and ideologies. Efforts to encourage and foster social and cultural transformation require State intervention at the individual, community and State level.[1396] The individual level primarily revolves around empowering

---

Explanatory Report to the Council of Europe Convention on preventing and combating violence against women and domestic violence, para. 107.

1389 Istanbul Convention, Article 16.

1390 Recommendation Rec(2002)5 of the Committee of Ministers to member states on the protection of women against violence, p. 12.

1391 CEDAW, *General Recommendation No. 35 on gender-based violence against women, updating General Recommendation No. 19*, para. 34.

1392 See subchapter 7.6.

1393 Committee on the Elimination of Discrimination Against Women, *Karen Tayag Vertido v. the Philippines*, 16 July 2010, Communication No. 18/2008, para. 8.4.

1394 Ertürk, *Integration of the human rights of women and the gender perspective: violence against women – The due diligence standard as a tool for the elimination of violence against women*, paras. 15, 46.; Manjoo, *Report of the Special Rapporteur on violence against women, its causes and consequences (2013)*, para. 19.

1395 Holtmaat *Article 5*, p. 148.

1396 Ertürk, *Integration of the human rights of women and the gender perspective: violence against women – The due diligence standard as a tool for the elimination of violence against women*, paras. 75–76.

victims of VAW and more generally women. The empowerment of women requires the strengthening of women's autonomy[1397], awareness, self-reliance and self-confidence. In order to enable women to ascertain and possess these properties, women and victims of VAW – more specifically – should be guaranteed access to critical resources and available services, including legal services.[1398]

Furthermore, States are encouraged to develop an infrastructure that facilitates women's access to opportunities for receiving education and training, developing their skills and gaining information on the available services and resources.[1399] When women are empowered to freely exercise their autonomy, they are able to contribute to bringing about social transformation by resisting oppression and participating in the deconstruction and reconstruction of cultural norms, values and beliefs.[1400]

At the community level, the Special Rapporteur on violence against women suggested adopting a discourse of 'cultural negotiations'. This entails a State and community effort which consists of multiple layers. Firstly, it requires that the root causes of VAW, which are entrenched in all cultures and traditions, are identified, challenged and condemned, while at the same time drawing on and maintaining the positive cultural elements which promote respect for human rights.[1401] Moreover, the wording of Article 5(a) CEDAW also clearly directs States to '*modify social and cultural patterns*', and specifically to '*eliminate*', prejudices and customs that are founded in stereotypical roles or a belief of hierarchy between women and men. Thus, Article 5 (a) CEDAW does not require the elimination or the condemnation of a culture as such. In fact, culture may form a positive force in the reconstruction of gender identities and societal norms.[1402] Article 5(a) CEDAW merely requires that certain prejudices, customs and practices that are harmful to women are eliminated.[1403] Secondly, an approach of cultural negotiation requires acknowledging the simple fact that cultures, traditions and even religion are mutable and that they possess flexible properties that are susceptible to change.[1404] Thirdly, a cultural negations approach should lead to questioning and challenging the legitimacy and authority of those speaking on behalf of a culture or religion, the validity of their interpretations as well as the power dynamics upon which such authority and legitimacy are based.[1405] With regards to the third layer, the Special Rapporteur on

1397 Holtmaat *Article 5*, p. 145.

1398 CEDAW, *General Recommendation No. 35 on gender-based violence against women, updating General Recommendation No. 19*, para. 41.

1399 Id., para. 43.

1400 Id., paras. 41, 43.

1401 Ertürk, *Integration of the human rights of women and the gender perspective: violence against women – The due diligence standard as a tool for the elimination of violence against women*, para. 85.

1402 Holtmaat *Article 5*, p. 150.

1403 Id., pp. 144, 147–149.

1404 Id., p. 150.; Ertürk, *Integration of the human rights of women and the gender perspective: violence against women – The due diligence standard as a tool for the elimination of violence against women*, para. 85.

1405 Id.

violence against women has stressed that it '*is not culture per se that dictates women to be beaten, mutilated or killed, rather it is those that monopolize the right to speak on behalf of culture*'.[1406] Encouraging dialogue between and within communities and fostering the conditions for participation in such dialogues by all members of society, particularly women, is an imperative precondition for realising the obligations contained in Article 2(f) *juncto* Article 5(a) CEDAW.[1407] In addition, awareness-raising campaigns, media, education and other modes of transmitting information are crucial mediums for furthering a process of cultural negotiation.[1408]

At the State level, legislative as well as non-legislative measures that address the structural and underlying causes of VAW should also be adopted and implemented.[1409] This includes the recognition by all State actors of their role in generating social and cultural transformation, not only by their actions and support in fostering change, but also in their reactions to VAW and their treatment of victims of gender-based violence.[1410] Reactions and public statements that are made by judges, prosecutors and law enforcement officials naturally carry weight in society. The condemnation of gender-based violence and harmful practices that are legitimised by culture, tradition or religion, can contribute to challenging stereotypical myths, cultural practices and patriarchal social constructions.[1411] Similarly, the condoning and/or acceptance of stereotypical roles and myths, harmful practices, patriarchal values or discriminatory norms by these agencies can have the adverse effect of reinforcing the structural factors that exacerbate VAW. In turn, this can have the effect of enabling VAW to persist. Therefore, in their activities and responses to instances of VAW, authorities are expected to adopt a gender-sensitive approach and to refrain from relying on or legitimising gendered stereotypes and myths that disadvantage women.[1412]

7.6.1.2. The duty to protect

The duty to protect requires measures for both short-term emergencies as well as long-term measures that minimise women's chances of victimisation.[1413] In this regard,

---

1406 Id., para. 88.

1407 Holtmaat *Article 5*, p. 160.

1408 Ertürk, *Integration of the human rights of women and the gender perspective: violence against women – The due diligence standard as a tool for the elimination of violence against women*, paras. 85, 87.

1409 CEDAW, *General Recommendation No. 35 on gender-based violence against women, updating General Recommendation No. 19*, para. 34.

1410 Ertürk, *Integration of the human rights of women and the gender perspective: violence against women – The due diligence standard as a tool for the elimination of violence against women*, para. 89.

1411 Id., para. 90.

1412 Committee on the Elimination of Discrimination Against Women, *Karen Tayag Vertido v. the Philippines,* 16 July 2010, Communication No. 18/2008, para. 8.4.; Committee on the Elimination of Discrimination Against Women, *Isatou Jallow v. Bulgaria,* 23 July 2012, Communication No. 32/2011, para. 8.6.

1413 Ertürk, *Integration of the human rights of women and the gender perspective: violence against women – The due diligence standard as a tool for the elimination of violence against women*, para. 49; Istanbul

States' efforts have mostly involved short-term measures.[1414] These include, but are not limited to, establishing telephone hotlines, providing medical and health care services which should include psychological care and counselling, providing forensic medical examination, providing legal assistance, establishing safe and adequately equipped shelters, providing other material assistance (e.g. clothing, child care), imposing and enforcing restraining orders, providing financial aid for victims of violence, detaining perpetrators and immediate response mechanisms by law enforcement officers to report incidences of VAW.[1415] States are recommended to ensure that the services offered to victims are available and accessible to them free of charge.[1416] Where appropriate, States should strive to combine multiple sources of protection and to offer support services in the same premises.[1417] Long-term measures should aim to improve the situation of victims, to empower them and to remove factors that increase the risk of (re)victimisation. These may include measures that safeguard and facilitate access to education, employment, land and housing opportunities.[1418]

Furthermore, in developing legislative measures, policing systems and judicial means to address and respond to acts of VAW, the State should guarantee that the rights and safety of women, witnesses and victims are protected. It is not unthinkable that victims of VAW may refrain from reporting incidents of VAW, due to them fearing for their safety or of escalating the violent environment they are already in. For example, in the case of *Opuz v. Turkey*, the court had to assess whether the authorities had struck a fair balance between the right to life and protection from ill-treatment of the victim, and the victim's right to private life. In this case, the authorities refrained from prosecuting the perpetrators of repeated domestic violence after the victim had withdrawn her complaints several times. The decision not to prosecute the perpetrator was based on the authority's consideration that the persecution would infringe upon the victims private and family life. In other words, the authorities did not want to interfere in a 'family matter'. Without prioritising either rights, the ECtHR stressed that a proper balance had to be struck between the victims' rights, considering all the facts and the seriousness of

Convention, Articles 18 (1), (3) and 22.

1414 Ertürk, *Integration of the human rights of women and the gender perspective: violence against women – The due diligence standard as a tool for the elimination of violence against women*, para. 49.

1415 Id., paras. 47, 49, 83.; See also Istanbul Convention, Articles 19–21, 23–26.; Recommendation Rec(2002)5 of the Committee of Ministers to member states on the protection of women against violence, pp. 9–10.; CEDAW, *General Recommendation No. 35 on gender-based violence against women, updating General Recommendation No. 19*, para. 40.; Committee on the Elimination of Discrimination Against Women, *Goekce v. Austria*, 06 August 2007, Communication No. 5/2005, para. 12.1.4.

1416 Recommendation Rec(2002)5 of the Committee of Ministers to member states on the protection of women against violence, p. 9.

1417 Istanbul Convention, Article 18 (3).

1418 Ertürk, *Integration of the human rights of women and the gender perspective: violence against women – The due diligence standard as a tool for the elimination of violence against women*, para. 83.; CEDAW, *General Recommendation No. 35 on gender-based violence against women, updating General Recommendation No. 19*, para. 40.; Council of Europe, *Explanatory Report to the Council of Europe Convention on preventing and combating violence against women and domestic violence*, para. 126.

the case.[1419] Noteworthy, in cases involving domestic violence, the ECtHR did establish that the act of not providing assistance to victims of domestic violence, due to the authority's considerations that it concerned a 'private matter', was incompatible with the positive obligations incumbent on States to secure the victims' rights.[1420] In fact, the ECtHR reasserted that '*in some instances, the national authorities' interference with the private or family life of the individuals might be necessary in order to protect the health and rights of others or to prevent commission of criminal acts*'.[1421] States should, thus, ensure that women can demand protection via these systems without the risk of being victimised.[1422] This requires that the judicial as well as law enforcement organisations and officials are sensitive and able to respond to gender-based violence. In this respect, states are encouraged to adopt a gender-sensitive approach, respond timely and adequately to requests for assistance and to adopt suitable interim measures.[1423] Furthermore, breaches of interim measures by the perpetrator should also be penalised.[1424]

Notably, in protecting from violations by non-state actors the CEDAW Committee and the ECtHR have also firmly established that '*perpetrators rights cannot supersede victims' human rights to life and to physical and mental integrity*'[1425] in cases of domestic violence. In the case *A.T. v. Hungary* the CEDAW committee reiterated this position that '*women's human rights to life and to physical and mental integrity cannot be superseded by other rights, including the right to property and the right to privacy*.[1426] In other words, consideration of the perpetrator's rights (e.g. the freedom of movement, the freedom of religion etc.) may not be invoked by States to defend inadequate responses.

The State's obligation to protect also extends to promulgating the use of alternative dispute resolution mechanisms. Women and victims of VAW may revert to

1419 European Court of Human Rights, *Opuz v. Turkey*, 9 June 2009, Application No. 33401/01, para. 138.

1420 Id., para.144.

1421 Id.

1422 Ertürk, *Integration of the human rights of women and the gender perspective: violence against women – The due diligence standard as a tool for the elimination of violence against women*, para. 82.; Hasselbacher, *State obligations regarding domestic violence: The European Court of Human Rights, due diligence, and international legal minimums of protection*, p. 202.; Recommendation Rec(2002)5 of the Committee of Ministers to member states on the protection of women against violence, pp. 11–12.

1423 CEDAW, *General Recommendation No. 35 on gender-based violence against women, updating General Recommendation No. 19*, para. 40.; Recommendation Rec(2002)5 of the Committee of Ministers to member states on the protection of women against violence, pp. 9,12.; See also Istanbul Convention, Articles 52–53.

1424 Hasselbacher, *State obligations regarding domestic violence: The European Court of Human Rights, due diligence, and international legal minimums of protection*, p. 202.; Recommendation Rec(2002)5 of the Committee of Ministers to member states on the protection of women against violence, para. 58 (f).

1425 European Court of Human Rights *Opuz v. Turkey*, 9 June 2009, Application No. 33401/01, para. 147.; Committee on the Eliminaton of Discrimination against Women *Fatma Yildirim v. Austria*, 1 October 2007 Communication No. 6/2005, para. 12.1.5.; see also Committee on the Elimination of Discrimination against Women *A.T. v. Hungary*, 26 January 2005, Communication No. 2/2003, para. 9.3.; Committee on the Elimination of Discrimination against Women *Goekce v. Austria*, 06 August 2007, Communication No. 5/2005, para. 12.1.5.

1426 Committee on the Elimination of Discrimination against Women *A.T. v. Hungary*, 26 January 2005, Communication No. 2/2003, para. 9.3.

alternative mechanisms or internal modes in their attempt to de-escalate the risks of VAW. Even when these are not regulated or provided by the State as such, the obligation to protect requires that such mechanisms, particularly in cases that involve VAW, should not be made mandatory.[1427] States should ensure that any participation in alternative dispute settlement mechanisms is based on free and informed consent and that women's rights are respected during such proceedings. States should also ensure that these proceedings are conducted by professionals that are trained to deal with cases involving VAW and that it is done in a judicious and appropriate manner.[1428] Lastly, recourse to formal proceedings should be made available at all times.[1429]

7.6.1.3. The duty to investigate alleged violence and to punish those responsible

The duty to investigate requires that all situations involving human rights violations are thoroughly and effectively investigated. Investigations contribute to enforcing national laws, protecting victims and also holding perpetrators of VAW accountable, including the State where the violation can be directly attributed to the State.[1430] Failing to investigate timely, effectively and adequately is considered as enabling an environment of impunity to persist, for which the State can be held accountable.[1431]

According to the Inter-American Court in *Rodriguez v. Honduras,* an investigation '*must have an objective and be assumed by the State as its own legal duty, not as a step taken by private interests that depends upon the initiative of the victim of his family or upon their offer of proof, without an effective search for the truth by the government*'.[1432] Thus, an adequate investigation involves active engagement by the State to retrieve the truth on a specific matter. However, as uncovering the truth may in certain circumstances be difficult, the inability to fully uncover all the evidence or the fact that the investigation has led to an undesirable or unfavourable conclusion, does not in itself imply a failure to investigate on the part of the State.[1433] Likewise, the ECtHR, in the case of *Z. and Others v. the United Kingdom,* requires that an investigation is conducted thoroughly and effectively so that it may lead to the '*identification and*

[1427] CEDAW, *General Recommendation No. 35 on gender-based violence against women, updating General Recommendation No. 19*, para. 45.; Istanbul Convention, Article 48 (1).

[1428] CEDAW, *General Recommendation No. 35 on gender-based violence against women, updating General Recommendation No. 19*, para. 45.

[1429] Id.

[1430] European Court of Human Rights, *Opuz v. Turkey*, 9 June 2009, Application No. 33401/01, para. 150.; Ertürk, *Integration of the human rights of women and the gender perspective: violence against women – The due diligence standard as a tool for the elimination of violence against women*, para. 50.
CEDAW, *General Recommendation No. 35 on gender-based violence against women, updating General Recommendation No. 19*, para. 44.

[1431] Inter-American Court of Human Rights, *Velasquez Rodriguez v. Honduras*, 29 July 1988, Series C No. 4, para. 177.

[1432] Id.

[1433] Id.

punishment of those responsible'.[1434] In another case, *Opuz v. Turkey*, the ECtHR concluded that investigations to ongoing criminal proceedings that had lasted six years and for which the perpetrator had confessed to the crime were incompatible with States' positive obligations.[1435] The Istanbul Convention promotes the prompt and appropriate response of law enforcement to incidents of VAW.[1436] In the same fashion, the CEDAW Committee also requires a 'suitable and timely investigation' by authorities from the moment they obtain knowledge of a case involving VAW.[1437] In addition, complainants should be granted access to the investigation procedure.[1438]

Besides having to carry out investigations, the obligation to exercise due diligence to protect against acts of VAW imposes a duty on States to develop and establish a system for punishing perpetrators of VAW.[1439] All acts of VAW should be punishable, and in particular acts of sexual violence and all forms of violence occurring within the family should be criminalised.[1440] Sanctions should be established so that they are proportionate to the seriousness of the crime for which they have been established.[1441] Additionally, the prosecutor is encouraged to regard the commission of VAW as an aggravating factor in criminal proceedings and as a decisive factor in deciding whether or not to prosecute.[1442] Finally, in order to comply with both the duty to investigate as well as the duty to punish, States should examine their legislation and adopt or modify them where necessary (e.g. enabling police officers to enter the residence of the potential victim, to bar the perpetrator from entering the residence of the victim, the removal of unnecessary procedural obstacles for arresting perpetrators, etc.) in order to strengthen the capacity and power of law enforcement and the judiciary, and to enable them to respond adequately and in accordance with the law.[1443]

1434 European Court of Human Rights, *Z and Others v. the United Kingdom*, 10 May 2001, Application No. 29392/95, para. 108.; European Court of Human Rights, *Opuz v. Turkey*, 9 June 2009, Application No. 33401/01, para. 150. This obligation has been interpreted as deriving from Article 13 ECHR on the right to effective domestic remedies, and Article 2 ECHR.

1435 European Court of Human Rights, *Opuz v. Turkey*, 9 June 2009, Application No. 33401/01, para. 150.

1436 Istanbul Convention, Article 50.

1437 CEDAW, *General Recommendation No. 35 on gender-based violence against women, updating General Recommendation No. 19*, para. 44.; Committee on the Elimination of Discrimination Against Women, *Isatou Jallow v. Bulgaria*, 23 July 2012, Communication No. 32/2011, para. 8.4.

1438 European Court of Human Rights, *Z and Others v. the United Kingdom*, 10 May 2001, Application No. 29392/95, para. 108.

1439 European Court of Human Rights, *Opuz v. Turkey*, 9 June 2009, Application No. 33401/01, para. 145.

1440 Recommendation Rec(2002)5 of the Committee of Ministers to member states on the protection of women against violence, pp. 11,13.

1441 Istanbul Convention, Article 45.; CEDAW, *General Recommendation No. 35 on gender-based violence against women, updating General Recommendation No. 19*, para. 29.

1442 Istanbul Convention, Article 46.; Recommendation Rec(2002)5 of the Committee of Ministers to member states on the protection of women against violence, p. 11.

1443 Istanbul Convention, Article 52.; Ertürk, *Integration of the human rights of women and the gender perspective: violence against women – The due diligence standard as a tool for the elimination of violence against women*, para. 50.; Recommendation Rec(2002)5 of the Committee of Ministers to member states on the protection of women against violence, p. 11.

7.6.1.4. Providing reparations

According to the Special Rapporteur on violence against women, the duty to provide reparations remains the most underdeveloped duty.[1444] The duty to provide reparations requires States to establish a system for offering financial compensation and ensuring that the victims of VAW are guaranteed reparations which are proportional to the harm suffered.[1445] Compensation should be provided for the physical, material, non-pecuniary and other intangible damage and harm that victims suffer as consequence of the violent acts.[1446] While financial compensation is among the measures that States can implement, the duty to provide reparations extends beyond this mode of reparations and requires States to provide for other means of reparation, such as guarantees of non-repetition, satisfaction, restorative justice, the provision of crucial support services for victims etc.[1447] Information on the reparations and other available resources, services and support systems (e.g. health care facilities, safehouses etc.) should be made easily accessible to victims.

7.6.1.5. Monitoring, data collection and international cooperation?

The assessment of the adopted measures, data collection and international cooperation between States and intergovernmental organisations are emerging areas of focus that are increasingly being considered as conditions of the due diligence standard. Despite the fact that these areas are barely mentioned in any of the formulations of treaties and soft-law instruments[1448], the goal of protecting women from acts of violence and to prevent these from occurring requires that the adopted and implemented measures are monitored and regularly assessed *vis-à-vis* their effectiveness.[1449] Monitoring and studying VAW is crucial in order to raise awareness and to generate a greater

---

1444 Ertürk, *Integration of the human rights of women and the gender perspective: violence against women – The due diligence standard as a tool for the elimination of violence against women*, para. 55.

1445 Istanbul Convention, Article 30.; Ertürk, *Integration of the human rights of women and the gender perspective: violence against women – The due diligence standard as a tool for the elimination of violence against women*, para. 84.; CEDAW, *General Recommendation No. 35 on gender-based violence against women, updating General Recommendation No. 19*, para. 46.

1446 Id.; Recommendation Rec(2002)5 of the Committee of Ministers to member states on the protection of women against violence, p. 11.

1447 CEDAW, *General Recommendation No. 35 on gender-based violence against women, updating General Recommendation No. 19*, para. 46.; Ertürk, *Integration of the human rights of women and the gender perspective: violence against women – The due diligence standard as a tool for the elimination of violence against women*, para. 84.; Council of Europe, *Explanatory Report to the Council of Europe Convention on preventing and combating violence against women and domestic violence*, para. 59.

1448 In its most recent general recommendation, the CEDAW Committee recognised and included these areas within the framework of the due diligence standard. The Istanbul Convention also contains provisions on establishing inter-State cooperation in Chapter VIII thereof.

1449 Ertürk, *Integration of the human rights of women and the gender perspective: violence against women – The due diligence standard as a tool for the elimination of violence against women*, para. 37.; CEDAW, *General Recommendation No. 35 on gender-based violence against women, updating General Recommendation No. 19*, para. 52.

understanding of how to address and respond to diverse forms of VAW within different contexts and circumstances. International cooperation, but also proficient cooperation at the national level (e.g. cooperation and exchange of information between the police force, the scientific community, health care workers, decision makers and the judiciary)[1450], very much contributes to advancing the goal of eradicating all forms of VAW.

The duty to collect data necessitates that States should establish a system to regularly collect data on violence against women. In this respect, States are encouraged to support the establishment of education programmes and research on violence against women, as well as equality-related issues.[1451] Furthermore, States should aim to compile disaggregated statistical data on violence against women, in order to (a) evaluate the scale of violence, (b) identify the various forms of VAW, (c) deduce the specific factors and combination of factors that exacerbate VAW and (d) expose the failures and inefficiencies in the adopted measures and compose indicators for studying and measuring VAW.[1452] The information that should be collected includes, among others, the causes of VAW, the type of violence involved, the number of complaints, the relationship between the victim and the perpetrator, the medium and long-term consequences of assault on victims, the consequence of violence on witnesses in the direct environment of the victim, the social, economic and health-related costs of VAW, efficiency of the judicial and legal system in eradicating VAW and intersecting forms of discrimination.[1453] Collecting and analysing data enables States to generate reliable empirical data, which in turn serves to facilitate the process of monitoring and evaluating the impact and effectiveness of adopted measures. The collected data also contributes to the process of designing and improving measures.[1454] Furthermore, for education, training and awareness-raising purposes, the compiled data and analysis should be made available, in an appropriate manner, to the general public.[1455]

1450 Recommendation Rec(2002)5 of the Committee of Ministers to member states on the protection of women against violence, p. 5.

1451 Id.

1452 CEDAW, *General Recommendation No. 35 on gender-based violence against women, updating General Recommendation No. 19*, para. 49.

1453 Recommendation Rec(2002)5 of the Committee of Ministers to member states on the protection of women against violence, p. 7.; CEDAW, *General Recommendation No. 35 on gender-based violence against women, updating General Recommendation No. 19*, para. 49.

1454 Recommendation Rec(2002)5 of the Committee of Ministers to member states on the protection of women against violence p. 7.; Ertürk, *Integration of the human rights of women and the gender perspective: violence against women – The due diligence standard as a tool for the elimination of violence against women*, para. 37.; CEDAW, *General Recommendation No. 35 on gender-based violence against women, updating General Recommendation No. 19*, para. 49.

1455 Recommendation Rec(2002)5 of the Committee of Ministers to member states on the protection of women against violence p. 7.; CEDAW, *General Recommendation No. 35 on gender-based violence against women, updating General Recommendation No. 19*, para. 49.

Lastly, national and international cooperation, not only in cases of VAW occurring in a transitional continuum (e.g. human trafficking, women migrant workers, female refugees etc.), but also more generally on violence against women, is encouraged.[1456] States are encouraged to cooperate in developing transnational solutions, for example in the area of regulating migration and multinational corporations and enabling victims of offences committed in a host country to seek remedies with the competent authorities of that State.[1457] Furthermore, States should also seek support from specialised agencies, such as the UN, as and when this is necessary.[1458]

7.6.2. STATES' OBLIGATIONS IN THE CONTEXT OF MARITAL CAPTIVITY

With respect to the forms of marital captivity that constitute VAW, States have an obligation to exercise due diligence. The due diligence standard requires States to respond reasonably and appropriately to situations of marital captivity that arise and to take appropriate measures to prevent and protect from the consequences of marital captivity. Whether the State has or has not complied with this obligation is a matter that can only be established on a case by case basis taking into account all circumstances of the specific case, as not all specific situations of marital captivity will be identical. Whether the State knew or ought to have known of the specific case, and whether the State responded reasonably and appropriate to mitigate situations of marital captivity are also factors that will determine whether or not the State has failed to comply with its due diligent obligation in a given case. It should be born in mind that the occurrence of situations of marital captivity is, by definition, not indicative of State's failure to exercise its due diligence obligations in preventing and ending situations of marital captivity as this is not an obligation of results but one of means.

While no general conclusions can be drawn regarding States' compliance or non-compliance with the due diligence obligations, general conclusions can be drafted concerning the State duties that arise from the obligation to exercise due diligence. This section briefly addresses these duties more specifically within the context of marital captivity. These are outlined in the following subsections as guidelines and measures that States are recommended to consider in their endeavour to comply with their human rights obligations, prevent situations of marital captivity from arising and protect trapped spouses. The obligations that rest upon States that have been discussed in the previous section 7.6.1 are elaborated and given further substance within the context of

[1456] Istanbul Convention, Article 62(1).

[1457] Id., Article 62 (2).; Ertürk, *Integration of the human rights of women and the gender perspective: violence against women – The due diligence standard as a tool for the elimination of violence against women*, para. 94.

[1458] CEDAW, *General Recommendation No. 35 on gender-based violence against women, updating General Recommendation No. 19*, para. 54.

marital captivity. This is achieved by tailoring the discussed obligations to situations of marital captivity as these have been observed in practice, taking into account relevant factors that influence how situations of marital captivity are manifested and resolved (e.g. the involved actors, the status of religious tribunals, non-secular solutions etc.). The enumerated State obligations provided in the previous section 7.6.1. are assembled and categorised into four areas, namely: measures on the individual level, measures for religious communities, measures for State agents and professionals and measures for enhancing cooperation between agencies on both the national and international level. This approach enables to clearly identify measures that can be adopted within each setting.

Notably the reports of van Eijk[1459] and Kruiniger[1460] are very insightful and they provide an enumeration of legal and non-legal measures that can be used to address and prevent marital captivity in the Netherlands. The suggested guidelines and measures in this contribution, however, are considered from a global perspective and they also include measures that are relevant for non-secular States.

7.6.2.1. Measures on the individual level

On the individual level, State measures should aim to empower women in religious communities and in particular trapped spouses. In this respect, the State should develop and support awareness-raising efforts, including educational material, so as to inform the public in general, and more specifically to target women and men in religious communities.[1461] Information should be disseminated not only on the phenomenon of marital captivity and its various forms and causes, but also on the harmful consequences for trapped spouses, the available resources and services (including health care services) and the available (legal) solutions. Furthermore, awareness-raising and educational efforts should aim to generate an understanding of marital captivity as an unacceptable phenomenon that violates the trapped spouses' rights and to acknowledge that in given circumstances it constitutes a form of violence against women. Awareness-raising campaigns and other modes for informing the public should take into account the religious dimension and religious views on divorce and ensure that the provided information does not demonise religions, offend religious groups or reinforce stereotypes of certain migrant and minority groups.

Additionally, information on the available judicial means and other means to exercise pressure on the recalcitrant spouses and to prevent marital captivity should be made easily accessible to women that find themselves in a situation of marital captivity (e.g. prenups, contractual agreements, involvement of State recognised religious tribunals, tort and liability actions adopted in some secular States, or the judge's

1459 Van Eijk, *Wel gescheiden, niet gescheiden? Een empirisch onderzoek naar huwelijkse gevangenschap in Nederland.*

1460 Kruiniger, *Niet langer geketend aan het huwelijk! Juridische instrumenten die huwelijkse gevangenschap kunnen voorkomen of oplossen.*

1461 See subsection 7.6.1.1. and 7.6.1.2.; See also paragraphs 7.6.1.1.2. and 7.6.1.1.3.

discretion to withhold a civil divorce until religious barriers are removed).[1462] Existing solutions should also be complemented with a system of judicial and financial assistance for spouses who cannot easily access these means due to material barriers, such as a lack of financial means, language barriers and insufficient knowledge of the legal system.[1463]

Where religious tribunals and other forms of informal dispute settlement mechanisms are not recognised by the State, enforcing and ensuring cooperation to a religious divorce by a non-cooperative spouse can be challenging. Furthermore, and particularly for secular States, national authorities should make efforts to inform all actors whom make use of these mechanisms, in particular women, of the fact that these are not mandatory, do not and cannot provide binding decisions on matters of divorce and that recourse can be made to the secular judge at any time if this is required.

As for the recalcitrant spouse, attention should also be given to informing and educating the recalcitrant spouses of the fact that by creating a situation of marital captivity, they are essentially infringing upon the human rights of the trapped spouse.[1464] Emphasis should be placed on the unacceptability and condemnation of marital captivity and the act of forcing a relationship unto someone against their will. Furthermore, where States have implemented civil and criminal laws to combat marital captivity, recalcitrant spouses should also be informed of the legal consequences of non-cooperation and that such practices may constitute unlawful and criminal offences.

7.6.2.2. Measures for the religious communities

State measures to prevent and protect against marital captivity should not only target the actual actions that create a situation of marital captivity i.e. the non-cooperation to a religious divorce in individual cases of marital captivity, but they should also aim to address the factors that allow for this phenomenon to exist. States have, both under the CEDAW and the Istanbul Convention, the obligation to foster cultural and social transformation and to adopt appropriate measures to eliminate gender-based discrimination, including VAW. This requires the State to actively make efforts to modify laws and cultural practices, including those which are linked to religion and which are harmful to and discriminate against women. States are required to actively pursue the goal of eradicating all stereotypes, ideologies and beliefs that proclaim the existence of a hierarchy between women and men and to promote gender inequality,

---

1462 See subsections 7.6.1.2., 7.6.1.4. and 7.6.1.5. For example, the marriage toolkit proposed by Kruiniger. This would not only facilitate informing intending spouses about the (legal) implications of civil and religious marriages, but it would also be a great source to inform spouses on measures to prevent and end situations of marital captivity. Kruiniger, *Niet langer geketend aan het huwelijk! Juridische instrumenten die huwelijkse gevangenschap kunnen voorkomen of oplossen*. pp. 54–55.

1463 See subsections 7.6.1.2., 7.6.1.4. and 7.6.1.5.

1464 See paragraph 7.6.1.1.2.

regardless of whether these are prescribed by religion or not.[1465] In fact, the religious dimension that is pertinent to situations of marital captivity, as well as the private sphere in which this phenomenon occurs, may not serve as justifications or reasons for the State authorities not to address the issue in general or to intervene in specific cases. Thus, even if a situation of marital captivity cannot be directly attributable to the State, responsibility may nevertheless be established on the basis of these positive obligations that exist to (a) address the structural factors pertaining marital captivity, (b) foster compliance with the principle of equality within religious groups and (c) eliminate practices of marital captivity.

Encouraging a shift of mindset and a cultural transformation within religious communities requires States to cooperate with religious authorities. The inclusion of religious authorities is crucial, particularly for addressing discriminatory practices and interpreting religious norms. Their cooperation in fostering religious interpretations and beliefs of women's position within the family and society ought, therefore, not to be underestimated. Governments should aim to encourage religious authorities to commit to addressing the religious practices, processes and interpretations that enable situations of marital captivity to arise in the first place. Cooperation with religious authorities should aim to encourage the process of challenging the prevailing discourse on marriage, divorce and gender equality, as well as the practices and interpretations of religious norms that enable husbands to hold their partners in a marriage against their will. In this regard, encouraging the cooperation of religious authorities with jurists[1466], and developing training programmes for religious authorities on the social and legal implications of a situation of marital captivity, are measures that should be considered and implemented where possible. States should consider developing government agencies to work exclusively with religious leaders in order to promote cultural practices that are commensurate with human rights and which discourage discrimination against women within the religious communities.[1467]

Furthermore, States should encourage religious communities to engage in a discourse of cultural negotiation and to facilitate open and progressive dialogues on the topics of divorce, marital captivity and gender equality, while at the same time drawing upon the positive aspects within the concerned religions and cultures.[1468] The Dutch Self-Determination Action Plan 2015–2017 (*Actie plan-zelfbeschikking 2015–2017)* is an example of how States can encourage an open dialogue within religious groups. This national action plan offered, among others, a training programme on sensitive

[1465] Convention on the Elimination of All of Discrimination Against Women, Article 5 (a).; Istanbul Convention, Article 12(1).; See also subchapter 7.6. and paragraph 7.6.1.1.3.

[1466] Van Eijk, *Wel gescheiden, niet gescheiden? Een empirisch onderzoek naar huwelijkse gevangenschap in Nederland*, p. 82.

[1467] *High-level round table on the elimination and prevention of all forms of violence against women and girls- Chair's summary*, (Commission on the Status of Women, 2013), para. 14.

[1468] See paragraph 7.6.1.1.3.; See also subsection 7.6.1.5. on cooperation with multiple actors on international as well as national level.

topics such as forced marriages, homosexuality, honour-related crimes and marital captivity to 160 individuals belonging to different migrant and religious groups. Upon finishing this training programme, the attendees were then supported and encouraged to organise several meetings within their respective community in order to discuss these issues. This has helped to reach and engage more persons within the respective communities and it has facilitated an open dialogue on these serious issues, that would otherwise have remained unaddressed.[1469]

A discourse on cultural negotiation should enable all community members to challenge existing gender roles, interpretations of religious rules on divorce and the way in which they are implemented by the religious authorities. Women and men, including trapped spouses and recalcitrant spouses, should be encouraged to participate in the deconstruction and reconstruction of social identities, cultural norms and values on divorce within the community.

Additionally, as cultural and social transformation requires a rigorous and continuous process of cultural negotiation, the existing platforms for dialogue within and between religious communities should continue to expand and extend for longer periods. The continual assessment of implemented measures to foster social and cultural transformation is also necessary in order to study their effectiveness. This requires the establishment of mechanisms that allow those within the communities and women's organisations to report back on the progress and problems they have encountered, as well as the successes thereof. Community members and women's organisations should also be enabled and included within the development of new measures, strategies and policies that address marital captivity.[1470] Sufficient funding and resources should also be made available to this end.[1471]

Where matters of personal status, such as marriage and divorce, are subjected to religious authorities, States should guarantee that the latter are well trained and informed on matters of gender equality and violence against women, including marital captivity.[1472] In their activities, religious authorities may also be confronted with situations of domestic violence. Where marriage is perceived primarily as a private matter that is subjugated to religious norms, violence occurring within the marriage may be perceived as a sub-category of the issues, which impair peaceful conjugal relations between the spouse. Therefore, violence within the marriage may be treated as primarily a private family matter that is to be resolved between the spouses and may be perceived less as a public matter that requires State intervention or involvement by public bodies.[1473] In addition, the inclination by religious authorities to condone practices

1469 'Brief van de Minister van Sociale Zaken en Werkgelegenheid, Kamerstukken II, 2014/2015, 32 175, nr. 54', 2015, pp. 8–9.

1470 See paragraph 7.6.1.1.2.

1471 See paragraph 7.6.1.1.1.

1472 See paragraph 7.6.1.1.2.

1473 See for example Griffiths, *Sharia and Beth Din courts in the UK: is legal pluralism nothing more than a necessary political fiction*, p. 46.

of chastisement of wives can have the effect that acts of violence are marginalised. If left unreported, cases of domestic violence may proceed unnoticed and even escalate, particularly where the spouses are encouraged to remain in violent relationships or when they are blamed for the violent situation. Furthermore, in acting in accordance with their religious duties to reconcile, the religious authorities may exacerbate violent situations by persistently demanding spouses to reconcile, thereby encouraging victims to remain in a violent relationship or by withholding a divorce, which in essence allows the violent relationship to persist.[1474] Consequently, incidents of domestic violence and marital captivity may progress and escalate unnoticed and unaddressed where the State authorities are not informed thereof, which only places the victims of violence at greater risk and danger. In addition, religious sanctions for acts of VAW may differ from State sanctions for domestic violence (e.g. restraint order, imprisonment) and religious adjudication.[1475] In their endeavour to adjudicate over matters of marriage and divorce, religious authorities may thus prove to be counterproductive and they may even undermine the State's efforts to address violence against women within the family.[1476] Thus, creating clear boundaries and informing and training religious authorities to report acts of VAW is necessary in order to eliminate all forms of VAW, including marital captivity. It is important that States coordinate and cooperate with religious authorities in the area of violence against women in order to prevent and protect against VAW.

7.6.2.3. Measures for State agents and professionals

State parties that prescribe and implement discriminatory divorce laws which allow the practices of repudiation or which deny or limit the women's right to divorce should be eliminated, regardless of whether these are premised in religion. Such practices perpetuate prejudices, reinforce inequality between women and men and they are incompatible with articles 2 (f) *juncto* Article 5(a) CEDAW.[1477] National legislators should review discriminatory divorce laws and amend these to comply with the principle of equality. Similarly, these principles should be enforced within divorce proceedings so that women are not subject to discriminatory standards or are confronted with gender stereotypes. In this respect, sensitising and training judges on the consequences of marital captivity, the impaired human rights and how to weigh these against any other competing interests is necessary. In fact, specifically on the issue

1474 Levitt and Ware, *Religious leaders' perspectives on marriage, divorce, and intimate partner violence*, p. 218.

1475 Ashley Nickel, 'Abusing the system: Domestic violence judgments from Sharia arbitration tribunals create parallel legal structures in the United Kingdom', 4 *The Arbitration Brief* 92–120, (2014), p. 97.

1476 Proudman, *Equal and free? Evidence in support of Baroness Cox's arbitration and dediation services (Equality) Bill*, pp. 19–21.; Levitt and Ware, *Religious leaders' perspectives on marriage, divorce, and intimate partner violence*, p. 218.

1477 See paragraph 7.6.1.1.1.; Heiner Bielefeldt, *Interim report of the Special Rapporteur on freedom of religion or belief* (UN General Assembly, 7 August 2013), [A/68/290], para. 38.

of marital captivity, the CEDAW Committee has recommended the State to adopt and carry out awareness-raising campaigns and to provide training for the judiciary and law enforcement officials on this issue and the available solutions (e.g. the tort- action in the Netherlands).[1478]

Besides judges, education and training programmes for, among others, law enforcement officers, social and health care workers, lawyers and other professionals that encounter marital captivity in their professional activities, should be developed.[1479] These programmes should aim to generate an understanding of marital captivity as an unacceptable issue, as a form of discrimination against women and, in certain circumstances, as constituting an act of violence against women. The rights that are undermined by an ongoing situation of marital captivity should be specified and guidelines should be developed for professionals on how to adequately respond to instances of marital captivity for each different sector.[1480] Furthermore, content on the religious dimension of marital captivity should be included so as to sensitise all involved professionals and State officials to the prevailing religious interpretations and religious divorce procedures. Against this backdrop, judges should proceed with caution and avoid placing the non-cooperative spouse's rights above the trapped wife's rights to be free from VAW. Furthermore, judges should also be versed in human rights law in general so that they can better identify the violated human rights when they are confronted with situations of marital captivity to formal and informal marriages.

States are also encouraged to continue supporting and expanding education programmes and research on marital captivity and violence against women in general.[1481] Studies should aim to expand on the current knowledge on marital captivity by studying the measures that have been developed and adopted in religious communities, as well as the solutions adopted in other legal systems. States should also assess the effectiveness and compatibility of such measures with the existing human rights law.

Furthermore, absolute inaction may be perceived, in society, as permitting practices that promote gender inequality in marital matters and as condoning situations of marital captivity. Therefore, State authorities should adopt a clear stance on the phenomenon of marital captivity as an unacceptable phenomenon and they should

---

1478 Committee on the Elimination of Discrimination Against Women, *Concluding Observations the Netherlands 2016*, para. 44 (d).

1479 Id. See also paragraph 7.6.1.1.2.

1480 Kruiniger suggests several specific measures which can be considered when developing educational and training programmes for professionals (e.g. the developing a marriage toolkit for professionals, providing information on the available (legal) solutions, training professionals and how to use the available solutions strategically in order to prevent or end situations of marital captivity, providing information on the transnational implications of religious marriages, providing assistance and information to (divorcing) spouses who are abroad etc.). Kruiniger, *Niet langer geketend aan het huwelijk! Juridische instrumenten die huwelijkse gevangenschap kunnen voorkomen of oplossen*. pp. 43, 54–55, 57–59, 182–189.

1481 See subsection 7.6.1.5. and paragraph 7.6.1.1.2.

adopt appropriate preventative measures, as well as protective measures, so as to protect spouses in individual cases.[1482]

Additionally, the State's judicial and legislative measures, equally, need to be monitored and assessed in their effectiveness in order to prevent and end situations of marital captivity.[1483] The tort action has been relatively successful in generating pressure on the recalcitrant spouses. So too has imposing financial sanctions on recalcitrant spouses to remedy the damage they have caused by maintaining a situation of marital captivity (as is the case in France). Another successful method has been to enable the secular judge to withhold a civil divorce until all religious barriers to remarrying have been removed. Criminalising marital captivity, as has been done in the Netherlands, is a new avenue that requires further assessment. In the Netherlands, no recalcitrant spouse has yet been prosecuted under the offence of coercion, which also criminalises marital captivity.[1484]

Finally, it is not unthinkable that in situations of marital captivity, the trapped wife may have other interests that also demand protection. For example, the fear of being victimised or harassed by the recalcitrant or opposing husband has shown to be a reason for a spouse not to pursue the dissolution of the religious divorce.[1485] Thus, State intervention to facilitate the dissolution of the religious marriage must simultaneously ensure the protection of the trapped wife's safety, privacy and anonymity.[1486] Trapped women should not have to choose between their personal security and finding solutions to end situations of marital captivity.

7.6.2.4. Cooperation on national and international level

Cooperation between all the agencies that encounter situations of marital captivity should be strengthened and the exchange of information between the different agencies should be facilitated.[1487] For those cases which have a transnational element, the national authorities are encouraged to establish cooperation with the countries of origin of the trapped spouses. Such cooperation should envisage, among others, (a) to facilitate the recognition of a legal divorce that has been pronounced in another country, (b) to guarantee the trapped spouse's safety when travelling within to and from the country of origin, (c) to ensure that the trapped spouse can obtain the necessary travel documents and (d) to encourage the country of origin to recognise the special situation of women in situations of marital captivity, particularly where a divorce has been realised elsewhere or incidents of violence or threats thereof, by the recalcitrant spouse, have been reported in another jurisdiction.

1482 See parapgraph 7.6.1.1.3.
1483 See subsection 7.6.1.5.
1484 See section. 3.4.3. for more detail in this regard.
1485 See at *supra* notes 28 and 33.
1486 See also subsection 7.6.1.2.
1487 See also subsection 7.6.1.5.

7.7. CONCLUDING REMARKS

As has previously been concluded, certain forms of marital captivity qualify as violence against women and thus constitute discrimination against women, as well as a human rights violation. This concerns situations where women are restricted in their opportunities to initiate and obtain a religious divorce, are required to secure the cooperation of their husbands and are placed at the mercy of their (former) spouse. By being forced to remain married against their will, trapped women are impaired in their autonomy and they cannot freely shape their lives as they deem appropriate. Furthermore, husbands are guaranteed exclusive rights and/or entitlements. These not only exempt them from the negative consequences of a situation of marital captivity but also enable husbands to maintain a degree of control over their (former) spouse, by denying her a religious divorce. As practice shows, husbands may abuse their privileged position to harass or punish the trapped woman, who wishes to terminate all links with their (former) partner. In essence, the power imbalance between the spouses lies at the very core of situations of marital captivity that also qualify as VAW.

Both human rights treaties as well as customary international law impose obligations on States to exercise due diligence in preventing, responding to and protecting against all forms of violence. The qualification of these forms of marital captivity as a form of VAW, therefore, triggers the State's obligation to exercise due diligence in preventing, responding to and protecting against marital captivity. States should respond to and address marital captivity in both individual cases, as well as in general. The negative obligations require that the State refrains from creating or maintaining the conditions that enable situations of marital captivity to exist and persist. States that incorporate religious laws that prescribe unequal divorce rights between women and men and that restrict women's opportunity to initiate and obtain a religious divorce, should review and amend these laws. Where these States fail to do so, they are then accountable for the situations of marital captivity that arise and for the situations of marital captivity that continue to exist as a consequence of such laws. It also means that the State can be held accountable for discriminating against married women, as well as for the human rights violations that occur within a situation of marital captivity.

The positive obligations require States to take appropriate and adequate legislative, as well as non-legislative measures, to prevent and protect against acts of marital captivity, including those that are enabled and committed by recalcitrant spouses and religious groups. The fact that a State is secular or non-secular does not alleviate the State from this obligation. In doing so, State efforts should not only focus on facilitating the dissolution of a religious marriage, but they should also be directed to prevent situations of marital captivity from occurring in the first place. Addressing the inherent power imbalance between women and men at the dissolution of the religious marriage and discrimination against women within religious divorce procedures is crucial. States should, in this respect, actively work to encourage the harmonisation of religious views and interpretations on women's equality and divorce with human rights and human rights principles.

CHAPTER 8
CONCLUSIONS

The aim of this contribution has been to provide a human rights perspective on the phenomenon of marital captivity. The forms of marital captivity that have been addressed in this contribution concern situations in which religious doctrines or practices create impediments to the dissolution of a religious marriage. Consequently, one or both spouses may be forced to remain married against their will.

A situation of marital captivity may arise in those communities that either adhere to their own rites for divorce or explicitly adhere to the belief that divorce is non-existent. For example, Catholicism adheres to the doctrine that a marriage, in principle, is indissoluble. However, adherents may terminate a marriage by way of an annulment or divorce. The latter is permitted in limited circumstances (i.e. in the case of an unconsummated marriage or the Pauline privilege). In Protestantism, the civil dissolution of a marriage is mostly also accepted to include the dissolution of the religious marriage, although as has been observed in other religions, divorce should be sought after as a last resort. This perception may create pressure for spouses to maintain an otherwise unhealthy and at times even violent relationship. The existence of divorce in Hinduism remains a nebulous subject. While divorce is recognised in Judaism and Islam, women and men are awarded unequal rights to initiate a divorce. In Judaism, both the women and the men are required to cooperate to the divorce. The man must grant a writ of divorce and the woman must accept it in order for the divorce to be validly concluded. Non-cooperation by either of the spouses, in principle, will create a situation of marital captivity. In Islam, husbands can repudiate their wives. Wives, on the other hand, must secure the cooperation of their husbands for the divorce or demand the religious authorities to dissolve the marriage. Grounds for divorce by religious authorities, however, are very limited.

Notably, in both Judaism and Islam women and men experience situations of marital captivity in different ways. In limited circumstances, the trapped husband may be permitted to entertain a new relationship/marriage. This is a privilege that trapped women do not enjoy as they are only entitled to be married to one spouse at a time. Consequently, the unequal rights to initiate a divorce and the restricted grounds for divorce found in Judaism and Islam means that women are more likely to become victims of marital captivity, where their husbands refuse to cooperate or demand exorbitant requests from the wife, in exchange for a divorce. The ability of husbands to take on more wives further exacerbates the inequality between spouses. Non-cooperative husbands can then engage in a bigamous marriage and they are not affected by the restrictions that are caused by a situation of marital captivity.[1488] Thus, situations of marital captivity arise due to the application of religious laws that do not recognise divorce or that restrict the divorce rights of women and enable the other spouse to obstruct the dissolution of the religious marriage.

More specifically, where grounds for divorce are limited and the cooperation of the husband is required, women are more likely to be subjected to their (ex)husbands' control, not only in respect of the existing marriage but also in relation to many other aspects of their lives. Furthermore, a situation of marital captivity may invoke serious social, religious and at times even economic consequences for the trapped spouse. Trapped spouses may have to endure, religious sanctions, financial extortions and restrictions on the ability to establish new relationships, remarry and shape their lives as they see fit. A trapped spouse may also experience enormous mental and physical suffering by the ongoing situation of marital captivity, including violence, stigmatisation and social isolation. Some situations of marital captivity in a religious marriage, in particular those occurring in Jewish and Muslim communities, may also have legal consequences, irrespective of the spouses' actual religious beliefs. This is the case when the religious marriage is recognised in multiple States. Among the consequences are that spouses may be divorced civilly in one State, but still be legally married in the other State where the civil divorce is not recognised. Consequently, an uncertain legal status arises where the trapped spouse is still legally married against her will. As a consequence, trapped wives may experience, *inter alia*, travelling restrictions, criminal prosecution for adultery, fear of losing custody rights over the children of the marriage and the inability or prohibition to remarry.

Essentially, trapped spouses are prevented from moving on with their lives and in exercising their fundamental rights. Yet inclusion and reference to the human rights legal framework has been scarce in the process of finding holistic and effective solutions to prevent and end marital captivity. The current study has, therefore, sought to offer a human rights perspective of the phenomenon of marital captivity. The research question adopted in this contribution has been:

In what ways does a human rights approach contribute to the process of finding solutions to prevent and end situations of marital captivity?

Four aspects are implied in this question, which are expressed in the sub-questions. Namely, what specific human rights are at stake in a situation of marital captivity? What are the State obligations that flow from the affected human rights? How should competing rights and interests within situations of marital captivity be balanced? What are the implications of adopting a human rights-based approach and what is the

[1488] For more on the religious doctrines and views on marriage and divorce see Chapter 2.

relevance of a human rights discourse for the process of finding solutions? The findings on these aspects are discussed in the following subchapters. Subchapters 8.1 and 8.2 summarise the main findings in the previous Chapters and deal with the first two sub-questions that concern the identification of the affected rights and the implied State obligations. These are followed up by a balancing exercise of the competing interests within a situation of marital captivity (i.e. the third sub-question) in subchapter 8.3. A balance must be found in order to guarantee and protect the rights of the trapped spouse, while simultaneously respecting the religious freedom of the religious communities and possibly of the non-cooperative spouse. This is particularly more relevant for secular States, who also are challenged with responding in a manner that aligns with their secular character and that is within their competences. The last sub-questions, which concern the implications and added value of adopting a human rights approach to marital captivity, is elaborated upon in subchapter 8.4. Finally, subchapter 8.5. concludes this contribution with a set of measures both secular and non-secular States should consider when responding to marital captivity. These are constructed and summarised from the State obligations that are implied within the substantive human rights analysed in Chapters 4 to 7. The specific recommendations on marital captivity by the CEDAW committee are also included. It should be kept in mind that these are by no means an exhaustive set of measures and that their implementation may require further specification and tailoring to the specific context of each country.

8.1. HUMAN RIGHTS THAT ARE AFFECTED IN A SITUATION OF MARITAL CAPTIVITY

Marital captivity is a phenomenon that is found in many parts of the world. The perception and consequences of marital captivity may differ between States due to the diversity of legal systems and the political organisation that is unique to each State. Nevertheless, a common denominator remains that trapped spouses are left with no choice other than to face impediments and restrictions to their rights, in varying degrees, as a consequence of having to remain married against their will. As a core principle pertaining to human rights law, personal autonomy is a prerequisite for the effective and full enjoyment of the broad spectrum of specific human rights. The denial or obstruction of personal autonomy results in the deprivation and restriction of substantive human rights.[1489]

This contribution has shown that a situation of marital captivity undermines women's right to equality during the marriage and at its dissolution, and it impairs the trapped spouse's autonomy. Other rights that are likely to be affected by a situation of marital captivity include, among others, the right to remarry, the right to respect for private

1489 Subchapter 6.1.

life, the right to health and the right to freely travel to, from and within the country of origin.[1490] Some situations of marital captivity may also constitute violence against women.[1491] It is imperative to point out that this enumeration of rights does not entail an exhaustive list of all the rights that may be at stake in a situation of marital captivity, nor does it imply that all these rights will always be adversely affected in each situation of marital captivity. For example, not all trapped spouses will experience travelling restrictions to their country of origin, where the religious marriage is not recognised. Every situation of marital captivity is unique and thus the degree and severity of infringement of these rights will vary. Consequently, the State's obligations in each situation of marital captivity may vary, depending on the specific circumstances of the case and the specific human rights that are affected.

The right to initiate a divorce exists in all countries with the exception of the Philippines and the Vatican. However, none of the human rights instruments, on the international and regional level, explicitly or implicitly recognise a right to divorce. Notably, UN treaty bodies have not been explicit in the exclusion of such a right within UN human rights treaties. The ECtHR, on the other hand, has been more vocal in this regard. The position of the ECtHR remains that a right to initiate and obtain a divorce cannot be derived from the ECHR.[1492] Notwithstanding, this contribution has, in subchapter 5.4., shown that there are compelling reasons to recognise a right to divorce in human rights law. The recognition of a right to divorce could be an instrumental tool for addressing situations of marital captivity to a formal religious marriage. A right to divorce would empower trapped spouses to claim their right to end the formal religious marriage. A right to divorce would also prompt States to address the unequal divorce rights between women and men that are entrenched within their legal systems and it would direct States to harmonise their domestic laws with the principle of equality.

The continued existence of a religious marriage has also been shown to form a barrier to the trapped spouse's choices and ability to remarry, both civilly and religiously. The right to remarry is guaranteed in human rights treaties and it concerns a marriage that is considered as having legal effect within a given legal system. The right to remarry informally, on the other hand, does not seem to be implied in the provisions on the right to marry. However, it may be a protected conduct that falls within the ambit of the protected interests of the freedom of religion.[1493]

Furthermore, a situation of marital captivity infringes upon the social aspects that are guaranteed by the right to respect for private life. Trapped spouses are guaranteed effective participation in social life, a right to entertain social interaction and a right to develop and entertain relationships of different kinds. These are activities which

1490 These rights are discussed in Chapter 6.

1491 Subchapter 7.4.

1492 To date, both the ECmHR and the ECtHR have maintained that a right to request or obtain a divorce cannot be derived from Article 8 ECHR (right to private life) and Article12 ECHR (right to marry). Details of the relevant cases concerning the right to divorce are discussed in subsection 5.2.1.2.

1493 Subsection 6.2.1.2.

benefit an individuals' personal development.[1494] However, the continued existence of a religious marriage may lead to the disapproval of any new relationships with new partners within the religious community. These may even be labelled as acts of adultery.[1495] A situation of marital captivity may also restrict the trapped spouse's effective participation in social life as a divorcee. Where the spouse is still considered to be married, she is expected to uphold her marital obligations towards the marriage. This has consequences for the personal development of the trapped spouses, as they are expected to behave in a way that does not reflect their own reality.

For situations of marital captivity that have transnational aspects, the freedom of movement of the trapped spouse may also be restricted. The freedom of movement guarantees a trapped spouse the right to leave, enter, and travel within, the territory of a State.[1496] The right to leave includes the right to acquire the necessary travel documents. However, obtaining those documents is at times made conditional upon the consent of the (ex) spouse. In more extreme cases, travel documents may be confiscated by family members. Where this is the case, the trapped spouse is then not only physically trapped within the religious marriage, but he or she may become trapped in a foreign country as well.[1497]

Furthermore, health risks brought about by situations of marital captivity have hitherto received minimum attention by experts, academics and public officials. As some case studies have revealed, an ongoing situation of marital captivity may cause severe mental suffering. Feelings of being trapped, unable to control one's life fully or feeling helpless or taken advantage of or the fear of violence and escalation of such violence, are not uncommon among trapped spouses. The health risks brought about by a situation of marital captivity will vary from case to case and may range from physical health implications (e.g. as a consequence of domestic violence) to mental and emotional suffering which is a form of suffering that is often overlooked and underestimated.[1498]

Some situations of marital captivity also constitute violence against women. This concerns situations in which only the woman's options to initiate divorce proceedings are restricted and the obtaining of a divorce is made conditional to the cooperation of the husband. Within these situations, women are effectively deprived of their free and full personal autonomy, while the husbands are enabled to hold a certain degree of control over their (ex-)partners. This control not only concerns the ability and possibility to terminate an irretrievable, and at times physically violent, relationship but it also concerns other aspects of the trapped wife's life and may incentivise other forms of violence (e.g. extortion, intimidation, honour-related crimes etc). The consequence is that these forms of marital captivity may cause physical, mental and/or economic harm and suffering to the trapped wife. These situations of marital captivity constitute

[1494] Subsection 6.2.2.2.
[1495] See the cases of Laila and Chiara discussed in section 1.3.2. and subsection 6.2.3.2.
[1496] Subsection 6.2.3.4.
[1497] See the cases of Farzaneh, Chiara and Sarah discussed in Section 6.2.3.
[1498] Section 6.2.4.

gender-based discrimination, as well as a human rights violation and it is therefore imperative to recognise and address them as such.[1499]

Finally, the freedom of religion also comes into play, particularly where State authorities intervene or are required to intervene in the effort to facilitate the dissolution of a religious marriage. Religious groups, communities and individuals derive entitlements from the freedom of religion. They are entitled to organise their internal affairs free from external interference and to be governed by their own rules insofar as this does not conflict with the law. This may arguably include the regulation of religious matters *vis-à-vis* marriage and divorce.[1500] Similarly, individuals have the right to manifest their religion in observance or practice. In principle, States are required to adopt a restrictive approach when assessing what activities constitute religious manifestations and practices.[1501] Opposition to a civil divorce or the non-cooperation to a religious divorce may in very limited circumstances constitute a religious manifestation. This is the case when a husband or wife withholds their cooperation to the religious divorce or when either of the spouses opposes a civil divorce on the grounds of genuine and sincere religious convictions (e.g. when the opposing spouse considers the marriage as indissoluble).

However, as concluded in Chapter 4, in intervening to mitigate situations of marital captivity, States have not interfered with the guarantees that religious communities are entitled to regulate their internal and doctrinal affairs.[1502] Where it involves a spouse who opposes a civil divorce, a decree of divorce from the competent court, will not affect the religious freedom of the opposing spouse. A civil divorce does neither affect nor regulate the religious marriage which is indissoluble. Where it involves a non-cooperative spouse, a legal obligation compelling her/him to cooperate in religious divorce can be argued to be an interference with her/his religious freedom where the non-cooperation is based on genuine and sincere religious convictions.[1503] Although this conclusion should be drawn cautiously as recognising non-cooperation in a religious divorce as a religious manifestation overlooks the devastating consequences that are the result of such conduct i.e. a situation of marital captivity and violations of the trapped spouse's rights.[1504] Additionally, it should be borne in mind that the recalcitrant spouse's religious freedom can be restricted in order to protect other competing interests. The right to manifest one's religion is a relative right which may be subjected to restrictions.[1505]

Notably, the refusal to comply with legal obligations on the basis of one's religion (i.e. conscientious objection) is for the most part, not a guaranteed right. The only exception

---

1499 Subchapters 7.3–7.4.

1500 Section 4.3.2.

1501 See *supra* note 441.

1502 Subsection 4.3.2.2.

1503 Subsection 4.4.2.3.

1504 Subsection 4.4.2.4.

1505 Id.

that has thus far been made is with respect to legal obligations that require individuals to engage in military activities. Thus, where the State imposes legal obligations which require spouses to cooperate in or facilitate the dissolution of a marriage, a recalcitrant spouse cannot evade compliance with such obligations by appealing to her/his right to conscientious objection.[1506]

8.2. STATE'S HUMAN RIGHTS OBLIGATIONS

All of the above-mentioned rights imply negative and positive obligations for the State. Positive obligations require the State to respond and adopt protective measures to ensure the actual exercise and enjoyment of these rights.

Despite there not being an explicit right to divorce in human rights law, in the past decades, human rights monitoring bodies have encouraged States to adopt legal means by which individuals may terminate their legal marriage. States that do not allow divorce or only allow divorce in accordance with personal laws are encouraged to introduce a civil form of divorce. Furthermore, States are also obliged to ensure that the principles of equality and non-discrimination are respected within the family, the marriage and at its dissolution.[1507] When introducing the possibility of divorce, States should guarantee that this occurs on the basis of equality for both spouses. Discriminatory personal laws and practices should be reviewed and modified in order to ensure equality in the dissolution of marriage.[1508]

For those countries where a religious marriage is considered as having legal effect and where personal laws form part of the legal system, the provisions on divorce, that award men more rights at and during the divorce, have been found to contravene the principles of non-discrimination and equality. Thus, these countries should ensure equality between women and men at the dissolution of marriage. Discriminatory provisions and practices during the divorce should be abolished or harmonised so as to comply with Article 16 CEDAW. In this regard, States are obliged to prohibit and eliminate the possibility for husbands to repudiate their wives, to exploit the disadvantageous situation of their wives, and the possibility for recalcitrant spouses to enter into bigamous or polygamous marriages.[1509] States that do allow the retroactive invalidation of a divorce, have been recommended to bring this practice to an end. The CEDAW Committee has even gone so far as to recommend limiting the jurisdiction of religious tribunals on matters of marriage and divorce so that they do not preside over these matters exclusively.[1510] Additionally, the fact that it concerns religious doctrines,

---

1506 Section 4.4.3.
1507 Subsection 6.2.1.1.
1508 Section 5.2.2.
1509 Id.
1510 See *supra* note 761.

rules or interpretation does not discharge or alleviate the State from its obligations to guarantee equality between women and men.[1511] Likewise, the fact that in certain countries religious courts may have jurisdiction over matters of marriage and divorce does not absolve the concerned State from its human rights obligation to ensure equality at the dissolution of the marriage.[1512]

With regard to the trapped spouse's rights, States are obliged to make the right to remarry effectively available for divorcees. This implies that States should refrain from infringing the right to remarry subsequent to a divorce, by for example imposing unreasonable or discriminatory restrictions on divorcees that seek to remarry.[1513] Practices that obscure the very essence of the right to remarry, including those that award women limited rights in the initiation of a divorce (e.g. repudiation, practice of levirate marriages, unequal waiting periods for divorced women), should be eliminated. The right to remarry should effectively be accessible for both women and men on an equal basis. States are obliged to review and modify domestic laws, customs and practices which impair the trapped spouse's right to remarry.[1514]

Additionally, the effective exercise of the right to remarry, at times, requires that any pre-existing marriage is dissolved. In other words, the dissolution of the legal marriage may become a precondition to the effective exercise and enjoyment of the right to remarry. On this subject matter, this contribution has argued that the obligations to guarantee the right to remarry imposes a duty on the States to remove unjustifiable obstacles to a divorce and to ensure that spouses to an involuntary and fictitious marriage are not deprived of their right to establish a valid and legal marriage with the person of their choice.[1515] Measures for removing obstacles to the right to remarry should be applied for women and men on the basis of equality. This obligation also extends to the situations in which the right to remarry is undermined by the actions of private actors.[1516] In essence, this comes down to the regulation of individual conduct and behaviour in a manner that secures the conditions for the trapped spouse to effectively enjoy the right to remarry. The tort action in the Netherlands is an example thereof.[1517] Where successful, compelling the husband to cease a tortious situation (i.e. a situation of marital captivity) by cooperating in the religious divorce results in the dissolution of the religious marriage. The trapped wife is then free to remarry if she wishes to do so.

As for remarrying in accordance with religious rituals, States are obliged to ensure and protect the right to freedom of religion. This right, among others, guarantees that individuals should be able to manifest their religion in the area of marriage. In other

1511 Section 5.2.2.
1512 Id.
1513 Subsection 6.2.1.1.
1514 Subsection 6.3.1.1.
1515 Subsection 5.3.3.2. and subchapter 5.4.
1516 Subsection 5.3.3.2.
1517 See section 3.4.1.

words, the right to freedom of religion also guarantees that adherents may marry in accordance with their religious beliefs and convictions. For this reason, States are encouraged to make both civil and religious forms of marriage available to those under their jurisdiction.

The positive obligations implied in the right to private life require that the State guarantees the effective participation of individuals in society and ensures that they are able to develop their personality. The State is obliged to protect trapped spouse's right to private life from violations by private parties. In doing so, (legislative) measures to regulate the conduct of individuals so as to ensure their compliance with human rights principles should be considered (e.g. provisions that require the removal of any barriers to remarry or cooperation in a religious divorce).[1518] Additionally, States should take the necessary steps to adopt remedial measures for trapped spouses, so that they can enforce their right to private life, as well as other rights that are infringed by a situation of marital captivity.[1519]

With regard to the right to freedom of movement, States have an obligation to protect the right to move within the territory, the right to leave, as well as the right to enter, from interference by private actors. This obligation includes ensuring that travelling restrictions are not caused by the confiscation of the travel documents of the trapped wife (e.g. by family members) or by the refusal of the husband to give his consent to the wife's travelling activities. The subjection of women's free movement to the consent of others should be avoided in law and in practice and States should bring such laws and such practices to an end. Furthermore, the State has a positive obligation to issue travel documents. Where the national is abroad, both the country of origin and the country of residence have obligations in relation to the nationals who are seeking to leave the host State.[1520]

States must also consider the special ways in which trapped women experience health-related issues. In this respect, States should ensure that goods, facilities and services meet the trapped spouse's specific needs. Special attention should not only be placed on the physical impairments, but also on the mental implications and the stressful conditions which situations of marital captivity give rise to. Account should be taken of such health-related issues which may affect spouses in exercising their human rights.[1521]

With respect to those situations of marital captivity that constitute violence against women, human rights law as well as customary international law requires the State to respond with due diligence to prevent and protect against actions of violence that are

1518 For example, the New York Domestic Relation Law, paras. 236 and 253.; United Kingdom Divorce (Religious Marriages) Act 2002, Chapter 27.; Canadian Divorce Act, Section 21.1.
1519 Subsection 6.3.1.2.
1520 Id.
1521 Subsections 6.3.1.2., 6.3.2.4.

directed towards women. This obligation requires the State to exercise due diligence in preventing, protecting, investigating and punishing gender-based violence, as well as providing victims with appropriate reparations. Measures should include, *inter alia,* awareness-raising efforts on all levels and educational and training programmes for all actors that encounter marital captivity (e.g. the judiciary, law enforcement, religious authorities, professionals, legislators, social workers, civil society). Where necessary legislative measures to address marital captivity should be introduced. States should also invest in enhancing cooperation with and between relevant actors and in establishing effective and accessible remedies for trapped spouses. State intervention to facilitate the dissolution of a religious marriage should also take into account that trapped women may have additional interests, besides dissolving the religious marriage, which also need to be protected (e.g. safety, security, privacy, anonymity, de-escalation of a violent relationship etc.).[1522] Thus, the facilitation of the dissolution of a religious marriage may have to be complemented with additional measures which guarantee better protection of the safety and privacy of the trapped women.

Additionally, in addressing marital captivity it is of paramount importance to also address the root causes of marital captivity, which find their basis in interpretations and application of religious rules. Articles 2 (f) *juncto* 5(a) CEDAW, require States to address discriminatory cultural norms and practices and to eliminate negative gender-based ideologies, stereotypes and prejudices which undermine women's rights. Culture is interpreted broadly so as to include traditions, customs and religion. This obligation extends to all activities and practices, whether occurring in the public or private spheres and irrespective of the prevailing legal system in a given State. Thus, the fact that religious normative systems and practices have no formal recognition does not alleviate the State from its obligation to eliminate discrimination that occurs within private spheres. In fact, the State has a positive obligation to intervene in activities and practices of private actors, including those undertaken by religious groups, which are harmful to women.[1523]

Besides the obligation to protect the trapped spouse's rights, States also have obligations to respect and protect the right to freedom of religion of individuals and religious groups. States are required to ensure that individuals and communities can manifest and interpret their religion without unjustified interference by the State and/or private persons. The State may not ban, prohibit or impose specific religious doctrines, interpretations or manifestations. More specifically for marital captivity, States should refrain from claiming the authority to dissolve a religious marriage and from compelling religious communities and authorities to assimilate norms and values that are not their own. Similarly, States should also be cautious to respect the collective freedom of religion and refrain from interfering in the internal doctrinal affairs of

[1522] Subsections 7.6.1.2, 7.6.2.3.
[1523] Subchapter 7.6.

religious groups.[1524] A State may, however, restrict the right to freedom of religion in accordance with the limitation clauses.

8.3. STRIKING A BALANCE BETWEEN COMPETING RIGHTS AND INTERESTS

The religious dimension that is inherent in situations of marital captivity necessitates that any strategy to address marital captivity takes into account the freedom of religion of the spouses and of the religious community in order to avoid creating unjustified interferences to this right. The secular character of a State may be another factor that requires attention as it may impact the way in which a State may respond to marital captivity. Similarly, the protection of the institute of marriage has also shown, in the cases of *Johnston and others v. Ireland, Ivanov and Petrova v. Bulgaria, Piotrowski v. Poland* and *Babiarz v. Poland*, to be an interest that States may consider as worthy of protection. On the other hand, States must also guarantee and protect the trapped spouses' rights from violations by private actors. Protecting against violations of human rights by non-State actors and remedying such violations requires active State intervention. States are also obliged to work towards advancing equality and eliminating discrimination. On top of that, States, as per the CEDAW convention, must also enact measures to foster cultural change and eliminate structural inequalities and discriminatory practices, customs, regulations and laws that reinforce stereotypes and beliefs of women's subordination, including those happening within private spheres.

In a situation of marital captivity, there are thus multiple competing rights and interests which all need to be contemplated by States when complying with their human rights obligations and when adopting measures to end and prevent situations of marital captivity.

However, in general there is no hierarchy of human rights. All human rights are interrelated, interdependent and indivisible. Where there is a clash of competing rights, it is thus imperative to balance these rights and interests. How to weigh these rights and interests is to be determined on a case by case basis, due to the fact that specific situations of marital captivity are not identical. Additionally, not all rights investigated in this contribution will be engaged in all situations of marital captivity. For example, not all situations of marital captivity constitute VAW. Similarly, not all trapped spouses will be impaired in their right to freedom of movement. Likewise, the national context and legal system of a State should be taken into account in this assessment. Nevertheless, several general observations may be made on how to weigh the rights and interests that may be conflicting within situations of marital captivity.

[1524] Sections. 4.3.2. and 4.5.2.

The following sections discuss the competing interests within situations of marital captivity. These can be summed up as: respecting the right to freedom of religion and the State's limitations to interfere in religious matters (the secular argument) *versus* the State's obligations to protect the rights of trapped spouses, guarantee the underlying principles of gender equality and non-discrimination and to address harmful practices, such as marital captivity which undermine women's rights. The purpose of this exercises is to generate a greater understanding of how to weigh the competing interests and to determine where to strike the balance. This is realised by drawing upon the analysis of all the interests, rights, State obligations and human rights principles that were addressed in Chapters 3 to 7. Consideration is taken of how these interests are addressed in the treaties and by human rights monitoring and expert bodies.

8.3.1. RELIGIOUS MANIFESTATIONS THAT UNDERMINE WOMEN'S RIGHTS AND GENDER EQUALITY

Starting with the right to freedom of religion for the non-cooperative and opposing spouses, the discussed case law of the ECtHR, as well as that of the national courts, reveal that in most cases, non-cooperation or opposition to a divorce is motivated by non-religious reasons and may at times even be motivated by bad faith.[1525] Where this is the case, the non-cooperative or opposing spouse cannot rely on the right to freedom of religion. Not cooperating or opposing the divorce cannot then be regarded as a religious manifestation or expression.

However, in some cases a spouse may refuse to cooperate in the dissolution of the religious marriage when this is perceived to be incompatible with their religious convictions and views on divorce. The non-cooperation with the divorce can then be considered as an expression of their genuine and sincere religious convictions. Compelling the spouses to cooperate in the dissolution of the religious marriage may, then, be experienced as an impairment to their religious freedom.[1526] Therefore, the non-cooperative spouse's right to manifest their religion must be considered in relation to the trapped spouse's rights and freedoms, which are impaired by having to remain married against their will.

However, it should be kept in mind that the freedom of religion is a relative right and may have to give way to other impeding interests, such as the rights of others.[1527] Additionally, human rights monitoring bodies have established that religion may not be relied upon to discriminate against women or to commit acts of violence against women.[1528] The State's human rights obligations, furthermore, require that States

1525 Section 4.4.2.

1526 Id.

1527 The criteria for legitimate State interference with the right to freedom of religion are discussed in Section 4.5.2.

1528 See subsection 4.4.1.1.

address practices which deny or restrict women's right to divorce and to eliminate the ability of husbands to unilaterally divorce their wives.[1529] Therefore, accepting or tolerating practices that undermine women's rights and equality as religious manifestations, may constitute a failure of the State to comply with its human rights obligations. In other words, although the non-cooperation to a divorce may in certain cases be a genuine expression of one's religious convictions, it is nevertheless conduct which is not worthy of protection under the freedom of religion, especially where it results in undermining women's rights and equality.

Where it concerns a spouse whom opposes a civil divorce the concerned spouse's freedom of religion is not affected by the effectuation of a civil divorce as has been concluded in 4.4.2.3. A civil divorce does not affect nor dissolve the religious marriage, so that the concerned spouse is not restricted in manifesting and acting in accordance with her/his religious convictions that are related to the religious marriage.

8.3.2. RESPECTING RELIGIOUS GROUPS THAT ENGAGE IN DISCRIMINATORY PRACTICES AGAINST WOMEN

The right to freedom of religion also has a collective dimension. This guarantees individuals the possibility to manifest their religion within their community. Religious groups are entitled to be governed by their own rules, establish their own places of worship, govern their internal affairs and doctrinal matters etc. Religious groups are not obliged to ensure the religious freedom of their adherents and, as reality shows, they can enforce religious interpretations and practices that are discriminatory and harmful to women. As long as individuals are guaranteed the freedom to leave the religion, the negative obligation to respect the individual and the collective freedom of religion places a constraint on the State's ability to intervene in strictly religious matters.[1530] States are required to adopt a restrictive approach when assessing religious manifestations, practices and conduct.[1531] However, this does not mean that religious groups can discriminate and unconditionally mistreat adherents. In fact, States are obliged to address cultural, religious, traditional norms and practices which discriminate against women and they must take measures to eliminate ideologies, beliefs and stereotypes that subordinate women. States must also undertake measures to encourage the transformation of cultural and traditional norms, values and views so that these align with human rights norms and principles. This obligation extends to the activities and practices of religious groups. States, thus, have an obligation to address harmful practices, such as marital captivity, that occur within religious groups and to ensure compliance with human rights standards and principle by religious

[1529] See also section 5.2.2.
[1530] See subsection 4.5.2.1.
[1531] See section 4.3.1.; subsection 4.3.2.2.

groups.[1532] The secular or non-secular character of a State does not alter or affect these obligations.

Noteworthy, the discussed national case law and legislative initiatives on marital captivity[1533] show that State's interventions to facilitate the dissolution of a religious marriage are possible without interfering with the right to freedom of religion. States have occasionally deployed legal measures to facilitate the dissolution of a religious marriage (e.g. the tort-action in the Netherlands). Generally, these interventions do not prescribe a specific outcome of the religious divorce proceedings. They also do not dictate how religious authorities should examine a situation of marital captivity or the trapped spouse's request for a divorce. These are indirect solutions. The actual dissolution of the marriage is still dependant on whether or not the other spouse will eventually cooperate and whether such a divorce will be considered as valid by the religious communities and authorities. Despite this, State interventions have shown to facilitate the dissolution of a religious marriage. An additional bonus of State intervention is that it can strengthen the decisions of religious authorities, by creating (much needed) pressure on the husband to cooperate with the divorce. In particular, in secular States this pressure is lacking as religious authorities and bodies have limited means to effectively pressurise non-cooperative husbands. Financial intervention should also not be overlooked. As the case of *Staatkundig Gereformeerde Partij v. The Netherlands* illustrates, financial subsidies, or the withholding thereof, can also incentivise religious groups to reassess and modify their practices, views and norms, particularly where they discriminate against women.[1534] There are also non-legal measures that can be employed to foster awareness of and compliance with human rights standards by religious communities, without necessarily interfering with the right to freedom of religion. The strategic use of awareness-raising campaigns and training programmes, such as the Self- Determination Action Plan 2015–2017 and the *(H)echt verbonden* project which were implemented in the Netherlands[1535], can massively benefit the efforts to encourage dialogue within religious groups, especially on marital captivity and the religious interpretations, doctrines and views on divorce. Thus, States not only have a duty to intervene in activities by religious groups and bodies that discriminate against women, but they also have effective means at their disposal to do so without infringing upon the right to freedom of religion, as the judicial and legislative measures in some secular States have revealed.[1536]

[1532] Subchapter 7.6.

[1533] Subsection 4.4.2.2.

[1534] Cook, *State Responsibility for Violations of Women's Human Rights*, p. 168. For more on this case, see subsection 4.3.2.2. and subchapter 7.6.

[1535] The Self- Determination Action Plan 2015–2017' (*Actie plan-zelfbeschikking 2015–2017)* and *(H)echt verbonden* project were elaborated upon in section 3.4.3. and subsection 7.6.2.2.

[1536] Subchapter 3.4.; subsection 7.4.2.2.

8.3.3. GENDER EQUALITY VS. THE FREEDOM OF RELIGION AND THE RIGHTS OF OTHERS

Entangled within the phenomenon of marital captivity is also the issue of inequality. This is particularly the case where religious norms, (a) interpretations and practices award the husband the right to unilaterally divorce his wife, (b) enable the husband to frustrate the wives' efforts to realise a divorce, (c) restrict the women's access to divorce and (d) allow for the husband to entertain bigamous or polygamous marriages. These conditions undermine women's rights within the marriage and at its dissolution, and they deprive them of their autonomy to decide and plan their own lives and futures. These conditions also create power imbalances and inequalities between the husband and wife. In turn the power imbalances enable the husband to maintain control over his (ex-) wife by holding her hostage in the religious marriage.

Equality and the prohibition of non-discrimination are both principles and rights that are fundamental in human rights law and they are contained in all of the documents that have been analysed in this contribution. More specifically, the advancement of gender equality and the prohibition of gender discrimination are goals that should be given considerable weight. Where it concerns a conflict between ensuring equality, non-discrimination and women's dignity *vis-à-vis* protecting religious manifestations that are harmful and undermine women's rights, the CEDAW Committee has asserted that priority needs to be given to the protection of women's rights and freedoms.[1537] Furthermore, States are obliged to promote and advance gender equality and to prohibit and eliminate gender discrimination in both the public and private spheres.[1538] In fact, the wording in article 5(a) CEDAW and 12(1) Istanbul Convention do implicitly incorporate a hierarchy. Namely, where cultural, traditional, customary or religious norms or attitudes are discriminatory towards women, the human rights obligations contained in the CEDAW[1539] and Istanbul Convention[1540] require States to address and modify these in order to advance gender equality. In other words, advancing gender equality and non-discrimination and protecting the trapped women's rights and freedoms are interests which prevail over the interest to protect religious manifestations and practices that undermine women's rights, restrict women's rights to seek divorce and enable situations of marital captivity to arise and persist.

Moreover, where it concerns situations of marital captivity that constitute VAW, the rights of the non-cooperative husband (e.g. the right to manifest one's religion) do not prevail over the victim's right to life and right to physical and mental integrity.[1541] It should also be borne in mind that religion cannot be invoked to justify discrimination

1537 Subchapter 7.6.
1538 Id.
1539 Convention on the Elimination of All forms of discrimination against women, Article 5(a).
1540 Istanbul Convention, Article 12 (5).
1541 Subchapter 7.6. at note 1358.

against women. Therefore, weighty reasons need to be provided in order to condone any differential treatment between men and women.

8.3.4. SECULARISM AS A BARRIER FOR STATE INTERVENTION?

For secular States, in particular, the obligation to address the structural causes of marital captivity (religious doctrines which establish power imbalances and inequalities between spouses) and to facilitate the dissolution of a religious marriage may be perceived as requiring interference in the internal and doctrinal affairs of religious groups.

This argument, however, does not hold up and is misguided. Firstly, all of the human rights investigated in this contribution impose obligations on States to protect the trapped spouse's rights and to advance the principles of gender equality and non-discrimination. This includes protection from violations and discrimination that are perpetrated by non-State actors, as well as harm caused by the State or its agents. The obligation to protect against violation by non-State actors implies, *inter alia*, that States must ensure observance with human rights principles by individuals and within the context of horizontal relationships. The secular or non-secular character of the State does not affect these obligations or alleviate States from their human rights obligations.[1542] Thus, secular States are obliged to protect trapped spouse's rights and to adopt all measures at their disposal to adequately and appropriately address this phenomenon.

Secondly, the national case law discussed in subsection 4.4.2.2. reveals that secular States can intervene in situations of marital captivity and address the structural factors pertaining to marital captivity, without interfering in religious doctrinal matters, trespassing the State's competences or jeopardising the State's secular principles. For example, the tort action as it is applied in the Netherlands generally compels the non-cooperative spouse to cooperate in the dissolution of a religious marriage.[1543] Similarly, the Divorce (Religious Marriages) Act in the UK has also been found to not infringe upon religious freedoms and was even deemed necessary in order to guarantee the trapped spouse's rights.[1544] Thus, the State's secular structure does not make intervention impossible or prevent the State from responding to and intervening in situations of marital captivity. Concluding remarks

From the above, it may be concluded that within the context of marital captivity, it is unthinkable that the recalcitrant spouse's rights will take precedence over the State's obligations to ensure and protect the rights of the trapped spouses and to guarantee

1542 Subchapter 6.3.; paragraph 7.6.1.1.1.

1543 See section 3.4.1.; paragraph 4.4.2.2.1.

1544 See paragraph 4.4.2.2.3.

and realise the fundamental principles of personal autonomy and gender equality. Religious manifestations which essentially undermine women's rights and impairs their autonomy are not worthy of protection. State intervention to facilitate the dissolution of a religious marriage also does not infringe upon the competences of religious groups to govern and regulate divorce. Likewise, States can and have shown that intervention in situations of marital captivity is possible without trespassing the boundaries set by the right to freedom of religion and the principles of secularism. Thus, the right to freedom of religion is outweighed by the State's obligations to advance equality, to prohibit discrimination and to protect the trapped spouse's rights from infringements by the other spouse and the religious community. Competing interests that would require limited State responses to address gender-based discrimination, protect trapped women and to prevent situations of marital captivity are therefore unthinkable.

8.4. THE ADVANTAGES OF A HUMAN RIGHTS APPROACH TO MARITAL CAPTIVITY

Approaching marital captivity from a human rights perspective is not only recommended but it is also very effective. It allows for an understanding of the phenomenon as a public and State affair, it provides a strong base to push for solutions and demand active State's responses and it provides a recognised framework to weigh any competing interests. The following paragraphs elaborate further hereupon.

Firstly, a human rights approach enables a greater understanding of the underlying causes of marital captivity, its consequences and social impact. Marital captivity is neither a country or community-specific issue, nor is it only limited to migrant groups. It is widespread and it occurs in many different ways and forms. Moreover, the religious dimension that is present within situations of marital captivity does not make this solely a religious or private issue. Rather, it is a societal problem that negatively impacts the trapped spouses, particularly women, across the world. Its prevalence primarily targets and impairs the trapped spouses' autonomy to live and shape their lives according to their wishes. The consequences are that the trapped spouses' rights and the full enjoyment thereof are restricted for as long as the religious marriage continues to exist.[1545] The social implications are the acceptance that the spouses' autonomy and freedom should be restricted in order to maintain the institution of marriage by controlling and limiting the way in which spouses can dissolve a broken marriage.[1546] More specifically for trapped women who must first obtain the cooperation of their (former) partner or their approval in order to travel, the consequences are, essentially, that they are subjected to the will or whims of their husbands. At times religious authorities may intervene, nonetheless,

[1545] See section 6.1.2. and subchapter 6.2.

[1546] In some situations, spouses cannot dissolve the marriage, as they can only annul the marriage or have to obtain the cooperation of the other spouse. For more details, see Chapter 2.

trapped women remain dependent upon the lenience of these authorities. Simply put, women are not only denied full autonomy, but they are subjected to the control of others and subordinated to the will of their (former) spouse.

Secondly, marital captivity has for long been considered as a religious and private matter which should primarily be resolved within the religious communities. This approach is particularly strengthened by the fact that the phenomenon is inherently connected to religion and occurs within the religious communities and private settings. For centuries, marital captivity has and continues largely to be addressed within these settings, despite the fact that sustainable solutions to end and prevent marital captivity have yet to be developed. On top of that these settings are often perceived as areas where the State should have limited intervention and are in fact protected from unwarranted State intervention by, among others, the right to freedom of religion and the right to privacy.

However, the human rights analysis provided above reveals that marital captivity is not solely a religious or private matter. In fact, marital captivity is predominantly a human rights issue. Within a situation of marital captivity, multiple human rights are affected. Specifying the human rights that are implicated in situations of marital captivity allows the identification of the role of the State in responding to marital captivity. In other words, it allows to establish the corresponding obligations that rest upon the State since States are the subjects of international human rights law and carry the obligations to comply with the specified human rights standards. Related to this, a human rights approach allows States to be held indirectly accountable for violations of human rights that are the result of harmful conduct of private actors. Human rights violations that have been committed by non-state actors are, in principle, not directly attributable to the State. However, State's accountability may still be established on the basis of the State's failure to comply with its positive obligation to protect from human rights violations caused by private actors. For marital captivity, this means that States can be held accountable where they fail to comply with their human rights obligations to protect trapped spouse's rights from infringements by private actors.

Additionally, the affirmation that marital captivity constitutes, in certain circumstances, VAW strengthens the viewpoint of marital captivity as a predominantly human rights issue. VAW constitutes discrimination and is a human rights violation. Discrimination, whether occurring in the private or public sphere, is a State affair. This flows from the human rights obligation to eliminate discrimination on the basis of protected criteria, including discrimination by private non-state actors. With regards to the phenomenon of marital captivity, this means that, as a form of VAW, it qualifies as discrimination and a human rights violation in and of itself and is thus a State affair.

Essentially, a human rights approach enables to transform marital captivity in a public issue that requires States attention. States are obliged to protect the trapped spouses' rights from infringements by third actors, remedy any human rights violation and eliminate discrimination against women.

Thirdly and related to this, the prevailing State-Church model of a State and reservations to certain rights are factors which can influence the State's commitment to protect trapped spouses' rights and address marital captivity. Human rights law does not require or recommend a particular model. Rather States Parties, irrespective of the State-church model they adopt, must comply with their human rights obligations and guarantee human rights. Thus, human rights should be the starting point of discussions on marital captivity and the State-Church relationship does not alleviate States from their human rights obligations. In other words, States are not excused from their human rights obligations to protect the trapped spouse's rights and freedom irrespective of their State-Church model.

Fourthly, a human rights-based approach is solution based in that it is centred around the trapped spouses' rights and the need to realise effective solutions to prevent and end situations of marital captivity. Placing the trapped spouses' rights at the centre of this debate allows for a more objective discussion on marital captivity and its consequences for the trapped spouses. As the analysis has shown, several fundamental rights are infringed in a situation of marital captivity. On top of that, a situation of marital captivity undermines the human rights principles of equality, non-discrimination and personal autonomy.

The identification and acknowledgement of these consequences is crucial and should be given considerate and appropriate weight within the dialogue on marital captivity, judicial proceedings and all State efforts to address and redress marital captivity. Furthermore, framing the trapped spouses' rights as a human rights issue also makes it possible to avoid placing uneven attention on the religious aspects and challenges (e.g. the position and rights of women within religious doctrines, interpreting religious doctrines to be more in line with women's rights, resolution of marital captivity within religious communities, the legitimacy of the State in intervening in the internal affairs of religious communities etc.). That is not to say that the religious dimensions and aspects should be eliminated from the discussion. By way of contrast, these are important discussion points and their inclusion contributes greatly to addressing marital captivity. However, placing religion and the religious aspects at the centre of the debate tends to ignore the fact that the rights of individuals are being infringed and it also tends to overlook the potential of non-religious based solutions. A human rights approach, on the other hand, primarily centralises the discussion on the human rights infringements and the need to find solutions to prevent and remedy human rights violations which are the result of marital captivity. It also makes it possible to recognise the potential of religious as well as non-religious means to facilitate the dissolution of the religious marriage.

Fifthly, a human rights approach allows to also include and assess the religious dimension of marital captivity within the human rights framework. More specifically, the rights and freedoms that religious members and communities lend from the right to freedom of religion within the context of religious divorce practices are also acknowledged and considered. It is imperative to acknowledge the crucial role and potentials that religion and religious communities have, not only in creating situations of marital captivity, but also in ending and preventing them from arising in the first place. Particularly for secular States, the effective resolution of situations of marital captivity and addressing the root causes which find their basis in religious norms and interpretations is unlikely to be reached independently without the involvement of religious communities and leaders. Sustainable solutions must take the religious dimension as well as the social and individual impacts of marital captivity, into consideration. Adopting an approach that is premised on the protection of human rights, thus, promotes the inclusion of religious communities in the efforts of examining and re-assessing the available means to effectively redress situations of marital captivity.

Furthermore, taking the religious dimension of marital captivity from a human rights perspective enables to avoid misrepresenting religious groups and reinforcing negative perception of individuals and groups that adhere to these religions. Among the risks of giving prominent attention on marital captivity as occurring within certain religious, minority or migrant groups, is that this may reinforce the perception that marital captivity is primarily a migrant, minority, religious or private matter. This, however, does not allow one to fully understand the phenomenon, its root causes and mechanisms (i.e. restriction of spouses' autonomy and power imbalances between spouses), its social implications (i.e. control over women's lives) and its widespread and pervasive nature. Furthermore, this also does a disservice for the process of developing and implementing effective solutions to address existing instances of marital captivity as well as its root causes.

Sixthly, a human rights-based approach provides an objective framework of reference for striking a balance between the competing interests within situations of marital captivity. Where there is a clash of rights and interests (e.g. an infringement of the right to remarry vs. protection of the freedom of religion), States should aim to strike a fair balance between the competing rights and interests. This requires weighing the competing interests against each other, while taking all of the circumstances into consideration, including the necessity and appropriateness of intervening or not intervening. This framework is further complemented by statements and decisions of human right monitoring bodies, which have provided insightful considerations on how to weigh certain competing interests that are inherent in situations of marital captivity.[1547] In this respect, where cultural, traditional or religious attitudes and conduct undermine women's rights and equality, the CEDAW Committee has firmly

1547 See subchapter 7.6.

established a precedent of giving priority to the protection of women's rights and freedoms. In fact, when it comes to VAW, the CEDAW Committee has established that the right of women's life, physical and mental integrity cannot be superseded by the perpetrator's rights. This approach is aligned with and is reflected in the hierarchy that is implied in Article 5(a) CEDAW as well as Article 12(1) of the Istanbul. Within the context of marital captivity, the principles of gender equality, as well as women's rights to life and physical and mental integrity are attributed significant weight. Additionally, freedom of religion clearly does not give *carte blanche* to religious communities to reinforce gender discrimination, stereotypes and beliefs of women's subordination within the public or private sphere. Nor can freedom of religion be invoked to justify a manifestation which undermines the rights of married women and deprives them of their autonomy to end and leave the marriage. On the basis hereof, the conclusion has been reached that it is unthinkable for the right to freedom of religion, or any other right of the recalcitrant/opposing spouse, to be given precedence over the trapped spouse's rights and freedoms.

Finally, a human rights approach also benefits trapped spouses in more direct ways and can serve as a practical tool in specific cases of marital captivity. For example, in judicial proceedings against a non-cooperative spouse trapped spouses can claim a violation of their human rights as a consequence of an ongoing situation of marital captivity, appeal for the judicial body to remedy the infringements and harm they have suffered and request adequate protection from further violations. Likewise, lawyers can and should include a human rights discourse when handling a case of marital captivity. A human rights approach strengthens the demands for State authorities, which include courts, to comply with their human rights obligations to protect trapped spouses and to address the root causes of marital captivity. Besides the strategic use of available legal tools, a human rights discourse adds weight on the demands for judicial intervention in order to protect trapped spouses' rights.

Additionally, including a human rights approach in judicial, legislative and policy processes, equips judges, policymakers and legislators, with a framework to consider any competing interests. Furthermore, a human rights approach, as shown in this contribution, provides identifiable obligations and measures State authorities should adopt in order to address and redress situations of marital captivity. Advocacy endeavours by the State and civil society are also enriched by a human rights approach in that they educate and empower trapped spouses with regard to their rights and also facilitate the inclusion and promotion of human rights within the ongoing dialogue on marital captivity in the public discourse. The latter is more important where such efforts are focused on facilitating the dialogue within the communities in which situations of marital captivity occur. After all, marital captivity is a societal problem that concerns the spouses as well as their community, and it is thus important to promote a human rights discourse within these dialogues so as to facilitate the process of cultural negotiations within the respective communities.

8.5. MEASURES TO PROTECT FROM AND PREVENT MARITAL CAPTIVITY

This contribution has established that a situation of marital captivity violates the autonomy and human rights of the trapped spouse. Its prevalence is incompatible with States 'obligations to achieve gender equality and eliminate gender discrimination and practices that are harmful to women. As established, the State has obligations to:

a) respond to situations of marital captivity;
b) protect the trapped spouse's rights;
c) actively develop and implement measures to eradicate situations of marital captivity;
d) adopt measures to prevent new situations from arising and lastly;
e) encourage the elimination of ideologies, beliefs and stereotypes of women's subordination within religious groups and stimulate cultural transformation with regards to the topics of gender equality, divorce and marital captivity.

Sustainable solutions to marital captivity require the development, adoption and implementation of a holistic and comprehensive system of measures that include legal, political, administrative and cultural tools. Engaging all relevant actors and stakeholders on all levels is also crucial. Furthermore, State measures should not only target the actions that create situations of marital captivity, but they should also aim to address the factors that allow for this phenomenon to exist in the first place. This requires challenging the prevailing discourse and practices within religious communities, especially those which condone and enable husbands to hold their partners in a fictitious marriage and force them to remain married against their will.

The measures outlined in the following sections derive from and are inspired by the obligations that rest upon States that have been discussed in the previous Chapters. Further substance is given to these measures and these are tailored to marital captivity as occurring within a global context. However, the measures provided do not intend or aim to serve as an exhaustive list of measures for the phenomenon of marital captivity. States, being in a far better position to assess the domestic circumstances and the appropriateness of implemented measures, have discretion in determining which measures they adopt and how these are implemented and enforced within their national contexts. The following measures may, therefore, be perceived as recommendations and areas of focus that States should consider in order to combat the phenomenon of marital captivity and to prevent new situations from arising.

8.5.1. GENERAL MEASURES

To begin with, adopting a clear public statement on the phenomenon of marital captivity as a harmful phenomenon that violates trapped women's rights, and the dissemination of such statements on all levels of society is a step that should not be underestimated. These statements should explicitly condemn marital captivity, as well as discrimination against women, VAW and other harmful practices. Additionally, the recognition of marital captivity as a human rights issue should also be extended and included in national strategies and policies for implementing the ratified human rights treaties.

National authorities should also support and encourage institutions and professionals that are active in this area, or who encounter and/or assist trapped spouses. This includes ensuring that sufficient funding and resources are made available and allocated to such agencies, including NGOs and organisations of minority and migrant women so as to guarantee their participation in the efforts to redress marital captivity. Dialogue and consultation with relevant stakeholders, including NGOs, should be systematically maintained in the development and evaluation of measures for addressing marital captivity.

The collection of disaggregated data and conducting further studies on marital captivity, its causes, consequences, frequencies and interaction with other harmful practices and solutions is needed. In collecting disaggregated data on violence against women, those forms of marital captivity that constitute VAW should also be included so as to gain comprehensive insights on how these forms manifest and progress.

The existing legal and non-legal measures should also be monitored in respect of their impact and effectiveness for preventing and/or solving situations of marital captivity. This should include assessing measures that have been developed and adopted in religious communities as well as good practices and solutions that have been adopted in other legal systems. These should be assessed in light of their effectiveness and compatibility with human rights law. In the process of developing and designing measures, States should actively engage professionals, experts, civil society and social workers. Furthermore, actors within the communities, religious leaders and women's organisations should be encouraged and facilitated to participate in the development and design of measures and be enabled to report back on the progress and problems they encounter within the religious communities.

Additionally, States which only recognise marriage and divorce in accordance with personal laws should introduce the possibility for spouses to contract a civil marriage and request a civil divorce. Likewise, legal provisions that enable marital captivity to persist or which facilitate the continuation of a situation of marital captivity, provide husbands with the right to unilaterally end the marriage, restrict women's rights to seek divorce, restrict the trapped spouse's right to remarry or restrict the trapped women's ability to travel, should be examined and eliminated. This includes State recognised religious norms and practices which enable men to hold their wives hostage in a religious marriage and to control their participation in social life. Polygamy should also be prohibited so that recalcitrant spouses are not able to marry a second partner.

The generally little available information on the economic and health implications of marital captivity is of great concern. The economic consequences of a situation of marital captivity and the impact on the physical and mental wellbeing of the trapped spouses are aspects which deserve greater attention and are factors that should be given appropriate consideration and weight during civil divorce procedures. As certain case studies have revealed, the realisation of a religious divorce may come with excessive financial costs for the trapped spouses. Recalcitrant spouses have, at times, also imposed exorbitant demands or affected the division of matrimonial property by transferring property to foreign destinations or accounts.

8.5.2. PREVENTIVE MEASURES

Preventative measures greatly contribute to improving the identification and investigation of situations of marital captivity, the available (legal) solutions and the appropriate responses. The development of and dispersal of education and training material on the phenomenon of marital captivity and human rights law is an important step in this regard and has even been recommended by the CEDAW. These should be provided and made accessible to the judiciary, law enforcement officers, prosecutors, lawyers, experts, professionals, religious leaders, professionals and civil society. Subjects should not only include human rights education, but also the various forms of marital captivity, its causes and consequences and the (legal) measures that are available to assist in preventing and ending situations of marital captivity. Training programmes for the judiciary should foresee that judicial officials are not only familiar with the phenomenon of marital captivity, but also informed of the related human rights aspects so that they can better identify the violated human rights.

In particular, when dealing with informal marriages judges should be sensitised to the violated rights and, in reaching their conclusion, they should be trained to place the emphasis on the trapped spouse's wellbeing instead of attributing too much weight to the fact that a legal marriage has not been concluded. Furthermore, training and educational programmes should provide sufficient cover of the subject of gender-based violence and, more specifically, those situations of marital captivity that constitute VAW. Judicial training should ensure that instances of abuse, violence, coercion or extortion are considered when deciding on custody rights, marital property, maintenance and the divorce judgment itself.

Legal counsellors, who are directly involved in cases involving marital captivity, should be enabled and supported in receiving training on the existing domestic solutions, as well as on the solutions and good practices that have been adopted in other States. This benefits the trapped spouses, as legal counsellors are then in a better situation to assess and deal with transnational situations of marital captivity.

Religious authorities should also be included in the process of finding (legal) solutions to prevent and end situations of marital captivity. Thus, States should actively make efforts to establish cooperation with religious authorities. In this regard, States should create clear boundaries and assert their monopoly in addressing VAW so that that situations involving VAW are dealt with appropriately. Informational campaigns and training programmes should also be provided for religious authorities on the themes of VAW, gender equality and human rights standards and principles. Additionally, religious authorities should be obliged to report any incidents of VAW they encounter to State authorities.

Furthermore, State measures should include awareness-raising campaigns on marital captivity, the factors that contribute to the creation of situations of marital captivity, the different types of social and legal consequences of marital captivity and the available solutions and remedies. Campaigns should not only target trapped spouses, religious authorities and members of the religious communities, but also experts and professionals who have a direct role in addressing marital captivity.

Complementary awareness-raising campaigns and national action plans for eliminating gender-based discrimination, stereotypes and violence and ensuring gender equality are also needed. Addressing gender stereotypes, gender discrimination and harmful practices that occur in both the public and private sphere is necessary in order to eradicate marital captivity. In this regard, States should aim to empower trapped spouses, particularly trapped women, and to strengthen their autonomy by guaranteeing their access to the implemented legal and non-legal 'solutions', social services, essential material and financial resources. States should also provide legal assistance and information on other protective and preventive measures which spouses can invoke in order to prevent or end a situation of marital captivity. More generally, States should make every effort to stimulate the participation of women, in particular those from migrant and minority communities, in the solution finding process.

Furthermore, States should avoid framing the phenomenon of marital captivity as limited to certain minority, migrant and religious groups. For example, discussions on marital captivity have predominantly focused on marital captivity within Muslim and Jewish communities. Admittedly, these are the most familiar forms of marital captivity. Nevertheless, all information sources on marital captivity should avoid portraying this phenomenon as, exclusively or predominantly, a Muslim or Jewish issue or to reinforce stereotypes related to these religions. This implies ensuring that the portrayal of the trapped women does not reinforce gender, religious or ethnic stereotypes. Positive non-stereotypical representation of women in situations of marital captivity should be encouraged.

Additionally, a discourse of 'cultural negotiations'[1548] should be pursued which engages all members, including women as well as religious authorities. In this respect, States should foster ongoing dialogue within religious groups on harmful practices as well as on the ideologies, beliefs, stereotypes and views that result in or justify discrimination and mistreatment of women. A discourse of cultural negotiations should also aim to inform and educate non-cooperative spouses of the fact that creating a situation of marital captivity is not only unacceptable but is also incompatible with human rights law and violates fundamental human rights.

Finally, since cultural and social transformation is a slow and long process, States' compliance with their obligations requires promoting a high level of active engagement and commitment of all actors. It also requires adopting a comprehensive system, which includes both legislative as well as non-legislative measures, in order to identify, challenge and modify the existing power arrangements, gender stereotypes and prejudices.

8.5.3. PROTECTIVE MEASURES

Trapped spouses should be able to enforce their human rights and invoke remedial actions where their rights have been violated. States should, therefore, develop strategies to increase the awareness and accessibility, for intended spouses and trapped spouses, of the available remedies and services. Furthermore, States should also guarantee that trapped spouses can bring their cases before qualified and trained judges or other independent bodies. Trapped spouses should also receive qualified legal aid, so as to better assess all the available means to dissolve both the religious and the civil marriage. Moreover, for situations involving domestic violence, free legal aid should be made easily available and accessible for the victims.

States should also consider establishing a telephone hotline or other modes which enable trapped spouses to report a situation of marital captivity. This should be complemented by efforts to facilitate the cooperation and exchange of information between the different agencies and services so as to ensure that trapped spouses receive assistance in good time.

States should also monitor and ensure that any legal obligations requiring the cooperation of the recalcitrant spouse are enforced. In this respect, States should also provide appropriate and effective remedial actions where the spouses refuse to comply with their legal obligations to cooperate in the dissolution of a religious marriage.

Strong cooperation between all relevant stakeholders is necessary not only for protecting trapped spouses but also for the development of an effective and holistic

[1548] The notion of cultural negotiation is explained further in paragraph 7.6.1.1.3.

strategy to tackle marital captivity. Thus, cooperation between the judiciary, lawyers, social workers, health-care providers, law enforcement officers, legislators, civil society and religious authorities should be encouraged and fostered. This requires facilitating the exchange of information on instances of marital captivity and streamlining the services between different sectors and agencies so as to increase their complementarity and effectiveness. Where possible, support services should be combined on the same premises. Cooperation between all involved stakeholders should seek to go beyond ending specific instances of marital captivity and include strategies for bringing an end to marital captivity as a social phenomenon.

States should also develop a strategy for registering religious marriages and encourage spouses and religious authorities to register religious marriages. This does not imply that States should give such marriages legal recognition, where otherwise they do not recognise religious marriages. Moreover, in States that do give recognition to religious marriages, encouraging the registration of these marriages is equally recommended. The registration of informal marriages enables States not only to keep track of ongoing situations of marital captivity and the prevalence of the issue, but it also contributes to guaranteeing better protection for the trapped spouses.

For those cases which have a transnational element, the national authorities are encouraged to establish cooperation with the countries of origin of the trapped spouses as both the state of nationality and the host State have obligations to ensure the trapped spouse's freedom of movement.[1549] Cooperation should aim to facilitate the recognition of a divorce decision between States. States should also cooperate in order to avoid situations whereby an uncertain legal status is created and to consider giving special recognition to the peculiar situation of women in a situation of marital captivity. In this regard, States should consider exempting trapped women from the requirement of having to show the approval of their (ex-) husbands in order to travel. States should also refrain from sanctioning trapped women for allegedly having committed adultery, particularly where the concerned spouse is formally divorced within another legal system. Furthermore, research is needed on the human rights of spouses that are trapped abroad and what the States obligations, both under human rights law and international law, are to ensure their safe return to their country of residence.

[1549] See subsections 6.3.1.2. and 7.6.1.5.

BIBLIOGRAPHY

PRIMARY SOURCES

LEGAL DOCUMENTS

International documents

United Nations General Assembly, 24 January 2007, Convention on the Rights of Persons with Disabilities.
United Nations General Assembly, 17 July 1998, Rome Statute of the International Criminal Court (last amended 2010).
United Nations General Assembly, 20 December 1993, Declaration on the Elimination of Violence against Women.
United Nations General Assembly, 1985, Resolution on domestic violence
United Nations General Assembly, 25 November 1981, Declaration on the Elimination of All Forms of Intolerance and of Discrimination Based on Religion or Belief.
United Nations General Assembly, 18 December 1979, Convention on the Elimination of All Forms of Discrimination Against Women.
United Nations General Assembly, 23 May 1969, Vienna Convention on the Law of Treaties.
United Nations General Assembly, 16 December 1966, International Covenant on Civil and Political Rights.
United Nations General Assembly, 16 December 1966, International Covenant on Economic, Social and Cultural Rights.
United Nations General Assembly, 9 December 1948, Convention on the Prevention and Punishment of the Crime of Genocide.

Regional documents

African Union

African Union, 11 July 2003, Protocol to the African Charter on Human and People's Rights on the Rights of Women in Africa ("Maputo protocol").
Organization of African Unity, 27 June 1981, African Charter on Human and People's Rights.

Council of Europe

Council of Europe, 24 June 2013, Protocol No. 15 amending the Convention on the Protection of Human Rights and Fundamental Freedom.

Council of Europe, 11 May 2011, Convention on preventing and combating violence against women and domestic violence ("Istanbul Convention").
Council of Europe, 22 November 1984, Protocol No. 7 to the European Convention for the Protocol of Human Rights and Fundamental Freedoms.
Council of Europe, 4 November 1950, European Convention for the Protection of Human Rights and Fundamental Freedoms, as amended by Protocols Nos. 11 and 14.

European Union

European Union, 26 October 2012, Charter of Fundamental Rights of the European Union.

Organization of American States

Organization of American States, 09 June 1994, Inter-American Convention on the Prevention, Punishment and Eradication of Violence against Women ("Convention of Belém do Pará").
Organization of American States, 22 November 1969, American Convention on Human Rights ("Pact of San Jose").

GENERAL COMMENTS AND RECOMMENDATIONS

Human Rights Committee

UN Human Rights Committee, *General comment No. 31 [80] The nature of the general legal obligation imposed on States Parties to the Covenant*, 2004, CCPR/C/21/Rev.1/Add.13.
UN Human Rights Committee, *General Comment No. 28: Article 3 (The equality of rights between men and women)*, 2000, CCPR/C/21/Rev.1/Add.10.
UN Human Rights Committee, *General Comment No. 27: Freedom of movement (article 12)*, 1999.
UN Human Rights Committee, *General Comment No. 24: Issues relating to reservations made upon ratification or accession to the covenant or the Optional Protocols thereto, or in relation to declarations under article 41 of the covenant*, 1994, CCPR/C/21/Rev.1/Add.6.
UN Human Rights Committee, *General Comment No. 22: Article 18 (Freedom of thought, conscience or religion)*, 1993, CCPR/C/21/Rev.1/Add.4.
UN Human Rights Committee, *General Comment No. 19: Article 23 (The Family) Protection of the Family, the Right to Marriage and Equality of the Spouses*, 1990.
UN Human Rights Committee, *General Comment No. 16*, 1988.
UN Human Rights Committee, *General Comment No. 15: The Position of Aliens Under the Covenant*, 1986.

Committee on Economic, Social and Cultural Rights

UN Committee on Economic, Social and Cultural Rights, *General Comment No. 14 (2000) – The right to the highest attainable standard of health (article 12)*, 2000, E/C.12/2000/4.
UN Committee on Economic, Social and Cultural Rights, *General Comment No. 3: The Nature of States Parties' Obligations (Art. 2, Para. 1, of the Covenant)*, 1990, E/1991/23.

Committee on the Elimination of Discrimination Against Women

UN Committee on the Elimination of Discrimination Against Women, *General Recommendation No. 35 on gender-based violence against women, updating general recommendation No. 19*, 2017, nr. CEDAW/ C/GC/35.

UN Committee on the Elimination of Discrimination Against Women & UN Committee on the Rights of the Child, *Joint General Comment No. 31 of the Committee on the Elimination of Discrimination Against Women/ General comment No. 18 of the Committee on the Rights of the Child on harmful practices*,2014, CEDAW/C/GC/31-CRC/C/GC/18.

UN Committee on the Elimination of Discrimination Against Women, *General Recommendation on article 16 of the Convention on the Elimination of All Forms of Discrimination against Women (Economic consequences of marriage, family relations and their dissolution)*, 2013, CEDAW/C/GC/29.

UN Committee on the Elimination of Discrimination Against Women, *General Recommendation No. 28 on the core obligations of States parties under Article 2 of the Convention on the Elimination of All Forms of Discrimination against Women*, 2010.

UN Committee on the Elimination of Discrimination Against Women, *General Recommendation No. 24 on Article 12 of the Convention (Women and Health)*, 1999.

UN Committee on the Elimination of Discrimination Against Women, *General Recommendation No. 21 on Equality in marriage and family relations*, 1994, HRI/GEN/1/Rev.6.

UN Committee on the Elimination of Discrimination Against Women, *General Recommendation No. 19 on Violence against women*, 1992.

UN Committee on the Elimination of Discrimination Against Women, *General Recommendation No. 12 on Violence against women*, 1989.

Committee Against Torture

UN Committee Against Torture, *General Comment No. 2: Implementation of Article 2 by States Parties*, 2008, CAT/C/GC/2.

DECISIONS BY HUMAN RIGHTS MONITORING BODIES

Human Rights Committee

Human Rights Committee, *Nasyrlayev v. Turkmenistan*, 15 July 2016, (Communication No. 2219/2012).

Human Rights Committee, *Nurjanov v. Turkmenistan*, 15 July 2016, (Communication No. 2225/2012).

Human Rights Committee, *Uchetov v. Turkmenistan*, 15 July 2016, (Communication No. 2226/2012).

Human Rights Committee, *Yegendurdyyew v. Turkmenistan*, 14 July 2016, (Communication No. 2227/2012).

Human Rights Committee, *Mahmud Hudaybergenov v. Turkmenistan*, 22 December 2015, (Communication No. 2221/2012).

Human Rights Committee, *Japparow v. Turkmenistan*, 17 December 2015, (Communication No. 2223/2012).
Human Rights Committee, *Abdullayev v. Turkmenistan*, 19 May 2015, (Communication No. 2218/2012).
Human Rights Committee *Min-Kyu Jeong et al. v. the Republic of Korea*, 27 April 2011, (Communications No. 1642–1741/2007).
Human Rights Committee, *Rhaiman v. Latvia*, 30 October 2010, (Communication No. 1621/2007).
Human Rights Committee, *Prince v. South Africa*, 31 October 2007, (Communication No. 1474/2006).
Human Rights Committee, *Leonid Komarovski v. Turkmenistan*, 05 August 2008, (Communication No. 1450/2006).
Human Rights Committee *Yeo-Bum Yoon and Myung-Jin Choi v. Republic of Korea*, 23 January 2007, (Communications Nos. 1321/2004 and 1322/2004).
UN Human Rights Committee *Clement Boodoo v. Trinidad and Tobago*, 15 April 2002, (Communication No. 721/1996).
Human Rights Committee, *Malcolm Ross v. Canada*, 26 October 2000, (Communication No. 736/1997).
Human Rights Committee, *Salah Karker v. France*, 26 October 2000, (Communication No. 833/1998).
Human Rights Committee *Paul Westerman v. the Netherlands*, 13 December 1999, (Communication No. 682/1996).
Human Rights Committee, *Hopu and Bessert v. France*, 29 July 1997, (Communication No. 549/1993).
Human Rights Committee, *Stewart v. Canada*, 01 November 1996, (Communication No. 538/1993).
Human Rights Committee, *Coeriel and Aurik v. the Netherlands*, 31 October 1994, (Communication No. 453/1991).
Human Rights Committee, *Peltonen v. Finland*, 26 July 1994, (Communication No. 492/1992).
Human Rights Committee, *M.A.B., W.A.T. and J.-A.Y.T. v. Canada*, 8 April 1994 (Communication No. 570/1993).
Human Rights Committee, *Miguel Gonzalez del Rio v. Peru*, 28 October 1992, (Communication No. 263/1987).
Human Rights Committee, *J.v.K. and C.M.G.v.K.-S. v. the Netherlands*, 31 July 1992, (Communication No. 483/1991).
Human Rights Committee, *J.P. v. Canada*, 7 November 1991, (Communication No. 446/1991*/).
Human Rights Court, *Karnel Singh Bhinder v. Canada*, 25 October 1988, (Communication Nos. 208/1986).
Human Rights Committee, *Samuel Lichtensztejn v. Uruguay*, 31 March 1983, (Communication No. 77/1980).
Human rights committee, *Gordon C. Van Duzen v. Canada*, 07 April 1982, (Communication No. 50/1979).
Human Rights Committee, *Sophie Vidal Martins v. Uruguay*, 23 March 1982, (Communication No. R.13/57).
Human Rights Committee, *Sandra Lovelace v. Canada*, 29 December 1977, (Communication No. R.6/24).

Committee on the Elimination of Discrimination Against Women

Committee on the Elimination of Discrimination Against Women, *Isatou Jallow v. Bulgaria*, 23 July 2012, (Communication No. 32/2011).
Committee on the Elimination of Discrimination Against Women, *Karen Tayag Vertido v. the Philippines*, 16 July 2010, (Communication No. 18/2008).
Committee on the Elimination of Discrimination Against Women, *Fatma Yildirim v. Austria*, 1 October 2007, (Communication No. 6/2005).
Committee on the Elimination of Discrimination Against Women, *Goekce v. Austria*, (Communication No. 5/2005).
Committee on the Elimination of Discrimination Against Women, *A.T. v. Hungary*, 26 January 2005, (Communication No. 2/2003).

European Court of Human Rights & European Commission of Human Rights

European Court of Human Rights, *Babiarz v. Poland*, 10 January 2017, (Application No. 1955/10).
European Court of Human Rights, *Magyar Helsinki Bizottság v. Hungary*, 08 November 2016, (Application No. 18030/11).
European Court of Human Rights, *Fernández Martínez v. Spain*, 12 June 2016, (Application No. 56030/07).
European Court of Human Rights, *Jehovah's witnesses of Moscow and Others v. Russia*, 10 June 2016, (Application No. 302/02).
European Court of Human Rights, *L.E. v. Greece*, 21 January 2016, (Application No. 71545/12).
European Court of Human Rights, *Piotrowski v. Poland*, ECHR, 22 November 2016, (Application No. 8923/12).
European Court of Human Rights, *S.A.S. v. France*, 1 July 2014 (Application No. 43835/11).
European Court of Human Rights, *Khlyustov v. Russia*, 11 July 2013, (Application No. 28975/05).
European Court of Human Rights, *Eweida and Others v. the United Kingdom* 15 January 2013, (Application Nos. 48420/10, 36516/10, 51671/10, 59842/10).
European Court of Human Rights, *Staatkundig Gereformeerde Partij v. the Netherlands*, 10 July 2012, (Application No. 58369/10).
European Court of Human Rights, *Miazdzyk v. Poland*, 24 January 2012, (Application No. 23592/07).
European Court of Human Rights, *Ivanov and Petrova v. Bulgaria*, 14 June 2011, (Application No. 15001/04).
European Court of Human Rights, *Byatyan v. Armenia*, 27 July 2011, (Application No. 23459/03).
European Court of Human Rights, *Savez Crkava "Riječ života" and Others v. Croatia*, 09 December 2010, (Application No. 7798/08).
European Court of Human Rights, *Sinan Işık v. Turkey*, 2 February 2010, (Application No. 21924/05).
European Court of Human Rights, *Skugar and Others v. Russia*, 3 December 2009, (Application No. 40010/04).
European Court of Human Rights, *Opuz v. Turkey*, 9 June 2009, (Application No. 33401/01).
European Court of Human Rights, *Friend, Countryside Alliance and Others v. the United Kingdom*, 24 November 2009, (Application Nos. 16072/06, 27809/08).
European Court of Human Rights, *Kalacheva v. Russia*, 07 May 2009, (Application No. 3451/05).

European Court of Human Rights, *Demir and Baykara v. Turkey*, 12 November 2008, (Application No. 34503/97).
European Court of Human Rights, *Klaus Blumberg v. Germany*, 18 March 2008, (Application No. 14618/03).
European Court of Human Rights, *Pfeifer v. Austria*, 15 November 2007, (Application No. 12556/03).
European Court of Human Rights, *Ivanova v. Bulgaria*, 12 July 2007, (Application No. 52435/99).
European Court of Human Rights, *Evans v. the United Kingdom*, 10 April 2007, (Application No. 6339/05).
European Court of Human Rights, *Kosteski v. the former Yugoslav Republic*, 13 April 2006, (Application No. 55170/00).
European Court of Human Rights, *Sorensen and Rasmussen v. Denmark*, 11 January 2006, (Application Nos. 52562/99, 52620/99).
European Court of Human Rights, *K.A. et A.D. v. Belgium*, 06 July 2005, (Application Nos. 42758/98 and 45558/99).
European Court of Human Rights, *Antonenkov and Others v. Ukraine*, 22 November 2005, (Application No. 14183/02).
European Court of Human Rights, *M.C. v. Bulgaria*, 4 December 2003, (Application No. 3927/98).
European Court of Human Rights, *Odievre v. France*, 13 February 2003, (Application No. 42326/98).
European Court of Human Rights, *Luordo v. Italy*, 17 July 2003, (Application No. 32190/96).
European Court of Human Rights, *Pretty v. the United Kingdom*, 29 July 2002 (Application No. 2346/02).
European Court of Human Rights, *E. and Others v. the United Kingdom*, 26 November 2002, (Application No. 33218/96).
European Court of Human Rights, *Al-Adsani v. The United Kingdom*, 21 November 2001, (Application No. 35763/97).
European Court of Human Rights, *Refah Partisi (The Welfare Party) and Others v. Turkey*, 31 July 2001, (Application Nos. 41340/98, 41342/98, 41343/98).
European Court of Human Rights, *Z and Others v. the United Kingdom*, 10 May 2001, (Application No. 29392/95).
European Court of Human Rights, *Metropolitan Church of Bessarabia and Others v. Moldova*, 13 December 2001, (No. 45701/99).
European Court of Human Rights, *Pellegrini v. Italy*, 20 July 2001, (Application No. 30882/96).
European Court of Human Rights, *Hasan and Chaush v. Bulgaria*, 26 October 2000, (Application No. 30985/96).
European Court of Human Rights, *Chassagnou and Others v. France*, 29 April 1999, (Application Nos. 25088/94, 28331/95, 28443/95).
European Court of Human Rights, *Osman v. the United Kingdom*, 28 October 1998, (Application No. 87/1997/871/1083).
European Court of Human Rights, *Larissis and Others v. Greece*, 24 February 1998, (Application Nos. 23372/94, 26377/94, 26378/94).
European Court of Human Rights, *Botta v. Italy*, 24 February 1998, (Application No. 21439/93).
European Commission of Human Rights, *Botta v. Italy*, 15 January 1996, (Application No. 21439/93).

European Court of Human Rights, *Sigurdur A. Sigurjónsson v. Iceland*, 30 June 1993, (Application No. 16130/90).

European Court of Human Rights, *Kokkinakis v. Greece*, 25 May 1993, (Application No. 14307/88).

European Court of Human Rights, *Niemietz v. Germany*, 16 December 1992, (Application No. 13710/88).

European Commission of Human Rights, *Wakefield v. the United Kingdom of Great Britain and Nothern Ireland*, 1 October 1990, (Application No. 15817/89).

European Commission of Human Rights, *Paul Revert and Denis Legallais v. France*, 8 September 1989, (Application Nos. 14331/88, 14332/88).

European Court of Human Rights, *F. v. Switzerland*, ECHR 18 December 1987, (Application No. 11329/85).

European Court of Human Rights, *Johnston and Others v. Ireland*, 18 December 1986, (Application No.9697/82).

European Court of Human Rights, *Khan v. the United Kingdom*, 17 July 1986, (Application No. 1579/85).

European Commission of Human Rights, *Knudsen v. Norway*, 8 March 1985, (Application No. 11045/84).

European Commission of Human Rights, *R. Johnston and others against Ireland*, 5 March 1985, (Application No. 9697/82).

European Commission of Human Rights, *C. v. the United Kingdom*, 15 December 1983, (Application No. 10358/83).

European Commission of Human Rights, *D. v. France*, 6 December 1983, (Application No. 10180/82).

Human Rights Committee, *Mabel Pereira Montero v. Uruguay*, 31 March 1983, (Communication No. 106/1981).

European Court of Human Rights, *Campbell and Cosans v. the United Kingdom*, 25 February 1982, (Application No. 7511/76; 7743/76).

European Commission of Human Rights, *X. v. the Federal Republic of Germany*, 10 March 1981, (Application No. 8741/79).

European Commission of Human Rights, *X. and Church of Scientology v. Sweden*, 5 May 1979, (Application No. 7805/77).

European Court of Human Rights, *Airey v. Ireland*, 9 October 1979, (Application No. 6289/73).

European Commission of Human Rights, *X. v. the United Kingdom*, 12 July 1978, (Application No. 7992/77).

European Commission of Human Rights, *Bruggman and Scheuten v. the Federal Republic of Germany*, 17 July 1977, (Application No. 6959/75).

European Commission of Human Rights, *Arrowsmith v. the United Kingdom*, 16 May 1977, (Application No. 7050/75).

European Commission of Human Rights, *X. v. Iceland*, 18 May 1976, (Application No. 6825/74).

European Court of Human Rights, *Engel and Others v. The Netherlands*, 8 June 1976, (Application Nos. 5100/71; 5101/71; 5102/71; 5354/72; 5370/72).

European Court of Human Rights, X. V. Federal Republic of Germany, 18 December 1974, (Application No. 6167/73).

European Commission of Human Rights, *European Commission of Human Rights, Austria v. Italy*, 11 January 1961, (Application No. 788/60).

Inter-American Court of Human Rights

Inter-American Court of Human Rights, *Miguel Castro- Castro Prison v. Peru*, 25 November 2006, (Series C No. 160).
Inter-American Court of Human Rights, *Mayagna (Sumo) Awas Tingni Community v. Nicaragua*, 31 August 2001, (Series C No. 79).
Inter-American Court of Human Rights, *Velasquez Rodriguez v. Honduras*, 29 July 1988, (Series C No. 4).

Other

International Criminal Tribunal for Rwanda, *Prosecutor v. Jean-Paul Akayesu*, 2 September 1998, (ICTR-96–4-T).

CONCLUDING OBSERVATIONS

Human Rights Comittee

Human Rights Committee, *Concluding Observations Kyrgyzstan 2014*, CCPR/C/C/KGZ/2.
Human Rights Committee, *Concluding Observations Philippines 2012*, CCPR/C/PHL/CO/4.
Human Rights Committee, *Concluding Observations on Mali 2003*, CCPR/CO/77/MLI.
Human Rights Committee, *Concluding Observations Ukraine 2001*, CCPR/CO/73/UKR.
Human Rights Committee, *Concluding Observations Morocco 2000*, A/55/40 vol. I (2000) 24.
Human Rights Committee, *Concluding Observations Chile 1999*, CCPR/C/79/Add.104.
Human Rights Committee, *Concluding Observations Libyan Arab Jamahiriya 1999*, A/54/40 vol. I (1999) 32.
Human Rights Committee, *Concluding Observations Mexico 1999*, CCPR/C/79/Add.109.
Human Rights Committee, *Concluding Observations Israel 1998*, A/53/40 vol. I (1998) 45.
Human Rights Committee, *Concluding Observations Japan 1998*, CCPR/C/79/Add.102.
Human Rights Committee, *Concluding Observations United Republic of Tanzania 1998*, A/53/40 vol. I (1998) 57.
Human Rights Committee, *Concluding Observations India 1997*, A/52/40 vol. I (1997) 67.
Human Rights Committee, *Concluding Observations Lebanon 1997*, CCPR/C/79/Add.78.
Human Rights Committee, *Concluding Observations Sudan 1997*, CCPR/C/79/Add.85.
Human Rights Committee, *Concluding Observations Gabon 1996*, CCPR/C/79/Add. 71.
Human Rights Committee, *Concluding Observations Sudan 1995*, CCPR, A/53/40 vol. I.
Human Rights Committee, *Concluding Observations Ukraine 1995*, A/50/40.
Human Rights Committee, *Concluding Observations Ireland 1993*, A/48/40 vol. I (1993) 119.

Committee on Economic, Social and Cultural Rights

Committee on Economic, Social and Cultural Rights, *Concluding Observations Israel 2003*, E/C.12/1/Add.90.
Committee on Economic, Social and Cultural Rights, *Concluding Observations Philippines 1995*, E/C.12/1995/7.

Committee on the Elimination of Discrimination Against Women

Committee on the Elimination of Discrimination Against Women, *Concluding Observations the Netherlands 2016*, CEDAW/C/NLD/CO/6.
Committee on the Elimination of Discrimination Against Women, *Concluding Observations Pakistan 2013*, CEDAW/C/Pak/CO/4.
Committee on the Elimination of Discrimination Against Women, *Concluding Observations Israel 2011*, CEDAW/C/ISR/CO/5.
Committee on the Elimination of Discrimination Against Women, *Concluding Observations Turkey, 2010*, CEDAW/C/TUR/CO/6.
Committee on the Elimination of Discrimination Against Women, *Concluding Observations Madagascar 2008*, CEDAW/C/MDG/CO/5.
Committee on the Elimination of Discrimination Against Women, *Concluding Observations Kazakhstan 2007*, CEDAW/C/KAZ/CO/2.
Committee on the Elimination of Discrimination Against Women, *Concluding Observations Togo 2006*, CEDAW/C/TGO/CO/5.
Committee on the Elimination of Discrimination Against Women, *Concluding Observations Japan 2003*, A/58/3 (Supp No.38).
Committee on the Elimination of Discrimination Against Women, *Concluding observations Zambia 2002*, A/57/38 part II.
Committee on the Elimination of Discrimination Against Women, Concluding *Observations Algeria 1999*, A/54/38/Rev.1 part I (1999) 12.
Committee on the Elimination of Discrimination Against Women, *Concluding Observations Chile 1999*, A/54/38/Rev.1 part II (1999) 64.
Committee on the Elimination of Discrimination Against Women, *Concluding Observations Czech Republic 1998*, A/53/38/Rev.1 part I (1998) 16.
Committee on the Elimination of Discrimination Against Women, *Concluding Observations Indonesia 1998*, A/53/38/Rev.1 part I (1998) 24.
Committee on the Elimination of Discrimination Against Women, *Concluding Observations Luxembourg 1997*, A/52/38/Rev.1 part II.
Committee on the Elimination of Discrimination Against Women, *Concluding Observations Chile 1995*, A/50/38 (1995) 35.

Committee Against Torture

Committee Against Torture, *Concluding Observations on Ecuador 2006*, CAT/C/ECU/CO/3.
Committee Against Torture, *Concluding Observations on Bahrain 2005*, CAT/C/CR/34/ BHR.
Committee Against Torture, *Concluding Observations on Nepal 2005*, CAT/C/NPL/CO/2.
Committee Against Torture, *Concluding Observations on Argentina 2004*, CAT/C/CR/33/1.
Committee Against Torture, *Concluding Observations on Cameroon 2004*, CAT/C/CR/31/6.
Committee Against Torture, Concluding Observations on Greece 2004, CAT/C/CR/33/2.

SOFT-LAW DOCUMENTS

Concluding Document of the Vienna Meeting 1986 of Representatives of the participating States of the Conference on Security and Co-operation in Europe, held on the basis of the provisions of the final act relating to the follow-up to the conference, 19 January 1989.

Constitution of the World Health Organization as amended at the forty-fifth World Health Assembly, October 2006.

Commission on the Status of Women, *International instruments relating to the status of women. Draft Convention on the elimination of Discrimination Against Women-Working Paper Prepared by the Secretary-General-Corrigendum* (United Nations 1976).

Draft IAC working document prepared by the Secretariat of the Inter-American Commission on Human Rights, in: T. Buergenthal & R. E. Norris (red.), *Human Rights: the Inter-American System* (Dobbs Ferry: Oceana Publications 1982).

International Law Commission, *Draft articles on Responsibility of States for Internationally Wrongful Acts, with commentaries,* 2001.

Principles and Guidelines on the implementation of economic, social and cultural rights in the African Charter on Human and People's Rights, 2010.

Recommendation Rec (2002) 5 of the Committee of Ministers to member states on the protection of women against violence, 30 April 2002.

United Nations, *Beijing Platform of Action, adopted at the Fourth World Conference on Women,* 15 September 1995.

United Nations, *Draft articles on diplomatic protection,* 2006.

United Nations General Assembly, *Universal Declaration of Human Rights,* 10 December 1948.

PREPARATORY WORKS

Bossuyt 1987
Marc J. Bossuyt, 'Guide to the "Travaux Préparatiores" of the International Covenant on Civil and Political Rights', (Dordrecht: Martinus Nijhoff Publishers 1987).

Council of Europe 1985
Council of Europe, 'Collected edition of the "Travaux Préparatoires" of the European Convention on Human Rights', (The Hague: Martinus Nijhoff Publishers 1985).

European Commission of Human Rights 1956
European Commission of Human Rights, 'Preparatory work on article 9 of the European Convention on Human Rights', (1956), [DH(56)] 14, *at* <https://www.echr.coe.int/Documents/Library_TravPrep_Table_ENG.pdf> last accessed 12 October 2018.

European Commission of Human Rights 1956
European Commission of Human Rights, 'Preparatory work on article 11 of the European Convention on Human Rights' (1956), [DH (56) 16 *at* < https://www.echr.coe.int/LibraryDocs/Travaux/ECHRTravaux-ART11-DH(56)16-EN1693924.PDF > last accessed 12 October 2019.

Rehof 1993
Lars Adam Rehof, 'Guide to the travaux préparatoires of the United Nations Convention on the Elimination of All Forms of Discrimination Against Women', (Dordrecht: Martinus Nijhoff Publishers 1993).

Schabas 2013
William A. Schabas (red.), 'The Universal Declaration of Human Rights: The Travaux Préparatoires', (Cambridge: Cambridge University Press 2013).

NATIONAL CASE LAW

Canada

Supreme Court of Canada, *Bruker v. Marcovitz,* 14 December 2007, (3 S.C.R. 607, 2007 SCC 54).

France

Cour de Cassation, Chambre civile 1, 17 January 2006, [03–19.879].
Cour de Cassation, Chambre civile 2, 13 March 2003, [01–14.616].
Cour de Cassation, Chambre civile 2, 24 October 2002, [01–12.431].
Cour de Cassation, Chambre civile 2, 20 January 2000, [97–14.750].
Cour de Cassation, Chambre civile 2, 21 November 1990, [89–17659].
Cour de Cassation, Chambre civile 2, 21 May 1990, [89–12.512].
Cour de Cassation, Chambre civile 2, 15 June 1988, [86–15.476].
Cour de Cassation, Chambre civile 2, 21 April 1982, [81–11.775].
Cour de Cassation, Chambre civile 2, 13 December 1972, [71–12.043].
Cour d'Appel de Versailles, 16 February 2012, [10/04809].
Cour d'Appel de Paris, 16 March 2011, [10/01413].
Cour d'Appel de Reims, 27 June 2002, [**2001/00587**].

South Africa

High Court of South Africa, *Singh v. Ramparsad* ((KZN564/2002) ZAKZHC 1).

The Netherlands

Hoge Raad, 29 April 2016, ECLI:NL:HR:2016:767.
Hoge Raad, 09 April 2010, ECLI:NL:HR:2010:BK4549.
Hoge Raad, Conclusion of the attorney general, 09 December 2005, ECLI:NL:PHR:2005:AU5285.
Hoge Raad, Conclusion of the attorney general, 27 June 2003, ECLI:NL:PHR:2003AF7681.
Hoge Raad, 12 July 2002, ECLI:NL:HR:2002:AE4037.
Hoge Raad, 10 November 1989, ECLI:NL:HR:1989:AC1683.
Hoge Raad, Conclusion of the high general, 10 November 1989, ECLI:NL:PHR:1989:AC1683.
Hoge Raad, 22 January 1982, ECLI: NL:HR:1982:AG4319.

Gerechtshof Den Haag, 21 November 2017, ECLI:NL:GHDHA:2017:3297.
Gerechtshof Leeuwarden, 23 September 2008, LIJN: BF4943.
Gerechtshof 's-Gravenhage, 20 December 2007, LIJN: BC0619.
Gerechtshof Amsterdam, 31 August 1989, ECLI:NL:GHAMS:1989:AD0874.
Raad van State, 05 December 2007, LJN: BB9493.
Rechtbank Amsterdam, 04 December 2017, ECLI:NL:RBAMS:2017:8910.
Rechtbank Rotterdam, 09 September 2016, ELCI:NL:RBROT:2016:6943.
Rechtbank Oost-Brabant, 03 August 2016, ECLI:NL:RBOBR:2016:4140.
Rechtbank Rotterdam, 04 February 2016, ECLI:NL:RBROT:2016:898.
Rechtbank Rotterdam, 06 January 2016, ECLI:NL:RBROT:2016:8.
Rechtbank Den Haag, 21 October 2014, ECLI:NL:RBDHA:2014:14191.
Rechtbank Amsterdam, 2 April 2014, ECLI:NL:RBAMS:2014:1644.
Rechtbank Overijssel, 24 December 2013, ECLI:NL:RBOVE:013: 4269.
Rechtbank Amsterdam, 10 April 2012, ECLI:NLRBAMS:2012:BW2800.
Rechtbank Rotterdam, 8 December 2010, ECLI:NL:RBROT:2010:BP8396.
Rechtbank Groningen, 11 October 2010, ECLI:NL:RBGRO:2010:BO0132.
Rechtbank Haarlem, 17 February 1989, ECLI:NL:RBHAA:1989:AH2605.
Rechtbank Amsterdam, 17 November 1983, ECLI:NL:RBAMS:1983:AH0155.

United Kingdom

High Court Justice, *AI v. MT*, 30 January 2013, ([2013] EWHC 100 (Fam)).
High Court of Justice (Family Division), *Sulaiman v. Juffali*, 09 November 2001, ([2001] EWHC556 (Fam)).
Court of Appeal of the United Kingdom, *Brett v. Brett*, 5 December 1968, ([1969] 1 All ER 1007).

GOVERNMENT DOCUMENTS

The Netherlands

Antwoorden kamervragen inzake shariarechtbanken, 02 July 2009.
Antwoorden op de Kamervragen van het lid Bergman (D66) over huwelijksdwang en huwelijkse gevangenschap, 26 September 2016.
Besluit van14 mei 2013 tot vaststelling van het tijdstip van inwerkingtreding van de wet van 7 maart 2013 tot wijziging van het Wetboek van Strafrecht, het Wetboek van Strafvordering en het Wetboek van Strafrecht BES met het oog op de verruiming van de mogelijkheden tot strafrechtelijke aanpak van huwelijksdwang, polygamie en vrouwelijke genitale verminking, 2013, Stb. 2013, 187.
Brief Motie Kooiman, 10 July 2013.
Brief Tweede Kamer: Schriftelijk overleg over shariarechtbanken, 1 Septmeber 2009.
Brief van de Minister van Sociale Zaken en Werkgelegenheid, Kamerstukken II, 2015/2016, 32 175, nr. 60, 2016.
Brief van de Minister van Sociale Zaken en Werkgelegenheid, Kamerstukken II, 2014/2015, 32 175, nr. 54, 2015.

Brief van de Minister van Sociale Zaken en Werkgelegenheid, Kamerstukken II, 2014/2015, 32 175, nr. 53, 2014.

Huwelijks- en gezinsmigratie; Brief regering; Reactie op de brief van de organisatie Femmes for Freedom inzake huwelijkse gevangenschap, Kamerstukken II, 2011/2012, 32 175, nr. 31, 2012.

Huwelijkse gevangenschap, Kamerstukken II 2018/2019 nr. 79 9, 2019.

Memorie van Toelichting – Wet van xxxx tot wijziging van met name het Wetboek van Burgerlijke Rechtsvordering en het Burgerlijk Wetboek (tegengaan huwelijkse gevangenschap), 2018 *at* <https://www.internetconsultatie.nl/huwelijksegevangenschaptegengaan> last accessed 23 January 2019.

Memorie van toelichting – Wijziging van het Wetboek van Strafrecht, het Wetboek van Strafvordering en het Wetboek van Strafrecht BES met het oog op de verruiming van de mogelijkheden tot strafrechtelijke aanpak van huwelijksdwang, polygamie en vrouwelijke genitale verminking, Tweede Kamer der Staten-Generaal 2011.

Motie van de Leden van Nispen en Karbulut, Kamerstukken II, 2016/2017, 33 836, nr. 11, 2016.

Motie van het lid Yücel c.s. over voorkomen dat een vrouw gevangen blijft in een religieus huwelijk, Kamerstukken II, 2015/2016 33 836, nr. 9, 2016.

Response of the Kingdom of the Netherlands to the List of issues (CEDAW/C/NLD/Q/6) in relation to the sixth periodic report submitted by the Netherlands under Article 18 of the Convention on the Elimination of All Forms of Discrimination against Women, June 2016.

Voorkomen geweld tegen vrouwen, Kamerstukken II, 2014/2015, nr. 91, 2015.

Vragen gesteld door de leden der Kamer, met de daarop door de regering gegeven antwoorden, Kamerstukken II, 2016/ 2017, 1785, 2017.

Vragen gesteld door de leden der Kamer, met de daarop door de regering gegeven antwoorden, Kamerstukken II, 2011/2012, 3114, aanhangsel, 2012.

Wet van xxxx tot wijziging van met name het Wetboek van Burgerlijke Rechtsvordering en het Burgerlijk Wetboek (tegengaan huwelijkse gevangenschap), 2018, WGK009515.

United Kingdom

House of Commons debate on the Divorce (Religious Marriages) Bill, Hansard Debates text for Friday 12 Apr 2002, Vol. 383, *at* <www.publications.parliament.uk/pa/cm200102/cmhansrd/vo020412/debtext/20412-02.htm#20412-02_spnew0> last accessed 23 September 2016.

House of Lords debate on the Divorce (Religious Marriages) Bill, Lords sitting of 10 June 2002, *at* < http://hansard.millbanksystems.com/lords/2002/may/10/divorce-religious-marriages-bill > last accessed 23 September 2016.

House of Lords debate on the Divorce (Religious Marriages), Lord siting of 30 June 2000, vol. 614, *at* < http://hansard.millbanksystems.com/lords/2000/jun/30/divorce-religious-marriages-bill-hl l > last accessed 23 September 2016.

RELIGIOUS DOCUMENTS

Christianity

Catechism of the Catholic Church 2003
Catechism of the Catholic Church, Vatican City: Libreria Editrice Vaticana 2003.

Code Canon
Code of Canon Law, Libreria Editrice Vaticana.
Dienstboek II 2004

Dienstboek II (2004), *digitale edition at* < https://www.preekwijzer.nl/liturgie/dienstboek-ii-pdf/7992> last accessed 03 April 2018.

Francis 2015
Pope Francis, *Apostolic Letter Motu Proprio of the supreme pontiff Francis, Mitis iudex Dominus Iesus* Libreria Editrice Vaticana 2015.

Kerkorde van de Protestantse Kerk in Nederland 2013
Kerkorde en ordinanties van de Protestantse Kerk in Nederland inclusief de overgangsbepalingen, (Zoetemeer: Uitgevery Boekencentrum 2013).

Kerkorde van de Christelijke Gereformeerde Kerken 2011
Kerkorde van de Christelijke Gereformeerde Kerken in Nederland – het laatst gewijzigd en aangevuld door de de generale synode van Huizen/Nunspeet (2010), (Amsterdam: Buijten & Schipperheijn Motief 2011).

Paul II 2011
Pope John Paul II, *Apostolic Constitution Fidei Depositum on the publication of the Catechism of the Catholic Church prepared following the Second Vatican Ecumenical Council,* 1992.

The Holy Bible 2011
The Holy Bible, New International Version, (Biblica Inc. 2011).

Hinduism

Bühler 1969
Georg Bühler, *The laws of Manu,* (Library of Alexandria 1969).

de Sola & Raphall 1843
David A. de Sola & Morris J. Raphall, *Eighteen Treatises from the Mishna,*(London: Sherwood, Gilbert and Piper, 1843) *at* < https://onlinebooks.library.upenn.edu/authors.html> (Search on: D.A. de Sola) last accessed 03 April 2018.

Islam

The Qur'an
The Qur'an (English translation by Sahih International) *at* < https://quran.com/> last accessed 03 April 2018.

Judaism

Reglement betreffende de inrichting en het bestuur van het Nederland-Israeliëtisch kerkgenootschap
Reglement betreffende de inrichting en het bestuur van het Nederland-Israeliëtisch kerkgenootschap at < www.nik.nl/wp-content/uploads/2015/12/VERORD-159–2016.pdf> last accessed 01 June 2018.

The Complete Tanakh
The Complete Tanakh -With Rashi commentary (Online English translation by Rabbi A.J. Rosenberg), *at* <www.chabad.org/library/bible_cdo/aid/63255/jewish/The-Bible-with-Rashi.htm> last accessed 27 December 2015.

Touger
Eliyahu Touger, *The Rambam's Mishneh Torah* (English translation by Eliyahu Touger) *at* <https://www.chabad.org/library/article_cdo/aid/682956/jewish/Mishneh-Torah.htm> last accessed 01 June 2018.
Secondary sources

Books and journals

Abbink 2000
G. J. Abbink, 'Preface: Violation and violence as cultural phenomena', in: G. Aijmer & G. J. Abbink (1red.), Meanings of violence: a cross-cultural perspective, (Oxford, New York: Berg 2000).

Adams 1986
Jay E. Adams, 'Marriage, divorce, and remarriage in the Bible', (Michigan: Zondervan 1986).

Akandji-Kombe 2007
Jean-François Akandji-Kombe, 'Positive obligations under the European Convention on Human Rights – A guide to the implementation of the European Convention on Human Rights', (Strasbourg: Council of Europe 2007).

Akita 2010
Edward M. Akita, *Hegemony, patriarchy and Human rights: The representation of Ghanaian women in politics* (Diss. University of Ohio 2010).

de Silva de Alwis & Klugman 2015
Rangita de Silva de Alwis & Jeni Klugman, 'Freedom from violence and the law: A global perspective in light of the Chinese Domestic Violence Law', *University of Pennsylvania Journal of International Law* (37) 2015-1, pp. 1–52.

Amato & Shelly 2013
Paul R. Amato & Irvin Shelly, 'Historical trends in divorce in the United States', in: M. A. Fine & J. H. Harvey (red.), *Handbook of Historical trends in divorce in the United States,* (New York, Oxon: Routledge, Taylor & Francis Group 2013), pp. 41–58.

Amerasinghe 2008
Chittharanjan F. Amerasinghe, 'Diplomatic Protection', (Oxford: Oxford University Press 2008).

Bagaric & Allan
Mirko Bagaric & James Allan, 'The Vacuous Concept of Dignity', *Journal of Human Rights* (5) 2006-2 pp. 257–270.

Bernhardt 1999
Rudolf Bernhardt. 'Evolutive treaty interpretation, especially of the European Convention on Human Rights.' *German Yearbook Book of International Law* (42) 1999, pp. 11–25.

Bielefeldt et al. 2016
H. Bielefeldt, N. Ghanea & M. Wiener, 'Freedom of Religion or Belief: An International Law Commentary', (Oxford: Oxford University Press 2016).

van Bijsterveld 2015
Sophie van Bijsterveld, 'Religion and Law in the Netherlands', *Insight Turkey* (17) 2015-1, pp. 121–141.

van Bijsterveld 2012
Sophie van Bijsterveld, 'Religion and the Secular State in the Netherlands', *Neuere Entwiclungen im Religionsrecht europaeischer Staaten* 2013-61, pp. 93–112.

van Bijsterveld 2006
Sophie van Bijsterveld, 'Scheiding van Kerk en Staat: een klassieke norm in een moderne tijd', in: W.B.H.J van de Donk et al. (red.), *Geloven in het publieke domein, (*Den Haag: Wetenschappelijke Raad voor het regeringsbeleid 2006).

de Blois 2010
Mattijs de Blois, 'Religious law versus secular law: The example of the Gett refusal in Dutch and English and Israeli law', *Utrecht Law Review* (6) 2010-2, pp. 93–114.

Boyle & Shah 2014
Kevin Boyle & Sangeeta Shah, 'Thought, expression, association, and assembly', in: D. Moeckli, S. Shah& S. Sivakumaran (red.), *International human rights law, (*Oxford: Oxford University Press 2014), pp. 53–74.

Brems 2006
Eva Brems, 'Article 14: The right to freedom of thought, conscience and religion', (Leiden: Martinus Nijhoff Publishers 2006).

Broyde 2001
Michael J. Broyde, 'Marriage, divorce, and the abandoned wife in Jewish Law: A conceptual understanding of the agunah problems in America', (Hoboken: KTAV Publishing House 2001).

van der Burg 2004
Corstiaan van der Burg, 'The Hindu diaspora in the Netherlands: Halfway between local structures and global ideologies', in: K. A. Jacobsen, & P. P. Kumar (red.), *South Asians in the Diaspora: Histories and Religious Traditions* (Leiden: Brill 2004), pp. 97–115.

van der Burg 1990
Corstiaan van der Burg, Theo Damsteegt, Krishna Autar, 'Hindoestanen in Nederland', (Leuven, Apledoorn: Garant Uitgevers 1990).

Byrnes 2012
Andrew Byrnes, 'Article 2', in: M. A. Freeman, C. Chinkin & B. Rudolf (red.), *The UN Convention on the Elimination of All Forms of Discrimination Against Women: A Commentary, (*New York: Oxford University Press Inc. 2012), pp. 71–99.

Chetial 2014
Vincent Chetail, 'The transnational movement of persons under general International Law. Mapping the Customary Law foundations of International Migration Law', (Cheltenham: Edward Elgar Publishing 2014).

Chinkin 2012
Christine Chinkin, 'Violence against Women', in: M. A. Freeman, C. Chinkin & B. Rudolf (red.), *The UN Convention on the Elimination of All Forms of Discrimination Against Women: A Commentary, (*New York: Oxford University Press Inc. 2012), pp. 443–474.

Chirwa 2004
Danwood M. Chirwa, 'The Doctrine of State responsibility as a potential means of holding private actors accountable for human rights', *Melbourne Journal in International Law* (5) 2004-1, pp. 1–36.

Clayton & Tomlinson 2000
Richard Clayton & Hugh Tomlinson, 'The law of human rights', (Oxford: Oxford University Press 2000).

Cook 1994
Rebeca J. Cook, 'State Responsibility for Violations of Women's Human Rights', *Havard Human Rights Journal* (7) 1994, pp. 125–175.

Crabb 1994
John H. Crabb, 'The French civil code: Revised Edition (as amended to 1 July `994)', (Deventer: Fred B. Rothman & Co. 1994).

Crowell & Burgess 1996
Nancy A. Crowell & Ann W. Burgess, 'Understanding violence against women', (Washington D.C.: National Academy Press 1996).

Dekeseredy & Schwarz 2011
Walter S. DeKeseredy & Martin D. Schwarz, 'Theoretical and methodological issues in researching violence against women', in: C. M. Renzetti, J. L. Edleson & B. Rauel Kennedy (red.), *Sourcebook on violence against women,* (California: Sage Publications, Inc. 2011), pp. 3–21.

Dillon 1989
Kathleen M Dillon, 'Divorce and Remarriage as Human Rights: The Irish Constitution and the European Convention on Human Rights at Odds in Johnston v. Ireland', *Cornell International Law Journal* (22) 1989, pp. 63–90.

Doné 2016
Sylvie Langlaude Doné, 'Religious organisations, internal autonomy and other religious rights before the European Court of Human Rights and the OSCE', *Netherlands Quarterly of Human Rights* (34) 2016–1, pp. 8–40.

Dorsen, et al. 2010
Norman Dorsen, et al. 'Comparative constitutionalism: cases and materials', (St. Paul, Minnesota: Thomson Reuters 2010).

Edwards 2011
Alice Edwards, 'Violence against women under International Human Rights Law', (Cambridge: Cambridge University Press 2011).

El Alami & Hinchcliffe 1996
Dawoud Sudqi El Alami & Doreen Hinchcliffe, 'Islamic marriage and divorce of the Arab world', (London: Kluwer Law International 1996).

Ending violence against women 2007
'Ending violence against women: From words to action (Study of the Secretary-General)', (United Nations Publication 2007).

Engelen 2004
Frank Engelen, *Interpretation of Tax treaties under International Law,* (2004) (Diss. Erasmus Universiteit Rotterdam).

Epstein 2002
Alek D Epstein, 'The freedom of conscience and sociological perspectives on dilemmas of collective secular disobedience: the case of Israel', *Journal of Human Rights* (1) 2002–3, pp. 305–320.

Ernst & Schwartz 1997
Morris L. Ernst & Alan U. Schwartz, 'Privacy: The right to be let alone', (Westport, Connecticut: Greenwood Press 1977).

Evans 2001
Carolyn Evans, 'Freedom of religion under the European Convention on Human Rights', (Oxford Scholarship Online 2001).

Evers & Stodel 2011
L. Evers & J. Stodel, 'Jodendom in de praktijk', (Amsterdam: Meulenhoff Boekerij B.V. 2011).

Fina 2017
Valentina D. Fina, 'Article 3 [General Principle]', in: V. D. Fina, R. Cera & G. Palmisano. (red.), *The United Nations Convention on the Rights of Persons with Disabilities: A commentary*, (Cham: Springer International Publishing 2017).

Fitoussi 2007
Guy Fitoussi, *Essai comparatif et critique du rôle du juge dans le procédure de divorce entre le système judiciaire français et israélien (*Diss. Edituer Indépendant University of Paris 2007).

Fitzmaurice 2013
Malgosia Fitzmaurice, 'Interpretation of human rights treaties', in D. Shelton (red.), *The Oxford Handbook of International Law* (Oxford: Oxford University Press 2013), pp. 739–771.

Fournier 2014
Pascale Fournier, 'Secular portraits and religious shadows: An empirical study of religious women in France', in: J. Berlinerblau, S. Fainberg & A. Nou (red.), *Secularism on the edge: Contemporary Church-State relations in the United States, France and Israel, (*New York: Palgrave Macmillian 2014), pp. 219–236.

Freeman 2012
Marsha Freeman, 'Article 16', in: M. A. Freeman, C. Chinkin & B. Rudolf (red.), *The UN Convention on the Elimination of All Forms of Discrimination Against Women: A Commentary,* (New York: Oxford University Press Inc. 2012), pp. 409–442.

Gardiner 2015
Richard K. Gardiner, 'Treaty interpretation', (Oxford: Oxford University Press 2015).

Gatti 2013
Mauro Gatti, 'Autonomy of religious organisations in the European Convention on Human Rights and in the European Union Law', in: L. S. Rossi & G. Di Federica (red.), *Fundamental rights in Europe and China- Regional identities and universalism,* (Editoriale Scientifica 2013), pp. 132–153.

Gelles 1999
Richard J. Gelles, 'Male offenders: Our understanding from the data', in: M. Harway & J. M. O'Neil (red.), *What causes men's violence against women*, (Thousand Oaks, California: Sage Publications, Inc. 1999), pp. 39–50.

Gerards et al. 2006
J.H. Gerards et al., 'Europees Verdrag voor de Rechten van de Mens: Rechtspraak & Commentaar', (Den Haag: Sdu Uitgever 2006).

Glenn 1980
H. Patrick Glenn, 'Where Heavens Meetheavens meet: The compelling of religious divorces', *The American Journal of Comparative Law* (28) 1980–1, pp. 1–38.

González & Viitanen 2009
Libertad González &Tarja K. Viitanen, 'The effect of divorce laws on divorce rates in Europe', *European Economic Review* (53) 2009–2, pp. 127–138.

Goonesekere 2012
Savitri W.E. Goonesekere, 'Article 15', in: M. A. Freeman, C. Chinkin & B. Rudolf (red.), *The UN Convention on the Elimination of All Forms of Discrimination Against Women: A Commentary*, (New York: Oxford University Press Inc. 2012), pp. 409–442.

Grabenwarter 2014
Christoph Grabenwarter, 'European Convention on Human Rights: Commentary', (München, Oxford, Baden-Baden, Basel: C.H. Beck, Hart, Nomos, Helbing Lichtenhahn 2014).

Gray 2009
Hillel. C. Gray, *Foreign features in Jewish law: How Christian and secular moral discourses permeate Halakhah* Chicago (Diss. University of Chicago 2009).

Greene 1999
Anthony F. Greene, 'Biological perspectives on violence against women', in: M. Harway & J. M. O'Neil (red.), *What causes men's violence against women*, (Thousand Oaks, California: Sage Publications, Inc. 1999), pp. 51–60.

Griffiths 2004
Cerian C. Griffiths, 'Sharia and Beth Din courts in the UK: is legal pluralism nothing more than a necessary political fiction', *Studia Iuridica Torniensia* (15) 2004, pp. 39–51.

Gumbis et al. 2008
Jaunius Gumbis, Vytaute Bacianskaite & Jurgita Randakeviciute, 'Do human rights guarantee autonomy?', *Cuadernos constitucionales de la Cátedra Fadrique Furió Ceriol* 2008–62, pp. 77–93.

de Haan 2008
Willem de Haan, 'Violence as an essentially contested concept', in: S. Body-Gendrot & P. Spierenburg (red.), *Violence in Europe: Historical and contemporary perspectives,* (Dordrecht, New York: Springer 2008).

Hacohen 2004
Aviad Hacohen, 'Tears of the oppressed: An examination of the agunah problem: background and Halakhic Sources', (Jersey City: KTAV Publishing House, Inc. 2004).

Hannum 1996
Hurst, Hannum, 'The status of the Universal Declaration of Human Rights in National and International Law.' *Georgia Journal of International & Comparative Law* (25) 1996, pp. 287–397.

Hannum 1987
Hurst Hannum, 'The right to leave and return in international law and practice', (Dorderecht: Springer Netherlands 1987).

Hanson 2004
Karl Hanson, 'Vrijheid van gedachte, geweten en godsdienst', in: J. vande Lanotte & Y. Haeck (red.), *Hanboek EVRM- Deel 2 Artikelsgewijze commentaar,* (Antwerpen, Oxford: Intersentia 2004), pp. 811.-812.

Hasselbacher 2009
Lee Hasselbacher, 'State obligations regarding domestic violence: The European Court of Human Rights, due diligence, and international legal minimums of protection', *Northwestern Journal of Human Rights* (8) 2009–2, pp. 190.

Hassoun 2008
Nicole Hassoun, 'Human rights, needs, and autonomy', *KiltHub Carnegie Mellon University,* 2008 *at* < www. kilthub.figshare.com> last accessed 1 April 2018 (Search on: Hassoun).

Heelsum 2002
Anja van Heelsum and Eske Voorthuysen,'Surinaamse organisaties in Nederland: Een netwerkanalyse' (Amsterdam: Aksant 2002).

Heth 2002
William A. Heth, 'Jesus on divorce: how my mind has changed', *The Southern Baptist Journal of Theology* (6) 2002, pp. 4–29.

van den Heuvel 2004
P. van den Heuvel (red.), *De toelichting op de kerkorde van de Protestantse Kerk in Nederland* (Zoetermeer: Uitgeverij Boekencentrum 2004).

Holden 2008
Livia Holden, 'Hindu divorce: A legal anthropology', (Hampshire, Burlington: Ashgate Publishing, Ltd. 2008).

Holtmaat 2012
Riki Holtmaat, 'Article 5', in: M. Freeman, C. Chinkin & B. Rudolf (red.), *The UN Convention on the Elimination of All forms of Discrimination against women: A commentary,* (Oxford: Oxford University Press 2012), pp. 141–167.

Humprey 1986
John P. Humphrey, 'Political and Related Rights', in: T. Meron (red.), *Human Rights in International Law: Legal and Policy Issues,* (Oxford Scholarship Online Oxford University Press 1986).

Hunnicutt 2009
Gwen Hunnicutt, 'Varieties of patriarchy and violence against women: Resurrecting "patriarchy" as a theoretical tool', *Violence against Women* (15) 2009–5.

Igra 2007
Anna R. Igra, 'Wives without husbands: Marriage, desertion, and welfare in New York, 1900–1935', (University of North Carolina Press 2007).

Jay 2005
L. Zagorsky Jay, 'Marriage and divorce's impact on wealth', *Journal of Sociology* (41) 2005–4, pp. 406–424.

Jayawickrama 2002
Nihal Jayawickrama, 'The judicial application of Human Rights Law: National, regional and international jurisprudence', (Cambridge: Cambridge University Press 2002).

Johnson 1987
Nancy Johnson, 'Recent Developments: The Breadth of Family Law Review Under the European Convention on Human Rights', *Havard International Law Journal* (36) 1995–2, pp. 513–570.

de Jong 2000
Cornelis D. de Jong, 'The freedom of thought, conscience and religion or belief in the United Nations (1946–1992)', (Antwerpen: Intersentia 2000).

Joseph et al. 2004
Sarah Joseph, Jenny Schultz & Melissa Castan, 'The International Covenant on Civil and Political Rights- Cases, materials and commentary', (New York: Oxford University Press Inc. 2004).

Kapinus & Flowers 2008
Carolyn A. Kapinus & Daniel R. Flowers, 'An Examination of Gender Differences in Attitudes Toward Divorce', *Journal of Divorce & Remarriage* (49) 2008–3–4, pp. 239–257.

Kalter 1987
Neil Kalter, 'Long-term effects of divorce on children: A developmental vulnerability model', *American Journal of Orthopsychiatry* (57) 1987–4, pp. 587–600.

Kaufman 1992
Michael Kaufman, 'Love, marriage, and family in Jewish law and tradition', (New Jersey: Jason Aronson 1992).

Kaufman 1996
Michael Kaufman, 'Love, marriage, and family in Jewish law and tradition', (New Jersey: Jason Aronson 1996).

Kibria 1990
Nazli Kibria, 'Power, patriarchy, and gender conflict in the Vietnamese immigrant community', *Gender & Society* (4) 1990–1, pp. 9–24.

Killander 2010
Magnus Killander, 'Interpreting regional human rights treaties', *SUR-International Journal on Human Rights* (7) 2010–13, pp. 145–169.

Kippenberg 2006
Hans Kippenberg, 'The changing relationship between state and church/religion in the Netherlands', *GEO journal* (67) 2006, pp. 317–330.

Klug 2001
Francesca Klug, 'The Human Rights Act – a "third way" or "third wave" Bill of Rights', *European Human Rights Law Review* 2001–4, pp. 361–372.

Knox 2007
John H. Knox, 'Horizontal Human Rights Law', *American Journal of International Law* (102) 2007–1, pp. 1–47.

Koivurova 2009
Timo Koivurova, 'Due Diligence', *Max Planck Encyclopedia of Public International Law* 2010.

Koski 2017
Alissa Koski and Jody Heymann, 'Thirty-year trends in the prevalence and severity of female genital mutilation: a comparison of 22 countries', *BMJ Global Health* (2) 2017, pp. 1–8.

Kruiniger 2014
Pauline M. Kruiniger, *Islamic divorce in Europe: Bridging the gap between European and Islamic legal orders* (Diss. Maastricht University 2014).

Labovitz 2015
Gail Labovitz, 'Contemporary Approaches to Qiddushin', in: S. B. Fishman (red.), *Love, Marriage, and Jewish Families: Paradoxes of a Social Revolution,* (Waltham: Brandeis University Press 2015).

Lavrysen 2014
Laurens Lavrysen, 'The scope of rights and the scope of obligations', in: E. Brems & J. Gerards (red.), *Shaping Rights in the ECHR: The role of the European Court of Human Rights in determining the scope of human rights,* (Cambridge: Cambridge University Press 2014).

Leichter 2009
Alexandra Leichter, 'The effect of Jewish divorce law on family law litigation', *Journal of the International Academy of Matrimonial Lawyers* (2) 2009–4, pp. 1–18.

Lenaerts 2013
Mariken Lenaerts, 'De voorstellen tot herziening van het Nederlandse echtscheidingsrecht tijdens de Duitse bezetting', *Family & Law* 2013, pp. 214–216.

Letsas 2007
George Letsas, 'A theory of interpretation of the European Convention on Human Rights', (Oxford: Oxford University Press 2007).

Levitt & Ware 2006
Heidi M. Levitt & Kimberly N. Ware, 'Religious leaders' perspectives on marriage, divorce, and intimate partner violence', *Psychology of Women Quarterly* (30) 2006–2, pp. 212–222.

Linderfalk 2007
Ulf Linderfalk, 'Is the hierarchical structure of articles 31 and 32 of the Vienna Convention real or not? Interpreting the rules of interpretation', *Netherlands International Law Review* (54) 2007–1, pp. 133–154.

Lixinski 2017
Lucas Lixinski, 'The Consensus Method of Interpretation by the Inter- American Court of Human Rights', 3 *Canadian Journal of Comparative and Contemporary Law* (3) 2017–1, pp. 65–96.

Lorenz et al. 2006
Frederick Lorenz et al, 'The short-term and decade-long effects of divorce on women's midlife health, *Journal of Health and Social Behavior* (47) 2006–2, pp. 111–125.

Marin & Russo 1999
Amy J. Marin & Nancy F. Russo, 'Feminist perspectives on male violence against women: Critiquing O'Neil and Harway's model', in: M. Harway & J. M. O'Neil (red.), *What causes men's violence against women,* (Thousand Oaks, California: Sage Publications, Inc. 1999), pp. 18–35.

Marshall 2009
Jill Marshall, 'Personal freedom through human rights law?Autonomy, identity and integrity under the European Convention on Human Rights', (Leiden: Martinus Nijhoff Publishers 2009).

McCrudden 2008
Christopher McCrudden, 'Human dignity and judicial interpretation of human rights', *The European Journal of International Law* (19) 2008–4, pp. 655–724.

Mechlem 2009
Kirsten Mechlem,'Treaty Bodies and the Interpretation of Human Rights', *Vanderbilt Journal of Transnational* Law (42) 2009, pp. 905–947.

Menski 2012
Werner Menski, 'Hindu law: beyond tradition and modernity', (Oxford Scholarship Online 2012).

Millett 1969
Kate Millett, *Theory of sexual politics,* (Granada Publishing 1969).

Montoya 2013
Celeste Montoya, 'From Global to Grassroots: The European Union, Transnational Advocacy, and Combating Violence Against Women', (New York: Oxford University Press 2013).

Morsink 2010
Johannes Morsink, 'The Universal Declaration of Human Rights: Origins, drafting, and intent', (Philadelphia: University of Pennsylvania Press, Incorporated 2010).

Mortenson 2013
Julian Davis Mortenson, 'The Travaux of Travaux: Is the Vienna Convention Hostile to Drafting History?', *American Journal of International Law* (107) 2013–4, pp. 780–822.

Munir 2013
Arshad Munir & Ghulam Ali Khan, 'A Social Custom "Vani": Introduction and Critical Analysis', *Al- Azwa* (28) 2013–40.

Nasir 2009
Jamal J. Ahmad Nasir, 'The Status of Women under Islamic Law and Modern Islamic Legislation', (Leiden, Boston: Brill 2009).

Neil & Nadeau 1999
James M. O'Neil & Rodney A. Nadeau, 'Men's gender-role conflict defense mechanisms, and self protective defensive strategies: Explaining men's violence against women from a gender-role socialization perspective', in: M. Harway & J. M. O'Neil (red.), *What causes men's violence against women,* (Thousand Oaks, California: Sage Publications, Inc. 1999), p. 39–50.

Nicholas 1995
Ralph W. Nicholas, 'The effectiveness of the Hindu sacrament (Samskära): Caste, marriage, and divorce in Bengali culture', in: L. Harlan & P. B. Courtright (red.), *From the margins of Hindu marriage: Essays on gender, religion, and culture,* (New York: Oxford University Press Inc. 1995), pp. 137–159.

Nickel 2014
Ashley Nickel, 'Abusing the system: Domestic violence judgments from Sharia arbitration tribunals create parallel legal structures in the United Kingdom', *The Arbitration Brief* (4) 2014-1, pp. 92–120.

Norton 2016
Jane. C. Norton, 'Freedom of religious organizations', (Oxford: Oxford University Press 2016).

Nowak 2005
Manfred Nowak, 'U.N. Covenant on Civil and Political Rights: CCPR commentary', (Arlington: N.P. Engel, Publisher 2005).

Oldenhuis et al. 2007
F.T Oldenhuis et al, 'Schurende relaties tussen recht en religie', (Assen: Koninklijke van Gorcum BV 2007).

Olivelle & Olivelle 2005
Patrick Olivelle & Suman Olivelle, 'Manu's Code of Law', (New York: Oxford University Press, Inc. 2005).

Orakhelashvili 2003
Alexander Orakhelashvili, 'Restrictive interpretation of human rights treaties in the recent jurisprudence of the European Court of Human Rights', *European Journal of International Law* (14) 2003-3, pp. 529–568.

Packer 2002
Corinne A. A. Packer, 'Using human rights to change traditions and practices that are harmful to women's reproductive rights', (Antwerpen, Oxford: Intersentia 2002).

Peers 2014
Steve Peers et al., 'The EU Charter of Fundamental Rights: A Commentary', (Oxford: Hart Publishing 2014).

Proudman 2013
Charlotte Proudman, 'Religious Marriages: Staying a decree absolute in order to increase the chances of obtaining a religious divorce', *Family Law week* 2013.

Radačic 2007
Ivana Radačic, 'Human Rights of women and the private/public divide in International Human Rights Law', *Croatian Yearbook of European Law and Policy* (3) 2007, pp. 443–468.

Raday 2007
Frances Raday, 'Culture, religion, and CEDAW' s article 5(a)', in: H. B. Schöpp-Schilling & C. Flinterman (red.), *The Circle of empowerment*, (New York: The Feminist Press 2007), pp. 68–85.

Raday 2003
Frances Raday, 'Culture, religion and gender', *International Journal of Constitutional Law* (1) 2003–4, pp. 663–715.

Riaz 2013
Shamreeza Riaz, 'Shariah perspective on marriage contract and practice in contemporary Muslim societies', *International Journal of Social Science and Humanity* (3) 2013–3, pp. 263–267.

Richardson 2007
Belinda Richardson, *Christian Clergy Response to Intimate Partner Violence: Attitudes, Training, Or Religious Views?* (West Lafayette: Proquest Information and Learning Company Purdue University), 2007.

Rivers 2010
Julian Rivers, 'The law of organized religions: between establishment and secularism', (Oxford: Oxford University Press 2010).

Rizvi 2014
Sayyid Muhammad Rizvi, 'Marriage and morals of Islam', (Islamic Education & Information Center 2014).

Rosenberg 2010
Lisa Rosenberg, 'Praying for divorce: The abuse of Jewish women through Jewish divorce law', in: J. Fong (red.), *Out of the shadows: Woman abuse in ethnic, immigrant, and aboriginal communities*, (Toronto: Canadian Scholars' Press 2010), pp. 215–242.

Rutten 2010
Susan Rutten, 'Protection of spouses in informal marriages by human rights', *Utrecht Law Review* (6) 2010–2, pp. 77–92.

Rzepka- Hagion 2001
Christine Rzepka-Hagion, 'Religious views & domestic violence', *The Ripple Effect* 2002.

Schabas 2015
William A. Schabas, 'The European Convention on Human Rights: A commentary', (Oxford: Oxford University Press 2015).

de Schutter 2014
Olivier de Schutter, 'International Human Rights Law: cases, materials, commentary', (Cambridge: Cambridge University Press 2014).

Shannon- Lewy & Dull 2005
Colleen Shannon- Lewy & Valeria T. Dull, 'The response of Christian clergy to domestic violence: Help or Hindrance?', *Aggression and Violent behaviour* (10) 2005–6, pp. 647–659.

Shelton & Gould 2013
Dinah Shelton & Ariel Gould, 'Positive and negative obligations', in: D. Shelton (red.), *The Oxford handbook of international human rights law,* (Oxford: Oxford University Press 2013), pp. 562–283.

Shmueli 2012
Benjamin Shmueli, 'Civil actions for acts that are valid according to religious family law but harm women 's rights: Legal pluralism in cases of collision between two sets of laws', *Vanderbilt Journal of Transnational Law* (46) 2012, pp. 823–897.

Silverstein 1999
Louise B. Silverstein, 'The evolutionary origins of male violence against women'', in: M. Harway & J. M. O'Neil (red.), *What causes men's violence against women,* (Thousand Oaks, California: Sage Publications, Inc. 1999), pp. 61–84.

van der Sloot 2015
Bart van der Sloot, 'Privacy as personality right: Why the ECtHR's focus on ulterior interests might prove indispensable in the age of 'Big Data'', *Utrecht Journal of International and European Law* (32) 2015–80, pp. 25–50.

van der Sloot 2014
Bart van der Sloot, 'Privacy as human flourishing: Could a shift towards virtue ethics strengthen privacy protection in the age of Big Data?', *Journal of intellectual property, information technology and electronic commerce law,* (5) 2014–3, pp. 230–244.

Spierenburg 2008
Pieter Spierenburg, 'Violence: Reflections about a word', in: S. Body-Gendrot & P. Spierenburg (red.), *Violence in Europe: Historical and contemporary perspectives,* (New York: Springer 2008).

Stanko 2006
Elizabeth A. Stanko, 'Introduction: Conceptualizing the meaning of violence', in: E. A. Stanko (red.), *The Meanings of Violence, (*Taylor and Francis e-Library: Routledge 2005).

Takemura 2008
Hitomi Takemura, 'International Human Right to Conscientious Objection to Military Service and Individual Duties to Disobey Manifestly Illegal Orders', (Berlin, Heidelberg: Springer 2008).

Taylor 2005
Paul M. Taylor, 'Freedom of Religion: UN and European Human Rights Law and Practice', (New York: Cambridge University Press 2005).

The Division for the Advancement of Women 2010
The Division for the Advancement of Women, 'Handbook for legislation on violence against women', (New York: United Nations Publication 2010).

***The right to leave and the right to return* 1973**
'The right to leave and the right to return: A declaration adopted by the Uppsala Colloquium, Sweden, June 21, 1972', *The International Migration Review* (7) 1973-1, pp. 62–66.

Tobin 2012
John Tobin, 'The Right to Health in International Law', (Oxford: Oxford University Press 2012).

Toebes 1999
Brigit C. A. Toebes, 'The right to health as a human right in international law' (Antwerpen: Intersentia, Hart 1999).

Tracy 2007
Steven R. Tracy, 'Patriarchy and domestic violence: challenging common misconceptions', *The Journal of the Evangelical Theological Society* (50) 2007-3, pp. 573–594.

Vermeer-Künzli 2007
Anna Maria Helena Vermeer-Künzli, *The protection of individuals by means of diplomatic protection: diplomatic protection as a human rights instrument* (Diss. Leiden University 2007).

Viljoen 2004
Frans Viljoen, 'The African Charter on Human and People's Rights: The Travaux Préparatoires in the light of subsequent Practice', *Human Rights Law and Journal* (24) 2004-9-12, pp. 313–326.

Wardle 2010
Lynn D. Wardle, 'Marriage and religious liberty: Comparative law problems and conflict of laws solutions', *Journal of Law & Family Studies* (12) 2010-2, pp. 315–364.

Weiss & Gross-Horowitz 2013
Susan M. Weiss & Netty C. Gross-Horowitz, 'Marriage and divorce in the Jewish state: Israel's civil war', (Brandeis University Press 2013).

Weitzman 2012
Lenore J. Weitzman, 'The Politics of Jewish Divorce Law Reform', *Franke Institute Annual* (12) 2012, pp. 12–14.

White & Ovey 2010
Robin C.A. White & Clare Ovey, 'The European Convention on Human Rights', (New York: Oxford University Press 2010).

Witte 2012
John Witte, 'From sacrament to contract: Marriage, religion, and law in the western tradition', (Louisville: Westminister John Knox Press 2012).

Witte 1997
John Witte, 'From sacrament to contract: Marriage, religion, and law in the western tradition', (Louisville: Westminster John Knox Press 1997).

Yildirim 2015
Mine Yildirim, *The Collective Dimension of Freedom of Religion or Belief in International Law: The Application of Findings to the Case of Turkey* (Diss. Åbo Åbo Akademi University 2015).

Zee 2016
Machteld Zee, 'Choosing Sharia? Multiculturalism, Islamic Fundamentalism and Sharia Councils', (The Hague: Eleven International Publishing 2016).

NEWSPAPER ARTICLES & MULTIMEDIA

***Radio Netherlands Worldwide* 2012**
'Holiday in Somalia turns into nightmare', August 18, 2012, *Radio Netherlands WorldWide.*

***Joop Vara* 2012**
'Nederlandse ambassade laat bruidslavinnnen in de steek', 13 August 2012, *Joop Vara.*

***Nos* 2012**
'Ook Sharia raad in Nederland?', 11 January 2012, *NOS.*

De Volkskrant
'Pleidooi shariaraad stuit op verzet vrouwen', 12 June 2012, *de Volkskrant.*

van Beek 2016
Marije van Beek, 'Vrouw in het nadeel bij religieuze scheiding', 30 June 2016, *Trouw.*

Belleman 2016
Saskia Belleman, 'Adeel D. blijft eerwraakmoord ontekennen', 21 January 2016, *Telegraaf.*

Berkelder 2016
Nadia Berkelder, 'Adeel D. veroordeeld tot tien jaar cel voor dood Yasmeen', 09 May 2016, *Algemeen Dagblad.*

***Blitz Quotidiano* 2012**
'Chiara Invernizzi: dieci mesi ostaggio del marito arabo ', 24 December 2012, *Blitz Quotidiano.*

Blumberg 2014
Antonia Blumberg, 'Michel Gugenheim, French Chief Rabbi, Accused Of Extortion Over Religious Divorce', 12 May 2014, *Huffing Post.*

Boverhuis 2017
Joyce Boverhuis & Ferry Stoop, 'CDA en GroenLinks willen boete voor mannen die vrouwen gevangen houden in Islamitisch huwelijk', 29 November 2017, *EenVandaag*.

Corbin 2013
Jane Corbin, 'Secrets of Britain's Sharia Councils', broadcasted 22 April 2013, *BBC Panorama*.

Kirchgaessner 2015
Stephanie Kirchgaessner, 'Pope reforms Catholic church's marriage annulment process', 8 September 2015, *The Guardian*.

Mossano 2012
Silvana Mossano, 'Ostaggio del marito in Arabia Saudita libera dopo 10 mesi', 24 December 2012, *La Stampa Italia*.

Mossano 2012
Silvana Mossano, 'Vi racconto il mio inferno di sequestrata in Arabia', 12 September 2012, *La Stampa Italia*.

Organisatie voor Hindoe Media 2013
Organisatie voor Hindoe Media, 'Scheiden binnen het hindoeïsme', broadcasted 25 May 2013, *NPO*.

Safi 2016
Michael Safi, 'Talaq' and the battle to ban the three words that grant India's Muslim men instant divorce', 20 October 2016, *The Guardian*.

Sharrock 2011
David Sharrock, 'Malta votes yes to legalise divorce', 29 May 2011, *The Guardian*.

Smith 2015
Yehudis Smith, 'In this story, the Agunah was me', 23 March 2015, *Collive Community News Service*.

Times of India 2016
'AIMPLB supports triple talaq, forms women's wing', 20 November 2016, *Times of India*.

ENCYCLOPAEDIA AND DICTIONARIES

Charlesworth 2008
Hilary Charlesworth, *Universal Declaration of Human Rights (1948)*, Oxford University Press 2008.

Dryden 2018
Jane Dryden, *Autonomy*, Internet Encyclopedia of Philosophy- A peer-reviewed Academic Resource, *at* <www.iep.utm.edu/autonomy/> last accessed 17 February 2018.

Encyclopedia Britannica
Encyclopedia Britannica, *Manu-smriti*, Encyclopedia Britannica Inc.

Johnson & Cureton 2017
Robert Johnson & Adam Cureton, *Kant's Moral Philosophy*, Stanford Encyclopedia of Philosophy, Spring 2017 Edition.

Oxford 2015
Oxford Dictionary of English, version 2015 (Online).

Piper 2018
Mark Piper, *Autonomy: Normative*, Internet Encyclopedia of Philosophy- a peer-reviewed academic resource, *at* <www.iep.utm.edu/autonomy/> last accessed 17 February 2018.

Rabinowitz
Mayer E. Rabinowitz, 'Issues in Jewish ethics: *Agunot* – Abandoned wives', *Jewish Virtual Library.*

REPORTS

Amor 2002
Abdelfattah Amor, *Étude sur la liberté de religion ou de conviction et la condition de la femme au regard de la religion et des traditions*, Commission on Human Rights 2002.

Bakker et al. 2010
Laurens G.H. Bakker et al., *Sharia in Nederland: Een studie naar Islamitische advisering en geschillenbeslechting bij moslims in Nederland*, Instituut voor Culturele Antropologie en Ontwikkelingsstudies, Instituut voor Rechtssociologie & Radboud Universiteit Nijmegen 2010.

Benito 1986
Elizabeth. O. Benito *Elimination of all forms of intolerance and discrimination based on religion or belief: Study of the current dimension of the problems of intolerance and of discrimination on grounds of religion or belief*, Sub-Commission on Prevention of Discrimination and Protection of Minorities 31 August 1986.

Bennouna 1984
Mohamed Bennouna, *Preliminatry Report on diplomatic protection*, 4 February 1984.

Bernts 2006
Ton Bernts, Gert de Jong & Hasan Yar, *Een religieuze atlas van Nederland*, Wetenschappelijke Raad voor het Regeringsbeleid, Amsterdam University Press 2006.

Bielefeldt 2013
Heiner Bielefeldt, *Interim report of the Special Rapporteur on freedom of religion or belief*, UN General Assembly 7 August 2013.

Coker-Appiah 2009
Dorcas Coker-Appiah, *The CEDAW Convention and harmful practices against women: the work of the CEDAW Committee*, Committee on the Elimination of Discrimination Against Women 2009.

Commission on the Status of Women 2013
Elimination and prevention of all forms of violence against women and girls: Focus on prevention of violence against women and girls – Moderator's summary, Commission on the Status of Women 2013.

Commission on the Status of Women 2013
High-level round table on the elimination and prevention of all forms of violence against women and girls- Chair's summary, Commission on the Status of Women 2013.

Commission on the Status of Women 1976
Commission on the Status of Women: report on the 26th and resumed 26th sessions (13 September – 1 October and 6–17 December 1976), Commission on the Status of Women 1976.

Committee on the Elimination of Discrimination Against Women 2005
Report on Mexico produced by the Committee on the Elimination of Discrimination Against Women under article 8 of the Optional Protocol to the Convention, and reply from the Government of Mexico, Committee on the Elimination of Discrimination Against Women 2005.

Committee on the Elimination of Discrimination against Women 1998
Committee on the Elimination of Discrimination against Women, *Report of the Committee on the Elimination of Discrimination Against Women (Eighteenth and nineteenth sessions)* UN General Assembly 1998).

Coomaraswamy 2002
Radhika Coomaraswamy, *Report of the Special Rapporteur on violence against women, its causes and consequences: Cultural practices in the family that are violent towards women*, Economic and Social Council 2002.

Coomaraswamy 1996
Radhika Coomaraswamy, *A framework for model legislation on domestic violence*, Commission on Human Rights 1996.

Council of Europe 2013
Explanatory Report to the Protocol No. 15 amending the Convention for the Protection of Human Rights and Fundamental Freedoms, Council of Europe 2013.

Council of Europe 2011
Explanatory Report to the Council of Europe Convention on preventing and combating violence against women and domestic violence, Council of Europe 2011.

Council of Europe 1985
Explanatory Report of Protocol No. 7 to the Convention for the Protection of Human Rights and Fundamental Freedoms, Council of Europ 1985.

Council of Europe 1963
Explanatory Report to Protocol No. 4 to the Convention for the Protection of Human Rights and Fundamental Freedoms, securing certain rights and freedoms other than those already included in the Convention and in the First Protocol thereto, Council of Europe 1963.

Dubravka 2017
Šimonović Dubravka, *Adequacy of the international legal framework on violence against women – Report of the Special Rapporteur on violence against women, its causes and consequences on the adequacy of the international legal framework on violence against women,* United Nations General Assembly 19 July 2017.

Dugard 2000
John R. Dugard, *First Report on Diplomatic Protection,* International Law Commission April 2000.

van Eijk 2017
Esther van Eijk, *Wel gescheiden, niet gescheiden? Een empirisch onderzoek naar huwelijkse gevangenschap in Nederland,* Maastricht University 2017.

Ertürk 2006
Yakin Ertürk, *Integration of the human rights of women and the gender perspective: violence against women – The due diligence standard as a tool for the elimination of violence against women,* United Nations Economic and Social Council & Commission on Human Rights 2006.

Ertürk 2003
Yakin Ertürk, *Towards an effective implementation of international norms to end violence against women,* Economic and Social Council 2003.

Hart & Dekker 2006
Joep de Hart & Paul Dekker, *Kerken in de Nederlandse civil society: institutionele grondslag en individuele* inspiratiebron, Wetenschappelijke Raad voor het regeringsbeleid, Amsterdam University Press Press 2006.

Human Rights Council 2014
Preventing and eliminating child, early and forced marriage- Report of the Office of the United Nations High Commissioner for Human Rights, Human Rights Council 2014.

Human Rights Watch 204
Divorced from justice- Women's unequal access to divorce in Egypt, Human Rights Watch 2004.

Inter-American Court of Human Rights 1982
The effect of reservations on the entry into force of the American Convention on Human Rights, Advisory Opinion OC-2/82 of 24 September 1982 (Series A) No. 2, Inter-American Court of Human Rights 1982.

International Law Association 2004
International Human Rights Law and Practice – Final Report on the impact of findings of the United Nation human rights treaty bodies, International Law Association 2004.

International Law Commission 2006
Draft articles on diplomatic protection with commentaries 2006, International Law Commission 2006.

Jahangir 2009
Asma Jahangir, *Report of the Special Rapporteur on freedom of religion or belief Asma Jahangir – Mission to Israel and the Occupied Palestinian Territory,* Human Rights Council 12 January 2009.

Jahangir 2006
Asma Jahangir, *Civil and Political Rights, including the question of religious intolerance,* Commission on Human Rights 8 March 2006.

Jurisconsult 2015
Jurisconsult, *Guide to article 9 – Freedom of thought, conscience and religion,* Council of Europe, European Court of Human Rights 2015.

Jurisconsult 2015
Jurisconsult, *Thematic Report: Health-related issues in the case-law of the European Court of Human Rights,* Council of Europe & European Court of Human Rights 2015.

Koffeman 2010
N R. Koffeman, *(The right to) personal autonomy in the case law of the European Court of Human Rights,* Leiden University 2010.

Krishnaswami 1960
Arcot Krishnaswami, *Study of discrimination in the matter of religious rights and practices,* United Nations 1960.

Kruiniger 2018
Pauline Kruiniger, *Niet langer geketend aan het huwelijk! Juridische instrumenten die huwelijkse gevangenschap kunnen voorkomen of oplossen,* Maastricht University 2018.

MacEoin 2009
Denis MacEoin, *Sharia Law or 'one law for all?'* Institute for the Study of Civil Society London Civitas 2009.

Manjoo 2015
Rashida Manjoo, *Report of the Special Rapporteur on violence against women, its causes and consequences*, United Nations 2015.

Manjoo 2014
Rashida Manjoo, *Advancement of Women- Note by the Secretary-General: Report of the Special Rapporteur on violence against women, its causes and consequences*, United Nations 2011.

Manjoo 2014
Rashida Manjoo, *Report of the Special Rapporteur on violence against women, its causes and consequences*, United Nations 2014.

Manjoo 2013
Rashida Manjoo, *Report of the Special Rapporteur on violence against women, its causes and consequences*, United Nations 2013.

Manjoo 2011
Rashida Manjoo, *Addendum to the Human Rights Council Thematic report of the Special rapporteur on Violence, its Causes and Consequences*, United Nations 2015.

Manjoo 2011
Rashida Manjoo, *Report of the Special Rapporteur on violence against women, its causes and consequences* Human Rights Council 2011.

Mejdoubi 2016
Jamila Mejdoubi, *Factsheet- Wel gescheiden, niet gescheiden. Huwelijkse gevangenschap in Nederland*, Universiteit Maastricht, Atria & Kennisinstituut voor emancipatie en vrouwengeschiedenis 2016.

Mubanga- Chipoya 1998
Chama L.C. Mubanga- Chipoya, *Analysis of the current trends and developments regarding the right to leave any country including one's own, and to return to one's own country, and some other rights or considerations arising therefrom: final report prepared by C.L.C. Mubanga-Chipoya*, Economic and Social Council 20 June 1988.

Murdoch 2007
Jim Murdoch, *Freedom of thought, conscience and religion: A guide to the implementation of Article 9 of the European Convention on Human Rights*, Council of Europe 2007.

Netherlands Institute for Human Rights 2016
Netherlands Institute for Human Rights, *Written Contribution to the 65th session of the UN Committee on the Elimination of Discrimination Against Women (CEDAW) on behalf of the consideration of the sixth periodic report of the Netherlands*, College voor de Rechten van de Mens 2016.

Office of the United Nations High Commissioner 2017
Office of the United Nations High Commissioner for Human Rights, *Conscientious objection to military service: Analytical report of the Office of the United Nations High Commissioner for Human Rights*, Human Rights Council 2017.

Proudman 2012
Rachael Charlotte Proudman, *Equal and free? Evidence in support of Baroness Cox's arbitration and mediation services (Equality) Bill* 2012.

Puppinck 2014
Grégor Puppinck, *Third party intervention- Submission to the Fourth Section of the European Court of Human Rights in the cases Babiarz v. Poland, Gajewski v. Poland, and Piotrowski v. Poland,* European Center for Law and Justice 2014.

Renucci 2005
Jean-François Renucci, *Article 9 of the European Convention on Human Rights,* Council of Europe 2005.

***Report of the US delegation* 1982**
'Report of the US delegation to the Inter-American conference on protection of human rights', in: T. Buergenthal & R. E. Norris (red.), *Human Rights: the Inter-American System* (Dobbs Ferry: Oceana Publications 1982).

Russel & van de Ven 1990
Diana E.H. Russell & Nicole van de Ven, *Crimes Against Women: Proceedings of the International Tribunal,* International Tribunal on Crimes Against Women 1990.

Rutten et al. 2015
Susan Rutten et al., *Gewoon getrouwd: Een onderzoek naar kindhuwelijken en religieuze huwelijken in Nederland,* Universiteit Maastricht & Verwey-Jonker Instituut 2015.

Schmeets 2016
Hans Schmeets, *De religieuze kaart van Nederland, 2010–2015,* Centraal Bureau of Statistics 2016.

Shmeets 2014
Hans Schmeets, *De religieuze kaart van Nederland, 2010–2013,* Centraal Bureau of Statistics 2014.

Shahinian 2012
Gulnara Shahinian, *Report of the Special Rapporteur on contemporary forms of slavery, including its causes and consequences, Gulnara Shahinian -Thematic report on servile marriage,* United Nations General Assembly 2012.

South African Law Commission 1992
Working paper 45- Project 76: Jewish Divorces, **South African Law Commission 1992.**

United Nations 1985
Report of the World Conference to review and appraise the achievements of the united nations decade for women: Equality, development and peace, United Nations 1985.

United Nations 1976
Report of the World Conference of the International Women's, United Nations 1976.

United Nations Secretary-General 2006
United Nations Secretary-General, *In-depth study on all forms of violence against women: Report of the Secretary-General,* United Nations General Assembly 2006.

UN Division for Social Policy and Development on the Family 2003
UN Division for Social Policy and Development- Programme on the Family, *Major trends affecting families: A background document,* United Nations 2003.

UN Office of the High Commissioner for Human Rights 2008
The Right to Health – Fact sheet No. 31, UN Office of the High Commissioner for Human Rights & World Health Organization 2008.

UN Office of the High Commissioner for Human Rights 1995
Fact sheet No. 23, Harmful Traditional Practices Affecting the Health of Women and Childre, UN Office of the High Commissioner for Human Rights 1995.

Ursula 2001
Kilkelly Ursula, *Handbook No.1: The Right to respect for private and family life,* Council of Europe Council of Europe 2001.

van Waesberghe et al. 2014
Eliane Smits van Waesberghe et al., *Zo zijn we niet getrouwd: Een onderzoek naar omvang en aard van huwelijksdwang, achterlating en huwelijkse gevangenschap,* Universiteit Maastricht, Femmes For Freedom, Verwey-Jonker Instituut 2014.

Weiss 2011
Susan M. Weiss, *The tort of Get- abuse: How damage litigation has changed the course of family law in Israel,* The Center for Women's Justice 2011.

World Health Organisation 2010
Global strategy to stop health-care providers from performing female genital mutilation, World Health Organisation 2010.

UNPUBLISHED WORKS

***Question for written answer P-007842/12* 2012**
Question for written answer P-007842/12 to the Commission (Vice President/High Representative) 5 September 2012, p. 122.

Halperin- Kaddari 2013
Ruth Halperin-Kaddari, 'Agunot in Israel- A study', *JOFA – NYU Tikvah Agunah Summit (New York, 2013).*

Zehra et al. 2016
Asma Zehra, et al., Press Statement of the Muslim Women strongly objecting to the interference in the Shariah Laws guaranteed under the constitution of India, 27 October 2016 <www.aimplboard.in> last accessed 18 November 2016 (search on: *press statement of the Muslim Women, Triple talaq, India*).

WEB PAGE

Aanpak huwelijksdwang
'Aanpak huwelijksdwang', <www.rijksoverheid.nl> accessed 02 February 2017 (search on: *aanpak huwelijksdwang).*

Berger 2012
Maurits Berger, 'Juist blokkeren van Shariaraad is dom', 2012, <www.leiden-islamblog.nl> last accessed 02 February 2018. (search on: *shariaraad*).

Declarations, Reservations and Objections to CEDAW
'Declarations, Reservations and Objections to CEDAW ', <www.un.org/womenwatch/daw/cedaw/reservations-country.htm> last accessed 18 August 2017.

Femmes for Freedom
Femmes for Freedom, 'Huwelijkse gevangenschap ', <www.femmesforfreedom.com > last accessed 27 December 2015 (search on: *huwelijkse gevangenschap*).

Friedman
David. D. Friedman, 'Jewish Law: A very brief account', <www.daviddfriedman.com> accessed 27 December 2015 (Search on: *legal systems very different from ours, Jewish laws*).

Huwelijksdwang en achterlating 2013
'Huwelijksdwang en achterlating- Huwelijkse gevangenschap', 2013, <www.huiselijkgeweld.nl> last accessed 03 February 2018 (search on: *huwelijkse gevangeschap).*

Landelijke Organisatie
'Landelijke Organisatie', <www.nik.nl/dit-is-het-nik/landelijke-organisatie/> last accessed 13 March 2018.

Marital Captivity 2014
'Marital Captivity: Bridging the gap between religion and law (MARICAP)', 2014, <www.maastrichtuniversity.nl> last accessed 24 January 2017 (search on: *marital captivity*).

Ministerie van Volksgezondheid Welzijn en Sport
Ministerie van Volksgezondheid Welzijn en Sport, 'Huwelijkse gevangenschap – Huiselijk geweld', *at* <www.huiselijkgeweld.nl/dossiers/campagne_huwelijksdwang/beleid/huwelijkse-gevangenschap> last accessed 27 December 2015.

Shields
Jacqueline Shields, 'Modern Jewish History: The Tribes Today – Kohens, Levis & Yisraels', *Jewish Virtual Library*, <www.jewishvirtuallibrary.org > last accessed 20 May 2016 (search on: *Kohen, Levis*).

Sperber
Haim Sperber, 'Wanted: Missing Jewish husband', *614 HBI eZine*, <www.614ezine.com/wanted-missing-jewish-husband> last accessed 24 January 2017.

***The property relations between spouses* 1973**
'The property relations between spouses', 1973, <www.pereslaw.co.il/document/54,67,32.aspx> accessed 04 February 2018.

Weiss 2009
Susan M. Weiss, 'Divorce: The Halakhic perspective', *Jewish Women: A comprehensive historical encyclopedia*, 2009, <www. jwa.org/encyclopedia/article/divorce-halakhic-perspective> accessed 27 December 2015 (search on: *divorce*).

CURRICULUM VITAE

Benedicta Deogratias obtained her bachelor degree in European Law at Maastricht University in 2012, and her master degree in Globalisation and Law at Maastricht University in 2013. Hereafter, she joined the Law Faculty at Maastricht University in 2014 to start her dissertation on marital captivity. Her research focused on the human rights dimensions of marital captivity and studied how human rights law can be used to address this phenomenon. This research was a part of the NWO project: Marital Captivity: Bridging the Gap between Religion and Law that was funded by the Netherlands Organisation for Scientific Research and was coordinated by Prof. dr. S.W.E Rutten. Benedicta has also, in the course of her research activities on marital captivity, produced a short documentary titled 'Gevangen in het huwelijk'. The short documentary can be accessed at <https://youtube.com/ua2keyvIFBA>.

Human Rights Research Series

The Human Rights Research Series' central research theme is the nature and meaning of international standards in the fi eld of human rights, their application and promotion in the national legal order, their interplay with national standards, and the international supervision of such application. Anyone directly involved in the defi nition, study, implementation, monitoring, or enforcement of human rights will fi nd this series an indispensable reference tool.
The Series is published together with the world famous Netherlands Network for Human Rights Research (formerly School of Human Rights Research), a joint eff ort by human rights researchers in the Netherlands.

 For previous volumes in the series, please visit http://shr.intersentia.com.

Published titles within the Series:

73. Roland Moerland, *The Killing of Death* ISBN 978-1-78068-351-5
74. Andrea Broderick, *The Long and Winding Road to Disability Equality and Inclusion* ISBN 978-1-78068-358-4
75. Christina Peristeridou, *The Principle of Legality in European Criminal Law* ISBN 978-1-78068-357-7
76. Emilie Kuijt, Humanitarian Assistance and State Sovereignty in International Law ISBN 978-1-78068-366-9
77. Lize R. Glas, *The Theory, Potential and Practice of Procedural Dialogue in the European Convention on Human Rights System* ISBN 978-1-78068-375-1
78. Paulien de Morree, *Rights and Wrongs under the ECHR* ISBN 978-1-78068-418-5
79. Malu Beijer, *The Limits of Fundamental Rights Protection by the EU* ISBN 978-1-78068-455-0
80. Marie Elske Gispen, *Human Rights and Drug Control* ISBN 978-1-78068-454-3
81. Bart van der Sloot, *Privacy as Virtue: Moving Beyond the Individual in the Age of Big Data* ISBN 978-1-78068-505-2
82. Mohammad Hadi Zakerhossein, *Situation Selection Regime at the International Criminal Court* ISBN 978-1-78068-618-9
83. Yi Zhang, *Advancing the Right to Health Care in China. Towards Accountability* ISBN 978-1-78068-677-6
84. Diana Itza Odier-Contreras Garduño, *Collective Reparations.Tensions and Dilemmas Between Collective Reparations and the Individual Right to Receive Reparations* ISBN 978-1-78068-705-6
85. Daphina Misiedjan, *Towards a Sustainable Human Right to Water. Supporting vulnerable people and protecting water resources* ISBN 978-1-78068-612-7

www.ingramcontent.com/pod-product-compliance
Ingram Content Group UK Ltd.
Pitfield, Milton Keynes, MK11 3LW, UK
UKHW051919100926
8556IPUK00021B/1263

9 781780 688428